POSTMODERNISM AND THE CONTEMPORARY NOVEL

A READER

Edited by

Bran Nicol

EDINBURGH UNIVERSITY PRESS

For Jamie Nicol, 21st Century boy

© Selection and editorial material,
Bran Nicol, 2002

Edinburgh University Press Ltd
22 George Square, Edinburgh

Typeset in Sabon and Gill Sans
by Bibliocraft Ltd, Dundee, and
printed and bound in Great Britain by
MPG Books Ltd, Bodmin

A CIP record for this book is available from
the British Library

ISBN 0 7486 1478 8 (hardback)
ISBN 0 7486 1479 6 (paperback)

CONTENTS

ACKNOWLEDGEMENTS

Thanks to: Jackie Jones, Carol Macdonald and Peter Williams at Edinburgh University Press for their boundless patience and careful editing; EUP's anonymous readers for valuable comments on the selections and organisation of this anthology; Poe Cheung of the University of Portsmouth for her kind and invaluable assistance securing permissions; all those at University College Chichester who talked about postmodernism with me over the years; and, most of all, to Karen Stevens and Joseph Furness for ensuring that the link between postmodernism and psychopathology remains a research interest not an epitaph.

The editor and Edinburgh University Press would like to thank the following for permission to reproduce copyright material in this book:

Fredric Jameson for the extracts from 'The Cultural Logic of Late Capitalism', in *Postmodernism, or, the Cultural Logic of Late Capitalism* (Verso, 1991).
University of Minnesota Press/Manchester University Press for the extracts from Jean-François Lyotard, *The Postmodern Condition: A Report on Knowledge*, pages xxiii–41, 85–103, translated by Geoff Bennington and Brian Massumi (1984);
University of Texas Press for the extracts from 'Discourse and the Novel' by Mikhail Bakhtin, pp. 261–367, from *The Dialogic Imagination: Four Essays* by M. M. Bakhtin, edited by Michael Holquist, translated by Caryl Emerson and Michael Holquist, copyright © 1981, reprinted by permission;
Johns Hopkins University Press for Ihab Hassan, 'POSTmodernISM: A Paracritical Bibliography', originally published in *New Literary History* 3: 1 (1971), 5–30, © The University of Virginia, reprinted by permission;
University of Pennsylvania Press for the extracts from *Dissident Postmodernists* (1991) by Paul Maltby, copyright © University of Pennsylvania Press, reprinted with permission;

Taylor and Francis Books Ltd for the extracts from *Metafiction: The Theory and Practice of Self-Conscious Fiction* (1984) by Patricia Waugh, copyright © Routledge, reprinted with permission; the extracts from *A Poetics of Postmodernism* (1988) by Linda Hutcheon, copyright © Routledge, reprinted with permission; and the extracts from *The Politics of Postmodernism* (1989) by Linda Hutcheon, copyright © Routledge, reprinted with permission;

Blackwell Publishers for the extracts from *The Condition of Postmodernity* by David Harvey (1989), copyright © Blackwell Publishers, reprinted with permission;

Leslie Fiedler for permission to reprint his article 'Cross the Border – Close that Gap: Postmodernism', from Marcus Cunliffe (ed.), *American Literature Since 1900*. London: Sphere Books, 1975;

Southern Illinois University Press for the extracts from Stephano Tani, *The Doomed Detective: The Contribution of the Detective Novel to Postmodern American and Italian Fiction* (1984), © by the Board of Trustees, Southern Illinois University Press, reprinted by permission of the publisher;

Mosaic, a journal for the interdisciplinary study of literature for permission to reprint Veronica Hollinger, 'Cybernetic Deconstructions: Cyberpunk and Postmodernism', originally published in *Mosaic*, vol. 23, no. 2, pp. 29–44, Spring 1990;

University of Michigan Press for the extracts from *Simulation and Simulacra* by Jean Baudrillard (Ann Arbor: The University of Michigan Press, 1994), pp. 1–32;

London Review of Books for Slavoj Žižek, 'You May!', which first appeared in *The London Review of Books* vol. 21, no. 6. <www.lrb.co.uk>;

Duke University Press for William V. Spanos, 'The Detective and the Boundary', *boundary 2*, 1:1 (Fall, 1972) and Patrick O' Donnell, 'Engendering Paranoia in Contemporary Narrative', *boundary 2*, 19: 1 (Spring, 1992) All rights reserved. Reprinted by permission;

Chrysalis Books plc. for Thomas Docherty, 'Postmodern Characterization: The Ethics of Alterity', from *Postmodernism and Contemporary Fiction*, ed. by Edmund Smyth (London: Batsford, 1991);

John Benjamins Publishing Co. for Brian McHale, 'Change of Dominant from Modernist to Postmodernist Writing', in *Approaching Postmodernism*, Douwe Fokkema and Hans Bertens (eds);

Verso for extracts from Meaghan Morris, *The Pirate's Fiancée: Feminism, Reading, Postmodernism* (1991);

Palgrave Publishers Ltd. for extracts from 'Mapping the Postmodern' by Andreas Huyssen, in *After the Great Divide* (London: Macmillan, 1988), reprinted by permission;

Gerald Graff for permission to reprint his article, 'The Myth of the Postmodern Breakthrough', first published in *TriQuarterly* 26: 383–417 and reprinted in *Literature Against Itself: Literary Ideas and Modern Society* (Ivan R. Dee, 1995);

John Wiley and Sons, Ltd for the extract from Charles Jencks, *What is Post-Modernism?* (London: Academy, 1987);

Methuen for the extracts from Kwame Anthony Appiah, 'The Postcolonial and the Postmodern', from *In My Father's House: Africa in the Philosophy of Culture* (London: Methuen, 1992);

Jonathan Cape and Farrar, Strauss and Giroux, Inc. for selections from *S/Z* by Roland Barthes, translated by Richard Miller. Translation © 1986;

The Random House Group Ltd. for permission to reprint 'One Culture and the New Sensibility' by Susan Sontag, first published in *Against Interpretation and Other Essays* (Jonathan Cape);

The estate of Irving Howe for permission to reprint 'Mass Society and Postmodern Fiction' by Irving Howe, originally published in *Partisan Review* 26:3 420–36;

Turnaround Books for permission to reprint 'Postmodern Blackness' by bell hooks, in *Yearning: Race, Gender and Cultural Politics* (London: Turnaround, 1991) 23–31;

The Atlantic Monthly for permission to reprint John Barth's 'The Literature of Exhaustion', originally published in *The Atlantic*, 22: 2 (1967) 29–34;

Curtis Brown on behalf of David Lodge for permission to reprint 'Postmodernist Fiction' from David Lodge, *The Modes of Modern Writing* (London: Arnold, 1977);

The Random House Group and Harcourt, Inc. for permission to reprint the extract from Umberto Eco, *Reflections on* The Name of the Rose (London: Secker & Warburg, 1985);

Donna J. Haraway for permission to reprint extracts from her essay, 'The Cyborg Manifesto: Science, Technology and Socialist Feminism in the 1980s', originally published in *Socialist Review* 15(80) (1985) 65–107.

INTRODUCTION:
WHAT WE TALK ABOUT WHEN WE
TALK ABOUT POSTMODERNISM

> Once we knew that fiction was about life and criticism was about fiction –
> and everything was simple. Now we know that fiction is about other
> fiction, is criticism in fact, or metafiction. And we know that criticism is
> about the impossibility of anything being about life, really, or even about
> fiction, or, finally, about anything. Criticism has taken the very idea of
> 'aboutness' away from us. It has taught us that language is tautological, if it
> is not nonsense, and to the extent that it is about anything it is about itself.
> Mathematics is about mathematics, poetry is about poetry and criticism is
> about the impossibility of its own existence. (Robert Scholes, 1975)

Postmodernism is the most problematic concept in contemporary cultural
criticism. The term has featured prominently in an unusually wide range of
academic disciplines – literary study, visual arts and architecture, philosophy,
social theory, history, cultural studies – where it is used in different ways, to
designate apparently different things. The matter is complicated by the fact that,
in recent years, the term has entered more general cultural discourse, cropping
up regularly in broadsheet newspapers, style magazines, TV arts programmes
and non-academic books, where the meaning of the term is even less clear. To
put it more precisely, the problem that confronts anyone trying to understand
what is meant by postmodernism is that its *object* – that is, the various
phenomena the theory purports to explain – is unstable, because it keeps
changing according to the context in which the concept is being discussed.

No wonder, then, that it is almost standard practice for introductions to
postmodernism to begin with the rather paradoxical assertion that postmodernism is impossible to introduce satisfactorily. This introduction is going

I

to suggest something similar, and will briefly survey some differing uses of the term. Yet my overall argument is that the postmodernism debate in fact highlights *universal* problems with relating the language of criticism to its apparent object – and this gives it extra value in the field of literary criticism. But before I consider this, I want to suggest that there is now, in the early twenty-first century, a fair amount of consensus about what the term refers to. For all its problems, 'postmodernism' has become more or less established in critical discourse as a term that refers to a shift in what it means to be a subject in late twentieth-century society and to designate a related attitude of self-reflexivity or ironic knowingness that permeates our culture as a result. This might seem like I am making two contradictory claims: postmodernism is definable, and postmodernism is indefinable. But my point is that even though there are signs that the *theory* of postmodernism is becoming less contentious, there are still doubts to be raised about whether it can successfully manage to represent its object. Since the main part of this reader is full of examples of postmodern fiction, my account here will concentrate on the question of postmodernism on a wider cultural scale than simply the literary, before coming back to the specific question of literature and literary criticism.

POSTMODERNISM AS CULTURAL CONDITION

Part of the problem with defining the postmodern has always been that the discourse is, almost by definition, concerned with what is contemporary, and this makes it liable to change. Other terms used for artistic movements (like 'romanticism' and 'modernism', for example) became adopted, by and large, *after* the pioneering cultural practices and traditions they aimed to designate had begun to wane. This is not true of postmodernism. (Postmodernism is often rightly regarded as being peculiarly concerned with 'belatedness', with the anxiety of coming *after* a major movement like modernism, but this is one sense in which it is right on time.) Charles Jencks, the architectural theorist most associated with postmodernism, prefaces his attempt to answer 'What is Post-Modernism?' by offering the proviso that 'one must see that [postmodernism's] continual growth and movement mean that no definitive answer is possible – at least until it stops moving' (Jencks, 1986: 9).

Yet now, however, there is a sense that that the term is finally showing signs of 'stopping moving' – or at least that major new definitions of postmodernism have, for the time being, ceased appearing. In other words, precisely *how* we are to use the term seems no longer quite such a pressing matter across the humanities and social sciences. Academic work now frequently seems to be comfortable in using the term almost in passing, adjectivally: 'postmodern environment', 'postmodern space', 'postmodern paranoia'.[1] Limited to a set of familiar themes and addressed to a particular 'discursive community', that is (here, academics in the field of contemporary fiction), the term is less contentious than it once was. Another way of putting this is to say that the moment when postmodernism was at the forefront of academic analysis – as is inevitably the case with all era-defining concepts – has passed. But this is not to say that it is no longer valuable as a term in literary study – quite the contrary, as I shall suggest later. For one thing, it means that it is easier to grasp the parameters of the debate about postmodernism and the novel now we can look at it with at least a measure of historical distance.

The fact that the term has moved out of an exclusively academic arena to take its place in the more general cultural lexicon suggests that there is consensus about its definition on a wider scale too: *some* people, that is, think they know what it means. To test this out we could look at two examples chosen at random (because they were what I happened to be reading at the time) from recent, commercially successful, books aimed at, or marketed towards, the general reader. The first comes from a description in Michael Burleigh's acclaimed *The Third Reich: A New History* (2001) of the form of hysterically theatrical politics favoured by emerging fascist regimes in 1920s Italy and 1930s Germany. These, Burleigh suggests, were ' "post-modern", in that Europe's demagogues were archly aware of the manipulative techniques they needed to generate mass faith, knowing about the impact of masses, flags, song, symbols and colours. These men were artist-politicians' (Burleigh, 2001: 9). The second example comes from an episode in *45*, a memoir by 1980s and 1990s pop entrepreneur and sometime art terrorist, Bill Drummond, where he describes what he calls the 'fantasy nationalism' indulged in by Scottish football fans. His point is that the 'saving grace of all this bonnie flower of [Scotland], lion rampant, tartan-bonnet-with-ginger-nylon-hair-attached nationalism', he continues, 'is, we all know it's silly. It is a send-up – nationalism as a postmodern jape' (Drummond, 2001: 45).

In each case the term is used as an adjective, without further clarification, without any apparent desire on the part of the writer to define the term. Neither book is about postmodernism, nor does the term appear with any frequency in the rest of their pages. In the first example we can infer that a 'postmodern' politics is one which is less *about* anything (like emancipation, improving the wealth of the nation, the standard of living, democracy, etc.) than simply preserving power through image-making and manipulation. Postmodern politics is the politics of gesture, theatre, art – the implication being that the audience can be seduced into swallowing the illusion wholesale, as we do in the theatre. The second example implies that 'postmodern' nationalism is really a question of style rather than any real existential significance, like choosing to wear 1970s jacket lapels or carry a Playboy handbag. In both cases there is a sense that postmodernism refers to the cynical deployment of the substanceless image. What makes nationalism postmodern, whether it is in Europe in the 1930s or 1990s is that style triumphs over content. The major difference between the two examples is that, in Drummond's case, there is the sense that the user chooses the style *consciously*.

Both examples are indeed representative of a pervasive general definition of 'postmodernism'. Postmodernism can be regarded as a mode of cultural awareness informed by the conviction that everything *is*, in fact, *cultural*; that is, nothing in life – nationalism, value systems, identity, history, even reality – is natural or given. Rather, everything is constructed, mediated, put there *by* someone *for* a particular reason. This attitude is reflected in the philosopher Peter Sloterdijk's concept of 'cynical reason' (Sloterdijk, 1987). Where previously – according to a 'classical Marxist' perspective – ideology was something that cleverly tricked us, making us believe in something we didn't, making us conform to prescribed social norms of behaviour because we didn't know what we were *really* doing, now we are conscious of ideological persuasion: we know what we do is false but still do it anyway. Nowadays, according to Slavoj Žižek, who has taken up Sloterdijk's concept, we all know that presidents lie, yet we still support them. We know that advertisers exaggerate the value of their products, yet we still buy them (Žižek, 1994). Or, in Bill Drummond's example, we can be passionate about our country without really meaning it.

This kind of heightened self-consciousness manifests itself most obviously perhaps in popular culture. Popular culture is irrepressibly 'intertextual': it constantly refers to, comments on, expresses admiration for, shamelessly copies, previous pop culture texts. TV listings are full of programmes which play on references to films and other TV programmes (e.g. *The Simpsons*, *Spaced*, *The Adam and Joe Show*), seemingly designed by and for people who were born into an age where mass media reaches into every aspect of life, have never known reality unframed by mass media and are consquently unable to avoid relating everyday 'real' experience to everyday fictional experience, especially that which has been screened. Though many cultural commentators despair of the apparent inability or unwillingness of pop culture to be original, we could argue that its intertextuality and self-referentiality at least demonstrates our awareness of the degree to which our lives are constructed by mass media, discourse and ideology.

The natural form for this awareness to be expressed – perhaps the dominant mode in postmodern culture as a whole – is irony. The Italian literary semiotician and novelist Umberto Eco certainly thinks so (his witty formulation is included in Part I), believing that irony enables us to overcome a potential impasse caused by what Žižek calls (in an essay included here) our 'reflexivity' – or our endless capacity to reflect ironically on one's motivations for doing anything, and to acknowledge that any belief one might have is provisional and could just as easily be exchanged for another. In Eco's vision of postmodernity, we want to say things but are simultaneously aware – as a result of the intertextuality of contemporary experience – that they have been said by others *before*. Irony, all English students know, is a non-literal usage of language, which involves the subversion of the intended meaning of words by their *actual* meaning. It has a distinguished history in literary criticism, where there is a classical distinction between *verbal* and *structural* irony, the former where what is said clashes with what is meant (deliberately or unwittingly), the latter where what is said is undermined by the particular context in which it is said. But to understand how irony works in postmodernism we really need to regard it as an *attitude*, like Eco, or, as Linda Hutcheon does in her book *Irony's Edge* (Hutcheon, 1994) (a book which is itself ironic in that it is written by one of the most prominent theorists of postmodernism but only uses the term post-modernism once), less as an intentional literary trope than as something which is created by language by virtue of its social, interactive aspect. As *discourse*, in other words, irony revolves around the knowledge that there is no such thing as fixed meaning: any meaning is pregnant with others and can be altered subtly into something quite different through a modulation of tone or context.

POSTMODERNISM AND 'THE REAL'

Regarded as an *attitude*, then, which underscores our culture, postmodernism refers to a heightened degree of self-consciousness indicating our experience of *reality* has changed. Reality is no longer something we can take for granted, but is something that we suspect is continually organised and constructed for us by the twin apparatuses of the mass media and the global capitalist economy. The changed experience of 'the real' is also a feature of more ambitious theoretical accounts of postmodernism, which seek to portray it as evidence of a paradigm shift in society as a whole, not just in terms of cultural style – those advanced by the likes of Daniel Bell, Fredric Jameson, Jean-François Lyotard and David Harvey. As most of these theorists feature in Part I, all I will attempt here is a general summary of this aspect of their work, though I must emphasise that there are significant differences between their approaches, terminology and arguments.

The rhetorical thrust of postmodern social theory, taken as a whole, is that to live in postmodernity is to find oneself divorced from those aspects of life which are regarded as authentic, genuine, *real*. In postmodernity we are no longer able to appreciate the particularity of our historical location, we can no longer create original works of art, we live and work in 'virtual' space rather than reality. Although the environment in which most of us work is undoutedly 'real', it is real in a different way from the experience of working on the land (as it would be in a predominantly rural economy), or with machines and raw materials (in an industrial one). Most of the work we do involves processing information via digital technology. The advent of the digital world has meant that our separation from the tangible world has become more extreme. Money, for example, has always operated purely on a symbolic level (the value of a five pound note is not, of course, what the paper it is printed on is worth, but the value we attach to it symbolically) but recently this symbolic quality has become more pronounced with the advent of credit cards and Internet banking where, increasingly, we trade in amounts that are purely symbolic, figures on a screen without any tangible object standing in for them. And, of course, away from work, our physical and linguistic space has been colonised by the discourses of mass media, which constantly recycle images that have been completely detached from their original context and are thus rendered meaningless.

In stark contrast to theorists such as Hutcheon and Eco, whose work implies a potentially liberating knowingness about our changed experience of reality in postmodernity, the more sociologically inclined theorists of postmodernism tend to see the separation from the real as dangerous to the individual and collective psyche. It is striking how readily postmodern theory turns to the language of psychopathology – schizophrenia, hysteria, narcissism, paranoia, etc. – to explain the postmodern 'condition'. Christopher Lasch sees ours as the 'culture of narcissism' (Lasch, 1991), while, according to Teresa Brennan, it is the 'age of paranoia' (Brennan, 1991). This tendency is most overt in Fredric Jameson's famous essay (included in Part I of this reader) 'Postmodernism, or the Cultural Logic of Late Capitalism', which reads almost like an extended psychoanalytic case study of the postmodern subject, a variety of cultural texts figuring as its symptomatology. The risk of psychopathology also hovers over Jean Baudrillard's provocative conception of postmodern life, which takes the logic of the changed status of the real in postmodernity further than anyone else. (His classic essay 'The Precession of Simulacra' appears in Part I.)

Baudrillard holds that the characteristic feature of contemporary society is its domination by systems which are capable of perfect duplication (Baudrillard's term for these is 'the code'). Previously technology could produce copies of things – recorded music, for example, or artistic prints – but these were clearly *versions* of the original, and still recognisable as a copy. Now, however, science and technology have advanced to such a degree that copies can be made which are *indistinguishable* from the original: as with the cloning of animals, or the ability to 'burn' CDs, the difference between the original and the copy is eliminated. This is the process Baudrillard terms *simulation*. The sphere in which simulation operates most powerfully is in the mass media, which similarly reproduces reality in a way that means there is no difference between real and fake. To live in postmodernity is to experience fake things as real, and real things as fake. We experience *Big Brother* as if it were reality, and the bombing of the World Trade Center as if it were a Hollywood film. Baudrillard thus argues that a new definition of 'real' applies in postmodernity: *anything which can be copied absolutely* – which is to say, in the age of the code, absolutely everything. Reality is no longer real any more, in fact; it is hyperreal.

Baudrillard's is only the most hyperbolic version of a widespread concern with the disappearance of the real in postmodern theory which is also demonstrated by the contemporary novel. The most characteristic formal practice in postmodern fiction is what is known as *metafiction*, fiction that in some way foregrounds its own status as a fictional construct. Metafiction is essentially an ironic form in that it demonstrates that we cannot accept the 'reality' we are presented with in a novel at face value. The story is undermined by its form, by the *way* in which it is told. In fact this practice relates to one particular literary version of irony from a much earlier tradition, 'romantic irony'. As J. A. Cuddon defines the term:

The writer who employs what is called romantic irony [...] exhibits true presence of mind by showing an awareness, a sensibility, that he does not expect his work to be taken wholly seriously – and does not wish it to be. He conveys this tone and attitude (thus inviting a complementary tone and attitude in his reader) by being at once critically aware of what he is doing and why he is doing it, even while he may be impelled by a strong dynamic creative purpose. Thus he is fully conscious of the comic implication of his own seriousness. This form of irony is often at its best when the author is *showing* us what he is doing while he is doing it, so to speak. (Cuddon, 1982)

Though the notion of 'true presence of mind' seems to jar with a postmodern sensibility (and is precisely the kind of value we might expect a postmodernist to be ironic about) there is a sense in which postmodernism in fiction *is* motivated by a conviction that a false state of mind is one which accepts reality at face value, or believes that meaning is stable.

Metafiction continually reminds us – in a variety of ways which are explored in more detail in Part III of this reader – that the work is *only* a work of fiction, it is not real; the world that it portrays is *not* the real world that it resembles. This seems to be a facetious pointing out of what is quite obvious. As the American novelist William H. Gass says, 'That novels should be made of words, and merely words, is shocking, really. It's as though you had discovered that your wife were made of rubber: the bliss of all those years, the fears ... from sponge' (Gass, 1970: 27). But metafiction encourages us to pursue the implications of this obvious fact to their logical conclusion: fiction is fictional, but no more so than reality. The effect of metafiction is to momentarily collapse the distinction between fiction and reality by causing the 'outside world' to intrude into the world of the novel, as in classic examples where the author suddenly appears 'as himself', breaking the illusion of reality, as in John Fowles *The French Lieutenant's Woman* (1969) or Paul Auster's *City of Glass* (1985). But what follows from this is that the obverse also happens: the fictional world spills over into the real world. As Patricia Waugh makes clear in her book *Metafiction* (1984) (see the extract in Part III) the ultimate point is that reality as we experience it is always mediated through discursive frames.

POSTMODERNISM AND THE OBJECT OF CRITICISM

At this point we can return to the question of the relation between criticism and its object. For the fact is that the continued concern with the separation between language and the real explored so doggedly in metafiction mirrors the fundamental problem of postmodernist theory and criticism. Can criticism *really* grasp its object satisfactorily? Can we really use the term postmodernism with any degree of confidence when it supposedly refers to so many different things? Charles Jencks points to a tendency he calls 'Nothing Post-Modernism', where the term is used in so many different ways that 'it means almost everything and thus nearly nothing' (Jencks, 1986: 30). This nothingness has even been seen as the key characteristic of the concept as a whole. As Noel King has said in a reading of Don DeLillo's novel *White Noise*, 'one definition of the postmodern could consist in saying that it is the latest name given to an enduring problem in cultural commentary: "postmodernism" designates the latest appearance of the familiar gap which opens between certain kinds of critical discourse and the objects they purport to describe or explain' (King, 1990: 66).

As you might expect, this problem has not passed theorists of the postmodern novel by, who, perhaps by definition, are self-conscious about their critical endeavours. Many have wondered aloud whether the object of postmodernism is really nothing more than a figment of the critical imagination. Larry McCaffrey begins *Postmodern Fiction*, his 'Bio-Bibliographical Guide', with a warning to the reader: 'beware of labels, lest you be tempted into a fruitless search for something that in reality exists in language only' (McCaffrey, 1986: xi). Brian McHale has acknowledged that every critic 'constructs' postmodernism according to their own agenda, each construction ending up as no more than a 'fiction' in the end.

> Whatever we think of the term, however much or little we may be satisfied with it, one thing is certain: the referent of 'postmodernism', the *thing* to which the term claims to refer, *does not exist* ... precisely in the way that 'the Renaissance' or 'romanticism' do not exist. There is no postmodernism 'out there' in the world any more than there ever was a Renaissance or a romanticism out there.

He then makes a list of the different postmodern fictions created by various theorists: John Barth's 'literature of replenishment', Charles Newman's 'literature of an inflationary economy', Lyotard's 'general condition of knowledge in the contemporary informational regime', Hassan's 'stage on the road to the spiritual unification of humankind' (McHale, 1987: 4). Quoting this list of critical 'fictions' with approval, Linda Hutcheon adds her own: Jameson's 'cultural logic of late capitalism', Baudrillard's 'gloating' triumph of the simulacrum 'over the body of the deceased referent', Kroker and Cook's 'dark side of postmodernism', Sloterdijk's age of cynicism, Alan Wilde's 'literary "middle grounds" of the postmodern'. She concludes by adding her own 'paradoxical postmodernism of complicity and critique, of reflexivity and historicity' (Hutcheon, 1989: 11).

But, as I said earlier, the problem of representation in criticism is not confined to the discourse of postmodernism, however acute it may be in that particular field. Defining the object of study has never been a straightforward question in cultural criticism – especially in a discipline like literary criticism, where even 'literature' itself is surprisingly difficult to define. One of the most contentious practices in literary criticism is the use of 'periodising' terms which simultaneously delineate a historical moment and a sequence of literary features which developed in that time: romanticism, realism, modernism, postmodernism. On the one hand, these seem to be indispensible: a fundamental impulse behind the whole critical endeavour is to seek to categorise different works of literature according to differences and similarity. But just how possible is it to attempt to reduce something as diverse and polysemic as literature into overarching categories? Another especially complicated object of literary criticism is the novel. According to Mikhail Bakhtin, perhaps the theorist who most satisfactorily defined its essence (as we shall see in Part III), the novel is *the* indefinable genre *par excellence*: 'The study of the novel as a genre is distinguished by peculiar difficulties. This is due to the unique nature of the object itself: the novel is the sole genre that continues to develop, that is as yet uncompleted' (Bakhtin, 1981).

Criticism that attempts to deal with postmodernism *and* the novel, then, two notoriously elastic categories, highlights in a particularly dynamic way a problem which lies at the heart of *all* acts of criticism, even though most criticism – certainly most criticism of fiction – does not explicitly address it. Is it possible to represent a novel when we interpret it? Even if great care is taken to read it 'on its own terms', are we not just seeing our own critical agenda reflected in the text as if it were a mirror? Is our interpretation loaded from the start, fatally flawed by the things we *want* it to say, by how it might back up our theory?

POSTMODERNISM AND THE CONTEMPORARY NOVEL

The rationale behind this book is emphatically not to suggest that the contemporary novel is somehow reducible to postmodernism, or *vice versa*. Its title acknowledges that its subject is really two problematic areas of contemporary cultural criticism, not one. In the selections in this reader we can see examples of the critical apparatus – literary criticism – attempting to grasp and explain its object – the postmodern novel.

Just as emphatically, though, I must point out that exploring the status of criticism is not the major aim of this reader. Postmodernism and the contemporary novel have always enjoyed something of a special relationship, however complicated it has been. The postmodern debate has been particularly useful to anyone seeking to grasp the complexities and preoccupations of the fiction produced over the last few decades. The most important thematic concerns and formal innovations in the contemporary novel during this time, as well as the writers regarded as the most major in postwar fiction (Amis, Rushdie, Morrison, DeLillo, Pynchon, Carter, Fowles, Marquez, Cortazar, Robbe-Grillet, Grass, Calvino, etc.) have been discussed at some point in relation to postmodernism. And the influence has worked the other way as well, for fiction has been central to the wider debate about postmodernism. The field of literary study was where the concept first became the subject of extensive debate, in American criticism in the 1960s (see Part II), while fiction is never far away from the reference points of key postmodernist thinkers not explicitly or exclusively concerned with literature, like Jameson, Baudrillard and Donna Haraway – perhaps because the novel has always been the artistic form whose special ability is to somehow *represent* society at a given moment, to capture its rhythms and reflect its concerns.

This reader, then, has gathered together some of the most important and representative writings on postmodernism and the novel to have appeared over the last 40 years for two main reasons. Examining the novel in terms of its relation to postmodernism can give us a valuable overall view of the landscape of contemporary fiction in the late twentieth- and early twenty-first centuries. And in looking at postmodernism *through* the contemporary novel we can effectively regard one cultural form as symptomatic of late twentieth- and early twenty-first century cultural experience.

NOTES

1. These examples are taken from essays in the recent Special Issue of the literary journal *Modern Fiction Studies* devoted to the work of Don DeLillo (vol. 45, no. 3, Fall 1999), the novelist who is closest to canonic status in postmodern fiction. For the reasons why, see Part IV.

WORKS CITED

Bakhtin, M. M. (1981) 'Epic and Novel', in M. Holquist (ed.), *The Dialogic Imagination*. Austin, TX: University of Texas Press.

Brennan, Teresa (1991) 'The Age of Paranoia', *Paragraph*, 14 (1): 20–45.

Burleigh, Michael (2001) *The Third Reich: A New History*. London: Pan Macmillan.

Cuddon, J. A. (1982) *A Dictionary of Literary Terms*. Harmondsworth: Penguin.

Drummond, Bill (2001) *45*. London: Abacus.

Gass, William H. (1970) *Fiction and the Figures of Life*. New York: Alfred A. Knopf.

Holquist, Michael (ed.) (1981) *The Dialogic Imagination*. Austin, TX: University of Texas Press.

Hutcheon, Linda (1989) *The Politics of Postmodernism*. London: Routledge.

Hutcheon, Linda (1994) *Irony's Edge: The Theory and Politics of Irony*. London: Routledge.

Jencks, Charles (1986) *What is Post-Modernism?* London: Academy.

King, Noel (1990) 'Reading *White Noise*: Floating Remarks', *Critical Quarterly*, 33 (3): 66–83.

Lasch, Christopher (1991) *The Culture of Narcissism: American Life in an Age of Diminishing Expectations* [1979]. New York: W. W. Norton.

McCaffrey, Larry (ed.) (1986) 'Introduction', *Postmodern Fiction: A Bio-Bibliographical Guide*. New York and London. Greenwood Press.

McHale, Brian (1987) *Postmodernist Fiction*. London: Routledge.

Scholes, Robert (1975) 'The Fictional Criticism of the Future', *TriQuarterly*, 34 (Fall).

Sloterdijk, Peter (1987) *Critique of Cynical Reason*. London and New York: Verso.

Žižek, Slavoj (1994) *Tarrying with the Negative*. London and New York: Verso.

PART I
THE POSTMODERN CONDITION

THE POSTMODERN CONDITION: INTRODUCTION

This section includes extracts from some of the classic writings on postmodernism. Though these do not focus primarily on literature, they provide some sense of the social, cultural and intellectual context in which to place the discussions of the postmodern novel which make up the rest of the anthology.

Among the theorists featured here there is a general consensus that postmodernism is the consequence of a new social and economic formation that begins around the middle of the twentieth century and ushers in significant cultural changes as a result. Three concepts are repeatedly used in writings on postmodernism to describe this socio-economic order. 'Post-industrialism' is defined by the sociologists Daniel Bell and Alain Touraine (Bell, 1973; Touraine, 1974) as the move from a society where heavy industry generates wealth to an increasingly consumerist, 'programmed' and bureaucratic one. 'Post-Fordism' is a concept associated with the work of social geographer David Harvey, which refers to the supercession of a 'scientific' or rule-governed approach to industry pioneered by the Ford Motor Company throughout a 'golden age' of capitalism lasting from the 1940s to the 1970s, by a new ethos of flexibility and deregulation (affecting, for example, labour markets, products, patterns of consumption, geographical mobility). The third concept, 'late capitalism', is used most notably by the Marxist cultural theorist Fredric Jameson (though he takes it from the work of Ernest Mandel (Mandel, 1978)), and refers to the way that capital has expanded into areas which were previously uncommodified, such as the media, arts and education.

The first three extracts in this part, by Jameson, Harvey and Andreas Huyssen, are three of the most cogent and interesting attempts to offer a 'totalising' account of postmodernism, namely one that perceives postmodernism as the result of a profound shift across a number of different spheres – social, economic, philosophical and cultural – which all impact on each other. Rather than seeing postmodernism as *either* an aesthetic style *or* a historical period, a totalising account views postmodernism as both. The most ambitious piece here is undoubtedly Jameson's. His argument is neatly encapsulated in the title of his most famous essay (which Douglas Kellner has called 'probably the most quoted, discussed, and debated article' of the 1980s (Kellner, 1989)), 'Postmodernism, or the Cultural Logic of Late Capitalism'. For Jameson, postmodernism *equals*, purely and simply, the effects of late capitalism on contemporary culture. Nothing escapes its logic. This means that a postmodern text is not just shaped by, but also demands to be read *as a comment on*, the political and economic organisation of this period in history.

Jameson's frame of reference is extraordinarily broad in the essay – extending from Hollywood film to pop art to contemporary architecture to the Beatles and the Stones – but what adds to the insistent energy of his analysis is his efforts at grappling with the problems of totalisation. He is aware of the paradox that his argument leads to: by stating that the logic of late capitalism envelops each discourse and cultural practice within it, preventing the subject from enjoying full agency and pointing to a way outside late capitalism, it follows that his *own* discourse must be at risk of contamination. His solution is to attempt a kind of 'counter' totalisation, by which he can outdo the totalising impulses of late capitalism through the process of what he calls 'cognitive mapping', that is the dogged effort to locate and classify *all* its cultural effects. In this respect Jameson is like the academic counterpart of the hero of one of the conspiracy films he writes about in his book *The Geopolitical Aesthetic* (Jameson, 1992): furiously fighting a shadowy global organisation much bigger than he is, by trying to match it blow for blow.

The second extract is less dramatic, but just as impressive. Although David Harvey also theorises postmodernism as a 'historical-geographical condition of a certain sort' (Harvey, 1989), he attempts – and has largely been acclaimed for achieving – a total view of postmodernity which doesn't necessarily mean we have to accept its logic, nor resort to the kind of 'homeopathic' or 'fatal' strategies rather desperately advocated by Jameson and Baudrillard to counter it. As we can see from the extract, Harvey gives a detailed account of just how the social changes brought on by post-Fordism have affected everyday life where Jameson is more brief and concerned mainly with its effects. In his Preface, he summarises his argument as follows:

> There has been a sea-change in cultural as well as in political-economic practices since around 1972.
> This sea-change is bound up with the emergence of new dominant ways in which we experience space and time.

While simultaneity in the shifting dimensions of time and space is no proof of necessary or causal connection, strong a priori grounds can be adduced for the proposition that there is some kind of necessary relation between the rise of postmodernist cultural forms, the emergence of more flexible modes of capital accumulation, and a new round of 'time–space compression' in the organization of capitalism.

But these changes, when set against the basic rules of capitalistic accumulation, appear more as shifts in surface appearance rather than as signs of the emergence of some entirely new postcapitalist or even postindustrial society.

Andreas Huyssen's essay 'Mapping the Postmodern' is also a self-reflexive attempt to provide an overall account of postmodernism, though unlike Jameson and Harvey he deliberately confines his analysis to the cultural sphere, making little attempt to explore the social or economic roots to cultural change. This is because he feels that any claim 'that there is a wholesale paradigm shift of the cultural, social, and economic orders', such as Jameson makes, is 'overblown' (Huyssen, 1986). Yet Huyssen's argument is far-reaching, nonetheless. Postmodern culture is not something that can be regarded as 'anti-modernist' but is the continuation of a trend *within* modernism. Postmodernism emerges in the 1960s as a response to the 'high' cultural ethos of the modernist era, but in its challenge it is the continuation of an alternative artistic order within the modernist tradition, that of the avant-garde. Huyssen's essay is useful in making the point that so many explorations of postmodernism get stuck in a simplistic binary, where it is seen as either following on from or breaking with modernism. The real answer is that it is both.

In contrast to the first three theorists featured, Jean-François Lyotard and Jean Baudrillard – perhaps as a result of the French poststructuralist tradition to which they both relate to – are firmly anti-totalising, Lyotard most explicitly so, ending his essay 'Answering the Question: What is Postmodernism?' with a call to arms: 'Let us wage a war on totality' (Lyotard, 1979: 82). The extracts here, though, are taken from the book to which this essay was appended, *The Postmodern Condition* (1979) (and which has rather curious origins for a key text on postmodernism, as it was a report commissioned by the Quebecois government). Its starting premise is that Bell's and Touraine's view that postmodernism is the result of the transition to a post-industrial, 'computerised' society is right. In fact, the book develops a point made by Bell that one of the most important consequences of this transition is a change in the 'status of knowledge'. For Lyotard, where, in modernity, it was assumed that knowledge could be universally applicable, now, in postmodernity it is localised and partial.

Lyotard takes his inquiry, however, in a completely different direction from Bell, given his leftist political credentials and, most importantly, the philosophical context to which he belongs, which I shall briefly outline. *The Postmodern Condition* is a polemic against the tradition of 'Enlightenment' thinking which dates back to the work of German philosophers like Immanuel Kant and G. W. F. Hegel and the French philosopher Jean-Jacques Rousseau, the spirit of which is preserved in the work of Lyotard's contemporary Jürgen Habermas. Running through Enlightenment thinking is the idea of a narrative of development: that the human being is distinguished from any other being by its ability to *reason* – and this capacity is directed towards ends which are principally benign. In other words, politics and science proceed according to rational logic, and this logic is directed *naturally* towards preserving the freedom of the human being. What leads off from this is the idea that humanity is 'progressing' towards the ultimate emancipation of the human being. This is the goal of history – the 'happy ending' of the 'story' of modernity, or the idea that we shall one day secure an ultimate unity of human knowledge.

The idea of story is central to Lyotard's account. Enlightenment thinking has preserved itself by perpetuating what he calls 'metanarratives', which structure the discourses of modern religion, politics, philosophy and science. Metanarratives are a form of ideology which constrains and controls the individual subject. They are violent and tyrannous in the way that they falsely impose a sense of 'totality' and 'universality' on a set of disparate things, actions and events. Just like narratives in literature, metanarratives, in other words, provide a *form* into which a series of discrete elements can be ordered. Their function is to *legitimate* political positions and courses of action; legitimation is always a matter of maintaining power, and power is inseparable from violence. It works in science, for example, when scientists make a discovery and legitimate it by telling a kind of 'epic' narrative about it. Science can thus preserve its transcendent quality because '[t]he state spends large amounts of money to enable science to pass itself off as an epic: the State's own credibility is based on that epic' (27–8).

But the crucial point about Lyotard's analysis of this reliance on metanarratives is that postmodernity has thrown it into crisis. It is not just Lyotard himself who is suspicious of metanarratives, but there exists a *general* disbelief in them. In crucial areas of contemporary life – politics, for example – metanarratives have begun to disappear and be replaced by what the philosopher Wittgenstein referred to as 'language games', where truth is a matter of rhetoric and performativity.

Unlike Lyotard, Jean Baudrillard performs 'anti-totalisation' rather than speaks about it directly. He seems to work as hard as he can to avoid his work coming to seem like a project or a system. He never offers rigorously theorised definitions of his major terms, preferring instead to utter enigmatic, hyperbolic statements. This means that when it comes to the concept which has proved most important in postmodernism, simulation (as summarised in my Introduction), we can often appreciate his rhetoric and respond to his examples, but it is sometimes hard to smooth over the gaps in his theory. As rhetoric, however, his work is fascinating, and hugely influential in postmodern theory. The essay represented here, 'The Precession of Simulacra' (a kind of companion piece to his earlier 'The Order of Simulacra' (Baudrillard, 1993) which covers similar ground), presents us with Baudrillard in one of his most convincing guises, as cultural critic, surveying examples of the hyperreal. A measure of the pertinency of these examples is the fact that, even though the essay was written in the early 1980s about a cultural landscape which was subject to bewilderingly swift change – in fact because of some of the factors Baudrillard speaks of – we could add new examples to the ones he provides in this essay and its case would only be strengthened. For example, we can add Clinton quite comfortably to his list of hyperreal US presidents after Kennedy, and we can usefully apply his comments on '*TV vérité*' (what we know now as 'reality TV') to *Big Brother*.

The next two extracts both define postmodernism in similar ways, as a cultural style which demonstrates a complex relationship to the past. As a result, they remind us that postmodernism is an aesthetic practice as well as an academic theory. The first is a brief chapter from the Italian novelist and semiotician Umberto Eco's *Reflections on* The Name of the Rose. Eco's novel *The Name of the Rose* is commonly regarded as a classic postmodernist text, and by imposing a modern form – the detective novel – onto events in the Middle Ages so that the modern form becomes contaminated by a counter (anti-rationalist) logic to its own, it exhibits precisely the attitude to history he theorises in the later book. Unlike the previous essays in this section, Eco suggests that postmodernism is not a style typical of a particular period in cultural history, but an *attitude* which can be seen in texts from any period: 'We could say that every period has its own postmodernism'. The postmodern comes into being whenever what happens to be 'modern' in a particular era – that is the avant-garde, which typically 'destroys' the past – realises that it cannot cannot proceed any further without lapsing into silence. The only solution is therefore to engage with the past once again. Specifically this engagement is made through the use of irony, a paradoxical form of language which says something new, but only by acknowledging the fact that it has *already* been said elsewhere.

Charles Jencks does not share Eco's 'metahistorical' view of postmodernism, but quotes with approval his analysis of its style. Postmodernism in Jencks' formation is primarily a willingness to strike contradictory poses and mix a range of aesthetic styles. It is governed by what he calls 'double coding' – an ironic strategy which resembles Eco's postmodern attitude. In architectural practice double coding means 'the combination of Modern techniques with something else (usually traditional building) in order for architecture to communicate with the public and [. . .] other architects'. Thus it manages to combine the elite with the popular and the old with the new. Most provocatively, however, the logic of Jencks' argument is such that if we accept this, we must also accept that a third term is required to explain the relation between postmodernism and modernism: 'late modernism'. Lyotard, Baudrillard and Jameson are included in a long list of theorists who Charles Jencks thinks have got it wrong about postmodernism because they mistake the 'late modern' for what is properly *post*modern. Late modernism, Jencks argues, is 'still committed to the tradition of the new and does not have a complex relation to the past, or pluralism, or the transformation of western culture – a concern with meaning, continuity and symbolism' (Jencks, 1986: 33–4).

The final essay in this section comes from the Slovenian philosopher Slavoj Žižek. If Jameson is the Hollywood hero of postmodern theory, Žižek is its 'stand-up theorist'. He is one of a new breed of academic 'star', a fixture on the conference circuit and in the media, continually cited in a wide range of academic books and articles, present on our bookshelves in the form of an apparently endless stream of publications – approaching 20 books in just over ten years. Like Jameson Žižek's work precociously blends references to 'high' and popular culture. But where the energy of Jameson's work seems to emerge from precisely the kind of modernist anxiety he laments in his analyses of postmodern culture, so Žižek's springs from the euphoria of being fully immersed in the culture he diagnoses. Like Baudrillard, Žižek is a thoroughly postmodern theorist in terms of the style of his work. His case, though, seems to be the theoretical equivalent to the kind of ironic attitude Umberto Eco regards as central to postmodern fiction. That is to say that most of his major points are made via a reference to those theorists – especially the psychoanalyst Jacques Lacan – who have already said what he wants to say (Žižek's own 'manifesto', *The Ticklish Subject* (2000), for example, begins as an ironic pastiche of *The Communist Manifesto*). Žižek's work revolves around the idea that postmodern society and culture testify to a significant shift in the very nature of subjectivity (social identity). Where society used to function by obeisance to what Lacan calls 'the symbolic order' or ('Big Other'), that is the various rules, injunctions and prohibitions which make us into social beings, postmodernity is characterised by a disregard for these, or an *ironic* adherence to them. The situation is complicated by the operation of what we might call the 'postmodern superego', that part of the psyche which urges us to act according to normative moral codes. Where the symbolic issues a straightforward injunction, the superego backs this up by urging you to *enjoy* what you have to do. This emphasis on enjoyment characterises postmodern culture.

'You May!' is untypical of Žižek in a sense as it is essentially a work of journalism (it was published in the *London Review of Books*, and Žižek tends to publish in academic journals or books). But his awareness of its readership makes it one of his most accessible pieces for the uninitiated, and also the one which expresses most concisely some of his views on postmodern subjectivity. It is classic Žižek, though, in its audacious blend of diverse cultural references, its humour, and in the fact that he feels no need to suggest *how* this new cultural attitude came about. Popular culture is simply taken as the proof of the new sensibility without the need to explain exactly which wider social and economic forces inform it. In this respect Žižek is very unlike totalising theorists like Jameson, Harvey and Huyssen, and makes them seem very earnest, very *modernist*, indeed.

WORKS CITED

Baudrillard, Jean (1993) *Simulacra and Simulation.* Ann Arbor, MI: University of Michigan Press.

Bell, Daniel (1973) *The Coming of Post-Industrial Society.* New York: Basic Books.

Harvey, David (1989) *The Condition of Postmodernity: An Enquiry into the Origins of Cultural Change.* Oxford: Blackwell.

Huyssen, Andreas (1986) *After the Great Divide: Modernism, Mass Culture, Postmodernism.* Bloomington, IN: Indiana University Press.

Jameson, Fredric (1992) *The Geo-political Aesthetic.* London: British Film Institute Publishing.

Jencks, Charles (1986) *What is Post-Modernism?* London: Academy.

Kellner, Douglas (ed.) (1989) *Postmodernism/Jameson/Critique.* Washington, DC: Maisonneuve Press.

Lyotard, Jean-François (1984) *The Postmodern Condition* [1979]. Manchester: Manchester University Press/Madison, WI: University of Wisconsin Press.

Mandel, Ernest (1978) *Late Capitalism.* London: New Left Books.

Touraine, Alain (1974) *The Post-Industrial Society, Tomorrow's Social History: Classes, Conflicts and Culture in the Programmed Society* [1969], trans. Leonard F. X. Mayhew. London: Wildwood House.

Žižek, Slavoj (2000) *The Ticklish Subject.* London and New York: Verso.

MAPPING POSTMODERNISM

I

'THE CULTURAL LOGIC OF LATE CAPITALISM'

Fredric Jameson

The last few years have been marked by an inverted millenarianism in which premonitions of the future, catastrophic or redemptive, have been replaced by senses of the end of this or that (the end of ideology, art, or social class; the 'crisis' of Leninism, social democracy, or the welfare state, etc., etc.); taken together, all of these perhaps constitute what is increasingly called postmodernism. The case for its existence depends on the hypothesis of some radical break or *coupure*, generally traced back to the end of the 1950s or the early 1960s.

As the word itself suggests, this break is most often related to notions of the waning or extinction of the hundred-year-old modern movement (or to its ideological or aesthetic repudiation). Thus abstract expressionism in painting, existentialism in philosophy, the final forms of representation in the novel, the films of the great auteurs, or the modernist school of poetry (as institutionalized and canonized in the works of Wallace Stevens) all are now seen as the final, extraordinary flowering of a high-modernist impulse which is spent and exhausted with them. The enumeration of what follows, then, at once becomes empirical, chaotic, and heterogeneous: Andy Warhol and pop art, but also photorealism, and beyond it, the 'new expressionism'; the moment, in music, of John Cage, but also the synthesis of classical and 'popular' styles found in composers like Phil Glass and Terry Riley, and also punk and new wave rock (the Beatles and the Stones now standing as the high-modernist moment of that more recent and rapidly evolving tradition); in film, Godard, post-Godard, and

From Fredric Jameson (1991) *Postmodernism, or, The Cultural Logic of Late Capitalism*. London and New York: Verso.

experimental cinema and video, but also a whole new type of commercial film (about which more below); Burroughs, Pynchon, or Ishmael Reed, on the one hand, and the French *nouveau roman* and its succession, on the other, along with alarming new kinds of literary criticism based on some new aesthetic of textuality or *écriture* ... The list might be extended indefinitely; but does it imply any more fundamental change or break than the periodic style and fashion changes determined by an older high-modernist imperative of stylistic innovation?

It is in the realm of architecture, however, that modifications in aesthetic production are most dramatically visible, and that their theoretical problems have been most centrally raised and articulated [...]

Postmodernism in architecture [...] has at least the merit of drawing our attention to one fundamental feature of all the postmodernisms enumerated above: namely, the effacement in them of the older (essentially high-modernist) frontier between high culture and so-called mass or commercial culture, and the emergence of new kinds of texts infused with the forms, categories, and contents of that very culture industry so passionately denounced by all the ideologues of the modern, from Leavis and the American New Criticism all the way to Adorno and the Frankfurt School. The postmodernisms have, in fact, been fascinated precisely by this whole 'degraded' landscape of schlock and kitsch, of TV series and *Reader's Digest* culture, of advertising and motels, of the late show and the grade-B Hollywood film, of so-called paraliterature, with its airport paperback categories of the gothic and the romance, the popular biography, the murder mystery, and the science fiction or fantasy novel: materials they no longer simply 'quote,' as a Joyce or a Mahler might have done, but incorporate into their very substance.

Nor should the break in question be thought of as a purely cultural affair: indeed, theories of the postmodern – whether celebratory or couched in the language of moral revulsion and denunciation – bear a strong family resemblance to all those more ambitious sociological generalizations which, at much the same time, bring us the news of the arrival and inauguration of a whole new type of society, most famously baptized 'postindustrial society' (Daniel Bell) but often also designated consumer society, media society, information society, electronic society or high tech, and the like. Such theories have the obvious ideological mission of demonstrating, to their own relief, that the new social formation in question no longer obeys the laws of classical capitalism, namely, the primacy of industrial production and the omnipresence of class struggle. The Marxist tradition has therefore resisted them with vehemence, with the signal exception of the economist Ernest Mandel, whose book *Late Capitalism* sets out not merely to anatomize the historic originality of this new society (which he sees as a third stage or moment in the evolution of capital) but also to demonstrate that it is, if anything, a *purer* stage of capitalism than any of the moments that preceded it. I will return to this argument later; suffice it for the moment to anticipate a point that will be argued, late, namely, that every position on postmodernism in culture – whether apologia or stigmatization – is also at one and the same time, and *necessarily*, an implicitly or explicitly political stance on the nature of multinational capitalism today.

A last preliminary word on method: what follows is not to be read as stylistic description, as the account of one cultural style or movement among others. I have rather meant to offer a periodizing hypothesis, and that at a moment in which the very conception of historical periodization has come to seem most problematical indeed. I have argued elsewhere that all isolated or discrete cultural analysis always involves a buried or repressed theory of historical periodization; in any case, the conception of the 'genealogy' largely lays to rest traditional theoretical worries about so-called linear history, theories of 'stages,' and teleological historiography. In the present context, however, lengthier theoretical discussion of such (very real) issues can perhaps be replaced by a few substantive remarks.

One of the concerns frequently aroused by periodizing hypotheses is that these tend to obliterate difference and to project an idea of the historical period as massive homogeneity (bounded on either side by inexplicable chronological metamorphoses and punctuation marks). This is, however, precisely why it seems to me essential to grasp postmodernism not as a style but rather as a cultural dominant: a conception which allows for the presence and coexistence of a range of very different, yet subordinate, features.

Consider, for example, the powerful alternative position that postmodernism is itself little more than one more stage of modernism proper (if not, indeed, of the even older romanticism); it may indeed be conceded that all the features of postmodernism I am about to enumerate can be detected, full-blown, in this or that preceding modernism (including such astonishing genealogical precursors as Gertrude Stein, Raymond Roussel, or Marcel Duchamp, who may be considered outright postmodernists, avant la lettre). What has not been taken into account by this view, however, is the social position of the older modernism, or better still, its passionate repudiation by an older Victorian and post-Victorian bourgeoisie for whom its forms and ethos are received as being variously ugly, dissonant, obscure, scandalous, immoral, subversive, and generally 'antisocial.' It will be argued here, however, that a mutation in the sphere of culture has rendered such attitudes archaic. Not only are Picasso and Joyce no longer ugly; they now strike us, on the whole, as rather 'realistic,' and this is the result of a canonization and academic institutionalization of the modern movement generally that can be traced to the late 1950s. This is surely one of the most plausible explanations for the emergence of postmodernism itself, since the younger generation of the 1960s will now confront the formerly oppositional modern movement as a set of dead classics, which 'weigh like a nightmare on the brains of the living,' as Marx once said in a different context.

As for the postmodern revolt against all that, however, it must equally be stressed that its own offensive features – from obscurity and sexually explicit material to psychological squalor and overt expressions of social and political defiance, which transcend anything that might have been imagined at the most extreme moments of high modernism – no longer scandalize anyone and are not only received with the greatest complacency but have themselves become institutionalized and are at one with the official or public culture of Western society.

What has happened is that aesthetic production today has become integrated into commodity production generally: the frantic economic urgency of producing fresh waves of ever more novel-seeming goods (from clothing to airplanes), at ever greater rates of turnover, now assigns an increasingly essential structural function and position to aesthetic innovation and experimentation. Such economic necessities then find recognition in the varied kinds of institutional support available for the newer art, from foundations and grants to museums and other forms of patronage. Of all the arts, architecture is the closest constitutively to the economic, with which, in the form of commissions and land values, it has a virtually unmediated relationship. It will therefore not be surprising to find the extraordinary flowering of the new postmodern architecture grounded in the patronage of multinational business, whose expansion and development is strictly contemporaneous with it. Later I will suggest that these two new phenomena have an even deeper dialectical interrelationship than the simple one-to-one financing of this or that individual project. Yet this is the point at which I must remind the reader of the obvious; namely, that this whole global, yet American, postmodern culture is the internal and superstructural expression of a whole new wave of American military and economic domination throughout the world: in this sense, as throughout class history, the underside of culture is blood, torture, death, and terror.

The first point to be made about the conception of periodization in dominance, therefore, is that even if all the constitutive features of postmodernism were identical with and continuous to those of an older modernism – a position I feel to be demonstrably erroneous but which only an even lengthier analysis of modernism proper could dispel – the two phenomena would still remain utterly distinct in their meaning and social function, owing to the very different positioning of postmodernism in the economic system of late capital and, beyond that, to the transformation of the very sphere of culture in contemporary society.

[...]

I have felt, however, that it was only in the light of some conception of a dominant cultural logic or hegemonic norm that genuine difference could be measured and assessed. I am very far from feeling that all cultural production today is 'postmodern' in the broad sense I will be conferring on this term. The postmodern is, however, the force field in which very different kinds of cultural impulses – what Raymond Williams has usefully termed 'residual' and 'emergent' forms of cultural production – must make their way. If we do not achieve some general sense of a cultural dominant, then we fall back into a view of present history as sheer heterogeneity, random difference, a coexistence of a host of distinct forces whose effectivity is undecidable. At any rate, this has been the political spirit in which the following analysis was devised: to project some conception of a new systematic cultural norm and its reproduction in order to reflect more adequately on the most effective forms of any radical cultural politics today.

The exposition will take up in turn the following constitutive features of the postmodern: a new depthlessness, which finds its prolongation both in contemporary 'theory' and in a whole new culture of the image or the simulacrum; a consequent weakening of historicity, both in our relationship to public History and in the new forms of our private temporality, whose 'schizophrenic' structure (following Lacan) will determine new types of syntax or syntagmatic relationships in the more temporal arts; a whole new type of emotional ground tone – what I will call 'intensities' – which can best be grasped by a return to older theories of the sublime; the deep constitutive relationships of all this to a whole new technology, which is itself a figure for a whole new economic world system; and, after a brief account of postmodernist mutations in the lived experience of built space itself, some reflections on the mission of political art in the bewildering new world space of late or multinational capital.

I

[...]

This is perhaps the moment to say something about contemporary theory, which has, among other things, been committed to the mission of criticizing and discrediting this very hermeneutic model of the inside and the outside and of stigmatizing such models as ideological and metaphysical. But what is today called contemporary theory – or better still, theoretical discourse – is also, I want to argue, itself very precisely a postmodernist phenomenon. It would therefore be inconsistent to defend the truth of its theoretical insights in a situation in which the very concept of 'truth' itself is part of the metaphysical baggage which poststructuralism seeks to abandon. What we can at least suggest is that the poststructuralist critique of the hermeneutic, of what I will shortly call the depth model, is useful for us as a very significant symptom of the very postmodernist culture which is our subject here.

Overhastily, we can say that besides the hermeneutic model of inside and outside which Munch's painting develops, at least four other fundamental depth models have generally been repudiated in contemporary theory: (1) the dialectical one of essence and appearance (along with a whole range of concepts of ideology or false consciousness which tend to accompany it); (2) the Freudian model of latent and manifest, or of repression (which is, of course, the target of Michel Foucault's programmatic and symptomatic pamphlet *La Volonté de savoir* [*The History of Sexuality*]); (3) the existential model of authenticity and inauthenticity whose heroic or tragic thematics are closely related to that other great opposition between alienation and disalienation, itself equally a casualty of the poststructural or postmodern period; and (4) most recently, the great semiotic opposition between signifier and signified, which was itself rapidly unraveled and deconstructed during its brief heyday in the 1960s and 1970s. What replaces these various depth models is for the most part a conception of practices, discourses, and textual play, whose new syntagmatic structures we will examine later on; let it suffice now to observe that here too depth is replaced by surface, or by multiple surfaces (what is often called intertextuality is in that sense no longer a matter of depth).

Nor is this depthlessness merely metaphorical: it can be experienced physically and 'literally' by anyone who, mounting what used to be Raymond Chandler's Bunker Hill from the great Chicano markets on Broadway and Fourth Street in downtown Los Angeles, suddenly confronts the great free-standing wall of Wells Fargo Court (Skidmore, Owings and Merrill) – a surface which seems to be unsupported by any volume, or whose putative volume (rectangular? trapezoidal?) is ocularly quite undecidable. This great sheet of windows, with its gravity-defying two-dimensionality, momentarily transforms the solid ground on which we stand into the contents of a stereopticon, pasteboard shapes profiling themselves here and there around us. The visual effect is the same from all sides: as fateful as the great monolith in Stanley Kubrick's *2001* which confronts its viewers like an enigmatic destiny, a call to evolutionary mutation. If this new multinational downtown effectively abolished the older ruined city fabric which it violently replaced, cannot something similar be said about the way in which this strange new surface in its own peremptory way renders our older systems of perception of the city somehow archaic and aimless, without offering another in their place?

[...]

All of which suggests some more general historical hypothesis: namely, that concepts such as anxiety and alienation (and the experiences to which they correspond, as in *The Scream*) are no longer appropriate in the world of the postmodern. The great Warhol figures – Marilyn herself or Edie Sedgewick – the notorious cases of burnout and self-destruction of the ending 1960s, and the great dominant experiences of drugs and schizophrenia, would seem to have little enough in common any more either with the hysterics and neurotics of Freud's own day or with those canonical experiences of radical isolation and solitude, anomie, private revolt, Van Gogh-type madness, which dominated the period of high modernism. This shift in the dynamics of cultural pathology can be characterized as one in which the alienation of the subject is displaced by the latter's fragmentation.

Such terms inevitably recall one of the more fashionable themes in contemporary theory, that of the 'death' of the subject itself – the end of the autonomous bourgeois monad or ego or individual – and the accompanying stress, whether as some new moral ideal or as empirical description, on the *decentering* of that formerly centered subject or psyche. [...]

[...] The end of the bourgeois ego, or monad, no doubt brings with it the end of the psychopathologies of that ego – what I have been calling the waning of affect. But it means the end of much more – the end, for example, of style, in the sense of the unique and the personal, the end of the distinctive individual brush stroke (as symbolized by the emergent primacy of mechanical reproduction). As for expression and feelings or emotions, the liberation, in contemporary society, from the older *anomie* of the centered subject may also mean not merely a liberation from anxiety but a liberation from every other kind of feeling as well, since there is no longer a self present to do the feeling. This is not to say that the cultural products of the postmodern era are utterly devoid of feeling, but rather that such feelings – which it may be better and more accurate, following J.-F. Lyotard, to call 'intensities' – are now free-floating and impersonal and tend to be dominated by a peculiar kind of euphoria, a matter to which we will want to return later on.

The waning of affect, however, might also have been characterized, in the narrower context of literary criticism, as the waning of the great high modernist thematics of time and temporality, the elegiac mysteries of *durée* and memory (something to be understood fully as much as a category of the literary criticism associated with high modernism as with the works themselves). We have often been told, however, that we now inhabit the synchronic rather than the diachronic, and I think it is at least empirically arguable that our daily life, our psychic experience, our cultural languages, are today dominated by categories of space rather than by categories of time, as in the preceding period of high modernism.[1]

II

The disappearance of the individual subject, along with its formal consequence, the increasing unavailability of the personal style, engender the well-nigh universal practice today of what may be called pastiche. This concept, which we owe to Thomas Mann (in *Doktor Faustus*), who owed it in turn to Adorno's great work on the two paths of advanced musical experimentation (Schoenberg's innovative planification and Stravinsky's irrational eclecticism), is to be sharply distinguished from the more readily received idea of parody.

To be sure, parody found a fertile area in the idiosyncracies of the moderns and their 'inimitable' styles: the Faulknerian long sentence, for example, with its breathless gerundives; Lawrentian nature imagery punctuated by testy colloquialism; Wallace Stevens's inveterate hypostasis of nonsubstantive parts of speech ('the intricate evasions of as'); the fateful (but finally predictable) swoops in Mahler from high orchestral pathos into village accordion sentiment; Heidegger's meditative-solemn practice of the false etymology as a mode of 'proof' ... All these strike one as somehow characteristic, insofar as they ostentatiously deviate from a norm which then reasserts itself, in a not necessarily unfriendly way, by a systematic mimicry of their willful eccentricities.

Yet in the dialectical leap from quantity to quality, the explosion of modern literature into a host of distinct private styles and mannerisms has been followed by a linguistic fragmentation of social life itself to the point where the norm itself is eclipsed: reduced to a neutral and reified media speech (far enough from the Utopian aspirations of the inventors of Esperanto or Basic English), which itself then becomes but one more idiolect among many. Modernist styles thereby become postmodernist codes. And that the stupendous proliferation of social codes today into professional and disciplinary jargons (but also into the badges of affirmation of ethnic, gender, race, religious, and class-factional adhesion) is also a political phenomenon, the problem of micropolitics suffi- ciently demonstrates. If the ideas of a ruling class were once the dominant (or hegemonic) ideology of bourgeois society, the advanced capitalist countries today are now a field of stylistic and discursive heterogeneity without a norm. Faceless masters continue to inflect the economic strategies which constrain our existences, but they no longer need to impose their speech (or are henceforth unable to); and the postliteracy of the late capitalist world reflects not only the absence of any great collective project but also the unavailability of the older national language itself.

In this situation parody finds itself without a vocation; it has lived, and that strange new thing pastiche slowly comes to take its place. Pastiche is, like parody, the imitation of a peculiar or unique, idiosyncratic style, the wearing of a linguistic mask, speech in a dead language. But it is a neutral practice of such mimicry, without any of parody's ulterior motives, amputated of the satiric impulse, devoid of laughter and of any conviction that alongside the abnormal tongue you have momentarily borrowed, some healthy linguistic normality still exists. Pastiche is thus blank parody, a statue with blind eyeballs: it is to parody what that other interesting and historically original modern thing, the practice of a kind of blank irony, is to what Wayne Booth calls the 'stable ironies' of the eighteenth century.

It would therefore begin to seem that Adorno's prophetic diagnosis has been realized, albeit in a negative way: not Schœnberg (the sterility of whose achieved system he already glimpsed) but Stravinsky is the true precursor of postmodern cultural production. For with the collapse of the high-modernist ideology of style – what is as unique and unmistakable as your own fingerprints, as incomparable as your own body (the very source, for an early Roland Barthes, of stylistic invention and innovation) – the producers of culture have nowhere to turn but to the past: the imitation of dead styles, speech through all the masks and voices stored up in the imaginary museum of a now global culture.

This situation evidently determines what the architecture historians call 'historicism,' namely, the random cannibalization of all the styles of the past, the play of random stylistic allusion, and in general what Henri Lefebvre has called the increasing primacy of the 'neo.' This omnipresence of pastiche is not incompatible with a certain humor, however, nor is it innocent of all passion: it is at the least compatible with addiction – with a whole historically original consumers' appetite for a world transformed into sheer images of itself and for pseudoevents and 'spectacles' (the term of the situationists). It is for such objects that we may reserve Plato's conception of the 'simulacrum,' the identical copy for which no original has ever existed. Appropriately enough, the culture of the simulacrum comes to life in a society where exchange value has been generalized to the point at which the very memory of use value is effaced, a society of which Guy Debord has observed, in an extraordinary phrase, that in it 'the image has become the final form of commodity reification' (*The Society of the Spectacle*).

The new spatial logic of the simulacrum can now be expected to have a momentous effect on what used to be historical time. The past is thereby itself modified: what was once, in the historical novel as Lukács defines it, the organic genealogy of the bourgeois collective project – what is still, for the redemptive historiography of an E. P. Thompson or of American 'oral history,' for the resurrection of the dead of anonymous and silenced generations, the retrospective dimension indispensable to any vital reorientation of our collective future – has meanwhile itself become a vast collection of images, a multitudinous photographic simulacrum. Guy Debord's powerful slogan is now even more apt for the 'prehistory' of a society bereft of all historicity, one whose own putative past is little more than a set of dusty spectacles. In faithful conformity to poststructuralist linguistic theory, the past as 'referent' finds itself gradually bracketed, and then effaced altogether, leaving us with nothing but texts.

Yet it should not be thought that this process is accompanied by indifference: on the contrary, the remarkable current intensification of an addiction to the photographic image is itself a tangible symptom of an omnipresent, omnivorous, and well-nigh libidinal historicism. As I have already observed, the architects use this (exceedingly polysemous) word for the complacent eclecticism of postmodern architecture, which randomly and without principle but with gusto cannibalizes all the architectural styles of the past and combines them in overstimulating ensembles. Nostalgia does not strike one as an altogether satisfactory word for such fascination (particularly when one thinks of the pain of a properly modernist nostalgia with a past beyond all but aesthetic retrieval), yet it directs our attention to what is a culturally far more generalized manifestation of the process in commercial art and taste, namely the so-called nostalgia film (or what the French call *la mode rétro*).

Nostalgia films restructure the whole issue of pastiche and project it onto a collective and social level, where the desperate attempt to appropriate a missing past is now refracted through the iron law of fashion change and the emergent ideology of the generation. The inaugural film of this new aesthetic discourse, George Lucas's *American Graffiti* (1973), set out to recapture, as so many films have attempted since, the henceforth mesmerizing lost reality of the Eisenhower era; and one tends to feel, that for Americans at least, the 1950s remain the privileged lost object of desire – not merely the stability and prosperity of a pax Americana but also the first naïve innocence of the countercultural impulses of early rock and roll and youth gangs (Coppola's *Rumble Fish* will then be the contemporary dirge that laments their passing, itself, however, still contradictorily filmed in genuine nostalgia film style). With this initial breakthrough, other generational periods open up for aesthetic colonization: as witness the stylistic recuperation of the American and the Italian 1930s, in Polanski's *Chinatown* and Bertolucci's *Il Conformista*, respectively. More interesting, and more problematical, are the ultimate attempts, through this new discourse, to lay siege either to our own present and immediate past or to a more distant history that escapes individual existential memory.

Faced with these ultimate objects – our social, historical, and existential present, and the past as 'referent' – the incompatibility of a postmodernist 'nostalgia' art language with genuine historicity becomes dramatically apparent. The contradiction propels this mode, however, into complex and interesting new formal inventiveness; it being understood that the nostalgia film was never a matter of some old-fashioned 'representation' of historical content, but instead approached the 'past' through stylistic connotation, conveying 'pastness' by the glossy qualities of the image, and '1930s-ness' or '1950s-ness' by the attributes of fashion [...]

As for 'real history' itself – the traditional object, however it may be defined, of what used to be the historical novel – it will be more revealing now to turn back to that older form and medium and to read its postmodern fate in the work of one of the few serious and innovative leftist novelists at work in the United States today, whose books are nourished with history in the more traditional sense and seem, so far, to stake out successive generational moments in the 'epic' of American history, between which they alternate. E. L. Doctorow's *Ragtime* gives itself officially as a panorama of the first two decades of the century (like *World's Fair*); his most recent novel, *Billy Bathgate*, like *Loon Lake* addresses the thirties and the Great Depression, while *The Book of Daniel* holds up before us, in painful juxtaposition, the two great moments of the Old Left and the New Left, of thirties and forties communism and the radicalism of the 1960s (even his early western may be said to fit into this scheme and to designate in a less articulated and formally self-conscious way the end of the frontier of the late nineteenth century).

The Book of Daniel is not the only one of these five major historical novels to establish an explicit narrative link between the reader's and the writer's present and the older historical reality that is the subject of the work; the astonishing last page of *Loon Lake*, which I will not disclose, also does this in a very different way; it is a matter of some interest to note that the first version of *Ragtime*[2] positions us explicitly in our own present, in the novelist's house in New Rochelle, New York, which at once becomes the scene of its own (imaginary) past in the 1900s. This detail has been suppressed from the published text, symbolically cutting its moorings and freeing the novel to float in some new world of past historical time whose relationship to us is problematical indeed. The authenticity of the gesture, however, may be measured by the evident existential fact of life that there no longer does seem to be any organic relationship between the American history we learn from schoolbooks and the lived experience of the current multinational, high-rise, stagflated city of the newspapers and of our own everyday life.

A crisis in historicity, however, inscribes itself symptomatically in several other curious formal features within this text. Its official subject is the transition from a pre-World War I radical and working-class politics (the great strikes) to the technological invention and new commodity production of the 1920s (the rise of Hollywood and of the image as commodity): the interpolated version of Kleist's *Michael Kohlhaas*, the strange, tragic episode of the black protagonist's revolt, may be thought of as a moment related to this process. That *Ragtime* has political content and even something like a political 'meaning' seems in any case obvious and has been expertly articulated by Linda Hutcheon in terms of

> its three paralleled families: the Anglo-American establishment one and the marginal immigrant European and American black ones. The novel's action disperses the center of the first and moves the margins into the multiple 'centers' of the narrative, in a formal allegory of the social demographics of urban America. In addition, there is an extended critique of American democratic ideals through the presentation of class conflict rooted in capitalist property and moneyed power. The black Coalhouse, the white Houdini, the immigrant Tateh are all working class, and because of this – not in spite of it – all can therefore work to create new aesthetic forms (ragtime, vaudeville, movies).[3]

But this does everything but the essential, lending the novel an admirable thematic coherence few readers can have experienced in parsing the lines of a verbal object held too close to the eyes to fall into these perspectives. Hutcheon is, of course, absolutely right, and this is what the novel would have meant had it not been a postmodern artifact. For one thing, the objects of representation, ostensibly narrative characters, are incommensurable and, as it were, of incomparable substances, like oil and water – Houdini being a *historical* figure, Tateh a *fictional* one, and Goalhouse an *intertextual* one – something very difficult for an interpretive comparison of this kind to register. Meanwhile, the theme attributed to the novel also demands a somewhat different kind of scrutiny, since it can be rephrased into a classic version of the Left's 'experience of defeat' in the twentieth century, namely, the proposition that the depoliticization of the workers' movement is attributable to the media or culture generally (what she here calls 'new aesthetic forms'). This is, indeed, in my opinion, something like the elegiac backdrop, if not the meaning, of *Ragtime*, and perhaps of Doctorow's work in general; but then we need another way of describing the novel as something like an unconscious expression and associative exploration of this left doxa, this historical opinion or quasi-vision in the mind's eye of 'objective spirit.' What such a description would want to register is the paradox that a seemingly realistic novel like

Ragtime is in reality a nonrepresentational work that combines fantasy signifiers from a variety of ideologemes in a kind of hologram.

My point, however, is not some hypothesis as to the thematic coherence of
this decentered narrative but rather just the opposite, namely, the way in which
the kind of reading this novel imposes makes it virtually impossible for us to
reach and thematize those official 'subjects' which float above the text but
cannot be integrated into our reading of the sentences. In that sense, the novel
not only resists interpretation, it is organized systematically and formally to
short-circuit an older type of social and historical interpretation which it
perpetually holds out and withdraws. When we remember that the theoretical
critique and repudiation of interpretation as such is a fundamental component
of poststructuralist theory, it is difficult not to conclude that Doctorow has
somehow deliberately built this very tension, this very contradiction, into the
flow of his sentences.

The book is crowded with real historical figures – from Teddy Roosevelt to
Emma Goldman, from Harry K. Thaw and Stanford White to J. Pierpont
Morgan and Henry Ford, not to mention the more central role of Houdini –
who interact with a fictive family, simply designated as Father, Mother, Older
Brother, and so forth. All historical novels, beginning with those of Sir Walter
Scott himself, no doubt in one way or another involve a mobilization of
previous historical knowledge generally acquired through the schoolbook
history manuals devised for whatever legitimizing purpose by this or that
national tradition – thereafter instituting a narrative dialectic between what
we already 'know' about The Pretender, say, and what he is then seen to be
concretely in the pages of the novel. But Doctorow's procedure seems much
more extreme than this; and I would argue that the designation of both types of
characters – historical names and capitalized family roles – operates powerfully
and systematically to reify all these characters and to make it impossible for us
to receive their representation without the prior interception of already
acquired knowledge or doxa – something which lends the text an extraordinary
sense of déjà vu and a peculiar familiarity one is tempted to associate with
Freud's 'return of the repressed' in 'The Uncanny' rather than with any solid
historiographic formation on the reader's part.

Meanwhile, the sentences in which all this is happening have their own
specificity, allowing us more concretely to distinguish the moderns' elaboration
of a personal style from this new kind of linguistic innovation, which is no
longer personal at all but has its family kinship rather with what Barthes long
ago called 'white writing.' In this particular novel, Doctorow has imposed upon
himself a rigorous principle of selection in which only simple declarative
sentences (predominantly mobilized by the verb 'to be') are received. The effect
is, however, not really one of the condescending simplification and symbolic
carefulness of children's literature, but rather something more disturbing, the
sense of some profound subterranean violence done to American English, which
cannot, however, be detected empirically in any of the perfectly grammatical

sentences with which this work is formed. Yet other more visible technical 'innovations' may supply a clue to what is happening in the language of *Ragtime*: it is, for example, well known that the source of many of the characteristic effects of Camus's novel *The Stranger* can be traced back to that author's willful decision to substitute, throughout, the French tense of the *passé composé* for the other past tenses more normally employed in narration in that language.[4] I suggest that it is as if something of that sort were at work here: *as though* Doctorow had set out systematically to produce the effect or the equivalent, in his language, of a verbal past tense we do not possess in English, namely, the French preterite (or *passé simple*), whose 'perfective' movement, as Émile Benveniste taught us, serves to separate events from the present of enunciation and to transform the stream of time and action into so many finished, complete, and isolated punctual event objects which find themselves sundered from any present situation (even that of the act of story telling or enunciation).

E. L. Doctorow is the epic poet of the disappearance of the American radical past, of the suppression of older traditions and moments of the American radical tradition: no one with left sympathies can read these splendid novels without a poignant distress that is an authentic way of confronting our own current political dilemmas in the present. What is culturally interesting, however, is that he has had to convey this great theme formally (since the waning of the content is very precisely his subject) and, more than that, has had to elaborate his work by way of that very cultural logic of the postmodern which is itself the mark and symptom of his dilemma. *Loon Lake* much more obviously deploys the strategies of the pastiche (most notably in its reinvention of Dos Passos); but *Ragtime* remains the most peculiar and stunning monument to the aesthetic situation engendered by the disappearance of the historical referent. This historical novel can no longer set out to represent the historical past; it can only 'represent' our ideas and stereotypes about that past (which thereby at once becomes 'pop history'). Cultural production is thereby driven back inside a mental space which is no longer that of the old monadic subject but rather that of some degraded collective 'objective spirit': it can no longer gaze directly on some putative real world, at some reconstruction of a past history which was once itself a present; rather, as in Plato's cave, it must trace our mental images of that past upon its confining walls. If there is any realism left here, it is a 'realism' that is meant to derive from the shock of grasping that confinement and of slowly becoming aware of a new and original historical situation in which we are condemned to seek History by way of our own pop images and simulacra of that history, which itself remains forever out of reach.

III

The crisis in historicity now dictates a return, in a new way, to the question of temporal organization in general in the postmodern force field, and indeed, to the problem of the form that time, temporality, and the syntagmatic will be able to take in a culture increasingly dominated by space and spatial logic. If, indeed, the subject has lost its capacity actively to extend its pro-tensions and re-tensions across the temporal manifold and to organize its past and future into coherent experience, it becomes difficult enough to see how the cultural productions of such a subject could result in anything but 'heaps of fragments' and in a practice of the randomly heterogeneous and fragmentary and the aleatory. These are, however, very precisely some of the privileged terms in which postmodernist cultural production has been analyzed (and even defended, by its own apologists). They are, however, still privative features; the more substantive formulations bear such names as textuality, *écriture*, or schizophrenic writing, and it is to these that we must now briefly turn.

[...]

Very briefly, Lacan describes schizophrenia as a breakdown in the signifying chain, that is, the interlocking syntagmatic series of signifiers which constitutes an utterance or a meaning. I must omit the familial or more orthodox psycho-analytic background to this situation, which Lacan transcodes into language by describing the Oedipal rivalry in terms not so much of the biological individual who is your rival for the mother's attention but rather of what he calls the Name-of-the-Father, paternal authority now considered as a linguistic function.[5] His conception of the signifying chain essentially presupposes one of the basic principles (and one of the great discoveries) of Saussurean structuralism, namely, the proposition that meaning is not a one-to-one relationship between signifier and signified, between the materiality of language, between a word or a name, and its referent or concept. Meaning on the new view is generated by the movement from signifier to signifier. What we generally call the signified – the meaning or conceptual content of an utterance – is now rather to be seen as a meaning-effect, as that objective mirage of signification generated and projected by the relationship of signifiers among themselves. When that relationship breaks down, when the links of the signifying chain snap, then we have schizophrenia in the form of a rubble of distinct and unrelated signifiers. The connection between this kind of linguistic malfunction and the psyche of the schizophrenic may then be grasped by way of a twofold proposition: first, that personal identity is itself the effect of a certain temporal unification of past and future with one's present; and, second, that such active temporal unification is itself a function of language, or better still of the sentence, as it moves along its hermeneutic circle through time. If we are unable to unify the past, present, and future of the sentence, then we are similarly unable to unify the past, present, and future of our own biographical experience or psychic life. With the breakdown of the signifying chain, therefore, the schizophrenic is reduced to an experience of pure material signifiers, or, in other words, a series of pure and unrelated presents in time. We will want to ask questions about the aesthetic or cultural results of such a situation in a moment; let us first see what it feels like:

I remember very well the day it happened. We were staying in the country and I had gone for a walk alone as I did now and then. Suddenly, as I was passing the school, I heard a German song; the children were having a singing lesson. I stopped to listen, and at that instant a strange feeling came over me, a feeling hard to analyze but akin to something I was to know too well later – a disturbing sense of unreality. It seemed to me that I no longer recognized the school, it had become as large as a barracks; the singing children were prisoners, compelled to sing. It was as though the school and the children's song were set apart from the rest of the world. At the same time my eye encountered a field of wheat whose limits I could not see. The yellow vastness, dazzling in the sun, bound up with the song of the children imprisoned in the smooth stone school-barracks, filled me with such anxiety that I broke into sobs. I ran home to our garden and began to play 'to make things seem as they usually were,' that is, to return to reality. It was the first appearance of those elements which were always present in later sensations of unreality: illimitable vastness, brilliant light, and the gloss and smoothness of material things.[6]

In our present context, this experience suggests the following: first, the breakdown of temporality suddenly releases this present of time from all the activities and intentionalities that might focus it and make it a space of praxis; thereby isolated, that present suddenly engulfs the subject with undescribable vividness, a materiality of perception properly overwhelming, which effectively dramatizes the power of the material – or better still, the literal – signifier in isolation. This present of the world or material signifier comes before the subject with heightened intensity, bearing a mysterious charge of affect, here described in the negative terms of anxiety and loss of reality, but which one could just as well imagine in the positive terms of euphoria, a high, an intoxicatory or hallucinogenic intensity.

What happens in textuality or schizophrenic art is strikingly illuminated by such clinical accounts, although in the cultural text, the isolated signifier is no longer an enigmatic state of the world or an incomprehensible yet mesmerizing fragment of language but rather something closer to a sentence in free-standing isolation. Think, for example, of the experience of John Cage's music, in which a cluster of material sounds (on the prepared piano, for example) is followed by a silence so intolerable that you cannot imagine another sonorous chord coming into existence and cannot imagine remembering the previous one well enough to make any connection with it if it does. Some of Beckett's narratives are also of this order, most notably *Watt*, where a primacy of the present sentence in time ruthlessly disintegrates the narrative fabric that attempts to reform around it. [...]

IV

Now we need to complete this exploratory account of postmodernist space and time with a final analysis of that euphoria or those intensities which seem so often to characterize the newer cultural experience. Let us reemphasize the enormity of a transition which leaves behind it the desolation of Hopper's buildings or the stark Midwest syntax of Sheeler's forms, replacing them with the extraordinary surfaces of the photorealist cityscape, where even the automobile wrecks gleam with some new hallucinatory splendor. The exhilaration of these new surfaces is all the more paradoxical in that their essential content – the city itself – has deteriorated or disintegrated to a degree surely still inconceivable in the early years of the twentieth century, let alone in the previous era. How urban squalor can be a delight to the eyes when expressed in commodification, and how an unparalleled quantum leap in the alienation of daily life in the city can now be experienced in the form of a strange new hallucinatory exhilaration – these are some of the questions that confront us in this moment of our inquiry. Nor should the human figure be exempted from investigation, although it seems clear that for the newer aesthetic the representation of space itself has come to be felt as incompatible with the representation of the body: a kind of aesthetic division of labor far more pronounced than in any of the earlier generic conceptions of landscape, and a most ominous symptom indeed. The privileged space of the newer art is radically antianthropomorphic, as in the empty bathrooms of Doug Bond's work. The ultimate contemporary fetishization of the human body, however, takes a very different direction in the statues of Duane Hanson: what I have already called the simulacrum, whose peculiar function lies in what Sartre would have called the *derealization* of the whole surrounding world of everyday reality. Your moment of doubt and hesitation as to the breath and warmth of these polyester figures, in order words, tends to return upon the real human beings moving about you in the museum and to transform them also for the briefest instant into so many dead and flesh-colored simulacra in their own right. The world thereby momentarily loses its depth and threatens to become a glossy skin, a stereoscopic illusion, a rush of filmic images without density. But is this now a terrifying or an exhilarating experience?

It has proved fruitful to think of such experiences in terms of what Susan Sontag, in an influential statement, isolated as 'camp.' I propose a somewhat different cross-light on it, drawing on the equally fashionable current theme of the 'sublime,' as it has been rediscovered in the works of Edmund Burke and Kant; or perhaps one might want to yoke the two notions together in the form of something like a camp or 'hysterical' sublime. The sublime was for Burke an experience bordering on terror, the fitful glimpse, in astonishment, stupor, and awe, of what was so enormous as to crush human life altogether: a description then refined by Kant to include the question of representation itself, so that the object of the sublime becomes not only a matter of sheer power and of the physical incommensurability of the human organism with Nature but also of the limits of figuration and the incapacity of the human mind to give representation to such enormous forces. Such forces Burke, in his historical moment at the dawn of the modern bourgeois state, was only able to conceptualize in terms of the divine, while even Heidegger continues to entertain a phantasmatic relationship with some organic precapitalist peasant landscape and village society, which is the final form of the image of Nature in our own time.

Today, however, it may be possible to think all this in a different way, at the moment of a radical eclipse of Nature itself: Heidegger's 'field path' is, after all, irredeemably and irrevocably destroyed by late capital, by the green revolution, by neocolonialism and the megalopolis, which runs its superhighways over the older fields and vacant lots and turns Heidegger's 'house of being' into condominiums, if not the most miserable unheated, rat-infested tenement buildings. The *other* of our society is in that sense no longer Nature at all, as it was in precapitalist societies, but something else which we must now identify.

I am anxious that this other thing not overhastily be grasped as technology per se, since I will want to show that technology is here itself a figure for something else. Yet technology may well serve as adequate shorthand to designate that enormous properly human and anti-natural power of dead human labor stored up in our machinery – an alienated power, what Sartre calls the counterfinality of the practico-inert, which turns back on and against us in unrecognizable forms and seems to constitute the massive dystopian horizon of our collective as well as our individual praxis.

Technological development is however on the Marxist view the result of the development of capital rather than some ultimately determining instance in its own right. It will therefore be appropriate to distinguish several generations of machine power, several stages of technological revolution within capital itself. I here follow Ernest Mandel, who outlines three such fundamental breaks or quantum leaps in the evolution of machinery under capital:

> The fundamental revolutions in power technology – the technology of the production of motive machines by machines – thus appears as the determinant moment in revolutions of technology as a whole. Machine production of steam-driven motors since 1848; machine production of electric and combustion motors since the 90s of the 19th century; machine production of electronic and nuclear-powered apparatuses since the 40s of the 20th century – these are the three general revolutions in technology engendered by the capitalist mode of production since the 'original' industrial revolution of the later 18th century.[7]

This periodization underscores the general thesis of Mandel's book *Late Capitalism*; namely, that there have been three fundamental moments in capitalism, each one marking a dialectical expansion over the previous stage. These are market capitalism, the monopoly stage or the stage of imperialism, and our own, wrongly called postindustrial, but what might better be termed multinational, capital. I have already pointed out that Mandel's intervention in the postindustrial debate involves the proposition that late or multinational or consumer capitalism, far from being inconsistent with Marx's great nineteenth-century analysis, constitutes, on the contrary, the purest form of capital yet to have emerged, a prodigious expansion of capital into hitherto uncommodified areas. This purer capitalism of our own time thus eliminates the enclaves of precapitalist organization it had hitherto tolerated and exploited in a tributary way. One is tempted to speak in this connection of a new and historically original penetration and colonization of Nature and the Unconscious: that is, the destruction of precapitalist Third World agriculture by the Green Revolution, and the rise of the media and the advertising industry. At any rate, it will also have been clear that my own cultural periodization of the stages of realism, modernism, and postmodernism is both inspired and confirmed by Mandel's tripartite scheme.

We may therefore speak of our own period as the Third Machine Age; and it is at this point that we must reintroduce the problem of aesthetic representation already explicitly developed in Kant's earlier analysis of the sublime, since it would seem only logical that the relationship to and the representation of the machine could be expected to shift dialectically with each of these qualitatively different stages of technological development.

It is appropriate to recall the excitement of machinery in the moment of capital preceding our own, the exhilaration of futurism, most notably, and of Marinetti's celebration of the machine gun and the motorcar. These are still visible emblems, sculptural nodes of energy which give tangibility and figuration to the motive energies of that earlier moment of modernization. The prestige of these great streamlined shapes can be measured by their metaphorical presence in Le Corbusier's buildings, vast Utopian structures which ride like so many gigantic steamship liners upon the urban scenery of an older fallen earth.[8] Machinery exerts another kind of fascination in the works of artists like Picabia and Duchamp, whom we have no time to consider here; but let me mention, for completeness' sake, the ways in which revolutionary or communist artists of the 1930s also sought to reappropriate this excitement of machine energy for a Promethean reconstruction of human society as a whole, as in Fernand Léger and Diego Rivera.

It is immediately obvious that the technology of our own moment no longer possesses this same capacity for representation: not the turbine, nor even Sheeler's grain elevators or smokestacks, not the baroque elaboration of pipes and conveyor belts, nor even the streamlined profile of the railroad train – all vehicles of speed still concentrated at rest – but rather the computer, whose outer shell has no emblematic or visual power, or even the casings of the various media themselves, as with that home appliance called television which articulates nothing but rather implodes, carrying its flattened image surface within itself.

Such machines are indeed machines of reproduction rather than of production, and they make very different demands on our capacity for aesthetic representation than did the relatively mimetic idolatry of the older machinery of the futurist moment, of some older speed-and-energy sculpture. Here we have less to do with kinetic energy than with all kinds of new reproductive processes; and in the weaker productions of postmodernism the aesthetic embodiment of such processes often tends to slip back more comfortably into a mere thematic representation of content – into narratives which are *about* the processes of reproduction and include movie cameras, video, tape recorders, the whole technology of the production and reproduction of the simulacrum. (The shift from Antonioni's modernist *Blow-Up* to DePalma's postmodernist *Blow-out* is here paradigmatic.) When Japanese architects, for example, model a building on the decorative imitation of stacks of cassettes, then the solution is at best thematic and allusive, although often humorous.

Yet something else does tend to emerge in the most energetic postmodernist texts, and this is the sense that beyond all thematics or content the work seems somehow to tap the networks of the reproductive process and thereby to afford us some glimpse into a postmodern or technological sublime, whose power or authenticity is documented by the success of such works in evoking a whole new postmodern space in emergence around us. Architecture therefore remains in this sense the privileged aesthetic language; and the distorting and fragmenting reflections of one enormous glass surface to the other can be taken as paradigmatic of the central role of process and reproduction in postmodernist culture.

As I have said, however, I want to avoid the implication that technology is in any way the 'ultimately determining instance' either of our present-day social life or of our cultural production: such a thesis is, of course, ultimately at one with the post-Marxist notion of a postindustrial society. Rather, I want to suggest that our faulty representations of some immense communicational and computer network are themselves but a distorted figuration of something even deeper, namely, the whole world system of a present-day multinational capitalism. The technology of contemporary society is therefore mesmerizing and fascinating not so much in its own right but because it seems to offer some privileged representational shorthand for grasping a network of power and control even more difficult for our minds and imaginations to grasp: the whole new decentered global network of the third stage of capital itself. This is a figural process presently best observed in a whole mode of contemporary entertainment literature – one is tempted to characterize it as 'high-tech paranoia' – in which the circuits and networks of some putative global computer hookup are narratively mobilized by labyrinthine conspiracies of autonomous but deadly interlocking and competing information agencies in a complexity often beyond the capacity of the normal reading mind. Yet conspiracy theory (and its garish narrative manifestations) must be seen as a degraded attempt – through the figuration of advanced technology – to think the impossible totality of the contemporary world system. It is in terms of that enormous and threatening, yet only dimly perceivable, other reality of economic and social institutions that, in my opinion, the postmodern sublime can alone be adequately theorized.

Such narratives, which first tried to find expression through the generic structure of the spy novel, have only recently crystallized in a new type of science fiction, called *cyberpunk*, which is fully as much an expression of transnational corporate realities as it is of global paranoia itself: William Gibson's representational innovations, indeed, mark his work as an exceptional literary realization within a predominantly visual or aural postmodern production.

[...]

NOTES

1. This is the moment to confront a significant translation problem and to say why, in my opinion, the notion of a postmodern spatialization is not incompatible with Joseph Frank's influential attribution of an essentially 'spatial form' to the high modern. In hindsight, what he describes is the vocation of the modern work to invent a kind of spatial mnemonics, reminiscent of Frances Yates's *Art of Memory* – 'totalizing' construction in the stricter sense of the stigmatized, autonomous work, whereby the particular somehow includes a battery of re- and pre-tensions linking the sentence or the detail to the Idea of the total form itself. Adorno quotes a remark about Wagner by the conductor Alfred Lorenz in precisely this sense: 'If you have completely mastered a major work in all its details, you sometimes experience moments in which your consciousness of time suddenly disappears and the entire work seems to be what one might call "spatial," that is, with everything present simultaneously in the mind with precision' [...]. But such mnemonic spatiality could never characterize postmodern texts, in which 'totality' is eschewed virtually by definition. Frank's modernist spatial form is thus synedochic, whereas it is scarcely even a beginning to summon up the word *metonymic* for postmodernism's universal urbanization, let alone its nominalism of the here-and-now.
2. 'Ragtime,' *American Review* no. 20 (April 1974): 1–20.
3. Linda Hutcheon, *A Poetics of Postmodernism* (1988), pp. 61–2.
4. Jean-Paul Sartre, 'L'Etranger de Camus,' in *Situations II* (Paris, Gallimard, 1948).
5. See my 'Imaginary and Symbolic in Lacan,' in *The Ideologies of Theory*, volume I (Minnesota, 1988), pp. 75–115.
6. Marguerite Séchehaye, *Autobiography of a Schizophrenic Girl*, G. Rubin-Rabson, trans. (New York, 1968), p. 19.
7. Ernest Mandel, *Late Capitalism* (London, 1978), p. 118.
8. See, particularly on such motifs in Le Corbusier, Gert Kähler, *Architektur als Symbolverfall: Das Dampfermotiv in der Boukunst* (Brunswick, 1981).

2

'TIME–SPACE COMPRESSION AND THE POSTMODERN CONDITION'

David Harvey

How have the uses and meanings of space and time shifted with the transition from Fordism to flexible accumulation? I want to suggest that we have been experiencing, these last two decades, an intense phase of time–space compression that has had a disorienting and disruptive impact upon political–economic practices, the balance of class power, as well as upon cultural and social life. While historical analogies are always dangerous, I think it no accident that postmodern sensibility evidences strong sympathies for certain of the confused political, cultural, and philosophical movements that occurred at the beginning of this century (in Vienna for example) when the sense of time–space compression was also peculiarly strong. I also note the revival of interest in geopolitical theory since around 1970, the aesthetics of place, and a revived willingness (even in social theory) to open the problem of spatiality to a general reconsideration (see, e.g., Gregory and Urry, 1985, and Soja, 1988).

The transition to flexible accumulation was in part accomplished through the rapid deployment of new organizational forms and new technologies in production. Though the latter may have originated in the pursuit of military superiority, their application had everything to do with bypassing the rigidities of Fordism and accelerating turnover time as a solution to the grumbling problems of Fordism – Keynesianism that erupted into open crisis in 1973. Speed-up was achieved in production by organizational shifts towards vertical disintegration – sub-contracting, outsourcing, etc. – that reversed the Fordist

From David Harvey (1989) *The Condition of Postmodernity: An Enquiry into the Origins of Cultural Change*. Oxford: Blackwell.

tendency towards vertical integration and produced an increasing roundabout-ness in production even in the face of increasing financial centralization. Other organizational shifts – such as the 'just-in-time' delivery system that reduces stock inventories – when coupled with the new technologies of electronic control, small-batch production, etc., all reduced turnover times in many sectors of production (electronics, machine tools, automobiles, construction, clothing, etc.). For the labourers this all implied an intensification (speed-up) in labour processes and an acceleration in the de-skilling and re-skilling required to meet new labour needs. [...]

Accelerating turnover time in production entails parallel accelerations in exchange and consumption. Improved systems of communication and information flow, coupled with rationalizations in techniques of distribution (packaging, inventory control, containerization, market feed-back, etc.), made it possible to circulate commodities through the market system with greater speed. Electronic banking and plastic money were some of the innovations that improved the speed of the inverse flow of money. Financial services and markets (aided by computerized trading) likewise speeded up, so as to make, as the saying has it, 'twenty-four hours a very long time' in global stock markets.

Of the many developments in the arena of consumption, two stand out as being of particular importance. The mobilization of fashion in mass (as opposed to elite) markets provided a means to accelerate the pace of consumption not only in clothing, ornament, and decoration but also across a wide swathe of life-styles and recreational activities (leisure and sporting habits, pop music styles, video and children's games, and the like). A second trend was a shift away from the consumption of goods and into the consumption of services – not only personal, business, educational, and health services, but also into enter-tainments, spectacles, happenings, and distractions. The 'lifetime' of such services (a visit to a museum, going to a rock concert or movie, attending lectures or health clubs), though hard to estimate, is far shorter than that of an automobile or washing machine. If there are limits to the accumulation and turnover of physical goods (even counting the famous six thousand pairs of shoes of Imelda Marcos), then it makes sense for capitalists to turn to the provision of very ephemeral services in consumption. This quest may lie at the root of the rapid capitalist penetration, noted by Mandel and Jameson [...] of many sectors of cultural production from the mid-1960s onwards.

Of the innumerable consequences that have flowed from this general speed-up in the turnover times of capital, I shall focus on those that have particular bearing on postmodern ways of thinking, feeling, and doing.

The first major consequence has been to accentuate volatility and ephemer-ality of fashions, products, production techniques, labour processes, ideas and ideologies, values and established practices. The sense that 'all that is solid melts into air' has rarely been more pervasive (which probably accounts for the volume of writing on that theme in recent years). The effect of this on labour markets and skills has already been considered [...]. My interest here is to look at the more general society-wide effects.

In the realm of commodity production, the primary effect has been to emphasize the values and virtues of instantaneity (instant and fast foods, meals, and other satisfactions) and of disposability (cups, plates, cutlery, packaging, napkins, clothing, etc.). The dynamics of a 'throwaway' society, as writers like Alvin Toffler (1970) dubbed it, began to become evident during the 1960s. It meant more than just throwing away produced goods (creating a monumental waste-disposal problem), but also being able to throw away values, life-styles, stable relationships, and attachments to things, buildings, places, people, and received ways of doing and being. These were the immediate and tangible ways in which the 'accelerative thrust in the larger society' crashed up against 'the ordinary daily experience of the individual' (Toffler, p. 40). Through such mechanisms (which proved highly effective from the standpoint of accelerating the turnover of goods in consumption) individuals were forced to cope with disposability, novelty, and the prospects for instant obsolescence. 'Compared to the life in a less rapidly changing society, more situations now flow through the channel in any given interval of time – and this implies profound changes in human psychology.' This transcience, Toffler goes on to suggest, creates 'a temporariness in the structure of both public and personal value systems' which in turn provides a context for the 'crack-up of consensus' and the diversification of values within a fragmenting society. The bombardment of stimuli, simply on the commodity front, creates problems of sensory overload that makes Simmel's dissection of the problems of modernist urban living at the turn of the century seem to pale into insignificance by comparison. Yet, precisely because of the relative qualities of the shift, the psychological responses exist roughly within the range of those which Simmel identified – the blocking out of sensory stimuli, denial, and cultivation of the blasé attitude, myopic specialization, reversion to images of a lost past (hence the importance of mementoes, museums, ruins), and excessive simplification (either in the presentation of self or in the interpretation of events). In this regard, it is instructive to see how Toffler (pp. 326–9), at a much later moment of time–space compression, echoes the thinking of Simmel, whose ideas were shaped at a moment of similar trauma more than seventy years before.

The volatility, of course, makes it extremely difficult to engage in any long-term planning. Indeed, learning to play the volatility right is now just as important as accelerating turnover time. This means either being highly adaptable and fast-moving in response to market shifts, or masterminding the volatility. The first strategy points mainly towards short-term rather than long-term planning, and cultivating the art of taking short-term gains wherever they are to be had. This has been a notorious feature of US management in recent times. The average tenure of company executive officers has come down to five years, and companies nominally involved in production frequently seek short-term gains through mergers, acquisitions, or operations in financial and currency markets. The tension of managerial performance in such an environ-ment is considerable, producing all kinds of side-effects, such as the so-called 'yuppie flu' (a psychological stress condition that paralyses the performance of talented people and produces long-lasting flu-like symptoms) or the frenzied life-style of financial operators whose addiction to work, long hours, and the rush of power makes them excellent candidates for the kind of schizophrenic mentality that Jameson depicts.

Mastering or intervening actively in the production of volatility, on the other hand, entails manipulation of taste and opinion, either through being a fashion leader or by so saturating the market with images as to shape the volatility to particular ends. This means, in either case, the construction of new sign systems and imagery, which is itself an important aspect of the postmodern condition – one that needs to be considered from several different angles. To begin with, advertising and media images [...] have come to play a very much more integrative role in cultural practices and now assume a much greater importance in the growth dynamics of capitalism. Advertising, moreover, is no longer built around the idea of informing or promoting in the ordinary sense, but is increasingly geared to manipulating desires and tastes through images that may or may not have anything to do with the product to be sold [...] If we stripped modern advertising of direct reference to the three themes of money, sex, and power there would be very little left. Furthermore, images have, in a sense, themselves become commodities. This phenomenon has led Baudrillard (1981) to argue that Marx's analysis of commodity production is outdated because capitalism is now predominantly concerned with the production of signs, images, and sign systems rather than with commodities themselves. The transition he points to is important, though there are in fact no serious difficulties in extending Marx's theory of commodity production to cope with it. To be sure, the systems of production and marketing of images (like markets for land, public goods, or labour power) do exhibit some special features that need to be taken into account. The consumer turnover time of certain images can be very short indeed (close to that ideal of the 'twinkling of an eye' that Marx saw as optimal from the standpoint of capital circulation). Many images can also be mass-marketed instantaneously over space. Given the pressures to accelerate turnover time (and to overcome spatial barriers), the commodifica-tion of images of the most ephemeral sort would seem to be a godsend from the standpoint of capital accumulation, particularly when other paths to relieve over accumulation seem blocked. Ephemerality and instantaneous communic-ability over space then become virtues to be explored and appropriated by capitalists for their own purposes.

But images have to perform other functions. Corporations, governments, political and intellectual leaders, all value a stable (though dynamic) image as part of their aura of authority and power. The mediatization of politics has now become all pervasive. This becomes, in effect, the fleeting, superficial, and illusory means whereby an individualistic society of transients sets forth its nostalgia for common values. The production and marketing of such images of permanence and power require considerable sophistication, because the continuity and stability of the image have to be retained while stressing the adaptability, flexibility, and dynamism of whoever or whatever is being imaged. Moreover, image becomes all-important in competition, not only through name-brand recognition but also because of various associations of 'respectability,' 'quality,' 'prestige,' 'reliability,' and 'innovation.' Competition in the image-building trade becomes a vital aspect of inter-firm competition. Success is so plainly profitable that investment in image-building (sponsoring the arts, exhibitions, television productions, new buildings, as well as direct marketing) becomes as important as investment in new plant and machinery. The image serves to establish an identity in the market place. This is also true in labour markets. The acquisition of an image (by the purchase of a sign system such as designer clothes and the right car) becomes a singularly important element in the presentation of self in labour markets and, by extension, becomes integral to the quest for individual identity, self-realization, and meaning. Amusing yet sad signals of this sort of quest abound. A California firm manufactures imitation car telephones, indistinguishable from the real ones, and they sell like hot cakes to a populace desperate to acquire such a symbol of importance. Personal image consultants have become big business in New York City, the *International Herald Tribune* has reported, as a million or so people a year in the city region sign up for courses with firms called Image Assemblers, Image Builders, Image Crafters, and Image Creators. 'People make up their minds about you in around one tenth of a second these days,' says one image consultant. 'Fake it till you make it,' is the slogan of another.

It has always been the case, of course, that symbols of wealth, status, fame, and power as well as of class have been important in bourgeois society, but probably nowhere near as widely in the past as now. The increasing material affluence generated during the postwar Fordist boom posed the problem of converting rising incomes into an effective demand that satisfied the rising aspirations of youth, women, and the working class. Given the ability to produce images as commodities more or less at will, it becomes feasible for accumulation to proceed at least in part on the basis of pure image production and marketing. The ephemerality of such images can then be interpreted in part as a struggle on the part of the oppressed groups of whatever sort to establish their own identity (in terms of street culture, musical styles, fads and fashions made up for themselves) and the rush to convert those innovations to commercial advantage (Carnaby Street in the late 1960s proved an excellent pioneer). The effect is to make it seem as if we are living in a world of ephemeral created images. The psychological impacts of sensory overload, of the sort that Simmel and Toffler identify, are thereby put to work with a redoubled effect.

The materials to produce and reproduce such images, if they were not readily to hand, have themselves been the focus for innovation – the better the replication of the image, the greater the mass market for image making could become. This is in itself an important issue and it brings us more explicitly to consider the role of the 'simulacrum' in postmodernism. By 'simulacrum' is meant a state of such near perfect replication that the difference between the original and the copy becomes almost impossible to spot. The production of images as simulacra is relatively easy, given modern techniques. Insofar as identity is increasingly dependent upon images, this means that the serial and recursive replications of identities (individual, corporate, institutional, and political) becomes a very real possibility and problem. We can certainly see it at work in the realm of politics as the image makers and the media assume a more powerful role in the shaping of political identities. But there are many more tangible realms where the simulacrum has a heightened role. With modern building materials it is possible to replicate ancient buildings with such exactitude that authenticity or origins can be put into doubt. The manufacture of antiques and other art objects becomes entirely possible, making the high-class forgery a serious problem in the art collection business. We not only possess, therefore, the capacity to pile images from the past or from other places eclectically and simultaneously upon the television screen, but even to transform those images into material simulacra in the form of built environments, events and spectacles, and the like, which become in many respects indistinguishable from the originals. What happens to cultural forms when the imitations become real, and the real takes on many of the qualities of an imitation, is a question to which we shall return.

The organization and conditions of labour prevailing within what we might broadly refer to as the 'image production industry' are also quite special. An industry of this sort has to rely, after all, upon the innovative powers of the direct producers. The latter have an insecure existence, tempered by very high rewards for the successful and at least a semblance of command over their own labour process and creative powers. The growth of cultural output has in fact been phenomenal. Taylor (1987, 77) contrasts the art market condition in New York in 1945, when there were a handful of galleries and no more than a score of artists regularly exhibiting, and the two thousand or so artists who practised in or around Paris in the mid-nineteenth century, with the 150,000 artists in the New York region who claim professional status, exhibiting at some 680 galleries, producing more than 15 million art-works in a decade (compared to 200,000 in late nineteenth-century Paris). And this is only the tip of an iceberg of cultural production that encompasses local entertainers and graphic designers, street and pub musicians, photographers, as well as the more established and recognized schools for teaching art, music, drama, and the like. Dwarfing all of this, however, is what Daniel Bell (1978, 20) calls 'the cultural mass' defined as:

> not the creators of culture but the transmitters: those working in higher
> education, publishing, magazines, broadcast media, theater, and
> museums, who process and influence the reception of serious cultural

products. It is in itself large enough to be a market for culture, purchase books, prints and serious music recordings. And it is also the group which, as writers, magazine editors, movie-makers, musicians, and so forth, produce the popular materials for the wider mass-culture audience.

This whole industry specializes in the acceleration of turnover time through the production and marketing of images. This is an industry where reputations are made and lost overnight, where big money talks in no uncertain terms, and where there is a ferment of intense, often individualized, creativity poured into the vast vat of serialized and recursive mass culture. It is the organizer of fads and fashions and, as such, it actively produces the very ephemerality that has always been fundamental to the experience of modernity. It becomes a social means to produce that sense of collapsing time horizons which it in turn so avidly feeds upon.

The popularity of a work like Alvin Toffler's *Future shock* lay precisely in its prescient appreciation of the speed with which the future has come to be discounted into the present. Out of that, also, comes a collapse of cultural distinctions between, say, 'science' and 'regular' fiction (in the works of, for example, Thomas Pynchon and Doris Lessing), as well as a merging of the cinema of distraction with the cinema of futuristic universes. We can link the schizophrenic dimension to postmodernity which Jameson emphasizes [...] with accelerations in turnover times in production, exchange, and consumption that produce, as it were, the loss of a sense of the future except and insofar as the future can be discounted into the present. Volatility and ephemerality similarly make it hard to maintain any firm sense of continuity. Past experience gets compressed into some overwhelming present. Italo Calvino (1981, 8) reports the effect on his own craft of novel writing this way:

> long novels written today are perhaps a contradiction: the dimension of time had been shattered, we cannot live or think except in fragments of time each of which goes off along its own trajectory and immediately disappears. We can rediscover the continuity of time only in the novels of that period when time no longer seemed stopped and did not yet seem to have exploded, a period that lasted no more than a hundred years.

Baudrillard (1986), never afraid to exaggerate, considers the United States as a society so given over to speed, motion, cinematic images, and technological fixes as to have created a crisis of explanatory logic. It represents, he suggests, 'the triumph of effect over cause, of instantaneity over time as depth, the triumph of surface and of pure objectivization over the depth of desire.' This, of course, is the kind of environment in which deconstructionism can flourish. If it is impossible to say anything of solidity and permanence in the midst of this ephemeral and fragmented world, then why not join in the [language] game? Everything, from novel writing and philosophizing to the experience of labouring or making a home, has to face the challenge of accelerating turnover time and the rapid write-off of traditional and historically acquired values. The temporary contract in everything, as Lyotard remarks [...], then becomes the hallmark of postmodern living.

But, as so often happens, the plunge into the maelstrom of ephemerality has provoked an explosion of opposed sentiments and tendencies. To begin with, all sorts of technical means arise to guard against future shocks. Firms sub-contract or resort to flexible hiring practices to discount the potential unemployment costs of future market shifts. Futures markets in everything, from corn and pork bellies to currencies and government debt, coupled with the 'securitization' of all kinds of temporary and floating debts, illustrate techniques for discounting the future into the present. Insurance hedges of all kinds against future volatility become much more widely available.

Deeper questions of meaning and interpretation also arise. The greater the ephemerality, the more pressing the need to discover or manufacture some kind of eternal truth that might lie therein. The religious revival that has become much stronger since the late sixties, and the search for authenticity and authority in politics (with all of its accoutrements of nationalism and localism and of admiration for those charismatic and 'protean' individuals with their Nietzschian 'will to power') are cases in point. The revival of interest in basic institutions (such as the family and community), and the search for historical roots are all signs of a search for more secure moorings and longer-lasting values in a shifting world. Rochberg-Halton (1986, 173), in a sample study of North Chicago residents in 1977, finds, for example, that the objects actually valued in the home were not the 'pecuniary trophies' of a materialist culture which acted as 'reliable indices of one's socio-economic class, age, gender and so on,' but the artefacts that embodied 'ties to loved ones and kin, valued experiences and activities, and memories of significant life events and people.' Photographs, particular objects (like a piano, a clock, a chair), and events (the playing of a record of a piece of music, the singing of a song) become the focus of a contemplative memory, and hence a generator of a sense of self that lies outside the sensory overloading of consumerist culture and fashion. The home becomes a private museum to guard against the ravages of time–space compression. At the very time, furthermore, that postmodernism proclaims the 'death of the author' and the rise of anti-auratic art in the public realm, the art market becomes ever more conscious of the monopoly power of the artist's signature and of questions of authenticity and forgery (no matter that the Rauschenberg is itself a mere reproduction montage). It is, perhaps, appropriate that the post-modernist developer building, as solid as the pink granite of Philip Johnson's AT & T building, should be debt-financed, built on the basis of fictitious capital, and architecturally conceived of, at least on the outside, more in the spirit of fiction than of function.

The spatial adjustments have been no less traumatic. The satellite communications systems deployed since the early 1970s have rendered the unit cost and time of communication invariant with respect to distance. It costs the same to communicate over 500 miles as it does over 5,000 via satellite. Air freight rates on commodities have likewise come down dramatically, while containerization has reduced the cost of bulk sea and road transport. It is now possible for a large multinational corporation like Texas Instruments to operate plants with simultaneous decision-making with respect to financial, market, input costs, quality control, and labour process conditions in more than fifty different locations across the globe (Dicken, 1986, 110–13). Mass television ownership coupled with satellite communication makes it possible to experience a rush of images from different spaces almost simultaneously, collapsing the world's spaces into a series of images on a television screen. The whole world can watch the Olympic Games, the World Cup, the fall of a dictator, a political summit, a deadly tragedy ... while mass tourism, films made in spectacular locations, make a wide range of simulated or vicarious experience of what the world contains available to many people. The image of places and spaces becomes as open to production and ephemeral use as any other.

We have, in short, witnessed another fierce round in that process of annihilation of space through time that has always lain at the center of capitalism's dynamic [...]. Marshall McLuhan described how he thought the 'global village' had now become a communications reality in the mid-1960s:

> After three thousand years of explosion, by means of fragmentary and mechanical technologies, the Western World is imploding. During the mechanical ages we had extended our bodies in space. Today, after more than a century of electronic technology, we have extended our central nervous system itself in a global embrace, abolishing both space and time as far as our planet is concerned.

In recent years a whole spate of writing has taken this idea on board and tried to explore, as for example Virilio (1980) does in his *Esthétique de la disparition*, the cultural consequences of the supposed disappearance of time and space as materialized and tangible dimensions to social life.

But the collapse of spatial barriers does not mean that the significance of space is decreasing. Not for the first time in capitalism's history, we find the evidence pointing to the converse thesis. Heightened competition under conditions of crisis has coerced capitalists into paying much closer attention to relative locational advantages, precisely because diminishing spatial barriers give capitalists the power to exploit minute spatial differentiations to good effect. Small differences in what the space contains in the way of labour supplies, resources, infrastructures, and the like become of increased significance. Superior command over space becomes an even more important weapon in class struggle. It becomes one of the means to enforce speed-up and the redefinition of skills on recalcitrant work forces. Geographical mobility and decentralization are used against a union power which traditionally concentrated in the factories of mass production. Capital flight, deindustrialization of some regions, and the industrialization of others, the destruction of traditional working-class communities as power bases in class struggle, become leitmotifs of spatial transformation under more flexible conditions of accumulation (Martin and Rowthorn, 1986; Bluestone and Harrison, 1982; Harrison and Bluestone, 1988).

As spatial barriers diminish so we become much more sensitized to what the world's spaces contain. Flexible accumulation typically exploits a wide range of seemingly contingent geographical circumstances, and reconstitutes them as structured internal elements of its own encompassing logic. For example, geographical differentiations in the mode and strengths of labour control together with variations in the quality as well as the quantity of labour power assume a much greater significance in corporate locational strategies. New industrial ensembles arise, sometimes out of almost nothing (as the various silicon valleys and glens) but more often on the basis of some pre-existing mix of skills and resources. The 'Third Italy' (Emilia-Romagna) builds upon a peculiar mix of co-operative entrepreneurialism, artisan labour, and local communist administrations anxious to generate employment, and inserts its clothing products with incredible success into a highly competitive world economy. Flanders attracts outside capital on the basis of a dispersed, flexible, and reasonably skilled labour supply with a deep hostility to unionism and social-ism. Los Angeles imports the highly successful patriarchal labour systems of South-East Asia through mass immigration, while the celebrated paternalistic labour control system of the Japanese and Taiwanese is imported into California and South Wales. The story in each case is different, making it appear as if the uniqueness of this or that geographical circumstance matters more than ever before. Yet it does so, ironically, only because of the collapse of spatial barriers.

While labour control is always central, there are many other aspects of geographical organization that have risen to a new prominence under condi-tions of more flexible accumulation. The need for accurate information and speedy communication has emphasized the role of so-called 'world cities' in the financial and corporate system (centres equipped with teleports, airports, fixed communication links, as well as a wide array of financial, legal, business, and infrastructural services). The diminution of spatial barriers results in the reaffirmation and realignment of hierarchy within what is now a global urban system. The local availability of material resources of special qualities, or even at marginally lower costs, starts to be ever more important, as do local variations in market taste that are today more easily exploited under conditions of small-batch production and flexible design. Local differences in entrepre-neurial ability, venture capital, scientific and technical know-how, social attitudes, also enter in, while the local networks of influence and power, the accumulation strategies of local ruling elites (as opposed to nation state policies) also become more deeply implicated in the regime of flexible accumulation.

But this then raises another dimension to the changing role of spatiality in contemporary society. If capitalists become increasingly sensitive to the spatially differentiated qualities of which the world's geography is composed, then it is possible for the peoples and powers that command those spaces to alter them in such a way as to be more rather than less attractive to highly mobile capital. Local ruling elites can, for example, implement strategies of local labour control, of skill enhancement, of infrastructural provision, of tax policy, state regulation, and so on, in order to attract development within their particular space. The qualities of place stand thereby to be emphasized in the midst of the increasing abstractions of space. The active production of places with special qualities becomes an important stake in spatial competition between localities, cities, regions, and nations. Corporatist forms of governance can flourish in such spaces, and themselves take on entrepreneurial roles in the production of favourable business climates and other special qualities. And it is in this context that we can better situate the striving [...] for cities to forge a distinctive image and to create an atmosphere of place and tradition that will act as a lure to both capital and people 'of the right sort' (i.e. wealthy and influential). Heightened inter-place competition should lead to the production of more variegated spaces within the increasing homogeneity of international exchange. But to the degree that this competition opens up cities to systems of accumulation, it ends up producing what Boyer (1988) calls a 'recursive' and 'serial' monotony, 'producing from already known patterns or molds places almost identical in ambience from city to city: New York's South Street Seaport, Boston's Quincy Market, Baltimore's Harbor Place.'

We thus approach the central paradox: the less important the spatial barriers, the greater the sensitivity of capital to the variations of place within space, and the greater the incentive for places to be differentiated in ways attractive to capital. The results has been the production of fragmentation, insecurity, and ephemeral uneven development within a highly unified global space economy of capital flows. The historic tension within capitalism between centralization and decentralization is now being worked out in new ways. Extraordinary decentralization and proliferation of industrial production ends up putting Benetton or Laura Ashley products in almost every serially produced shopping mall in the advanced capitalist world. Plainly, the new round of time–space compression is fraught with as many dangers as it offers possibilities for survival of particular places or for a solution to the overaccumulation problem.

The geography of devaluation through deindustrialization, rising local unemployment, fiscal retrenchment, write-offs of local assets, and the like, is indeed a sorry picture. But we can at least see its logic within the frame of the search for a solution to the overaccumulation problem through the push into flexible and more mobile systems of accumulation. But there are also a priori reasons to suspect (as well as some material evidence to support the idea) that regions of maximum churning and fragmentation are also regions that seem best set to survive the traumas of devaluation in the long run. There is more than a hint that a little devaluation now is better than massive devaluation later in the scramble for local survival in the world of severely constrained opportunities for positive growth. Reindustrializing and restructuring cannot be accomplished without deindustrializing and devaluing first.

None of these shifts in the experience of space and time would make the sense or have the impact they do without a radical shift in the manner in which value gets represented as money. Though long dominant, money has never been a clear or unambiguous representation of value, and on occasion it becomes so muddled as to become itself a major source of insecurity and uncertainty. Under the terms of the postwar settlement, the question of world money was put on a fairly stable basis. The US dollar became the medium of world trade, technically backed by a fixed convertibility into gold, and backed politically and economically by the overwhelming power of the US productive apparatus. The space of the US production system became, in effect, the guarantor of international value. But, as we have seen, one of the signals of the breakdown of the Fordist – Keynesian system was the breakdown of the Bretton Woods agreement, of convertibility of US dollars to gold, and the shift to a global system of floating exchange rates. The breakdown in part occurred because of the shifting dimensionalities of space and time generated out of capital accumulation. Rising indebtedness (particularly within the United States), and fiercer international competition from the reconstructed spaces of the world economy under conditions of growing accumulation, had much to do with undermining the power of the US economy to operate as an exclusive guarantor of world money.

The effects have been legion. The question of how value should now get represented, what form money should take, and the meaning that can be put upon the various forms of money available to us, has never been far from the surface of recent concerns. Since 1973, money has been 'de-materialized' in the sense that it no longer has a formal or tangible link to precious metals (though the latter have continued to play a role as one potential form of money among many others), or for that matter to any other tangible commodity. Nor does it rely exclusively upon productive activity within a particular space. The world has come to rely, for the first time in its history, upon immaterial forms of money – i.e. money of account assessed quantitatively in numbers of some designated currency (dollars, yen, Deutsch Marks, sterling, etc.). Exchange rates between the different currencies of the world have also been extremely volatile. Fortunes could be lost or made simply by holding the right currency during the right phases. The question of which currency I hold is directly linked to which place I put my faith in. That may have something to do with the competitive economic position and power of different national systems. That power, given the flexibility of accumulation over space, is itself a rapidly shifting magnitude. The effect is to render the spaces that underpin the determination of value as unstable as value itself. This problem is compounded by the way that speculative shifts bypass actual economic power and performance, and then trigger self-fulfilling expectations. The de-linking of the financial system from active production and from any material monetary base

calls into question the reliability of the basic mechanism whereby value is supposed to be represented.

These difficulties have been most powerfully present in the process of devaluation of money, the measure of value, through inflation. The steady inflation rates of the Fordist – Keynesian era (usually in the 3 per cent range, and rarely above 5 per cent) gave way from 1969 onwards, and then accelerated in all the major capitalist countries during the 1970s into double-digit rates [. . .]. Worse still, inflation became highly unstable, between as well as within countries, leaving everyone in doubt as to what the true value (the buying power) of a particular money might be in the near future. Money consequently became useless as a means of storing value for any length of time (the real rate of interest, measured as the money rate of interest minus the rate of inflation, was negative for several years during the 1970s, so dispossessing savers of the value they were seeking to store). Alternative means had to be found to store value effectively. And so began the vast inflation in certain kinds of asset prices – collectibles, art objects, antiques, houses, and the like. Buying a Degas or Van Gogh in 1973 would surely outstrip almost any other kind of investment in terms of capital gain. Indeed it can be argued that the growth of the art market (with its concern for authorial signature) and the strong commercialization of cultural production since around 1970 have had a lot to do with the search to find alternative means to store value under conditions where the usual money forms were deficient. Commodity and general price inflation, though to some degree brought under control in the advanced capitalist countries during the 1980s, has by no means diminished as a problem. It is rampant in countries like Mexico, Argentina, Brazil, and Israel (all with recent rates in hundreds of per cent), and the prospect of generalized inflation looms in the advanced capitalist countries, where it is in any case arguable that the inflation of asset prices (housing, works of art, antiques, etc.) has taken over where commodity and labour market inflation left off in the early 1980s.

The breakdown of money as a secure means of representing value has itself created a crisis of representation in advanced capitalism. It has also been reinforced by, and added its very considerable weight to, the problems of time–space compression which we earlier identified. The rapidity with which currency markets fluctuate across the world's spaces, the extraordinary power of money capital flow in what is now a global stock and financial market, and the volatility of what the purchasing power of money might represent, define, as it were, a high point of that highly problematic intersection of money, time, and space as interlocking elements of social power in the political economy of postmodernity.

It is, furthermore, not hard to see how all of this might create a more general crisis of representation. The central value system, to which capitalism has always appealed to validate and gauge its actions, is dematerialized and shifting, time horizons are collapsing, and it is hard to tell exactly what space we are in when it comes to assessing causes and effects, meanings or values. The intriguing exhibition at the Pompidou Centre in 1985 on 'The Immaterial' (an exhibition for which none other than Lyotard acted as one of the consultants) was perhaps a mirror image of the dissolution of the material representations of value under conditions of more flexible accumulation, and of the confusions as to what it might mean to say, with Paul Virilio, that time and space have disappeared as meaningful dimensions to human thought and action.

There are, I would submit, more tangible and material ways than this to go about assessing the significance of space and time for the condition of post-modernity. It should be possible to consider how, for example, the changing experience of space, time, and money has formed a distinctive material basis for the rise of distinctive systems of interpretation and representation, as well as opening a path through which the aestheticization of politics might once more reassert itself. If we view culture as that complex of signs and significations (including language) that mesh into codes of transmission of social values and meanings, then we can at least begin upon the task of unravelling its complex-ities under present-day conditions by recognizing that money and commodities are themselves the primary bearers of cultural codes. Since money and com-modities are entirely bound up with the circulation of capital, it follows that cultural forms are firmly rooted in the daily circulation process of capital. It is, therefore, with the daily experience of money and the commodity that we should begin, no matter if special commodities or even whole sign systems may be extracted from the common herd and made the basis of 'high' culture or that specialized 'imaging' which we have already had cause to comment upon.

The annihilation of space through time has radically changed the commodity mix that enters into daily reproduction. Innumerable local food systems have been reorganized through their incorporation into global commodity exchange. French cheeses, for example, virtually unavailable except in a few gourmet stores in large cities in 1970, are now widely sold across the United States. And if this is thought a somewhat elite example, the case of beer consumption suggests that the internationalization of a product, that traditional location theory always taught should be highly market-oriented, is now complete. Baltimore was essentially a one-beer town (locally brewed) in 1970, but first the regional beers from places like Milwaukee and Denver, and then Canadian and Mexican beers followed by European, Australian, Chinese, Polish, etc. beers became cheaper. Formerly exotic foods became commonplace while popular local delicacies (in the Baltimore case, blue crabs and oysters) that were once relatively inexpensive jumped in price as they too became integrated into long-distance trading.

The market place has always been an 'emporium of styles' (to quote Raban's phrase) but the food market, just to take one example, now looks very different from what it was twenty years ago. Kenyan haricot beans, Californian celery and avocados, North African potatoes, Canadian apples, and Chilean grapes all sit side by side in a British supermarket. This variety also makes for a pro-liferation of culinary styles, even among the relatively poor. Such styles have always migrated, of course, usually following the migration streams of different groups before diffusing slowly through urban cultures. The new waves of immigrants (such as the Vietnamese, Koreans, Filipinos, Central Americans, etc. that have added to the older groups of Japanese, Chinese, Chicanos, and all the European ethnic groups that have also found their culinary heritage can be revived for fun and profit) make a typical United States city such as New York, Los Angeles, or San Francisco (where the last census showed the majority of the population to be made up of minorities) as much an emporium of culinary styles as it is an emporium of the world's commodities. But here, too, there has been an acceleration, because culinary styles have moved faster than the immigration streams. It did not take a large French immigration to the United States to send the croissant rapidly spreading across America to challenge the traditional doughnut, nor did it take a large immigration of Americans to Europe to bring fast-food hamburgers to nearly all medium-sized European cities. Chinese takeaways, Italian pizza-parlours (run by a US chain), Middle Eastern felafel stalls, Japanese sushi bars the list is now endless in the Western world.

The whole world's cuisine is now assembled in one place in almost exactly the same way that the world's geographical complexity is nightly reduced to a series of images on a static television screen. This same phenomenon is exploited in entertainment palaces like Epcott and Disneyworld; it becomes possible, as the US commercials put it, 'to experience the Old World for a day without actually having to go there.' The general implication is that through the experience of everything from food, to culinary habits, music, television, entertainment, and cinema, it is now possible to experience the world's geography vicariously, as a simulacrum. The interweaving of simulacra in daily life brings together different worlds (of commodities) in the same space and time. But it does so in such a way as to conceal almost perfectly any trace of origin, of the labour processes that produced them, or of the social relations implicated in their production.

The simulacra can in turn become the reality. Baudrillard (1986) in L'Amérique even goes so far, somewhat exaggeratedly in my view, to suggest that US reality is now constructed as a giant screen: 'the cinema is everywhere, most of all in the city, incessant and marvellous film and scenario.' Places portrayed in a certain way, particularly if they have the capacity to attract tourists, may begin to 'dress themselves up' as the fantasy images prescribe. Mediaeval castles offer mediaeval weekends (food, dress, but not of course the primitive heating arrangements). Vicarious participation in these various worlds has real effects on the ways in which these worlds get ordered. Jencks (1984, 127) proposes that the architect should be an active participant in this:

> Any middle class urbanite in any large city from Teheran to Tokyo is bound to have a well-stocked, indeed over-stocked 'image bank' that is continually restuffed by travel and magazines. His musée imaginaire may mirror the pot-pourri of the producers but it is nonetheless natural to his way of life. Barring some kind of totalitarian reduction in the

heterogeneity of production and consumption, it seems to be desirable that architects learn to use this inevitable heterogeneity of languages. Besides, it is quite enjoyable. Why, if one can afford to live in different ages and cultures, restrict oneself to the present, the locale? Eclecticism is the natural evolution of a culture with choice.

Much the same can be said of popular music styles. Commenting on how collage and eclecticism have recently come to dominate, Chambers (1987) goes on to show how oppositional and subcultural musics like reggae, Afro-American and Afro-Hispanic have taken their place 'in the museum of fixed symbolic structures' to form a flexible collage of 'the already seen, the already worn, the already played, the already heard.' A strong sense of 'the Other' is replaced, he suggests, by a weak sense of 'the others.' The loose hanging together of divergent street cultures in the fragmented spaces of the contemporary city re-emphasizes the contingent and accidental aspects of this 'otherness' in daily life. This same sensibility exists in postmodern fiction. It is, says McHale (1987), concerned with 'ontologies,' with a potential as well as an actual plurality of universes, forming an eclectic and 'anarchic landscape of worlds in the plural.' Dazed and distracted characters wander through these worlds without a clear sense of location, wondering, 'Which world am I in and which of my personalities do I deploy?' Our postmodern ontological landscape, suggests McHale, 'is unprecedented in human history – at least in the degree of its pluralism.' Spaces of very different worlds seem to collapse upon each other, much as the world's commodities are assembled in the supermarket and all manner of sub-cultures get juxtaposed in the contemporary city. Disruptive spatiality triumphs over the coherence of perspective and narrative in postmodern fiction, in exactly the same way that imported beers coexist with local brews, local employment collapses under the weight of foreign competition, and all the divergent spaces of the world are assembled nightly as a college of images upon the television screen.

There seem to be two divergent sociological effects of all of this in daily thought and action. The first suggests taking advantage of all of the divergent possibilities, much as Jencks recommends, and cultivating a whole series of simulacra as milieux of escape, fantasy, and distraction:

> All around us – on advertisement hoardings, bookshelves, record covers, television screens – these miniature escape fantasies present themselves. This, it seems, is how we are destined to live, as split personalities in which the private life is disturbed by the promise of escape routes to another reality. (Cohen and Taylor, 1978, quoted in McHale, 1987, 38)

From this standpoint I think we have to accept McHale's argument that postmodern fiction is mimetic of something, much as I have argued that the emphasis upon ephemerality, collage, fragmentation, and dispersal in philosophical and social thought mimics the conditions of flexible accumulation. And it should not be surprising either to see how all of this fits in with the emergence since 1970 of a fragmented politics of divergent special and regional interest groups.

But it is exactly at this point that we encounter the opposite reaction that can best be summed up as the search for personal or collective identity, the search for secure moorings in a shifting world. Place-identity, in this collage of super-imposed spatial images that implode in upon us, becomes an important issue, because everyone occupies a space of individuation (a body, a room, a home, a shaping community, a nation), and how we individuate ourselves shapes identity. Furthermore, if no one 'knows their place' in this shifting collage world, then how can a secure social order be fashioned or sustained?

There are two elements within this problem that deserve close consideration. First, the capacity of most social movements to command place better than space puts a strong emphasis upon the potential connection between place and social identity. This is manifest in political action. The defensiveness of muni-cipal socialism, the insistence on working-class community, the localization of the fight against capital, become central features of working-class struggle within an overall patterning of uneven geographical development. The con-sequent dilemmas of socialist or working-class movements in the face of a universalizing capitalism are shared by other oppositional groups – racial minorities, colonized peoples, women, etc. – who are relatively empowered to organize in place but disempowered when it comes to organizing over space. In clinging, often of necessity, to a place-bound identity, however, such oppo-sitional movements become a part of the very fragmentation which a mobile capitalism and flexible accumulation can feed upon. 'Regional resistances,' the struggle for local autonomy, place-bound organization, may be excellent bases for political action, but they cannot bear the burden of radical historical change alone. 'Think globally and act locally' was the revolutionary slogan of the 1960s. It bears repeating.

The assertion of any place-bound identity has to rest at some point on the motivational power of tradition. It is difficult, however, to maintain any sense of historical continuity in the face of all the flux and ephemerality of flexible accumulation. The irony is that tradition is now often preserved by being commodified and marketed as such. The search for roots ends up at worst being produced and marketed as an image, as a simulacrum or pastiche (imitation communities constructed to evoke images of some folksy past, the fabric of traditional working-class communities being taken over by an urban gentry). The photograph, the document, the view, and the reproduction become history precisely because they are so overwhelmingly present. The problem, of course, is that none of these are immune from tampering or downright faking for present purposes. At best, historical tradition is reorganized as a museum culture, not necessarily of high modernist art, but of local history, of local production, of how things once upon a time were made, sold, consumed, and integrated into a long-lost and often romanticized daily life (one from which all trace of oppressive social relations may be expunged). Through the presentation of a partially illusory past it becomes possible to signify something of local identity and perhaps to do it profitably.

The second reaction to the internationalism of modernism lies in the search to construct place and its meanings qualitatively. Capitalist hegemony over space puts the aesthetics of place very much back on the agenda. But this, as we have seen, meshes only too well with the idea of spatial differentiations as lures for a peripatetic capital that values the option of mobility very highly. Isn't this place better than that place, not only for the operations of capital but also for living in, consuming well, and feeling secure in a shifting world? The construction of such places, the fashioning of some localized aesthetic image, allows the construction of some limited and limiting sense of identity in the midst of a collage of imploding spatialities.

[...]

This should alert us to the acute geopolitical dangers that attach to the rapidity of time–space compression in recent years. The transition from Fordism to flexible accumulation, such as it has been, ought to imply a transition in our mental maps, political attitudes, and political institutions. But political thinking does not necessarily undergo such easy transformations, and is in any case subject to the contradictory pressures that derive from spatial integration and differentiation. There is an omni-present danger that our mental maps will not match current realities. The serious diminution of the power of individual nation states over fiscal and monetary policies, for example, has not been matched by any parallel shift towards an internationalization of politics. Indeed, there are abundant signs that localism and nationalism have become stronger precisely because of the quest for the security that place always offers in the midst of all the shifting that flexible accumulation implies. The resurgence of geopolitics and of faith in charismatic politics (Thatcher's Falklands War, Reagan's invasion of Grenada) fits only too well with a world that is increasingly nourished intellectually and politically by a vast flux of ephemeral images.

Time–space compression always exacts its toll on our capacity to grapple with the realities unfolding around us. Under stress, for example, it becomes harder and harder to react accurately to events. The erroneous identification of an Iranian airbus, ascending within an established commercial flight corridor, with a fighter-bomber descending towards a targeted US warship – an incident that resulted in many civilian deaths – is typical of the way that reality gets created rather than interpreted under conditions of stress and time–space compression. The parallel with Kern's account of the outbreak of World War I [...] is instructive. If 'seasoned negotiators cracked under the pressure of tense confrontations and sleepless nights, agonizing over the probable disastrous consequences of their snap judgements and hasty actions,' then how much more difficult must decision-making now be? The difference this time is that there is not even time to agonize. And the problems are not confined to the realms of political and military decision-making, for the world's financial markets are on the boil in ways that make a snap judgement here, an unconsidered word there, and a gut reaction somewhere else the slip that can unravel the whole skein of fictitious capital formation and of interdependency.

The conditions of postmodern time–space compression exaggerate in many respects the dilemmas that have from time to time beset capitalist procedures of modernization in the past (1848 and the phase just before the First World War spring particularly to mind). While the economic, cultural, and political responses may not be exactly new, the range of those responses differs in certain important respects from those which have occurred before. The intensity of time–space compression in Western capitalism since the 1960s, with all of its congruent features of excessive ephemerality and fragmentation in the political and private as well as in the social realm, does seem to indicate an experiential context that makes the condition of postmodernity somewhat special. But by putting this condition into its historical context, as part of a history of successive waves of time–space compression generated out of the pressures of capital accumulation with its perpetual search to annihilate space through time and reduce turnover time, we can at least pull the condition of postmodernity into the range of a condition accessible to historical materialist analysis and interpretation. [...]

WORKS CITED

Baudrillard, Jean (1981) *For a Critique of the Political Economy of the Sign*. St Louis, MO.
Baudrillard, Jean (1986) *L'Amérique*. Paris.
Bluestone, B. and Harrison B. (1982) *The Deindustrialization of America*. New York.
Boyer, R. (1986) *La théorie de regulation: une analyse critique*. Paris.
Chambers, Ian (1987) 'Maps for the Metropolis: A Possible Guide to the Present', *Cultural Studies*, 1: 1–22.
Dicken, P. (1986) *Global Shift: Industrial Change in a Turbulent World*. London.
Gregory, D. and Urry, J. (eds) (1985) *Social Relations and Spatial Structures*. London.
Harrison, B. and Bluestone, B (1988) *The Great U-Turn: Capital Restructuring and the Polarizing of America*. New York.
Heisenberg, W. K. (1972) 'The Representation of Nature in Contemporary Physics', in Sallie Sears and Georgianna W. Lord (eds), *The Discontinuous Universe*. London and New York.
Jencks, Charles (1984) *The Language of Post-Modern Architecture*. London.
Kern, S. (1983) *The Culture of Time and Space, 1880–1918*. London.
McHale, Brian (1987) *Postmodernist Fiction*. London.
McLuhan, Marshall (1966) *Understanding Media: The Extensions of Man*. New York.
Martin, R. and Rowthorn, B. (eds) *The Geography of Deindustrialisation*. London.
Rochberg-Halton, E. (1986) *Meaning and Modernity*. Chicago, IL.
Soja, Edward (1988) *Postmodern Geographies*. London.
Taylor, B. (1987) *The Principles of Scientific Management*. New York.
Toffler, Alvin (1970) *Future Shock*. New York.
Touraine, Alain (1974) *The Post-Industrial Society, Tomorrow's Social History: Classes, Conflicts and Culture in the Programmed Society* [1974], trans. Leonard F. X. Mayhew. London.
Virilio, Paul (1980) *L'ésthetique de la disparition*. Paris.

3

'MAPPING THE POSTMODERN'

Andreas Huyssen

THE PROBLEM

[...] While the recent media hype about postmodernism in architecture and the arts has propelled the phenomenon into the limelight, it has also tended to obscure its long and complex history. Much of my ensuing argument will be based on the premise that what appears on one level as the latest fad, advertising pitch, and hollow spectacle is part of a slowly emerging cultural transformation in Western societies, a change in sensibility for which the term 'postmodernism' is actually, at least for now, wholly adequate. The nature and depth of that transformation are debatable, but transformation it is. I don't want to be misunderstood as claiming that there is a wholesale paradigm shift of the cultural, social, and economic orders;[1] any such claim clearly would be overblown. But in an important sector of our culture there is a noticeable shift in sensibility, practices, and discourse formations which distinguishes a postmodern set of assumptions, experiences, and propositions from that of a preceding period. What needs further exploration is whether this transformation has generated genuinely new aesthetic forms in the various arts or whether it mainly recycles techniques and strategies of modernism itself, reinscribing them into an altered cultural context.

[...]

In much of the postmodernism debate, a very conventional thought pattern has asserted itself. Either it is said that postmodernism is continuous with

From Andreas Huyssen (1988) 'Mapping the Postmodern' [1984], in *After the Great Divide: Modernism, Mass Culture, Postmodernism*. London: Macmillan, pp. 178–221.

modernism, in which case the whole debate opposing the two is specious; or, it is claimed that there is a radical rupture, a break with modernism, which is then evaluated in either positive or negative terms. But the question of historical continuity or discontinuity simply cannot be adequately discussed in terms of such an either/or dichotomy. To have questioned the validity of such dichotomous thought patterns is of course one of the major achievements of Derridean deconstruction. But the poststructuralist notion of endless textuality ultimately cripples any meaningful historical reflection on temporal units shorter than, say, the long wave of metaphysics from Plato to Heidegger or the spread of *modernité* from the mid-10th century to the present. The problem with such historical macro-schemes, in relation to postmodernism, is that they prevent the phenomenon from even coming into focus.

I will therefore take a different route. I will not attempt here to define what postmodernism *is*. The term '*post*modernism' itself should guard us against such an approach as it positions the phenomenon as relational. Modernism as that from which postmodernism is breaking away remains inscribed into the very word with which we describe our distance from modernism. Thus keeping in mind postmodernism's relational nature. I will simply start from the *Selbstverständnis* of the postmodern as it has shaped various discourses since the 1960s. What I hope to provide in this essay is something like a large-scale map of the postmodern which surveys several territories and on which the various postmodern artistic and critical practices could find their aesthetic and political place. Within the trajectory of the postmodern in the United States I will distinguish several phases and directions. My primary aim is to emphasize some of the historical contingencies and pressures that have shaped recent aesthetic and cultural debates but have either been ignored or systematically blocked out in critical theory *à l'américaine*. While drawing on developments in architecture, literature, and the visual arts, my focus will be primarily on the critical discourse about the postmodern: postmodernism in relation to, respectively, modernism, the avantgarde, neo-conservatism, and poststructuralism. Each of these constellations represents a somewhat separate layer of the postmodern and will be presented as such. And, finally, central elements of the *Begriffsgeschichte* of the term will be discussed in relation to a broader set of questions that have arisen in recent debates about modernism, modernity, and the historical avantgarde.[2] A crucial question for me concerns the extent to which modernism and the avantgarde as forms of an adversary culture were nevertheless conceptually and practically bound up with capitalist modernization and/or with communist vanguardism, that modernization's twin brother. As I hope this essay will show, postmodernism's critical dimension lies precisely in its radical questioning of those presuppositions which linked modernism and the avantgarde to the mindset of modernization.

[...]

I will now suggest a historical distinction between the postmodernism of the 1960s and that of the 1970s and early 1980s. My argument will roughly be this: 1960s' and 1970s' postmodernism both rejected or criticized a certain version of modernism. Against the codified high modernism of the preceding decades, the postmodernism of the 1960s tried to revitalize the heritage of the European avantgarde and to give it an American form along what one could call in short-hand the Duchamp-Cage-Warhol axis. By the 1970s, that avantgardist post-modernism of the 1960s had in turn exhausted its potential, even though some of its manifestations continued well into the new decade. What was new in the 1970s was, on the one hand, the emergence of a culture of eclecticism, a largely affirmative postmodernism which had abandoned any claim to critique, trans-gression or negation; and, on the other hand, an alternative postmodernism in which resistance, critique, and negation of the status quo were redefined in non-modernist and non-avantgardist terms, terms which match the political devel-opments in contemporary culture more effectively than the older theories of modernism. [...]

I would now like to sketch four major characteristics of the early phase of postmodernism which all point to postmodernism's continuity with the inter-national tradition of the modern, yes, but which – and this is my point – also establish American postmodernism as a movement *sui generis*.[3]

First, the postmodernism of the 1960s was characterized by a temporal imagination which displayed a powerful sense of the future and of new frontiers, of rupture and discontinuity, of crisis and generational conflict, an imagination reminiscent of earlier continental avantgarde movements such as Dada and surrealism rather than of high modernism. Thus the revival of Marcel Duchamp as godfather of 1960s postmodernism is no historical acci-dent. And yet, the historical constellation in which the postmodernism of the 1960s played itself out (from the Bay of Pigs and the civil rights movement to the campus revolts, the anti-war movement and the counter-culture) makes this avantgarde specifically American, even where its vocabulary of aesthetic forms and techniques was not radically new.

Secondly, the early phase of postmodernism included an iconoclastic attack on what Peter Bürger has tried to capture theoretically as the 'institution art.' By that term Bürger refers first and foremost to the ways in which art's role in society is perceived and defined, and, secondly, to ways in which art is produced, marketed, distributed, and consumed. In his book *Theory of the Avantgarde* Bürger has argued that the major goal of the historical European avantgarde (Dada, early surrealism, the postrevolutionary Russian avant-garde[4]) was to undermine, attack and transform the bourgeois institution art and its ideology of autonomy rather than only changing artistic and literary modes of representation. Bürger's approach to the question of art as institution in bourgeois society goes a long way toward suggesting useful distinctions between modernism and the avantgarde, distinctions which in turn can help us place the American avantgarde of the 1960s. In Bürger's account the European avantgarde was primarily an attack on the highness of high art and on art's separateness from everyday life as it had evolved in 19-century aestheticism and its repudiation of realism. Bürger argues that the avantgarde attempted to reintegrate art and life or, to use his Hegelian-Marxist formula, to sublate art into life, and he sees this reintegration attempt, I think correctly, as a major break with the aestheticist tradition of the later 19th century. The value of Bürger's account for contemporary American debates is that it permits us to distinguish different stages and different projects within the trajectory of the modern. The usual equation of the avantgarde with modernism can indeed no longer be maintained. Contrary to the avantgarde's intention to merge art and life, modernism always remained bound up with the more traditional notion of the autonomous art work, with the construction of form and meaning (however estranged or ambiguous, displaced or undecidable such meaning might be), and with the specialized status of the aesthetic.[5] The politically important point of Bürger's account for my argument about the 1960s is this: The historical avantgarde's iconoclastic attack on cultural institutions and on traditional modes of representation presupposed a society in which high art played an essential role in legitimizing hegemony, or, to put it in more neutral terms, to support a cultural establishment and its claims to aesthetic knowledge. It had been the achievement of the historical avantgarde to demystify and to under-mine the legitimizing discourse of high art in European society. The various modernisms of this century, on the other hand, have either maintained or restored versions of high culture, a task which was certainly facilitated by the ultimate and perhaps unavoidable failure of the historical avantgarde to reinte-grate art and life. And yet, I would suggest that it was this specific radicalism of the avantgarde, directed against the institutionalization of high art as a dis-course of hegemony and a machinery of meaning, that recommended itself as a source of energy and inspiration to the American postmodernists of the 1960s. Perhaps for the first time in American culture an avantgardist revolt against a tradition of high art and what was perceived as its hegemonic role made political sense. High art had indeed become institutionalized in the burgeoning museum, gallery, concert, record, and paperback culture of the 1950s. Mod-ernism itself had entered the mainstream via mass reproduction and the culture industry. And, during the Kennedy years, high culture even began to take on functions of political representation with Robert Frost and Pablo Casals, Malraux and Stravinsky at the White House. The irony in all of this is that the first time the U.S. had something resembling an 'institution art' in the emphatic European sense, it was modernism itself, the kind of art whose purpose had always been to resist institutionalization. In the form of happen-ings, pop vernacular, psychedelic art, acid rock, alternative and street theater, the postmodernism of the 1960s was groping to recapture the adversary ethos which had nourished modern art in its earlier stages, but which it seemed no longer able to sustain. Of course, the 'success' of the pop avantgarde, which itself had sprung full-blown from advertising in the first place, immediately made it profitable and thus sucked it into a more highly developed culture industry than the earlier European avantgarde ever had to contend with. But despite such cooption through commodification the pop avantgarde retained a certain cutting edge in its proximity to the 1960s culture of confrontation.[6] No matter how deluded about its potential effectiveness, the attack on the institution art was always also an attack on hegemonic social institutions, and the raging battles of the 1960s over whether or not pop was legitimate art prove the point.

Thirdly, many of the early advocates of postmodernism shared the technological optimism of segments of the 1920s avantgarde. What photography and film had been to Vertov and Tretyakov, Brecht, Heartfield, and Benjamin in that period, television, video, and the computer were for the prophets of a technological aesthetic in the 1960s. McLuhan's cybernetic and technocratic media eschatology and Hassan's praise for 'runaway technology,' the 'boundless dispersal by media,' 'the computer as substitute consciousness' – all of this combined easily with euphoric visions of a postindustrial society. Even if compared to the equally exuberant technological optimism of the 1920s, it is striking to see in retrospect how uncritically media technology and the cybernetic paradigm were espoused in the 1960s by conservatives, liberals, and leftists alike.[7]

The enthusiasm for the new media leads me to the fourth trend within early postmodernism. There emerged a vigorous, though again largely uncritical attempt to validate popular culture as a challenge to the canon of high art, modernist or traditional. This 'populist' trend of the 1960s with its celebration of rock 'n' roll and folk music, of the imagery of everyday life and of the multiple forms of popular literature gained much of its energy in the context of the counter-culture and by a next to total abandonment of an earlier American tradition of a critique of modern mass culture. Leslie Fiedler's incantation of the prefix 'post' in his essay 'The New Mutants' had an exhilarating effect at the time.[8] The postmodern harbored the promise of a 'post-white,' 'post-male,' 'post-humanist,' 'post-Puritan' world. It is easy to see how all of Fiedler's adjectives aim at the modernist dogma and at the cultural establishment's notion of what Western Civilization was all about. Susan Sontag's camp aesthetic did much the same. Even though it was less populist, it certainly was as hostile to high modernism. There is a curious contradiction in all this. Fiedler's populism reiterates precisely that adversarial relationship between high art and mass culture which, in the accounts of Clement Greenberg and Theodor W. Adorno, was one of the pillars of the modernist dogma Fiedler had set out to undermine. Fiedler just takes his position on the other shore, opposite Greenberg and Adorno, as it were, validating the popular and pounding away at 'elitism.' And yet, Fiedler's call to cross the border and close the gap between high art and mass culture as well as his implied political critique of what later came to be called 'eurocentrism' and 'logocentrism' can serve as an important marker for subsequent developments within postmodernism. A new creative relationship between high art and certain forms of mass culture is, to my mind, indeed one of the major marks of difference between high modernism and the art and literature which followed it in the 1970s and 1980s both in Europe and the United States. And it is precisely the recent self-assertion of minority cultures and their emergence into public consciousness which has undermined the modernist belief that high and low culture have to be categorically kept apart; such rigorous segregation simply does not make much sense *within* a given minority culture which has always existed outside in the shadow of the dominant high culture.

In conclusion, I would say that from an American perspective the postmodernism of the 1960s had some of the makings of a genuine avantgarde movement, even if the overall political situation of 1960s' America was in no way comparable to that of Berlin or Moscow in the early 1920s when the tenuous and short-lived alliance between avantgardism and vanguard politics was forged. For a number of historical reasons the ethos of artistic avantgardism as iconoclasm, as probing reflection upon the ontological status of art in modern society, as an attempt to forge another life was culturally not yet as exhausted in the U.S. of the 1960s as it was in Europe at the same time. From a European perspective, therefore, it all looked like the endgame of the historical avantgarde rather than like the breakthrough to new frontiers it claimed to be. My point here is that American postmodernism of the 1960s was both: an American avantgarde *and* the endgame of international avantgardism. And I would go on to argue that it is indeed important for the cultural historian to analyze such *Ungleichzeitigkeiten* within modernity and to relate them to the very specific constellations and contexts of national and regional cultures and histories. The view that the culture of modernity is essentially internationalist – with its cutting edge moving in space and time from Paris in the later 19th and early 20th centuries to Moscow and Berlin in the 1920s and to New York in the 1940s – is a view tied to a teleology of modern art whose unspoken subtext is the ideology of modernization. It is precisely this teleology and ideology of modernization which has become increasingly problematic in our postmodern age, problematic not so much perhaps in its descriptive powers relating to past events, but certainly in its normative claims.

[...]

HABERMAS AND THE QUESTION OF NEO-CONSERVATISM

Both in Europe and the U.S., the waning of the 1960s was accompanied by the rise of neo-conservatism, and soon enough there emerged a new constellation characterized by the terms postmodernism and neo-conservatism. Even though their relationship was never fully elaborated, the left took them to be compatible with each other or even identical, arguing that postmodernism was the kind of affirmative art that could happily coexist with political and cultural neo-conservatism. Until very recently, the question of the postmodern was simply not taken seriously on the left,[9] not to speak of those traditionalists in the academy or the museum for whom there is still nothing new and worthwhile under the sun since the advent of modernism. The left's ridiculing of postmodernism was of a piece with its often haughty and dogmatic critique of the counter-cultural impulses of the 1960s. During much of the 1970s, after all, the thrashing of the 1960s was as much a pastime of the left as it was the gospel according to Daniel Bell.

Now, there is no doubt that much of what went under the label of postmodernism in the 1970s is indeed affirmative, not critical, in nature, and often, especially in literature, remarkably similar to tendencies of modernism which it so vocally repudiates. But not all of it is simply affirmative, and the wholesale writing off of postmodernism as a symptom of capitalist culture in decline is reductive, unhistorical and all too reminiscent of Lukács' attacks on modernism in the 1930s. Can one really make such clear-cut distinctions as to uphold modernism, today, as the only valid form of 20th-century 'realism,'[10] an art that is adequate to the *condition moderne*, while simultaneously reserving all the old epitheta – inferior, decadent, pathological – to postmodernism? And isn't it ironic that many of the same critics who will insist on this distinction are the first ones to declare emphatically that modernism already had it all and that there is really nothing new in postmodernism...

I would instead argue that in order not to become the Lukács of the postmodern by opposing, today, a 'good' modernism to a 'bad' postmodernism, we try to salvage the postmodern from its assumed total collusion with neo-conservatism wherever possible; and that we explore the question whether postmodernism might not harbor productive contradictions, perhaps even a critical and oppositional potential. If the postmodern is indeed a historical and cultural condition (however transitional or incipient), then oppositional cultural practices and strategies must be located *within* postmodernism, not necessarily in its gleaming façades, to be sure, but neither in some outside ghetto of a properly 'progressive' or a correctly 'aesthetic' art. Just as Marx analyzed the culture of modernity dialectically as bringing both progress and destruction,[11] the culture of postmodernity, too, must be grasped in its gains as well as in its losses, in its promises as well as in its deprivations; and yet, it may be precisely one of the characteristics of the postmodern that the relationship between progress and destruction of cultural forms, between tradition and modernity can no longer be understood today the same way Marx understood it at the dawn of modernist culture.

[...]

WHITHER POSTMODERNISM?

The cultural history of the 1970s still has to be written, and the various postmodernisms in art, literature, dance, theater, architecture, film, video, and music will have to be discussed separately and in detail. All I want to do now is to offer a framework for relating some recent cultural and political changes to postmodernism, changes which already lie outside the conceptual network of 'modernism/avantgardism' and have so far rarely been included in the postmodernism debate.[12]

I would argue that the contemporary arts – in the widest possible sense, whether they call themselves postmodernist or reject that label – can no longer be regarded as just another phase in the sequence of modernist and avantgardist movements which began in Paris in the 1850s and 1860s and which maintained an ethos of cultural progress and vanguardism through the 1960s. On this level, postmodernism cannot be regarded simply as a sequel to modernism, as the latest step in the never-ending revolt of modernism against itself. The postmodern sensibility of our time is different from both modernism *and* avantgardism precisely in that it raises the question of cultural tradition and conservation in the most fundamental way as an aesthetic and a political issue. It doesn't always do it successfully, and often does it exploitatively. And yet, my main point about contemporary postmodernism is that it operates in a field of tension between tradition and innovation, conservation and renewal, mass culture and high art, in which the second terms are no longer automatically privileged over the first; a field of tension which can no longer be grasped in categories such as progress vs. reaction, left vs. right, present vs. past, modernism vs. realism, abstraction vs. representation; avantgarde vs. Kitsch. The fact that such dichotomies, which after all are central to the classical accounts of modernism, have broken down is part of the shift I have been trying to describe. I could also state the shift in the following terms: Modernism and the avantgarde were always closely related to social and industrial modernization. They were related to it as an adversary culture, yes, but they drew their energies, not unlike Poe's *Man of the Crowd*, from their proximity to the crises brought about by modernization and progress. Modernization – such was the widely held belief, even when the word was not around – had to be traversed. There was a vision of emerging on the other side. The modern was a world-scale drama played out on the European and American stage, with mythic modern man as its hero and with modern art as a driving force, just as Saint-Simon had envisioned it already in 1825. Such heroic visions of modernity and of art as a force of social change (or, for that matter, resistance to undesired change) are a thing of the past, admirable for sure, but no longer in tune with current sensibilities, except perhaps with an emerging apocalyptic sensibility as the flip side of modernist heroism.

Seen in this light, postmodernism at its deepest level represents not just another crisis within the perpetual cycle of boom and bust, exhaustion and renewal, which has characterized the trajectory of modernist culture. It rather represents a new type of crisis *of* that modernist culture itself. Of course, this claim has been made before, and fascism indeed was a formidable crisis *of* modernist culture. But fascism was never the alternative to modernity it pretended to be, and our situation today is very different from that of the

Weimar Republic in its agony. It was only in the 1970s that the historical limits of modernism, modernity, and modernization came into sharp focus. The growing sense that we are not bound to *complete* the project of modernity (Habermas' phrase) and still do not necessarily have to lapse into irrationality or into apocalyptic frenzy, the sense that art is not exclusively pursuing some telos of abstraction, non-representation, and sublimity – all of this has opened up a host of possibilities for creative endeavors today. And in certain ways it has altered our views of modernism itself. Rather than being bound to a one-way history of modernism which interprets it as a logical unfolding toward some imaginary goal, and which thus is based on a whole series of exclusions, we are beginning to explore its contradictions and contingencies, its tensions and internal resistances to its own 'forward' movement. Postmodernism is far from making modernism obsolete. On the contrary, it casts a new light on it and appropriates many of its aesthetic strategies and techniques inserting them and making them work in new constellations. What has become obsolete, however, are those codifications of modernism in critical discourse which, however subliminally, are based on a teleological view of progress and modernization. Ironically, these normative and often reductive codifications have actually prepared the ground for that repudiation of modernism which goes by the name of the postmodern. Confronted with the critic who argues that this or that novel is not up to the latest in narrative technique, that it is regressive, behind the times and thus uninteresting, the postmodernist is right in rejecting modernism. But such rejection affects only that trend within modernism which has been codified into a narrow dogma, not modernism as such. In some ways, the story of modernism and postmodernism is like the story of the hedgehog and the hare: the hare could not win because there always was more than just one hedgehog. But the hare was still the better runner.

The crisis of modernism is more than just a crisis of those trends within it which tie it to the ideology of modernization. In the age of late capitalism, it is also a new crisis of art's relationship to society. At their most emphatic, modernism and avantgardism attributed to art a privileged status in the processes of social change. Even the aestheticist withdrawal from the concern of social change is still bound to it by virtue of its denial of the status quo and the construction of an artificial paradise of exquisite beauty. When social change seemed beyond grasp or took an undesired turn, art was still privileged as the only authentic voice of critique and protest, even when it seemed to withdraw into itself. The classical accounts of high modernism attest to that fact. To admit that these were heroic illusions – perhaps even necessary illusions in art's struggle to survive in dignity in a capitalist society – is not to deny the importance of art in social life.

But modernism's running feud with mass society and mass culture as well as the avantgarde's attack on high art as a support system of cultural hegemony always took place on the pedestal of high art itself. And certainly that is where the avantgarde has been installed after its failure, in the 1920s, to create a more encompassing space for art in social life. To continue to demand today that high art leave the pedestal and relocate elsewhere (wherever that might be) is to pose the problem in obsolete terms. The pedestal of high art and high culture no longer occupies the privileged space it used to, just as the cohesion of the class which erected its monuments on that pedestal is a thing of the past; recent conservative attempts in a number of Western countries to restore the dignity of the classics of Western Civilization, from Plato via Adam Smith to the high modernists, and to send students back to the basics, prove the point. I am not saying here that the pedestal of high art does not exist any more. Of course it does, but it is not what it used to be. Since the 1960s, artistic activities have become much more diffuse and harder to contain in safe categories or stable institutions such as the academy, the museum or even the established gallery network. To some, this dispersal of cultural and artistic practices and activities will involve a sense of loss and disorientation; others will experience it as a new freedom, a cultural liberation. Neither may be entirely wrong, but we should recognize that it was not only recent theory or criticism that deprived the univalent, exclusive and totalizing accounts of modernism of their hegemonic role. It was the activities of artists, writers, film makers, architects, and performers that have propelled us beyond a narrow vision of modernism and given us a new lease on modernism itself.

In political terms, the erosion of the triple dogma modernism/modernity/ avantgardism can be contextually related to the emergence of the problematic of 'otherness,' which has asserted itself in the sociopolitical sphere as much as in the cultural sphere. I cannot discuss here the various and multiple forms of otherness as they emerge from differences in subjectivity, gender and sexuality, race and class, temporal *Ungleichzeitigkeiten* and spatial geographic locations and dislocations. But I want to mention at least four recent phenomena which, in my mind, are and will remain constitutive of postmodern culture for some time to come.

Despite all its noble aspirations and achievements, we have come to recognize that the culture of enlightened modernity has also always (though by no means exclusively) been a culture of inner and outer imperialism, a reading already offered by Adorno and Horkheimer in the 1940s and an insight not unfamiliar to those of our ancestors involved in the multitude of struggles against rampant modernization. Such imperialism, which works inside and outside, on the micro and macro levels, no longer goes unchallenged either politically, economically, or culturally. Whether these challenges will usher in a more habitable, less violent and more democratic world remains to be seen, and it is easy to be skeptical. But enlightened cynicism is as insufficient an answer as blue-eyed enthusiasm for peace and nature.

The women's movement has led to some significant changes in social structure and cultural attitudes which must be sustained even in the face of the recent grotesque revival of American machismo. Directly and indirectly, the women's movement has nourished the emergence of women as a self-confident and creative force in the arts, in literature, film, and criticism. The ways in which we now raise questions of gender and sexuality, reading and writing, subjectivity and enunciation, voice and performance are unthinkable without the impact of feminism, even though many of these activities may take place on the margin or even outside the movement proper. Feminist critics have also contributed substantially to revisions of the history of modernism, not just by unearthing forgotten artists, but also by approaching the male modernists in novel ways. This is true also of the 'new French feminists' and their theorization of the feminine in modernist writing, even though they often insist on maintaining a polemical distance from an American-type feminism.[13]

During the 1970s, questions of ecology and environment have deepened from single-issue politics to a broad critique of modernity and modernization, a trend which is politically and culturally much stronger in West Germany than in the U.S. A new ecological sensibility manifests itself not only in political and regional subcultures, in alternative life-styles, and the new social movements in Europe, but it also affects art and literature in a variety of ways: the work of Joseph Beuys, certain land art projects, Christo's California running fence, the new nature poetry, the return to local traditions, dialects, and so on. It was especially due to the growing ecological sensibility that the link between certain forms of modernism and technological modernization has come under critical scrutiny.

There is a growing awareness that other cultures, non-European, non-Western cultures must be met by means other than conquest or domination, as Paul Ricoeur put it more than twenty years ago, and that the erotic and aesthetic fascination with 'the Orient' and 'the primitive' – so prominent in Western culture, including modernism – is deeply problematic. This awareness will have to translate into a type of intellectual work different from that of the modernist intellectual who typically spoke with the confidence of standing at the cutting edge of time and of being able to speak for others. Foucault's notion of the local and specific intellectual as opposed to the 'universal' intellectual of modernity may provide a way out of the dilemma of being locked into our own culture and traditions while simultaneously recognizing their limitations.

In conclusion, it is easy to see that a postmodernist culture emerging from these political, social, and cultural constellations will have to be a postmodernism of resistance, including resistance to that easy postmodernism of the 'anything goes' variety. Resistance will always have to be specific and contingent upon the cultural field within which it operates. It cannot be defined simply in terms of negativity or non-identity à la Adorno, nor will the litanies of a totalizing, collective project suffice. At the same time, the very notion of resistance may itself be problematic in its simple opposition to affirmation. After all, there are affirmative forms of resistance and resisting forms of affirmation. But this may be more a semantic problem than a problem of practice. And it should not keep us from making judgments. How such resistance can be articulated in art works in ways that would satisfy the needs of the political *and* those of the aesthetic, of the producers and of the recipients, cannot be prescribed, and it will remain open to trial, error and debate. But it is time to abandon that dead-end dichotomy of politics and aesthetics which for too long has dominated accounts of modernism, including the aestheticist trend within poststructuralism. The point is not to eliminate the productive tension between the political and the aesthetic, between history and the text, between engagement and the mission of art. The point is to heighten that tension, even to rediscover it and to bring it back into focus in the arts as well as in criticism. No matter how troubling it may be, the landscape of the postmodern surrounds us. It simultaneously delimits and opens our horizons. It's our problem and our hope.

NOTES

1. On this question see Fredric Jameson, 'Postmodernism or the Cultural Logic of Capitalism,' *New Left Review*, 146 (July–August 1984), 53–92, whose attempt to identify postmodernism with a new stage in the developmental logic of capital, I feel, overstates the case.
2. For an earlier attempt to give a *Begriffsgeschichte* of postmodernism in literature, see the various essays in *Amerikastudien*, 22:1 (1977), 9–6 (includes a valuable bibliography). Cf. also Ihab Hassan, *The Dismemberment of Orpheus*, second edition (Madison: University of Wisconsin Press, 1982), especially the new 'Postface 1982: Toward a Concept of Postmodernism,' pp. 259–271 – The debate about modernity and modernization in history and the social sciences is too broad to document here; for an excellent survey of the pertinent literature, see Hans-Ulrich Wehler, *Modernisierungstheorie und Geschichte* (Göttingen: Vandenhoeck & Ruprecht, 1975). – On the question of modernity and the arts, see Matei Calinescu, *Faces of Modernity* (Bloomington: Indiana University Press, 1977); Marshall Berman, *All That Is Solid Melts Into Air: The Experience of Modernity* (New York: Simon & Schuster, 1982); Eugene Lunn, *Marxism and Modernism* (Berkeley and Los Angeles: University of California Press, 1982); Peter Bürger. *Theory of the Avantgarde* (Minneapolis: University of Minnesota Press, 1984). Also important for this debate is the recent work by cultural historians on specific cities and their culture, e.g., Carl Schorske's and Robert Waissenberger's work on fin-de-siècle Vienna, Peter Gay's and John Willett's work on the Weimar Republic, and, for a discussion of American anti-modernism at the turn of the century, T. J. Jackson Lear's *No Place of Grace* (New York: Pantheon, 1981).
3. The following section will draw on arguments developed less fully in the preceding article entitled 'The Search for Tradition: Avantgarde and Postmodernism in the 1970s.'
4. Peter Bürger, *Theory of the Avant-Garde* (Minneapolis: University of Minnesota Press, 1984). The fact that Bürger reserves the term avantgarde for mainly these three movements may strike the American reader as idiosyncratic or as unnecessarily limited unless the place of the argument within the tradition of 20th-century German aesthetic thought from Brecht and Benjamin to Adorno is understood.
5. This difference between modernism and the avantgarde was one of the pivotal points of disagreement between Benjamin and Adorno in the late 1930s, a debate to which Bürger owes a lot. Confronted with the successful fusion of aesthetics, politics, and everyday life in fascist Germany, Adorno condemned the avantgarde's intention to merge art with life and continued to insist, in best modernist fashion, on the autonomy of art; Benjamin, on the other hand, looking backward to the radical experiments in Parìs, Moscow, and Berlin in the 1920s, found a messianic promise in the avantgarde, especially in surrealism, a fact which may help explain Benjamin's strange (and, I think, mistaken) appropriation in the U.S. as a postmodern critic *avant la lettre*.

6. Cf. my essay, 'The Cultural Politics of Pop.' From a different perspective, Dick Hebdige developed a similar argument about British pop culture at a talk he gave last year at the Center for Twentieth Century-Studies at the University of Wisconsin-Milwaukee.

7. The Left's fascination with the media was perhaps more pronounced in Germany than it was in the United States. Those were the years when Brecht's radio theory and Benjamin's 'The Work of Art in the Age of Mechanical Reproduction' almost became cult texts. See, for example, Hans Magnus Enzensberger, 'Baukasten zu einer Theorie der Medien,' *Kursbuch*, 20 (March 1970), 159–86. Reprinted in H. M. E., *Palaver* (Frankfurt am Main: Sulirkamp, 1974). The old belief in the democratizing potential of the media is also intimated on the last pages of Lyotard's *The Postmodern Condition*, not in relation to radio, film or television, but in relation to computers.

8. Leslie Fidler, 'The New Mutants' (1965), *A Fiedler Reader* (New York: Stein and Day, 1977), pp. 189–10.

9. It is with the recent publications of Fred Jameson and of Hal Foster's *The Anti-Aesthetic* that things have begun to change.

10. Of course, those who hold this view will not utter the word 'realism' as it is tarnished by its traditionally close association with the notions of 'reflection,' 'representation,' and a transparent reality; but the persuasive power of the modernist doctrine owes much to the underlying idea that only modernist art and literature are somehow adequate to our time.

11. For a work that remains very much in the orbit of Marx's notion of modernity and tied to the political and cultural impulses of the American 1960s see Marshall Berman, *All That Is Solid Melts Into Air: The Experience of Modernity* (New York: Simon & Schuster, 1982). For a critique of Berman see David Bathrick, 'Marxism and Modernism,' *New German Critique*, 33 (Fall 1984), 207–18.

12. The major exception is Craig Owens, 'The Discourse of Others,' in Hal Foster, ed., *The Anti-Aesthetic*, p. 65–98.

13. Cf. Elaine Marks and Isabelle de Courtivron, eds., *New French Feminisms* (Amherst: University of Massachusetts Press, 1980). For a critical view of French theories of the feminine cf. Alice Jardine's essay 'Gynesis,' *diacritics*, 12:2 (Summer 1982), 54–65.

NARRATIVE, KNOWLEDGE, REPRESENTATION

4

FROM *THE POSTMODERN CONDITION: A REPORT ON KNOWLEDGE*

Jean-François Lyotard

The object of this study is the condition of knowledge in the most highly developed societies. I have decided to use the word *postmodern* to describe that condition. The word is in current use on the American continent among sociologists and critics; it designates the state of our culture following the transformations which, since the end of the nineteenth century, have altered the game rules for science, literature, and the arts. The present study will place these transformations in the context of the crisis of narratives.

Science has always been in conflict with narratives. Judged by the yardstick of science, the majority of them prove to be fables. But to the extent that science does not restrict itself to stating useful regularities and seeks the truth, it is obliged to legitimate the rules of its own game. It then produces a discourse of legitimation with respect to its own status, a discourse called philosophy. I will use the term *modern* to designate any science that legitimates itself with reference to a metadiscourse of this kind making an explicit appeal to some grand narrative, such as the dialectics of Spirit, the hermeneutics of meaning, the emancipation of the rational or working subject, or the creation of wealth. For example, the rule of consensus between the sender and addressee of a statement with truth-value is deemed acceptable if it is cast in terms of a possible unanimity between rational minds: this is the Enlightenment narrative, in which the hero of knowledge works toward a good ethico-political end – universal peace. As can be seen from this example, if a metanarrative implying a

From Jean-François Lyotard (1984) *The Postmodern Condition: A Report on Knowledge* [1979] Minneapolis, MN: University of Minnesota Press; Manchester: Manchester University Press.

philosophy of history is used to legitimate knowledge, questions are raised concerning the validity of the institutions governing the social bond: these must be legitimated as well. Thus justice is consigned to the grand narrative in the same way as truth.

Simplifying to the extreme, I define *postmodern* as incredulity toward metanarratives. This incredulity is undoubtedly a product of progress in the sciences: but that progress in turn presupposes it. To the obsolescence of the metanarrative apparatus of legitimation corresponds, most notably, the crisis of metaphysical philosophy and of the university institution which in the past relied on it. The narrative function is losing its functors, its great hero, its great dangers, its great voyages, its great goal. It is being dispersed in clouds of narrative language elements – narrative, but also denotative, prescriptive, descriptive, and so on. Conveyed within each cloud are pragmatic valencies specific to its kind. Each of us lives at the intersection of many of these. However, we do not necessarily establish stable language combinations, and the properties of the ones we do establish are not necessarily communicable.

Thus the society of the future falls less within the province of a Newtonian anthropology (such as stucturalism or systems theory) than a pragmatics of language particles. There are many different language games – a heterogeneity of elements. They only give rise to institutions in patches – local determinism.

The decision makers, however, attempt to manage these clouds of sociality according to input/output matrices, following a logic which implies that their elements are commensurable and that the whole is determinable. They allocate our lives for the growth of power. In matters of social justice and of scientific truth alike, the legitimation of that power is based on its optimizing the system's performance – efficiency. The application of this criterion to all of our games necessarily entails a certain level of terror, whether soft or hard: be operational (that is, commensurable) or disappear.

The logic of maximum performance is no doubt inconsistent in many ways, particularly with respect to contradiction in the socio-economic field: it demands both less work (to lower production costs) and more (to lessen the social burden of the idle population). But our incredulity is now such that we no longer expect salvation to rise from these inconsistencies, as did Marx.

Still, the postmodern condition is as much a stranger to disenchantment as it is to the blind positivity of delegitimation. Where, after the metanarratives, can legitimacy reside? The operativity criterion is technological; it has no relevance for judging what is true or just. Is legitimacy to be found in consensus obtained through discussion, as Jürgen Habermas thinks? Such consensus does violence to the heterogeneity of language games. And invention is always born of dissension. Postmodern knowledge is not simply a tool of the authorities; it refines our sensitivity to differences and reinforces our ability to tolerate the incommensurable. Its principle is not the expert's homology, but the inventor's paralogy.

Here is the question: is a legitimation of the social bond, a just society, feasible in terms of a paradox analogous to that of scientific activity? What would such a paradox be?

[...]

3. THE METHOD: LANGUAGE GAMES

The reader will already have noticed that in analyzing this problem within the framework set forth I have favored a certain procedure: emphasizing facts of language and in particular their pragmatic aspect.[1] To help clarify what follows it would be useful to summarize, however briefly, what is meant here by the term *pragmatic*.

A denotative utterance[2] such as 'The university is sick,' made in the context of a conversation or an interview, positions its sender (the person who utters the statement), its addressee (the person who receives it), and its referent (what the statement deals with) in a specific way: the utterance places (and exposes) the sender in the position of 'knower' (he knows what the situation is with the university), the addressee is put in the position of having to give or refuse his assent, and the referent itself is handled in a way unique to denotatives, as something that demands to be correctly identified and expressed by the statement that refers to it.

If we consider a declaration such as 'The university is open,' pronounced by a dean or rector at convocation, it is clear that the previous specifications no longer apply. Of course, the meaning of the utterance has to be understood, but that is a general condition of communication and does not aid us in distinguishing the different kinds of utterances or their specific effects. The distinctive feature of this second, 'performative,'[3] utterance is that its effect upon the referent coincides with its enunciation. The university is open because it has been declared open in the above-mentioned circumstances. That this is so is not subject to discussion or verification on the part of the addressee, who is immediately placed within the new context created by the utterance. As for the sender, he must be invested with the authority to make such a statement. Actually, we could say it the other way around: the sender is dean or rector – that is he is invested with the authority to make this kind of statement – only insofar as he can directly affect both the referent (the university) and the addressee (the university staff) in the manner I have indicated.

A different case involves utterances of the type, 'Give money to the university'; these are prescriptions. They can be modulated as orders, commands, instructions, recommendations, requests, prayers, pleas, etc. Here, the sender is clearly placed in a position of authority, using the term broadly (including the authority of a sinner over a god who claims to be merciful): that is, he expects the addressee to perform the action referred to. The pragmatics of prescription entail concomitant changes in the posts of addressee and referent.[4]

Of a different order again is the efficiency of a question, a promise, a literary description, a narration, etc. I am summarizing. Wittgenstein, taking up the study of language again from scratch, focuses his attention on the effects of different modes of discourse; he calls the various types of utterances he identifies along the way (a few of which I have listed) *language games*.[5] What he means by this term is that each of the various categories of utterance can be defined in terms of rules specifying their properties and the uses to which they can be put – in exactly the same way as the game of chess is defined by a set of rules determining the properties of each of the pieces, in other words, the proper way to move them.

It is useful to make the following three observations about language games. The first is that their rules do not carry within themselves their own legitimation, but are the object of a contract, explicit or not, between players (which is not to say that the players invent the rules). The second is that if there are no rules, there is no game,[6] that even an infinitesimal modification of one rule alters the nature of the game, that a 'move' or utterance that does not satisfy the rules does not belong to the game they define. The third remark is suggested by what has just been said: every utterance should be thought of as a 'move' in a game.

This last observation brings us to the first principle underlying our method as a whole: to speak is to fight, in the sense of playing, and speech acts[7] fall within the domain of a general agonistics.[8] This does not necessarily mean that one plays in order to win. A move can be made for the sheer pleasure of its invention: what else is involved in that labor of language harassment undertaken by popular speech and by literature? Great joy is had in the endless invention of turns of phrase, of words and meanings, the process behind the evolution of language on the level of *parole*. But undoubtedly even this pleasure depends on a feeling of success won at the expense of an adversary – at least one adversary, and a formidable one: the accepted language, or connotation.[9]

This idea of an agonistics of language should not make us lose sight of the second principle, which stands as a complement to it and governs our analysis: that the observable social bond is composed of language 'moves.' An elucidation of this proposition will take us to the heart of the matter at hand.

[...]

6. THE PRAGMATICS OF NARRATIVE KNOWLEDGE

[...] I leveled two objections against the unquestioning acceptance of an instrumental conception of knowledge in the most highly developed societies. Knowledge is not the same as science, especially in its contemporary form; and science, far from successfully obscuring the problem of its legitimacy, cannot avoid raising it with all of its implications, which are no less sociopolitical than epistemological. Let us begin with an analysis of the nature of 'narrative' knowledge; by providing a point of comparison, our examination will clarify at least some of the characteristics of the form assumed by scientific knowledge in contemporary society. In addition, it will aid us in understanding how the question of legitimacy is raised or fails to be raised today.

Knowledge, [*savoir*] in general cannot be reduced to science, nor even to learning [*connaissance*]. Learning is the set of statements which, to the exclusion of all other statements, denote or describe objects and may be declared true of false.[10] Science is a subset of learning. It is also composed of denotative statements, but imposes two supplementary conditions on their acceptability: the objects to which they refer must be available for repeated access, in other words, they must be accessible in explicit conditions of observation; and it must be possible to decide whether or not a given statement pertains to the language judged relevant by the experts.[11]

But what is meant by the term *knowledge* is not only a set of denotative statements, far from it. It also includes notions of 'know-how,' 'knowing how to live,' 'how to listen' [*savoir-faire, savoir-vivre, savoir-écouter*], etc. Knowledge, then, is a question of competence that goes beyond the simple determination and application of the criterion of truth, extending to the determination and application of criteria of efficiency (technical qualification), of justice and/or happiness (ethical wisdom), of the beauty of a sound or color (auditory and visual sensibility), etc. Understood in this way, knowledge is what makes someone capable of forming 'good' denotative utterances but also 'good' prescriptive and 'good' evaluative utterances. . . . It is not a competence relative to a particular class of statements (for example, cognitive ones) to the exclusion of all others. On the contrary, it makes 'good' performances in relation to a variety of objects of discourse possible: objects to be known, decided on, evaluated, transformed. . . . From this derives one of the principal features of knowledge: it coincides with an extensive array of competence-building measures and is the only from embodied in a subject constituted by the various areas of competence composing it.

Another characteristic meriting special attention is the relation between this kind of knowledge and custom. What is a 'good' prescriptive or evaluative utterance, a 'good' performance in denotative or technical matters? They are all judged to be 'good' because they conform to the relevant criteria (of justice, beauty, truth, and efficiency respectively) accepted in the social circle of the 'knower's' interlocutors. The early philosophers called this mode of legitimating statements opinion.[12] The consensus that permits such knowledge to be circumscribed and makes it possible to distinguish one who knows from one who doesn't (the foreigner, the child) is what constitutes the culture of a people.[13]

This brief reminder of what knowledge can be in the way of training and culture draws on ethnological description for its justification.[14] But anthropological studies and literature that take rapidly developing societies as their object can attest to the survival of this type of knowledge within them, at least in some of their sectors.[15] The very idea of development presupposes a horizon of nondevelopment where, it is assumed, the various areas of competence remain enveloped in the unity of a tradition and are not differentiated according to separate qualifications subject to specific innovations, debates, and inquiries. This opposition does not necessarily imply a difference in nature between 'primitive' and 'civilized' man,[16] but is compatible with the premise of a formal identity between 'the savage mind' and scientific thought;[17] it is even compatible with the (apparently contrary) premise of the superiority of customary knowledge over the contemporary dispersion of competence.[18]

It is fair to say that there is one point on which all of the investigations agree, regardless of which scenario they propose to dramatize and understand the distance separating the customary state of knowledge from its state in the scientific age: the preeminence of the narrative form in the formulation of traditional knowledge. Some study this form for its own sake;[19] others see it as the diachronic costume of the structural operators that, according to them, properly constitute the knowledge in question;[20] still others bring to it an 'economic' interpretation in the Freudian sense of the term.[21] All that is important here is the fact that its form its narrative. Narration is the quintessential form of customary knowledge, in more ways than one.

First the popular stories themselves recount what could be called positive or negative apprenticeships (*Bildungen*): in other words, the successes or failures greeting the hero's undertakings. These successes or failures either bestow legitimacy upon social institutions (the function of myths), or represent positive or negative models (the successful or unsuccessful hero) of integration into established institutions (legends and tales). Thus the narratives allow the society in which they are told, on the one hand, to define its criteria of competence and, on the other, to evaluate according to those criteria what is performed or can be performed within it.

Second, the narrative form, unlike the developed forms of the discourse of knowledge, lends itself to a great variety of language games. Denotative statements concerning, for example, the state of the sky and the flora and fauna easily slip in; so do deontic statements prescribing what should be done with respect to these same referents, or with respect, to kinship, the difference between the sexes, children, neighbors, foreigners, etc. Interrogative statements are implied, for example, in episodes involving challenges (respond to a question, choose one from a number of things); evaluative statements also enter in, etc. The areas of competence whose criteria the narrative supplies or applies are thus tightly woven together in the web it forms, ordered by the unified viewpoint characteristic of this kind of knowledge.

We shall examine in somewhat more detail a third property, which relates to the transmission of narratives. Their narration usually obeys rules that define the pragmatics of their transmission. I do not mean to say that a given society institutionally assigns the role of narrator to certain categories on the basis of age, sex, or family or professional group. What I am getting at is a pragmatics of popular narratives that is, so to speak, intrinsic to them. For example, a

Cashinahua[22] storyteller always begins his narration with a fixed formula: 'Here is the story of—, as I've always heard it told. I will tell it to you in my turn. Listen.' And he brings it to a close with another, also invariable, formula: 'Here ends the story of—. The man who has told it to you is—. (Cashinahua name), or to the Whites— (Spanish or Portuguese name).'[23]

A quick analysis of this double pragmatic instruction reveals the following: the narrator's only claim to competence for telling the story is the fact that he has heard it himself. The current narratee gains potential access to the same authority simply by listening. It is claimed that the narrative is a faithful transmission (even if the narrative performance is highly inventive) and that it has been told 'forever': therefore the hero, a Cashinahuan, was himself once a narratee, and perhaps a narrator, of the very same story. This similarity of condition allows for the possibility that the current narrator could be the hero of a narrative, just as the Ancestor was. In fact, he is necessarily such a hero because he bears a name, declined at the end of his narration, and that name was given to him in conformity with the canonic narrative legitimating the assignment of patronyms among the Cashinahua.

The pragmatic rule illustrated by this example cannot, of course, be universalized.[24] But it gives insight into what is a generally recognized property of traditional knowledge. The narrative 'posts' (sender, addressee, hero) are so organized that the right to occupy the post of sender receives the following double grounding: it is based upon the fact of having occupied the post of addressee, and of having been recounted oneself, by virtue of the name one bears, by a previous narrative – in other words, having been positioned as the diegetic reference of other narrative events.[25] The knowledge transmitted by these narrations is in no way limited to the functions of enunciation; it determines in a single stroke what one must say in order to be heard, what one must listen to in order to speak, and what role one must play (on the scene of diegetic reality) to be the object of a narrative.

Thus the speech acts[26] relevant to this form of knowledge are performed not only by the speaker, but also by the listener, as well as by the third party referred to. The knowledge arising from such an apparatus may seem 'condensed' in comparison with what I call 'developed' knowledge. Our example clearly illustrates that a narrative tradition is also the tradition of the criteria defining a threefold competence – 'know-how,' 'knowing how to speak,' and 'knowing how to hear' [*savoir-faire, savoir-dire, savoir-entendre*] – through which the community's relationship to itself and its environment is played out. What is transmitted through these narratives is the set of pragmatic rules that constitutes the social bond.

A fourth aspect of narrative knowledge meriting careful examination is its effect on time. Narrative form follows a rhythm; it is the synthesis of a meter beating time in regular periods and of accent modifying the length or amplitude of certain of those periods.[27] This vibratory, musical property of narrative is clearly revealed in the ritual performance of certain Cashinahua tales: they are handed down in initiation ceremonies, in absolutely fixed form, in a language whose meaning is obscured by lexical and syntactic anomalies, and they are sung as interminable, monotonous chants.[28] It is a strange brand of knowledge, you may say, that does not even make itself understood to the young men to whom it is addressed!

And yet this kind of knowledge is quite common; nursery rhymes are of this type, and repetitive forms of contemporary music have tried to recapture or at least approximate it. It exhibits a surprising feature: as meter takes precedence over accent in the production of sound (spoken or not), time ceases to be a support for memory to become an immemorial beating that, in the absence of a noticeable separation between periods, prevents their being numbered and consigns them to oblivion.[29] Consider the form of popular sayings, proverbs, and maxims: they are like little splinters of potential narratives, or molds of old ones, which have continued to circulate on certain levels of the contemporary social edifice. In their prosody can be recognized the mark of that strange temporalization that jars the golden rule of our knowledge: 'never forget.'

Now there must be a congruence between this lethal function of narrative knowledge and the functions, cited earlier, of criteria formation, the unification of areas of competence, and social regulation. By way of a simplifying fiction, we can hypothesize that, against all expectations, a collectivity that takes narrative as its key form of competence has no need to remember its past. It finds the raw material for its social bond not only in the meaning of the narratives it recounts, but also in the act of reciting them. The narratives' reference may seem to belong to the past, but in reality it is always contemporaneous with the act of recitation. It is the present act that on each of its occurrences marshals in the ephemeral temporality inhabiting the space between the 'I have heard' and the 'you will hear.'

The important thing about the pragmatic protocol of this kind of narration is that it betokens a theoretical identity between each of the narrative's occurrences. This may not in fact be the case, and often is not, and we should not blind ourselves to the element of humor or anxiety noticeable in the respect this etiquette inspires. The fact remains that what is emphasized is the metrical beat of the narrative occurrences, not each performance's differences in accent. It is in this sense that this mode of temporality can be said to be simultaneously evanescent and immemorial.[30]

Finally, a culture that gives precedence to the narrative form doubtless has no more of a need for special procedures to authorize its narratives than it has to remember its past. It is hard to imagine such a culture first isolating the post of narrator from the others in order to give it a privileged status in narrative pragmatics, then inquiring into what right the narrator (who is thus disconnected from the narratee and diegesis) might have to account what he recounts, and finally undertaking the analysis or anamnesis of its own legitimacy. It is even harder to imagine it handing over the authority for its narratives to some incomprehensible subject of narration. The narratives themselves have this authority. In a sense, the people are only that which actualizes the narratives: once again, they do this not only by recounting them, but also by listening to them and recounting themselves through them; in other words, by putting them into 'play' in their institutions – thus by assigning themselves the posts of narratee and diegesis as well as the post of narrator.

There is, then, an incommensurability between popular narrative pragmatics, which provides immediate legitimation, and the language game known to the West as the question of legitimacy – or rather, legitimacy as a referent in the game of inquiry. Narratives, as we have seen, determine criteria of competence and/or illustrate how they are to be applied. They thus define what has the right to be said and done in the culture in question, and since they are themselves a part of that culture, they are legitimated by the simple fact that they do what they do.

7. THE PRAGMATICS OF SCIENTIFIC KNOWLEDGE

Let us attempt to characterize, if only in summary fashion, the classical conception of the pragmatics of scientific knowledge. In the process, we will distinguish between the research game and the teaching game.

Copernicus states that the path of the planets is circular.[31] Whether this proposition is true or false, it carries within it a set of tensions, all of which affect each of the pragmatic posts it brings into play: sender, addressee, and referent. These 'tensions' are classes of prescriptions which regulate the admissibility of the statement as 'scientific.'

First, the sender should speak the truth about the referent, the path of the planets. What does this mean? That on the one hand he is supposed to be able to provide proof of what he says, and on the other hand he is supposed to be able to refute any opposing or contradictory statements concerning the same referent.

Second, it should be possible for the addressee validly to give (or refuse) his assent to the statement he hears. This implies that he is himself a potential sender, since when he formulates his agreement or disagreement he will be subject to the same double requirement (or proof or refutation) that Copernicus was. He is therefore supposed to have potentially, the same qualities as Copernicus: he is his equal. But this will only become known when he speaks and under the above conditions. Before that, it will be impossible to say whether or not he is a scientific scholar.

Third, the referent (the path of the planets) of which Copernicus speaks is supposed to be 'expressed' by his statement in conformity with what it actually is. But since what it is can only be known through statements of the same order as that of Copernicus, the rule of adequation becomes problematical. What I say is true because I prove that it is – but what proof is there that my proof is true?

The scientific solution of this difficulty consists in the observance of two rules. The first of these is dialectical or even rhetorical in the forensic sense:[32] a referent is that which is susceptible to proof and can be used as evidence in a debate. Not: I can prove something because reality is the way I say it is. But: as long as I can produce proof, it is permissible to think that reality is the way I say it is.[33] The second rule is metaphysical; the same referent cannot supply a plurality of contradictory or inconsistent proofs. Or stated differently: 'God' is not deceptive.[34]

These two rules underlie what nineteenth-century science calls verification and twentieth-century science, falsification.[35] They allow a horizon of consensus to be brought to the debate between partners (the sender and the addressee). Not every consensus is a sign of truth; but it is presumed that the truth of a statement necessarily draws a consensus.

That covers research. It should be evident that research appeals to teaching as its necessary complement: the scientists needs an addressee who can in turn become the sender; he needs a partner. Otherwise, the verification of his statements would be impossible, since the nonrenewal of the requisite skills would eventually bring an end to the necessary, contradictory debate. Not only the truth of a scientist's statement, but also his competence, is at stake in that debate. One's competence is never an accomplished fact. It depends on whether or not the statement proposed is considered by one's peers to be worth discussion in a sequence of argumentation and refutation. The truth of the statement and the competence of its sender are thus subject to the collective approval of a group of persons who are competent on an equal basis. Equals are needed and must be created.

Didactics is what ensures that this reproduction takes place. It is different from the dialectical game of research. Briefly, its first presupposition is that the addressee, the student, does not know what the sender knows: obviously, that is why he has something to learn. Its second presupposition is that the student can learn what the sender knows and become an expert whose competence is equal to that of his master.[36] This double requirement supposes a third: that there are statements for which the exchange of arguments and the production of proof constituting the pragmatics of research are considered to have been sufficient, and which can therefore be transmitted through teaching as they stand, in the guise of indisputable truths.

In other words, you teach what you know: such is the expert. But as the student (the addressee of the didactic process) improves his skills, the expert can confide to him what he does not know but is trying to learn (at least if the expert is also involved in research). In this way, the student is introduced to the dialectics of research, or the game of producing scientific knowledge.

If we compare the pragmatics of science to that of narrative knowledge, we note the following properties:

1. Scientific knowledge requires that one language game, denotation, be retained and all others excluded. A statement's truth-value is the criterion determining its acceptability. Of course, we find other classes of statements, such as interrogatives ('How can we explain that . . .?') and prescriptives ('Take a finite series of elements . . .'). But they are only present as turning points in the

dialectical argumentation, which must end in a denotative statement.[37] In this context, then, one is 'learned' if one can produce a true statement about a referent, and one is a scientist if one can produce verifiable or falsifiable statements about referents accessible to the experts.

2. Scientific knowledge is in this way set apart from the language games that combine to form the social bond. Unlike narrative knowledge, it is no longer a direct and shared component of the bond. But it is indirectly a component of it, because it develops into a profession and gives rise to institutions, and in modern societies language games consolidate themselves in the form of institutions run by qualified partners (the professional class). The relation between knowledge and society (that is, the sum total of partners in the general agonistics, excluding scientists in their professional capacity) becomes one of mutual exteriority. A new problem appears – that of the relationship between the scientific institution and society. Can this problem be solved by didactics, for example, by the premise that any social atom can acquire scientific competence?

3. Within the bounds of the game of research, the competence required concerns the post of sender alone. There is no particular competence required of the addressee (it is required only in didactics – the student must be intelligent). And there is no competence required of the referent. Even in the case of the human sciences, where it is an aspect of human conduct, the referent is in principle external to the partners engaged in scientific dialectics. Here, in contrast to the narrative game, a person does not have to know how to be what knowledge says he is.

4. A statement of science gains no validity from the fact of being reported. Even in the case of pedagogy, it is taught only if it is still verifiable in the present through argumentation and proof. In itself, it is never secure from 'falsification.'[38] The knowledge that has accumulated in the form of already accepted statements can always be challenged. But conversely, any new statement that contradicts a previously approved statement regarding the same referent can be accepted as valid only if it refutes the previous statement by producing arguments and proofs.

5. The game of science thus implies a diachronic temporality, that is, a memory and a project. The current sender of a scientific statement is supposed to be acquainted with previous statements concerning its referent (bibliography) and only proposes a new statement on the subject if it differs from the previous ones. Here, what I have called the 'accent' of each performance, and by that token the polemical function of the game, takes precedence over the 'meter.' This diachrony, which assumes memory and a search for the new, represents in principle a cumulative process. Its 'rhythm,' or the relationship between accent and meter, is variable.[39]

These properties are well known. But they are worth recalling for two reasons. First, drawing a parallel between science and nonscientific (narrative) knowledge helps us understand, or at least sense, that the former's existence is no more – and no less – necessary than the latter's. Both are composed of sets of statements; the statements are 'moves' made by the players within the frame-work of generally applicable rules; these rules are specific to each particular kind of knowledge, and the 'moves' judged to be 'good' in one cannot be of the same type as those judged 'good' in another, unless it happens that way by chance.

It is therefore impossible to judge the existence or validity of narrative knowledge on the basis of scientific knowledge and vice versa: the relevant criteria are different. All we can do is gaze in wonderment at the diversity of discursive species, just as we do at the diversity of plant or animal species. Lamenting the 'loss of meaning' in postmodernity boils down to mourning the fact that knowledge is no longer principally narrative. Such a reaction does not necessarily follow. Neither does an attempt to derive or engender (using operators like development) scientific knowledge from narrative knowledge, as if the former contained the latter in an embryonic state.

Nevertheless, language species, like living species, are interrelated, and their relations are far from harmonious. The second point justifying this quick reminder on the properties of the language game of science concerns, precisely, its relation to narrative knowledge. I have said that narrative knowledge does not give priority to the question of its own legitimation and that it certifies itself in the pragmatics of its own transmission without having recourse to argu-mentation and proof. This is why its incomprehension of the problems of scientific discourse is accompanied by a certain tolerance: it approaches such discourse primarily as a variant in the family of narrative cultures.[40] The opposite is not true. The scientist questions the validity of narrative statements and concludes that they are never subject to argumentation or proof.[41] He classifies them as belonging to a different mentality: savage, primitive, under-developed, backward, alienated, composed of opinions, customs, authority, prejudice, ignorance, ideology. Narratives are fables, myths, legends, fit only for women and children. At best, attempts are made to throw some rays of light into this obscurantism, to civilize, educate, develop.

This unequal relationship is an intrinsic effect of the rules specific to each game. We all know its symptoms. It is the entire history of cultural imperialism from the dawn of Western civilization. It is important to recognize its special tenor, which sets it apart from all other forms of imperialism: it is governed by the demand for legitimation.

[...]

10. DELEGITIMATION

In contemporary society and culture – postindustrial society, postmodern culture[42] – the question of the legitimation of knowledge is formulated in different terms. The grand narrative has lost its credibility, regardless of what mode of unification it uses, regardless of whether it is a speculative narrative or a narrative of emancipation.

The decline of narrative can be seen as an effect of the blossoming of techniques and technologies since the Second World War, which has shifted emphasis from the ends of action to its means; it can also be seen as an effect of the redeployment of advanced liberal capitalism after its retreat under the protection of Keynesianism during the period 1930–60, a renewal that has eliminated the communist alternative and valorized the individual enjoyment of goods and services.

Anytime we go searching for causes in this way we are bound to be disappointed. Even if we adopted one or the other of these hypotheses, we would still have to detail the correlation between the tendencies mentioned and the decline of the unifying and legitimating power of the grand narratives of speculation and emancipation.

It is, of course, understandable that both capitalist renewal and prosperity and the disorienting upsurge of technology would have an impact on the status of knowledge. But in order to understand how contemporary science could have been susceptible to those effects long before they took place, we must first locate the seeds of 'delegitimation'[43] and nihilism that were inherent in the grand narratives of the nineteenth century.

First of all, the speculative apparatus maintains an ambigious relation to knowledge. It shows that knowledge is only worthy of that name to the extent that it reduplicates itself ('lifts itself up,' *hebt sich auf*; is sublated) by citing its own statements in a second-level discourse (autonymy) that functions to legitimate them. This is as much as to say that, in its immediacy, denotative discourse bearing on a certain referent (a living organism, a chemical property, a physical phenomenon, etc.) does not really know what it thinks it knows. Positive science is not a form of knowledge. And speculation feeds on its suppression. The Hegelian speculative narrative thus harbors a certain skepticism toward positive learning, as Hegel himself admits.[44]

A science that has not legitimated itself is not a true science; if the discourse that was meant to legitimate it seems to belong to a prescientific form of knowledge, like a 'vulgar' narrative, it is demoted to the lowest rank, that of an ideology or instrument of power. And this always happens if the rules of the science game that discourse denounces as empirical are applied to science itself.

Take for example the speculative statement: 'A scientific statement is knowledge if and only if it can take its place in a universal process of engendering.' The question is: Is this statement knowledge as it itself defines it? Only if it can take its place in a universal process of engendering. Which it can. All it has to do is to presuppose that such a process exists (the Life of spirit) and that it is itself an expression of that process. This presupposition, in fact, is indispensable to the speculative language game. Without it, the language of legitimation would not be legitimate; it would accompany science in a nosedive into nonsense, at least if we take idealism's word for it.

But this presupposition can also be understood in a totally different sense, one which takes us in the direction of postmodern culture: we could say, in keeping with the perspective we adopted earlier, that this presupposition defines the set of rules one must accept in order to play the speculative game.[45] Such an appraisal assumes first that we accept that the 'positive' sciences represent the general mode of knowledge and second, that we understand this language to imply certain formal and axiomatic presuppositions that it must always make explicit. This is exactly what Nietzsche is doing, though with a different terminology, when he shows that 'European nihilism' resulted from the truth requirement of science being turned back against itself.[46]

There thus arises an idea of perspective that is not far removed, at least in this respect, from the idea of language games. What we have here is a process of delegitimation fueled by the demand for legitimation itself. The 'crisis' of scientific knowledge, signs of which have been accumulating since the end of the nineteenth century, is not born of a chance proliferation of sciences, itself an effect of progress in technology and the expansion of capitalism. It represents, rather, an internal erosion of the legitimacy principle of knowledge. There is erosion at work inside the speculative game, and by loosening the weave of the encyclopedic net in which each science was to find its place, it eventually sets them free.

The classical dividing lines between the various fields of science are thus called into question – disciplines disappear, overlappings occur at the borders between sciences, and from these new territories are born. The speculative hierarchy of learning gives way to an immanent and, as it were, 'flat' network of areas of inquiry, the respective frontiers of which are in constant flux. The old 'faculties' splinter into institutes and foundations of all kinds, and the universities lose their function of speculative legitimation. Stripped of the responsibility for research (which was stifled by the speculative narrative), they limit themselves to the transmission of what is judged to be established knowledge, and through didactics they guarantee the replication of teachers rather than the production of researchers. This is the state in which Nietzsche finds and condemns them.[47]

The potential for erosion intrinsic to the other legitimation procedure, the emancipation apparatus flowing from the *Aufklärung*, is no less extensive than the one at work within speculative discourse. But it touches a different aspect. Its distinguishing characteristic is that it grounds the legitimation of science and truth in the autonomy of interlocutors involved in ethical, social, and political praxis. As we have seen, there are immediate problems with this form of legitimation: the difference between a denotative statement with cognitive value and a prescriptive statement with practical value is one of relevance, therefore of competence. There is nothing to prove that if a statement describing a real situation is true, it follows that a prescriptive statement based upon it (the effect of which will necessarily be a modification of that reality) will be just.

Take, for example, a closed door. Between 'The door is closed' and 'Open the door' there is no relation of consequence as defined in propositional logic. The two statements belong to two autonomous sets of rules defining different kinds of relevance, and therefore of competence. Here, the effect of dividing reason into cognitive or theoretical reason on the one hand, and practical reason on the other, is to attack the legitimacy of the discourse of science. Not directly, but indirectly, by revealing that it is a language game with its own rules (of which the a priori conditions of knowledge in Kant provide a first glimpse) and that it has no special calling to supervise the game of praxis (nor the game of aesthetics, for that matter). The game of science is thus put on a par with the others.

If this 'delegitimation' is pursued in the slightest and if its scope is widened (as Wittgenstein does in his own way, and thinkers such as Martin Buber and Emmanuel Lévinas in theirs)[48] the road is then open for an important current of postmodernity: science plays its own game; it is incapable of legitimating the other language games. The game of prescription, for example, escapes it. But above all, it is incapable of legitimating itself, as speculation assumed it could.

The social subject itself seems to dissolve in this dissemination of language games. The social bond is linguistic, but is not woven with a single thread. It is a fabric formed by the intersection of at least two (and in reality an indeterminate number) of language games, obeying different rules. Wittgenstein writes: 'Our language can be seen as an ancient city: a maze of little streets and squares, of old and new houses, and of houses with additions from various periods; and this surrounded by a multitude of new boroughs with straight regular streets and uniform houses.'[49] And to drive home that the principle of unitotality – or synthesis under the authority of a metadiscourse of knowledge – is inapplicable, he subjects the 'town' of language to the old sorites paradox by asking: 'how many houses or streets does it take before a town begins to be a town?'[50]

New languages are added to the old ones, forming suburbs of the old town: 'the symbolism of chemistry and the notation of the infinitesimal calculus.'[51] Thirty-five years later we can add to the list: machine languages, the matrices of game theory, new systems of musical notation, systems of notation for non-denotative forms of logic (temporal logics, deontic logics, modal logics), the language of the genetic code, graphs of phonological structures, and so on.

We may form a pessimistic impression of this splintering: nobody speaks all of those languages, they have no universal metalanguage, the project of the system-subject is a failure, the goal of emancipation has nothing to do with science, we are all stuck in the positivism of this or that discipline of learning, the learned scholars have turned into scientists, the diminished tasks of research have become compartmentalized and no one can master them all.[52] Speculative or humanistic philosophy is forced to relinquish its legitimation duties,[53] which explains why philosophy is facing a crisis wherever it persists in arrogating such functions and is reduced to the study of systems of logic or the history of ideas where it has been realistic enough to surrender them.[54]

Turn-of-the-century Vienna was weaned on this pessimism: not just artists such as Musil, Kraus, Hofmannsthal, Loos, Schönberg, and Broch, but also the

philosophers Mach and Wittgenstein.[55] They carried awareness of and theoretical and artistic responsibility for delegitimation as far as it could be taken.
We can say today that the mourning process has been completed. There is no
need to start all over again. Wittgenstein's strength is that he did not opt for the
positivism that was being developed by the Vienna Circle,[56] but outlined in his
investigation of language games a kind of legitimation not based on performativity. That is what the postmodern world is all about. Most people have lost the
nostalgia for the lost narrative. It in no way follows that they are reduced to
barbarity. What saves them from it is their knowledge that legitimation can only
spring from their own linguistic practice and communicational interaction.
Science 'smiling into its beard' at every other belief has taught them the harsh
austerity of realism.[57]

[...]

NOTES

1. In the wake of Peirce's semiotics, the distinction of the syntactic, semantic, and
   pragmatic domains is made by Charles W. Morris, 'Foundations of the Theory of
   Signs,' in Otto Neurath, Rudolph Carnap, and Charles Morris, eds., *International
   Encyclopedia of Unified Science*, vol. 1, pt. 2 (1938): 77–137. For the use of this term
   I refer especially to: Ludwig Wittgenstein, *Philosophical Investigations* [trans. G. E.
   M. Anscombe (New York: Macmillan, 1953)]; J. L. Austin, *How to Do Things with
   Words* (Oxford: Oxford University Press, 1962); J. R. Searle, *Speech Acts* (Cam-
   bridge: Cambridge University Press, 1969); Jürgen Habermas, 'Unhereitende Ber-
   merkungen zu einer Theorie der kommunikativen Kompetens,' in Habermas and
   Luhmann, *Theorie der gesellschaft oder Sozialtechnologie* (Stuttgart: Suhrkamp,
   1971); Oswald Ducrot, *Dire et ne pas dire* (Paris: Hermann, 1972); J. Poulain, 'Vers
   une pragmatique nucléaire de la communication' (typescript, Université de Mon-
   tréal, 1977). See too Paul Watzlawick, Janet Helmick Beavin and Don. D. Jackson,
   Pragmatics of Human *Communication: A Study of Inter-actional Patterns, Pathol-
   ogies and Paradoxes* (London: Faber, 1968).
2. 'Denotation' corresponds here to 'description' in the classical usage of logicians.
   Quine replaces 'denotation' by 'true of'; see W. V. Quine, *Word and Object*
   (Cambridge, Mass.: MIT Press, 1960). J. L. Austin, *How to Do Things with Words*,
   p. 39, prefers 'constative' to 'descriptive.'
3. The term *performative* has taken on a precise meaning in language theory since
   Austin, Later in this book, the concept will reappear in association with the term
   performativity (in particular, of a system) in the new current sense of efficiency
   measured according to an input/output ratio. The two meanings are not far apart.
   Austin's performative realizes the optimal performance.
4. A recent analysis of these categories is to be found in Habermas, 'Unbereitende
   Bemerkungen,' and is discussed by J. Poulain, 'Vers une pragmatique nucléaire.'
5. *Philosophical Investigations*, sec. 23.
6. John Von Neumann and Oskar Morgenstern, *Theory of Games and Economic
   Behavior* (Princeton University Press, 1944), p. 49; 'The *game* is simply the totality
   of the rules which describe it.' This formulation is foreign to the spirit of Wittgenstein,
   for whom the concept of the game cannot be mastered by a definition, since definition
   is already a language game (*Philosophical Investigations*, especially secs. 65–84).
7. The term comes from Searle: 'Speech acts ..., are the basic or minimal units of
   linguistic communication' [*Speech Acts*, p. 16]. I place them within the domain of the
   agon (the joust) rather than that of communication.

8. Agonistics is the basis of Heraclitus's ontology and of the Sophists' dialectic, not to mention the early tragedians. A good part of Aristotle's reflections in the *Topics* and the *Sophistici Elenchi* is devoted to it. See F. Nietzsche, 'Homer's Contest' [trans. Maximilian A. Mügge, in *Complete Works*, vol. 2 (London: T. N. Fowlis, 1911; reprint, New York: Gordon Press, 1974)].

9. In the sense established by Louis Hjelmslev, in *Prolegomena to a Theory of Language* (Madison: University of Wisconsin Press, 1963), and taken up by Roland Barthes, *Eléments de sémiologie* (1964) (Paris: Seuil, 1966), 4:1 [Eng. trans. Annette Lavers and Colin Smith, *Elements of Semiology* (New York: Hill and Wang, 1968)].

10. The object of knowledge in Aristotle is strictly circumscribed by what he defines as apophantics: 'While every sentence has meaning (*semantikos*) ... not all can be called propositions (*apophantikos*). We call propositions those only that have truth or falsity in them. A prayer is, for instance, a sentence, but neither has truth nor has falsity.' 'De Interpretatione.' 4, 17a. *The Organon*, vol. 1, trans. Harold Cooke and Hugh Tredennick (Cambridge, Mass.: Harvard, 1938), 121. [TRANS: The translation of *connaissance* as 'learning is not uniform. It was sometimes necessary to translate it as 'knowledge' (especially where it occurs in the plural): it should be clear from the context whether it is a question of *connaissance* (in Lyotard's usage, a body of established denotive statements) or *savoir* (knowledge in the more general sense). *Savoir* has been uniformly translated as 'knowledge.']

11. See Karl Popper, *Logik der Forschung* (Wien: Springer, 1935) [Eng. trans. Popper et al., *The Logic of Scientific Discovery* (New York: Basic Books, 1949)], and 'Normal Science and its Dangers,' in Imre Lakatos and Alan Musgrave, eds., *Criticism and the Growth of Knowledge* (Cambridge: Cambridge University Press, 1970).

12. See Jean Beaufret, *Le Poème de Parménide* (Paris: Presses Universitaires de France, 1955).

13. Again in the sense of *Bildung* (or, in English, 'culture'), as accredited by culturalism. The term is preromantic and romantic: cf. Hegel's *Volksgeist*.

14. See the American culturalist school: Cora DuBois, Abram Kardiner, Ralph Linton, Margaret Mead.

15. See studies of the institution of European folklore traditions from the end of the eighteenth century in their relation to romanticism, for example, the brothers Grimm and Vuk Karadic (Serbian folktales).

16. This was, briefly stated, Lucien Lévy-Bruhl's thesis in *La Mentalité primitive* (Paris: Alcan, 1922) [Eng. trans. Lillian Clare, *Primitive Mentality* (New York: Macmillan, 1923)].

17. Claude Lévi-Strauss, *La Pensée sauvage* (Paris: Plon, 1962) [Eng. trans. *The Savage Mind* (Chicago, University of Chicago, 1966)].

18. Robert Jaulin, *La paix blanche* (Paris: Seuil, 1970).

19. Vladimir Propp, *Morphology of the Folktale*, trans. Laurence Scott with intro. by Suatana Pirkora-Jakobson [Publications of the American Folklore Society, Bibliographical and Special Series, no. 9 (Bloomington, Ind., 1958); 2d ed. rev. (Austin, Tex. University of Texas Press, 1968).

20. Claude Lévi-Strauss, 'La Structure des Mythes' (1955), in *Anthropologie Structurale* (Paris: Plon, 1958) [Eng. trans. Claire Jacobson and Brooke Grundfest Schoepf, *Structural Anthropology* (New York: Basic Books, 1963)], and 'La Structure et la forme: Réflexions sur un ouvrage de Vladimir Propp, *Cahiers de l'Institut de science èconomique appliquèe*, 99, series M, 7 (1960) [in Claude Lévi-Strauss, *Structural Anthropology II*, trans. Monique Layton (New York: Basic Books, 1976). The essay will also be included in Vladimir Propp, *Theory and History of Folklore*, trans. Ariadna and Richard Martin, intro. by Anatoly Liberman, Theory and History of Literature, vol. 5 (Minneapolis: University of Minnesota Press, forthcoming)].

21. Geza Róbeim, *Psychoanalysis and Anthropology* (New York: International Universities Press, 1959).

22. André M. d'Ans, *Le Dit des vrais hommes* (Paris: Union Générale d'Edition, 1978).

23. Ibid., p. 7.

24. I have made use of it here because of the pragmatic 'etiquette' surrounding the transmission of the narratives; the anthropologist details it with great care. See Pierre Clastres, *Le grand Parler: Mytbes et chants sacrés des Indiens Guarani* (Paris: Scuil, 1972).

25. For a narratology that treats the pragmatic dimension, see Gérard Genette, *Figures III* (Paris: Seuil, 1972) [Eng. trans. Jane E. Lewin, *Narrative Discourse* (New York: Cornell University Press, 1980).

26. See note 7.

27. The relationship between meter and accent, which constitutes and dissolves rhythm, is at the center of Hegel's reflection on speculation. See sec. 4 of the preface to the *Phenomenology of Spirit.*

28. I would like to thank André M. d'Ans for kindly providing this information.

29. See Daniel Charles's analyses in *Le Temps de la voix* (Paris: Delarge, 1978) and those of Dominique Avron in *L'Appareil musical* (Paris: Union Générale d'Edition, 1978).

30. See Mircea Eliade, *Le Mythe de l'éternel retour: Archétypes et répétitions* (Paris: Gallimard, 1949) [Eng. trans. Willard R. Trask, *The Myth of the Eternal Return* (New York: Panthcon Books, 1954)].

31. The example is borrowed from Frege, 'Über Sinn und Bedeutung' (1892) [Eng. trans. Max Black and Peter Geach, 'On Sense and Reference,' in *Translations from the Philosophical Writings of Gottlob Frege* (Oxford: Blackwell, 1960)].

32. Bruno Latour and Paolo Fabbri, 'Rhétorique de la science,' *Actes de la recherche en sciences sociales* 13 (1977): 81–95.

33. Gaston Bachelard, *Le Nouvel Esprit scientifique* (Paris: Presses Universitaires de France, 1934).

34. Descartes, *Méditations métaphysiques* (1641), Méditation 4.

35. See for example Karl G. Hempel, *Philosophy of Natural Science* (Englewood Cliffs, N.J.: Prentice-Hall, 1966).

36. There is no space here to discuss the difficulties raised by this double presupposition. See Vincent Descombes, *L'Inconscient malgré lui* (Paris: Editions de Minuit, 1977).

37. This remark avoids a major difficulty, one that would also arise in the examination of narration: the distinction between language games and discursive games. I will not discuss it here.

38. In the sense indicated in note 35.

39. Thomas Kuhn, *The Structure of Scientific Revolutions* (Chicago: University of Chicago Press, 1962).

40. Cf. children's attitude toward their first science lessons, or the way natives interpret the ethnologist's explanations (see Lévi-Strauss, *The Savage Mind* [note 17], chap. 1).

41. That is why Métraux commented to Clastres, 'To be able to study a primitive society, it already has to be a little decayed.' In effect, the native informant must be able to see his own society through the eyes of the ethnologist; he must be able to question the functioning of its institutions and therefore their legitimacy. Reflecting on his failure with the Achè tribe, Clastres concludes, 'And so the Achè' accepted presents they had not asked for while at the same time refusing attempts at a dialogue, because they were strong enough not to need it: we would start talking when they were sick' [quoted by M. Cartry in 'Pierre Clastres,' *Libre* 4 (1978)].

42. Certain scientific aspects of postmodernism are inventoried by Ihab Hassan in 'Culture, Indeterminacy and Immanence: Margins of the (Postmodern) Age,' *Humanities in Society* 1 (1978): 51–85.

43. Claus Mueller uses the expression 'a process of delegitimation' in *The Politics of Communication* (New York: Oxford University Press, 1973), p. 164.

44. 'Road of doubt . . . road of despair . . . skepticism,' writes Hegel in the preface to the *Phenomenology of Spirit* to describe the effect of the speculative drive on natural knowledge.

45. For fear of encumbering this account, I have postponed until a later study the exposition of this group of rules. [See 'Analyzing Speculative Discourse as Language-Game,' *The Oxford Literary Review* 4, no. 3 (1981): 59–67.]

46. Nietzsche, 'Der europäische Nihilismus' (MS. N VII 3); 'der Nihilism, ein normaler Zustand' (MS. W II 1); 'Kritik der Nihilism' (MS. W VII 3); 'Zum Plane' (MS. W II 1), in *Nietzsches Werke kritische Gesamtausgabe*, vol. 7, pts. 1 and 2 (1887–89) (Berlin: De Gruyter, 1970). These texts have been the object of a commentary by K. Ryjik, *Nietzsche, le manuscrit de Lenzer Heide* (typescript, Département de philosophie, Université de Paris VIII [Vincennes]).

47. 'On the future of our educational institutions,' in *Complete Works* (note 8), vol. 3.

48. Martin Buber, *Ich und Du* (Berlin: Schocken Verlag, 1922) [Eng. trans. Ronald G. Smith, *I and Thou* (New York: Charles Scribner's Sons, 1937)], and *Dialogisches Leben* (Zürich: Müller, 1947); Emmanuel Lévinas, *Totalité et Infinité* (La Haye: Nijhoff, 1961) [Eng. trans. Alphonso Lingis, *Totality and Infinity: An Essay on Exteriority* (Pittsburgh: Duquesne University Press, 1969)], and 'Martin Buber und die Erkenntnis theorie' (1958), in *Philosophen des 20. Jahrhunderts* (Stuttgart: Kohlhammer, 1963) [Fr. trans. 'Martin Buber et la théorie de la connaissance,' in *Noms Propres* (Montpellier: Fata Morgana, 1976)].

49. *Philosophical Investigations*, sec. 18, p. 8.

50. Ibid.

51. Ibid.

52. See for example, 'La taylorisation de la recherche,' in A. Jaubert and J.-M. Lévy-Lebk eds. *(Auto) critique de la science* (Paris: Seuil, 1973), Pt. 1, pp. 291–3. And especially D. J. de Solla Price, *Little Sccience, Big Science* (New York: Columbia University Press, 1963), who emphasizes the split between a small number of highly productive researchers (evaluated in terms of publication) and a large mass of researchers with low productivity. The number of the latter grows as the square of the former, so that the number of high productivity researchers only really increases every twenty years. Price concludes that science considered as a social entity is 'undemocratic' (p. 59) and that 'the eminent scientist' is a hundred years ahead of 'the minimal one' (p. 56).

53. See J. T. Desanti, 'Sur le rapport traditionnel des sciences et de la philosophie,' in *La Philosophie silenciense, ou critique des philosophies de la science* (Paris: Seuil, 1975).

54. The reclassification of academic philosophy as one of the human sciences in this respect has a significance far beyond simply professional concerns. I do not think that philosophy as legitimation is condemned to disappear, but it is possible that it will not be able to carry out this work, or at least advance it, without revising its ties to the university institution. See on this matter the preamble to the *Project d'un institut polytechnique de philosophie* (typescript, Départment de philosophie, Universite de Paris VIII [Vincennes], 1979).

55. See Allan Janik and Stephan Touhnin, *Wittgenstein's Vienna* (New York: Simon & Schuster, 1973), and J. Piel, ed., 'Vienne début d'un siècle,' *Critique*, 339–40 (1975).

56. See Jürgen Habermas, 'Dogmatismus, Vernunft unt Entscheidung – Zu Theorie und Praxis in der verwissenschaftlichen Zivilisation' (1963), in *Theorie und Praxis* [*Theory and Practice*, abr. ed. of 4th German ed., trans. John Viertel (Boston: Beacon Press, 1971)].

57. 'Science Smiling into its Beard' is the title of chap. 72, vol. 1 of Musil's *The Man Without Qualities*. Cited and discussed by J. Bouveresse, 'La Problématique du sujet dans *L'homme sans qualirés*', *Noroît* (Arras) 234 and 235 (December 1978 and January 1979).

5

'THE PRECESSION OF SIMULACRA'

Jean Baudrillard

The simulacrum is never what hides the truth – it is truth that hides the fact that there is none.

The simulacrum is true.

– Ecclesiastes

If once we were able to view the Borges fable in which the cartographers of the Empire draw up a map so detailed that it ends up covering the territory exactly (the decline of the Empire witnesses the fraying of this map, little by little, and its fall into ruins, though some shreds are still discernible in the deserts – the metaphysical beauty of this ruined abstraction testifying to a pride equal to the Empire and rotting like a carcass, returning to the substance of the soil, a bit as the double ends by being confused with the real through aging) – as the most beautiful allegory of simulation, this fable has now come full circle for us, and possesses nothing but the discrete charm of second-order simulacra.[1]

Today abstraction is no longer that of the map, the double, the mirror, or the concept. Simulation is no longer that of a territory, a referential being, or a substance. It is the generation by models of a real without origin or reality: a hyperreal. The territory no longer precedes the map, nor does it survive it. It is nevertheless the map that precedes the territory – *precession of simulacra* – that engenders the territory, and if one must return to the fable, today it is the territory whose shreds slowly rot across the extent of the map. It is the real, and

From Jean Baudrillard (1994) 'The Precession of Simulacra' [1981], in *Simulacra and Simulation*, trans. Sheila Faria Glaser. Ann Arbor, MI: University of Michigan Press.

not the map, whose vestiges persist here and there in the deserts that are no longer those of the Empire, but ours. *The desert of the real itself*.

In fact, even inverted, Borges's fable is unusable. Only the allegory of the Empire, perhaps, remains. Because it is with this same imperialism that present-day simulators attempt to make the real, all of the real, coincide with their models of simulation. But it is no longer a question of either maps or territories. Something has disappeared: the sovereign difference, between one and the other, that constituted the charm of abstraction. Because it is difference that constitutes the poetry of the map and the charm of the territory, the magic of the concept and the charm of the real. This imaginary of representation, which simultaneously culminates in and is engulfed by the cartographer's mad project of the ideal coextensivity of map and territory, disappears in the simulation whose operation is nuclear and genetic, no longer at all specular or discursive. It is all of metaphysics that is lost. No more mirror of being and appearances, of the real and its concept. No more imaginary coextensivity: it is genetic miniaturization that is the dimension of simulation. The real is produced from miniaturized cells, matrices, and memory banks, models of control – and it can be reproduced an indefinite number of times from these. It no longer needs to be rational, because it no longer measures itself against either an ideal or negative instance. It is no longer anything but operational. In fact, it is no longer really the real, because no imaginary envelops it anymore. It is a hyperreal, produced from a radiating synthesis of combinatory models in a hyperspace without atmosphere.

By crossing into a space whose curvature is no longer that of the real, nor that of truth, the era of simulation is inaugurated by a liquidation of all referentials – worse: with their artificial resurrection in the systems of signs, a material more malleable than meaning, in that it lends itself to all systems of equivalences, to all binary oppositions, to all combinatory algebra. It is no longer a question of imitation, nor duplication, nor even parody. It is a question of substituting the signs of the real for the real, that is to say of an operation of deterring every real process via its operational double, a programmatic, metastable, perfectly descriptive machine that offers all the signs of the real and short-circuits all its vicissitudes. Never again will the real have the chance to produce itself – such is the vital function of the model in a system of death, or rather of anticipated resurrection, that no longer even gives the event of death a chance. A hyperreal henceforth sheltered from the imaginary, and from any distinction between the real and the imaginary, leaving room only for the orbital recurrence of models and for the simulated generation of differences.

THE DIVINE IRREFERENCE OF IMAGES

To dissimulate is to pretend not to have what one has. To simulate is to feign to have what one doesn't have. One implies a presence, the other an absence. But it is more complicated than that because simulating is not pretending: 'Whoever fakes an illness can simply stay in bed and make everyone believe he is ill.

Whoever simulates an illness produces in himself some of the symptoms'
(Littre). Therefore, pretending, or dissimulating, leaves the principle of reality
intact: the difference is always clear, it is simply masked, whereas simulation
threatens the difference between the 'true' and the 'false,' the 'real' and the
'imaginary.' Is the simulator sick or not, given that he produces 'true' symptoms? Objectively one cannot treat him as being either ill or not ill. Psychology
and medicine stop at this point, forestalled by the illness's henceforth undiscoverable truth. For if any symptom can be 'produced,' and can no longer be
taken as a fact of nature, then every illness can be considered as simulatable and
simulated, and medicine loses its meaning since it only knows how to treat 'real'
illnesses according to their objective causes. Psychosomatics evolves in a
dubious manner at the borders of the principle of illness. As to psychoanalysis,
it transfers the symptom of the organic order to the unconscious order: the latter
is new and taken for 'real' more real than the other – but why would simulation
be at the gates of the unconscious? Why couldn't the 'work' of the unconscious
be 'produced' in the same way as any old symptom of classical medicine?
Dreams already are.

Certainly, the psychiatrist purports that 'for every form of mental alienation
there is a particular order in the succession of symptoms of which the simulator
is ignorant and in the absence of which the psychiatrist would not be deceived.'
This (which dates from 1865) in order to safeguard the principle of a truth at all
costs and to escape the interrogation posed by simulation – the knowledge that
truth, reference, objective cause have ceased to exist. Now, what can medicine
do with what floats on either side of illness, on either side of health, with the
duplication of illness in a discourse that is no longer either true or false? What
can psychoanalysis do with the duplication of the discourse of the unconscious
in the discourse of simulation that can never again be unmasked, since it is not
false either?[2]

What can the army do about simulators? Traditionally it unmasks them and
punishes them, according to a clear principle of identification. Today it can
discharge a very good simulator as exactly equivalent to a 'real' homosexual, a
heart patient, or a madman. Even military psychology draws back from
Cartesian certainties and hesitates to make the distinction between true and
false, between the 'produced' and the authentic symptom. 'If he is this good at
acting crazy, it's because he is.' Nor is military psychology mistaken in this
regard: in this sense, all crazy people simulate, and this lack of distinction is the
worst kind of subversion. It is against this lack of distinction that classical
reason armed itself in all its categories. But it is what today again outflanks
them, submerging the principle of truth.

Beyond medicine and the army, favored terrains of simulation, the question
returns to religion and the simulacrum of divinity: 'I forbade that there be any
simulacra in the temples because the divinity that animates nature can never be
represented.' Indeed it can be. But what becomes of the divinity when it reveals
itself in icons, when it is multiplied in simulacra? Does it remain the supreme

power that is simply incarnated in images as a visible theology? Or does it volatilize itself in the simulacra that, alone, deploy their power and pomp of fascination – the visible machinery of icons substituted for the pure and intelligible Idea of God? This is precisely what was feared by Iconoclasts, whose millennial quarrel is still with us today.[3] This is precisely because they predicted this omnipotence of simulacra, the faculty simulacra have of effacing God from the conscience of man, and the destructive, annihilating truth that they allow to appear – that deep down God never existed, that only the simulacrum ever existed, even that God himself was never anything but his own simulacrum – from this came their urge to destroy the images. If they could have believed that these images only obfuscated or masked the Platonic Idea of God, there would have been no reason to destroy them. One can live with the idea of distorted truth. But their metaphysical despair came from the idea that the image didn't conceal anything at all, and that these images were in essence not images, such as an original model would have made them, but perfect simulacra, forever radiant with their own fascination. Thus this death of the divine referential must be exorcised at all costs.

One can see that the iconoclasts, whom one accuses of disdaining and negating images, were those who accorded them their true value, in contrast to the iconolaters who only saw reflections in them and were content to venerate a filigree God. On the other hand, one can say that the icon worshipers were the most modern minds, the most adventurous, because, in the guise of having God become apparent in the mirror of images, they were already enacting his death and his disappearance in the epiphany of his representations (which, perhaps, they already knew no longer represented anything, that they were purely a game, but that it was therein the great game lay – knowing also that it is dangerous to unmask images, since they dissimulate the fact that there is nothing behind them).

This was the approach of the Jesuits, who founded their politics on the virtual disappearance of God and on the worldly and spectacular manipulation of consciences – the evanescence of God in the epiphany of power – the end of transcendence, which now only serves as an alibi for a strategy altogether free of influences and signs. Behind the baroqueness of images hides the éminence grise of politics.

This way the stake will always have been the murderous power of images, murderers of the real, murderers of their own model, as the Byzantine icons could be those of divine identity. To this murderous power is opposed that of representations as a dialectical power, the visible and intelligible mediation of the Real. All Western faith and good faith became engaged in this wager on representation: that a sign could refer to the depth of meaning, that a sign could be exchanged for meaning and that something could guarantee this exchange – God of course. But what if God himself can be simulated, that is to say can be reduced to the signs that constitute faith? Then the whole system becomes weightless, it is no longer itself anything but a gigantic simulacrum – not unreal, but a simulacrum, that is to say never exchanged for the real, but exchanged for itself, in an uninterrupted circuit without reference or circumference.

Such is simulation, insofar as it is opposed to representation. Representation stems from the principle of the equivalence of the sign and of the real (even if this equivalence is utopian, it is a fundamental axiom). Simulation, on the contrary, stems from the utopia of the principle of equivalence, *from the radical negation of the sign as value*, from the sign as the reversion and death sentence of every reference. Whereas representation attempts to absorb simulation by interpreting it as a false representation, simulation envelops the whole edifice of representation itself as a simulacrum.

Such would be the successive phases of the image:

it is the reflection of a profound reality;
it masks and denatures a profound reality;
it masks the *absence* of a profound reality;
it has no relation to any reality whatsoever: it is its own pure simulacrum.

In the first case, the image is a *good* appearance – representation is of the sacramental order. In the second, it is an evil appearance – it is of the order of maleficence. In the third, it plays at being an appearance – it is of the order of sorcery. In the fourth, it is no longer of the order of appearances, but of simulation.

The transition from signs that dissimulate something to signs that dissimulate that there is nothing marks a decisive turning point. The first reflects a theology of truth and secrecy (to which the notion of ideology still belongs). The second inaugurates the era of simulacra and of simulation, in which there is no longer a God to recognize his own, no longer a Last Judgment to separate the false from the true, the real from its artificial resurrection, as everything is already dead and resurrected in advance.

When the real is no longer what it was, nostalgia assumes its full meaning. There is a plethora of myths of origin and of signs of reality – a plethora of truth, of secondary objectivity, and authenticity. Escalation of the true, of lived experience, resurrection of the figurative where the object and substance have disappeared. Panic-stricken production of the real and of the referential, parallel to and greater than the panic of material production: this is how simulation appears in the phase that concerns us – a strategy of the real, of the neoreal and the hyperreal that everywhere is the double of a strategy of deterrence.

RAMSES, OR THE ROSY-COLORED RESURRECTION

Ethnology brushed up against its paradoxical death in 1971, the day when the Philippine government decided to return the few dozen Tasaday who had just been discovered in the depths of the jungle, where they had lived for eight centuries without any contact with the rest of the species, to their primitive state, out of the reach of colonizers, tourists, and ethnologists. This at the suggestion of the anthropologists themselves, who were seeing the indigenous people disintegrate immediately upon contact, like mummies in the open air.

In order for ethnology to live, its object must die; by dying, the object takes its revenge for being 'discovered' and with its death defies the science that wants to grasp it.

Doesn't all science live on this paradoxical slope to which it is doomed by the evanescence of its object in its very apprehension, and by the pitiless reversal that the dead object exerts on it? Like Orpheus, it always turns around too soon, and, like Eurydice, its object falls back into Hades.

It is against this hell of the paradox that the ethnologists wished to protect themselves by cordoning off the Tasaday with virgin forest. No one can touch them anymore: as in a mine the vein is closed down. Science loses precious capital there, but the object will be safe, lost to science, but intact in its 'virginity.' It is not a question of sacrifice (science never sacrifices itself, it is always murderous), but of the simulated sacrifice of its object in order to save its reality principle. The Tasaday, frozen in their natural element, will provide a perfect alibi, an eternal guarantee. Here begins an antiethnology that will never end and to which Jaulin, Castaneda, Clastres are various witnesses. In any case, the logical evolution of a science is to distance itself increasingly from its object, until it dispenses with it entirely: its autonomy is only rendered even more fantastic – it attains its pure form.

The Indian thus returned to the ghetto, in the glass coffin of the virgin forest, again becomes the model of simulation of all the possible Indians *from before ethnology*. This model thus grants itself the luxury to incarnate itself beyond itself in the 'brute' reality of these Indians it has entirely reinvented – Savages who are indebted to ethnology for still being Savages: what a turn of events, what a triumph for this science that seemed dedicated to their destruction!

[...]

In the same way, with the pretext of saving the original, one forbade visitors to enter the Lascaux caves, but an exact replica was constructed five hundred meters from it, so that everyone could see them (one glances through a peephole at the authentic cave, and then one visits the reconstituted whole). It is possible that the memory of the original grottoes is itself stamped in the minds of future generations, but from now on there is no longer any difference: the duplication suffices to render both artificial.

In the same way science and technology were recently mobilized to save the mummy of Ramses II, after it was left to rot for several dozen years in the depths of a museum. The West is seized with panic at the thought of not being able to save what the symbolic order had been able to conserve for forty centuries, but out of sight and far from the light of day. Ramses does not signify anything for us, only the mummy is of an inestimable worth because it is what guarantees that accumulation has meaning. Our entire linear and accumulative culture collapses if we cannot stockpile the past in plain view. To this end the pharaohs must be brought out of their tomb and the mummies out of their silence. To this end they must be exhumed and given military honors. They are prey to both science and worms. Only absolute secrecy assured them this millennial power – the mastery over putrefaction that signified the mastery of the complete cycle of exchanges with death. *We* only know how to place our science in service of *repairing* the mummy, that is to say restoring a *visible* order, whereas embalming was a mythical effort that strove to immortalize a *hidden* dimension.

We require a visible past, a visible continuum, a visible myth of origin, which reassures us about our end. Because finally we have never believed in them. Whence this historic scene of the reception of the mummy at the Orly airport. Why? Because Ramses was a great despotic and military figure? Certainly. But mostly because our culture dreams, behind this defunct power that it tries to annex, of an order that would have had nothing to do with it, and it dreams of it because it exterminated it by exhuming it *as its own past*.

[...]

THE HYPERREAL AND THE IMAGINARY

Disneyland is a perfect model of all the entangled orders of simulacra. It is first of all a play of illusions and phantasms: the Pirates, the Frontier, the Future World, etc. This imaginary world is supposed to ensure the success of the operation. But what attracts the crowds the most is without a doubt the social microcosm, the *religious*, miniaturized pleasure of real America, of its constraints and joys. One parks outside and stands in line inside, one is altogether abandoned at the exit. The only phantasmagoria in this imaginary world lies in the tenderness and warmth of the crowd, and in the sufficient and excessive number of gadgets necessary to create the multitudinous effect. The contrast with the absolute solitude of the parking lot – a veritable concentration camp – is total. Or, rather: inside, a whole panoply of gadgets magnetizes the crowd in directed flows – outside, solitude is directed at a single gadget: the automobile. By an extraordinary coincidence (but this derives without a doubt from the enchantment inherent to this universe), this frozen, childlike world is found to have been conceived and realized by a man who is himself now cryogenized: Walt Disney, who awaits his resurrection through an increase of 180 degrees centigrade.

Thus, everywhere in Disneyland the objective profile of America, down to the morphology of individuals and of the crowd, is drawn. All its values are exalted by the miniature and the comic strip. Embalmed and pacified. Whence the possibility of an ideological analysis of Disneyland (L. Marin did it very well in *Utopiques, jeux d'espace* [Utopias, play of space]): digest of the American way of life, panegyric of American values, idealized transposition of a contradictory reality. Certainly. But this masks something else and this 'ideological' blanket functions as a cover for a *simulation of the third order*: Disneyland exists in order to hide that it is the 'real' country, all of 'real' America that is Disneyland (a bit like prisons are there to hide that it is the social in its entirety, in its banal omnipresence, that is carceral). Disneyland is presented as imaginary in order to make us believe that the rest is real, whereas all of Los Angeles and the America that surrounds it are no longer real, but belong to the hyperreal order and to the order of simulation. It is no longer a question of a false representation of reality (ideology) but of concealing the fact that the real is no longer real, and thus of saving the reality principle.

The imaginary of Disneyland is neither true nor false, it is a deterrence machine set up in order to rejuvenate the fiction of the real in the opposite camp. Whence the debility of this imaginary, its infantile degeneration. This world wants to be childish in order to make us believe that the adults are elsewhere, in the 'real' world, and to conceal the fact that true childishness is everywhere – that it is that of the adults themselves who come here to act the child in order to foster illusions as to their real childishness.

Disneyland is not the only one, however. Enchanted Village, Magic Mountain, Marine World: Los Angeles is surrounded by these imaginary stations that feed reality, the energy of the real to a city whose mystery is precisely that of no longer being anything but a network of incessant, unreal circulation – a city of incredible proportions but without space, without dimension. As much as electrical and atomic power stations, as much as cinema studios, this city, which is no longer anything but an immense scenario and a perpetual pan shot, needs this old imaginary like a sympathetic nervous system made up of childhood signals and faked phantasms.

Disneyland: a space of the regeneration of the imaginary as waste-treatment plants are elsewhere, and even here. Everywhere today one must recycle waste, and the dreams, the phantasms, the historical, fairylike, legendary imaginary of children and adults is a waste product, the first great toxic excrement of a hyperreal civilization. On a mental level, Disneyland is the prototype of this new function. But all the sexual, psychic, somatic recycling institutes, which proliferate in California, belong to the same order. People no longer look at each other, but there are institutes for that. They no longer touch each other, but there is contactotherapy. They no longer walk, but they go jogging, etc. Everywhere one recycles lost faculties, or lost bodies, or lost sociality, or the lost taste for food. One reinvents penury, asceticism, vanished savage naturalness: natural food, health food, yoga. Marshall Sahlins's idea that it is the economy of the market, and not of nature at all, that secretes penury, is verified, but at a secondary level: here, in the sophisticated confines of a triumphal market economy is reinvented a penury/sign, a penury/simulacrum, a simulated behavior of the underdeveloped (including the adoption of Marxist tenets) that, in the guise of ecology, of energy crises and the critique of capital, adds a final esoteric aureole to the triumph of an esoteric culture. Nevertheless, maybe a mental catastrophe, a mental implosion and involution without precedent lies in wait for a system of this kind, whose visible signs would be those of this strange obesity, or the incredible coexistence of the most bizarre theories and practices, which correspond to the improbable coalition of luxury, heaven, and money, to the improbable luxurious materialization of life and to undiscoverable contradictions.

POLITICAL INCANTATION

Watergate. The same scenario as in Disneyland (effect of the imaginary concealing that reality no more exists outside than inside the limits of the artificial perimeter): here the scandal effect hiding that there is no difference between the facts and their denunciation (identical methods on the part of the CIA and of the *Washington Post* journalists). Same operation, tending to regenerate through scandal a moral and political principle, through the imaginary, a sinking reality principle.

The denunciation of scandal is always a homage to the law. And Watergate in particular succeeded in imposing the idea that Watergate was a scandal – in this sense it was a prodigious operation of intoxication. A large dose of political morality reinjected on a world scale. One could say along with Bourdieu: 'The essence of every relation of force is to dissimulate itself as such and to acquire all its force only because it dissimulates itself as such,' understood as follows: capital, immoral and without scruples, can only function behind a moral superstructure, and whoever revives this public morality (through indignation, denunciation, etc.) works spontaneously for the order of capital. This is what the journalists of the *Washington Post* did.

But this would be nothing but the formula of ideology, and when Bourdieu states it, he takes the 'relation of force' for the *truth* of capitalist domination, and he himself *denounces* this relation of force as *scandal* – he is thus in the same deterministic and moralistic position as the *Washington Post* journalists are. He does the same work of purging and reviving moral order, an order of truth in which the veritable symbolic violence of the social order is engendered, well beyond all the relations of force, which are only its shifting and indifferent configuration in the moral and political consciences of men.

All that capital asks of us is to receive it as rational *or* to combat it in the name of rationality, to receive it as moral *or* to combat it in the name of morality. Because *these are the same*, which *can be thought of in another way*: formerly one worked to dissimulate scandal – today one works to conceal that there is none.

Watergate is not a scandal, this is what must be said at all costs, because it is what everyone is busy concealing, this dissimulation masking a strengthening of morality, of a moral panic as one approaches the primitive *(mise en) scene* of capital: its instantaneous cruelty, its incomprehensible ferocity, its fundamental immorality – that is what is scandalous, unacceptable to the system of moral and economic equivalence that is the axiom of leftist thought, from the theories of the Enlightenment up to Communism. One imputes this thinking to the contract of capital, but it doesn't give a damn – it is a monstrous unprincipled enterprise, nothing more. It is 'enlightened' thought that seeks to control it by imposing rules on it. And all the recrimination that replaces revolutionary thought today comes back to incriminate capital for not following the rules of the game. 'Power is unjust, its justice is a class justice, capital exploits us, etc.' – as if capital were linked by a contract to the society it rules. It is the Left that holds out the mirror of equivalence to capital hoping that it will comply, comply with this phantasmagoria of the social contract and fulfill its obligations to the whole of society (by the same token, no need for revolution: it suffices that capital accommodate itself to the rational formula of exchange).

Capital, in fact, was never linked by a contract to the society that it dominates. It is a sorcery of social relations, it is a *challenge to society*, and it must be responded to as such. It is not a scandal to be denounced according to moral or economic rationality, but a challenge to take up according to symbolic law.

MOBIUS-SPIRALING NEGATIVITY

Watergate was thus nothing but a lure held out by the system to catch its adversaries – a simulation of scandal for regenerative ends. In the film, this is embodied by the character of 'Deep Throat,' who was said to be the eminence grise of the Republicans, manipulating the left-wing journalists in order to get rid of Nixon – and why not? All hypotheses are possible, but this one is superfluous: the Left itself does a perfectly good job, and spontaneously, of doing the work of the Right. Besides, it would be naive to see an embittered good conscience at work here. Because manipulation is a wavering causality in which positivity and negativity are engendered and overlap, in which there is no longer either an active or a passive. It is through the *arbitrary* cessation of this spiraling causality that a principle of political reality can be saved. It is through the *simulation* of a narrow, conventional field of perspective in which the premises and the consequences of an act or of an event can be calculated, that a political credibility can be maintained (and of course 'objective' analysis, the struggle, etc.). If one envisions the entire cycle of any act or event in a system where linear continuity and dialectical polarity no longer exist, in a field *unhinged by simulation*, all determination evaporates, every act is terminated at the end of the cycle having benefited everyone and having been scattered in all directions.

Is any given bombing in Italy the work of leftist extremists, or extreme-right provocation, or a centrist *mise-en-scène* to discredit all extreme terrorists and to shore up its own failing power, or again, is it a police-inspired scenario and a form of blackmail to public security? All of this is simultaneously true, and the search for proof, indeed the objectivity of the facts does not put an end to this vertigo of interpretation. That is, we are in a logic of simulation, which no longer has anything to do with a logic of facts and an order of reason. Simulation is characterized by a *precession of the model*, of all the models based on the merest fact – the models come first, their circulation, orbital like that of the bomb, constitutes the genuine magnetic field of the event. The facts no longer have a specific trajectory, they are born at the intersection of models, a single fact can be engendered by all the models at once. This anticipation, this precession, this short circuit, this confusion of the fact with its model (no more divergence of meaning, no more dialectical polarity, no more negative electricity, implosion of antagonistic poles), is what allows each time for all possible interpretations, even the most contradictory – all true, in the sense that their truth is to be exchanged, in the image of the models from which they derive, in a generalized cycle.

The Communists attack the Socialist Party as if they wished to shatter the union of the Left. They give credence to the idea that these resistances would come from a more radical political need. In fact, it is because they no longer want power. But do they not want power at this juncture, one unfavorable to the Left in general, or unfavorable to them within the Union of the Left – or do they no longer want it, by definition? When Berlinguer declares: 'There is no need to be afraid to see the Communists take power in Italy,' it simultaneously signifies:

> that there is no need to be afraid, since the Communists, if they come to power, will change nothing of its fundamental capitalist mechanism;
> that there is no risk that they will ever come to power (because they don't want to) – and even if they occupy the seat of power, they will never exercise it except by proxy;
> that in fact, power, genuine power no longer exists, and thus there is no risk whoever seizes power or seizes it again;
> but further: I, Berlinguer, am not afraid to see the Communists take power in Italy – which may seem self-evident, but not as much as you might think, because
> it could mean the opposite (no need for psychoanalysis here): *I am afraid* to see the Communists take power (and there are good reasons for that, even for a Communist).

All of this is simultaneously true. It is the secret of a discourse that is no longer simply ambiguous, as political discourses can be, but that conveys the impossibility of a determined position of power, the impossibility of a determined discursive position. And this logic is neither that of one party nor of another. It traverses all discourses without them wanting it to.

[...]

THE STRATEGY OF THE REAL

The impossibility of rediscovering an absolute level of the real is of the same order as the impossibility of staging illusion. Illusion is no longer possible, because the real is no longer possible. It is the whole *political* problem of parody, of hypersimulation or offensive simulation, that is posed here.

For example: it would be interesting to see whether the repressive apparatus would not react more violently to a simulated holdup than to a real holdup. Because the latter does nothing but disturb the order of things, the right to property, whereas the former attacks the reality principle itself. Transgression and violence are less serious because they only contest the *distribution* of the real. Simulation is infinitely more dangerous because it always leaves open to supposition that, above and beyond its object, *law and order themselves might be nothing but simulation.*

But the difficulty is proportional to the danger. How to feign a violation and put it to the test? Simulate a robbery in a large store: how to persuade security that it is a simulated robbery? There is no 'objective' difference: the gestures, the signs are the same as for a real robbery, the signs do not lean to one side or another. To the established order they are always of the order of the real.

Organize a fake holdup. Verify that your weapons are harmless, and take the most trustworthy hostage, so that no human life will be in danger (or one lapses into the criminal). Demand a ransom, and make it so that the operation creates as much commotion as possible – in short, remain close to the 'truth,' in order to test the reaction of the apparatus to a perfect simulacrum. You won't be able to do it: the network of artificial signs will become inextricably mixed up with real elements (a policeman will really fire on sight; a client of the bank will faint and die of a heart attack; one will actually pay you the phony ransom), in short, you will immediately find yourself once again, without wishing it, in the real, one of whose functions is precisely to devour any attempt at simulation, to reduce everything to the real – that is, to the established order itself, well before institutions and justice come into play.

It is necessary to see in this impossibility of isolating the process of simulation the weight of an order that cannot see and conceive of anything but the real, because it cannot function anywhere else. The simulation of an offense, if it is established as such, will either be punished less severely (because it has no 'consequences') or punished as an offense against the judicial system (for example if one sets in motion a police operation 'for nothing') – but *never as simulation* since it is precisely as such that no equivalence with the real is possible, and hence no repression either. The challenge of simulation is never admitted by power. How can the simulation of virtue be punished? However, as such it is as serious as the simulation of crime. Parody renders submission and transgression equivalent, and that is the most serious crime, because it *cancels out the difference upon which the law is based.* The established order can do nothing against it, because the law is a simulacrum of the second order, whereas simulation is of the third order, beyond true and false, beyond equivalences, beyond rational distinctions upon which the whole of the social and power depend. Thus, *lacking the real*, it is there that we must aim at order.

This is certainly why order always opts for the real. When in doubt, it always prefers this hypothesis (as in the army one prefers to take the simulator for a real madman). But this becomes more and more difficult, because if it is practically impossible to isolate the process of simulation, through the force of inertia of the real that surrounds us, the opposite is also true (and this reversibility itself is part of the apparatus of simulation and the impotence of power): namely, it is *now impossible to isolate the process of the real*, or to prove the real.

This is how all the holdups, airplane hijackings, etc. are now in some sense simulation holdups in that they are already inscribed in the decoding and orchestration rituals of the media, anticipated in their presentation and their possible consequences. In short, where they function as a group of signs dedicated exclusively to their recurrence as signs, and no longer at all to their 'real' end. But this does not make them harmless. On the contrary, it is as hyperreal events, no longer with a specific content or end, but indefinitely refracted by each other (just like so-called historical events: strikes, demonstrations, crises, etc.),[4] it is in this sense that they cannot be controlled by an order that can only exert itself on the real and the rational, on causes and ends, a referential order that can only reign over the referential, a determined power that can only reign over a determined world, but that cannot do anything against this indefinite recurrence of simulation, against this nebula whose weight no longer obeys the laws of gravitation of the real, power itself ends by being dismantled in this space and becoming a simulation of power (disconnected from its ends and its objectives, and dedicated to the *effects of power* and mass simulation).

The only weapon of power, its only strategy against this defection, is to reinject the real and the referential everywhere, to persuade us of the reality of the social, of the gravity of the economy and the finalities of production. To this end it prefers the discourse of crisis, but also, why not? that of desire. 'Take your desires for reality!' can be understood as the ultimate slogan of power since in a nonreferential world, even the confusion of the reality principle and the principle of desire is less dangerous than contagious hyperreality. One remains among principles, and among those power is always in the right.

Hyperreality and simulation are deterrents of every principle and every objective, they turn against power the deterrent that it used so well for such a long time. Because in the end, throughout its history it was capital that first fed on the destructuration of every referential, of every human objective, that shattered every ideal distinction between true and false, good and evil, in order to establish a radical law of equivalence and exchange, the iron law of its power. Capital was the first to play at deterrence, abstraction, disconnection, deterritorialization, etc., and if it is the one that fostered reality, the reality principle, it was also the first to liquidate it by exterminating all use value, all real equivalence of production and wealth, in the very sense we have of the unreality of the stakes and the omnipotence of manipulation. Well, today it is this same logic that is even more set against capital. And as soon as it wishes to combat this disastrous spiral by secreting a last glimmer of reality, on which to establish a last glimmer of power, it does nothing but multiply the *signs* and accelerate the play of simulation.

As long as the historical threat came at it from the real, power played at deterrence and simulation, disintegrating all the contradictions by dint of producing equivalent signs. Today when the danger comes at it from simulation (that of being dissolved in the play of signs), power plays at the real, plays at crisis, plays at remanufacturing artificial, social, economic, and political stakes. For power, it is a question of life and death. But it is too late.

Whence the characteristic hysteria of our times: that of the production and reproduction of the real. The other production, that of values and commodities, that of the belle epoque of political economy, has for a long time had no specific meaning. What every society looks for in continuing to produce, and to overproduce, is to restore the real that escapes it. That is why *today this 'material' production is that of the hyperreal itself*. It retains all the features, the whole discourse of traditional production, but it is no longer anything but its scaled-down refraction (thus hyperrealists fix a real from which all meaning and charm, all depth and energy of representation have vanished in a hallucinatory resemblance). Thus everywhere the hyperrealism of simulation is translated by the hallucinatory resemblance of the real to itself.

Power itself has for a long time produced nothing but the signs of its resemblance. And at the same time, another figure of power comes into play: that of a collective demand for *signs* of power – a holy union that is reconstructed around its disappearance. The whole world adheres to it more or less in terror of the collapse of the political. And in the end the game of power becomes nothing but the *critical* obsession with power – obsession with its death, obsession with its survival, which increases as it disappears. When it has totally disappeared, we will logically be under the total hallucination of power – haunting memory that is already in evidence everywhere, expressing at once the compulsion to get rid of it (no one wants it anymore, everyone unloads it on everyone else) and the panicked nostalgia over its loss. The melancholy of societies without power: this has already stirred up fascism, that overdose of a strong referential in a society that cannot terminate its mourning.

With the extenuation of the political sphere, the president comes increasingly to resemble that *Puppet of Power* who is the head of primitive societies (Clastres).

All previous presidents pay for and continue to pay for Kennedy's murder as if they were the ones who had suppressed it – which is true phantasmatically, if not in fact. They must efface this defect and this complicity with their simulated murder. Because, now it can only be simulated. Presidents Johnson and Ford were both the object of failed assassination attempts which, if they were not staged, were at least perpetrated by simulation. The Kennedys died because they incarnated something: the political, political substance, whereas the new presidents are nothing but caricatures and fake film – curiously, Johnson, Nixon, Ford, all have this simian mug, the monkeys of power.

Death is never an absolute criterion, but in this case it is significant: the era of James Dean, Marilyn Monroe, and the Kennedys, of those who really died simply because they had a mythic dimension that implies death (not for romantic reasons, but because of the fundamental principle of reversal and exchange) – this era is long gone. It is now the era of murder by simulation, of the generalized aesthetic of simulation, of the murder-abibi – the allegorical resurrection of death, which is only there to sanction the institution of power, without which it no longer has any substance or an autonomous reality.

[...]

THE END OF THE PANOPTICON

It is still to this ideology of lived experience – exhumation of the real in its fundamental banality, in its radical authenticity – that the American TV verité experiment attempted on the Loud family in 1971 refers: seven months of uninterrupted shooting, three hundred hours of nonstop broadcasting, without a script or a screenplay, the odyssey of a family, its dramas, its joys, its unexpected events, nonstop – in short, a 'raw' historical document, and the 'greatest television performance, comparable, on the scale of our day-to-day life, to the footage of our landing on the moon.' It becomes more complicated because this family fell apart during the filming: a crisis erupted, the Louds separated, etc. Whence that insoluble controversy: was TV itself responsible? What would have happened *if TV hadn't been there?*

More interesting is the illusion of filming the Louds *as if TV weren't there.* The producer's triumph was to say: 'They lived as if we were not there.' An absurd, paradoxical formula – neither true nor false: utopian. The 'as if *we* were not there' being equal to 'as if *you* were there.' It is this utopia, this paradox that fascinated the twenty million viewers, much more than did the 'perverse' pleasure of violating someone's privacy. In the 'verité' experience it is not a question of secrecy or perversion, but of a sort of frisson of the real, or of an aesthetics of the hyperreal, a frisson of vertiginous and phony exactitude, a frisson of simultaneous distancing and magnification, of distortion of scale, of an excessive transparency. The pleasure of an excess of meaning, when the bar of the sign falls below the usual waterline of meaning: the nonsignifier is exalted by the camera angle. There one sees what the real never was (but 'as if you were there'), without the distance that gives us perspectival space and depth vision (but 'more real than nature'). Pleasure in the microscopic simulation that allows the real to pass into the hyperreal. (This is also somewhat the case in porno, which is fascinating more on a metaphysical than on a sexual level.)

Besides, this family was already hyperreal by the very nature of its selection: a typical ideal American family, California home, three garages, five children, assured social and professional status, decorative housewife, upper-middle-class standing. In a way it is this statistical perfection that dooms it to death. Ideal heroine of the American way of life, it is, as in ancient sacrifices, chosen in order to be glorified and to die beneath the flames of the medium, a modern *fatum.* Because heavenly fire no longer falls on corrupted cities, it is the camera lens that, like a laser, comes to pierce lived reality in order to put it to death. 'The Louds: simply a family who agreed to deliver themselves into the hands of television, and to die by it,' the director will say. Thus it is a question of a sacrificial process, of a sacrificial spectacle offered to twenty million Americans. The liturgical drama of a mass society.

TV verité. A term admirable in its ambiguity, does it refer to the truth of this family or to the truth of TV? In fact, it is TV that is the truth of the Louds, it is

TV that is true, it is TV that renders true. Truth that is no longer the reflexive truth of the mirror, nor the perspectival truth of the panoptic system and of the gaze, but the manipulative truth of the test that sounds out and interrogates, of the laser that touches and pierces, of computer cards that retain your preferred sequences, of the genetic code that controls your combinations, of cells that inform your sensory universe. It is to this truth that the Loud family was subjected by the medium of TV, and in this sense it amounts to a death sentence (but is it still a question of truth?).

End of the panoptic system. The eye of TV is no longer the source of an absolute gaze, and the ideal of control is no longer that of transparency. This still presupposes an objective space (that of the Renaissance) and the omnipotence of the despotic gaze. It is still, if not a system of confinement, at least a system of mapping. More subtly, but always externally, playing on the opposition of seeing and being seen, even if the panoptic focal point may be blind.

Something else in regard to the Louds. 'You no longer watch TV, it is TV that watches you (live)' or again: 'You are no longer listening to Don't Panic, it is Don't Panic that is listening to you' – a switch from the panoptic mechanism of surveillance (*Discipline and Punish* [Surveiller et punir]) to a system of deterrence, in which the distinction between the passive and the active is abolished. There is no longer any imperative of submission to the model, or to the gaze 'YOU are the model!' 'YOU are the majority!' Such is the watershed of a hyperreal sociality, in which the real is confused with the model, as in the statistical operation, or with the medium, as in the Louds' operation. Such is the last stage of the social relation, ours, which is no longer one of persuasion (the classical age of propaganda, of ideology, of publicity, etc.) but one of deterrence: 'YOU are information, you are the social, you are the event, you are involved, you have the word, etc.' An about-face through which it becomes impossible to locate one instance of the model, of power, of the gaze, of the medium itself, because *you* are always already on the other side. No more subject, no more focal point, no more center or periphery: pure flexion or circular inflexion. No more violence or surveillance: only 'information,' secret virulence, chain reaction, slow implosion, and simulacra of spaces in which the effect of the real again comes into play.

We are witnessing the end of perspectival and panoptic space (which remains a moral hypothesis bound up with all the classical analyses on the 'objective' essence of power), and thus to the *very abolition of the spectacular*. Television, for example in the case of the Louds, is no longer a spectacular medium. We are no longer in the society of the spectacle, of which the situationists spoke, nor in the specific kinds of alienation and repression that it implied. The medium itself is no longer identifiable as such, and the confusion of the medium and the message (McLuhan)[5] is the first great formula of this new era. There is no longer a medium in the literal sense: it is now intangible, diffused, and diffracted in the real, and one can no longer even say that the medium is altered by it.

Such a blending, such a viral, endemic, chronic, alarming presence of the medium, without the possibility of isolating the effects – spectralized, like these advertising laser sculptures in the empty space of the event filtered by the medium – dissolution of TV in life, dissolution of life in TV – indiscernible chemical solution: we are all Louds doomed not to invasion, to pressure, to violence and blackmail by the media and the models, but to their induction, to their infiltration, to their illegible violence.

But one must watch out for the negative turn that discourse imposes: it is a question neither of disease nor of a viral infection. One must think instead of the media as if they were, in outer orbit, a kind of genetic code that directs the mutation of the real into the hyperreal, just as the other micromolecular code controls the passage from a representative sphere of meaning to the genetic one of the programmed signal.

It is the whole traditional world of causality that is in question: the perspectival, determinist mode, the 'active,' critical mode, the analytic mode – the distinction between cause and effect, between active and passive, between subject and object, between the end and the means. It is in this sense that one can say: TV is watching us, TV alienates us, TV manipulates us, TV informs us … In all this, one remains dependent on the analytical conception of the media, on an external active and effective agent, on 'perspectival' information with the horizon of the real and of meaning as the vanishing point.

Now, one must conceive of TV along the lines of DNA as an effect in which the opposing poles of determination vanish, according to a nuclear contraction, retraction, of the old polar schema that always maintained a minimal distance between cause and effect, between subject and object: precisely the distance of meaning, the gap, the difference, the smallest possible gap (PPEP!),[6] irreducible under pain of reabsorption into an aleatory and indeterminate process whose discourse can no longer account for it, because it is itself a determined order.

It is this gap that vanishes in the process of genetic coding, in which indeterminacy is not so much a question of molecular randomness as of the abolition, pure and simple, of the *relation*. In the process of molecular control, which 'goes' from the DNA nucleus to the 'substance' that it 'informs,' there is no longer the traversal of an effect, of an energy, of a determination, of a message. 'Order, signal, impulse, message': all of these attempt to render the thing intelligible to us, but by analogy, retranscribing in terms of inscription, of a vector, of decoding, a dimension, of which we know nothing – it is no longer even a 'dimension,' or perhaps it is the fourth (which is defined, however, in Einsteinian relativity by the absorption of the distinct poles of space and time). In fact, this whole process can only be understood in its negative form: nothing separates one pole from another anymore, the beginning from the end; there is a kind of contraction of one over the other, a fantastic telescoping, a collapse of the two traditional poles into each other: *implosion* – an absorption of the radiating mode of causality, of the differential mode of determination, with its positive and negative charge – an implosion of meaning. *That is where simulation begins*.

Everywhere, in no matter what domain – political, biological, psychological, mediatized – in which the distinction between these two poles can no longer be maintained, one enters into simulation, and thus into absolute manipulation – not into passivity, but into *the indifferentiation of the active and the passive*. DNA realizes this aleatory reduction at the level of living matter, Television, in the case of the Louds, also reaches this *indefinite* limit in which, vis-à-vis TV, they are neither more nor less active or passive than a living substance is vis-à-vis its molecular code. Here and there, a single nebula whose simple elements are indecipherable, whose truth is indecipherable.

[…]

NOTES

1. Cf. J. Baudrillard, 'L'ordre des simulacres' (The order of simulacra), in *L'échange symbolique et la mort* (Symbolic exchange and death) (Paris: Gallimard, 1976).
2. A discourse that is itself not susceptible to being resolved in transference. It is the entanglement of these two discourses that renders psychoanalysis interminable.
3. Cf. M. Perniola, *Icónes, visions, simulacres* (Icons, visions, simulacra), 39.
4. Taken together, the energy crisis and the ecological *mise-en-scène* arc themselves a *disaster movie*, in the same style (and with the same value) as those that currently comprise the golden days of Hollywood. It is useless to laboriously interpret these films in terms of their relation to an 'objective' social crisis or even to an 'objective' phantasm of disaster. It is in another sense that it must be said that it is *the social itself that*, in contemporary discourse, *is organized along the lines of a disaster-movie script*. (Cf. M. Makarius, *La stratégie de la catastrophe* [The strategy of disaster], 115.)
5. The medium/message confusion is certainly a corollary of that between the sender and the receiver, thus sealing the disappearance of all dual, polar structures that formed the discursive organization of language, of all determined articulation of meaning reflecting Jakobson's famous grid of functions. That discourse 'circulates' is to be taken literally: that is, it no longer goes from one point to another, but it traverses a cycle that *without distinction* includes the positions of transmitter and receiver, now unlocatable as such. Thus there is no instance of power, no instance of transmission – power is something that circulates and whose source can no longer be located, a cycle in which the positions of the dominator and the dominated are exchanged in an endless reversion that is also the end of power in its classical definition. The circularization of power, of knowledge, of discourse puts an end to any localization of instances and poles. In the psychoanalytic interpretation itself, the 'power' of the interpreter does not come from any outside instance but from the interpreted himself. This changes everything, because one can always ask of the traditional holders of power where they get their power from. Who made you duke? The king. Who made you king? God. Only God no longer answers. But to the question: who made you a psychoanalyst? the analyst can well reply: You. Thus is expressed, by an inverse simulation, the passage from the 'analyzed' to the 'analysand,' from passive to active, which simply describes the spiraling effect of the shifting of poles, the effect of circularity in which power is lost, is dissolved, is resolved in perfect manipulation (it is no longer of the order of directive power and of the gaze, but of the order of tactility and commutation). See also the state/family circularity assured by the fluctuation and metastatic regulation of the images of the social and the private (J. Donzelot, *La police des familles* [The policing of families]).
   Impossible now to pose the famous question: 'From what position do you speak?' – 'How do you know?' 'From where do you get your power?' without hearing the

immediate response: 'But it is *of* you (from you) that I speak' – meaning, it is you who are speaking, you who know, you who are the power. Gigantic circumvolution, circumlocution of the spoken word, which is equal to a blackmail with no end, to a deterrence that cannot be appealed of the subject presumed to speak, leaving him without a reply, because to the question that he poses one ineluctably replies: but *you are* the answer, or: your question is already an answer, etc. – the whole strangulatory sophistication of intercepting speech, of the forced confession in the guise of freedom of expression, of trapping the subject in his own interrogation, of the precession of the reply to the question (all the violence of interpretation lies there, as well as that of the conscious or unconscious management of the 'spoken word' [*parole*]).

This simulacrum of the inversion or the involution of poles, this clever subterfuge, which is the secret of the whole discourse of manipulation and thus, today, in every domain, the secret of any new power in the erasure of the scene of power, in the assumption of all words from which has resulted this fantastic silent majority characteristic of our time – all of this started without a doubt in the political sphere with the democratic simulacrum, which today is the substitution for the power of God with the power of the people as the source of power, and of power as *emanation* with power as *representation*. Anti-Copernican revolution: no transcendental instance either of the sun or of the luminous sources of power and knowledge – everything comes from the people and everything returns to them. It is with this magnificent recycling that the universal simulacrum of manipulation, from the scenario of mass suffrage to the present-day phantoms of opinion polls, begins to be put in place.

6. PPEP is an acronym for smallest possible gap, or 'plus petit écart possible.' – Trans.

IRONY AND 'DOUBLE CODING'
6

'POSTMODERNISM, IRONY, THE ENJOYABLE'

Umberto Eco

Between 1965 and today, two ideas have been definitively clarified: that plot could be found also in the form of quotation of other plots, and that the quotation could be less escapist than the plot quoted. In 1972 I edited the *Almanacco Bompiani*, celebrating 'The Return to the Plot,' though this return was via an ironic re-examination (not without admiration) of Ponson du Terrail and Eugène Sue, and admiration (with very little irony) of some of the great pages of Dumas. The real problem at stake then was, could there be a novel that was not escapist and, nevertheless, still enjoyable?

This link, and the rediscovery not only of plot but also of enjoyability, was to be realized by the American theorists of postmodernism.

Unfortunately, 'postmodern' is a term *bon à tout faire*. I have the impression that it is applied today to anything the user of the term happens to like. Further, there seems to be an attempt to make it increasingly retroactive: first it was apparently applied to certain writers or artists active in the last twenty years, then gradually it reached the beginning of the century, then still further back. And this reverse procedure continues; soon the postmodern category will include Homer.

Actually, I believe that postmodernism is not a trend to be chronologically defined, but, rather, an ideal category – or, better still, a *Kunstwollen*, a way of operating. We could say that every period has its own postmodernism, just as every period would have its own mannerism (and, in fact, I wonder if

From Umberto Eco (1985) *Reflections on* The Name of the Rose. London: Secker & Warburg.

postmodernism is not the modern name for mannerism as metahistorical category). I believe that in every period there are moments of crisis like those described by Nietzsche in his *Thoughts Out of Season*, in which he wrote about the harm done by historical studies. The past conditions us, harries us, blackmails us. The historic avant-garde (but here I would also consider avant-garde a metahistorical category) tries to settle scores with the past. 'Down with moonlight' – a futurist slogan – is a platform typical of every avant-garde; you have only to replace 'moonlight' with whatever noun is suitable. The avant-garde destroys, defaces the past: *Les Demoiselles d'Avignon* is a typical avant-garde act. Then the avant-garde goes further, destroys the figure, cancels it, arrives at the abstract, the informal, the white canvas, the slashed canvas, the charred canvas. In architecture and the visual arts, it will be the curtain wall, the building as stele, pure parallelepiped, minimal art; in literature, the destruction of the flow of discourse, the Burroughs-like collage, silence, the white page; in music, the passage from atonality to noise to absolute silence (in this sense, the early Cage is modern).

But the moment comes when the avant-garde (the modern) can go no further, because it has produced a metalanguage that speaks of its impossible texts (conceptual art). The postmodern reply to the modern consists of recognizing that the past, since it cannot really be destroyed, because its destruction leads to silence, must be revisited: but with irony, not innocently. I think of the postmodern attitude as that of a man who loves a very cultivated woman and knows he cannot say to her, 'I love you madly,' because he knows that she knows (and that she knows that he knows) that these words have already been written by Barbara Cartland. Still, there is a solution. He can say, 'As Barbara Cartland would put it, I love you madly.' At this point, having avoided false innocence, having said clearly that it is no longer possible to speak innocently, he will nevertheless have said what he wanted to say to the woman: that he loves her, but he loves her in an age of lost innocence. If the woman goes along with this, she will have received a declaration of love all the same. Neither of the two speakers will feel innocent, both will have accepted the challenge of the past, of the already said, which cannot be eliminated; both will consciously and with pleasure play the game of irony. . . . But both will have succeeded, once again, in speaking of love.

Irony, metalinguistic play, enunciation squared. Thus, with the modern, anyone who does not understand the game can only reject it, but with the postmodern, it is possible not to understand the game and yet to take it seriously. Which is, after all, the quality (the risk) of irony. There is always someone who takes ironic discourse seriously. I think that the collages of Picasso, Juan Gris, and Braque were modern: this is why normal people would not accept them. On the other hand, the collages of Max Ernst, who pasted together bits of nineteenth-century engravings, were postmodern: they can be read as fantastic stories, as the telling of dreams, without any awareness that they amount to a discussion of the nature of engraving, and perhaps even of collage. If 'postmodern' means this, it is clear why Sterne and Rabelais were postmodern, why Borges surely is, and why in the same artist the modern moment and the postmodern moment can coexist, or alternate, or follow each other closely. Look at Joyce. The *Portrait* is the story of an attempt at the modern. *Dubliners*, even if it comes before, is more modern than *Portrait*. *Ulysses* is on the borderline. *Finnegans Wake* is already postmodern, or at least it initiates the postmodern discourse: it demands, in order to be understood, not the negation of the already said, but its ironic rethinking.

On the subject of the postmodern nearly everything has been said, from the very beginning (namely, in essays like 'The Literature of Exhaustion' by John Barth, which dates from 1967). Not that I am entirely in agreement with the grades that the theoreticians of postmodernism (Barth included) give to writers and artists, establishing who is postmodern and who has not yet made it. But I am interested in the theorem that the trend's theoreticians derive from their premises: 'My ideal postmodernist author neither merely repudiates nor merely imitates either his twentieth-century modernist parents or his nineteenth-century premodernist grandparents. He has the first half of our century under his belt, but not on his back. . . . He may not hope to reach and move the devotees of James Michener and Irving Wallace – not to mention the lobotomized mass-media illiterates. But he *should* hope to reach and delight, at least part of the time, beyond the circle of what Mann used to call the Early Christians: professional devotees of high art. . . . The ideal postmodernist novel will somehow rise above the quarrel between realism and irrealism, formalism and "contentism," pure and committed literature, coterie fiction and junk fiction. . . . My own analogy would be with good jazz or classical music: one finds much on successive listenings or close examination of the score that one didn't catch the first time through; but the first time through should be so ravishing – and not just to specialists – that one delights in the replay.'

This is what Barth wrote in 1980, resuming the discussion, but this time under the title 'The Literature of Replenishment: Postmodernist Fiction.' Naturally, the subject can be discussed further, with a greater taste for paradox; and this is what Leslie Fiedler does. In 1980 *Salmagundi* (no. 50–51) published a debate between Fiedler and other American authors. Fiedler, obviously, is out to provoke. He praises *The Last of the Mohicans*, adventure stories, Gothic novels, junk scorned by critics that was nevertheless able to create myths and capture the imagination of more than one generation. He wonders if something like *Uncle Tom's Cabin* will ever appear again, a book that can be read with equal passion in the kitchen, the living room, and the nursery. He includes Shakespeare among those who knew how to amuse, along with *Gone with the Wind*. We all know he is too keen a critic to believe these things. He simply wants to break down the barrier that has been erected between art and enjoyability. He feels that today reaching a vast public and capturing its dreams perhaps means acting as the avant-garde, and he still leaves us free to say that capturing readers' dreams does not necessarily mean encouraging escape: it can also mean haunting them.

7

'POST-MODERNISM DEFINED'

Charles Jencks

Post-Modernism, like Modernism, varies for each art both in its motives and time-frame, and here I shall define it just in the field with which I am most involved – architecture. The responsibility for introducing it into the architectural subconscious lies with Joseph Hudnut who, at Harvard with Walter Gropius, may have wished to give this pioneer of the Modern Movement a few sleepless nights. At any rate, he used the term in the title of an article published in 1945 called 'the post-modern house' (all lower case, as was Bauhaus practice), but didn't mention it in the body of the text or define it polemically. Except for an occasional slip here and there, by Philip Johnson or Nikolaus Pevsner, it wasn't used until my own writing on the subject which started in 1975.[1] In that first year of lecturing and polemicising in Europe and America. I used it as a temporising label, as a definition to describe where we had left rather than where we were going. The observable fact was that architects as various as Ralph Erskine, Robert Venturi, Lucien Kroll, the Krier brothers and Team Ten had all departed from Modernism and set off in different directions which *kept a trace of their common departure*. To this day I would define Post-Modernism as I did in 1978 as *double coding: the combination of Modern techniques with something else (usually traditional building) in order for architecture to communicate with the public and a concerned minority, usually other architects*. The point of this double coding was itself double. Modern architecture had failed to remain credible partly

From Charles Jencks (1986) 'Post-Modernism Defined', in *What Is Post-Modernism?* London: Academy.

because it didn't communicate effectively with its ultimate users – the main argument of my book *The Language of Post-Modern Architecture* – and partly because it didn't make effective links with the city and history. Thus the solution I perceived and defined as Post-Modern: an architecture that was professionally based *and* popular as well as one that was based on new techniques *and* old patterns. Double coding to simplify means both elite/popular and new/old and there are compelling reasons for these opposite pairings. Today's Post-Modern architects were trained by Modernists, and are committed to using contemporary technology as well as facing current social reality. These commitments are enough to distinguish them from revivalists or traditionalists, a point worth stressing since it creates their hybrid language, the style of Post-Modern architecture. The same is not completely true of Post-Modern artists and writers who may use traditional techniques of narrative and representation in a more straightforward way. Yet all the creators who could be called Post-Modern keep something of a Modern sensibility – some intention which distinguishes their work from that of revivalists – whether this is irony, parody, displacement, complexity, eclecticism, realism or any number of contemporary tactics and goals. As I mentioned in the foreword. Post-Modernism has the essential double meaning: the continuation of Modernism and its transcendence.

The main motive for Post-Modern architecture is obviously the social failure of Modern architecture, its mythical 'death' announced repeatedly over ten years. In 1968, an English tower block of housing, Ronan Point, suffered what was called 'cumulative collapse' as its floors gave way after an explosion. In 1972, many slab blocks of housing were intentionally blown up at Pruitt-Igoe in St Louis. By the mid 1970s, these explosions were becoming a quite frequent method of dealing with the failures of Modernist building methods: cheap prefabrication, lack of personal 'defensible' space and the alienating housing estate. The 'death' of Modern architecture and its ideology of progress which offered technical solutions to social problems was seen by everyone in a vivid way. The destruction of the central city and historical fabric was almost equally apparent to the populace and again these popular, social motives should be stressed because they aren't quite the same in painting, film, dance or literature. There is no similar, vivid 'death' of Modernism in these fields, nor perhaps the same social motivation that one finds in Post-Modern architecture. But even in Post-Modern literature there is a social motive for using past forms in an ironic way. Umberto Eco has described this irony or double coding: 'I think of the postmodern attitude as that of a man who loves a very cultivated woman and knows he cannot say to her, "I love you madly" '[2] [. . .]

Thus Eco underlines the lover's use of Post-Modern double coding and extends it, of course, to the novelist's and poet's social use of previous forms. Faced with a restrictive Modernism, a minimalism of means and ends, writers such as John Barth have felt just as restricted as architects forced to build in the International Style, or using only glass and steel. The most notable, and perhaps the best, use of this double coding in architecture is James Stirling's addition to the Staatsgalerie in Stuttgart. Here one can find the fabric of the city and the existing museum extended in amusing and ironic ways. The U-shaped palazzo form of the old gallery is echoed and placed on a high plinth, or 'Acropolis', above the traffic. But this classical base holds a very real and necessary parking garage, one that is ironically indicated by stones which have 'fallen', like ruins, to the ground. The resultant holes show the real construction – not the thick marble blocks of the real Acropolis, but a steel frame holding stone cladding which allows the air required by law. One can sit on these false ruins and ponder the truth of our lost innocence: that we live in an age which can build with beautiful, expressive masonry as long as we make it skin-deep and hang it on a steel skeleton. A Modernist would of course deny himself and us this pleasure for a number of reasons: 'truth to materials', 'logical consistency', 'straight-forwardness', 'simplicity' – all the values and rhetorical tropes celebrated by such Modernists as Le Corbusier and Mies van der Rohe.

Stirling, by contrast and like the lovers of Umberto Eco, wants to communicate more and different values. To signify the permanent nature of the museum, he has used traditional rustication and classical forms including an Egyptian cornice, an open-air Pantheon, and segmental arches. These are beautiful in an understated and conventional way, but they aren't revivalist either because of small distortions, or the use of a modern material such as reinforced concrete. They say, 'We are beautiful like the Acropolis or Panthcon, but we are also based on concrete technology and deceit.' The extreme form of this double coding is visible at the entry points: a steel temple outline which announces the taxi drop-off point, and the Modernist steel canopies which tell the public where to walk in. These forms and colours are reminiscent of De Stijl, that quintessentially modern language, but they are collaged onto the traditional background. Thus Modernism confronts Classicism to such an extent that both Modernists and Classicists would be surprised, if not offended. There is not the simple harmony and consistency of either language or world view. It's as if Stirling were saying through his hybrid language and uneasy confrontations that we live in a complex world where we can't deny either the past and conventional beauty, or the present and current technical and social reality. Caught between this past and present, unwilling to oversimplify our situation. Stirling has produced the most 'real' beauty of Post-Modern architecture to date.

As much of this reality has to do with taste as it does with technology. Modernism failed as mass-housing and city building partly because it failed to communicate with its inhabitants and users who might not have liked the style, understood what it meant or even known how to use it. Hence the double coding, the essential definition of Post-Modernism, has been used as a strategy of communicating on various levels at once. Virtually every Post-Modern architect – Robert Venturi, Hans Hollein, Charles Moore, Robert Stern, Michael Graves, Arata Isozaki are the notable examples – use popular *and* elitist signs in their work to achieve quite different ends, and their styles are essentially hybrid. To simplify, at Stuttgart the blue and red handrails and vibrant polychromy fit in with the youth that uses the museum – they literally resemble their dayglo hair and anoraks – while the Classicism appeals more to the lovers of Schinkel. This is a very popular building with young and old and when I interviewed people there – a group of *plein air* painters, schoolchildren and businessmen – I found their different perceptions and tastes were accommodated and stretched. The pluralism which is so often called on to justify Post-Modernism is here a tangible reality.

This is not the place to recount the history of Post-Modern architecture, but I want to stress the ideological and social intentions which underlie this history because they are so often overlooked in the bitter debate with Modernists.[3] Even traditionalists often reduce the debate to matters of style, and thus the symbolic intentions and morality are overlooked. If one reads the writings of Robert Venturi, Denise Scott Brown, Christian Norberg-Schulz, or myself, one will find the constant notion of pluralism, the idea that the architect must design for different 'taste cultures' (in the words of the sociologist Herbert Gans) and for differing views of the good life. In any complex building, in any large city building such as an office, there will be varying tastes and functions that have to be articulated and these will inevitably lead, if the architect follows these hints, towards an eclectic style. He may pull this heterogeneity together under a Free-Style Classicism, as do many Post-Modernists today, but a trace of the pluralism will and should remain. I would even argue that 'the true and proper style' is not as they said Gothic, but some form of eclecticism, because only this can adequately encompass the pluralism that is our social and metaphysical reality.

Many people would disagree with this last point and some of them, such as the visionary and urbanist Leon Krier, are almost Post-Modern. I bring him up as a borderline case and because he shows how different traditions may influence each other in a positive way. Krier worked for James Stirling in the early 1970s and since then has evolved his own form of Vernacular Classicism. In his schemes for the reconstruction of cities such as Berlin and Washington DC, he shows how the destroyed fabric of the historic city could be repaired and a traditional set of well-scaled spaces added to this core. The motivations are urbanistic and utopian (in the sense that they are unlikely to be realised). They are also traditional and idealistic in the straightforward manner that Post-Modernism is not. The way of life implied is paternalistic and monistic, but the plans would entail not the totalitarianism that his critics aver when they compare him with Albert Speer but an integrated culture led by a determined and sensitive elite. In this sense, Krier hasn't lost the innocence which Umberto Eco and the Post-Modernists believe is gone for good, but has returned to a pre-industrial golden age where singular visions could be imagined for everyone. Again, critics will say he's kept his innocence precisely because he hasn't built and faced the irreducibly plural reality.

This may be true and yet Krier has had a beneficent effect on Post-Modernists, as on others, because his ideal models act as a critique of current planning in the same way as do such surviving fragments as the centres of Siena and Venice. His nostalgia, like that of the French Revolution, is of a very positive and creative kind because it shows what a modern city might be if built with traditional streets, arcades, lakes and squares. Moreover – and this does make him a Post-Modernist – his drawing manner derived equally from Le Corbusier and the École des Beaux-Arts, is based on practical urban knowledge. He is not simply a mannerist, sprinkling bi-planes and 1920s technology through the sky, but someone who thinks through all the public buildings and private fabric before he draws. His bi-planes are of course ironic Post-Modern comments on the desirability of technical regression.

There are, inevitably, many more strands of Post-Modern architecture than the two major ones which the work of Stirling and Krier represent, and I have tried to show the plurality as consisting of six basic traditions or 'species'. There is some overlap between these identifiable species, within the evolutionary tree of my diagram, and architects, unlike animals, can jump from one category to another, or occupy several strands at once. The diagram shows two fundamental aspects which have to be added to our former definition of Post-Modernism: it is a movement that starts *roughly in 1960 as a set of plural departures from Modernism*. Key definers are a pluralism both philosophical and stylistic, and a dilaectical or critical relation to a pre-existing ideology. There is no one Post-Modern style, although there is a dominating Classicism, just as there was no one Modern mode, although there was a dominating International Style. Furthermore, if one is going to classify anything as complex as an architectural movement, one has to use *many* definers: Anthony Blunt, in a key text on Baroque and Rococo, shows the necessity for using ten definers, and in distinguishing Post-Modernism from Modern and Late-Modern architecture. I have used thirty.[4] Most of these definers concern differences over symbolism, ornament, humour, technology and the relation of the architect to existing and past cultures. Modernists and Late-Modernists tend to emphasise technical and economic solutions to problems, whereas Post-Modernists tend to emphasise contextual and cultural additions to their inventions.

Many of these points could be made about Post-Modern art. It also started roughly in 1960 with a succession of departures from Modernism – notably Pop Art, Hyperrealism, Photo Realism, Allegorical and Political Realism, New Image Painting, *La Transavanguardia*, Neo-Expressionism and a host of other more or less fabricated movements. Pressure from the art market to produce new labels and synthetic schools has, no doubt, increased the tempo and heat of this change. And the influence of the international media, so emphasised as a defining aspect of the post-industrial society, has made these movements cross over national boundaries. Post-Modern art, like architecture, is influenced by the 'world village' and the sensibility that comes with this: an ironic cosmopolitanism. If one looks at three Italian Post-Modernists, Carlo Maria Mariani, Sandro Chia and Mimmo Paladino, one sees their 'Italianness' always in quotation marks, an ironic fabrication of their roots made as much for the New York they occasionally inhabit as from inner necessity. Whereas a mythology was given to the artist in the past by tradition and by patron, in the Post-Modern world it is chosen and invented.

Mariani, in the mid 1970s, created his fictional academy of eighteenth-century peers – Goethe, Winckelmann, Mengs, etc. – and then painted some missing canvasses to fill out a mythic history. In the early 1980s he transferred this mythology to the present day and painted an allegory of Post-Modern Parnassus with friends, enemies, critics and dealers collected around himself in the centre – a modern-day version of Raphael's and Meng's versions of the traditional subject. We see here a series of texts layered one on top of another as an enigmatic commentary, like the structure of a myth. Is it serious, or parody, or more likely, the combination ironic allegory? The facial expressions and detail would suggest this double reading. Mariani both solemn and supercilious sits below Ganymede being abducted to heaven by Zeus: Ganymede is not only the beautiful boy of Greek mythology being captured in the erotic embrace of the eagle Zeus, but a portrait of the performance artist Luigi Ontani, hence the hoop and stick. To the right, Francesco Clemente gazes past a canvas held by Sandro Chia; Mario Merz is Hercules in an understated bathtub; a well-known New York dealer waddles to the water personified as a turtle; critics write and admire their own profiles. All this is carried out in the mock heroic style of the late eighteenth century, the style of *la pittura colta* which Mariani has made his own. No one who gives this 'cultured painting' an extended analysis would call it eighteenth-century, or straight revivalist, although many critics unsympathetic to Post-Modernism have again branded the work as 'fascist'. The representational conventions had been dismissed by Modernists as taboo, as frigid academic art.

If Mariani adapts and invents his mythology then so do many Post-Modernists who are involved in allegory and narrative. This concern for content and subject matter is in a sense comparable to architects' renewed concern for symbolism and meaning. Whereas Modernism and particularly Late-Modernism concentrated on the autonomy and expression of the individual art form – the aesthetic dimension – Post-Modernists focus on the semantic aspect. This generalisation is true of such different artists as David Hockney, Malcolm Morley, Eric Fischl, Lennart Anderson and Paul Georges, some of whom have painted enigmatic allegories, others a combination of sexual and classical narratives. The so-called 'return to painting' of the 1980s is also a return to a traditional concern with content, although it is content with a difference from pre-Modern art.

First, because these Post-Modernists have had a Modern training, they are inevitably concerned with abstraction and the basic reality of modern life, that is, a secular mass-culture dominated by economic and pragmatic motives. This gives their work the same complexity, mannerism and double coding present in Post-Modern architecture, and also an eclectic or hybrid style. For instance Ron Kitaj, who is the artist most concerned with literary and cultural subject matter, combines Modernist techniques of collage and a flat, graphic composition with

Renaissance traditions. His enigmatic allegory *If Not, Not* is a visual counterpart of T.S. Eliot's *The Wasteland*, on which it is partly based. Survivors of war crawl through the desert towards an oasis, survivors of civilisation (Eliot himself) are engaged in quizzical acts, some with representatives of exotic culture. Lamb, crow, palm tree, turquoise lake and a Tuscan landscape consciously adapted from the classical tradition resonate with common overtones. They point towards a western and Christian background overlaid by Modernism, the cult of primitivism and disaster. The classical barn/monument at the top so reminiscent of Aldo Rossi and Post-Modern face buildings, also suggests the death camps, which it represents. Indeed the burning inferno of the sky, the corpse and broken pier, the black and truncated trees all suggest life after the Second World War: plural, confused and tortured on the whole, but containing islands of peace (and a search for wholeness). The title, with its double negative – *If Not, Not* – was taken from an ancient political oath which meant roughly: if you the King do not uphold our liberties and laws, then we do not uphold you. Thus the consequences of broken promises and fragmented culture are the content of this gripping drama, one given a classical *gravitas* and dignity.

Examples could be multiplied of this type of hidden moralistic narrative: Robert Rauschenberg, David Salle, Hans Haacke, Ian Hamilton Finlay and Stephen McKenna all make use of the classical tradition in portraying our current cultural situation. Their political and ethical views are often opposed, but their intention to revive the tradition of moralistic art is shared. Thus the definition of Post-Modernism that I've given above for architects also holds true for artists and, I believe, such literary figures as Umberto Eco, David Lodge, John Barth, John Gardner and Jorge Luis Borges among many others. It does not hold true, however, for so many artists lumped together under a Post-Modern label for whom there are much better appellations.

NOTES

1. My own writing and lecturing on Post-Modernism in architecture started in 1975 and 'The Rise of Post-Modern Architecture' was published in a Dutch book and a British magazine, *Architecture – Inner Town Government*, Eindhoven, July 1975, and *Architecture Association Quarterly*. No. 4, 1975. Subsequently Eisenman and Stern started using the term and by 1977 it had caught on. For a brief history see the 'Footnote on the Term' in *The Language of Post-Modern Architecture*, fourth edition, Academy Editions. London/Rizzoli, New York 1984, p. 8.
2. Umberto Eco, *Postscript to The Name of the Rose*, Harcourt Brace Jovanovich. New York, 1984, pp. 67–8. [See previous extract, p. 111 – Ed.]
3. Besides my own *The Language of Post-Modern Architecture*, *op. cit.*, and *Current Architecture*, Academy Editions, London/Rizzoli, New York 1982, and *Modern Movements in Architecture*, second edition, Penguin Books, Harmondsworth, 1985, see Paolo Portoghesi, *After Modern Architecture*, Rizzoli, New York 1982, and its updated version, *Postmodern*, Rizzoli, New York 1983, and *Immagini del Post-Moderno*, Edizioni Chiva, Venice 1983. See also Heinrich Klotz, *Die Revision der Moderne, Postmoderne Architektur, 1960–1980* and *Moderne und Postmoderne Architektur der Gegenwart 1960–1980*, Friedr. Vieweg & Sohn. Braunschweig/Wiesbaden 1984. We have debated his notion of Post-Modern architecture as

'fiction' and this has been published in *Architectural Design* 7/8 1984, *Revision of the Modern*. See also my discussion of users and abusers of Post-Modern in 'La Bataille des étiquettes', *Nouveaux plaisirs d'architecture*, Centre Georges Pompidou, Paris 1985, pp. 25–33.

4. Anthony Blunt, *Some Uses and Misuses of the Terms Baroque and Rococo as applied to Architecture*, Oxford 1973; Charles Jencks, *Late-Modern Architecture*, Academy Editions, London/Rizzoli, New York 1980, p. 32.

DIAGNOSING POSTMODERNISM
8

'YOU MAY!'

Slavoj Žižek

'Rule Girls' are heterosexual women who follow precise rules as to how they let themselves be seduced (accept a date only if you are asked at least three days in advance etc.). Although the rules correspond to customs which used to regulate the behaviour of old-fashioned women actively pursued by old-fashioned men, the Rule Girls phenomenon does not involve a return to conservative values: women now freely choose their own rules – an instance of the 'reflexivisation' of everyday customs in today's 'risk society'. According to the risk society theory of Anthony Giddens, Ulrich Beck and others, we no longer live our lives in compliance with Nature or Tradition; there is no symbolic order or code of accepted fictions (what Lacan calls the 'Big Other') to guide us in our social behaviour. All our impulses, from sexual orientation to ethnic belonging, are more and more often experienced as matters of choice. Things which once seemed self-evident – how to feed and educate a child, how to proceed in sexual seduction, how and what to eat, how to relax and amuse oneself – have now been 'colonised' by reflexivity, and are experienced as something to be learned and decided on.

The retreat of the accepted Big Other accounts for the prevalence of code-cracking in popular culture. New Age pseudo-scientific attempts to use computer technology to crack some recondite code – in the Bible, say, or the pyramids – which can reveal the future of humanity offer one example of this. Another is provided by the scene in cyberspace movies in which the hero (or

From Slavoj Žižek (1999) 'You May!', *London Review of Books*, 21 (6).

often the heroine), hunched over a computer and frantically working against time, has his/her 'access denied', until he/she cracks the code and discovers that a secret government agency is involved in a plot against freedom and democracy. Believing there is a code to be cracked is of course much the same as believing in the existence of some Big Other: in every case what is wanted is an agent who will give structure to our chaotic social lives.

Even racism is now reflexive. Consider the Balkans. They are portrayed in the liberal Western media as a vortex of ethnic passion – a multiculturalist dream turned into a nightmare. The standard reaction of a Slovene (I am one myself) is to say: 'Yes, this is how it is in the Balkans, but Slovenia is not part of the Balkans; it is part of Mitteleuropa; the Balkans begin in Croatia or in Bosnia; we Slovenes are the last bulwark of European civilisation against the Balkan madness.' If you ask, 'Where do the Balkans begin?' you will always be told that they begin *down there*, towards the south-east. For Serbs, they begin in Kosovo or in Bosnia where Serbia is trying to defend civilised Christian Europe against the encroachments of this Other. For the Croats, the Balkans begin in Orthodox, despotic and Byzantine Serbia, against which Croatia safeguards Western democratic values. For many Italians and Austrians, they begin in Slovenia, the Western outpost of the Slavic hordes. For many Germans, Austria is tainted with Balkan corruption and inefficiency; for many Northern Germans, Catholic Bavaria is not free of Balkan contamination. Many arrogant Frenchmen associate Germany with Eastern Balkan brutality – it lacks French finesse. Finally, to some British opponents of the European Union, Continental Europe is a new version of the Turkish Empire with Brussels as the new Istanbul – a voracious despotism threatening British freedom and sovereignty.

We are dealing with an imaginary cartography, which projects onto the real landscape its own shadowy ideological antagonisms, in the same way that the conversion-symptoms of the hysterical subject in Freud project onto the physical body the map of another, imaginary anatomy. Much of this projection is racist. First, there is the old-fashioned, unabashed rejection of the Balkan Other (despotic, barbarian, Orthodox, Muslim, corrupt, Oriental) in favour of true values (Western, civilised, democratic, Christian). But there is also a 'reflexive', politically correct racism: the liberal, multiculturalist perception of the Balkans as a site of ethnic horrors and intolerance, of primitive, tribal, irrational passions, as opposed to the reasonableness of post-nation-state conflict resolution by negotiation and compromise. Racism is a disease of the Balkan Other, while we in the West are merely observers, neutral, benevolent and righteously dismayed. Finally, there is reverse racism, which celebrates the exotic authenticity of the Balkan Other, as in the notion of Serbs who, by contrast with inhibited, anaemic Western Europeans, still exhibit a prodigious lust for life. Reverse racism plays a crucial role in the success of Emir Kusturica's films in the West.

Because the Balkans are part of Europe, they can be spoken of in racist clichés which nobody would dare to apply to Africa or Asia. Political struggles in the

Balkans are compared to ridiculous operetta plots; Ceauşescu was presented as a contemporary reincarnation of Count Dracula. Slovenia is most exposed to this displaced racism, since it is closest to Western Europe: when Kusturica, talking about his film *Underground*, dismissed the Slovenes as a nation of Austrian grooms, nobody reacted: an 'authentic' artist from the less developed part of former Yugoslavia was attacking the most developed part of it. When discussing the Balkans, the tolerant multiculturalist is allowed to act out his repressed racism.

Perhaps the best example of the universalised reflexivity of our lives is the growing inefficiency of interpretation. Traditional psychoanalysis relied on a notion of the unconscious as the 'dark continent', the impenetrable substance of the subject's being, which had to be probed by interpretation: when its content was brought to light a liberating new awareness would follow. Today, the formations of the unconscious (from dreams to hysterical symptoms) have lost their innocence: the 'free associations' of a typical educated patient consist for the most part of attempts to provide a psychoanalytic explanation of his own disturbances, so we have not only Annafreudian, Jungian, Kleinian, Lacanian interpretations of the symptoms, but symptoms which are themselves Annafreudian, Jungian, Kleinian, Lacanian – they don't exist without reference to some psychoanalytic theory. The unfortunate result of this reflexivisation is that the analyst's interpretation loses its symbolic efficacy and leaves the symptom intact in its idiotic *jouissance*. It's as though a neo-Nazi skinhead, pressed to give reasons for his behaviour, started to talk like a social worker, sociologist or social psychologist, citing diminished social mobility, rising insecurity, the disintegration of paternal authority, the lack of maternal love in his early childhood.

'When I hear the word "culture", I reach for my gun,' Goebbels is supposed to have said. 'When I hear the word "culture", I reach for my cheque-book,' says the cynical producer in Godard's *Le Mépris*. A leftist slogan inverts Goebbels's statement: 'When I hear the word "gun", I reach for culture.' Culture, according to that slogan, can serve as an efficient answer to the gun: an outburst of violence is a *passage à l'acte* rooted in the subject's ignorance. But the notion is undermined by the rise of what might be called 'Post-Modern racism', the surprising characteristic of which is its insensitivity to reflection – a neo-Nazi skinhead who beats up black people knows what he's doing, but does it anyway.

Reflexivisation has transformed the structure of social dominance. Take the public image of Bill Gates. Gates is not a patriarchal father-master, nor even a corporate Big Brother running a rigid bureaucratic empire, surrounded on an inaccessible top floor by a host of secretaries and assistants. He is instead a kind of Small Brother, his very ordinariness an indication of a monstrousness so uncanny that it can no longer assume its usual public form. In photos and drawings he looks like anyone else, but his devious smile points to an underlying evil that is beyond representation. It is also a crucial aspect of Gates as icon that he is seen as the hacker who made it (the term 'hacker' has, of course, subversive/marginal/anti-establishment connotations; it suggests someone who sets out to disturb the smooth functioning of large bureaucratic corporations). At the level of fantasy, Gates is a small-time, subversive hooligan who has taken over and dressed himself up as the respectable chairman. In Bill Gates, Small Brother, the average ugly guy coincides with and contains the figure of evil genius who aims for total control of our lives. In early James Bond movies, the evil genius was an eccentric figure, dressed extravagantly, or alternatively in the grey uniform of the Maoist commissar. In the case of Gates, this ridiculous charade is no longer needed – the evil genius turns out to be the boy next door.

Another aspect of this process is the changed status of the narrative tradition that we use to understand our lives. In *Men are from Mars, Women are from Venus* (1992), John Gray proposed a vulgarised version of narrativist-deconstructionist psychoanalysis. Since we ultimately 'are' the stories we tell ourselves about ourselves, the solution to a psychic deadlock resides, he proposes, in a 'positive' rewriting of the narrative of our past. What he has in mind is not only the standard cognitive therapy of changing negative 'false beliefs' about oneself into an assurance that one is loved by others and capable of creative achievements, but a more 'radical', pseudo-Freudian procedure of regressing back to the scene of the primordial traumatic wound. Gray accepts the psychoanalytic notion of an early childhood traumatic experience that forever marks the subject's further development, but he gives it a pathological spin. What he proposes is that, after regressing to, and thus confronting, his primal traumatic scene, the subject should, under the therapist's guidance, 'rewrite' this scene, this ultimate phantasmatic framework of his subjectivity, as part of a more benign and productive narrative. If, say, the primordial trau-matic scene existing in your unconscious, deforming and inhibiting your creative attitude, is that of your father shouting at you, 'You are worthless! I despise you! Nothing good will come of you,' you should rewrite the scene so that a benevolent father smiles at you and says: 'You're OK! I trust you fully.' (Thus the solution for the Wolf Man would have been to 'regress' to the parental *coitus a tergo* and then rewrite the scene so that what he saw was merely his parents lying on the bed, his father reading a newspaper and his mother a sentimental novel.) It may seem a ridiculous thing to do, but there is a widely accepted, politically correct version of this procedure in which ethnic, sexual and other minorities rewrite their past in a more positive, self-assertive vein (African Americans claiming that long before European modernity, ancient African empires had a sophisticated understanding of science and technology etc.). Imagine a rewriting of the Decalogue along the same lines. Is one of the Commandments too severe? Well then, let's regress to Mount Sinai and rewrite it: adultery – fine, provided it is sincere and serves the goal of profound self-realisation. What disappears is not 'hard fact' but the Real of a traumatic encounter whose organising role in the subject's psychic economy resists its symbolic rewriting.

In our post-political liberal-permissive society, human rights can be seen as expressing the right to violate the Ten Commandments. The right to privacy is, in effect, the right to commit adultery, in secret, without being observed or investigated. The right to pursue happiness and to possess private property is, in effect, the right to steal (to exploit others). Freedom of the press and of expression – the right to lie. The right of free citizens to possess weapons – the right to kill. Freedom of religious belief – the right to celebrate false gods. Human rights do not, of course, directly condone the violation of the Commandments, but they preserve a marginal 'grey zone' which is out of the reach of religious or secular power. In this shady zone, I can violate the Commandments, and if the Power catches me with my pants down and tries to prevent my violation, I can cry: 'Assault on my basic human rights!' It is impossible for the Power to prevent a 'misuse' of human rights without at the same time impinging on their proper application. Lacan draws attention to a resistance to the use of lie-detectors in crime investigations – as if such a direct 'objective' verification somehow infringes the subject's right to the privacy of his thoughts.

A similar tension between rights and prohibitions determines heterosexual seduction in our politically correct times. Or, to put it differently, there is no seduction which cannot at some point be construed as intrusion or harassment because there will always be a point when one has to expose oneself and 'make a pass'. But, of course, seduction doesn't involve incorrect harassment through-out. When you make a pass, you expose yourself to the Other (the potential partner), and her reaction will determine whether what you just did was harassment or a successful act of seduction. There is no way to tell in advance what her response will be (which is why assertive women often despise 'weak' men, who fear to take the necessary risk). This holds even more in our pc times: the pc prohibitions are rules which, in one way or another, are to be violated in the seduction process. Isn't the seducer's art to accomplish the violation in such a way that, afterwards, by its acceptance, any suggestion of harassment has disappeared?

Although psychoanalysis is one of the victims of reflexivisation, it can also help us to understand its implications. It does not lament the disintegration of the old stability or locate in its disappearance the cause of modern neuroses, compelling us to rediscover our roots in traditional wisdom or a deeper self-knowledge. Nor is it just another version of modern reflexive knowledge which teaches us how to master the secrets of our psychic life. What psychoanalysis properly concerns itself with are the unexpected consequences of the disinte-gration of the structures that have traditionally regulated libidinal life. Why does the decline of paternal authority and fixed social and gender roles generate new guilts and anxieties, instead of opening up a brave new world in which we can enjoy shifting and reshaping our multiple identities?

The Post-Modern constellation in which the subject is bent on experimenting with his life encourages the formation of new 'passionate attachments' (to use

Judith Butler's term), but what if the disintegration of patriarchal symbolic authority is counterbalanced by an even stronger 'passionate attachment' to subjection? This would seem to explain the increasing prevalence of a strict and severely enacted master/slave relationship among lesbian couples. The one who gives the orders is the 'top', the one who obeys is the 'bottom' and, in order for the 'top' to be attained, an arduous apprenticeship has to be completed. This 'top/bottom' duality is neither a sign of direct 'identification with the (male) aggressor' nor a parodic imitation of the patriarchal relations of domination. Rather, it expresses the genuine paradox of a freely chosen master/slave form of coexistence which provides deep libidinal satisfaction.

Everything is turned back to front. Public order is no longer maintained by hierarchy, repression and strict regulation, and therefore is no longer subverted by liberating acts of transgression (as when we laugh at a teacher behind his back). Instead, we have social relations among free and equal individuals, supplemented by 'passionate attachment' to an extreme form of submission, which functions as the 'dirty secret', the transgressive source of libidinal satisfaction. In a permissive society, the rigidly codified, authoritarian master/slave relationship becomes transgressive. This paradox or reversal is the proper topic of psychoanalysis: psychoanalysis does not deal with the authoritarian father who prohibits enjoyment, but with the obscene father who enjoins it and thus renders you impotent or frigid. The unconscious is not secret resistance to the law, but the law itself.

The psychoanalytic response to the 'risk-society' theory of the reflexivisation of our lives is not to insist on a pre-reflexive substance, the unconscious, but to suggest that the theory neglects another mode of reflexivity. For psychoanalysis, the perversion of the human libidinal economy is what follows from the prohibition of some pleasurable activity: not a life led in strict obedience to the law and deprived of all pleasure but a life in which exercising the law provides a pleasure of its own, a life in which performance of the ritual destined to keep illicit temptation at bay becomes the source of libidinal satisfaction. The military life, for example, may be governed as much by an unwritten set of obscene rules and rituals (homoerotically charged beatings and humiliations of younger comrades) as by official regulations. This sexualised violence does not undermine order in the barracks: it functions as its direct libidinal support. Regulatory power mechanisms and procedures become 'reflexively' eroticised: although repression first emerges as an attempt to regulate any desire considered 'illicit' by the predominant socio-symbolic order, it can only survive in the psychic economy if the desire for regulation is there – if the very activity of regulation becomes libidinally invested and turns into a source of libidinal satisfaction.

This reflexivity undermines the notion of the Post-Modern subject free to choose and reshape his identity. The psychoanalytic concept that designates the short-circuit between the repression and what it represses is the superego. As Lacan emphasised again and again, the essential content of the superego's injunction is 'Enjoy!' A father works hard to organise a Sunday excursion, which has to be postponed again and again. When it finally takes place, he is fed up with the whole idea and shouts at his children: 'Now you'd better enjoy it!' The superego works in a different way from the symbolic law. The parental figure who is simply 'repressive' in the mode of symbolic authority tells a child: 'You must go to grandma's birthday party and behave nicely, even if you are bored to death – I don't care whether you want to, just do it!' The superego figure, in contrast, says to the child: 'Although you know how much grandma would like to see you, you should go to her party only if you really want to – if you don't, you should stay at home.' The trick performed by the superego is to seem to offer the child a free choice, when, as every child knows, he is not being given any choice at all. Worse than that, he is being given an order and told to smile at the same time. Not only: 'You must visit your grandma, whatever you feel,' but: 'You must visit your grandma, and you must be glad to do it!' The superego orders you to enjoy doing what you have to do. What happens, after all, if the child takes it that he has a genuinely free choice and says 'no'? The parent will make him feel terrible. 'How can you say that!' his mother will say: 'How can you be so cruel! What did your poor grandma do to make you not want to see her?'

'You can do your duty, because you must do it' is how Kant formulated the categorical imperative. The usual negative corollary of this formula serves as the foundation of moral constraint: 'You cannot, because you should not.' The argument of those who oppose human cloning, for example, is that it cannot be allowed because it would involve the reduction of a human being to an entity whose psychic properties can be manipulated. Which is another variation on Wittgenstein's 'Whereof one cannot speak thereof one must be silent.' In other words, we should say that we can't do it, because otherwise we may do it, with catastrophic ethical consequences. If the Christian opponents of cloning believe in the immortality of the soul and the uniqueness of the personality – i.e. that I am not just the result of the interaction between my genetic code and my environment – why oppose cloning? Is it possible that they do in fact believe in the ability of genetics to reach the very core of our personality? Why do some Christians oppose cloning with talk of the 'unfathomable mystery of the conception' as if by cloning my body I am at the same time cloning my immortal soul?

The superego inverts the Kantian 'You can, because you must' in a different way, turning it into 'You must, because you can.' This is the meaning of Viagra, which promises to restore the capacity of male erection in a purely biochemical way, bypassing all psychological problems. Now that Viagra can take care of the erection, there is no excuse: you should have sex whenever you can; and if you don't you should feel guilty. New Ageism, on the other hand, offers a way out of the superego predicament by claiming to recover the spontaneity of our 'true' selves. But New Age wisdom, too, relies on the superego imperative: 'It is your duty to achieve full self-realisation and self-fulfilment, because you can.' Isn't this why we often feel that we are being terrorised by the New Age language of liberation?

Although submission within a lesbian sado-masochistic relationship and the submission of an individual to a fundamental religious or ethnic belief are both generated by modern reflexivisation, their libidinal economies are quite different. The lesbian master/slave relationship is a theatrical enactment, based on accepted rules and a contract that has been freely entered into. As such, it has a tremendous liberating potential. In contrast, a fundamentalist devotion to an ethnic or religious cause denies the possibility of any form of consent. It is not that sado-masochists are only playfully submissive, while in the 'totalitarian' political community, submission is real. If anything, the opposite is the case: in the sadomasochistic contract, the performance is definitely for real and taken absolutely seriously, while the totalitarian submission, with its mask of fanatical devotion, is ultimately fake, a pretence of its opposite. What reveals it as fake is the link between the figure of the totalitarian Master and the superego's injunction: 'Enjoy!'

A good illustration of the way the 'totalitarian' master operates is provided by the logo on the wrapper around German fat-free salami. 'Du darfst!' it says – 'You may!' The new fundamentalisms are not a reaction against the anxiety of excessive freedom that accompanies liberal late capitalism; they do not provide strong prohibitions in a society awash with permissiveness. The cliché' about 'escaping from freedom' into a totalitarian haven is profoundly misleading. Nor is an explanation found in the standard Freudo-Marxian thesis according to which the libidinal foundation of totalitarian (fascist) regimes is the 'authoritarian personality' – i.e. someone who finds satisfaction in compulsive obedience. Although, on the surface, the totalitarian master also issues stern orders compelling us to renounce pleasure and to sacrifice ourselves in some higher cause, his effective injunction, discernible between the lines, is a call to unconstrained transgression. Far from imposing on us a firm set of standards to be complied with, the totalitarian master suspends (moral) punishment. His secret injunction is: 'You may.' He tells us that the prohibitions which regulate social life and guarantee a minimum of decency are worthless, just a device to keep the common people at bay – we, on the other hand, are free to let ourselves go, to kill, rape, plunder, but only in so far as we follow the master. (The Frankfurt School discerned this key feature of totalitarianism in its theory of repressive desublimation.) Obedience to the master allows you to transgress everyday moral rules: all the dirty things you were dreaming of, everything you had to renounce when you subordinated yourself to the traditional, patriarchal, symbolic Law you are now allowed to indulge in without punishment, just as you may eat fat-free salami without any risk to your health.

The same underlying suspension of moral prohibitions is characteristic of Post-Modern nationalism. The cliché according to which in a confused, secular, global society, passionate ethnic identification restores a firm set of values should be turned upside down: nationalist fundamentalism works as a barely concealed 'you may'. Our Post-Modern reflexive society which seems hedonistic and permissive is actually saturated with rules and regulations which are intended to serve our well-being (restrictions on smoking and eating, rules against sexual harassment). A passionate ethnic identification, far from further restraining us, is a liberating call of 'you may': you may violate (not the Decalogue, but) the stiff regulations of peaceful coexistence in a liberal tolerant society; you may drink and eat whatever you want, say things prohibited by political correctness, even hate, fight, kill and rape. It is by offering this kind of pseudo-liberation that the superego supplements the explicit texture of the social symbolic law.

The superficial opposition between pleasure and duty is overcome in two different ways. Totalitarian power goes even further than traditional author-itarian power. What it says, in effect, is not, 'Do your duty, I don't care whether you like it or not,' but: 'You must do your duty, and you must enjoy doing it.' (This is how totalitarian democracy works: it is not enough for the people to follow their leader, they must love him.) Duty becomes pleasure. Second, there is the obverse paradox of pleasure becoming duty in a 'permissive' society. Subjects experience the need to 'have a good time', to enjoy themselves, as a kind of duty, and, consequently, feel guilty for failing to be happy. The superego controls the zone in which these two opposites overlap – in which the command to enjoy doing your duty coincides with the duty to enjoy yourself.

PART II
THE POSTMODERN TURN

THE POSTMODERN TURN:
INTRODUCTION

This section features some of the key essays produced in the formative period and location of the debate about postmodernism in literature, the 1960s and early 1970s in America.

The selections reflect a general awareness that *something* new was happening in fiction (or that some critics were investing a great deal in claiming that there was, which is the same thing) brought on by the flowering of anti-realist, experimental writing in America, France and, to a lesser extent, Britain in the 1950s and 1960s. Not everyone called this postmodernism, however, and the uncertainty about categories and labels which has beset the postmodern debate is suggested clearly here by the wide number of different novelists cited as embodying the new aesthetic, none of whom would be likely to figure in a retrospective survey of postmodernism in criticism produced today: Irving Howe co-opts J. D. Salinger, Saul Bellow and Bernard Malamud into his cause; Leslie Fiedler cites Boris Vian, Norman Mailer and Philip Roth; William Spanos points to Alain Robbe-Grillet and Nathalie Sarraute. But though the essays can seem a little dated in this sense (the authoritative tone of Howe's and Fiedler's in particular recalling a time when cultural criticism was better able to set the tone of public debate than it is now, in a more advanced 'information age') it is true that almost all of the major issues to be explored in the postmodern debate over the next few decades are considered in these writings: the extent to which the new social order prompts changes in the novel, the merging of 'high' and 'low' forms of culture, the postmodern emphasis on form rather than content, literary self-consciousness, the death of originality, the problem of interpretation, the complex relation between modernism and postmodernism. As Umberto Eco remarks, 'On the subject of the postmodern nearly everything has been said, from the very beginning' (Eco, 1985: 70–1).

The essay Eco cites to support this claim is John Barth's 'The Literature of Exhaustion', which begins this section. Its main focus is the work of the Argentinian short story writer and essayist Jorge Luis Borges (whose work appeared in the 1950s and early 1960s) who Barth presents as a kind of founding father for the new writing because of his exploration of the notion of 'the ultimate'. Much contemporary fiction follows Barth in demonstrating 'how an artist may paradoxically turn the felt ultimacies of our time into material and means for his work – *paradoxically* because by doing so he transcends what had appeared to be his refutation' (Barth, 1967: 79). In other words, though the various forms of fiction have all been 'used up' by writers, they are able to continue writing by focusing on the very question of exhaustion. Thirteen years later Barth published a sequel to 'The Literature of Exhaustion', called 'The Literature of Replenishment', which takes his earlier essay to task for its imprecision: it was, he says, really about 'the effective "exhaustion" not of language or of literature but of the aesthetic of high modernism' (Barth, 1980). (An extensive quotation from this essay appears in Eco's 'Postmodernism, Irony, the Enjoyable', in Part I.) Nevertheless his first essay is valuable as it attempts to explain the increased self-consciousness of contemporary fiction, and in doing so prefigures some of the important later work on the death of originality by Barthes, Baudrillard, Jameson and Eco.

Following Barth's essay is Irving Howe's 'Mass Society and Postmodern Fiction' (1959), one of the first attempts to define a category called 'postmodern fiction'. Though it seems a little dated now in some of its observations and in the authors it labels as postmodern, its value is not just as a museum piece. In linking together a new social formation – mass society – and new anti-representational currents in the novel, Howe might be regarded as initiating one of the characteristic moves of the entire debate about postmodernism in art and culture.

Also keen to explain how art has changed as a result of the changes in our society is Susan Sontag in her essay 'One Culture and the New Sensibility'. Rather than lapse into the kind of hysterical proclamations about the end of art or the death of the novel current at the time, Sontag offers a coolly rational argument that the social and technological advances simply mean that the function of art has changed. It is at once a less sweeping and more radical conclusion. As a result of the growth of science and technology, changes like 'extreme social and physical mobility', 'crowdedness', physical speed and speed of images, and the mass reproduction of art objects have transformed art into 'an instrument for modifying consciousness and organizing new modes of sensibility' rather than what it used to be, 'a technique for depicting and commenting on secular reality' (Sontag, 1965: 296). More specifically, this means that there is a new emphasis on form rather than content in the arts, something which must be acknowledged by criticism. What is important is not what a novel, say, can tell us *about* something, it is what the work itself *does* to us, how it makes us feel – though a consequence of the changed function of art is that the novel will no longer be the privileged artistic form.

Central to Sontag's work in this period is the conviction that interpretation – the practice of penetrating through the 'surface' of a text until we discover its 'deep' meaning, a practice at the heart of the classical style of literary criticism – is unsuited to dealing with the kind of art she outlines. The new art must be approached through form rather than content, 'erotically' instead of 'herme-neutically' (to borrow her terms in 'Against Interpretation' (Sontag, 1964: 14)). A similar argument is run in William Spanos's 1972 essay 'The Detective and the Boundary: Some Notes on the Postmodern Literary Imagination'. Spanos would be important in any account of the critical culture of this period in America even if he hadn't written anything, as he was the editor of *boundary 2*, one of the academic journals of the time (along with others, like *TriQuarterly*) which gave extensive space to the postmodernism debate. Yet his essay is a very influential one in itself, as it remains one of the most successful attempts to map shifts in twentieth-century philosophy onto those in fiction.

Spanos begins by linking the postmodern worldview to that of absurdism and existentialism (literary-philosophical movements which immediately preceded postmodernism historically, and held that the most significant fact about existence was that it was meaningless, without God or reason). Strangely perhaps, given the similarities between postmodernism and existentialism, this is not a move made very often by postmodern theorists (though another inter-esting example would be the work of Robert Scholes (Scholes, 1979)), but Spanos makes it the foundation for a persuasive demonstration of how post-modern literature makes the same point as anti-rationalist philosophy, more powerfully, if anything, because it does so *formally*, so that the reader 'feels' the point before he or she understands it cognitively. Simply put, Spanos equates the satisfactory closure of the conventional detective novel with the Enlightenment faith in teleology (progress leading to a decisive, enlightening ending) with the new postmodern 'anti-detective' novel. Where the detective successfully recon-structs the complete narrative of the crime in the classic (modernist) detective novel, the postmodern version results in no such satisfactory outcome and problematises the whole idea of closure as a result.

Leslie Fiedler's essay 'Cross the Border – Close that Gap' (1967) turns to another aspect of the postmodern novel, the way it contributes to one of the dominant symptoms of cultural change in the 1960s, a 'closing of the gap between elite and mass culture' (Fiedler, 1975: 351). The 'New Novel', as he calls it, rejects the elitism and seriousness of modernism by turning to popular genres, especially the western, science fiction and pornography.[1] Fiedler's insights anticipate the emphasis on double-coding in later formulations of the postmodern (like Jencks's and Hutcheon's) in that his 'new novel' moves forward by incorporating previously established genres, and 'crosses the border' between 'serious' literary forms and popular culture.

His essay, incidentally, is one of surprisingly few accounts of the postmodern novel to deal with the question of popular fiction – a fact that implies that postmodern literary criticism did not become as populist and ironic as Fiedler hoped it would in 'Cross the Border'. Having said this, Fiedler's own conventionally written essay shies away from becoming the new form of criticism he feels that postmodern literature begs. (The most radical thing about the *form* of his essay is perhaps that it first appeared in *Playboy Magazine*, an unusual source for a key essay on postmodernism that eclipses the claim of Lyotard's government report, *The Postmodern Condition*.) That 'Cross the Border' raises the question of a more appropriate form of criticism, though, reflects an anxiety felt by critics at the time: if postmodern fiction was to be championed as a radical new form capable of ushering in political change, surely it was unreasonable to celebrate this fiction in an old-fashioned dogmatic critical form? The one critic who attempted successfully to grasp this nettle was Ihab Hassan, one of the most important figures in the postmodernism debate in the 1970s and 1980s (though his work is less commonly referenced now). His form of 'paracriticism' attempts, through a visually arresting pattern of experimental typography, listings, allusions, etc. to blend the objective and the subjective, the analytical and the intuitive and the conceptual and empirical, and thereby mirror the kind of fiction he was writing about (see Hassan, 1975). The essay included here, 1973's 'POSTmodernISM' (the title of which emphasises the problematic prefix and suffix of the term) attempts to put together a definition of postmodernism 'paracritically' rather than through conventional academic argument.

Most of the essays in this part regard postmodernism as marking a break with the aesthetics and ethics of modernism, especially in so far as modernism equates to a particular kind of elitism and seriousness in art. Hassan's is more ambivalent on this matter, portraying postmodernism as a radical break on the one hand, and as something which emerged out of modernism on the other. But the final essay here, Gerald Graff's 'The Myth of the Postmodern Breakthrough', originally published in 1973, mounts a sustained critique against this view of modernism. It challenges what it sees as the assumption contained in work by the likes of Fiedler and Sontag that 'a logical evolution [...] connects the romantic and post-romantic cult of the creative self to the cult of the disintegrated, disseminated, dispersed self and of the decentred, undecidable, indeterminate text' (Graff, 1979: 51). Graff takes an extensive and quite rigorous excursion into literary history (most of which I have had to leave out for reasons of space) to make this point. His overall conclusion, though, is not unlike the point Andreas Huyssen would later make in 'Mapping the Postmodern' (though Graff positions his argument more firmly in a literary-historical context): what is apparently radical in the postmodern was already part of the modernist tradition, though there it was attached to an accompanying idea – worth preserving, according to Graff – that art was serious and meaningful.

NOTE

1. Fiedler's term for this – the 'New Novel' – is misleading, as it translates into French as *nouveau roman*, the name of a contemporaneous but different kind of novel to the one Fiedler is championing. While Robbe-Grillet is included in some classifications of the postmodern, Fiedler makes the point that the *nouveau roman* is too 'serious' and 'neo-neo-classical' to be called postmodern. I agree with this point – if ever there was an artist who required the label 'late modernist' Robbe-Grillet is the one – and this is why, as fascinating as I find Robbe-Grillet's pronouncements on the novel, his work is not included in this reader.

WORKS CITED

Barth, John (1980) 'The Literature of Replenishment', *Atlantic Monthly*, 245, 1: 65–71.

Barth, John (1990) 'The Literature of Exhaustion' [1967], in Malcom Bradbury (ed.), *The Novel Today*, 2nd edn. London: Fontana.

Eco, Umberto (1985) *Reflections on* The Name of the Rose. London: Weidenfeld & Nicholson.

Fiedler, Leslie (1975) 'Cross the Border – Close that Gap', Marcus Cunliffe (ed.), *American Literature Since 1900*. London: Sphere.

Graff, Gerald (1979) 'The Myth of the Postmodern Breakthrough' [1973], in *Literature Against Itself: Literary Ideas in Modern Society*. Chicago and London: University of Chicago Press.

Hassan, Ihab (1975) *Paracriticisms: Seven Speculations of the Times*. Urbana, IL: University of Illinois Press.

Scholes, Robert (1979) *Fabulation and Metafiction*. Urbana, IL, Chicago and London: University of Illinois Press.

Sontag, Susan (1994) 'Against Interpretation' [1965], in *Against Interpretation*. London: Vintage, pp. 3–14.

Sontag, Susan (1994) 'One Culture and the New Sensibility' [1965], in *Against Interpretation*. London: Vintage, pp. 293–304.

9

'THE LITERATURE OF EXHAUSTION'

John Barth

> The fact is that every writer *creates* his own precursors. His work modifies our conception of the past, as it will modify the future.
>
> <div align="right">JORGE LUIS BORGES, <i>Labyrinths</i></div>

> You who   listen   give me life   in a
> manner   of speaking.   I won't hold you
> responsible.   My first words weren't my first words. I wish
> I'd begun differently.
>
> <div align="right">JOHN BARTH, <i>Lost in the Fun House</i></div>

I want to discuss three things more or less together: first, some old questions raised by the new intermedia arts; second, some aspects of the Argentine writer Jorge Luis Borges, whom I greatly admire; third, some professional concerns of my own, related to these other matters and having to do with what I'm calling 'the literature of exhausted possibility' – or, more chicly, 'the literature of exhaustion'.

By 'exhaustion' I don't mean anything so tired as the subject of physical, moral, or intellectual decadence, only the used-upness of certain forms or exhaustion of certain possibilities – by no means necessarily a cause for despair. That a great many Western artists for a great many years have quarrelled with received definitions of artistic media, genres, and forms goes without saying: pop art, dramatic and musical 'happenings', the whole range of 'intermedia' or

From John Barth (1967) 'The Literature of Exhaustion', *The Atlantic*, 220 (2): 29–34.

'mixed-means' art, bear recentest witness to the tradition of rebelling against Tradition. A catalogue I received some time ago in the mail, for example, advertises such items as Robert Filliou's *Ample Food for Stupid Thought*, a box full of postcards on which are inscribed 'apparently meaningless questions', to be mailed to whomever the purchaser judges them suited for; Ray Johnson's *Paper Snake*, a collection of whimsical writings, 'often pointed', once mailed to various friends (what the catalogue describes as The New York Correspondence School of Literature); and Daniel Spoerri's *Anecdoted Typography of Chance*, 'on the surface' a description of all the objects that happen to be on the author's parlour table – 'in fact, however … a cosmology of Spoerri's existence'.

'On the surface', at least, the document listing these items is a catalogue of The Something Else Press, a swinging outfit. 'In fact, however', it may be one of their offerings, for all I know: The New York Direct-Mail Advertising School of Literature. In any case, their wares are lively to read about, and make for interesting conversation in fiction-writing classes, for example, where we discuss Somebody-or-other's unbound, unpaginated, randomly assembled novel-in-a-box and the desirability of printing *Finnegans Wake* on a very long roller-towel. It's easier and sociabler to talk technique than it is to make art, and the area of 'happenings' and their kin is mainly a way of discussing aesthetics, really; illustrating 'dramatically' more or less valid and interesting points about the nature of art and the definition of its terms and genres.

One conspicuous thing, for example, about the 'intermedia' arts is their tendency (noted even by *Life* magazine) to eliminate not only the traditional audience – 'those who apprehend the artists' art' (in 'happenings' the audience is often the 'cast', as in 'environments', and some of the new music isn't intended to be performed at all) – but also the most traditional notion of the artist: the Aristotelian conscious agent who achieves with technique and cunning the artistic effect; in other words, one endowed with uncommon talent, who has moreover developed and disciplined that endowment into virtuosity. It's an aristocratic notion on the face of it, which the democratic West seems eager to have done with; not only the 'omniscient' author of older fiction, but the very idea of the controlling artist, has been condemned as politically reactionary, even fascist.

Now, personally, being of the temper that chooses to 'rebel along traditional lines', I'm inclined to prefer the kind of art that not many people can *do*: the kind that requires expertise and artistry as well as bright aesthetic ideas and/or inspiration. I enjoy the pop art in the famous Albright-Knox collection, a few blocks from my house in Buffalo, like a lively conversation for the most part, but was on the whole more impressed by the jugglers and acrobats at Baltimore's old Hippodrome, where I used to go every time they changed shows: genuine *virtuosi* doing things that anyone can dream up and discuss but almost no one can do.

I suppose the distinction is between things worth remarking – preferably over beer, if one's of my generation – and things worth doing. 'Somebody ought to make a novel with scenes that pop up, like the old children's books,' one says, with the implication that one isn't going to bother doing it oneself.

However, art and its forms and techniques live in history and certainly do change. I sympathize with a remark attributed to Saul Bellow, that to be technically up to date is the least important attribute of a writer, though I would have to add that this least important attribute may be nevertheless essential. In any case, to be technically *out* of date is likely to be a genuine defect: Beethoven's Sixth Symphony or the Chartres Cathedral if executed today would be merely embarrassing. A good many current novelists write turn-of-the-century-type novels, only in more or less mid-twentieth-century language and about contemporary people and topics; this makes them considerably less interesting (to me) than excellent writers who are also technically contemporary: Joyce and Kafka, for instance, in their time, and in ours, Samuel Beckett and Jorge Luis Borges. The intermedia arts, I'd say, tend to be intermediary too, between the traditional realms of aesthetics on the one hand and artistic creation on the other; I think the wise artist and civilian will regard them with quite the kind and degree of seriousness with which he regards good shoptalk: he'll listen carefully, if non-committally, and keep an eye on his intermedia colleagues, if only the corner of his eye. They may very possibly suggest something usable in the making or understanding of genuine works of contemporary art.

The man I want to discuss a little here, Jorge Luis Borges, illustrates well the difference between a technically old-fashioned artist, a technically up-to-date civilian, and a technically up-to-date artist. In the first category I'd locate all those novelists who for better or worse write not as if the twentieth century didn't exist, but as if the great writers of the last sixty years or so hadn't existed (*nota bene* that our century's more than two-thirds done; it's dismaying to see so many of our writers following Dostoevsky or Tolstoy or Flaubert or Balzac, when the real technical question seems to me to be how to succeed not even Joyce and Kafka, but those who've *succeeded* Joyce and Kafka and are now in the evenings of their own careers). In the second category are such folk as an artist-neighbour of mine in Buffalo who fashions dead Winnie-the-Poohs in sometimes monumental scale out of oilcloth stuffed with sand and impaled on stakes or hung by the neck. In the third belong the few people whose artistic thinking is as hip as any French new-novelist's, but who manage nonetheless to speak eloquently and memorably to our still-human hearts and conditions, as the great artists have always done. Of these, two of the finest living specimens that I know of are Beckett and Borges, just about the only contemporaries of my reading acquaintance mentionable with the 'old masters' of twentieth-century fiction. In the unexciting history of literary awards, the 1961 International Publishers' Prize, shared by Beckett and Borges, is a happy exception indeed.

One of the modern things about these two is that in an age of ultimacies and 'final solutions' – at least *felt* ultimacies, in everything from weaponry to theology, the celebrated dehumanization of society, and the history of the novel – their work in separate ways reflects and deals with ultimacy, both technically and thematically, as, for example, *Finnegans Wake* does in its different manner. One notices, by the way, for whatever its symptomatic worth, that Joyce was virtually blind at the end, Borges is literally so, and Beckett has become virtually mute, musewise, having progressed from marvellously constructed English sentences through terser and terser French ones to the unsyntactical, unpunctuated prose of *Comment C'est* and 'ultimately' to wordless mimes. One might extrapolate a theoretical course for Beckett: language, after all, consists of silence as well as sound, and the mime is still communication – 'that nineteenth-century idea', a Yale student once snarled at me – but by the language of action. But the language of action consists of rest as well as movement, and so in the context of Beckett's progress, immobile, silent figures still aren't altogether ultimate. How about an empty, silent stage, then, or blank pages (an ultimacy already attained in the nineteenth century by that *avant-gardiste* of East Aurora, New York, Elbert Hubbard, in his *Essay on Silence*) – a 'happening' where nothing happens, like Cage's 4' 33" performed in an empty hall? But dramatic communication consists of the absence as well as the presence of the actors; 'we have our exists and our entrances'; and so even that would be imperfectly ultimate in Beckett's case. Nothing at all, then, I suppose: but Nothingness is necessarily and inextricably the background against which Being et cetera; for Beckett, at this point in his career, to cease to create altogether would be fairly meaningful: his crowning work, his 'last word'. What a convenient corner to paint yourself into! 'And now I shall finish,' the valet Arsene says in *Watt*, 'and you will hear my voice no more.' Only the silence *Molloy* speaks of, 'of which the universe is made'.

After which, I add on behalf of the rest of us, it might be conceivable to rediscover validly the artifices of language and literature – such far-out notions as grammar, punctuation ... even characterization! Even *plot*! – if one goes about it the right way, aware of what one's predecessors have been up to.

Now J. L. Borges is perfectly aware of all these things. Back in the great decades of literary experimentalism he was associated with *Prisma*, a 'muralist' magazine that published its pages on walls and billboards; his later *Labyrinths* and *Ficciones* not only anticipate the farthest-out ideas of The Something Else Press crowd – not a difficult thing to do – but being marvellous works of art as well, illustrate in a simple way the difference between the *fact* of aesthetic ultimacies and their artistic *use*. What it comes to is that an artist doesn't merely exemplify an ultimacy; he employs it.

Consider Borges's story 'Pierre Menard, Author of the Quixote': the hero, an utterly sophisticated turn-of-the-century French Symbolist, by an astounding effort of imagination, produces – not *copies* or *imitates*, mind, but *composes* – several chapters of Cervantes's novel.

It is a revelation [Borges's narrator tells us] to compare Menard's *Don Quixote* with Cervantes's. The latter, for example, wrote (part one, chapter nine):

> ...truth, whose mother is history, rival of time, depository of deeds, witness of the past, exemplar and adviser to the present, the future's counsellor.

Written in the seventeenth century, written by the 'lay genius' Cervantes, this enumeration is a mere rhetorical praise of history. Menard, on the other hand, writes:

> ...truth, whose mother is history, rival of time, depository of deeds, witness of the past, exemplar and adviser to the present, the future's counsellor.

History, the *mother* of truth: the idea is astounding. Menard, a contemporary of William James, does not define history as an enquiry into reality but as its origin...

Et cetera. Now, this is an interesting idea, of considerable intellectual validity. I mentioned earlier that if Beethoven's Sixth were composed today, it would be an embarrassment; but clearly it wouldn't be, necessarily, if done with ironic intent by a composer quite aware of where we've been and where we are. It would have then potentially, for better or worse, the kind of significance of Warhol's Campbell's Soup ads, the difference being that in the former case a work of art is being reproduced instead of a work of non-art, and the ironic comment would therefore be more directly on the genre and history of the art than on the state of the culture. In fact, of course, to make the valid intellectual point one needn't even re-compose the Sixth Symphony any more than Menard really needed to recreate the *Quixote*. It would've been sufficient for Menard to have *attributed* the novel to himself in order to have a new work of art, from the intellectual point of view. Indeed, in several stories Borges plays with this very idea, and I can readily imagine Beckett's next novel, for example, as *Tom Jones*, just as Nabokov's last was that multivolume annotated translation of Pushkin. I myself have always aspired to write Burton's version of *The 1001 Nights*, complete with appendices and the like, in twelve volumes, and for intellectual purposes I needn't even write it. What evenings we might spend (over beer) discussing Saarinen's Parthenon, D. H. Lawrence's *Wuthering Heights*, or the Johnson Administration by Robert Rauschenberg!

The idea, I say, is intellectually serious, as are Borges's other characteristic ideas, most of a metaphysical rather than an aesthetic nature. But the important thing to observe is that Borges doesn't attribute the *Quixote* to himself, much less re-compose it like Pierre Menard; instead, he writes a remarkable and original work of literature, the implicit theme of which is the difficulty, perhaps the unnecessity, of writing original works of literature. His artistic victory, if you like, is that he confronts an intellectual dead end and employs it against itself to accomplish new human work. If this corresponds to what mystics do – 'every moment leaping into the infinite', Kierkegaard says, 'and every moment falling surely back into the finite' – it's only one more aspect of that old analogy. In homelier terms, it's a matter of every moment throwing out the bath water without for a moment losing the baby.

Another way of describing Borges's accomplishment is in a pair of his own favourite terms, *algebra* and *fire*. In his most often anthologized story, 'Tlön, Uqbar, Orbis Tertius', he imagines an entirely hypothetical world, the invention of a secret society of scholars who elaborate its every aspect in a surreptitious encyclopaedia. This *First Encyclopaedia of Tlön* (what fictionist would not wish to have dreamed up the *Britannica*?) describes a coherent alternative to this world complete in every aspect from its algebra to its fire, Borges tells us, and of such imaginative power that, once conceived, it begins to obtrude itself into and eventually to supplant our prior reality. My point is that neither the algebra nor the fire, metaphorically speaking, could achieve this result without the other. Borges's algebra is what I'm considering here – algebra is easier to talk about than fire – but any intellectual giant could equal it. The imaginary authors of the *First Encyclopaedia of Tlön* itself are not artists, though their work is in a manner of speaking fictional and would find a ready publisher in New York nowadays. The author of the story 'Tlön, Uqbar, Orbis Tertius', who merely *alludes* to the fascinating *Encyclopaedia*, is an artist; what makes him one of the first rank, like Kafka, is the combination of that intellectually profound vision with great human insight, poetic power, and consummate mastery of his means, a definition which would have gone without saying, I suppose, in any century but ours.

Not long ago, incidentally, in a footnote to a scholarly edition of Sir Thomas Browne (*The Urn Burial*, I believe it was), I came upon a perfect Borges datum, reminiscent of Tlön's self-realization: the actual case of a book called *The Three Impostors*, alluded to in Browne's *Religio Medici* among other places. *The Three Impostors* is a non-existent blasphemous treatise against Moses, Christ, and Mohammed, which in the seventeenth century was widely held to exist, or to have once existed. Commentators attributed it variously to Boccaccio, Pietro Aretino, Giordano Bruno, and Tommaso Campanella, and though no one, Browne included, had ever seen a copy of it, it was frequently cited, refuted, railed against, and generally discussed as if everyone had read it – until, sure enough, in the *eighteenth* century a spurious work appeared with a forged date of 1598 and the title *De Tribus Impostoribus*. It's a wonder that Borges doesn't mention this work, as he seems to have read absolutely everything, including all the books that don't exist, and Browne is a particular favourite of his. In fact, the narrator of 'Tlön, Uqbar, Orbis Tertius' declares at the end:

> ...English and French and mere Spanish will disappear from the globe. The world will be Tlön. I pay no attention to all this and go on revising, in

the still days at the Adrogué hotel, an uncertain Quevedian translation (which I do not intend to publish) of Browne's *Urn Burial*.

(Moreover, on rereading 'Tlön', etc., I find now a remark I'd swear wasn't in it last year: that the eccentric American millionaire who endows the *Encyclopaedia* does so on condition that 'the work will make no pact with the impostor Jesus Christ'.)

This 'contamination of reality by dream', as Borges calls it, is one of his pet themes, and commenting upon such contaminations is one of his favourite fictional devices. Like many of the best such devices, it turns the artist's mode or form into a metaphor for his concerns, as does the diary-ending of *Portrait of the Artist as a Young Man* or the cyclical construction of *Finnegans Wake*. In Borges's case, the story 'Tlön', etc., for example, is a real piece of imagined reality in our world, analogous to those Tlönian artifacts called *hronir*, which imagine themselves into existence. In short, it's a paradigm of or metaphor for itself; not just the *form* of the story but the *fact* of the story is symbolic; 'the medium is the message'.

Moreover, like all of Borges's work, it illustrates in other of its aspects my subject: how an artist may paradoxically turn the felt ultimacies of our time into material and means for his work – *paradoxically* because by doing so he transcends what had appeared to be his refutation, in the same way that the mystic who transcends finitude is said to be enabled to live, spiritually and physically, in the finite world. Suppose you're a writer by vocation – a 'print-oriented bastard', as the McLuhanites call us – and you feel, for example, that the novel, if not narrative literature generally, if not the printed word altogether, has by this hour of the world just about shot its bolt, as Leslie Fiedler and others maintain. (I'm inclined to agree, with reservations and hedges. Literary forms certainly have histories and historical contingencies, and it may well be that the novel's time as a major art form is up, as the 'times' of classical tragedy, grand opera, or the sonnet sequence came to be. No necessary cause for alarm in this at all, except perhaps to certain novelists, and one way to handle such a feeling might be to write a novel about it. Whether historically the novel expires or persists seems immaterial to me; if enough writers and critics *feel* apocalyptical about it, their feeling becomes a considerable cultural fact, like the feeling that Western civilization, or the world, is going to end rather soon. If you took a bunch of people out into the desert and the world didn't end, you'd come home shame-faced, I imagine; but the persistence of an art form doesn't invalidate work created in the comparable apocalyptic ambience. That's one of the fringe benefits of being an artist instead of a prophet. There are others.) If you happened to be Vladimir Nabokov you might address that felt ultimacy by writing *Pale Fire*: a fine novel by a learned pedant, in the form of a pedantic commentary on a poem invented for the purpose. If you were Borges you might write *Labyrinths*: fictions by a learned librarian in the form of footnotes, as he describes them, to imaginary or hypothetical books. And I'll add, since I believe Borges's idea is rather more interesting, that if you were the author of this paper, you'd have written something like *The Sot-Weed Factor* or *Giles Goat-Boy*: novels which imitate the form of the Novel, by an author who imitates the role of Author.

If this sort of thing sounds unpleasantly decadent, nevertheless it's about where the genre began, with *Quixote* imitating *Amadis of Gaul*, Cervantes pretending to be the Cid Hamete Benengeli (and Alonso Quijano pretending to be Don Quixote), or Fielding parodying Richardson. 'History repeats itself as farce' – meaning, of course, in the form or mode of farce, not that history is farcical. The imitation (like the Dadaist echoes in the work of the 'intermedia' types) is something new and *may be* quite serious and passionate despite its farcical aspect. This is the important difference between a proper novel and a deliberate imitation of a novel, or a novel imitative of other sorts of documents. The first attempts (has been historically inclined to attempt) to imitate actions more or less directly, and its conventional devices – cause and effect, linear anecdote, characterization, authorial selection, arrangement, and interpretation – can be and have long since been objected to as obsolete notions, or metaphors for obsolete notions: Robbe-Grillet's essays *For a New Novel* come to mind. There are replies to these objections, not to the point here, but one can see that in any case they're obviated by imitations-of-novels, which attempt to represent not life directly but a representation of life. In fact such works are no more removed from 'life' than Richardson's or Goethe's epistolary novels are: both imitate 'real' documents, and the subject of both, ultimately, is life, not the documents. A novel is as much a piece of the real world as a letter, and the letters in *The Sorrows of Young Werther* are, after all, fictitious.

One might imaginably compound this imitation, and though Borges doesn't he's fascinated with the idea: one of his frequenter literary allusions is to the 602nd night of *The 1001 Nights*, when, owing to a copyist's error, Scheherezade begins to tell the King the story of the 1001 nights, from the beginning. Happily, the King interrupts; if he didn't there'd be no 603rd night ever, and while this would solve Scheherezade's problem – which is every story-teller's problem: to publish or perish – it would put the 'outside' author in a bind. (I suspect that Borges dreamed this whole thing up: the business he mentions isn't in any edition of *The 1001 Nights* I've been able to consult. Not *yet*, anyhow: after reading 'Tlön, Uqbar', etc., one is inclined to recheck every semester or so.)

Now Borges (whom someone once vexedly accused *me* of inventing) is interested in the 602nd night because it's an instance of the story-within-the-story turned back upon itself, and his interest in such instances is threefold: first, as he himself declares, they disturb us metaphysically: when the characters in a work of fiction become readers or authors of the fiction they're in, we're reminded of the fictitious aspect of our own existence, one of Borges's cardinal themes, as it was of Shakespeare, Calderón, Unamuno, and other folk. Second, the 602nd night is a literary illustration of the *regressus in infinitum*, as are almost all Borges's principal images and motifs. Third, Scheherezade's accidental gambit, like Borges's other versions of the *regressus in infinitum*, is an image of the exhaustion, or attempted exhaustion, of possibilities – in this case literary possibilities – and so we return to our main subject.

What makes Borges's stance, if you like, more interesting to me than, say, Nabokov's or Beckett's is the premise with which he approaches literature; in the words of one of his editors: 'For [Borges] no one has claim to originality in literature; all writers are more or less faithful amanuenses of the spirit, translators and annotators of pre-existing archetypes.' Thus his inclination to write brief comments on imaginary books: for one to attempt to add overtly to the sum of 'original' literature by even so much as a conventional short story, not to mention a novel, would be too presumptuous, too naïve; literature has been done long since. A librarian's point of view! And it would itself be too presumptuous, if it weren't part of a lively, passionately relevant metaphysical vision and slyly employed against itself precisely, to make new and original literature. Borges defines the Baroque as 'that style which deliberately exhausts (or tries to exhaust) its possibilities and borders upon its own caricature'. While his own work is *not* Baroque, except intellectually (the Baroque was never so terse, laconic, economical), it suggests the view that intellectual and literary history has been Baroque, and has pretty well exhausted the possibilities of novelty. His *ficciones* are not only footnotes to imaginary texts, but postscripts to the real corpus of literature.

This premise gives resonance and relation to all his principal images. The facing mirrors that recur in his stories are a dual *regressus*. The doubles that his characters, like Nabokov's, run afoul of suggest dizzying multiples and remind one of Browne's remark that 'every man is not only himself . . . men are lived over again'. (It would please Borges, and illustrate Browne's point, to call Browne a precursor of Borges. 'Every writer,' Borges says in his essay on Kafka, 'creates his own precursors.' Borges's favourite third-century heretical sect is the Histriones – I think and hope he invented them – who believe that repetition is impossible in history and therefore live viciously in order to purge the future of the vices they commit: in other words, to exhaust the possibilities of the world in order to bring its end nearer.

The writer he most often mentions, after Cervantes, is Shakespeare; in one piece he imagines the playwright on his deathbed asking God to permit him to be one and himself, having been everyone and no one; God replies from the whirlwind that He is no one either; He has dreamed the world like Shakespeare, and including Shakespeare. Homer's story in Book IV of the *Odyssey*, of Menelaus on the beach at Pharos, tackling Proteus, appeals profoundly to Borges: Proteus is he who 'exhausts the guises of reality' while Menelaus – who, one recalls, disguised his own identity in order to ambush him – holds fast. Zeno's paradox of Achilles and the Tortoise embodies a *regressus in infinitum* which Borges carries through philosophical history, pointing out that Aristotle uses it to refute Plato's theory of forms, Hume to refute the possibility of cause and effect, Lewis Carroll to refute syllogistic deduction, William James to refute the notion of temporal passage, and Bradley to refute the general possibility of logical relations; Borges himself uses it, citing Schopenhauer, as evidence that the world is our dream, our idea, in which 'tenuous and eternal crevices of unreason' can be found to remind us that our creation is false, or at least fictive.

The infinite library of one of the most popular stories is an image particularly pertinent to the literature of exhaustion; the 'Library of Babel' houses every possible combination of alphabetical characters and spaces, and thus every possible book and statement, including your and my refutations and vindications, the history of the actual future, the history of every possible future, and, though he doesn't mention it, the encyclopaedias not only of Tlön but of every imaginable other world – since, as in Lucretius's universe, the number of elements, and so of combinations, is finite (though very large), and the number of instances of each element and combination of elements is infinite, like the library itself.

That brings us to his favourite image of all, the labyrinth, and to my point. *Labyrinths* is the name of his most substantial translated volume, and the only full-length study of Borges in English, by Ana Maria Barrenechea, is called *Borges the Labyrinth-Maker*. A labyrinth, after all, is a place in which, ideally, all the possibilities of choice (of direction, in this case) are embodied, and – barring special dispensation like Theseus's – must be exhausted before one reaches the heart. Where, mind, the Minotaur waits with two final possibilities: defeat and death, or victory and freedom. Now, in fact, the legendary Theseus is non-Baroque; thanks to Ariadne's thread he can take a shortcut through the labyrinth at Knossos. But Menelaus on the beach at Pharos, for example, is genuinely Baroque in the Borgesian spirit, and illustrates a positive artistic morality in the literature of exhaustion. He is not there, after all, for kicks (any more than Borges and Beckett are in the fiction racket for their health): Menelaus is *lost*, in the larger labyrinth of the world, and has got to hold fast while the Old Man of the Sea exhausts reality's frightening guises so that he may extort direction from him when Proteus returns to his 'true' self. It's a heroic enterprise, with salvation as its object – one recalls that the aim of the Histriones is to get history done with so that Jesus may come again the sooner, and that Shakespeare's heroic metamorphoses culminate not merely in a theophany but in an apotheosis.

Now, not just any old body is equipped for this labour, and Theseus in the Cretan labyrinth becomes in the end the aptest image of Borges after all. Distressing as the fact is to us liberal Democrats, the commonality, alas, will *always* lose their way and their souls; it's the chosen remnant, the virtuoso, the Thesean *hero*, who, confronted with Baroque reality, Baroque history, the Baroque state of his art, need *not* rehearse its possibilities to exhaustion, any more than Borges needs actually to *write* the *Encyclopaedia of Tlön* or the books in the Library of Babel. He need only be aware of their existence or possibility, acknowledge them, and with the aid of *very special* gifts – as extraordinary as saint- or hero-hood and not likely to be found in The New York Correspondence School of Literature – go straight through the maze to the accomplishment of his work.

10

'MASS SOCIETY AND POSTMODERN FICTION'

Irving Howe

[...]

In the last two decades there has occurred a series of changes in American life, the extent, durability, and significance of which no one has yet measured. No one can. We speak of the growth of a 'mass society,' a term I shall try to define in a moment; but at best this is merely a useful hypothesis, not an accredited description. It is a notion that lacks common consent, for its does not yet merit common consent. Still, one can say with some assurance that the more sensitive among the younger writers, those who feel that at whatever peril to their work and careers they must grapple with something new in contemporary experience, even if, like everyone else, they find it extremely hard to say what that 'newness' consists of – such writers recognize that the once familiar social categories and place marks have now become as uncertain and elusive as the moral imperatives of the nineteenth century seemed to novelists of fifty years ago. And the something new which they notice or stumble against is, I would suggest, the mass society.

By the mass society we mean a relatively comfortable, half-welfare and half-garrison society in which the population grows passive, indifferent, and atomized; in which traditional loyalties, ties, and associations become lax or dissolve entirely; in which coherent publics based on definite interests and opinions gradually fall apart; and in which man becomes a consumer, himself mass-produced like the products, diversions, and values that he absorbs.

From Irving Howe (1959) 'Mass Society and Postmodern Fiction', *Partisan Review*, 26: 420–36.

No social scientist has yet come up with a theory of mass society that is entirely satisfying; no novelist has quite captured its still amorphous symptoms – a peculiar blend of frenzy and sluggishness, amiability, and meanness. I would guess that a novelist unaware of the changes in our experience to which the theory of mass society points, is a novelist unable to deal successfully with recent American life; while one who focused only upon those changes would be unable to give his work an adequate sense of historical depth and social detail.

This bare description of the mass society can be extended by noting a few traits or symptoms:

1) Social classes continue to exist, and the society cannot be understood without reference to them; yet the visible tokens of class are less obvious than in earlier decades and the correlations between class status and personal condition, assumed both by the older sociologists and the older novelists, become elusive and problematic – which is not, however, to say that such correlations no longer exist.

2) Traditional centers of authority, like the family, tend to lose some of their binding-power upon human beings; vast numbers of people now float through life with a burden of freedom they can neither sustain nor legitimately abandon to social or religious groups.

3) Traditional ceremonies that have previously marked moments of crisis and transition in human life, thereby helping men to accept such moments, are now either neglected or debased into mere occasions for public display.

4) Passivity becomes a widespread social attitude: the feeling that life is a drift over which one has little control and that even when men do have shared autonomous opinions they cannot act them out in common.

5) As perhaps never before, opinion is manufactured systematically and 'scientifically.'

6) Opinion tends to flow unilaterally, from the top down, in measured quantities: it becomes a market commodity.

7) Disagreement, controversy, polemic are felt to be in bad taste; issues are 'ironed out' or 'smoothed away'; reflection upon the nature of society is replaced by observation of its mechanics.

8) Direct and first-hand experience seems to evade human beings, though the quantity of busy-ness keeps increasing and the number of events multiplies with bewildering speed.

9) The pressure of material need visibly decreases, yet there follows neither a sense of social release nor a feeling of personal joy; instead, people become increasingly aware of their social dependence and powerlessness.

Now this is a social cartoon and by no means a description of American society; but it is a cartoon that isolates an aspect of our experience with a suggestiveness that no other mode of analysis is likely to match. Nor does it matter that no actual society may ever reach the extreme condition of a 'pure' mass society; the value of the theory lies in bringing to our attention a major historical drift.

If there is any truth at all in these speculations, they should help illuminate the problems faced by the novelists whose work began to appear shortly after World War II. They had to confront not merely the chronic confusion of values which has gripped our civilization for decades. In a sense they were quite prepared for that – the whole of modern literature taught them to expect little else. But they had also to face a problem which, in actually composing a novel, must have been still more troublesome: our society no longer lent itself to assured definition, one could no longer assume as quickly as in the recent past that a spiritual or moral difficulty could find a precise embodiment in a social conflict. [...]

How to give shape to a world increasingly shapeless and an experience increasingly fluid; how to reclaim the central assumption of the novel that telling relationships can be discovered between a style of social behavior and a code of moral judgment, or if that proves impossible, to find ways of imaginatively projecting the code in its own right – these were the difficulties that faced the young novelists. It was as if the guidelines of both our social thought and literary conventions were being erased. Or, as a young German writer has recently remarked:

> There's no longer a society to write about. In former years you knew where you stood: the peasants read the Bible; the maniacs read *Mein Kampf*. Now people no longer have any opinions; they have refrigerators. Instead of illusions we have television, instead of tradition, the Volkswagen. The only way to catch the spirit of the times is to write a handbook on home appliances.

[...]

A whole group of novelists, among the best of recent years, found itself responding to immediate American experience by choosing subjects and locales apparently far removed from that experience yet, through their inner quality, very close to it. These writers were sensitive to the moods and tones of postwar American life; they knew that something new, different, and extremely hard to describe was happening to us. Yet they did not usually write about postwar experience *per se*: they did not confront it as much as they tried to ambush it. The film critic Stanley Kauffmann has noted a similar phenomenon:

> When Vittorio de Sica was asked why so many of his films deal with adultery, he is said to have replied, 'But if you take adultery out of the lives of the *bourgeoisie*, what drama is left?' It is perhaps this belief that has impelled Tennessee Williams into the areas that his art inhabits. He has recognized that most of contemporary life offers limited dramatic opportunities ... so he has left 'normal' life to investigate the highly neurotic, the

violent and the grimy. It is the continuing problem of the contemporary writer who looks for great emotional issues to move him greatly. The anguish of the advertising executive struggling to keep his job is anguish indeed, but its possibilities in art are not large-scale. The writer who wants to 'let go' has figuratively to leave the urban and suburban and either go abroad, go into the past, or go into those few pockets of elemental emotional life left in this country.

Abroad, the past, or the few pockets of elemental emotional life – many of our writers pursued exactly these strategies in order to convey their attitudes toward contemporary experience. In *The Assistant* Bernard Malamud wrote a somber story about a Jewish family during the Depression years, yet it soon becomes clear that one of his impelling motives is a wish to recapture intensities of feeling we have apparently lost but take to be characteristic of an earlier time. Herbert Gold's *The Man Who Was Not With It* is an account of marginal figures in a circus as they teeter on the edge of *lumpen* life; but soon one realizes that he means his story to indicate possibilities for personal survival in a world increasingly compressed. The precocious and bewildered boy in J. D. Salinger's *Catcher in the Rye* expresses something of the moral condition of adolescents during the forties and fifties – or so they tell us; but clearly his troubles are not meant to refer to his generation alone. In *A Walk on the Wild Side* Nelson Algren turns to down-and-outers characteristic of an earlier social moment, but if we look to the psychic pressures breaking through the novel we see that he is really searching for a perspective for estrangement that will continue to be relevant. In *The Field of Vision* Wright Morris moves not backward in time but sideways in space: he contrives to bring a dreary Nebraskan middle-class family to a Mexican bullfight so that the excitement of the blood and ritual will stir it to self-awareness. And while, on the face of it, Saul Bellow's *The Adventures of Augie March* is a picaresque tale about a cocky Jewish boy moving almost magically past the barriers of American society, it is also a kind of paean to the idea of personal freedom in hostile circumstances. Bellow's next novel, *Henderson the Rain King*, seems an even wilder tale about an American millionaire venturing into deepest Africa, in part, the deepest Africa of boys' books; but when he writes that men need a shattering experience to 'wake the spirit's sleep' we soon realize that his ultimate reference is to America, where many spirits sleep.

Though vastly different in quality, these novels of the fifties have in common a certain obliqueness of approach. They do not represent directly the postwar American experience, yet refer to it constantly. They tell us rather little about the surface tone, the manners, the social patterns of recent American life, yet are constantly projecting moral criticisms of its essential quality. They approach that experience on the sly, yet are colored and shaped by it throughout. And they gain from it their true subject: the recurrent search – in America, almost a national obsession – for personal identity and freedom. In their distance from fixed social categories and their concern with the metaphysical implications of that distance, these novels constitute what I would call postmodern fiction.

But the theme of personal identity, if it is to take on fictional substance, needs some kind of placement, a setting in the world of practical affairs. And it is here that the postmodern novelists ran into serious troubles: the connection between subject and setting cannot always be made, and the 'individual' of their novels, because he lacks social definition and is sometimes a creature of literary or ideological flat, tends to be not very individualized. Some of the best postwar novels, like *The Invisible Man* and *The Adventures of Augie March*, are deeply concerned with the fate of freedom in a mass society; but the assertiveness of idea and vanity of style which creep into such books are the result, I think, of willing a subject onto a novel rather than allowing it to grow out of a sure sense of a particular moment and place. These novels merit admiration for defending the uniqueness of man's life, but they suffer from having to improvise the terms of this uniqueness. It is a difficulty that seems to have been unavoidable and I have no wish to disparage writers who faced it courageously. Still, it had better be said that the proclamation of personal identity in postwar American fiction tends, if I may use a fashionable phrase, to be more a product of the will than of the imagination.

11

'ONE CULTURE AND THE NEW SENSIBILITY'

Susan Sontag

In the last few years there has been a good deal of discussion of a purported chasm which opened up some two centuries ago, with the advent of the Industrial Revolution, between 'two cultures,' the literary-artistic and the scientific. According to this diagnosis, any intelligent and articulate modern person is likely to inhabit one culture to the exclusion of the other. He will be concerned with different documents, different techniques, different problems; he will speak a different language. Most important, the type of effort required for the mastery of these two cultures will differ vastly. For the literary-artistic culture is understood as a general culture. It is addressed to man insofar as he is man; it is culture or, rather, it promotes culture, in the sense of culture defined by Ortega y Gasset: that which a man has in his possession when he has forgotten everything that he has read. The scientific culture, in contrast, is a culture for specialists; it is founded on remembering and is set down in ways that require complete dedication of the effort to comprehend. While the literary-artistic culture aims at internalization, ingestion – in other words, cultivation – the scientific culture aims at accumulation and externalization in complex instruments for problem-solving and specific techniques for mastery.

Though T. S. Eliot derived the chasm between the two cultures from a period more remote in modern history, speaking in a famous essay of a 'dissociation of sensibility' which opened up in the 17th century, the connection of the problem with the Industrial Revolution seems well taken. There is a historic antipathy on

From Susan Sontag (1994) 'One Culture and the New Sensibility' [1965], in *Against Interpretation*. London: Vintage.

the part of many literary intellectuals and artists to those changes which characterize modern society – above all, industrialization and those of its effects which everyone has experienced, such as the proliferation of huge impersonal cities and the predominance of the anonymous style of urban life. It has mattered little whether industrialization, the creature of modern 'science,' is seen on the 19th and early 20th century model, as noisy smoky artificial processes which defile nature and standardize culture or on the newer model, the clean automated technology that is coming into being in the second half of the 20th century. The judgment has been mostly the same. Literary men, feeling that the status of humanity itself was being challenged by the new science and the new technology, abhorred and deplored the change. But the literary men, whether one thinks of Emerson and Thoreau and Ruskin in the 19th century, or of 20th century intellectuals who talk of modern society as being in some new way incomprehensible, 'alienated,' are inevitably on the defensive. They know that the scientific culture, the coming of the machine, cannot be stopped.

The standard response to the problem of 'the two cultures' – and the issue long antedates by many decades the crude and philistine statement of the problem by C. P. Snow in a famous lecture some years ago – has been a facile defense of the function of the arts (in terms of an ever vaguer ideology of 'humanism') or a premature surrender of the function of the arts to science. By the second response, I am not referring to the philistinism of scientists (and those of their party among artists and philosophers) who dismiss the arts as imprecise, untrue, at best mere toys. I am speaking of serious doubts which have arisen among those who are passionately engaged in the arts. The role of the individual artist, in the business of making unique objects for the purpose of giving pleasure and educating conscience and sensibility, has repeatedly been called into question. Some literary intellectuals and artists have gone so far as to prophesy the ultimate demise of the art-making activity of man. Art, in an automated scientific society, would be unfunctional, useless.

But this conclusion, I should argue, is plainly unwarranted. Indeed, the whole issue seems to me crudely put. For the question of 'the two cultures' assumes that science and technology are changing, in motion, while the arts are static, fulfilling some perennial generic human function (consolation? edification? diversion?). Only on the basis of this false assumption would anyone reason that the arts might be in danger of becoming obsolete.

Art does not progress, in the sense that science and technology do. But the arts do develop and change. For instance, in our own time, art is becoming increasingly the terrain of specialists. The most interesting and creative art of our time is not open to the generally educated; it demands special effort; it speaks a specialized language. The music of Milton Babbitt and Morton Feldman, the painting of Mark Rothko and Frank Stella, the dance of Merce Cunningham and James Waring demand an education of sensibility whose difficulties and length of apprenticeship are at least comparable to the difficulties of mastering physics or engineering. (Only the novel, among the arts, at least in America, fails to provide similar examples.) The parallel between the abstruseness of contemporary art and that of modern science is too obvious to be missed. Another likeness to the scientific culture is the history-mindedness of contemporary art. The most interesting works of contemporary art are full of references to the history of the medium; so far as they comment on past art, they demand a knowledge of at least the recent past. As Harold Rosenberg has pointed out, contemporary paintings are themselves acts of criticism as much as of creation. The point could be made as well of much recent work in the films, music, the dance, poetry, and (in Europe) literature. Again, a similarity with the style of science – this time, with the accumulative aspect of science – can be discerned.

The conflict between 'the two cultures' is in fact an illusion, a temporary phenomenon born of a period of profound and bewildering historical change. What we are witnessing is not so much a conflict of cultures as the creation of a new (potentially unitary) kind of sensibility. This new sensibility is rooted, as it must be, in our experience, experiences which are new in the history of humanity – in extreme social and physical mobility; in the crowdedness of the human scene (both people and material commodities multiplying at a dizzying rate); in the availability of new sensations such as speed (physical speed, as in airplane travel; speed of images, as in the cinema); and in the pan-cultural perspective on the arts that is possible through the mass reproduction of art objects.

What we are getting is not the demise of art, but a transformation of the function of art. Art, which arose in human society as a magical-religious operation, and passed over into a technique for depicting and commenting on secular reality, has in our own time arrogated to itself a new function – neither religious, nor serving a secularized religious function, nor merely secular or profane (a notion which breaks down when its opposite, the 'religious' or 'sacred,' becomes obsolescent). Art today is a new kind of instrument, an instrument for modifying consciousness and organizing new modes of sensibility. And the means for practicing art have been radically extended. Indeed, in response to this new function (more felt than clearly articulated), artists have had to become self-conscious aestheticians: continually challenging their means, their materials and methods. Often, the conquest and exploitation of new materials and methods drawn from the world of 'non-art' – for example, from industrial technology, from commercial processes and imagery, from purely private and subjective fantasies and dreams – seems to be the principal effort of many artists. Painters no longer feel themselves confined to canvas and paint, but employ hair, photographs, wax, sand, bicycle tires, their own toothbrushes and socks. Musicians have reached beyond the sounds of the traditional instruments to use tampered instruments and (usually on tape) synthetic sounds and industrial noises.

All kinds of conventionally accepted boundaries have thereby been challenged: not just the one between the 'scientific' and the 'literary-artistic' cultures, or the one between 'art' and 'non-art'; but also many established distinctions within the world of culture itself – that between form and content, the frivolous and the serious, and (a favorite of literary intellectuals) 'high' and 'low' culture.

The distinction between 'high' and 'low' (or 'mass' or 'popular') culture is based partly on an evaluation of the difference between unique and mass-produced objects. In an era of mass technological reproduction, the work of the serious artist had a special value simply because it was unique, because it bore his personal, individual signature. The works of popular culture (and even films were for a long time included in this category) were seen as having little value because they were manufactured objects, bearing no individual stamp – group concoctions made for an undifferentiated audience. But in the light of contemporary practice in the arts, this distinction appears extremely shallow. Many of the serious works of art of recent decades have a decidedly impersonal character. The work of art is reasserting its existence as 'object' (even as manufactured or mass-produced object, drawing on the popular arts) rather than as 'individual personal expression.'

The exploration of the impersonal (and trans-personal) in contemporary art is the new classicism; at least, a reaction against what is understood as the romantic spirit dominates most of the interesting art of today. Today's art, with its insistence on coolness, its refusal of what it considers to be sentimentality, its spirit of exactness, its sense of 'research' and 'problems,' is closer to the spirit of science than of art in the old-fashioned sense. Often, the artist's work is only his idea, his concept. This is a familiar practice in architecture, of course. And one remembers that painters in the Renaissance often left parts of their canvases to be worked out by students, and that in the flourishing period of the concerto the cadenza at the end of the first movement was left to the inventiveness and discretion of the performing soloist. But similar practices have a different, more polemical meaning today, in the present post-romantic era of the arts. When painters such as Joseph Albers, Ellsworth Kelly, and Andy Warhol assign portions of the work, say, the painting in of the colors themselves, to a friend or the local gardener; when musicians such as Stockhausen, John Cage, and Luigi Nono invite collaboration from performers by leaving opportunities for random effects, switching around the order of the score, and improvisations – they are changing the ground rules which most of us employ to recognize a work of art. They are saying what art need not be. At least, not necessarily.

The primary feature of the new sensibility is that its model product is not the literary work, above all, the novel. A new non-literary culture exists today, of whose very existence, not to mention significance, most literary intellectuals are entirely unaware. This new establishment includes certain painters, sculptors, architects, social planners, film-makers, TV technicians, neurologists, musicians, electronics engineers, dancers, philosophers, and sociologists. (A few poets and prose writers can be included.) Some of the basic texts for this new cultural alignment are to be found in the writings of Nietzsche, Wittgenstein, Antonin Artaud, C. S. Sherrington, Buckminster Fuller, Marshall McLuhan,

John Cage, André Breton, Roland Barthes, Claude Lévi-Strauss, Siegfried Gidieon, Norman O. Brown, and Gyorgy Kepes.

Those who worry about the gap between 'the two cultures,' and this means virtually all literary intellectuals in England and America, take for granted a notion of culture which decidedly needs reexamining. It is the notion perhaps best expressed by Matthew Arnold (in which the central cultural act is the making of literature, which is itself understood as the criticism of culture). Simply ignorant of the vital and enthralling (so called 'avant-garde') developments in the other arts, and blinded by their personal investment in the perpetuation of the older notion of culture, they continue to cling to literature as the model for creative statement.

What gives literature its preeminence is its heavy burden of 'content,' both reportage and moral judgment. (This makes it possible for most English and American literary critics to use literary works mainly as texts, or even pretexts, for social and cultural diagnosis – rather than concentrating on the properties of, say, a given novel or a play, as an art work.) But the model arts of our time are actually those with much less content, and a much cooler mode of moral judgment – like music, films, dance, architecture, painting, sculpture. The practice of these arts – all of which draw profusely, naturally, and without embarrassment, upon science and technology – are the locus of the new sensibility.

The problem of 'the two cultures,' in short, rests upon an uneducated, uncontemporary grasp of our present cultural situation. It arises from the ignorance of literary intellectuals (and of scientists with a shallow knowledge of the arts, like the scientist-novelist C. P. Snow himself) of a new culture, and its emerging sensibility. In fact, there can be no divorce between science and technology, on the one hand, and art, on the other, any more than there can be a divorce between art and the forms of social life. Works of art, psychological forms, and social forms all reflect each other, and change with each other. But, of course, most people are slow to come to terms with such changes – especially today, when the changes are occurring with an unprecedented rapidity. Marshall McLuhan has described human history as a succession of acts of technological extension of human capacity, each of which works a radical change upon our environment and our ways of thinking, feeling, and valuing. The tendency, he remarks, is to upgrade the old environment into art form (thus Nature became a vessel of aesthetic and spiritual values in the new industrial environment) 'while the new conditions are regarded as corrupt and degrading.' Typically, it is only certain artists in any given era who 'have the resources and temerity to live in immediate contact with the environment of their age ... That is why they may seem to be 'ahead of their time' ... More timid people prefer to accept the ... previous environment's values as the continuing reality of their time. Our natural bias is to accept the new gimmick (automation, say) as a thing that can be accommodated in the old ethical order.' Only in the terms of what McLuhan calls the old ethical order does the problem of 'the two cultures' appear to be a genuine problem. It is not a problem for most of the creative artists of our time (among whom one could include very few novelists) because most of these artists have broken, whether they know it or not, with the Matthew Arnold notion of culture, finding it historically and humanly obsolescent.

The Matthew Arnold notion of culture defines art as the criticism of life – this being understood as the propounding of moral, social, and political ideas. The new sensibility understands art as the extension of life – this being understood as the representation of (new) modes of vivacity. There is no necessary denial of the role of moral evaluation here. Only the scale has changed; it has become less gross, and what it sacrifices in discursive explicitness it gains in accuracy and subliminal power. For we are what we are able to see (hear, taste, smell, feel) even more powerfully and profoundly than we are what furniture of ideas we have stocked in our heads. Of course, the proponents of 'the two cultures' crisis continue to observe a desperate contrast between unintelligible, morally neutral science and technology, on the one hand, and morally committed, human-scale art on the other. But matters are not that simple, and never were. A great work of art is never simply (or even mainly) a vehicle of ideas or of moral sentiments. It is, first of all, an object modifying our consciousness and sensibility, changing the composition, however slightly, of the humans that nourishes all specific ideas and sentiments. Outraged humanists, please note. There is no need for alarm. A work of art does not cease being a moment in the conscience of mankind, when moral conscience is understood as only one of the functions of consciousness.

Sensations, feelings, the abstract forms and styles of sensibility count. It is to these that contemporary art addresses itself. The basic unit for contemporary art is not the idea, but the analysis of and extension of sensations. (Or if it is an 'idea,' it is about the form of sensibility.) Rilke described the artist as someone who works 'toward an extension of the regions of the individual senses'; McLuhan calls artists 'experts in sensory awareness.' And the most interesting works of contemporary art (one can begin at least as far back as French symbolist poetry) are adventures in sensation, new 'sensory mixes.' Such art is, in principle, experimental – not out of an elitist disdain for what is accessible to the majority, but precisely in the sense that science is experimental. Such an art is also notably apolitical and undidactic, or, rather, infra-didactic.

When Ortega y Gasset wrote his famous essay *The Dehumanization of Art* in the early 1920s, he ascribed the qualities of modern art (such as impersonality, the ban on pathos, hostility to the past, playfulness, willful stylization, absence of ethical and political commitment) to the spirit of youth which he thought dominated our age.[1] In retrospect, it seems this 'dehumanization' did not signify the recovery of childlike innocence, but was rather a very adult, knowing response. What other response than anguish, followed by anesthesia and then by wit and the elevating of intelligence over sentiment, is possible as a response to the social disorder and mass atrocities of our time, and – equally important for our sensibilities, but less often remarked on – to the unprecedented change in what rules our environment from the intelligible and visible to that which is only with difficulty intelligible, and is invisible? Art, which I have characterized as an instrument for modifying and educating sensibility and consciousness, now operates in an environment which cannot be grasped by the senses.

Buckminster Fuller has written:

> In World War I industry suddenly went from the visible to the invisible base, from the track to the trackless, from the wire to the wireless, from visible structuring to invisible structuring in alloys. The big thing about World War I is that man went off the sensorial spectrum forever as the prime criterion of accrediting innovations ... All major advances since World War I have been in the infra and the ultrasensorial frequencies of the electromagnetic spectrum. All the important technical affairs of men today are invisible ... The old masters, who were sensorialists, have unleased a Pandora's box of non-sensorially controllable phenomena, which they had avoided accrediting up to that time ... Suddenly they lost their true mastery, because from then on they didn't personally understand what was going on. If you don't understand you cannot master ... Since World War I, the old masters have been extinct ...

But, of course, art remains permanently tied to the senses. Just as one cannot float colors in space (a painter needs some sort of surface, like a canvas, however neutral and textureless), one cannot have a work of art that does not impinge upon the human sensorium. But it is important to realize that human sensory awareness has not merely a biology but a specific history, each culture placing a premium on certain senses and inhibiting others. (The same is true for the range of primary human emotions.) Here is where art (among other things) enters, and why the interesting art of our time has such a feeling of anguish and crisis about it, however playful and abstract and ostensibly neutral morally it may appear. Western man may be said to have been undergoing a massive sensory anesthesia (a concomitant of the process that Max Weber calls 'bureaucratic rationalization') at least since the Industrial Revolution, with modern art functioning as a kind of shock therapy for both confounding and unclosing our senses.

One important consequence of the new sensibility (with its abandonment of the Matthew Arnold idea of culture) has already been alluded to – namely, that the distinction between 'high' and 'low' culture seems less and less meaningful. For such a distinction – inseparable from the Matthew Arnold apparatus – simply does not make sense for a creative community of artists and scientists engaged in programming sensations, uninterested in art as a species of moral journalism. Art has always been more than that, anyway.

Another way of characterizing the present cultural situation, in its most creative aspects, would be to speak of a new attitude toward pleasure. In one sense, the new art and the new sensibility take a rather dim view of pleasure.

(The great contemporary French composer, Pierre Boulez, entitled an important essay of his twelve years ago, 'Against Hedonism in Music.') The seriousness of modern art precludes pleasure in the familiar sense – the pleasure of a melody that one can hum after leaving the concert hall, of characters in a novel or play whom one can recognize, identify with, and dissect in terms of realistic psychological motives, of a beautiful landscape or a dramatic moment represented on a canvas. If hedonism means sustaining the old ways in which we have found pleasure in art (the old sensory and psychic modalities), then the new art is anti-hedonistic. Having one's sensorium challenged or stretched hurts. The new serious music hurts one's ears, the new painting does not graciously reward one's sight, the new films and the few interesting new prose works do not go down easily. The commonest complaint about the films of Antonioni or the narratives of Beckett or Burroughs is that they are hard to look at or to read, that they are 'boring.' But the charge of boredom is really hypocritical. There is, in a sense, no such thing as boredom. Boredom is only another name for a certain species of frustration. And the new languages which the interesting art of our time speaks are frustrating to the sensibilities of most educated people.

But the purpose of art is always, ultimately, to give pleasure – though our sensibilities may take time to catch up with the forms of pleasure that art in a given time may offer. And, one can also say that, balancing the ostensible anti-hedonism of serious contemporary art, the modern sensibility is more involved with pleasure in the familiar sense than ever. Because the new sensibility demands less 'content' in art, and is more open to the pleasures of 'form' and style, it is also less snobbish, less moralistic – in that it does not demand that pleasure in art necessarily be associated with edification. If art is understood as a form of discipline of the feelings and a programming of sensations, then the feeling (or sensation) given off by a Rauschenberg painting might be like that of a song by the Supremes. The brio and elegance of Budd Boetticher's *The Rise and Fall of Legs Diamond* or the singing style of Dionne Warwick can be appreciated as a complex and pleasurable event. They are experienced without condescension.

This last point seems to me worth underscoring. For it is important to understand that the affection which many younger artists and intellectuals feel for the popular arts is not a new philistinism (as has so often been charged) or a species of anti-intellectualism or some kind of abdication from culture. The fact that many of the most serious American painters, for example, are also fans of 'the new sound' in popular music is not the result of the search for mere diversion or relaxation; it is not, say, like Schoenberg also playing tennis. It reflects a new, more open way of looking at the world and at things in the world, our world. It does not mean the renunciation of all standards: there is plenty of stupid popular music, as well as inferior and pretentious 'avant-garde' paintings, films, and music. The point is that there are new standards, new standards of beauty and style and taste. The new sensibility is defiantly pluralistic; it is dedicated both to an excruciating seriousness and to fun and wit and nostalgia.

It is also extremely history-conscious; and the voracity of its enthusiasms (and of the supercession of these enthusiasms) is very high-speed and hectic. From the vantage point of this new sensibility, the beauty of a machine or of the solution to a mathematical problem, of a painting by Jasper Johns, of a film by Jean-Luc Godard, and of the personalities and music of the Beatles is equally accessible.

NOTE

1. Ortega remarks, in this essay: 'Were art to redeem man, it could do so only by saving him from the seriousness of life and restoring him to an unexpected boyishness.'

12

'CROSS THE BORDER – CLOSE THAT GAP: POST-MODERNISM'

Leslie A. Fiedler

[...]

Almost all living readers and writers are aware of a fact which they have no adequate words to express, not in English certainly, nor even in American. We are living, have been living for two decades – and have become acutely conscious of the fact since 1955 – through the death throes of Modernism and the birth pangs of Post-Modernism. The kind of literature which had arrogated to itself the name Modern (with the presumption that it represented the ultimate advance in sensibility and form, that beyond it newness was not possible), and whose moment of triumph lasted from a point just before the First World War until one just after the Second World War, is *dead*, i.e., belongs to history not actuality. In the field of the novel, this means that the age of Proust, Mann, and Joyce is over; just as in verse that of T. S. Eliot, Paul Valéry, Montale and Seferis is done with.

[...]

In any case, it seems evident that writers not blessed enough to be under thirty (or thirty-five, or whatever the critical age is these days) must be reborn in order to seem relevant to the moment, and those who inhabit it most comfortably, i.e., the young. But no one has even the hope of being reborn unless he knows first that he is dead – dead, to be sure, for someone else; but a writer exists as a writer precisely for someone else. More specifically, no novelist can be reborn until he

From Leslie A. Fiedler (1975) 'Cross the Border – Close that Gap: Post-Modernism', in Marcus Cunliffe (ed.), *American Literature since 1900*. London: Sphere Books.

knows that insofar as he remains a novelist in the traditional sense, he is dead; since the traditional novel is dead – not dying, but dead. What was up to only a few years ago a diagnosis, a prediction (made, to be sure, almost from the moment of the invention of the novel: first form of pop literature, and therefore conscious that as compared to classic forms like epic or tragedy its lifespan was necessarily short) is now a fact. As certainly as God, i.e., the Old God, is dead, so the Novel, i.e., the Old Novel, is dead. To be sure, certain writers, still alive and productive (Saul Bellow, for instance, or John Updike, Mary McCarthy or James Baldwin), continue to write Old Novels, and certain readers, often with a sense of being quite up-to-date, continue to read them. But so do preachers continue to preach in the Old Churches, and congregations gather to hear them.

It is *not* a matter of assuming, like Marshall McLuhan, that the printed book is about to disappear, taking with it the novel – first form invented for print; only of realizing that in all of its forms – and most notably, perhaps, the novel – the printed book is being radically, functionally altered. No medium of communication ever disappears merely because a new, and more efficient one is invented. One thinks, for instance, of the lecture, presumably superannuated by the invention of moveable type, yet flourishing still after more than five centuries of obsolescence. What is demanded by functional obsolescence is learning to be less serious, more frivolous, a form of *entertainment*. Indeed, it could be argued that a medium begins to be felt as entertainment only at the point where it ceases to be a necessary or primary means of communication. [...]

[...] the truly New Novel must be anti-art as well as anti-serious. But this means, after all, that it must become more like what it was in the beginning, more what it seemed when Samuel Richardson could not be taken *quite* seriously, and what it remained in England (as opposed to France, for instance) until Henry James had justified himself as an artist against such self-declared 'entertainers' as Charles Dickens and Robert Louis Stevenson: popular, not quite reputable, a little dangerous – the one his loved and rejected cultural father, the other his sibling rival in art. [...]

This popular tradition the French may have understood once (in the days when Diderot praised Richardson extravagantly, and the Marquis de Sade emulated him in a dirtier book than the Englishman dared) but they long ago lost sight of it. And certainly the so-called '*nouveau roman*' is in its deadly earnest almost the opposite of anything truly new, which is to say, anti-art. Robbe-Grillet, for example, is still the prisoner of dying notions of the *avant-garde*; and though he is aware of half of what the new novelist must do (destroy the Old, destroy Marcel Proust), he is unaware of what he must create in its place. His kind of anti-novel is finally too arty and serious: a kind of neo-neo-classicism, as if to illustrate once more that in the end this is all the French can invent no matter how hard they try. [...]

[...] Boris Vian is in many ways a prototype of the New Novelist, though he has been dead for a decade or so and his most characteristic work belongs to the years just after the Second World War. He was, first of all, an Imaginary

American (as even writers born in the United States must be these days), who found himself in total opposition to the politics of America at the very moment he was most completely immersed in its popular culture; actually writing a detective novel called 'I Will Spit On Your Grave' under the pen-name of Vernon Sullivan, but pretending that he was only its translator into French. In fact, by virtue of this peculiar brand of mythological Americanism he managed to straddle the border, if not quite close the gap between high culture and low, *belles-lettres* and pop art. On the one hand, he was the writer of pop songs and a jazz trumpeter much influenced by New Orleans style; and on the other, the author of novels in which the thinly disguised figures of such standard French intellectuals as Jean-Paul Sarte and Simone de Beauvoir are satirized. But even in his fiction, which seems at first glance quite traditional or, at any rate, conventionally *avant-garde*, the characters move towards their fates through an imaginary city whose main thoroughfare is called Boulevard Louis Armstrong.

Only now, however, has Vian won the audience we all know he deserved, finding it first among the young of Paris, who know like their American counterparts that such a closing of the gap between elite and mass culture is precisely the function of the novel now – and not merely optional, as in Vian's day, but necessary. [...]

The young Americans who have succeeded Vian, on the other hand, have abandoned all concealment; and when they are most themselves, nearest to their central concerns, turn frankly to Pop forms – though not, to be sure, the detective story which has by our time become hopelessly compromised by middle-brow condescension: an affectation of Presidents and college professors. The forms of the novel which they prefer are those which seem now what the hard-boiled detective story once seemed to Vian: at the furthest possible remove from art and *avant-garde*, the greatest distance from inwardness, analysis, and pretension; and, therefore, immune to lyricism, on the one hand, or righteous social commentary, on the other. It is not compromise by the market-place they fear; on the contrary, they choose the genre most associated with exploitation by the mass media: notably, the Western, Science Fiction and Pornography.

Most congenial of all is the 'Western', precisely because it has for many decades now seemed to belong exclusively to pulp magazines, run-of-the-mill TV series and class B movies; which is to say, has been experienced almost purely as myth and entertainment rather than as 'literature' at all – and its sentimentality has, therefore, come to possess our minds so completely that it can now be mitigated without essential loss by parody, irony – and even critical analysis. In a sense, our mythological innocence has been preserved in the Western, awaiting the day when, no longer believing ourselves innocent in fact, we could decently return to claim it in fantasy. But such a return of the Western represents, of course, a rejection of laureates of the loss of innocence like Henry James and Hawthorne: those particular favourites of the Forties, who despite their real virtues turn out to have been too committed to the notion of European high art to survive as major influences in an age of Pop. And it implies as well momentarily turning aside from our beloved Herman Melville (compromised by his New Critical admirers and the countless Ph.D. dissertations they prompted), and even from Mark Twain. To Hemingway, Twain could still seem central to a living tradition, the Father of us all, but being Folk rather than Pop in essence, he has become ever more remote from an urban, industrialized world, for which any evocation of pre-Civil War, rural American seems a kind of pastoralism which complements rather than challenges the Art Religion. Folk Art knows and accepts its place in a class-structured world which Pop blows up, whatever its avowed intentions. What remain are only the possibilities of something closer to travesty than emulation – such a grotesque neo-Huck, for instance, as the foul-mouthed D.J. in Norman Mailer's *Why Are We in Vietnam?*, who, it is wickedly suggested, may *really* be a Black joker in Harlem pretending to be the White refugee from respectability. And, quite recently, Twain's book itself has been rewritten to please and mock its exegetes in John Seelye's *Huck Finn for The Critics*, which lops off the whole silly-happy ending, the deliverance of Nigger Jim (in which Hemingway, for instance, never believed); and puts back into the tale the cussing and sex presumably excised by the least authentic part of Samuel Clemens's mind – as well as the revelation, at long last, that what Huck and Jim were smoking on the raft was not tobacco but 'hemp', which is to say, marijuana. Despite all, however, Huck seems for the moment to belong not to the childhood we all continue to live, but to the one we have left behind.

Natty Bumppo, on the other hand, dreamed originally in the suburbs of New York City and in Paris, oddly survives along with his author. Contrary to what we had long believed, it is James Fenimore Cooper who now remains alive, or rather who has been reborn, perhaps not so much as he saw himself as in the form D. H. Lawrence re-imagined him en route to America; for Cooper understood that the dream which does not fade with the building of cities, but assumes in their concrete and steel environment the compelling vividness of a waking hallucination, is the encounter of Old World men and New in the wilderness, the meeting of the transplanted European and the Red Indian. No wonder Lawrence spoke of himself as 'Kindled by Fenimore Cooper'.

The Return of the Redskin to the centre of our art and our deep imagination, as we all of us have retraced Lawrence's trip to the mythical America, is based not merely on the revival of the oldest and most authentic of American Pop forms, but also projects certain meanings of our lives in terms more metapolitical than political, which is to say, meanings valid as myth is valid rather than as history. Writers of Westerns have traditionally taken sides for or against the Indians; and unlike the authors of the movies which set the kids to cheering at the Saturday matinees of the Twenties and Thirties, the new novelists have taken a clear stand with the Red Man. In this act of mythological renegacy they have not only implicitly declared themselves enemies of the Christian Humanism; but they have also rejected the act of genocide with which our nation began – and whose last reflection, perhaps, is to be found in the war in Vietnam.

It is impossible to write any Western which does not in some sense glorify violence; but the violence celebrated in the anti-White Western is guerrilla violence: the sneak attack on 'civilization' as practised first by Geronimo and Cochise and other Indian warrior chiefs, and more latterly prescribed by Ché Guevara or the spokesmen for North Vietnam. Warfare, however, is not the final vision implicit in the New Western, which is motivated on a deeper level by a nostalgia for the Tribe: a form of social organization thought of as preferable both to the tight two-generation bourgeois family, from which its authors come, and the soulless out-of-human-scale bureaucratic state, into which they are initiated via schools and universities. [...]

In any case, our best writers have been able to take up the Western again – playfully and seriously at once, quite like their ancestors who began the Revolution which made us a country by playing Indians in deadly earnest and dumping all that English tea into the salt sea that sundered them from their King. There are many writers still under forty, among them the most distinguished of their generation, who have written New Westerns which have found the hearts of the young, particularly in paperback form; since to these young readers, for reasons psychological as well as economic, the hard-cover book with its aspiration to immortality in libraries begins to look obsolete. John Barth's *The Sotweed Factor* represents the beginning of the wave which has been cresting ever since 1960; and which has carried with it not only Barth's near contemporaries like Thomas Berger (in *Little Big Man*), Ken Kesey (in both *One Flew Over the Cuckoo's Nest* and *Sometimes a Great Notion*), and most recently Leonard Cohen (in his extraordinarily gross and elegant *Beautiful Losers*) – but has won over older and more established writers like Norman Mailer whose newest novel, *Why Are We in Vietnam?*, is not as its title seems to promise a book about a war in the East as much as a book about the idea of the West. Even William Burroughs, expert in drug fantasies and homosexual paranoia, keeps promising to turn to the genre; though so far he has contented himself with another popular form, another way of escaping from personal to public or popular myth, of using dreams to close rather than open a gap: Science Fiction.

Science Fiction does not seem at first glance to have as wide and universal appeal as the Western, in book form at least; though perhaps it is too soon to judge, for it is a very young genre, having found its real meaning and scope only after the Second World War, after tentative beginnings in Jules Verne, H. G. Wells, etc. At that point, two things became clear: first, that the future was upon us, that the pace of technological advance had become so swift that a distinction between present and future would get harder and harder to maintain; and second, that the end of Man, by annihilation or mutation, was a real, even an immediate possibility. But these are the two proper subjects of Science Fiction: the Present Future and the End of Man – not time travel or the penetration of outer space, except as the latter somehow symbolizes the former.

Perhaps only in quite advanced technologies which also have a tradition of self-examination and analysis, bred by Puritanism or Marxism or whatever, can Science Fiction at its most explicit, which is to say, expressed in words on the page, really flourish. In any case, only in America, England and the Soviet Union does the Science Fiction Novel or Post-Novel seem to thrive; though Science Fiction cartoon strips and comic books, as well as Science Fiction TV programmes and especially films (where the basic imagery is blissfully wed to electronic music, and words are kept to a minimum) penetrate everywhere. In England and America, at any rate, the prestige and influence of the genre are sufficient not only to allure Burroughs (in *Nova Express*), but also to provide a model for William Golding (in *Lord of the Flies*), Anthony Burgess (in *The Clockwork Orange*), and John Barth (whose second major book, *Giles Goatboy*, abandoned the Indian in favour of the Future).

Quite unlike the Western, which asserts the differences between England and America, Science Fiction reflects what still makes the two mutually distrustful communities one; as, for instance, a joint effort (an English author, an American director) like the movie, *2001: A Space Odyssey*, testifies. If there is still a common 'Anglo-Saxon' form, it is Science Fiction. Yet even here, the American case is a little different from the English; for only in the United States is there a writer of first rank whose preferred mode has been from the first Science Fiction in its unmitigated Pop form. Kurt Vonnegut, Jr., did not begin by making some sort of traditional bid for literary fame and then shift to Science Fiction, but was so closely identified with that popular, not-quite-respectable form from the first, that the established critics were still ignoring him completely at a time when younger readers, attuned to the new rhythm of events by Marshall McLuhan or Buckminster Fuller, had already made underground favourites of his *The Sirens of Titan* and *Cat's Cradle*. That Vonnegut now, after years of neglect, teaches writing in a famous American university and is hailed in lead reviews in the popular press, is a tribute not to the critics' acuity but to the persuasive powers of the young.

The revival of pornography in recent days, its moving from the periphery to the centre of the literary scene, is best understood in this context, too; for it, like the Western and Science Fiction, is a form of Pop Art – ever since Victorian times, indeed, the *essential* form of Pop Art, which is to say, the most unredeemable of all kinds of sub-literature, understood as a sort of entertainment closer to the pole of Vice than that of Art. Many of the more notable recent works of the genre have tended to conceal this fact, often because the authors themselves did not understand what they were after, and have tried to disguise their work as earnest morality (Hubert Selby's *Last Exit to Brooklyn*, for instance) or parody (Terry Southern's *Candy*). But whatever the author's conscious intent, all those writers who have helped move Porn from the underground to the foreground have in effect been working towards the liquidation of the very conception of pornography; since the end of Art on one side means the end of Porn on the other. And that end is now in sight, in the area of films and Pop songs and poetry, but especially in that of the novel which seemed, initially at least, more congenial than other later Pop Art forms to the sort of private masturbatory reverie which is essential to pornography.

[…]

[…] Reversing the process typical of Modernism – under whose aegis an unwilling, ageing elite audience was bullied and cajoled slowly, slowly, into accepting the most vital art of its time – Post-Modernism provides an example of a young, mass audience urging certain ageing, reluctant critics onwards towards the abandonment of their former elite status in return for a freedom the prospect of which more terrifies than elates them. In fact, Post-Modernism implies the closing of the gap between critic and audience, too, if by critic one understands 'leader of taste' and by audience 'follower'. But more importantly of all, it implies the closing of the gap between artist and audience, or at any rate, between professional and amateur in the realm of art.

[…]

13

'THE DETECTIVE AND THE BOUNDARY: SOME NOTES ON THE POSTMODERN LITERARY IMAGINATION'

William V. Spanos

[...]

I

[...] What I wish to suggest at the outset is that, unlike the early modern imagination – indeed, in partial reaction against its refusal of historicity – the postmodern imagination, agonized as it has been by the on-going boundary situation which is contemporary history, is an existential imagination. Its anti-Aristotelianism – its refusal to fulfill causally oriented expectations, to create fictions and in extreme cases, sentences with beginnings, middles, and ends – has its source, not so much in an aesthetic as in an existential critique of the traditional Western view of man in the world, especially as it has been formulated by positivistic science and disseminated by the vested interests of the modern – technological – City. It is not, in other words, the ugliness, the busyness, the noisiness of a world organized on the principle of utility that has called forth postmodern anti-Aristotelianism, it is rather, though the two are not mutually exclusive, the anthropomorphic objectification of a world in which God is dead or has withdrawn.

[...]

According to the implications of existential philosophy, then, the problem-solution perspective of the 'straightforward' Western man of action, as Dostoevsky's denizen of the underground calls the exponents of the Crystal Palace,

From William V. Spanos (1995) 'The Detective and the Boundary: Some Notes on the Postmodern Literary Imagination' [1972], in Paul A. Bové (ed.), *Early Postmodernism: Foundational Essays*. Durham, NC: Duke University Press.

has its ground in more than merely a belief in the susceptibility of nature to rational explanation. It is based, rather on a monolithic certainty that immediate psychic or historical experience is part of a comforting, even exciting and suspenseful well-made cosmic drama or novel – more particularly, a detective story (the French term is *policière*) in the manner of Poe's *The Murders in the Rue Morgue* or Conan Doyle's *The Hound of the Baskervilles*. For just as the form of the detective story has its source in the comforting certainty that an acute 'eye,' private or otherwise, can solve the crime with resounding finality by inferring causal relationships between clues which point to it (they are 'leads,' suggesting the primacy of rigid linear narrative sequence), so the 'form' of the well-made positivistic universe is grounded in the equally comforting certainty that the scientist and/or psychoanalyst can solve the immediate problem by the inductive method, a process involving the inference of relationships between discontinuous 'facts' that point to or lead straight to an explanation of the 'mystery,' the 'crime' of contingent existence. ' "This is most important," said [Holmes in *The Hound of the Baskervilles*] ... "It fills up a gap which I had been unable to bridge in this most complex affair." '

Far from being arbitrary, this way of defining the structure of consciousness into which modern Western man has coerced his humanistic inheritance from the Renaissance is, as we shall see, amply justified, especially by the evidence of his popular arts and public-political life. Though, on the whole, scientists and psychologists no longer are inclined to view existence in this rigidly positivistic and deterministic way, it is nevertheless this structure of consciousness, which assumes the universe, the 'book of nature,' to be a well-made cosmic drama, that determines the questions and thus the expectations and answers – in language and in action – of the 'silent majority,' *das Man* of the modern technological City and of the political executors of its will.

II

As the profound influence of certain kinds of literature on existential philosophy suggests, the impulse of the Western writer to refuse to fulfill causal expectations, to refuse to provide 'solutions' for the 'crime' of existence, historically precedes the existential critique of Westernism. We discover it in, say, Euripides' *Orestes*, Shakespeare's problem plays, the tragi-comedies of the Jacobeans, Wycherley's *The Plain Dealer*, Dickens's *Edwin Drood*, and more recently in Tolstoy's *The Death of Ivan Ilych*, Dostoevsky's *Notes from Underground*, Alfred Jarry's *Ubu Roi*, Kafka's *The Trial*, Pirandello's *Six Characters in Search of an Author*, and even in T. S. Eliot's *Sweeney Agonistes*. (These are works, it is worth observing, the radical temporality of which does not yield readily to the spatial methodology of the New Criticism, which has its source in the iconic art of symbolist modernism.) In *Notes from Underground*, for example, Dostoevsky as editor 'concludes' this antinovel: 'The "notes" of this paradoxalist do not end here. However, he could not resist and continued them. But it also seems to me that we may stop here.' Fully conscious of the psychological need of the 'straightforward' Gentleman of the hyper-Westernized St. Petersburg – the 'most international city in the whole world – Dostoevsky refuses to transform the discordant experience of this terrible voice into a 'sublime and beautiful,' that is, 'straightforward' and distancing *story*. So also in *Six Characters in Search of an Author*. Seeking relief from the agony of their ambiguous relationships, the characters express their need to give artistic shape to the 'infinite absurdities' of their lives. But when the Director (I want to emphasize the coercive implications of the word) – who hates their authorless, that is, inconclusive drama ('it seems to me you are trying to imitate the manner of a certain author whom I heartily detest') – tries to make a well-made play, a melodrama in the manner of Eugène Scribe or Alexander Dumas *fils* of their dreadful experience ('What we've got to do is to combine and group up all the facts in one simultaneous close-knit action'), they refuse to be coerced into that comforting but fraudulent 'arrangement.' Similarly in *Sweeney Agonistes*, just as Sweeney will not allow his anxious listeners to package the terrible 'anti-Aristotelian' murder story he tells them ('Well here again that don't apply/But I've gotta use words when I talk to you'), so Eliot in his great antidetective play will not allow his audience of middle class fugitives to fulfill their positivistically conditioned need to experience the explanatory and cathartic conclusion. Rather, like Dostoevsky, he ends the play inconclusively with the dreadful knocking at the door.

But in each of these earlier works, one has the feeling that the writer has only reluctantly resisted the conventional ending. It is actually the unconscious pressure of the powerfully felt content – the recognition and acknowledgment of contingency, or what I prefer to call the ontological invasion – that has driven him into undermining the traditional Aristotelian dramatic or fictional form. The existential diagnosis and critique of the humanistic tradition had not yet emerged to suggest the formal implications of metaphysical disintegration. Only after the existentialist philosophers revealed that the perception of the universe as a well-made fiction, obsessive to the Western consciousness, is in reality a self-deceptive effort to evade the anxiety of contingent existence by objectifying and taking hold of 'it,' did it become clear to the modern writer that the ending-as-solution is the literary agency of this evasive objectification. And it is the discovery of the 'anti-formal' imperatives of absurd time for fiction and drama and poetry (though poetry, which in our time means lyric poetry, as Sartre has said in *What is Literature!*, tends by its natural amenability to spatialization to be nonhistorical) that constitutes the most dynamic thrust of the contemporary Western literary imagination and differentiates the new from symbolist modernism.

Taking their lead from the existentialists, the postmodern absurdists – writers like the Sartre of *Nausea* and *No Exit*, the Beckett of *Watt* and the Molloy trilogy as well as *Waiting for Godot*, *Endgame*, and *Krapp's Last Tape* (the titles should not be overlooked), Ionesco, Genet, Pinter, Frisch, Sarraute, Pynchon, etc. – thus view the well-made play or novel (*la pièce bien faite*), the post-Shakespearian allotrope of the Aristotelian form, as the inevitable analogue of the well-made positivistic universe delineated by the post-Renaissance humanistic structure of consciousness. More specifically, they view the rigid deterministic plot of the well-made fiction, like that of its metaphysical counterpart, as having its source in bad faith. I mean (to appropriate the metaphor Heidegger uses to remind us of the archetypal flight of the Apollonian Orestes from the *Erinyes*) the self-deceptive effort of the 'fallen "they"' (*das verfallene 'Man'*) 'to flee in the face of death' and the ominous absurd by finding objects for the dread of Nothing, that is, *by imposing coercively a distancing and tranquillizing ending or* telos *from the beginning on the invading contingencies of existence*. What Roquentin says in Sartre's *Nausea* about *l'aventure* (which is the aesthetic equivalent of the Bouville merchants' arrogant positivism – their certain 'right to exist') in distinguishing it from *la vie* is precisely what the postmodern absurdists seem to imply in their 'de-composed' drama and fiction about the modern humanistic structure of consciousness and its metaphysical and aesthetic paradigms:

> everything changes when you tell about life [*raconte la vie:* Sartre seems to be pointing here to the relationship between the mathematical associations of the etymology and the concept of story or well-made plot and, ultimately, the recounting of existence from the vantage point of the end], it's a change no one notices: ... Things happen one way and we tell about them in the opposite sense. You seem to start at the beginning: 'It was a fine autumn evening in 1922. I was a notary clerk in Marommes.' And in reality you have started at the end. It was there, invisible and present, it is the one which gives to words the pomp and value of a beginning. 'I was out walking, I had left the town without realizing it, I was thinking about my money troubles.' This sentence, taken simply for what it is, means that the man was absorbed, morose, a hundred leagues from adventure, exactly in the mood to let things happen without noticing them. But the end is there, transforming everything. For us, the man is already the hero of the story. His moroseness, his money troubles are much more precious than ours, they are all gilded by the light of future passions. And the story goes on in the reverse: instants have stopped piling themselves in a lighthearted way one on top of the other [as in life], they are snapped up by the end of the story which draws them and each one of them in turn, draws out the preceding instant: 'It was night, the street was deserted.' *The phrase is cast out negligently, it seems superfluous* [*superflue:* an equivalent of *de trop*, Sartre's term for the condition of man in the primordial realm of existence which is prior to essence]; *but we do not let ourselves be caught and put it aside: this is a piece of information whose value we shall subsequently appreciate.* And we feel that the hero has lived all the details of this night like annunciations, promises, or even that he lives only those that were promises, blind and deaf to all that did not herald adventure...

> I wanted the moments of my life to follow and order themselves like those of a life remembered. You might as well try and catch time by the tail. (My emphasis).

In short, the postmodern absurdists interpret this obsession for what Roland Barthes, perhaps with Sartre in mind, calls the fiction of 'the preterite mode,' for the rigidly causal plot of the well-made work of the humanistic tradition, as catering to and thus further hardening the expectation of – and aggravating the need for – the rational solution generated by the scientific analysis of man-in-the-world. As the reference to the technique of the detective story in the passage from *Nausea* suggests, these expectations demand the kind of fiction and drama that achieves its absolute fulfillment in the utterly formularized clockwork certainties of plot in the innumerable detective drama series – *Perry Mason, The FBI, Hawaii 5–0, Mannix, Mission Impossible*, etc. – which use up, or rather, 'kill,' prime television time. Ultimately they also demand the kind of social and political organization that finds its fulfillment in the imposed certainties of the well-made world of the totalitarian state, where investigation or inquisition on behalf of the achievement of a total, that is, preordained or teleologically determined structure – 'final solution' – is the defining activity. It is, therefore, no accident that the paradigmatic archetype of the postmodern literary imagination is the antidetective story (and its antipsychoanalytical analogue), the formal purpose of which is to evoke the impulse to 'detect' and/or to psychoanalyze in order to violently frustrate it by refusing to solve the crime (or find the cause of the neurosis). I am referring, for example, to works like Kafka's *The Trial*, T. S. Eliot's *Sweeney Agonistes* (subtitled significantly *Fragments of an Aristophanic Melodrama*), Graham Greene's *Brighton Rock*, Arthur Koestler's *Arrival and Departure*, Beckett's *Watt* and *Molloy* (especially the Moran section), Ionesco's *Victims of Duty*, Robbe-Grillet's *The Erasers*, and Nathalie Sarraute's *Portrait of a Man Unknown* (which Sartre, in his characteristically seminal way, refers to as an 'anti-novel that reads like a detective story' and goes on to characterize as 'a parody on the novel of "quest" into which the author has introduced a sort of impassioned amateur detective' who 'doesn't find anything … and gives up the investigation as a result of a metamorphosis, just as though Agatha Christie's detective, on the verge of unmasking the villain, had himself suddenly turned criminal').

In *Victims of Duty*, for example, the Detective, like Sherlock Holmes, is certain in the beginning that 'everything hangs together, everything can be comprehended in time' and thus 'keeps moving forward … one step at a time, tracking down the extraordinary': 'Mailot, with a t at the end, or Mallod with a d.' Holmes, of course, eventually gets his man (though the foregone certainty, especially of the monstrous evilness of the criminal, should not obscure the grimness of the metaphor that characterizes Conan Doyle's fictional and real universe): 'This chance of the picture has supplied us with one of our most obvious missing links. We have him, Watson, we have him, and I dare swear that before tomorrow he will be fluttering in our net as helpless as one of his own butterflies. A pin, a cork, and a card, and we add him to the Baker Street collection!' But the Detective in the process of Ionesco's play cannot make Choubert 'catch hold of' the elusive Mallot. Despite his brutal efforts to 'plug the gaps [of his wayward memory]' by stuffing food down his throat, what he 'finds' is only the bottomless hole of Choubert's being: that is, Nothing. And so, instead of ending with 'A Retrospective' that ties everything together (clarifies the mystery) as in *The Hound of the Baskervilles, Victims of Duty* 'ends' in verbal, formal and, analogously, ontological disintegration. The disturbing mystery still survives the brutal coercion.

What I am suggesting is that it was the recognition of the ultimately 'totalitarian' implications of the Western structure of consciousness – of the expanding analogy that encompasses art, politics, and metaphysics in the name of the security of rational order – that compelled the postmodern imagination to undertake the deliberate and systematic subversion of plot – the beginning, middle, and end structure – which has enjoyed virtually unchallenged supremacy in the Western literary imagination ever since Aristotle or, at any rate, since the Renaissance interpreters of Aristotle claimed it to be the most important of the constitutive elements of literature. In the familiar language of Aristotle's *Poetics*, then, the postmodern strategy of de-composition exists to generate rather than to purge pity and terror; to disintegrate, to atomize rather than to create a community. In the more immediate language of existentialism, it exists to generate anxiety or dread: to dislodge the tranquilized individual from the 'at-home of publicness,' from the domesticated, the scientifically charted and organized familiarity of the totalized world, to make him experience what Roquentin sees from the top of a hill overlooking the not so 'solid, bourgeois city,' Bouville:

> They come out of their offices after their day of work, they look at the houses and the squares with satisfaction, they think it is *their* city, a good, solid, bourgeois city. They aren't afraid, they feel at home ... They have proof, a hundred times a day, that everything happens mechanically, that the world obeys fixed, unchangeable laws. In a vacuum all bodies fall at the same rate of speed, the public park is closed at 4 p.m. in winter, at 6 p.m. in summer, lead melts at 335 degrees centigrade ... And all this time, great, vague nature has slipped into their city, it has infiltrated everywhere, in their house, in their office, in themselves. It doesn't move, it stays quietly and they are full of it inside, they breathe it, and they don't see it, they imagine it to be outside, twenty miles from the city. I *see* it, I *see* this nature ... I know that its obedience is idleness, I know it has no laws: what they take for constancy is only habit and it can change tomorrow.
>
> What if something were to happen? What if something suddenly started throbbing? Then they would notice it was there and they'd think their hearts were going to burst. Then what good would their dykes, bulwarks, power houses, furnaces and pile drivers be to them?

This aesthetic of de-composition is not, as is too often protested, a purely negative one. For the *depaysment* – the ejection from one's 'homeland' – as Ionesco calls it after Heidegger, which is effected by the carefully articulated discontinuities of absurdist literary form, reveals the *Urgrund*, the primordial not-at-home, where dread, as Kierkegaard and Heidegger and Sartre and Tillich tell us, becomes not just the agency of despair but also and simultaneously of hope, that is, of freedom and infinite possibility:

> [If] a man were a beast or an angel [Kierkegaard, echoing Pascal, writes in *The Concept of Dread*], he would not be able to be in dread. Since he is a synthesis he can be in dread, and the greater the dread, the greater the man. And no Grand Inquisitor has in readiness such terrible tortures as has dread, and no spy knows how to attack more artfully the man he suspects, choosing the instant when he is weakest, nor knows how to lay traps where he will be caught and ensnared as dread knows how, and no sharpwitted judge knows how to interrogate, to examine the accused, as dread does, which never lets him escape, neither by diversion nor by noise, neither at work not at play, neither by day nor by night.
>
> Dread is the possibility of freedom. Only this dread is by the aid of faith absolutely educative, *laying bare as it does all finite aims and discovering all their deceptions . . .*
>
> He who is educated by dread is educated by possibility, and only the man who is educated by possibility is educated in accordance with his infinity. (My emphasis.)

Thus on the psychological level too this dislodgement not only undermines the confident positivistic structure of consciousness that really demands answers it already has (i.e., the expectation of *catharsis*). It also compels the new self to ask, like Orestes or Job – the Job who, against the certain advice of his comforters, the advocates of the Law, 'spoke of God that which is right' – the ultimate, the authentically humanizing questions: *die Seinfragen*, as Heidegger puts it. To evoke the buried metaphor I have hinted at in the passage from *The Concept of Dread*, the postmodern antiliterature of the absurd exists to strip its audience of positivized fugitives of their protective garments of rational explanation and leave them standing naked and unaccommodated – poor, bare, forked animals – before the encroaching Nothingness. Here, to add another dimension to the metaphor, in the precincts of their last evasions, in the realm of silence, where the language that objectifies (clothes), whether the syntax of plot or of sentence, as Sweeney says, 'don't apply' (is seen to be mere noise), they must choose authentically (*eigentlich*: in the context of the naked my-ownness of death and Nothingness) whether to capitulate to Nothingness, to endure it (this is what Tillich calls the courage to be in the face of despair), to affirm the Somethingness of Nothingness 'by virtue of the absurd,' or to risk letting Being be. It is this metaphor of divestment and silence, which finds its most forceful premodern expression in such works as *King Lear, Fear and*

Trembling, Crime and Punishment, and *The Death of Ivan Ilych*, that gives postmodern antinovels and antiplays like Sartre's *Nausea* and *No Exit*, Ionesco's *Victims of Duty*, Tardieu's *The Keyhole* (*La Serrure*), Beckett's *Watt* and *Molloy*, Genet's *The Maids*, Pinter's *The Homecoming*, and Sarraute's *Tropisms* their special ambience.

III

We have seen during the twentieth century the gradual emergence of an articulate minority point of view – especially in the arts – that interprets Western technological civilization as a progress not toward the Utopian *polis* idealized by the Greeks, but toward a rationally mass-produced City which, like the St. Petersburg of Dostoevsky's and Tolstoy's novels, is a microcosm of universal madness. This point of view involves a growing recognition of one of the most significant paradoxes of modern life: that in the pursuit of order the positivistic structure of consciousness, having gone beyond the point of equilibrium, generates radical imbalances in nature which are inversely proportional to the intensity with which it is coerced. However, it has not been able to call the arrogant anthropomorphic Western mind and its well-made universe into serious question.

As I have suggested, this is largely because the affirmative formal strategy of symbolist modernism was one of religio-aesthetic withdrawal from existential time into the eternal simultaneity of essential art. The symbolist movement, that is, tried to deconstruct language, to drive it out of its traditional temporal orbit – established by the humanistic commitment to *kinesis* and utility and given its overwhelming socioliterary authority, as Marshall McLuhan has shown, by the invention of the printing press – in order to achieve iconic or, more inclusively, spatial values. Its purpose was to undermine its utilitarian function in order to disintegrate the reader's linear-temporal orientation and to make him *see* synchronically – as one sees a painting or a circular mythological paradigm – what the temporal words express. In other words, its purpose was to *reveal* (in the etymological sense of 'unveil') the whole and by so doing raise the reader above the messiness or, as Yeats calls the realm of existence in 'Phases of the Moon,' 'that raving tide,' into a higher and more permanent reality.

This impulse to transcend the historicity of the human condition in the 'allatonceness' (the term is McLuhan's) of the spatialized work of symbolist literary art is brought into remarkably sharp focus when one perceives the similarity between the poetic implicit in W. B. Yeats's 'Sailing to Byzantium' with Stephen Dedalus's aesthetic of *stasis* in *Portrait of the Artist as a Young Man*, which has often been taken, especially by the New Critics, as a theoretical definition of modern symbolist literary form:

> You see I use the word *arrest*. I mean that the tragic emotion is static. Or rather the dramatic emotion is. The feelings excited by improper art are kinetic, desire and loathing. Desire urges us to possess, to go to something,

loathing urges us to abandon, to go from something. These are kinetic emotions. The arts which excite them, pornographical or didactic, are therefore improper arts. The esthetic emotion (I use the general term) is therefore static. The mind is arrested and raised above desire and loathing.

> O sages standing in God's holy fire
> As in the gold mosaic of a wall,
> Come from the holy fire, perne in a gyre,
> And be the singing-masters of my soul.
> Consume my heart away; sick with desire
> And fastened to a dying animal
> It knows not what it is; and gather me
> Into the artifice of eternity.
>
> Once out of nature I shall never take
> My bodily form from any natural thing,
> But such a form as Grecian goldsmiths make
> Of hammered gold and gold enamelling
> To keep a drowsy Emperor awake;
> Or set upon a golden bough to sing
> To lords and ladies of Byzantium
> Of what is past, or passing, or to come.

For Stephen, growing up has been a terrible process of discovering the paradox that the City – for Plato, for Virgil, for Augustine, for Justinian, for Dante, for Plethon, for Campanella, the image of beauty, of order, of repose – has become in the modern world the space of radical ugliness and disorder. To put it in Heidegger's terms, it has been a process of discovering that the at-home of the modern world has in fact become the realm of the not-at-home. This process, that is, has been one of *dislocation*. Thus for Stephen the ugliness and disorder, the 'squalor' and 'sordidness,' that assault his sensitive consciousness after his 'Ptolemaic' universe (which he diagrams on the fly-leaf of his geography book) has been utterly shattered during the catastrophic and traumatic Christmas dinner, is primarily or, at any rate, ontologically, a matter of random motion:

> He sat near them [his numerous brothers and sisters] at the table and asked where his father and mother were. One answered:
> – Goneboro toboro lookboro atboro aboro houseboro.
> Still another removal! A boy named Fallon in Belvedere had often asked him with a silly laugh why they moved so often...
> He asked:
> – Why are we on the move again, if it's a fair question?
> The sister answered:
> – Becauseboro theboro landboro lordboro willboro putboro usboro outboro...

> He waited for some moments, listening [to the children sing 'Oft in the Stilly Night'], before he too took up the air with them. He was listening with pain of spirit to the overtones of weariness behind their frail fresh innocent voices. Even before they set out on life's journey they seemed weary already of the way.
>
> ...All seemed weary of life even before entering upon it. And he remembered that Newman had heard this note also in the broken line of Virgil *giving utterance, like the voice of Nature herself, to that pain and weariness yet hope of better things which has been the experience of her children in every time.*

(Walter Pater too had heard this sad Virgilian note and in quoting the passage in *Marius the Epicurean*, another novel having its setting in a disintegrating world, established the nostalgia for rest as the essential motive of the aesthetic movement in England.)

Seen in the light of his discovery that random motion is the radical category of modern urban life – that existence is prior to essence, which the postmodern writer will later present as the Un-Naming in the Garden-City – Stephen's well-known aesthetic or rather (to clarify what persistent critical reference to Stephen's 'aesthetic' has obscured) his iconic poetics of stasis, both its volitional ground and its formal character, becomes clear. He wants, like T. E. Hulme, like Proust, like Virginia Woolf and like most other symbolists, a poetry the iconic – and autotelic – nature of which *arrests* the mind – neutralizes the anguish, the schism in the spirit – and *raises* it above desire and loathing, which is to say, the realm of radical motion, of contingency, of historicity, in the distancing moment when the whole is seen simultaneously.

The 'epiphanic' – one is tempted to say 'Oriental' – nature of this iconic poetic is further clarified in Stephen's amplification of the principle of *stasis* in terms of Saint Thomas's '*ad pulcritudinem tria requiruntur, integritas, consonantia, claritas,*' especially the first and, above all, the most important third categories. *Integritas* or 'wholeness,' Stephen observes, is the apprehension of 'a bounding line drawn about the object' no matter whether it is in space or in time: 'temporal or spatial, the esthetic image is first luminously apprehended as selfbounded and selfcontained upon the immeasurable background of space or time which is not it. You apprehend it as *one* thing. You see it as one whole.' *Consonantia* or 'harmony' is the apprehension of the 'rhythm of its structure', the feeling that 'it is a *thing*,' 'complex, multiple, divisible, separable, made up of parts, the result of its parts and their sum, harmonious.' Finally, and most important for Stephen, *claritas* or 'radiance' (the etymology of his translation – 'radiance' is the light emitted in rays from a center or *logos* – and his analysis of the term clearly suggest its relation with revelation) is the apprehension of 'that thing which it is and no other thing. The radiance of which [Saint Thomas] speaks is the scholastic *quidditas*, the *whatness* of a thing. This supreme quality is felt by the artist when the esthetic image is first conceived in his imagination ... The instant wherein that supreme quality of beauty, the clear radiance of the esthetic image, is apprehended *luminously by the mind which has been arrested by its wholeness* and fascinated by its harmony in the *luminous silent stasis of esthetic pleasure*' (my emphasis).

So also in 'Sailing to Byzantium' – though the metaphysical context is more ontological than social in orientation – Yeats's speaker, like Stephen, is articulating, both in the content and form of the poem, an iconic poetic that has its source in an impulse for epiphanic transcendence – what Wilhelm Worringer (the proponent of primitive and oriental, including Byzantine, artistic models who influenced T. E. Hulme) in *Abstraction and Empathy* calls the 'urge to abstraction.' As fully, if more implicitly, conscious of the paradoxical horror of the modern Western City as Stephen, the poet has come to the City of the iconic imagination – the City of Phase 15 – to pray his mosaic models to teach him *an art of poetry* that will 'consume my heart away' – heart like Stephen's which, 'sick with desire/And fastened to a dying animal/ ... knows not what it is.' Such a heart is ignorant because, as Yeats says here and reiterates in innumerable ways throughout his early and middle poetry, its *immediate* relationship to history makes everything appear to be random motion, that is, absurd. Clearly, to continue with the phenomenological language of existentialism, this heart is a synecdoche for the dislodged and thus anguish-ridden man-in-the-world, the alienated man in the dreadful realm of *das Unheimliche*. And, as in Stephen's iconic poetic, Yeats's moment of consummation (the parallel with 'radiance' should not be overlooked) which negates the human heart and neutralizes (arrests) desire – the Western, the empathetic urge 'to possess, to go to something' – is the consummation of the creative act, the metamorphosis of kinesis into stasis, becoming into being, the uncertain temporal life into assured iconic artifact, 'selfbounded and selfcontained upon the immeasurable background of space or time which is not it.' (Similarly, the image of a Byzantine mosaic Panaghia or Saint is sharply articulated upon a depthless and vast gold space that suggests the absolute purity of eternity.) Like Stephen's 'instant' of 'luminous silent stasis,' Yeats's moment of consummation is thus the distancing moment when all time can be seen simultaneously. Whereas the real birds of the first stanza – 'those dying generations' – know not what they are because they are 'caught' *in* time, the poet in this moment of consummation, having assumed the form 'as Grecian goldsmiths make/Of hammered gold and gold enamelling,' can sing in *full knowledge* from a perspective beyond or 'out of nature' of the world below, which is to say, of history seen all at once, that is, spatially: 'Of what is past, or passing, or to come.' In the words that Yeats's myth or rather his 'sacred book' insists on, this burning moment, like that of Joyce's 'priest of the eternal imagination,' and of so many other symbolist poets and novelists, is, in Ortega's term, the 'dehumanizing' epiphanic moment of transcendence.

IV

Committed to an iconic poetic of transcendence, the literature of early modernism thus refused to engage itself in the history of modern man. Though it was able to reveal the squalor of the 'Unreal City' of the West, where, as one of T. S. Eliot's Thames daughters puts it, 'I can connect/Nothing with nothing,' and even point with Dickens and Dostoevsky to the ontological invasion that had already begun, it did not challenge the positivistic structure of consciousness which organizes and sustains it. Despite, therefore, the terrible lessons of World War I and again World War II, especially of the genocidal holocaust perpetrated in the name of 'the final solution,' it is still the positivistic frame of reference that determines the questions-and-answers, that delineates the Western image of the universe and creates Western man's values. From the governing bodies and the scientific-industrial-military complex and even our educational and religious institutions to the so-called hard hat and blue collar workers, it is this well-made world, the world pointing toward a materialist utopia, toward a Crystal Palace end, that appears real. And as Sartre suggests in his assault on *les salauds* in *Nausea* and 'The Childhood of a Leader,' it is the certainty of the *rightness* of this fictional image of the macrocosm that continues to justify the coercion of the unique and disturbing deviant into its predetermined role – or its elimination ('liquidation' or 'wasting') – when it does not fulfill the rigid and inexorable expectations established by a preconceived end. Indeed, this world-picture, as a book like Lewis Mumford's *The Pentagon of Power* suggests, becomes more rigid and inclusive, that is, totalitarian, in proportion to the irrationality it generates. The investigator and monstrous proliferation: these are the *presences* of contemporary life. And this is no accident.

As I have already suggested, my definition of the Western structure of consciousness as one which perceives the world as a well-made melodrama is not a *tour de force* of the critical imagination. It is discoverable everywhere in the language and the shape of action of men from all social levels of the Western City. All that is necessary to perceive it is attention. It is impossible in this limited space to support this claim in any detail. But perhaps a quotation from an editorial on the subject of literature that appeared some time ago in the *Daily News*, the New York tabloid with a circulation of over two million, may suggest how rooted and inclusive this perspective is:

Winner and Still Champ

For generations William Shakespeare has been recognized as the greatest English master of the drama, and quite possibly the greatest handler of the English language, that ever yet has trod this earthly ball . . .

Shakespeare and Dickens had several things in common. They . . . composed stage or fictional pieces which had definite beginnings, unmistakable climaxes and positive endings.

> Neither Dickens nor Shakespeare wrote so-what tripe that gets nowhere and is in some fashion nowadays. Nor did they glorify characters whom even the ablest of modern psychiatrists couldn't help.
> *End* of today's discussion of matters literary.

This obsession for the 'positive' and comforting *ending* in the face of Shakespeare's – and even Dickens's – disturbing ambiguities, to say nothing of the uncertainties of contingent existence, I submit, lies behind this newspaper's editorial support of all causes 'grounded' in a storybook patriotism (such as United States involvement in Vietnam, President Nixon's invasion of Cambodia, Vice-President Agnew's political rhetoric) and vilification of all others 'grounded' in storybook treachery (such as the peace movement, senatorial opposition to unilateral policy-making by the executive branch, and even Scandinavian anti-Americanism). More pernicious, because its implications are harder to perceive, this structure of consciousness also lies behind this newspaper's *presentation* of the news, whether a tenement murder, a campus uprising, or an international incident, as sensational melodrama whose problem-solution form not only neutralizes the reader's anxieties but even makes him a voyeur. To forestall the objection that this evidence is unreliably partisan, let me parenthetically refer to the parallel with, say, *Time* or *Newsweek*, where the narrative structure of every article is conceived as a well-made fiction, that is, written – manipulated – from the end.

Further, as even the most cursory examination of 'The Pentagon Papers' clearly suggests, this positivistic structure of consciousness also lies behind the actions that constitute the news. It has governed the United States' involvement in Vietnam from the overthrow of Diem, the Tonkin Bay incident, and the ensuing large-scale 'retaliatory' bombing of North Vietnam to the Vietnamization – which means the Americanization or rather the Westernization – of Vietnam. It is, then, no accident that *everywhere* in these secret documents the Southeast Asian situation is seen by their American authors as a problem to be solved, that the planning to solve the problem – to achieve conclusive American objectives – is referred to in the metaphor of plotting a scenario, that the execution – the acting out – of the *scenario* in this recalcitrant theater of operations is to be accomplished, first, by the CIA – the international detective agency whose job it is to coerce the reality under investigation to conform to a preconceived order – and, then, by the military arm by way of a massive assault on the 'criminal' enemy. In short, what emerges in these disturbing documents, if we pay critical attention to the language (especially to its trite metaphors), is an image of an action in which virtually everyone involved in this terrible human disaster – from the executive branch and its councils to the intelligence agencies and the military and the American press and its public – speaks and acts as if he is playing a role in a well-made fiction in the utterly dehumanized mode of a play by Eugène Scribe, a novel by Sir Arthur Conan Doyle, or closest of all, an episode of *Mission Impossible*.

I will refer specifically to only one concrete but representative action of the war in Vietnam: the large-scale interservice rescue operation staged against the Son Tay prisoner-of-war camp in North Vietnam in December 1970. Seen in the light of my discussion, this melodramatic action constitutes an illuminating paradigm not only of the war that America has been waging against Southeast Asia since 1954, but also – and more fundamentally, for it is not so much politics as ontology that concerns me here – of the war that the West has been waging against the world, indeed against Nature itself, ever since the seventeenth century. It reveals, that is, how embedded – how *located* – in the Western consciousness is the metaphor of the well-made universe and how intense the conditioned psychological need behind it. This elaborately plotted action, the 'scenario' of which, according to the *New York Times* report, 'was rehearsed for a month in a stage-set replica of the objective on the Florida Gulf Coast,' did not achieve its objective, that is, did not end, because, despite the split-second timing with which all the roles were acted out, there was no one there to rescue at the climactic moment. 'It was like hollering in an empty room,' one of the bewildered actors in this dreadful experience put it. 'When we realized that there was no one in the compound,' said another – his language should be marked well – 'I had the most horrible feeling of my life.' And *Time* summed up in language that unintentionally recalls Watt's agonized quest for or rather his futile effort to take hold of the elusive Knott in Beckett's novel: 'All the courage, the long training, the perfectly executed mission, had come to naught.'

Despite these revelatory glimpses into the horror, the secretary of defense was driven to declare reiteratively in the following days that the Son Tay affair was a successfully completed operation. It is this metamorphosis of the absurd into manageable object, into fulfilled objective, into an accomplishment, which is especially revealing. For the obvious incommensurability between the assertion of successful completion and the absurd and dreadful non-end constitutes a measure of the intensity of the need that the power complex and the people that depend on it feel for definite conclusions. Returning to the ontological level, it is a measure of modern Western man's need *to take hold of the Nothing* that despite, or perhaps because of; his technics is crowding in on him. To put it in the central metaphor of the existential imagination, it is the measure of his need to flee from the Furies of the not-at-home and its implications for freedom.

V

In the past decade or so there have emerged a variety of 'postmodern' modes of writing and critical thought that, despite certain resemblances to aspects of the existential imagination, are ultimately extensions of early iconic modernism. I am referring, for example, to the structuralist criticism of Roland Barthes, the phenomenological criticism of consciousness of Georges Poulet and Jean-Pierre Richard, and the neo-imagism of Marshall McLuhan, the 'field poetry' of Charles Olson and the concrete poetry of Pierre Garnier, Ferdinand Kriwet, and Franz Mon; the *roman nouveau* of Robbe-Grillet and Michel Butor, the

'Happenings' of Allan Kaprow and Claes Oldenburg; and the Pop Art literature advocated by critics such as Leslie Fiedler (who, it is worth observing, wants to reconcile the sensibilities of Henry Wadsworth Longfellow and Stephen Foster with those of the Beatles, Bob Dylan, Leonard Cohen, etc., all of whom have in common not only the clichés and the assertive end rhymes he admires for their expression of childlike innocence, but also, and in a way at the source of these characteristics, the desire to go home again: the nostalgia for the hearth). These modes of creativity and critical speculation attest to the variety of the post-modern scene, but this pluralism has also tended to hide the fact that, in tendency, they are all oriented beyond history or, rather, they all aspire to the spatialization of time. As a result the existential sources of the primary thrust of the postmodern literary imagination have been obscured, thus jeopardizing the encouraging post-World War II impulse to recover the temporality of the literary medium from the plastic arts, which is to say, to engage literature in an ontological dialogue with the world in behalf of the recovery of the authentic historicity of modern man.

Seen in this light, the 'Pentagon Papers' not only emerge as a stark reminder that the totalizing structure of consciousness of the 'straightforward' Gentlemen who built the modern City continues to coerce history with missionary certainty into well-made fictions. Because they resemble so closely the kind of fiction and drama associated with the rise of science, technology, and middle-class culture in the nineteenth century, they also emerge as a paradigm capable of teaching both the contemporary writer and critic a great deal about the Western mind and the popular arts and the media that nourish it. In so doing, finally, they suggest a way of discriminating between modernisms and of clarifying the direction that the main impulse of the postmodern sensibility has taken and, I think, should continue to take in the immediate future.

Ultimately, one would like a literature of generosity, a literature, like Chaucer's or Shakespeare's or Dickens's or George Eliot's or Tolstoy's, that acknowledges, indeed celebrates, the 'messiness' of existence, as Iris Murdoch puts it, in the context of discovered form. But at the moment, Western man as a cultural community or rather public is simply incapable of responding to the generosity – the humane impulse, having its source in the humility of acknowledged uncertainty, to let Being be – that, on occasion, infuses Shakespeare's stage and his world as stage. (As the editorial quoted above suggests, the ungenerous effort of the 'Enlightenment' to rewrite the 'endings' of Shakespeare's 'inconclusive' plays continues down to the present, though it takes the form of accepting the rewritten version as myth while the plays themselves are locked up in university libraries.) For, to put the point in the familiar language of the historical critical debate, unlike the Western past, when Art (*The Odyssey*, for example) was justifiably a taxonomic model for ordering a brutal and terrifying Nature (existence) or a mode of psychological consolation in the face of its catastrophic power, the Western present, as the 'Pentagon Papers' and the Son Tay 'scenario' and the *Mission Impossible* series and the

Daily News and *Time* suggest, is a time that bears witness to a Nature whose brutal and terrifying forces have been coerced – and domesticated – into a very well-made and therefore very dangerous work of Art.

The Western structure of consciousness is bent, however inadvertently, on unleashing chaos in the name of the order of a well-made world. If this is true, contemporary literature cannot afford the luxury of the symbolist, or, as I prefer to call it, the iconic literary aesthetic nor of its 'postmodern' variants. For ours is no time for psychic flights, for Dedalean 'seraphic embraces,' however enticing they may be. Neither, for that matter, despite its more compelling claim as an authentic possibility, can it afford the luxury of the aesthetic implicit in the concept of the later Heidegger's *Gelassenheit* (that receptivity which might disclose the Being of Not-being and thus the sacramental at-homeness of the not-at-home), the aesthetic of 'letting be' or, perhaps, of letting Being be, that Nathan Scott seems to be recommending in his important recent books, *Negative Capability* and *The Wild Prayer of Longing*. For, in the monolithic well-made world that the positivistic structure of consciousness perceives – and perceiving, creates – it is the Detective who has usurped the place not only of God but of Being too as the abiding presence and, therefore, has first to be confronted.

Our time calls for an existence-Art, one which, by refusing to resolve discords into the satisfying concordances of a *telos*, constitutes an assault against an *artificialized* Nature in behalf of the recovery of its primordial terrors. The most immediate task, therefore, in which the contemporary writer must engage himself – it is, to borrow a phrase ungratefully from Yeats, the most difficult task not impossible – is that of undermining the detective-like expectations of the positivistic mind, of unhoming Western man, by evoking rather than purging pity and terror – anxiety. It must, that is, continue the *iconoclastic* revolution begun in earnest after World War II to dislodge or, to be absolutely accurate, to *dis-occident*, the objectified modern Western man, the weighty, the solid citizen, to drive him out of the fictitious well-made world, not to be gathered into the 'artifice of eternity,' but to be exposed to the existential realm of history, where Nothing is certain. For only in the precincts of our last evasions, where 'dread strikes us dumb,' only in this silent realm of dreadful uncertainty, are we likely to discover the ontological and aesthetic possibilities of generosity.

In this image-breaking enterprise, therefore, the contemporary writer is likely to find his 'tradition,' not in the 'anti-Aristotelian' line that goes back from the Concrete poets to Proust, Joyce, the imagists, Mallarme Gautier, and Pater, but in the 'anti-Aristotelianism' that looks back from Beckett, Ionesco, and the Sartre of *Nausea* and *No Exit* through the Eliot of *Sweeney Agonistes*, some of the surrealists, Kafka, Pirandello, Dostoevsky and the 'loose and baggy monsters' of his countrymen, Dickens, Wycherley, and – with all due respect to the editor of the *Daily News* – the Shakespeare of *King Lear, Measure for Measure*, and the ironically entitled *All's Well that Ends Well*, in which one of the characters says:

They say miracles are past, and we have our philosophical persons to make modern and familiar things supernatural and causeless. Hence it is that we make trifles of terrors, ensconcing ourselves into seeming knowledge when we should submit ourselves to an unknown fear.

14

'POSTmodernISM: A PARACRITICAL
BIBLIOGRAPHY'

Ihab Hassan

I. CHANGE

Dionysus and Cupid are both agents of change. First *The Bacchae*, destruction of the city, then *The Metamorphoses*, mischievous variations of nature. Some might say that change is violence, and violence is continuous whether it be Horror or High Camp. But sly Ovid simply declares:

> My intention is to tell of bodies changed
> To different forms; the gods, who made the changes,
> Will help me – or I hope so – with a poem
> That runs from the world's beginning to our own days.

To our own days, the bodies natural or politic wax and wane, *carpen perpetuam*. Something warms Galatea out of ivory; even rock turns into spiritual forms. Perhaps love is one way we experience change.

How then can we live without love of change?

> Evolution has its enemies, that quiet genius, Owen Barfield, knows. In *Unancestral Voices*, he calls them by name: Lucifer and Ahriman. Most often, they coexist in us. Lucifer preserves the past utterly from dissolution. Ahriman destroys the past utterly for the sake of his own inventions.

From Ihab Hassan (1971) 'POSTmodernISM: A Paracritical Bibliography', *New Literary History*, 3, 1 (Autumn): 5–30.

a. Thus in one kind of history, chronicles of continuity, we deny real change. Even endings become part of a history of endings. From schism to paradigm; from apocalypse to archetype. Warring empires, catastrophe and famine, immense hopes, faraway names – Cheops, Hammurabi, David, Darius, Alcibiades, Hannibal, Caesar – all fall into place on numbered pages.

Yet continuities, 'the glory that was Greece, the grandeur that was Rome,' must prevail in Story, on a certain level of narrative abstraction, obscuring change.

b. Thus, too, in another kind of history, we reinvent continually the past. Without vision, constant revision, the Party chronicles of 1984. Or individually, each man dreams his ancestors to remake himself. The Black Muslim takes on a new name, ignoring the deadly dawn raids, cries of Allah among slave traders, journeys across Africa in Arab chains.

Yet relevances must persist in Story, on a certain level of fictional selectivity, veiling change.

Behind all history, continuous or discrete, abstract or autistic, lurks the struggle of identity with death. Is history often the secret biography of historians? The recorded sense of our own mortality?

Thou, silent form, dost tease us out of thought
As doth eternity: Cold Pastoral!

II. Periods

When will the Modern Period end?

Has ever a period waited so long? Renaissance? Baroque? Neo-Classical? Romantic? Victorian?

When will Modernism cease and what comes thereafter?

What will the twenty-first century call us? and will its voice come from the same side of our graves?

Does Modernism stretch merely to stretch out our lives? Or, ductile, does it give a new sense of time? The end of periodization? The slow arrival of simultaneity?

If change changes ever more rapidly, and the future jolts us now, do men, paradoxically, resist both endings and beginnings?

Childhood is huge and youth golden. Few recover. Critics are no exception. Like everyone else, they recall the literature of their youth brilliantly; they do not think it can ever tarnish.

Let us consider where the great men are
Who will obsess the child when he can read.

So Delmore Schwartz wrote, naming Joyce, Eliot, Pound, Rilke, Yeats, Kafka, Mann. He could have added: Proust, Valéry, Gide, Conrad, Lawrence, Woolf, Faulkner, Hemingway, O'Neill.

A walker in the city of that literature will not forget. Nor will he forgive. How can contemporaries of Mailer, Pinter, or Grass dare breathe in this ancestral air? Yet it is possible that we will all remain Invisible Men until each becomes his own father.

III. INNOVATION

All of us devise cunning ceremonies of ancestor worship. Yet there is a fable for us in the lives of two men: Proteus and Picasso, mentors of shapes.

Masters of possibility, ponder this. They used to say: the kingdom of the dead is larger than any kingdom. But the earth has now exploded. Soon the day may come when there will be more people alive than ever lived.

When the quick are more populous than all the departed, will history reverse itself? End?

We resist the new under the guise of judgment. 'We must have standards.' But standards apply only where they are applicable. This has been the problem with the Tradition of the New (Harold Rosenberg).

Standards are inevitable, and the best of these will create themselves to meet, to *create*, new occasions. Let us, therefore, admit standards. But let us also ask how many critics of literature espouse, even selectively, the new, speak of it with joyous intelligence? Taking few risks, the best known among them wait for men of lesser reputations to clear the way.

Reaction to the new has its own reasons that reason seldom acknowledges. It also has its rhetoric of dismissal.

   a. *The Fad*
- 'It's a passing fashion, frivolous; if we ignore it now, it will quietly go away.'
- This implies permanence as absolute value. It also implies the ability to distinguish between fashion and history without benefit of time or creative intuition. How many judgments of this kind fill the Purgatorio of letters?

   b. *The Old Story*
- 'It's been done before, there's nothing new in it; you can find it in Euripides, Sterne, or Whitman.'
- This implies prior acquaintance, rejection on the basis of unestablished similarity. It also implies that nothing really changes. Therefore, why unsettle things, require a new response?

   c. *The Safe Version*
- 'Yes, it seems new, but in the same genre, I prefer Duchamp; he really did it better.'
- This implies a certain inwardness with the tradition of the avant-garde. The entrance fee has been paid, once and forever. Without seeming in the least Philistine, one can disdain the intrusions of the present.

   d. *The Newspeak of Art*
- 'The avant-garde is just the new academicism.'
- This may imply that art which *seems* conventional can be more genuinely innovative, which is sometimes true. It may also imply mere irritation: the oxymoron as means of discreditation.

About true innovation we can have no easy preconceptions. Prediction is mere extrapolation, the cool whisper of RAND. But prophecy is akin to madness or the creative imagination; its path, seldom linear, breaks, turns, disappears in mutations or quantum jumps.

Therefore, we can not expect the avant-garde of past, present, and future to obey the same logic, assume the same forms. For instance, the new avant-garde need not have a historical consciousness, express recognizable values, or endorse radical politics. It need not shock, surprise, protest.

Footnote

Consult Renato Poggioli, *The Theory of the Avant-Garde* (Cambridge, Mass, 1968).

What the avant-garde probably still needs to do for a time is serve as the agent of change, which is recognizable when still newer change is in progress.

And yet everything I have said here could lend, has lent, itself to serious abuses. The rage for change can be a form of self-hatred or spite.

IV. DISTINCTIONS

The change in Modernism may be called Postmodernism. Looking at the former with later eyes, we begin to discern in it fringe figures closer to us now than the great Moderns who 'will obsess the child' someday.

Thus the classic text of Modernism is Edmund Wilson's *Axel's Castle: A Study in the Imaginative Literature of 1870–1930* (1931). Contents: Symbolism, Yeats, Valéry, Eliot, Proust, Joyce, Stein.

Thus, forty years later, my alternate view, *The Dismemberment of Orpheus: Toward a Postmodern Literature* (1971). Contents: Sade, 'Pata-physics to Surrealism, Hemingway, Kafka, Existentialism to Aliterature, Genet, Beckett.

Erratum: Gertrude Stein should have appeared in the latter work, for she contributed to both Modernism and Postmodernism.

But without a doubt, the crucial text is

```
                        F
          K                          I
        A                          N
        W             e             N
        S                          E
          N                      G
            A
```

If we can arbitrarily state that literary Modernism includes certain works between Jarry's *Ubu Roi* (1896) and Joyce's *Finnegans Wake* (1939), where will we arbitrarily say that Postmodernism begins? A year earlier than the *Wake*? With Sartre's *La nausée* (1938) or Beckett's *Murphy* (1938)? In any case, it includes works by writers as different as Barth, arthelme, eckett, orges, recht, roch, urroughs, utor.

V. CRITICS

The assumptions of Modernism, elaborated by formalist and mythopoeic critics especially, by the intellectual culture of the first half of the century as a whole, still define the dominant perspective on the study of literature.

Exception:
Karl Shapiro's *Beyond Criticism* (1953), *In Defence of Ignorance* (1960), works we acknowledge in a whisper. Why?

In England as in America, the known critics, different as they may seem in age or persuasion, share the broad Modernist view: Blackmur, Brooks, Connolly, Empson, Frye, Howe, Kazin, Kermode, Leavis, Levin, Pritchett, Ransom, Rahv, Richards, Schorer, Tate, Trilling, Warren, Wellek, Wilson, Winters, etc. In saying this, surely I take nothing away from their various distinctions.

No doubt, there are many passages in the writings of these critics – of Leavis, say, or Wilson – which will enlighten minds in every age. Yet is was Herbert Read who possessed the most active sympathy for the avant-garde. His generosity of intuition enabled him to sponsor the new, rarely embracing the trivial. He engaged the Postmodern spirit in his anarchic affinities, in his concern for the prevalence of suffering, in his sensuous apprehension of renewed being. He cried: behold the Child! To him, education through art meant a salutation to Eros. Believing that the imagination serves the purpose of moral good, Read hoped to implicate art into existence so fully that their common substance became as simple, as necessary, as bread and water. This is a sacramental hope, still alive though mute in our midst, which recalls Tolstoy's *What Is Art?* I can hardly think of another critic, younger even by several decades, who might have composed that extraordinary romance, *The Green Child*.

The culture of literary criticism is still ruled by Modernist assumptions. This is particularly true within the academic profession, excepting certain linguistic, structuralist, and hermeneutics schools. But it is also true within the more noisy culture of our media. *The New York Review of Books*, *Time* (the literary sections), and *The New York Times Book Review* share a certain aspiration to wit or liveliness, to intelligence really, concealing distaste for the new. All the more skeptical in periods of excess, the culture of the *logos* insists on old orders in clever or current guises, and, with the means of communication at hand, inhibits and restrains.

Self-Admonition:
Beware of glib condemnations of the media. They are playing a national role as bold, as crucial, as the Supreme Court played in the Fifties. Willful and arbitrary as they may be in their creation of public images – which preempt ourselves – they are still custodians of some collective sanity. Note, too, the rising quality of the very publications you cited.

VI. BIBLIOGRAPHY

Here is a curious chronology of some Postmodern criticism:

1. George Steiner, 'The Retreat from the Word,' *Kenyon Review* XXIII (Spring, 1961). See also his *Language and Silence* (New York, 1967), and *Extraterritorial* (New York, 1971).

2. Ihab Hassan, 'The Dismemberment of Orpheus,' *American Scholar* XXIII (Summer, 1963). See also his *Literature of Silence* (New York, 1967).

3. Hugh Kenner, 'Art in a Closed Field,' in *Learners and Discerners*, ed. Robert Scholes (Charlottesville, Va., 1964). See also his *Samuel Beckett* (New York, 1961, 1968), and *The Counterfeiters* (Bloomington, Indiana, 1968).

4. Leslie Fiedler, 'The New Mutants,' *Partisan Review* XXXII (Fall, 1965). See also his 'The Children's Hour: or, The Return of the Vanishing Longfellow,' in *Liberations*, ed. Ihab Hassan (Middletown, Conn., 1971), and *Collected Essays* (New York, 1971).

5. Susan Sontag, 'The Aesthetics of Silence,' *Aspen*, No. 5 & 6 (1967). See also her *Against Interpretation* (New York, 1966), and *Styles of Radical Will* (New York, 1969).

6. Richard Poirier, 'The Literature of Waste,' *New Republic*, May 20, 1967. See also his 'The Politics of Self-Parody,' *Partisan Review* XXXV (Summer, 1968), and *The Performing Self* (New York, 1971).

7. John Barth, 'The Literature of Exhaustion,' *Atlantic Monthly*, August, 1967. See also his *Lost in the Funhouse* (New York, 1968).

And here are some leitmotifs of that criticism: the literary act in quest and question of itself; self-subversion or self-transcendence of forms; popular mutations; languages of silence.

VII. ReVisions

A revision of Modernism is slowly taking place, and this is another evidence of Postmodernism. In *The Performing Self*, Richard Poirier tries to mediate between these two movements. We need to recall the doctrines of formalist criticism, the canons of classroom and quarterly in the last three decades, to savor such statements:

Three of the great and much used texts of twentieth century criticism, *Moby Dick*, *Ulysses*, *The Waste Land*, are written in mockery of system, written against any effort to harmonize discordant elements, against any mythic or metaphoric scheme ... But while this form of the literary imagination is radical in its essentially parodistic treatment of systems, its radicalism is in the interest of essentially conservative feelings...

*　　*　　*

The most complicated examples of twentieth-century literature, like *Ulysses* and *The Waste Land*, the end of which seems parodied by the end of *Giles* [*Goat-Boy* by Barth], are more than contemptuous of their own formal and stylistic elaborateness.

Certainly some profound philosophic minds of our century have concerned themselves with the disease of verbal systems: Heidegger, Sartre, Wittgenstein. And later writers as different as John Cage, Norman O. Brown, and Elie Wiesel have listened intently to the sounds of silence in art or politics, sex, morality, or religion. In this context, the perceptions of Poirier do not merely display a revisionist will; they strain toward an aesthetic of Postmodernism.

We are still some way from attaining such an aesthetic; nor is it clear that Postmodern art gives high priority to that end. Perhaps we can start by revisioning Modernism as well as revising the pieties we have inherited about it. In *Continuities*, Frank Kermode cautiously attempts that task. A critic of great civility, he discriminates well between types of modernism – what he calls 'palaeo- and neo-modern' corresponds perhaps to Modern and Postmodern – and takes note of the new 'anti-art' which he rightly traces back to Duchamp. But his preference for continuities tempts him to assimilate current to past things. Kermode, for instance, writes: 'Aleatory art is accordingly, for all its novelty, an extension of past art, indeed the hypertrophy of one aspect of that art.' Does not this statement close more possibilities than it opens? There is another perspective of things which Goethe described: 'The most important thing is always the contemporary element, because it is most purely reflected in ourselves, as we are in it.' I think that we will not grasp the cultural experience of our moment if we insist that the new arts are 'marginal developments of older modernism;' or that distinctions between 'art' and 'joke' are crucial to any future aesthetic.

Whether we tend to revalue Modernism in terms of Postmodernism (Poirier) or to reverse that procedure (Kermode), we will end by doing something of both since relations, analogies, enable our thought. New lines emerge from the past because our eyes every morning open anew. In a certain frame of mind, Michelangelo or Rembrandt, Goethe or Hegel, Nietzsche or Rilke, can reveal to us something about Postmodernism, as Erich Heller incidentally shows. Consider this marvelous passage from *The Artist's Journey to the Interior*:

> ... Michelangelo spent the whole of his last working day, six days before his death, trying to finish the Pietà which is known as the 'Pietà Rondanini.' He did not succeed. Perhaps it lies in the nature of stone that he had to leave unfinished what Rembrandt completed in paint: the employment of the material in the service of its own negation. For this sculpture seems to intimate that its maker was in the end determined to use only as much marble as was necessary to show that matter did not matter; what alone mattered was the pure inward spirit.

Here Michelangelo envisions, past any struggle with the obdurate material of existence, a state of consciousness to which we may be tending. Yet can we justifiably call him Postmodern?

Where Modern and Postmodern May Meet: Or, Make Your Own List:
1. Blake, Sade, Lautreamont, Rimbaud, Whitman, etc.
2. daDaDA
3. SURrealism
4. K A F K A
5. *Finnegans Wake*
6. *The Cantos*
7. ? ? ?

VIII. MODERNISM

This is no place to offer a comprehensive definition of Modernism. From Apollinaire and Arp to Valéry, Woolf, and Yeats – I seem to miss the letters X and Z – runs the alphabet of authors who have delivered themselves memorably on the subject; and the weighty work of Richard Ellmann and Charles Feidelson, Jr., *The Tradition of the Modern*, still stands as the best compendium of that 'large spiritual enterprise including philosophic, social, and scientific thought, and aesthetic and literary theories and manifestoes, as well as poems, novels, dramas.'

Expectations of agreement, let alone of definition, seem superlatively naive. This is true among stately and distinguished minds, not only rowdy critical tempers. Here, for instance, is Lionel Trilling, 'On the Modern Element in Modern Literature':

> I can identify it by calling it the disenchantment of our culture with culture itself ... the bitter line of hostility to civilization that runs through it [modern literature] ... I venture to say that the idea of losing oneself up to the point of self-destruction, of surrendering oneself to experience without regard to self-interest or conventional morality, of escaping wholly from the societal bonds, is an 'element' somewhere in the mind of every modern person ...

To this, Harry Levin counters in 'What Was Modernism?':[1]

> Insofar as we are still moderns, I would argue, we are the children of Humanism and the Enlightenment. To identify and isolate the forces of unreason, in a certain sense, has been a triumph for the intellect. In another sense it has reinforced that anti-intellectual undercurrent which, as it comes to the surface, I would prefer to call post-modern.

Yet the controversy of Modernism has still wider scope as Monroe K. Spears, in *Dionysus and the City*, with bias beneath his Apollonian lucidity, shows. Released as energy from the contradictions of history, Modernism makes contradiction its own.

> For my purpose, let Modernism stand for X: a window on human madness, the shield of Perseus against which Medusa glances, the dream of some frowning, scholarly muse. I offer, instead, some rubrics and spaces. Let readers fill them with their own queries or grimaces. We value what we choose.

a. Urbanism: Nature put in doubt, from Baudelaire's '*cité*' to Proust's Paris, Eliot's London, Joyce's Dublin. It is not a question of locale but of presence. The sanatorium of *The Magic Mountain* and the village of *The Castle* are 'cities' still. Exceptions, Faulkner's Yoknapatawpha or Lawrence's Midlands, recognize the City as pervasive threat.

_____

_____

_____

b. Technologism: City and Machine make and remake one another. Centralization, diffusion of the human will. Yet technology does not feature simply as a theme of Modernism; it is also as a form of its artistic struggle. Witness Cubism, Futurism, Dadaism. More subtle *reactions* to technology: Bergsonian time, mythical space, the occult image, the dissociation of sensibility, etc.

_____

_____

_____

c. 'Dehumanization': Ortega y Gasset really means Elitism, Irony, and Abstraction (*The Dehumanization of Art*). Style takes over: let life and the masses fend for themselves. 'Poetry has become the higher algebra of metaphor.' Instead of Vitruvian man, Leonardo's famous image of the human measure, we have Picasso's beings splintered on many planes. Not less human, just another idea of man.

_____

_____

_____

Elitism: Aristocratic or crypto-fascist: Rilke, Proust, Yeats, Eliot, Lawrence, Pound, D'Annunzio, Wyndham Lewis, etc.

Irony: Play, complexity, formalism. The aloofness of art but also sly hints of its radical incompleteness. *Dr. Faustus* and *Confessions of Felix Krull*. The irony of Nonbeing.

Abstraction: Impersonality, sophistical simplicity, reduction and construction, time decomposed or spatialized.
    Mondrian on Reductionism. 'To create pure reality plastically, it is necessary to reduce natural forms to the *constant elements* of form and natural colour to *primary colour*.' Gabo on Constructivism: 'It has revealed a universal law that the elements of a visual art such as lines, colours, shapes, possess their own forces of expression, independent of any association with the external aspects of the world...'

The literary equivalent of these ideas may be 'spatial time.' (See Joseph Frank, 'Spatial Form in Modern Literature,' *The Widening Gyre*.)

'Dehumanization' and the Nonhuman: There is more to it than 'another idea of man'; there is also a revulsion against the human, or a renewal of the sense of the superhuman. Rilke's 'Angels.' Lawrence's 'Fish':

> And my heart accused itself
> Thinking: I am not the measure of creation
> This is beyond me, this fish.
> His God stands outside my God.

d. Primitivism: The archetypes behind abstraction, behind civilization. An African mask, a beast slouching toward Bethlehem. Structure as ritual or myth, metaphors from the collective dream of mankind. Cunning palimpsests of time, ironic palingenesis of literary forms. Also Dionysus and the violent return of the repressed.

_____

_____

_____

e. Eroticism: All literature is erotic but Modernist sex scratches the skin from within. It is not merely the liberation of the libido, a new language of anger or desire; love now becomes an intimate of disease: sado-masochism, solipsism, nihilism, anomie. Consciousness seeks desperately to discharge itself in the world. A new and darker stage in the struggle between Eros and Thanatos. (See Lionel Trilling, 'The Fate of Pleasure.')

_____

_____

_____

f. Antinomianism: Beyond law, dwelling in paradox. Also discontinuity, alienation, *non serviam!* The pride of art, of the self, defining the conditions of its own grace. Iconoclasm, schism, excess. Beyond antinomianism, even, toward apocalypse. Therefore, decadence and renovation. (See Nathan A. Scott, Jr., *The Broken Center*.)

_____

_____

_____

g. Experimentalism: Innovation, dissociation, the brilliance of change in all its aesthetic shapes. New languages, new concepts of order. Also, the Word beginning to put its miracle to question in the midst of a miracle. Poem, novel, or play henceforth can never really bear the same name.

—————————————————————————————
—————————————————————————————
—————————————————————————————

In those seven rubrics, I seek not so much to define Modernism as to carry certain elements which I consider crucial, carry them forward toward Post-modernism.

IX. THE UNIMAGINABLE

The unimaginable lies somewhere between the Kingdom of Complacence and the Sea of Hysteria. It balks all geographies; bilks the spirit of the traveler who passes unwittingly through its spaceless realm; it boggles time. Yet anyone who can return from it to tell his tale may also know how to spell the destiny of man.

I know the near-infinite resources of man, and that his imagination may still serve as the teleological organ of his evolution. Yet I am possessed by the feeling that in the next few decades, certainly within half a century, the earth and all that inhabits it may be wholly other, perhaps ravaged, perhaps on the way to some strange utopia indistinguishable from nightmare. I have no language to articulate this feeling with conviction, nor imagination to conceive this special destiny. To live from hour to hour seems as maudlin as to invoke Last Things. In this feeling I find everyday that I am not alone.

The litany of our disasters is all too familiar, and we recite it in the name of that unholy trinity, Population, Pollution, Power (read genocide), hoping to appease our furies, turn our fate inside out. But soon our minds lull themselves to sleep again on this song of abstractions, and a few freak out. The deathly dreariness of politics brings us ever closer to death. Neither is the alteration of human consciousness at hand. And the great promise of technology – which? Fuller's? Skinner's? Dr. No's? Engineers of liberation or of control? – the promise is conditional on everything that we are, in this our ambiguous state.

Truly, we dwell happily in the Unimaginable. We also dwell at our task: Literature. I could learn to do pushups in a prison cell, but I can not bring myself to 'study literature' as if the earth were still in the orbit of our imagination. I hope this is Hope.

X. POSTMODERNISM

Postmodernism may be a response, direct or oblique, to the Unimaginable which Modernism glimpsed only in its most prophetic moments. Certainly it is not the Dehumanization of the Arts that concerns us now; it is rather the Denaturalization of the Planet and the End of Man. We are, I believe, inhabitants of another Time and another Space, and we no longer know what response is adequate to our reality. In a sense, we have all learned to become minimalists – of that time and space we can call our own – though the globe has become our village. This is why it seems bootless to compare Modern with Postmodern artists, range 'masters' against 'epigones.' The latter are closer to 'zero in the bone,' to silence or exhaustion, and the best of them brilliantly display the resources of the void. Thus the verbal omnipotence of Joyce yields to the impotence of Beckett, heir and peer, no less genuine, only more austere. Yet moving into the void, these artists also pass to the other side of silence, and discover the sacrament of plenum. The consummation of their art is a work which, though art still, pretends to abolish itself (Beckett, Tinguely, Robert Morris, Ad Reinhardt) or else to become indistinguishable from life (Cage, Rauschenberg, the Man Within Mailer's Fiction). Duchamp coolly pointed the way.

Nihilism is a word we often use, when we use it unhistorically, to designate values we dislike. It is applied to the children of Marcel Duchamp.

When John Cage, in 'HPSCHD' for instance, insists on Quantity rather than Quality, he does not surrender to nihilism – far, far from it – he requires:
- affluence and permission of being, generosity
- discovery in multitude, confusion of prior judgment
- mutation of perception, of consciousness, through randomness and diversity

Cage knows how to praise Duchamp: 'The rest of them were artists. Duchamp collects dust.'

I have not defined Modernism; I can define Postmodernism less; and the parallels and contrasts between these movements are least obvious to me. No doubt, the more we ponder, the more we will need to qualify all we say.[2] Perhaps elisions may serve to qualify these notes.

Modernist Rubrics	*Postmodernist Notes*
a. Urbanism	– – The City and also the Global Village (McLuhan) and Spaceship Earth (Fuller). The City as Cosmos.
	– – Meanwhile, the world breaks up into untold blocs, nations, tribes, clans, parties, languages, sects. Anarchy and fragmentation everywhere. A new diversity or prelude to world totalitarianism? Or to world unification?
	– – Nature recovered partly in ecological activism, the green revolution, urban renewal, etc.
	– – Meanwhile, Dionysus has entered the City: prison riots, urban crime, pornography, etc.
b. Technologism	– – Runaway technology, from genetic engineering and thought control to the conquest of space.
	– – All the physical materials of the arts changed. New media, new art forms.
	– – Art following the trend of ephemeralization. Also, boundless dispersal by media. The sensuous object disappearing into a concept?
	– – The computer as substitute consciousness or as extension of consciousness? Will it prove tautological, increased reliance on prior orders? Or will it help to create novel forms?

– – Human needs soon to be altered, perhaps on the most basic level, and the end of art? Hence sporadic artistic reactions against Technologism.

c. 'Dehumanization'   – – Anti-elitism, anti-authoritarianism. Diffusion of the ego. Participation. Art becomes communal, optional, gratuitous, or anarchic.

– – Irony becomes radical, self-consuming play. Black canvas or blank page. Silence. Also comedy of the absurd, black humor, insane parody and slapstick, Camp. (See Nathan A. Scott, Jr., *Negative Capability*.)

– – Abstraction taken to the limit and coming back as New Concreteness: the found object, the signed Brillo box or soup can, the non-fiction novel, the novel as history. The range from Concept Art (abstract) to Environmental Art (concrete).

– – Warhol: 'I want to be a machine;' Burroughs simulating insect life. From infrahumanism to posthumanism, beyond man and into the cosmos. Sci-fi. To love life and to love man are no longer the same.

'Dehumanization,' both in Modernism and Postmodernism, essentially means the end of the old Realism. Increasingly, Illusionism takes its place, not only in art but also in life. The media contribute egregiously to this process in Postmodern society. In *Act and the Actor Making the Self*, Harold Rosenberg says: 'History has been turned inside out; writing takes place in advance of its occurrence, and every statesman is an author in embryo.' Thus the Illusionism of politics matches that of Pop Art or Neo-Realism.

The end of the old Realism also affects the sense of the Self. Thus 'Dehumanization,' both in Modernism and Postmodernism, implies revision of the Self evidenced:

In Modernism – by doctrines of impersonality, the masks of Yeats, the tradition of Eliot, the dramatic objectivity of Joyce; or by the opposite, the stream of consciousness of Joyce, the allotropic ego of Lawrence. (See Robert Langbaum, *The Modern Tradition*, pp. 164–184.)

In Postmodernism – by phenomenology (Husserl, Sartre, Merleau-Ponty), Beckett's fiction of consciousness, varieties of the *nouveau roman* (Sarraute, Butor, Robbe-Grillet), the linguistic novel of *Tel Quel* (Sollers, Thibaudeau). (See Vivian Mercier, *The New Novel*, pp. 3–42.)

d. Primitivism	– – Away from the mythic, toward the existential. Beat and Hip. Energy and spontaneity of the White Negro (Mailer).
	– – The post-existential ethos, psychedelics (Leary), the Dionysian ego (Brown), Pranksters (Kesey), Hell's Angels, madness (Laing).
	– – The Hippie movement. Woodstock, rock music and poetry, communes. The culture of *The Whole Earth Catalogue*.
	– – The primitive Jesus.
e. Eroticism	– – Beyond the trial of *Lady Chatterley's Lover*. The repeal of censorship. Grove Press and the *Evergreen Review*.
	– – The new sexuality, from Reichian orgasm to Brownian polymorphous perversity and Esalen body consciousness.
	– – The homosexual novel (Burroughs, Vidal, Selby, Rechy, etc.). And the lesbian?

– – Camp and comic pornography.

f. Antinomianism   – – The Counter Cultures, political and otherwise. Free Speech Movement, S.D.S., Weathermen, Church Militants, Women's Lib, J.D.L., Black, Red, and Chicano Power, etc. Rebellion and Reaction! Not only aesthetic but also actual (guerilla) attacks on reason and history, science and society.

– – Beyond alienation from the whole culture, acceptance of discreteness and discontinuity. Evolution of radical empiricism in art as in politics or morality.

– – Counter Western 'ways' or metaphysics, Zen, Buddhism, Hinduism. But also Western mysticism, transcendentalism, witchcraft, the occult.

– – The widespread cult of apocalyptism, less as renovation than as destruction.

g. Experimentalism   – – Open, discontinuous, improvisational, indeterminate, or aleatory structures. Absurdist and neo-surrealist modes. But also reductive, minimalist forms. In general, anti-formalism. (See Calvin Tompkins, *The Bride and the Bachelor*.)

– – Simultaneism. Now. The impermanence of art (sculpture made of dry ice or a hole in Central Park filled with earth), the transcience of man. Absurd time.

– – Play, humor, happening, farce. (See 'Irony' above.)

– – Intermedia, the fusion of forms, the confusion of realms. An end to traditional aesthetics focused on the 'beauty' or 'uniqueness' of the art work?

Morse Peckham argues, in *Man's Rage for Chaos*, 'that art is a disjunctive category, established by convention, and that art is not a category of perceptual fields, but of roleplaying.' And in *The Art of Time*, Kirby White says: 'Traditional aesthetics asks a particular hermetic attitude or state of mind that concentrates on the sensory perception of the work ... [Postmodern] aesthetics makes use of no special attitude or set, and art is viewed just as anything else in life.'

Is this why Postmodern art, viewed in a Modernist perspective, creates more anxiety than it appeases?

XI. ALTERNATIVES

The reader, no doubt, will want to judge for himself how much Modernism permeates the present and how much the latter contains elements of a new reality. The judgment is not always made rationally; self-love and the fear of dissolution may enter into it as much as the conflict of literary generations. Yet it is already possible to note that whereas Modernism created its own forms of Authority, precisely because the center no longer held, Postmodernism has tended toward Anarchy, in deeper complicity with things falling apart. The ceremonies of Yeats' own work, indeed of his life, are to the point.

Speculating further, we may say that the Authority of Modernism – artistic, cultural, personal – rests on intense, elitist, self-generated orders in times of crisis, of which the Hemingway Code is perhaps the starkest exemplar, and Eliot's Tradition or Yeats' Mythology is a more devious kind. Such elitist orders, perhaps the last of the world's Eleusinean mysteries, may no longer have a place amongst us, threatened as we are, at the same instant, by extermination and totalitarianism.

Yet is the Anarchy of Postmodernism a deeper response, somehow more inward with our destiny? Though my sympathies are in the present, I can not believe this to be so. True, there is enhancement of life in certain anarchies of the spirit, in humor and play, in love released and freedom of the imagination to overreach itself, in a cosmic consciousness of variousness as of unity. I recognize these as values intended by Postmodern art, and see the latter as closer, not only in time but even more in tenor, to the transformation of hope itself. Still, I wonder if any art can help to engender the motives we must now acquire; or if we can long continue to value an art that fails us in such endeavor. These are not assertions; they are open questions. It is time for everyone to open up alternatives to the Unimaginable.

Who knows but that the only alternative man *does* possess is one to his 'human' consciousness?

Notes

1. More accurately, the quotation appears in a note preceding the essay. See Harry Levin, *Refractions* (New York, 1966), pp. 271–73.
2. New journals are now founded for the purpose of exploring Postmodernism. See, for instance, *Boundary 2*, Binghamton, New York.

15

'THE MYTH OF THE POSTMODERN BREAKTHROUGH'

Gerald Graff

The postmodern tendency in literature and literary criticism has been characterized as a 'breakthrough,' a significant reversal of the dominant literary and sociocultural directions of the last two centuries. Literary critics such as Leslie Fiedler, Susan Sontag, George Steiner, Richard Poirier, and Ihab Hassan have written about this reversal, differing in their assessments of its implications but generally agreeing in their descriptions of what is taking place. What is taking place, these critics suggest, is the death of our traditional Western concept of art and literature, a concept which defined 'high culture' as our most valuable repository of moral and spiritual wisdom. [...]

I want here to raise some critical questions about the postmodern breakthrough in the arts and about the larger implications claimed for it in culture and society. I want in particular to challenge the standard description of postmodernism as an overturning of romantic and modernist traditions. To characterize postmodernism as a 'breakthrough' – a cant term of our day – is to place a greater distance between current writers and their predecessors than is, I think, justified. There are distinctions to be drawn, of course, and both here and in the final chapter of this book I shall try to draw them. But this chapter argues that postmodernism should be seen not as a break with romantic and modernist assumptions but rather as a logical culmination of the premises of these earlier movements, premises not always clearly defined in discussions of these issues. [...]

From Gerald Graff (1979) 'The Myth of the Postmodern Breakthrough', in *Literature Against Itself: Literary Ideas in Modern Society*. Chicago, IL and London: University of Chicago Press.

[...] Romantic and modernist writing expressed a faith in the constitutive power of the imagination, a confidence in the ability of literature to impose order, value, and meaning on the chaos and fragmentation of industrial society. This faith seemed to have lapsed after World War II. Literature increasingly adopted an ironic view of its traditional pretensions to truth, high seriousness, and the profundity of 'meaning.' Furthermore, literature of the postwar period has seemed to have a different relation to criticism than that of the classic modernists. Eliot, Faulkner, Joyce, and their imitators sometimes seemed to be deliberately providing occasions for the complex critical explications of the New Critics. In contrast, much of the literature of the last several decades has been marked by the desire to remain invulnerable to critical analysis.

In an essay that asks the question, 'What Was Modernism?' Harry Levin identifies the 'ultimate quality' pervading the work of the moderns as 'its uncompromising intellectuality.'[1] The conventions of postmodern art systematically invert this modernist intellectuality by parodying its respect for truth and significance. In Donald Barthelme's anti-novel, *Snow White*, a questionnaire poses for the reader such mock questions as, '9. Has the work, for you, a metaphysical dimension? Yes ( ) No ( ) 10. What is it (twenty-five words or less)?'[2] Alain Robbe-Grillet produces and campaigns for a type of fiction in which 'obviousness, transparency preclude the existence of *higher worlds*, of any transcendence.'[3] Susan Sontag denounces the interpretation of works of art on the grounds that 'to interpret is to impoverish, to deplete the world – in order to set up a shadow world of "meanings." '[4] Leslie Fiedler, writing on modern poetry, characterizes one of its chief tendencies as a 'flight from the platitude of meaning.'[5] As Jacob Brackman describes this attitude in *The Put-On*, 'we are supposed to have learned by now that one does not ask what art means.'[6] And, as Brackman shows, this deliberate avoidance of interpretability has moved from the arts into styles of personal behavior. It appears that the term 'meaning' itself, as applied not only to art but to more general experience, has joined 'truth' and 'reality' in the class of words which can no longer be written unless apologized for by inverted commas.

Thus it is tempting to agree with Leslie Fiedler's conclusion that 'the Culture Religion of Modernism' is now dead.[7] The most advanced art and criticism of the last twenty years seem to have abandoned the modernist respect for artistic meaning. The religion of art has been 'demythologized.' A number of considerations, however, render this statement of the case misleading. Examined more closely, both the modernist faith in literary meanings and the postmodern repudiation of these meanings prove to be highly ambivalent attitudes, much closer to one another than may at first appear. The equation of modernism with 'uncompromising intellectuality' overlooks how much of this intellectuality devoted itself to calling its own authority into question.

[...]

FROM DEIFICATION TO DEMYSTIFICATION

Having been dispossessed of a rational world view, literature must be conceived as an 'organism' that somehow, in a fashion infinitely described but never successfully explained by several generations of literary theorists, 'contains' its meaning immanently within its concrete symbols or processes. Esthetic theory embarks on the attempt to explain how the concrete artistic structure can *mean* even though the structure does not rely on the now-discredited discursive, conceptual, referential forms of thought and expression. Though this appeal to nonconceptual models is supposed to help heal the divisions within culture, its actual tendency is to reinforce the isolation of art and its withdrawal from public accessibility.

The definition of literature as a nondiscursive, nonconceptual mode of communication has been proposed in a great variety of forms, closed, open, and mixed. It is a continuous impulse from the beginnings of romanticism to the latest postmodernisms. From Coleridge and his German predecessors to recent formalists, there runs a common theory of art as a *symbol* that contains or 'presents' its meanings intransitively, by contrast with discursive *signs* or concepts, which make statements 'about' external states of affairs. Despite mounting attacks, the theory shows no sign of losing confidence even today. Thus a recent critic, Leonard B. Meyer, can write with assurance: 'There is a profound and basic difference between scientific theories, which are *propositional*, and works of art, which are *presentational*'[8] – if it were necessary to choose between the propositional and the presentational, as if a work of art could not be both at the same time.

The denial of the propositional nature of literature makes it difficult for literary theory to make a place – as most theorists still wish to do – for a defensible notion of artistic *significance*. Rejecting the idea that literature is propositional, the critic is forced into a dilemma: on the one hand, he tries to elaborate a description of literary meaning that does not appeal to propositions, and plunges into obscurity and mystification; on the other hand, he tries to clarify that description by bringing it into line with our familiar notions of meaning and contradicts himself, since those notions are propositional. Furthermore, every time the critic tries to speak of the meaning or 'theme' or 'vision' of a particular, concrete work, he can hardly help sliding into a propositional conception of literature. Despite these difficulties, the critical refusal to see literature as propositional remains strong. In the main tradition of modern esthetics – which includes such figures as Croce, Richards, Dewey, Cassirer, Langer, Eliot, Jung, Frye, Jakobson, and Ingarden – literature and art deal with experience only as myth, psychology, or language, not as an object of conceptual understanding. A number of these theorists define art as the experiential complement of understanding without its content – as does Langer in her theory of art as 'virtual experience' or Eliot in his view that poetry does not assert beliefs but dramatizes 'what it feels like' to have them – again as if experience and ideas 'about' experience were incompatible.[9] The intention of these theorists is not to make art irrelevant to life; art in its own ways allegedly gives order and form to life. But this artistic ordering is not supposed to offer itself as understanding, and it does not solicit verification by anything external to the work or to the autonomous consciousness out of which the work arose.

It often follows that the *content* of a literary work, assuming it is even valid to attribute content to literary works, has no interest in itself but serves merely as a pretext, the 'bit of nice meat,' according to Eliot, that the burglar holds out to the house dog while going about his real work.[10] Consequently, the reader need 'believe' only provisionally, if at all, in the truth of the picture of reality presented by the work. Behind this thesis that belief is an inappropriate frame of mind in which to approach literature is the feeling that either there are no beliefs one can legitimately risk affirming, or that the belief-affirming modes of thought and expression have been hopelessly discredited. Often these theorists claim that art is a higher form of 'knowledge,' but since this knowledge is not conceptual knowledge 'about' the world, since it does not invite belief, its credentials are not clear. The various theories of art as nonconceptual knowledge fail to provide art with any stronger cognitive function than was provided by I. A. Richards's logical positivist theory of art as pseudo-statement.[11]

From the position that the literary symbol means no more than itself (autotelic art), it is only a step to the position that literature has *no* meaning (anti-teleological art), or that its meaning is totally indeterminate and 'open' to interpretation. The theory of the nondiscursive symbol, though capable of supporting Coleridge's affirmation of literature's transcendent truth, is equally capable of supporting the bleakest, most naturalistic denial of transcendence. Consider a brief illustration. Emerson, in a famous passage in 'Self-Reliance,' says that 'these roses under my window make no reference to former roses or to better ones; they are for what they are; they exist with God to-day. There is no time to them. There is simply the rose.'[12] Emerson's rose is a Coleridgean symbol – self-sufficient, complete in itself, untranslatable, yet an embodiment of the immanence of God in nature. Though the feeling-tone of Emerson's statement is far different, the underlying logic is the same as that of the following statement by Robbe-Grillet: 'the world is neither significant nor absurd. It *is* quite simply.'[13] Both Emerson and Robbe-Grillet are concerned with the intransitivity of natural objects, but the analogy with artistic objects is obvious. Neither nature nor art means anything apart from itself – they simply *are*. Behind Emerson's rose there is the Over-Soul, whereas behind Robbe-Grillet's inexpressive objects there are only hysteria and paranoia – the demystified postmodern equivalent of the Over-Soul. Emerson's object is intransitive because it means everything, Robbe-Grillet's because it means nothing. But whether it is affirmatively or negatively expressed, the esthetic of self-contained meaning is symptomatic of an intellectual situation in which intelligibility is being emptied from the world, so that objects and artworks appear only in their simple presence. The logic underlying the romantic glorification of literature as an autonomous lawgiver is identical to that underlying the postmodern repudiation of literature and its pretensions to interpret life.

The theorists who have adopted these positions rarely suppose that they are draining literature of meaning or cutting it off from life. Charged with doing so, they offer disclaimers: 'We are not draining literature of meaning but trying to get at the special character of that meaning; we don't mean to sever literature from life, only to redefine this extremely complex relation.' Such disclaimers are largely rhetorical, however, since the critics do not make clear how it is possible to avoid the apparent implications of what they say. The fact that we do not *want* a certain implication to follow from our statements does not in itself prevent it from following. If a critic asserts that literature is an autonomous creation that is not obliged to conform to any preestablished laws, he does not disarm the charge of irresponsibility by adding, 'of course I do not mean to suggest that "anything goes" in literature and that writers are totally free to violate fundamental dictates of common sense.' For one has to answer, 'Why *shouldn't* anything go, if your original proposition is taken seriously?'

[...]

A logical evolution, then, connects the romantic and postromantic cult of the creative self to the cult of the disintegrated, disseminated, disperesed self and of the decentered, undecidable, indeterminate text. Today's cultural battlefield is polarized between traditional humanists on one side and nihilistic 'schismatics,' in Frank Kermode's term, on the other.[14] Yet the humanists who celebrate the arts as the sovereign orderer of experience often seem nihilistic in their view of life. This nihilism is particularly overt in a critic like Northrop Frye, who praises Oscar Wilde for the view that 'as life has no shape and literature has, literature is throwing away its one distinctive quality when it tries to imitate life.'[15] How Frye came to know with such assurance that 'life has no shape' is not clear, but if he is right one wonders what difference it should make if literature throws away its distinctive quality, or how literature – or anything – can have a distinctive quality. But those like Frye and Kermode, who defend humanism as a necessary fiction that somehow permits us to make sense of a reality known in advance to be senseless, share the same presuppositions as schismatics such as Artaud, Foucault, Derrida, Barthes, and Robbe-Grillet. The schismatics conclude, with better logic, that, if humanism is indeed a fiction, we ought to quit this pretense that it can be taken seriously.

FROM MODERN TO POSTMODERN

If postmodern literature extends rather than overturns the premises of romanticism and modernism, we should expect this relation to be visible not only in the themes of literature but in its forms. Consider as an example the following passage from Barthelme's *Snow White*:

> 'Try to be a man about whom nothing is known,' our father said, when we
> were young. Our father said several other interesting things, but we have
> forgotten what they were Our father was a man about whom nothing was
> known. Nothing is known about him still. He gave us the recipes. He was
> not very interesting. A tree is more interesting. A suitcase is more
> interesting. A canned good is more interesting.[16]

Barthelme here parodies Henry James's advice to the aspiring fiction writer:
'Try to be one of the people on whom nothing is lost.'[17] Barthelme inverts the
assumptions about character, psychology, and the authority of the artist upon
which James, the father of the modernist 'recipe' for the novel, had depended. In
postmodern fiction, character, like external reality, is something 'about which
nothing is known,' lacking in plausible motive or discoverable depth. Whereas
James, had stressed the importance of artistic selection, defining the chief
obligation of the novelist as the obligation to be 'interesting,' Barthelme
operates by a law of equivalence according to which nothing is intrinsically
more interesting than anything else.[18] Such a law destroys the determinacy of
artistic selection and elevates canned goods to equal status with human moral
choice as artistic subject matter. In place of Jamesian dedication to the craft of
fiction, Barthelme adopts an irreverent stance toward his work, conceding the
arbitrary and artificial nature of his creation. Retracting any Jamesian claim to
deal seriously with the world, Barthelme's work offers – for wholly different
reasons – the sort of confession of the merely 'make-believe' status of fiction to
which James objected in Thackeray and Trollope. The novel's inability to
transcend the solipsism of subjectivity and language becomes the novel's chief
subject and the principle of its form.

It would seem that the Jamesian esthetic could not be stood on its head more
completely. But only a surface consideration of the comparison can be content
to leave it at that. James himself, in both his fiction and his criticism, contributed to the skepticism which Barthelme turns against him. T. S. Eliot wrote
that Paul Valéry was 'much too sceptical to believe even in art.'[19] The remark
applies, in greater or lesser degree, to all the great modernist worshippers at the
shrine of high art, not excluding James. Consider James's view of the infinite
elusiveness of experience, which is 'never limited, and never complete,'[20] an
elusiveness he dramatized in the interminable ambiguities of his later fiction.
James combined an intense dedication to unraveling the secrets of motive and
action with an acutely developed sense of the ultimate impossibility of such an
enterprise.

Perceiving that the modernist's seriousness rests on admittedly arbitrary
foundations, the postmodern writer treats this seriousness as an object of
parody. Whereas modernists turned to art defined as the imposition of human
order upon inhuman chaos – as an antidote for what Eliot called the 'immense
panorama of futility and anarchy which is contemporary history' – postmodernists conclude that, under such conceptions of art and history, art

provides no more consolation than any other discredited cultural institution. Postmodernism signifies that the nightmare of history, as modernist esthetic and philosophical traditions have defined history, has overtaken modernism itself.[21] If history lacks value, pattern, and rationally intelligible meaning, then no exertions of the shaping, ordering imagination can be anything but a refuge from truth. Alienation from significant external reality, from *all* reality, becomes an inescapable condition.

THE TWO POSTMODERNISMS

In carrying the logic of modernism to its extreme limits, postmodern literature poses in an especially acute fashion the critical problem raised by all experimental art: does this art represent a criticism of the distorted aspects of modern life or a mere addition to it? Georg Lukács has argued persuasively that the successful presentation of distortion as such presupposes the existence of an undistorted norm. 'Literature,' he writes, 'must have a concept of the normal if it is to "place" distortion correctly, that is to say, to see it *as* distortion.'[22] If life were really a solipsistic madness, we should have no means of knowing this fact or representing it. But once the concept of the normal is rejected as a vestige of an outmoded metaphysics or patronized as a myth, the concepts of 'distortion' and 'madness' lose their meanings. This observation provides a basis for some necessary distinctions between tendencies in postmodern writing.

In Jorge Luis Borges's stories, for example, techniques of reflexiveness and self-parody suggest a universe in which human consciousness is incapable of transcending its own mythologies. This condition of imprisonment, however, though seen from the 'inside,' is presented from a tragic or tragicomic point of view that forces us to see it *as* a problem. The stories generate a pathos at the absence of a transcendent order of meanings. As Borges's narrator in 'The Library of babel' declares, 'Let heaven exist, though my place be in hell. Let me be outraged and annihilated, but for one instant, in one being, let Your enormous Library be justified.'[23] The library contains all possible books and all possible interpretations of experience but none which can claim authority over the others; therefore, it cannot be 'justified.' Nevertheless, Borges affirms the indispensable nature of justification. As in such earlier writers as Kafka and Céline, the memory of a significant external reality that would justify human experience persists in the writer's consciousness and serves as his measure of the distorted, indeterminate world he depicts. Borges's kind of postmodern writing, even in presenting solipsistic distortion as the only possible perspective, nevertheless presents this distortion *as* distortion – that is, it implicitly affirms a concept of the normal, if only as a concept which has been tragically lost. The comic force of characters like 'Funes the Memorious' and of solipsistic worlds such as those of 'Tlön, Uqbar, Orbis Tertius' lies in the crucial fact that Borges, for all his imaginative sympathy, is *not* Funes, is not an inhabitant of Tlön, and is thus able to view the unreality of their worlds as a predicament. His work retains a link with traditional classical humanism by virtue of its sense of the pathos of this humanism's demise. The critical power of absence remains intact, giving Borges a perspective for judging the unreality of the present. His work affirms the sense of reality in a negative way by dramatizing its absence as a deprivation.

Whatever tendency toward subjectivism these Borges works may contain is further counteracted by their ability to suggest the historical and social causes of this loss of objective reality. Borges invites us to see the solipsistic plight of his characters as a consequence of the relativistic thrust of modern philosophy and modern politics. If reality has yielded to the myth-making of Tlön, as he suggests it has, 'the truth is that it longed to yield.' The mythologies of 'dialectical materialism, anti-Semitism, Nazism' were sufficient 'to entrance the minds of men.'[24] The loss of reality is made intelligible to the reader as an aspect of a social and historical evolution. At its best, the contemporary wave of self-reflexive fiction is not quite so totally self-reflexive as it is taken to be, since its very reflexivity implies a 'realistic' comment on the historical crisis which brought it about. Where such a comment is made, the conventions of anti-realism subserve a higher realism. Often, however, this fiction fails to make its reflexivity intelligible as a consequence of any recognizable cause. Estrangement from reality and meaning becomes detached from the consciousness of its causes – as in the more tediously claustrophobic and mannered experiments of Barthelme and the later Barth. Even in these works, however, the loss of reality and meaning is seen as a distortion of the human condition.

Far different is the attitude expressed in the more celebratory forms of postmodernism. Here there is scarcely any memory of an objective order of values in the past and no regret over its disappearance in the present. Concepts like 'significant external reality' and 'the human condition' figure only as symbols of the arbitrary authority and predetermination of a repressive past, and their disappearance is viewed as liberation. Dissolution of ego boundaries, seen in tragic postmodern works like *Invitation to a Beheading* as a terrifying disintegration of identity, is viewed as a bracing form of consciousness-expansion and a prelude to growth. Both art and the world, according to Susan Sontag, simply *are*. 'Both need no justification; nor could they possibly have any.'[25] The obsessive quest for justification which characterizes Borges's protagonists is thus regarded, if it is noticed at all, as a mere survival of outmoded thinking.

It is symptomatic of the critical climate that Borges has been widely read as a celebrant of apocalyptic unreality. Borges's current celebrity is predicated to a large degree on a view that sees him as a pure fabulator revelling in the happy indistinguishability of truth and fiction. Richard Poirier, for example, urges us in reading Borges to get rid of 'irrelevant distinctions between art and life, fiction and reality.'[26] But if distinctions between fiction and reality were really irrelevant, Borges's work would be pointless.

But then, in a world which simply *is*, pointlessness is truth. There is no ground for posing the question of justification as a question. We can no longer even speak of 'alienation' or 'loss' of perspective, for there never was anything to be alienated from, never any normative perspective to be lost. The realistic perspective that gives shape and point to works of tragicomic postmodernism, permitting them to present distortion *as* distortion, gives way to a celebration of *energy* – the vitalism of a world that cannot be understood or controlled. We find this celebration of energy in the poetry of the Beats, the 'Projective' poets, and other poetic continuators of the nativist line of Whitman, Williams, and Pound, in the short-lived vogue of the Living Theater, happenings, and pop art, and in a variety of artistic and musical experiments with randomness and dissonance. It is also an aspect of the writing of Mailer, Burroughs, and Pynchon, where despite the suggestion of a critical or satiric point of view, the style expresses a facile excitement with the dynamisms of technological process. Richard Poirier states the rationale for this worship of energy, making energy and literature synonymous: 'Writing is a form of energy not accountable to the orderings anyone makes of it and specifically not accountable to the liberal humanitarian values most readers want to find there.'[27] Literature, in short, is closer to a physical force than to an understanding or 'criticism of life,' both of which are tame and bourgeois. This celebration of energy frequently seems to hover somewhere between revolutionary politics and sophisticated acquiescence to the agreeably meaningless surfaces of mass culture.

[...]

The postmodern temper has carried the skepticism and antirealism of modern literary culture to an extreme beyond which it would be difficult to go. Though it looks back mockingly on the modernist tradition and professes to have got beyond it, postmodern literature remains tied to that tradition and unable to break with it. The very concepts through which modernism is demystified derive from modernism itself. The loss of significant external reality, its displacement by myth-making, the domestication and normalization of alienation – these conditions constitute a common point of departure for the writing of our period. Though for some of this writing they remain conditions to be somehow resisted, a great deal of it finds them an occasion for acquiescence and even celebration. Unable to imagine an alternative to a world that has for so long seemed unreal, we have begun to resign ourselves to this kind of world and to learn how to redescribe this resignation as a form of heroism. [...]

NOTES

1. Harry Levin, 'What Was Modernism?' *Refractions: Essays in Comparative Literature* (New York: Oxford University Press, 1966), 292.
2. Donald Barthelme, *Snow White* (New York: Bantam Books, 1968), 82.
3. Alain Robbe-Grillet, *For a New Novel: Essays on Fiction*, trans. R. Howard (New York: Grove Press, 1965), 87. Unless indicated, italics in quotations are not added.
4. Susan Sontag, *Against Interpretation* (New York: Delta Books, 1967), 7.
5. Leslie Fiedler, *Waiting for the End* (New York: Stein and Day, 1964), 227.
6. Jacob Brackman, *The Put-On: Modern Fooling and Modern Mistrust* (Chicago: Regnery, 1971), 68.

7. Fiedler, *Cross the Border – Close the Gap* (New York: Stein and Day, 1972), 64.
8. Leonard B. Meyer, 'Concerning the Sciences, the Arts, AND the Humanities,' *Critical Inquiry*, 1, no. 1 (September 1974), 166.
9. T. S. Eliot, 'The Social Function of Poetry,' in *Critiques and Essays in Criticism, 1920–1948*, ed. R. W. B. Stallman (New York: Ronald Press Co., 1949), 107; Susanne K. Langer, *Feeling and Form* (New York: Charles Scribner's Sons, 1953), 234.
10. Eliot, *The Use of Poetry and the Use of Criticism* (London: Faber and Faber, 1933), 151.
11. Once again, further documentation can be found in Gerald Graff, *Poetic Statement and Critical Dogma* (Chicago: University of Chicago Press, 1980).
12. R. W. Emerson, 'Self-Reliance,' *Selected Writings* (New York: Modern Library, 1950), 157.
13. Robbe-Grillet, *For a New Novel*, 19.
14. Frank Kermode, *The Sense of an Ending* (New York: Oxford University Press, 1965), 103. [. . .] Kermode himself seems to have become a 'schismatic' in his recent writings on textual interpretation.
15. Northrop Frye, *The Secular Scripture: A Study in the Structure of Romance* (Cambridge: Harvard University Press, 1976), 45–46.
16. Barthelme, *Snow White*, 18–19.
17. Henry James, 'The Art of Fiction,' in *Criticism: The Foundation of Modern Literary Judgment*, revised edition, ed. Schorer et al. (New York: Harcourt Brace and World, 1958), 49.
18. Ibid., 47.
19. Eliot, 'From Poe to Valéry,' *To Criticize the Critic* (New York: Farrar, Straus and Giroux, 1965), 39.
20. James, 'The Art of Fiction,' in Schorer, *Criticism: the Foundation*
21. Eliot, ' "Ulysses," Order, and Myth,' in *Selected Prose*, ed. Frank Kermode (New York: Harcourt Brace Jovanovich, 1975), 177.
22. Georg Lukács, *The Meaning of Contemporary Realism*, trans. J. and N. Mander (London: Merlin Press, 1963), 33.
23. Jorge Luis Borges, *Labyrinths: Selected Stories and Other Writings*, trans. J. Irby (New York: New Directions, 1964), 57.
24. Ibid., 17.
25. Sontag, *Against Interpretation*, 27.
26. Richard Poirier, *The Performing Self: Compositions and Decompositions in the Languages of Contemporary Life* (New York: Oxford University Press, 1971).
27. Poirier, *The Performing Self*, 40.

PART III
POSTMODERN POETICS

POSTMODERN POETICS:
INTRODUCTION

If the previous section contained essays which were representative of the first great 'moment' in the debate about postmodernism and the novel, the extracts in this section, coming for the most part from the mid- to late-1980s, represent the second. This narrative is of course misleading in a sense, as in the intervening years the term never really went away. But in this second period postmodernism came to be a fixture in intellectual discourse on a much wider scale. As far as the contemporary novel was concerned, the idea of just what postmodernism in fiction was began to become clearer.

The reason for this is that theories began to concentrate more intently on the formal properties of the postmodern novel. In other words, more studies appeared which attempted to show how the postmodern novel *worked*. The question of form is often raised in the essays in the previous section – in those by Sontag and Spanos, for example – but their method of analysis is not formalist to any systematic degree. One reason for this greater concentration on the stylistic features of postmodern fiction is clearly the fact that the earlier attempts to differentiate the postmodern novel from previous incarnations tended to get caught in a stalemate which resulted from simply pitting different *general* versions of modernism and postmodernism against one another. Another reason is, as Paul Maltby has said (see Part IV), because postmodernist writing is formally so complex. A third reason for the turn to formalism is no doubt the change in critical fashion that occurred in the late 1970s and 1980s with the wide-ranging impact of structuralism, the intellectual school which sought to analyse cultural forms by isolating the underlying codes and conventions by which they worked. Typical of structuralist literary criticism is the construction of a *poetics* of literature – a practice which rests on the idea that if we break down a series of related texts into their constituent parts, we can establish a taxonomy of features which can then stand as the *essential* properties of a particular genre or grouping of texts. This is clearly attractive to a critic approaching such a loose category as the postmodern novel. Not that any of the following texts are structuralist, pure and simple, however. Each of them (not surprisingly, given the nature of postmodernism) is acutely aware of the particular historical context of their object of study – unlike structuralism, which wanted to see the structures it analysed as universal and a historical.

The idea of poetics is important, too, because of the notorious elasticity of the novel form. Before we define what the postmodern novel is, in other words, we must first define what the *novel* is. This is no easy matter, as the development of the novel has never been restricted by generic convention the way that, say, poetry has. To quote Chris Baldick's ironic definition in *The Concise Oxford Dictionary of Literary Terms*, the novel 'is nearly always an extended fictional prose narrative, although some novels are very short, some are non-fictional, some have been written in verse, and some do not even tell a story' (Baldick, 1990). The inherent openness of the novel has led criticism – naturally, as its very purpose is to limit meaning – to close it down. It is hard, even now, to shake the ideological premise that the novel 'proper' is equal to a particular version of the genre written in the mid-nineteenth century, what is known as 'classic realism', and anything else is a departure. As Michael Holquist has pointed out, some of the most influential attempts to define the novel (such as Georg Lukács' *Theory of the Novel* in 1920, or Ian Watt's *The Rise of the Novel* in 1957) tend to be beset 'by the same shortcoming: they seek to elevate *one kind* of novel into a definition of the novel as such' (Holquist, 1981: xxvii).

The interest in postmodern fiction in 1980s and 1990s criticism can also be linked to the concern in literary study of the time (e.g. in Colin McCabe's 'Realism and the Cinema' (1979) and Catherine Belsey's *Critical Practice* (1980)) with the question of 'open' and 'closed' form in the novel. As the classic realist nineteenth-century novel is the model cultural form of a rationalist age organised around notions of social hierarchy, its form consequently seeks to limit the meanings it generates, so that its reader is essentially 'passive' (who interprets freely only when space is provided by the author for him or her to do so) and to absorb the dominant ideological message about the value of social cohesion (accept, do not question, know your place). Twentieth-century fiction, by contrast, is generally open: its poetic use of language and multiplicity of narrative perspective implies that any presentation of reality and any social organisation is partial.

Two of the major theoretical figures whose work informs this strain within literary criticism are Roland Barthes and Mikhail Bakhtin, and this is why I have included extracts from their work, even though neither was explicitly concerned with postmodernism (or even twentieth-century fiction). The first extract is from Barthes's extraordinary book *S/Z*, at once the most gloriously obsessive and pedantic inquiry into the act of reading ever produced. Barthes analyses Balzac's short 'Sarrasine' line by line in such precise detail that his book about it is over twice the length of the original story. But this apparent critical conceit is performed in order to prove his point (voiced over a number of works, most notably 'The Death of the Author' (1968) and *The Pleasure of the Text* (1973)) that it is really the reader who 'writes' a text, that is, makes it *mean* whatever it means. In the extract which follows, Barthes formalises this process by defining a couple of terms which have endured in critical discourse. He argues that where some texts attempt to constrain the reader's co-writing of the text, others actively encourage it. The first kind of text he calls '*lisible*' (French for 'readable': because the reader can *only* read it, that is, remain passive), and the second he calls '*scriptible*' ('writable', because the reader is effectively able – and even required to if the novel is to make any sense – to 'write' it himself). Barthes deftly avoids linking any particular works of literature to these categories, apart from 'Sarrasine' (and even that is ambigious) but successive critics have pointed out that Barthes's categories can usefully be mapped onto classic realist fiction and modernist and postmodernist fiction respectively. So although *S/Z* is really about reading, it gives us a valuable way of distinguishing between different kinds of novel formally.

Bakhtin approaches the difficult question 'what is a novel?' along more rigorously formalist lines. As his contemporaries and compatriots, the Russian Formalists, had done in trying to answer the question 'what is literature?' Bakhtin tries to grasp the very *essence* of the novel, those features which make it different from any other form. The Russian Formalists thought that a particular use of language made literature literature; for Bakhtin what makes a novel a novel is the fact that it contains different social types of speech. In this respect, it mirrors the society which produces it, as it is governed by the condition Bakhtin terms *heteroglossia*, 'different-speechness'. The novel is naturally a *social* form, because it contains different characters and voices. As a work of more or less continuous prose, it follows that each of these voices interacts with each of the others – that is, each discourse which features within its pages complements, counters and modifies the discourses of the others. As the different speech types are each representative of a different point of view on the world, these different viewpoints enter into dialogue with each other. For Bakhtin, meaning can never be stable or singular so long as it is expressed in language (which means always).

The historical scope of Bakhtin's work is much wider than Barthes's, but he makes a similar point. The novel is naturally and always a 'dialogic' (or 'polyphonic') form, even though some authors attempt to make it more *monologic*, by making it clear which of the voices contained within their text is most valuable according to their own point of view. Though Bakhtin never speaks of postmodernism either (for obvious reasons, as he wrote most of his work before it became a prominent concept), we can also, as with Barthes, use his conception of the novel as an insight into the liberal way postmodern fiction organises the discourses which constitute it.

The third extract in this part, from Patricia Waugh's book *Metafiction* (1984), also seeks to define what is an essential aspect of the novel. Metafiction – fiction which openly acknowedges its own status as an artificial construct – is not a 'new' strategy employed by writers in postmodernity but an integral part of the novel since its inception in the early eighteenth century. Waugh emphasises that it 'is a tendency or function inherent in *all* novels' and 'is worth studying not only because of the insights it offers into both the representational nature of all fiction and the literary history of the novel as a genre. By studying metafiction, one is, in effect, studying that which gives the novel its identity' (Waugh, 1984: 5). Nevertheless, she argues that there has been an increase in particular kinds of metafictional devices in the novel in the twentieth century and exploring these is crucial to understanding how postmodernism in fiction works.

Metafiction is central to the chapter of David Lodge's *The Modes of Modern Writing* (1977) which amounts to the first notable attempt to construct a taxonomy of postmodern features, and which is reproduced here. The book as a whole figures as a classic example of how critics set about constructing a poetics of a literary form. It begins with a claim that in order to determine 'what principles underlie the variety of literary forms, and the changes in literary fashion, in the modern era' it is necessary to develop 'a comprehensive typology of literary discourse – that is, one capable of describing and discriminating between all types of text without prejudging them' (Lodge, 1977: viiii). The typology that Lodge develops throughout his book is based on the linguist Roman Jakobson's view that 'all discourse tends towards either the metaphoric or the metonymic pole of language' (Lodge, 1977: 228). Lodge builds systematically on a suggestion in Jakobson that metaphor (the substitution of one term for another) and metonymy (the use of one aspect of a thing to imply its whole) are more than just figures of speech, but can be used to make sense of differences between entire literary modes and movements. So where drama, say, tends towards metaphor, film is largely metonymic; poetry is generally metaphoric, while prose is metonymic – but modernist and symbolist writing is more metaphoric than realism. What interests Lodge about postmodernism is the way it threatens to confound his system. Like all good critics, though, Lodge turns what is potentially the weak point in his theory into its strength, and catalogues the different ways postmodernist writing deploys both 'metaphoric and metonymic devices in radically new ways, and to defy [. . .] the obligation to choose between these two principles of connecting one topic with another'.

Right at the beginning of his book, *Postmodernist Fiction* (1987), Brian McHale acknowledges his debt to Lodge's *Modes of Modern Writing*, explaining that his study reflects his desire to build upon the typology of features Lodge sketches out and improve them. McHale's approach is similar, devoting each chapter to a different feature in the way that Lodge divides up his essay, even preserving some of Lodge's terms. What is different, though, is that McHale also has an overall model which makes sense of each of these typological features, and it is one which has proved very influential in theories of post-modern fiction. *Postmodernist Fiction*, McHale states in his Preface, 'is essentially a one-idea book – an admission that probably ought to embarrass me more than it in fact does. That idea is simply stated: postmodernist fiction differs from modernist fiction just as a poetics dominated by ontological issues differs from one dominated by epistemological issues' (McHale, 1987: xii). The advantage of this overall idea, as McHale explains in the following extract, is that it can account for precisely what unites the catalogue of distinctive features identified by the likes of Lodge (and others who have developed a typology of postmodern features, like Douwe Fokkema (1986)) and how the resulting system compares with previous systems (in this case, modernism). McHale's thesis also involves a rather provocative argument about how some of the key writers emerging from the modernist tradition – like Faulkner, Robbe-Grillet and Beckett – actually began to shift from a modernist poetics to a post-modernist one in the course of a writing career, sometimes even in the course of a novel. Though it was his book that had most impact, included in this part is an essay, 'Change of Dominant from Modernist to Postmodernist Writing', which is a version of a paper McHale delivered at a conference on postmodernism at the University of Utrecht in 1984 and which came to form much of the book. The advantage is that the essay serves as a kind of summary of the key ideas in the whole book, which is less singular in its focus than McHale claims.

Where McHale describes his book as a 'one-idea' book, Linda Hutcheon's project could be said to revolve around one main idea, too. Like McHale she endeavours to construct 'a "poetics" of postmodernism, a flexible conceptual structure which could at once constitute and contain postmodern culture and our discourses about and adjacent to it' (Hutcheon, 1988: ix). Postmodernism, Hutcheon has argued over the course of several books, is characterised by 'an inherently paradoxical structure' (Hutcheon, 1988: 222). This quality explains the peculiar contradictory nature of postmodernist works (something Lodge explores too) and also the tendency for the postmodern debate to become polarised: left-wing/right-wing, for/against. But her view is that postmodernism is not oppositional, nor even dialectical, but *double*, representing both sides of a binary at the same time. Postmodern art is simultaneously self-reflexive *and* referential, apolitical *and* strongly political, it continues with *and* breaks with modernism. A perfect postmodern form is parody, 'for it paradoxically both incorporates and challenges that which it parodies' (Hutcheon, 1988: 11). In her first book on postmodern fiction, *Narcissistic Narrative*, Hutcheon show how, in postmodern texts, the reader is invited to become 'co-writer' in the Barthesian sense, on the one hand free to interpret its plural signifiers freely, but on the other required to adhere to the imposed logic of the writer's (political) agenda. Postmodern fiction, in other words, is simultaneously didactic and liberating.

Hutcheon's logic of 'both … and …' has clear affinities with Charles Jencks's and Umberto Eco's conceptions of the postmodern. It presents postmodernism as primarily an ironic mode, which says one thing and another at the same time. Indeed one of the values of Hutcheon's work is that she states directly what Eco's theory only implies: postmodern irony is not an empty cynical gesture, but in fact a kind of 'necessary negotiation', a crucial move in order to say anything at all.

The section concludes with a formalist exploration of one particular sub-genre favoured by postmodern writers, the 'anti-detective novel'. Despite its emphasis on breaking the rules of form, and its tendency to create generic hybrids (as explored in Leslie Fiedler's 'Cross the Border – Close that Gap'), postmodern fiction, like any current within literary history, inevitably favours some *genres* over others. A number of genres have been linked to postmodern-ism, such as 'historiographic metafiction' or 'cyberpunk', for example, con-sidered in Linda Hutcheon's and Veronica Hollinger's pieces in Part IV respectively. Another is 'magic realism', the peculiar blend of fantastic and realistic events narrated in the objective, rationalist tone of the conventional realist narrator which is associated with a Spanish American tradition including Gabriel García Márquez, Carlos Fuentes and Isabel Allende, and also promi-nent British writers like Salman Rushdie, Angela Carter and D. M. Thomas). A third, newer postmodern genre might be the 'brat pack' fiction of Bret Easton Ellis, Jay McInerney and Douglas Coupland, novels which portray obsessively and ironically lives saturated in consumer culture. But the 'anti-detective' genre is the genre which has perhaps been most consistently linked to postmodernism, ever since William V. Spanos's essay 'The Detective and the Boundary' (in Part II; see also McHale, 1992). The extracts here from Stephano Tani's *The Doomed Detective: The Contribution of the Detective Novel to Postmodern American and Italian Fiction* (1984) are clearly a development of the basic premise of Spanos's essay: that the subversion of narrative closure in the anti-detective novel is symptomatic of the postmodern mindset. I consider the risk of overlap here worth taking because Tani's study offers a more systematic exploration of some writers more generally regarded as postmodern than those mentioned by Spanos. Taking the solution to the crime as the defining element of the detective genre (that which 'justifies its existence') Tani explores in detail three ways in which this is problematised in postmodernist writing: the innovative, the deconstructive and the metafictional. In his discussion of this third category, Tani gives a clue as to why the genre might have proved so interesting to postmodern theorists: there is an obvious link between the activity of the detective and the reader of a literary text, in that both aim to decode a series of signs and arrive at a final meaning – a practice the anti-detective novel reveals to be impossible.

WORKS CITED

Baldick, Chris (1990) *The Concise Oxford Dictionary of Literary Terms*. Oxford: Oxford University Press.
Belsey, Catherine (1980) *Critical Practice*. London: Methuen.

Fokkema, Douwe (1986) 'The Semantic and Syntactic Organization of Postmodernist Texts', in Douwe Fokkema and Hans Bertens (eds), *Approaching Postmodernism*. Amsterdam and Philadelphia, PA: John Benjamins, pp. 81–95.

Holquist, Michael (1981) 'Introduction' to Bakhtin, Mikhail, *The Dialogic Imagination: Four Essays*. Austin, TX: University of Texas Press.

Hutcheon, Linda (1988) *A Poetics of Postmodernism*. London: Routledge.

Lodge, David (1977) *The Modes of Modern Writing: Metaphor, Metonymy, and the Typology of Modern Literature*. London: Edward Arnold.

MacCabe, Colin (1974) 'Realism and the Cinema: Notes on Some Brechtian Theses', *Screen* 15, 2: 216–29.

McHale, Brian (1987) *Postmodernist Fiction*. London: Routledge.

McHale, Brian (1992) *Constructing Postmodernism*. London: Routledge.

Waugh, Patricia (1984) *Metafiction: The Theory and Practice of Self-Conscious Fiction*. London: Methuen.

THE NOVEL
16

FROM *S/Z*

Roland Barthes

I. Evaluation

There are said to be certain Buddhists whose ascetic practices enable them to see a whole landscape in a bean. Precisely what the first analysts of narrative were attempting: to see all the world's stories (and there have been ever so many) within a single structure: we shall, they thought, extract from each tale its model, then out of these models we shall make a great narrative structure, which we shall reapply (for verification) to any one narrative: a task as exhausting (ninety-nine percent perspiration, as the saying goes) as it is ultimately undesirable, for the text thereby loses its difference. This difference is not, obviously, some complete, irreducible quality (according to a mythic view of literary creation), it is not what designates the individuality of each text, what names, signs, finishes off each work with a flourish; on the contrary, it is a difference which does not stop and which is articulated upon the infinity of texts, of languages, of systems: a difference of which each text is the return. A choice must then be made: either to place all texts in a demonstrative oscillation, equalizing them under the scrutiny of an indifferent science, forcing them to rejoin, inductively, the Copy from which we will then make them derive; or else to restore each text, not to its individuality, but to its function, making it cohere, even before we talk about it, by the infinite paradigm of difference, subjecting it from the outset to a basic typology, to an evaluation. How then posit the value of a text? How establish a basic typology of texts? The primary evaluation of all

From Roland Barthes (1975) *S/Z* [1970], trans. Richard Miller. Oxford: Blackwell.

texts can come neither from science, for science does not evaluate, nor from ideology, for the ideological value of a text (moral, aesthetic, political, alethiological) is a value of representation, not of production (ideology 'reflects', it does not do work). Our evaluation can be linked only to a practice, and this practice is that of writing. On the one hand, there is what it is possible to write, and on the other, what it is no longer possible to write: what is within the practice of the writer and what has left it: which texts would I consent to write (to re-write), to desire, to put forth as a force in this world of mine? What evaluation finds is precisely this value: what can be written (rewritten) today: the *writerly*. Why is the writerly our value? Because the goal of literary work (of literature as work) is to make the reader no longer a consumer, but a producer of the text. Our literature is characterized by the pitiless divorce which the literary institution maintains between the producer of the text and its user, between its owner and its customer, between its author and its reader. This reader is thereby plunged into a kind of idleness – he is intransitive; he is, in short, *serious:* instead of functioning himself, instead of gaining access to the magic of the signifier, to the pleasure of writing, he is left with no more than the poor freedom either to accept or reject the text: reading is nothing more than a *referendum*. Opposite the writerly text, then, is its countervalue, its negative, reactive value: what can be read, but not written: the *readerly*. We call any readerly text a classic text.

II. INTERPRETATION

There may be nothing to say about writerly texts. First of all, where can we find them? Certainly not in reading (or at least very rarely: by accident, fleetingly, obliquely in certain limit-works): the writerly text is not a thing, we would have a hard time finding it in a bookstore. Further, its model being a productive (and no longer a representative) one, it demolishes any criticism which, once produced, would mix with it: to rewrite the writerly text would consist only in disseminating it, in dispersing it within the field of infinite difference. The writerly text is a perpetual present, upon which no *consequent* language (which would inevitably make it past) can be superimposed; the writerly text is *ourselves writing*, before the infinite play of the world (the world as function) is traversed, intersected, stopped, plasticized by some singular system (Ideology, Genus, Criticism) which reduces the plurality of entrances, the opening of networks, the infinity of languages. The writerly is the novelistic without the novel, poetry without the poem, the essay without the dissertation, writing without style, production without product, structuration without structure. But the readerly texts? They are products (and not productions), they make up the enormous mass of our literature. How differentiate this mass once again? Here, we require a second operation, consequent upon the evaluation which has separated the texts, more delicate than that evaluation, based upon the appreciation of a certain quantity – of the *more or less* each text can mobilize. This new operation is *interpretation* (in the Nietzschean sense of the word). To interpret a text is not to give it a (more or less justified, more or less free) meaning, but on the contrary to appreciate what *plural* constitutes it. Let us first posit the image of a triumphant plural, unimpoverished by any constraint of representation (of imitation). In this ideal text, the networks are many and interact, without any one of them being able to surpass the rest; this text is a galaxy of signifiers, not a structure of signifieds; it has no beginning; it is reversible; we gain access to it by several entrances, none of which can be authoritatively declared to be the main one; the codes it mobilizes extend *as far as the eye can reach*, they are indeterminable (meaning here is never subject to a principle of determination, unless by throwing dice); the systems of meaning can take over this absolutely plural text, but their number is never closed, based as it is on the infinity of language. The interpretation demanded by a specific text, in its plurality, is in no way liberal: it is not a question of conceding some meanings, of magnanimously acknowledging that each one has its share of truth; it is a question, against all in-difference, of asserting the very existence of plurality, which is not that of the true, the probable, or even the possible. This necessary assertion is difficult, however, for as nothing exists outside the text, there is never a *whole* of the text (which would by reversion form an internal order, a reconciliation of complementary parts, under the paternal eye of the representative Model): the text must simultaneously be distinguished from its exterior and from its totality. All of which comes down to saying that for the plural text, there cannot be a narrative structure, a grammar, or a logic; thus, if one or another of these are sometimes permitted to come forward, it is *in proportion* (giving this expression its full quantitative value) as we are dealing with incompletely plural texts, texts whose plural is more or less parsimonious.

[...]

V. READING, FORGETTING

I read the text. This statement, consonant with the 'genius' of the language (subject, verb, complement), is not always true. The more plural the text, the less it is written before I read it; I do not make it undergo a predicative operation, consequent upon its being, an operation known as *reading*, and I is not an innocent subject, anterior to the text, one which will subsequently deal with the text as it would an object to dismantle or a site to occupy. This 'I' which approaches the text is already itself a plurality of other texts, of codes which are infinite or, more precisely, lost (whose origin is lost). *Objectivity* and *subjectivity* are of course forces which can take over the text, but they are forces which have no affinity with it. Subjectivity is a plenary image, with which I may be thought to encumber the text, but whose deceptive plenitude is merely the wake of all the codes which constitute me, so that my subjectivity has ultimately the generality of stereotypes. Objectivity is the same type of replenishment: it is an imaginary system like the rest (except that here the castrating gesture is more fiercely characterized), an image which serves to name me advantageously, to make myself known, 'misknown', even to myself. Reading involves risks of objectivity or subjectivity (both are imaginary) only insofar as we define the text as an expressive object (presented for our own expression), sublimated under a morality of truth, in one instance laxist; in the other, ascetic. Yet reading is not a parasitical act, the reactive complement of a writing which we endow with all the glamour of creation and anteriority. It is a form of work (which is why it would be better to speak of a lexeological act – even a lexeographical act, since I write my reading), and the method of this work is topological: I am not hidden within the text, I am simply irrecoverable from it: my task is to move, to shift systems whose perspective ends neither at the text nor at the 'I': in operational terms, the meanings I find are established not by 'me' or by others, but by their *systematic* mark: there is no other *proof* of a reading than the quality and endurance of its systematics; in other words: than its functioning. To read, in fact, is a labor of language. To read is to find meanings, and to find meanings is to name them; but these named meanings are swept toward other names; names call to each other, reassemble, and their grouping calls for further naming: I name, I unname, I rename: so the text passes: it is a nomination in the course of becoming, a tireless approximation, a metonymic labor. – With regard to the plural text, forgetting a meaning cannot therefore be seen as a fault. Forgetting in relation to what? What is the *sum* of the text? Meanings can indeed be forgotten, but only if we have chosen to bring to bear upon the text a singular scrutiny. Yet reading does not consist in stopping the chain of systems, in establishing a truth, a legality of the text, and consequently in leading its reader into 'errors'; it consists in coupling these systems, not according to their finite quantity, but according to their plurality (which is a being, not a discounting): I pass, I intersect, I articulate, I release, I do not count. Forgetting meanings is not a matter for excuses, an unfortunate defect in performance; it is an affirmative value, a way of asserting the irresponsibility of the text, the pluralism of systems (if I closed their list, I would inevitably reconstitute a singular, theological meaning): it is precisely because I forget that I read.

VI. STEP BY STEP

If we want to remain attentive to the plural of a text (however limited it may be), we must renounce structuring this text in large masses, as was done by classical rhetoric and by secondary-school explication: no *construction* of the text: everything signifies ceaselessly and several times, but without being delegated to a great final ensemble, to an ultimate structure. Whence the idea, and so to speak the necessity, of a gradual analysis of a single text. Whence, it would seem, several implications and several advantages. The commentary on a single text is not a contingent activity, assigned the reassuring alibi of the 'concrete': the single text is valid for all the texts of literature, not in that it represents them (abstracts and equalizes them), but in that literature itself is never anything but a single text: the one text is not an (inductive) access to a Model, but entrance into a network with a thousand entrances; to take this entrance is to aim, ultimately, not at a legal structure of norms and departures, a narrative or poetic Law, but at a perspective (of fragments, of voices from other texts, other codes), whose vanishing point is nonetheless ceaselessly pushed back, mysteriously opened: each (single) text is the very theory (and not the mere example) of this vanishing, of this difference which indefinitely returns, insubmissive. Further, to study this text down to the last detail is to take up the structural analysis of narrative where it has been left till now: at the major structures; it is to assume the power (the time, the elbow room) of working back along the threads of meanings, of abandoning no site of the signifier without endeavoring to ascertain the code or codes of which this site is perhaps the starting point (or the goal); it is (at least we may hope as much, and work to this end) to substitute for the simple representative model another model, whose very gradualness would guarantee what may be productive in the classic text; for the *step-by-step* method, through its very slowness and dispersion, avoids penetrating, reversing the tutor text, giving an internal image of it: it is never anything but the *decomposition* (in the cinematographic sense) of the work of reading: a *slow motion*, so to speak, neither wholly image nor wholly analysis; it is, finally, in the very writing of the commentary, a systematic use of digression (a form ill-accommodated by the discourse of knowledge) and thereby a way of observing the reversibility of the structures from which the text is woven; of course, the classic text is incompletely reversible (it is modestly plural): the reading of this text occurs within a necessary order, which the gradual analysis will make precisely its order of writing; but the step-by-step commentary is of necessity a renewal of the entrances to the text, it avoids structuring the text *excessively*, avoids giving it that additional structure which would come from a dissertation and would close it: it stars the text, instead of assembling it.

17

FROM 'DISCOURSE IN THE NOVEL'

Mikhail Bakhtin

The novel as a whole is a phenomenon multiform in style and variform in speech and voice. In it the investigator is confronted with several heterogeneous stylistic unities, often located on different linguistic levels and subject to different stylistic controls.

We list below the basic types of compositional-stylistic unities into which the novelistic whole usually breaks down:

(1) Direct authorial literary-artistic narration (in all its diverse variants);
(2) Stylization of the various forms of oral everyday narration (*skaz*);
(3) Stylization of the various forms of semiliterary (written) everyday narration (the letter, the diary, etc.);
(4) Various forms of literary but extra-artistic authorial speech (moral, philosophical or scientific statements, oratory, ethnographic descriptions, memoranda and so forth);
(5) The stylistically individualized speech of characters.

These heterogeneous stylistic unities, upon entering the novel, combine to form a structured artistic system, and are subordinated to the higher stylistic unity of the work as a whole, a unity that cannot be identified with any single one of the unities subordinated to it.

The stylistic uniqueness of the novel as a genre consists precisely in the combination of these subordinated, yet still relatively autonomous, unities

From Mikhail Bakhtin (1981) 'Discourse in the Novel', in *The Dialogic Imagination*, ed. Michael Holquist, trans. Caryl Emerson and Michael Holquist. Austin, TX: University of Texas Press.

(even at times comprised of different languages) into the higher unity of the work as a whole: the style of a novel is to be found in the combination of its styles; the language of a novel is the system of its 'languages.' Each separate element of a novel's language is determined first of all by one such subordinated stylistic unity into which it enters directly – be it the stylistically individualized speech of a character, the down-to-earth voice of a narrator in *skaz*, a letter or whatever. The linguistic and stylistic profile of a given element (lexical, semantic, syntactic) is shaped by that subordinated unity to which it is most immediately proximate. At the same time this element, together with its most immediate unity, figures into the style of the whole, itself supports the accent of the whole and participates in the process whereby the unified meaning of the whole is structured and revealed.

The novel can be defined as a diversity of social speech types (sometimes even diversity of languages) and a diversity of individual voices, artistically organized. The internal stratification of any single national language into social dialects, characteristic group behavior, professional jargons, generic languages, languages of generations and age groups, tendentious languages, languages of the authorities, of various circles and of passing fashions, languages that serve the specific sociopolitical purposes of the day, even of the hour (each day has its own slogan, its own vocabulary, its own emphases) – this internal stratification present in every language at any given moment of its historical existence is the indispensable prerequisite for the novel as a genre. The novel orchestrates all its themes, the totality of the world of objects and ideas depicted and expressed in it, by means of the social diversity of speech types [*raznorečie*] and by the differing individual voices that flourish under such conditions. Authorial speech, the speeches of narrators, inserted genres, the speech of characters are merely those fundamental compositional unities with whose help heteroglossia [*raznorečie*] can enter the novel; each of them permits a multiplicity of social voices and a wide variety of their links and interrelationships (always more or less dialogized). These distinctive links and interrelationships between utterances and languages, this movement of the theme through different languages and speech types, its dispersion into the rivulets and droplets of social heteroglossia, its dialogization – this is the basic distinguishing feature of the stylistics of the novel.

[...]

The novel is an artistic genre. Novelistic discourse is poetic discourse, but one that does not fit within the frame provided by the concept of poetic discourse as it now exists. This concept has certain underlying presuppositions that limit it. The very concept – in the course of its historical formulation from Aristotle to the present day – has been oriented toward the specific 'official' genres and connected with specific historical tendencies in verbal ideological life. Thus a whole series of phenomena remained beyond its conceptual horizon.

[...]

At the time when major divisions of the poetic genres were developing under the influence of the unifying, centralizing, centripetal forces of verbal-ideological life, the novel – and those artistic-prose genres that gravitate toward it – was being historically shaped by the current of decentralizing, centrifugal forces. At the time when poetry was accomplishing the task of cultural, national and political centralization of the verbal-ideological world in the higher official socio-ideological levels, on the lower levels, on the stages of local fairs and at buffoon spectacles, the heteroglossia of the clown sounded forth, ridiculing all 'languages' and dialects; there developed the literature of the *fabliaux* and *Schwänke* of street songs, folksayings, anecdotes, where there was no language-center at all, where there was to be found a lively play with the 'languages' of poets, scholars, monks, knights and others, where all 'languages' were masks and where no language could claim to be an authentic, incontestable face.

Heteroglossia, as organized in these low genres, was not merely heteroglossia vis-à-vis the accepted literary language (in all its various generic expressions), that is, vis-à-vis the linguistic center of the verbal-ideological life of the nation and the epoch, but was a heteroglossia consciously opposed to this literary language. It was parodic, and aimed sharply and polemically against the official languages of its given time. It was heteroglossia that had been dialogized.

[...]

In any given historical moment of verbal-ideological life, each generation at each social level has its own language; moreover, every age group has as a matter of fact its own language, its own vocabulary, its own particular accentual system that, in their turn, vary depending on social level, academic institution (the language of the cadet, the high school student, the trade school student are all different languages) and other stratifying factors. All this is brought about by socially typifying languages, no matter how narrow the social circle in which they are spoken. It is even possible to have a family jargon define the societal limits of a language, as, for instance, the jargon of the Irtenevs in Tolstoy, with its special vocabulary and unique accentual system.

And finally, at any given moment, languages of various epochs and periods of socio-ideological life cohabit with one another. Even languages of the day exist: one could say that today's and yesterday's socio-ideological and political 'day' do not, in a certain sense, share the same language; every day represents another socio-ideological semantic 'state of affairs,' another vocabulary, another accentual system, with its own slogans, its own ways of assigning blame and praise. Poetry depersonalizes 'days' in language, while prose, as we shall see, often deliberately intensifies difference between them, gives them embodied representation and dialogically opposes them to one another in unresolvable dialogues.

Thus at any given moment of its historical existence, language is heteroglot from top to bottom: it represents the co-existence of socio-ideological contradictions between the present and the past, between differing epochs of the past, between different socio-ideological groups in the present, between tendencies, schools, circles and so forth, all given a bodily form. These 'languages' of heteroglossia intersect each other in a variety of ways, forming new socially typifying 'languages.'

[...]

Thus an illiterate peasant, miles away from any urban center, naively immersed in an unmoving and for him unshakable everyday world, nevertheless lived in several language systems: he prayed to God in one language (Church Slavonic), sang songs in another, spoke to his family in a third and, when he began to dictate petitions to the local authorities through a scribe, he tried speaking yet a fourth language (the official-literate language, 'paper' language). All these are *different languages*, even from the point of view of abstract socio-dialectological markers. But these languages were not dialogically coordinated in the linguistic consciousness of the peasant; he passed from one to the other without thinking, automatically: each was indisputably in its own place, and the place of each was indisputable. He was not yet able to regard one language (and the verbal world corresponding to it) through the eyes of another language (that is, the language of everyday life and the everyday world with the language of prayer or song, or vice versa).[1]

[...]

The poet is a poet insofar as he accepts the idea of a unitary and singular language and a unitary, monologically sealed-off utterance. These ideas are immanent in the poetic genres with which he works. In a condition of actual contradiction, these are what determine the means of orientation open to the poet. The poet must assume a complete single-personed hegemony over his own language, he must assume equal responsibility for each one of its aspects and subordinate them to his own, and only his own, intentions. Each word must express the poet's *meaning* directly and without mediation; there must be no distance between the poet and his word. The meaning must emerge from language as a single intentional whole: none of its stratification, its speech diversity, to say nothing of its language diversity, may be reflected in any fundamental way in his poetic work.

To achieve this, the poet strips the word of others' intentions, he uses only such words and forms (and only in such a way) that they lose their link with concrete intentional levels of language and their connection with specific contexts. Behind the words of a poetic work one should not sense any typical or reified images of genres (except for the given poetic genre), nor professions, tendencies, directions (except the direction chosen by the poet himself), nor world views (except for the unitary and singular world view of the poet himself), nor typical and individual images of speaking persons, their speech mannerisms or typical intonations. *Everything that enters the work must immerse itself in Lethe, and forget its previous life in any other contexts: language may remember only its life in poetic contexts (in such contexts, however, even concrete reminiscences are possible).*

Of course there always exists a limited sphere of more or less concrete contexts, and a connection with them must be deliberately evidenced in poetic discourse. But these contexts are purely semantic and, so to speak, accented in the abstract; in their linguistic dimension they are impersonal or at least no particularly concrete linguistic specificity is sensed behind them, no particular manner of speech and so forth, no socially typical linguistic face (the possible personality of the narrator) need peek out from behind them. Everywhere there is only one face – the linguistic face of the author, answering for every word as if it were his own. No matter how multiple and varied these semantic and accentual threads, associations, pointers, hints, correlations that emerge from every poetic word, one language, one conceptual horizon, is sufficient to them all; there is no need of heteroglot social contexts. What is more, the very movement of the poetic symbol (for example, the unfolding of a metaphor) presumes precisely this unity of language, an unmediated correspondence with its object. Social diversity of speech, were it to arise in the work and stratify its language, would make impossible both the normal development and the activity of symbols within it.

[...]

As a result of this work – stripping all aspects of language of the intentions and accents of other people, destroying all traces of social heteroglossia and diversity of language – a tension-filled unity of language is achieved in the poetic work. This unity may be naive, and present only in those extremely rare epochs of poetry, when poetry had not yet exceeded the limits of a closed, unitary, undifferentiated social circle whose language and ideology were not yet stratified. More often than not, we experience a profound and conscious tension through which the unitary poetic language of a work rises from the heteroglot and language-diverse chaos of the literary language contemporary to it.

This is how the poet proceeds. The novelist working in prose (and almost any prose writer) takes a completely different path. He welcomes the heteroglossia and language diversity of the literary and extraliterary language into his own work not only not weakening them but even intensifying them (for he interacts with their particular self-consciousness). It is in fact out of this stratification of language, its speech diversity and even language diversity, that he constructs his style, while at the same time he maintains the unity of his own creative personality and the unity (although it is, to be sure, unity of another order) of his own style.

The prose writer does not purge words of intentions and tones that are alien to him, he does not destroy the seeds of social heteroglossia embedded in words, he does not eliminate those language characterizations and speech mannerisms (potential narrator-personalities) glimmering behind the words and forms, each at a different distance from the ultimate semantic nucleus of his work, that is, the center of his own personal intentions.

The language of the prose writer deploys itself according to degrees of greater or lesser proximity to the author and to his ultimate semantic instantiation: certain aspects of language directly and unmediatedly express (as in poetry) the semantic and expressive intentions of the author, others refract these intentions; the writer of prose does not meld completely with any of these words, but rather accents each of them in a particular way – humorously, ironically, parodically and so forth[2] yet another group may stand even further from the author's ultimate semantic instantiation, still more thoroughly refracting his intentions; and there are, finally, those words that are completely denied any authorial intentions: the author does not express *himself* in them (as the author of the word) – rather, he *exhibits* them as a unique speech-thing, they function for him as something completely reified. Therefore the stratification of language – generic, professional, social in the narrow sense, that of particular world views, particular tendencies, particular individuals, the social speech diversity and language-diversity (dialects) of language – upon entering the novel establishs its own special order within it, and becomes a unique artistic system, which orchestrates the intentional theme of the author.

Thus a prose writer can distance himself from the language of his own work, while at the same time distancing himself, in varying degrees, from the different layers and aspects of the work. He can make use of language without wholly giving himself up to it, he may treat it as semi-alien or completely alien to himself, while compelling language ultimately to serve all his own intentions. The author does not speak in a given language (from which he distances himself to a greater or lesser degree), but he speaks, as it were, *through* language, a language that has somehow more or less materialized, become objectivized, that he merely ventriloquates.

[…]

The language used by characters in the novel, how they speak, is verbally and semantically autonomous; each character's speech possesses its own belief system, since each is the speech of another in another's language; thus it may also refract authorial intentions and consequently may to a certain degree constitute a second language for the author. Moreover, the character speech almost always influences authorial speech (and sometimes powerfully so), sprinkling it with another's words (that is, the speech of a character perceived as the concealed speech of another) and in this way introducing into it stratification and speech diversity.

Thus even where there is no comic element, no parody, no irony and so forth, where there is no narrator, no posited author or narrating character, speech diversity and language stratification still serve as the basis for style in the novel.

Even in those places where the author's voice seems at first glance to be unitary and consistent, direct and unmediatedly intentional, beneath that smooth single-languaged surface we can nevertheless uncover prose's three-dimensionality, its profound speech diversity, which enters the project of style and is its determining factor.

[...]

The plot itself is subordinated to the task of coordinating and exposing languages to each other. The novelistic plot must organize the exposure of social languages and ideologies, the exhibiting and experiencing of such languages: the experience of a discourse, a world view and an ideologically based act, or the exhibiting of the everyday life of social, historical and national worlds or micro-worlds (as is the case with novels concerned primarily with description, everyday life or travel), or of the socio-ideological worlds of epochs (the novel-memoir, or various types of historical novel) or of age groups and generations linked with epochs and socio-ideological worlds (the *Bildungsroman* and *Entwicklungsroman*). In a word, the novelistic plot serves to represent speaking persons and their ideological worlds. What is realized in the novel is the process of coming to know one's own language as it is perceived in someone else's language, coming to know one's own horizon within someone else's horizon. There takes place within the novel an ideological translation of another's language, and an overcoming of its otherness – an otherness that is only contingent, external, illusory. Characteristic for the historical novel is a positively weighted modernizing, an erasing of temporal boundaries, the recognition of an eternal present in the past. The primary stylistic project of the novel as a genre is to create images of languages.

Every novel, taken as the totality of all the languages and consciousnesses of language embodied in it, is a *hybrid*. But we emphasize once again: it is an intentional and conscious hybrid, one artistically organized, and not an opaque mechanistic mixture of languages (more precisely, a mixture of the brute elements of language). *The artistic image of a language* – such is the aim that novelistic hybridization sets for itself.

For this reason the novelist makes no effort at all to achieve a linguistically (dialectologically) exact and complete reproduction of the empirical data of those alien languages he incorporates into his text – he attempts merely to achieve an artistic consistency among the *images* of these languages.

An artistic hybrid demands enormous effort: it is stylized through and through, thoroughly premeditated, achieved, distanced. This is what distinguishes it from the frivolous, mindless and unsystematic mixing of languages – often bordering on simple illiteracy – characteristic of mediocre prose writers. In such hybrids there is no joining together of consistent language systems, merely a random combination of the brute elements out of which languages are made. This is not orchestration by means of heteroglossia, but in most cases merely a directly authorial language that is impure and incompletely worked out.

The novel not only labors, therefore, under the necessity of knowing literary language in all its depth and subtlety, but it must in addition know all the other languages of heteroglossia. The novel demands a broadening and deepening of the language horizon, a sharpening in our perception of socio-linguistic differentiations.

NOTES

1. We are of course deliberately simplifying: the real-life peasant could and did do this to a certain extent.
2. That is to say, the words are not his if we understand them as direct words, but they are his as things that are being transmitted ironically, exhibited and so forth, that is, as words that are understood from the distances appropriate to humor, irony, parody, etc.

18

FROM *METAFICTION*

Patricia Waugh

The term 'metafiction' itself seems to have originated in an essay by the American critic and self-conscious novelist William H. Gass (in Gass 1970). However, terms like 'metapolitics', 'metarhetoric' and 'metatheatre' are a reminder of what has been, since the 1960s, a more general cultural interest in the problem of how human beings reflect, construct and mediate their experience of the world. Metafiction pursues such questions through its formal self-exploration, drawing on the traditional metaphor of the world as book, but often recasting it in the terms of contemporary philosophical, linguistic or literary theory. If, as individuals, we now occupy 'roles' rather than 'selves', then the study of characters in novels may provide a useful model for understanding the construction of subjectivity in the world outside novels. If our knowledge of this world is now seen to be mediated through language, then literary fiction (worlds constructed entirely of language) becomes a useful model for learning about the construction of 'reality' itself.

The present increased awareness of 'meta' levels of discourse and experience is partly a consequence of an increased social and cultural self-consciousness. Beyond this, however, it also reflects a greater awareness within contemporary culture of the function of language in constructing and maintaining our sense of everyday 'reality'. The simple notion that language passively reflects a coherent, meaningful and 'objective' world is no longer tenable. Language is an independent, self-contained system which generates its own 'meanings'. Its

From Patricia Waugh (1984) *Metafiction: The Theory and Practice of Self-Conscious Fiction.* London: Routledge.

relationship to the phenomenal world is highly complex, problematic and regulated by convention. 'Meta' terms, therefore, are required in order to explore the relationship between this arbitrary linguistic system and the world to which it apparently refers. In fiction they are required in order to explore the relationship between the world *of* the fiction and the world *outside* the fiction.

In a sense, metafiction rests on a version of the Heisenbergian uncertainty principle: an awareness that 'for the smallest building blocks of matter, every process of observation causes a major disturbance' (Heisenberg 1972, p. 126), and that it is impossible to describe an objective world because the observer always changes the observed. However, the concerns of metafiction are even more complex than this. For while Heisenberg believed one could at least describe, if not a *picture* of nature, then a picture of one's *relation* to nature, metafiction shows the uncertainty even of this process. How is it possible to 'describe' anything? The metafictionist is highly conscious of a basic dilemma: if he or she sets out to 'represent' the world, he or she realizes fairly soon that the world, as such, cannot be 'represented'. In literary fiction it is, in fact, possible only to 'represent' the *discourses* of that world. Yet, if one attempts to analyse a set of linguistic relationships using those same relationships as the instruments of analysis, language soon becomes a 'prisonhouse' from which the possibility of escape is remote. Metafiction sets out to explore this dilemma.

The linguist L. Hjelmslev developed the term 'metalanguage' (Hjelmslev 1961). He defined it as a language which, instead of referring to non-linguistic events, situations or objects in the world, refers to *another* language: it is a language which takes another language as its object. Saussure's distinction between the signifier and the signified is relevant here. The signifier is the sound-image of the word or its shape on the page; the signified is the concept evoked by the word. A metalanguage is a language that functions as a signifier to *another language*, and this other language thus becomes its signified.[1]

In novelistic practice, this results in writing which consistently displays its conventionality, which explicity and overtly lays bare its condition of artifice, and which thereby explores the problematic relationship between life and fiction – both the fact that 'all the world is not of course a stage' and 'the crucial ways in which it isn't' (Goffman 1974, p. 53). The 'other' language may be either the registers of everyday discourse or, more usually, the 'language' of the literary system itself, including the conventions of the novel as a whole or particular forms of that genre.

Metafiction may concern itself, then, with particular conventions of the novel, to display the process of their construction (for example, John Fowles's use of the 'omniscient author' convention in *The French Lieutenant's Woman* (1969). It may, often in the form of parody, comment on a specific work or fictional mode (for example, John Gardner's *Grendel* (1971), which retells, and thus comments on, the *Beowulf* story from the point of view of the monster; or John Hawkes's *The Lime Twig* (1961), which constitutes both an example and a critique of the popular thriller. Less centrally metafictional, but still displaying 'meta' features, are fictions like Richard Brautigan's *Trout Fishing in America* (1967). Such novels attempt to create alternative linguistic structures or fictions which merely *imply* the old forms by encouraging the reader to draw on his or her knowledge of traditional literary conventions when struggling to construct a meaning for the new text.

[...]

MODERNISM AND POST-MODERNISM: THE REDEFINITION OF SELF-CONSCIOUSNESS

Metafiction is a mode of writing within a broader cultural movement often referred to as post-modernism. The metafictional writer John Barth has expressed a common feeling about the term 'post-modernism' as 'awkward and faintly epigonic, suggestive less of a vigorous or even interesting new direction in the old art of storytelling than of something anticlimactic, feebly following a very hard act to follow' (Barth 1980, p. 66). Post-modernism can be seen to exhibit the same sense of crisis and loss of belief in an external authoritative system of order as that which prompted modernism. Both affirm the constructive powers of the mind in the face of apparent phenomenal chaos. Modernist self-consciousness, however, though it may draw attention to the aesthetic construction of the text, does *not* 'systematically flaunt its own condition of artifice' (Alter 1975, p. x) in the manner of contemporary metafiction.

Modernism only occasionally displays features typical of post-modernism: the over-obtrusive, visibly inventing narrator (as in Barth's *Lost in the Funhouse* (1968), Robert Coover's *Pricksongs and Descants* (1969)); ostentatious typographic experiment (B. S. Johnson's *Travelling People* (1963), Raymond Federman's *Double or Nothing* (1971)); explicit dramatization of the reader. (Italo Calvino's *If on a Winter's Night a Traveller* (1979)); Chinese-box structures (Doris Lessing's *The Golden Notebook* (1962), John Barth's *Chimera* (1972)); incantatory and absurd lists (Donald Barthelme's *Snow White* (1967), Gabriel Josipovici's *The Inventory* (1968)); over-systematized or overtly arbitrarily arranged structural devices (Walter Abish's *Alphabetical Africa* (1974)); total breakdown of temporal and spatial organization of narrative (B. S. Johnson's 'A Few Selected Sentences' (1973)); infinite regress (Beckett's *Watt* (1953)); dehumanization of character, parodic doubles, obtrusive proper names (Pynchon's *Gravity's Rainbow* (1973)); self-reflexive images (Nabokov's mirrors, acrostics, mazes); critical discussions of the story within the story (Fowles's 'The Enigma' (1974), Barth's *Sabbatical* (1982)); continuous undermining of specific fictional conventions (Muriel Spark's quasi-omniscient author, Fowles's very un-Victorian ending in *The French Lieutenant's Woman* (1969)); use of popular genres (Richard Brautigan's *A Confederate General from Big Sur* (1964), Vonnegut's *Slaughter-house-Five* (1969)); and explicit parody of previous texts whether literary or non-literary (Gilbert Sorrentino's *Mulligan Stew* (1979), Alan Burns's *Babel* (1969)).

In all of these what is foregrounded is the writing of the text as the most fundamentally problematic aspect of that text. Although metafiction is just one form of post-modernism, nearly all contemporary experimental writing displays *some* explicitly metafictional strategies. Any text that draws the reader's attention to its process of construction by frustrating his or her conventional expectations of meaning and closure problematizes more or less explicitly the ways in which narrative codes – whether 'literary' or 'social' – artificially construct apparently 'real' and imaginary worlds in the terms of particular ideologies while presenting these as transparently 'natural' and 'eternal'.

In 1945 Joseph Frank explained the self-referential quality of modernist literature in these terms:

> Since the primary reference of any word group is to something inside the poem itself, language in modern poetry is really reflexive . . . instead of the instinctive and immediate reference of words and word groups to the objects and events they symbolize, and the construction of meaning from the sequence of these references, modern poetry asks its readers to suspend the process of individual reference temporarily until the entire pattern of internal references can be apprehended as a unity.
>
> (Frank 1958, p. 73)

the illusioned transparency of realist writing

In short, self-reflexiveness in modernist texts generates 'spatial form'. With realist writing the reader has the illusion of constructing an interpretation by referring the words of the text to objects in the real world. However, with texts like T. S. Eliot's *The Waste Land* (1922), in order to construct a satisfactory interpretation of the poem, the reader must follow the complex web of cross-references and repetitions of words and images which function independently of, or in addition to, the narrative codes of causality and sequence. The reader becomes aware that 'meaning' is constructed primarily through internal *verbal* relationships, and the poem thus appears to achieve a verbal autonomy: a 'spatial form'. Such organization persists in contemporary metafictional texts, but merely as *one* aspect of textual self-reflexivity. Indeed, 'spatial form' may *itself* function in these fictions as the object of self-conscious attention [. . .].

Post-modernism clearly does not involve the modernist concern with the mind as itself the basis of an aesthetic, ordered at a profound level and revealed to consciousness at isolated 'epiphanic' moments. At the end of Virginia Woolf's *To the Lighthouse* (1927), for example, Lily Briscoe suddenly perceives a higher (or deeper) order in things as she watches the boat return. Her realization is translated, directly and overtly, into aesthetic terms. Returning to her canvas, with intensity she draws the final line: 'It was finished. Yes she thought laying down her brush in extreme fatigue, I have had my vision' (p. 320). A post-modern 'line' is more likely to imitate that drawn by Tristram Shandy to represent the plot of his 'life and times' (resembling a diagram of the formation of an oxbow lake). In fact, if post-modernism shares some of the philosophies of modernism, its formal techniques seem often to have originated from novels like *Tristram Shandy* (1760), *Don Quixote* (1604) or *Tom Jones* (1749).

For Sterne, as for contemporary writers, the mind is not a perfect aestheticizing instrument. It is not free, and it is as much constructed out of, as constructed with, language. The substitution of a purely metaphysical system (as in the case of Proust) or mythical analogy (as with Joyce and Eliot) cannot be accepted by the metafictionist as final structures of authority and meaning. Contemporary reflexivity implies an awareness both of language *and* metalanguage, of consciousness *and* writing.

B. S. Johnson's 'A Few Selected Sentences', for example, is precisely what its title suggests: a series of fragments taken from a wide variety of discursive practices (ranging from a sixteenth-century description of the cacao fruit to absurd warnings) which, although resisting final totalization, can be arranged into a number of conventional narratives. The most obvious of these is a comment on what we are doing as we read: constructing a detective story. The style is reminiscent of Eliot's technique of fragmentation and montage in *The Waste Land*, but there the connections are present despite the fragmentary surface, to be recovered through the mythic consciousness as the reader partakes in the modern equivalent of the Grail search. The fragments which Johnson has shored against his ruins are not at all explicable by any such *a priori* transcendental system, only by his readers' knowledge of the conventions of stories. There is no longer a deep, structured collective unconscious to be relied upon, only the heavily italicized and multi-coded 'Life' with which the story ends (p. 80).

Whereas loss of order for the modernist led to the belief in its recovery at a deeper level of the mind, for metafictional writers the most fundamental assumption is that composing a novel is basically no different from composing or constructing one's 'reality'. Writing itself rather than consciousness becomes the main object of attention. Questioning not only the notion of the novelist as God, through the flaunting of the author's godlike role, but also the authority of consciousness, of the mind, metafiction establishes the categorization of the world through the arbitrary system of language. The modernist writer whose style fits closest with this essentially post-modernist mode of writing is; of course, James Joyce. Even in *A Portrait of the Artist as a Young Man* (1916), the epiphanic moments are usually connected with a self-reflexive response to language itself. The word 'foetus', for example, scratched on a desk, forces upon Stephen's consciousness a recognition of his whole 'monstrous way of life' (pp. 90–2).

Ulysses (1922) goes further in showing 'reality' to be a consequence of 'style'. However, despite parody, stylization and imitation of non-literary discourses, there is no overtly self-referential voice which systematically establishes, as the main focus of the novel, the problematic relationship of language and 'reality'. The only strictly metafictional line is Molly's 'Oh Jamesy let me up out of this Pooh' (p. 691), though there are many inherently self-conscious devices now widely used by metafictional writers, and the 'Oxen of the Sun' section is, of course, an extended piece of literary pastiche. Each of the parodies of literary styles in this section presents a direct and problematical relationship between style and content which draws attention to the fact that language is not simply a set of empty forms filled with meaning, but that it actually dictates and circumscribes what can be said and therefore what can be perceived. When a discussion of contraception, for example, creeps into the parody of the language of courtly love, the reader is made to see contraception in a new light. The realities of procreation in the twentieth century are thrown into a different perspective through their discussion within the linguistic parameters of the medieval world.

Ulysses has eighteen chapters and eighteen main styles. B. S. Johnson's *Travelling People* (1963), overtly both Shandyan and Joycean, has nine chapters and styles. Style is explicitly explored here in terms of negativity: how it represents certain aspects of experience only by excluding others. The novel begins by parodying the opening of *Tom Jones*, with Johnson setting out his 'bill of fare' and explaining that the style of each chapter should spring from its subject matter. Each shift of style is further accompanied by a Fieldingesque chapter heading, which, through its equally vacuous generality in Johnson's text, undermines the attempt of such verbal signposts to be comprehensive. The introduction, headings and 'interludes' complement the Joycean stylistic shifts through which the characters, the rootless 'travelling people' of the contemporary world, attempt to construct identities for themselves.

Henry, the protagonist, for example, is shown continually stylizing his existence, distancing unpleasant realities such as how many dogs are required to manufacture a certain amount of glue by communicating the information to himself in the language of a strident advertising slogan: 'See that your pet has a happy home in Henry's glue' (p. 12). The reader is thus made aware of how reality is *subjectively* constructed. But beyond this essentially modernist perspective, the text reveals a post-modernist concern with how it is itself *linguistically* constructed. Through continuous narrative intrusion, the reader is reminded that not only do characters verbally construct their own realities; they are themselves verbal constructions, *words* not *beings*.

[…]

THE ANALYSIS OF FRAMES: METAFICTION AND FRAME-BREAKING

A frame may be defined as a 'construction, constitution, build; established order, plan, system … underlying support or essential substructure of anything' (*Oxford English Dictionary*). Modernism and post-modernism begin with the view that both the historical world and works of art are organized and perceived through such structures or 'frames'. Both recognize further that the distinction between 'framed' and 'unframed' cannot in the end be made. Everything is framed, whether in life or in novels. Ortega y Gasset, writing on modernism, pointed out, however, that 'not many people are capable of adjusting their perceptive apparatus to the pane and the transparency that is the work of art. Instead they look right through it and revel in the human reality with which the work deals' (Ortega y Gasset 1948, p. 31). Contemporary metafiction, in particular, foregrounds 'framing' as a problem, examining frame procedures in the construction of the real world and of novels. The first problem it poses, of course, is: what is a 'frame'? What is the 'frame' that separates reality from 'fiction'? Is it more than the front and back covers of a book, the rising and lowering of a curtain, the title and 'The End'?

Modernist texts begin by plunging in *in medias res* and end with the sense that nothing is finished, that life flows on. Metafictional novels often begin with an explicit discussion of the arbitrary nature of beginnings, of boundaries, as in Graham Greene's *The End of the Affair* (1951): 'A story has no beginning or end: arbitrarily one chooses that moment of experience from which to look back or from which to look ahead' (p. 7). They often end with a choice of endings. Or they may end with a sign of the impossibility of endings. Julio Cortázar's *Hopscotch* (1967) presents the reader with two 'books': the book can be read according to the order in which it is printed, or it can be read according to an alternative order presented to the reader in the 'conclusion', the apparent 'end' of the first order. The first 'book' is read up to chapter 56; the second 'book' begins at chapter 73 and covers the whole novel except for chapter 55. The final 'end' is now apparently in chapter 58, but, when the reader gets there, it is to discover that he or she should go back to chapter 131, and so on and on and on. The final chapter printed is chapter 155 (which directs the reader back to 123), so the last printed words are: 'Wait'll I finish my cigarette' (*Hopscotch*, p. 564). We are still waiting . . .

Alternatively, such novels may end with a gloss upon the archetypal fictional ending, the 'happily ever after'. John Barth's *Sabbatical* (1982) poses the question whether the ending of the events begins the writing, or the ending of the writing begins the events. Susan decides that they should 'begin it at the end and end at the beginning, so we can go on forever. Begin with our living happily ever after' (p. 365); but her author has decided: 'we commence as we would conclude, that they lived

> Happily ever after, to the end of Fenwick and Susie . . .'
>
> (p. 366)

Contemporary metafiction draws attention to the fact that life, as well as novels, is constructed through frames, and that it is finally impossible to know where one frame ends and another begins. Contemporary sociologists have argued along similar lines. Erving Goffman in *Frame Analysis* has suggested that there is no simple dichotomy 'reality/fiction':

> When we decide that something is unreal, the real it isn't need not itself be very real, indeed, can just as well be a dramatization of events as the events

themselves – or a rehearsal of the dramatization, or a painting of the rehearsal or a reproduction of the painting. Any of these latter can serve as the original of which something is a mere mock-up, leading one to think that which is sovereign is relationship – not substance.

(Goffman 1974, pp. 560–1)

Frames in life operate like conventions in novels: they facilitate action and involvement in a situation. Goffman defines frames early in his book:

I assume that definitions of a situation are built up in accordance with principles which govern events – at least social ones – and our subjective involvement in them; frame is the word I use to refer to such of these basic elements as I am able to identify.

(ibid., p. 67)

Analysis of frames is the analysis, in the above terms, of the organization of experience. When applied to fiction it involves analysis of the formal conventional organization of novels. What both Goffman and metafictional novels highlight through the foregrounding and analysis of framing activities is the extent to which we have become aware that neither historical experiences nor literary fictions are unmediated or unprocessed or non-linguistic or, as the modernists would have it, 'fluid' or 'random'. Frames are essential in all fiction. They become more perceptible as one moves from realist to modernist modes and are explicitly laid bare in metafiction.

In metafictional novels, obvious framing devices range from stories within stories (John Irving's *The World According to Garp* (1976)), characters reading about their own fictional lives (Calvino's *If on a Winter's Night a Traveller*) and self-consuming worlds or mutually contradictory situations (Coover's 'The Babysitter', 'The Magic Poker' (1971)). The concept of 'frame' includes Chinese-box structures which contest the reality of each individual 'box' through a nesting of narrators (Flann O'Brien's *At Swim-Two-Birds* (1939), John Barth's *Chimera* (1972)). Similar are so-called 'fictions of infinity' such as Borges' 'Library of Babel', where 'In order to locate Book B, first consult Book C and so on *ad infinitum*' (*Labyrinths*, p. 84). Sometimes overt frames involve a confusion of ontological levels through the incorporation of visions, dreams, hallucinatory states and pictorial representations which are finally indistinct from the apparently 'real' (Alain Robbe-Grillet's *Dans le labyrinthe* (1959), Thomas Pynchon's *Gravity's Rainbow*, Doris Lessing's *The Memoirs of a Survivor* (1974) and *Briefing for a Descent into Hell* (1971)). Such infinities of texts within texts draw out the paradoxical relationship of 'framed' and 'unframed' and, in effect, of 'form' and 'content'. There is ultimately no distinction between 'framed' and 'unframed'. There are only levels of form. There is ultimately only 'content' perhaps, but it will never be discovered in a 'natural' unframed state.

One method of showing the function of literary conventions, of revealing their provisional nature, is to show what happens when they malfunction. Parody and inversion are two strategies which operate in this way as frame-breaks. The alternation of frame and frame-break (or the construction of an illusion through the imperceptibility of the frame and the shattering of illusion through the constant exposure of the frame) provides the essential deconstructive method of metafiction.

It seems that, according to Goffman, our sense of reality is strong enough to cope with minor frame-breaks, and in fact they reaffirm it, ensuring

> the continuity and viability of the established frame. Indeed the disattend track specifically permits the occurrence of many out-of-frame acts, provided only that they are 'properly' muted, that is, within the disattend capacity of the frame. ... Thus collusive exchanges between friends at stylish gatherings can be at once a means of breaking frame and a means of staying within it.
>
> (Goffman 1974, p. 382)

This comment is interesting because it offers support for an intuitive sense that although Fielding, Trollope and George Eliot, for example, often 'break the frame' of their novels they are by no means self-conscious novelists in the sense in which the term has been discussed here. Although the intrusive commentary of nineteenth-century fiction may at times be metalingual (referring to fictional codes themselves), it functions mainly to aid the readerly concretization of the world of the book by forming a bridge between the historical and the fictional worlds. It suggests that the one is merely a continuation of the other, and it is thus not metafictional.

In *Adam Bede* (1859), for example, George Eliot destroys the illusion of Hayslope's self-containedness by continually intruding moralistic commentary, interpretation and appeals to the reader. However, such intrusions do in fact *reinforce* the connection between the real and the fictional world, *reinforce* the reader's sense that one is a continuation of the other. In metafictional texts such intrusions *expose* the ontological distinctness of the real and the fictional world, *expose* the literary conventions that disguise this distinctness. In the chapter entitled 'The Rector', the narrative voice intrudes: 'Let me take you into their dining room ... we will enter, very softly ... the walls you see, are new. ... He will perhaps turn round by and by and in the meantime we can look at that stately old lady' (p. 63). Eliot is here using the convention of the reader's presence and the author's limitations – a pretence that neither knows what will happen next – to suggest through the collusive interchange that both are situated in ontologically undifferentiated worlds. Although this is a frame-break, therefore, it is of the minor variety which, in Goffman's terms, *reinforces* the illusion.

In order to clarify the implications of the difference between a minor and a major frame-break, and their respective uses in realistic and metafictional novels, *Adam Bede* can be compared with a metafictional novel, set at roughly the same time and in many ways involving similar moral issues. John Fowles's *The French Lieutenant's Woman* uses the device of authorial intimacy ultimately to *destroy* the illusion of reality. Throughout the fiction, real documents are referred to – as, for example, in the description of Sarah unpacking at Exeter. The narrator meticulously describes each article that she takes out:

> and then a Toby Jug, not one of those greenish-coloured monstrosities of Victorian manufacture, but a delicate little thing ... (certain experts may recognize a Ralph Leigh) ... the toby was cracked and was to be recracked in the course of time, as I can testify, having bought it myself a year or two ago for a good deal more than the three pennies Sarah was charged. But unlike her I fell for the Ralph Leigh part of it. She fell for the smile.
>
> (p. 241)

Sarah and the toby jug appear to have the same ontological status as the narrator. This brings the reader up against the paradoxical realization that normally we can read novels only because of our suspension of disbelief. Of course we *know* that what we are reading is not 'real', but we suppress the knowledge in order to increase our enjoyment. We tend to read fiction as if it were history. By actually appearing to treat the fiction as a historical document, Fowles employs the convention against itself. The effect of this, instead of *reinforcing* our sense of a continuous reality, is to split it open, to *expose* the levels of illusion. We are forced to recall that our 'real' world can *never* be the 'real' world of the novel. So the frame-break, while appearing to bridge the gap between fiction and reality, in fact lays it bare.

Throughout *The French Lieutenant's Woman* there is an abundance of frame-breaks more overt than this, particularly where the twentieth-century narrator suddenly appears as a character in the *histoire* as well as in the *discours*. The effect is one which Goffman has again discussed: 'When a character comments on a whole episode of activity in frame terms, he acquires a peculiar reality through the same words by which he undermines the one that was just performed' (Goffman 1974, p. 400). When Fowles discusses the fact that 'these characters I create never existed outside my own mind' (pp. 84–5), the peculiar reality forced upon the reader is that the character who is the apparent teller of the tale is its inventor and not a recorder of events that happened (this becomes the entire theme of Raymond Federman's novel *Double or Nothing*). Fowles goes on to argue, of course, that 'Fiction is woven into all. ... I find this new reality (or unreality) more valid' (pp. 86–7).

Despite this effect of exposure, however, it can be argued that metafictional novels simultaneously strengthen each reader's sense of an everyday real world while problematizing his or her sense of reality from a conceptual or philosophical point of view. As a consequence of their metafictional undermining of the conventional basis of existence, the reader may revise his or her ideas about the philosophical status of what is assumed to be reality, but he or she will presumably continue to believe and live in a world for the most part constructed out of 'common sense' and routine. What writers like Fowles are hoping is that each reader does this with a new awareness of how the meanings and values of that world have been constructed and how, therefore, they can be challenged or changed. To some extent each metafictional novel is a fictional *Mythologies* which, like Roland Barthes's work, aims to unsettle our convictions about the relative status of 'truth' and 'fiction'. As Goffman argues:

> The study of how to uncover deceptions is also by and large the study of how to build up fabrications ... one can learn how one's sense of ordinary reality is produced by examining something that is easier to become conscious of, namely, how reality is mimicked and/or how it is faked.
>
> (Goffman 1974, p. 251)

[...]

NOTE

1. See Fredric Jameson's *The Prisonhouse of Language* (Princeton and London, 1972), p. 159. Also useful is Jameson's essay 'Metacommentary', *PMLA*, 86 (1971).

WORKS CITED

Alter, Robert (1975) *Partial Magic: The Novel as a Self-Conscious Genre*. London and Berkeley, CA: University of California Press.

Barth, John (1980) 'The Literature of Replenishment', *Atlantic Monthly*, 245, 1: 65–71.

Frank, Joseph (1958) 'Spatial Form in Modern Literature', in Mark Schorer, J. Miles and G. McCenzie (eds), *Criticism: the Foundations of Modern Judgement*. Berkeley and Los Angeles, CA and London: University of California Press.

Gass, William H. (1970) *Fiction and the Figures of Life*. New York: Alfred A. Knopf.

Goffman, Irving (1974) *Frame Analysis*. Harmondsworth: Penguin.

Heisenberg, W. K. (1972) 'The Representation of Nature in Contemporary Physics', in Sallie Sears and Georgianna W. Lord (eds), *The Discontinuous Universe*. London and New York: Basic Books.

Hjelmslev, Louis (1961) *Prolegomena to a Theory of Language*. Madison, WI: University of Wisconsin Press.

Jameson, Fredric (1971) 'Metacommentary', *PMLA*, 86 [no page numbers in original].

Jameson, Fredric (1972) *The Prisonhouse of Language*. Princeton, NJ and London: Princeton University Press.

Ortega y Gasset, J. (1948) *The Dehumanization of Art and Notes on the Novel*. Princeton, NJ: Princeton University Press.

TOWARDS A POETICS OF POSTMODERN FICTION

19

'POSTMODERNIST FICTION'

David Lodge

The history of modern English literature [. . .] can be seen as an oscillation in the practice of writing between polarized clusters of attitudes and techniques: modernist, symbolist or mythopoeic, writerly and metaphoric on the one hand; antimodernist, realistic, readerly and metonymic on the other. What looks like innovation – a new mode of writing foregrounding itself against the background of the received mode when the latter becomes stale and exhausted – is therefore also in some sense a reversion to the principles and procedures of an earlier phase. If the critical pronouncements associated with each phase tend to be somewhat predictable, the actual creative work produced is not, such is the infinite variety and fertility of the human imagination working upon the fresh materials thrown up by secular history. But the metaphor/metonymy distinction explains why at the deepest level there is a cyclical rhythm to literary history, for there is nowhere else for discourse to go except between these two poles.

There is, however, a certain kind of contemporary avant-garde art which is said to be neither modernist nor antimodernist, but postmodernist; it continues the modernist critique of traditional mimetic art, and shares the modernist commitment to innovation, but pursues these aims by methods of its own. It tries to go beyond modernism, or around it, or underneath it, and is often as critical of modernism as it is of antimodernism. In the field of writing such a phenomenon obviously offers an interesting challenge to the explanatory power of the literary typology expounded above. The object of this chapter, then, is to

From David Lodge (1977) *The Modes of Modern Writing: Metaphor, Metonymy, and Typology of Modern Literature*. London: Edward Arnold.

attempt a profile of postmodernist fiction and to test the relevance of the metaphor/metonymy distinction to it. Postmodernism has established itself as an *écriture*, in Barthes's sense of the word – a mode of writing shared by a significant number of writers in a given period – most plausibly in the French *nouveau roman* and in American fiction of the last ten or fifteen years, and I shall be concerned here chiefly with the latter. But I shall make reference to texts by British writers where these seem relevant, and I begin with Samuel Beckett, who has a strong claim to be considered the first important postmodernist writer.

Beckett served his literary apprenticeship in the shadow of classical modernism. His earliest publications in prose were a contribution to a symposium on Joyce (1929) and a study of Proust (1930). The opening story, 'Dante and the Lobster', in his first book of fiction, *More Pricks than Kicks* (1934), shows him just beginning to detach himself from the modernist tradition, especially from the technique of Joyce, with whom, of all the modernist writers, Beckett has the closest affinity (and for whom he worked, for a time, as secretary). As it happens, this story deals with the same theme of life/death/time as the texts discussed in Part One. Belacqua, a Dublin student, performs various banal tasks in his day – makes himself a sandwich of burnt toast and gorgonzola cheese for his lunch, attends an Italian lesson, collects a lobster from the fishmonger for his aunt's and his own supper. Among the miscellaneous pieces of information that impinge on his consciousness is the fact that a convicted murderer is to be hanged the next day. Spectacles of pain and misery in the streets on his way home, combined with inner musings on Dante, especially the line from the *Inferno*, '*qui vive la pietà quando èben morta*' ('here pity lives when it is virtually dead' – Belacqua remarks that there is a 'superb pun' on pity/piety), provoke Belacqua to ask, 'Why not piety and pity both, even down below?', to pray for 'a little mercy in the stress of sacrifice' and to extend his compassion to the convicted murderer:

> Poor McCabe, he would get it in the neck at dawn. What was he doing now, how was he feeling? He would relish one more meal, one more night.[1]

This mood is, however, exposed as a sentimental illusion, for what really shocks Belacqua into a true awareness of pain and death is the discovery that the lobster is still alive and must be boiled in that state so that he may eat it.

> 'Christ!' he said 'it's alive.'
> His aunt looked at the lobster. It moved again. It made a faint nervous act of life on the oilcloth. They stood above it, looking down on it, exposed cruciform on the oilcloth. It shuddered again. Belacqua felt he would be sick.
> 'My God' he whined 'it's alive, what'll we do?'...
> 'You make a fuss' she said angrily 'and upset me and then lash into it for your dinner.'

> She lifted the lobster clear of the table. It had about thirty seconds to
> live. Well, thought Belcqua, it's a quick death, God help us all.
> It is not.[2]

This conclusion to the story (which I have much abridged) takes place in the
aunt's kitchen which, like Dante's Hell, is in 'the bowels of the earth'. The
Divine Comedy seems to function in Beckett's story much as Homer's *Odyssey*
does in *Ulysses*. Belacqua's name (as improbable as Dedalus) derives from
Purgatory; at the opening of the story he is wrestling with the interpretation of a
difficult passage in *Paradise*; and his conversation with his Italian teacher
touches on 'Dante's rare movements of compassion in Hell'.[3] The story seems
to indicate the ultimate irrelevance of the Christian metaphysic (supremely
articulated by Dante) to the problem of suffering and death. It thus reverses the
message of Oscar Wilde's 'The Ballad of Reading Gaol'; but Christian symbolism and allusion, especially to the Passion, permeate the climax of the story
even if largely disguised under 'low' diction ('Christ!' 'cruciform' 'My God'
'lash into'), evidently to underline the horror of the world when recognized for
what it is, a place where one creature lives by the cruel sacrifice of another, right
along the chain of being. The identification of the lobster with Christ is clearly
signalled earlier in the story when Belacqua, talking to a French teacher, is
obliged to use the word *poisson*. 'He did not know the French for lobster. Fish
would do very well. Fish had been good enough for Jesus Christ, Son of God,
Saviour. It was good enough for Mlle Glain.'[4] Even the hilarious business of
Belacqua's lunch fits into the same thematic scheme, inasmuch as Belcaqua's
toasting of the bread till it is black, and his handling of the cheese, are portrayed
as violent actions perpetrated upon innocent living matter:

> He laid his cheek against the soft of the bread, it was spongy and warm,
> *alive*. But he would very quickly take that fat white look off its face ...[5]
> [my italics]

> He looked sceptically at the cut of cheese. He turned it over on its back to
> see was the other side any better. The other side was worse. . . . He rubbed
> it. It was sweating. That was something. He stooped and smelt it. A faint
> fragrance of corruption. What good was that? He didn't want fragrance,
> he wasn't a bloody gourmet, he wanted a good stench. What he wanted
> was a good green stenching rotten lump of Gorgonzola cheese, *alive*, and
> by God he would have it.[6] [my italics]

The handling of the cheese is proleptic of the aunt's treatment of the lobster at
the end of the story: 'She caught up the lobster and laid it on its back. It
trembled. "They feel nothing" she said.'[7]

Up to a point, then, 'Dante and the Lobster' responds to the same kind of
reading as an episode of *Ulysses*, as a narrative of modern life which alludes to a
prior myth that is in some sense a key to its meaning, and in which a superficially
gratuitous sequence of banal events is guided towards a final thematic epiphany

by discreetly planted *leitmotifs*. But there is a good deal in the text that is not accountable in these terms. The manic, obsessional and eccentric behaviour of the hero, for instance (a long way from the endearing whims and fetishes of Bloom) is in no sense 'explained' by the story. It is funny, but it is also disconcerting. So is, in a different way, the last line of the story: 'It is not.' This is not the first occasion on which the author who 'speaks' the narrative is distinguishable from Belacqua, through whose eyes it is mainly seen, but it is certainly the most emphatically foregrounded – being, in effect, not merely a comment, but a flat contradiction and dismissal of the hero and his hollow epiphany. The author, as it were, scuttles his story in its last line, and this prevents the reader from leaving its uncomfortable implications safely enclosed within the category of 'literature' or 'fiction'. These are features which become progressively more marked in Beckett's fiction (and in postmodernist writing generally), while the 'mythical method' (exemplified by the Dantean parallels) 'of ordering, of giving a shape and significance to the immense panorama of futility and anarchy that is contemporary history' (as T. S. Eliot said of Joyce)[8] disappears, is displaced by a growing insistence that there is no order, no shape or significance to be found anywhere.

Beckett's next work of fiction, *Murphy* (1938) begins:

> The sun shone, having no alternative, on the nothing new. Murphy sat out of it, as though he were free, in a mew in West Brompton ... He sat naked in his rocking-chair of undressed teak, guaranteed not to crack, warp, corrode or creak at night. It was his own, it never left him. The corner in which he sat was curtained off from the sun, the poor old sun in the Virgin again for the billionth time. Seven scarves held him in position. Two fastened his shins to the rockers, one his things to the seat, two his breast and belly to the back, one his wrists to the strut behind. Only the most local movements were possible. Sweat poured off him, tightened the thongs. The breath was not perceptible. The eyes, cold and unwavering as a gull's, stared up at an irridescence splashed over the cornice moulding, shrinking and fading.[9]

This discourse raises a lot of questions in the reader's mind. Some are answered: for instance, Murphy constrains his body in this eccentric manner in order to live more completely in his mind – he is a dedicated solipsist. But how does Murphy manage to tie himself up unassisted? and where is the seventh scarf? More fundamentally, whose voice are we listening to? Who takes pity on 'the poor old sun', and who compares Murphy's eyes to a gull's, and what is the import of these tropes? It is difficult to answer these questions.

If 'Dante and the Lobster' reminds one of Joyce, *Murphy* is Beckett's '1930s' novel. Its drab, historically precise setting (London, 1935), and its subject matter (penniless, alienated young man having difficulties in finding acceptable employment and keeping his girlfriend) have certain affinities with the novels of Isherwood and Orwell (especially *Keep the Aspidistra Flying*) but the experience of reading it is very different. While renouncing the mythic parallelism of Joyce's treatment of Dublin, it also ignores or ridicules the conventions of realism adopted by the representative novelists of the 1930s. There is no local colour in *Murphy*, no evocative synecdochic detail in the descriptions of places and people. The opening of Chapter 2, describing Celia in a list of facts and figures –

Age	Unimportant
Head	Small and round
Eyes	Green
Complexion	White
Hair	Yellow
Features	Mobile
Neck	$13\frac{3}{4}''$

etc. – mocks the conventional novelistic description of physical appearance, as the description of Murphy's grotesque green suit parodies the realistic novelist's reliance on the code of clothing as an index to character.[10] The narrator is for the most part impersonal and aloof, but given to disconcerting interventions, addresses to the reader ('gentle skimmer') and metafictional comments ('Celia, thank God for a Christian name'. . . . 'The above passage is carefully calculated to deprave the cultivated reader'). The predictability of the style and development of the action is extremely low, and although it is a very funny book it is not at all easy to read for this reason. It *resists* reading by refusing to settle into a simply identifiable mode or rhythm, thus imitating, on the level of reading conventions, the resistance of the world to interpretation.

The latter idea becomes explicit in the next novel *Watt* (1953 – composed 1942–3), supremely in the episode of the Galls, who appear at the door of the house where Watt is working as a servant to Mr Knott:

> We are the Galls, father and son, and we are come, what is more, all the way from town, to choon the piano.
> They were two, and they stood, arm in arm, in this way, because the father was blind, like so many members of his profession. For if the father had not been blind, then he would not have needed his son to hold his arm, and guide him on his rounds, no, but he would have set his son free, to go about his own business. So Watt supposed, though there was nothing in the father's face to show that he was blind, nor in his attitude, either, except that he leaned on his son in a way expressive of a great need of support. But he might have done this, if he had been halt, or merely tired, on account of his great age. There was no family likeness between the two, as far as Watt could make out, and nevertheless he knew he was in the presence of a father and son, for had he not just been told so. Or were they not perhaps merely stepfather and stepson. We are the Galls stepfather and stepson – those were perhaps the words that should have been spoken.

> But it was natural to prefer the others. Not that they could not very well be a true father and son, without resembling each other in the least, for they could.[11]

Uncertainty spreads like the plague through the world of *Watt*. 'The incident of the Galls father and son,' observes the narrator, 'was followed by others of a similar kind, incidents that is to say of great formal brilliance and indeterminable purport. ... And Watt could not accept them for what they perhaps were, the simple games that time plays with space ... but was obliged, because of his peculiar character, to enquire into what they meant. ... But what was this pursuit of meaning, in this indifference to meaning? And to what did it tend? These are delicate questions.'[12] Indeed – but questions absolutely fundamental to Beckett's work. The often-asserted resistance of the world to meaningful interpretation would be a sterile basis for writing if it were not combined with a poignant demonstration of the human obligation to attempt such interpretation, especially by the process of organizing one's memories into narrative form. In the next stage of Beckett's narrative writing, the trilogy of *Molloy* (1951), *Malone Dies* (1951) and the *Unnamable* (1953) (all of which first appeared in French) the impersonal, erratically intrusive and rhetorically unpredictable narrator of the earlier fiction is displaced by a series of first-person narrators, increasingly isolated and deprived of sensory stimuli, desperately trying to make sense of their experience by recalling it. The contradiction between the futility of the effort and the compulsion to make it produces a longing for extinction and silence, which in turn provokes fear and a frantic clinging to the vestiges of consciousness – which is intolerable.

> ...if only there were a thing, but there it is, there is not, they took away things when they departed, they took away nature, there was never anyone, anyone but me, anything but me, talking to me of me, impossible to stop, impossible to go on, but I must go on, I'll go on, without anyone, without anything, but me, but my voice, that is to say I'll stop, I'll end, it's the end already, shortlived, what is it, a little hole, you go down into it, into the silence, it's worse than the noise, you listen, it's worse than talking, no, not worse, no worse, you wait, in anguish, have they forgotten me, no, yes, no, someone calls me, I crawl out again, what is it, a little hole, in the wilderness. It's the end that is the worst, no, it's the beginning that is the worst, then the middle, then the end, in the end it's the end that is the worst, this voice, that, I don't know, it's every second that is the worst...[13]

It would be quite false to suggest that all postmodernist writers share Beckett's particular philosophical preoccupations and obsessions. But the general idea of the world resisting the compulsive attempts of the human consciousness to interpret it, of the human predicament being in some sense 'absurd', does underlie a good deal of postmodernist writing. That is why it seeks to find formal alternatives to modernism as well as to antimodernism. The falsity of the patterns imposed upon experience in the traditional realistic novel is common ground between the modernists and the postmodernists, but to the latter it seems that the modernists, too, for all their experimentation, obliquity and complexity, oversimplified the world and held out a false hope of somehow making it at home in the human mind. *Finnegans Wake* (to take the most extreme product of the modernist literary imagination) certainly 'resists' reading, resists interpretation, by the formidable difficulty of its verbal style and narrative method, and perhaps it has yet to find that 'ideal reader suffering from ideal insomnia' for whom, Joyce said, it was designed. But we persist in trying to read it in the faith that it is ultimately susceptible of being understood – that we shall, eventually, be able to unpack all the meanings that Joyce put into it, and that these meanings will cohere into a unity. Postmodernism subverts that faith. 'Where is the figure in the carpet?' asks a character in Donald Barthelme's *Snow White* (1967), alluding to the title of a story by Henry James that has become proverbial among modern critics as an image of the goal of interpretation; but he adds disconcertingly: 'Or is it just … carpet?'[14] A lot of postmodernist writing implies that experience is 'just carpet' and that whatever patterns we discern in it are wholly illusory, comforting fictions.

The difficulty, for the reader, of postmodernist writing, is not so much a matter of obscurity (which might be cleared up) as of uncertainty, which is endemic, and manifests itself on the level of narrative rather than style. No amount of patient study could establish, for instance, whether the man with the heavy coat and hat and stick encountered by Moran in *Molloy* is the man Molloy designated as C, or Molloy himself, or someone else; and Hugh Kenner's description of Beckett 'filling the air with uncertainty, the uncertainty fiction usually dissipates',[15] will apply to a lot of postmodernist writers. We shall never be able to unravel the plots of John Fowles's *The Magus* (1966) or Alain Robbe-Grillet's *Le Voyeur* (1955) or Thomas Pynchon's *The Crying of Lot 49* (1966), for they are labyrinths without exits. Endings, the 'exits' of fictions, are particularly significant in this connection. Instead of the closed ending of the traditional novel, in which mystery is explained and fortunes are settled, and instead of the open ending of the modernist novel, 'satisfying but not final' as Conrad said of Henry James,[16] we get the multiple ending, the false ending, the mock ending or parody ending.

The classic type of the 'closed' ending is that of the crime story in which the detective solves the mystery, reduces to meaningful order the apparently meaningless confusion of clues, and ensures that justice is done. Muriel Spark parodies this convention, and implicitly criticizes the presumption of those (novelists as well as policemen) who play the part of Providence, in novels which disconcertingly readjust the roles of criminal, victim and witnesses. Thus in *The Driver's Seat* (1970) Lise scatters across Europe in the days before her death a trail of clues which make no sense at all until we grasp that she is in a sense the plotter as well as the victim of the crime. In the same author's *Not to*

Disturb (1971) the servants in a luxurious villa on Lake Geneva make their arrangements to profit by a *crime passionelle* which has not yet occurred. Journalists are alerted, statements prepared, contracts negotiated by transatlantic telephone, interviews recorded on tape and film, while the husband, wife and lover are still arguing in the library. The suave butler, Lister, who presides over the whole operation, observes of his employers that 'They have placed themselves, unfortunately, within the realm of predestation.'[17] He excludes two people from the house 'because they don't fit into the story' and the weather (always ready to cooperate with gods and novelists) obligingly eliminates them with a thunderbolt.

In *The French Lieutenant's Woman* (1969) John Fowles presents alternative endings to his story and invites the reader to choose between them. John Barth floats a whole series of possible endings to the title story of his collection *Lost in the Funhouse* (1968), but rejects them all except the most inconclusive and banal. Another story, 'Title', perceptibly influenced by Beckett, contrives not to end at all:

> It's about over. Let the dénouement be soon and unexpected, painless if possible, quick at least, above all soon. Now now! How in the world will it ever[18]

Richard Brautigan adds to the ending of *A Confederate General From Big Sur* (1964) 'A SECOND ENDING', then a third, a fourth and fifth.

> Then there are more and more endings: the sixth, the 53rd, the 131st, the 9,435th ending, endings going faster and faster, more and more endings, faster and faster until this book is having 186,000 endings per second.[19]

The same author concludes the penultimate chapter of *Trout Fishing in America* (1967), entitled 'PRELUDE TO THE "MAYONNAISE" CHAPTER': 'Expressing a human need I always wanted to write a book that ended with the word Mayonnaise.'[20] And accordingly the last chapter consists of the transcript of a letter written in 1952 from 'Mother and Nancy' to 'Florence and Harv' which has the P.S., 'Sorry I forgot to give you the mayonnaise [sic].'[21] There is the additional joke that this whimsical human need could have been fulfilled without the last chapter, since the penultimate chapter also ends with the word 'mayonnaise', and the 'MAYONNAISE CHAPTER' is no less arbitrary a way of ensuring that the book ends on that word, since the letter in no way relates to anything that has gone before. Indeed, insofar as the P.S. misspells the word, Brautigan has cheated himself of his intention by transcribing it.

Critical opinion varies about how significantly *new* postmodernism really is. Leslie Fiedler, for instance, thinks it is genuinely revolutionary;[22] Frank Kermode, on the other hand, thinks that it has achieved only 'marginal developments of older modernism'.[23] Both opinions are tenable – both are in a sense 'true'. It depends upon what you are looking for and where you are standing when you are looking. Fiedler is mainly concerned with American literature and culture (in the anthropological sense); Kermode with the international avantgarde in all the arts. Fiedler defines postmodernism primarily as a very recent 'posthumanist' phenomenon, hostile or indifferent to traditional aesthetic categories and values, offering a polymorphous hedonism to its (largely youthful) audience, and unamenable to formalist analysis. Its art is anti-art, and demands 'Death-of-Art criticism'.[24] Kermode, on the other hand, approaches postmodernism as a historian of art and aesthetics and has little difficulty in tracing its theoretical assumptions back to either classical modernism or to the Dadaist schism that developed as long ago as 1916; and he sees the latter tradition as an essentially marginal one, its products more akin to jokes than art, 'piquant allusions to what fundamentally interests us more than they do.'[25] The aim of this chapter is not to try and settle the disagreement, but to try and throw light on the formal principles underlying postmodernist writing.

If Jakobson is right, that all discourse tends towards either the metaphoric or the metonymic pole of language, it should be possible to categorize postmodernist writing under one heading or the other. The theory (crudely summarized) states that all discourse connects one topic with another, either because they are in some sense similar to each other, or because they are in some sense contiguous with each other; and implies that if you attempt to group topics according to some other principle, or absence of principle, the human mind will nevertheless persist in trying to make sense of the text thus produced by looking in it for relationships of similarity and/or contiguity; and insofar as a text succeeds in defeating such interpretation, it defeats itself. It would, I believe, be possible to analyse postmodernist writing in these terms, but perhaps not very profitable. For if we extend the term 'postmodernist' to cover all the writers to whom it seems applicable, we might identify them individually as either metaphoric or metonymic, but it would be difficult to show that their work, considered *collectively*, has any bias towards one pole or the other. Rather it would seem that we can best define the formal character of postmodernist writing by examining its efforts to deploy both metaphoric and metonymic devices in radically new ways, and to defy (even if such defiance is ultimately vain) the obligation to choose between these two principles of connecting one topic with another. What other alternatives might there be? The headings below are intended to indicate some of the possibilities.

CONTRADICTION

But what is the good of talking about what they will do as soon as Worm sets himself in motion, so as to gather himself without fail into their midst, since he cannot set himself in motion, though he often desires to, if when speaking of him one may speak of desire, and one may not, one should not, but there it is, that is the way to speak of him, as if he were alive, as if he could understand, as if he could desire, even if it serves no purpose, and it serves none.[26]

This passage from *The Unnamable* cancels itself out as it goes along, and is representative of a text in which the narrator is condemned to oscillate between irreconcilable desires and assertions. Famously, it ends, 'you must go on, I can't go on, I'll go on.' If that were rearranged slightly to read, 'I can't go on, you must go on, I'll go on', it would not be at all self-contradictory, but a quite logically motivated and 'uplifting' sequence of despair followed by self-admonishment followed by renewed resolve. As it stands, each clause negates the preceding one. Leonard Michaels approaches this radically contradictory basis for the practice of writing when he says in 'Dostoevsky', 'It is impossible to live with or without fictions.'[27] The religion of Bokonism in Kurt Vonnegut's *Cat's Cradle* (1963) is based on 'the cruel paradox of . . . the heartbreaking necessity of lying about reality and the heartbreaking impossibility of lying about it.'[28]

One of the most emotively powerful emblems of contradiction, one that affronts the most fundamental binary system of all, is the hermaphrodite; and it is not surprising that the characters of postmodernist fiction are often sexually ambivalent: for example, Gore Vidal's sex-changing Myra/Myron Breckinridge,[29] and the central character of Brigid Brophy's *In Transit* (1969), who is suffering from amnesia in an international airport and cannot remember what sex he/she is (the narrator cannot examine his/her private parts in public, but cannot retreat to the privacy of a public convenience without knowing what she/he desires to find out). Henry, the hero of the postmodernist half of Julian Mitchell's duplex novel *The Undiscovered Country* (1968) (the other half is realistic or autobiographical in mode – I have written about this work at some length in *The Novelist at the Crossroads, and Other Essays on Fiction and Criticism* (1971) pp. 26–32) is transformed into a woman, and then into a hermaphrodite, and is engaged in the pursuit of a beautiful creature of equally uncertain sex. At the climax of John Barth's allegorical fabulation *Giles Goat-boy* (1966) the caprine hero and his beloved Anastasia survive the dreaded inquisition of the computer WESCAC when, locked together in copulation, they answer the question 'ARE YOU MALE OR FEMALE?' with two simultaneous and contradictory answers, 'YES' and 'NO'.[30]

PERMUTATION

Both metaphoric and metonymic modes of writing involve selection, and selection involves leaving something out. Postmodernist writers often try to defy this law by incorporating alternative narrative lines in the same text – for example John Fowles' *The French Lieutenant's Woman* and John Barth's 'Lost in the Funhouse', already cited, Robert Coover's 'The Magic Poker' and 'The Babysitter' in *Pricksongs and Descants* (1969) and Raymond Federman's *Double or Nothing* (1971). This procedure is another kind of 'contradiction', though in practice we are usually able to resolve it by ranking the alternatives in an order of authenticity. A more radical way of denying the obligation to select is to exhaust all the possible combinations in a given field. In the imaginary world of 'Tlön, Uqbar, Orbis Tertius', one of the fables of Jorge Luis Borges that have exercised a potent fascination over many American postmodernist writers, 'Works of fiction contain a single plot, with all its imaginable permutations';[31] and the labyrinthine novel of Ts'ui Pen in Borges' 'The Garden of the Forking Paths' is constructed on similar principles:

> In all fictional works, each time a man is confronted with several alternatives, he chooses one and eliminates the others; in the fiction of Ts'ui Pen, he chooses – simultaneously – all of them. *He creates*, in this way, diverse futures, diverse times which themselves also proliferate and fork. Here, then, is the explanation of the novel's contradictions. Fang, let us say, has a secret; a stranger calls at his door; Fang resolves to kill him. Naturally, there are several possible outcomes: Fang can kill the intruder, the intruder can kill Fang, they both can escape, they both can die, and so forth. In the work of Ts'ui Pen, all possible outcomes occur; each one is the point of departure for other forkings.[32]

By plausibly imagining the impossible, Borges liberates the imagination. Beckett uses permutation in a more limited way and to more depressive effect:

> As for his feet, sometimes he wore on each a sock, or on the one a sock and on the other a stocking, or a boot, or a shoe, or a slipper, or a sock and boot, or a sock and shoe, or a sock and slipper, or a stocking and boot, or a stocking and shoe, or a stocking and slipper, or nothing at all. And sometimes he wore on each a stocking, or on the one a stocking and on the other a boot, or a shoe, or a slipper, or a sock and boot, or a sock and shoe. . . .[33]

and so on, for a page and a half. There are several similar passages in *Watt*, in which every possible combination of a set of variables is exhausted. Probably the most famous example of permutation in Beckett, however, is in *Molloy*, where the eponymous hero wrestles with the problem of distributing and circulating his sixteen sucking stones in his pockets in such a way as to guarantee that he will always suck them in the same order.[34] Beckett's characters seek desperately to impose a purely mathematical order upon experience in the absence of any metaphysical order. In *Murphy* the hero, making his lunch from a packet of mixed biscuits, is torn between his weakness for one particular kind of biscuit and the possibility of total permutability:

> were he to take the final step and overcome his infatuation with the ginger, then the assortment would spring to life before him, dancing the radiant measure of its total permutability, edible in a hundred and twenty ways![35]

When reduced to only two variables, permutation becomes simply alternation and expresses the hopelessness of the human condition. ' "For every symptom that is eased, another is worse," ' opines Wylie in *Murphy*. ' "The horse leech's daughter is a closed system. Her quantum of wantum cannot vary. . . . Humanity is a well with two buckets . . . one going down to be filled, the other coming up to be emptied." '[36] In Joseph Heller's *Catch 22* (1961) there is a wounded soldier in the hospital entirely swathed in bandages and connected to a drip-feed bottle and a bottle for waste fluid:

> When the jar on the floor was full, the jar feeding his elbow was empty, and the two were simply switched over quickly so that the stuff could drip back into him.[37]

DISCONTINUITY

One quality we expect of all writing is continuity. Writing is a one-sided conversation. As every student, and every critic, knows, the most difficult aspect of composing an essay or thesis or book is to put one's scattered thoughts into an ideal order which will appear to have a seamless logical inevitability in its progress from one topic to another, without distorting or omitting any important point. This book itself contains innumerable sentences and phrases included not primarily to convey information but to construct smooth links between one topic and another. In fiction, metonymic writing offers a very obvious and readily intelligible kind of continuity based on spatio-temporal contiguities; the continuity of metaphorical writing is more difficult, but not impossible to identify. And as it is by its continuity that a discursive text persuades the reader, implying that no other ordering of its data could be intellectually as satisfying, so it is by its continuity that a work of fiction, if successful, imposes its vision of the world upon the reader, displaces the 'real world' with an imagined world in which the reader (especially in the case of realistic fiction) lives vicariously. Postmodernism is suspicious of continuity. Beckett disrupts the continuity of his discourse by unpredictable swerves of tone, metafictional asides to the reader, blank spaces in the text, contradiction and permutation. Some recent American writers have gone a step further and *based* their discourse upon discontinuity. 'Interruption. Discontinuity. Imperfection. It can't be helped,' insists the authorial voice of Ronald Sukenick's *98.6*.[38]

98.6 illustrates the most obvious sign of discontinuity in contemporary fiction – the growing fashion for composing in very short sections, often only a paragraph in length, often quite disparate in content, the breaks between sections being sometimes further emphasized by capitalized headings (as in Richard Brautigan's *In Watermelon Sugar* [1968]), numbers (as in Robert Coover's 'The Gingerbread Man') or typographical devices (like the arrows in Vonnegut's *Breakfast of Champions* [1973]). Vonnegut's later novels and all of Brautigan's are built up in this way, out of sections too short to be recognized as conventional chapters. Donald Barthelme uses bizarre illustrations to break up the text of some of the pieces in *City Life* (1971), and Raymond Federman ingeniously varies the typographical layout of *Double or Nothing*, using techniques borrowed from concrete poetry to avoid the odium of

```
a very direct form of narration    without any distractions
                                    without any obstructions just plain
                                                            normal
                                                            regular
                                                            readable
                                                            realistic
                                                            leftoright
                                                            unequivocal
                                                            conventional
                                                            unimaginative
                                                            wellpunctuated
                                                            understandable
                                                            uninteresting
                                                            safetodigest
                                                            paragraphed
                                                            compulsive
                                                            anecdotal
                                                            salutory
                                                            textual
              PROSE         prose      prose             boring
      PROSE      PROSE            prose        PROSE  plain  PROSE³⁹
```

Leonard Michaels has recently developed what is virtually a new genre: the cluster (it is precisely *not* a sequence) of short passages – stories, anecdotes, reflections, quotations, prose-poems, jokes – each with an individual title in large type. Between these apparently discontinuous passages the bewildered but exhilarated reader bounces and rebounds like a ball in a pinball machine, illuminations flashing on and off, insights accumulating, till the author laconically signals TILT. One such cluster, 'I Would Have Saved Them If I Could', is concerned with the same life/death/time theme in the context of capital punishment – 'the condemned prisoner story', Michaels calls it – that we have encountered several times already in this study, but it is quite distinctive in form. It consists of seventeen sections: *Giving Notice*, a brief, bitter comedy of Jewish American life, turning on a son's loss of faith; *A Suspected Jew*, an interpretation of Borges's story 'The Secret Miracle' about a Jewish writer Jaromir Hladik, executed by the Gestapo, who was allowed by God enough time between the firing of the bullets and death to mentally complete his unfinished masterpiece; *The Subject at the Vanishing Point*, a memoir of the narrator's – and author's? – grandfather, a refugee from Polish pogroms; *Material Circumstances*, a hostile vignette of Karl Marx roused to historical wrath by a landlord's insolence; *Business Life*, a wry anecdote of the narrator's uncle who runs successful beauty parlours; *Shrubless Crags*, a quotation from Byron's *The Prisoner of Chillon* about a condemned prisoner; *Song*, a three-line gag about Russian folksongs; *Blossoms*, about the terrifying early experiences of the uncle in Europe; *The Screams of Children*, about Jesus, Hladik, Kafka, the Final Solution; *Heraclitus, Hegel, Giacometti, Nietzsche, Wordsworth, Stevens*, on philosophical systems; *Alienation*, about the relation of Marxism to Christianity; *Lord Byron's Letter*, the transcription of a letter in which the poet gives an eye-witness account of three criminals being guillotined ('the second and third (which shows how dreadfully soon things grow indifferent) I am ashamed to say, had no effect on me as a horror, though I would have saved them if I could'); *Species Being*, a critique of the letter; *Dostoevsky*, a brief account of Dostoevsky's story of being reprieved from sentence of death; *The Night I Became a Marxist*, a mock-Pauline account of conversion; and *Conclusion*, which points out that 'from a certain point of view [that of the dead] none of this shit matters any more'.[40] After several readings a kind of thematic coherence does begin to emerge from this textual collage, epitomized by the sentence quoted earlier from Dostoevsky, 'It is impossible to live with or without fictions.' Fictions, whether literary, theological, philosophical or political, can never make death acceptable, or even comprehensible, yet in a world 'incessantly created of incessant death' (*Conclusion*) we have no other resource. There are degrees of authenticity (Byron's honest exactitude is preferred to Borges's whimsy or Marx's theorizing) but in the end it makes no difference. Such a paraphrase, however, is more than usually misleading, since it is only in the actual reading experience, in the disorientation produced by the abrupt and unpredictable shifts of register from one section to another, that the effects of bafflement, anguish, contradiction are felt. Michaels's exploitation of discontinuity can be more conveniently illustrated by quoting the opening lines of a less complex story, 'In the Fifties':

> In the fifties I learned to drive a car. I was frequently in love. I had more friends than now.
>
> When Krushchev denounced Stalin my roommate shit blood, turned yellow and lost most of his hair.
>
> I attended the lectures of the excellent E. B. Burgum until Senator McCarthy ended his tenure. I imagined NYU would burn. Miserable students, drifting in the halls, looked at one another.
>
> In less than a month, working day and night, I wrote a bad novel.
>
> I went to school – NYU, Michigan, Berkeley – much of the time. I had witty, giddy conversation, four or five nights a week, in a homosexual bar in Ann Arbor.
>
> I read literary reviews the way people suck candy.
>
> Personal relationships were more important to me than anything else.
>
> I had a fight with a powerful fat man who fell on my face and was immovable.
>
> I had personal relationships with football players, jazz musicians, ass-bandits, nymphomaniacs, non-specialized degenerates, and numerous Jewish premedical students.

> I had personal relationships with thirty-five rhesus monkeys in an
> experiment on monkey addiction to morphine. They knew me as one
> who shot reeking crap out of cages with a hose.[41]

The 'story' (hardly the right word, but there is no other) continues in the same
mode: bald statements of fact which appear to have nothing to connect them
except that they belong to the life of the narrator in the 1950s, and seem to have
been selected at random from his total experience. There is a kind of recurrent
theme – the political impotence of the 1950s – but most of the statements made
have nothing to do with it. It's a very risky procedure, but it works because of
the casual brilliance of the writing and because the writer persuades us that the
discontinuity of his text *is* the truth of his experience. 'I used to think that
someday I would write a fictional version of my stupid life in the fifties,' says the
narrator at one point, and the implication is that the raw ingredients of that life
heaped in front of us constitute a more authentic record than would be any well-
made novel.

In the work of Donald Barthelme the principle of *non-sequitur* governs the
relationships between sentences as well as between paragraphs. 'Edward looked
at his red beard in the tableknife. Then Edward and Pia went to Sweden, to the
farm.'[42] The purely temporal continuity of these actions is overwhelmed by the
huge difference in scale between them and the absence of any causal connection.

> From his window Charles watched Hilda. She sat playing under the black
> pear tree. She bit deeply into a black pear. It tasted bad and Hilda looked
> at the tree inquiringly. Charles started to cry. He had been reading
> Bergson. He was surprised by his own weeping, and in a state of surprise,
> decided to get something to eat.[43]

This passage begins with a kind of logical continuity of motivation, but frays
out into disparate reactions of Charles – weeping, reading Bergson, feeling
hungry – which have nothing to do with Hilda or with each other. One of
Barthelme's favourite devices is to take a number of interrelated or contiguous
characters, or consciousness or conversations, and scramble them together to
produce an apparently random montage of bizarrely contrasting verbal fragments ('fragments are the only forms I trust,' a Barthelme character observes).[44]
For example, 'The Viennese Opera Ball':

> It is one of McCormack's proudest boasts, Carola heard over her lovely
> white shoulder, that he never once missed having dinner with his wife in
> their forty-one years of married life. She remembered Knocko at the
> Evacuation Day parade, and Baudelaire's famous remark. Mortality is
> the final evaluator of methods. An important goal is an intact sphincter.
> The greater the prematurity, the more generous should be the episiotomy.
> Yes, said Leon Jaroff, Detroit Bureau Chief for *Time*, at the Thomas
> Elementary School on warm spring afternoons I could look from my
> classroom into the open doors of the Packard plant. Ideal foster parents

are mature people who are not necessarily well off, but who have a good marriage and who love and understand children. The ninth day of the ninth month is the festival of the crysanthemum (Kiku No Sekku) when *sake* made from the crysanthemum is drunk.[45]

RANDOMNESS

The discontinuity of the discourse in Brautigan, Michaels, Barthelme, often looks like randomness, but it would be more accurate to say these writers compose according to a logic of the absurd. The human mind being what it is, true randomness can only be introduced into a literary text by mechanical means – for instance the cut-up method of William Burroughs. As he says, 'You cannot will spontaneity. But you can introduce the unpredictable spontaneous factor with a pair of scissors.'[46] The writer cuts up pieces of different texts, including his own, sticks them together in random order and transcribes the result. A similar method of introducing an element of genuine randomness into literature is to issue books in loose-leaf form, the reader being invited to shuffle the sheets to produce his own text (for example B. S. Johnson's *The Unfortunates* [1969]). Such experiments seem to me the least interesting, because most mechanical, way of trying to break out of the metaphor/metonymy system; and I have nothing to add to what I have already said about them elsewhere.[47]

EXCESS

Some postmodernist writers have deliberately taken metaphoric or metonymic devices to excess, tested them, as it were, to destruction, parodied and burlesqued them in the process of using them, and thus sought to escape from their tyranny. Thomas Pynchon's *Gravity's Rainbow* (1973), for example, takes the commonplace analogy between rocket and phallus and pursues its ramifications relentlessly and grotesquely through the novel's enormous length, while the V motif in the same author's first novel *V* (1963) mocks interpretation by the plurality of its manifestations. Donald Barthelme practices metaphoric overkill more locally, for example in this absurd cadenza of comparisons for the collection of moon rocks in the Smithsonian Institute:

> The moon rocks were as good as a meaningful and emotionally rewarding seduction that you had not expected. The moon rocks were as good as listening to what the members of the Supreme Court say to each other, in the Supreme Court Locker Room. They were as good as a war. The moon rocks were better than a presentation copy of the Random House Dictionary of the English Language signed by Geoffrey Chaucer himself. They were better than a movie in which the President refuses to tell the people what to do to save themselves from the terrible thing that is about to happen, although he knows what ought to be done and has written a secret memorandum about it. The moon rocks were better than a good

cup of coffee from an urn decorated with the change of Philomel, by the barbarous king. The moon rocks were better than a ¡huelga! led by Mongo Santamaria, with additional dialogue by St. John of the Cross and special effects by Melmoth the Wanderer.[48]

Richard Brautigan's *Trout Fishing in America* is notable for its bizarre similes, which are based on very idiosyncratic perceptions of resemblance and which frequently threaten to detach themselves from the narrative and develop into little self-contained stories – not quite like a heroic simile, because they are not returned to the original context at their conclusion. For example:

> The sun was like a huge fifty-cent piece that someone had poured kerosene on and then lit with a match and said, 'Here, hold this while I go get a newspaper' and put the coin in my hand, but never came back.[49]

> Eventually the seasons would take care of their wooden names [on grave markers] like a sleepy short-order cook cracking eggs over a grill next to a railroad station.[50]

> my body was like birds sitting on a telephone wire strung out down the world, clouds tossing the wires carefully.[51]

> His eyes were like the shoelaces of a harpsichord.[52]

> The light behind the trees was like going into a gradual and strange department store.[53]

> The creek was like 12,845 telephone booths in a row with high Victorian ceilings and all the doors taken off and all the backs of the booths knocked out.[54]

> The streets were white and dry like a collision at high speed between a cemetery and a truck loaded with sacks of flour.[55]

If these similes strain the principle of similarity to breaking point, the title of the book is used to take the principle of substitution to excess. Trout Fishing in America can be a person:

> And this is a very small cookbook for Trout Fishing in America as if Trout Fishing in America were a rich gourmet and Trout Fishing in America had Maria Callas for a girlfriend and they ate together on a marble table with beautiful candles.[56]

a corpse:

> This is the autopsy of Trout Fishing in America as if Trout Fishing in America had been Lord Byron and had died in Missolonghi, Greece, and afterwards never saw the shores of Idaho again.[57]

or the name of a hotel:

> Half a block away from Broadway and Columbus is Hotel Trout Fishing in America, a cheap hotel. It is very old and run by some Chinese.[58]

Trout Fishing in America receives letters, and sends replies signed 'Trout Fishing in America'. Trout Fishing in America can be an adjective:

> THE LAST MENTION OF TROUT FISHING IN AMERICA SHORTY[59]
> WITNESS FOR TROUT FISHING IN AMERICA PEACE[60]

Trout Fishing in America can be a pen nib:

> I thought to myself what a lovely nib trout fishing in America would make with a stroke of cool green trees along the river's shore, wild flowers and dark fins pressed against the paper.[61]

Trout Fishing in America, in short, can be anything Brautigan wants it to be.

One equivalent, on the axis of combination, to this excess of substitution, would be the permutation of variables already discussed. But any overloading of the discourse with specificity will have the same effect: by presenting the reader with more details than he can synthesize into a whole, the discourse affirms the resistance of the world to interpretation. The immensely detailed, scientifically exact and metaphor-free description of objects in Robbe-Grillet's writing actually prevents us from visualizing them. That this possibility was inherent in the metonymic method was demonstrated a long time ago by some of the late nineteenth-century realists. Jakobson cites the example of the Russian novelist Gleb Ivanovic Uspenskij, quoting the observation of Kamegulov that in his characterization, 'the reader is crushed by the multiplicity of detail unloaded on him in a limited verbal space, and is physically unable to grasp the whole, so that the portrait is often lost.'[62] The celebrated description of Charles Bovary's school cap in the first chapter of *Madame Bovary* is a more familiar example of what might be called 'metonymic overkill'. Robbe- Grillet not only overwhelms the reader with more detail than he wants or can handle, but also (I strongly suspect) ensures that the details will not cohere. Consider, for example, this description of the harbour which Mattias is approaching in the first chapter of *Le Voyeur*:

> La jetée, maintenant toute proche, dominait le pont d'une hauteur de plusiers mètres; la marée devait être basse. La cale qui allait servir pour l'accostage montrait à sa partie infèrieure une surface plus lisse, brunie par l'eau et couverte a moitié de mousses verdâtres. En regardant avec plus d'attention, on voyait le bord de pierre qui se rapprochait insensiblement.
>
> Le bord de pierre – une arrête vive, oblique, à l'intersection de deux plans perpendiculaires: la paroi verticale fuyant tout droit vers le quai et la rampe qui rejoint le haut de la digue – se prolonge à son extrèmite supérieure, en haut de la digue, par une ligne horizontale fuyant tout droit vers le quai.

Le quai, rendu plus lointain par l'effet de perspective, émet de part et d'autre de cette ligne principale un faisceau de parallèles qui délimitent, avec une netteté encore accentuée par l'éclairage du matin, une série de plans allongés, alternativement horizontaux et verticaux: le sommet du parapet massif protégeant le passage du côté du large, la paroi intérieure du parapet, la chausée sur le haut de la digue, le flanc sans garde-fou qui plonge dans l'eau du port. Les deux surfaces verticales sont dans l'ombre, les deux autres sont vivement éclairées par le soleil – le haut du parapet dans toute sa largeur et la chausée à l'exception d'une étroite blande obscure: l'ombre portée du parapet. Theéoretiquement on devrait voir encore dans l'eau du port l'image renversée de l'ensemble et, à la surface, toujours dans le même jeu de parallèles, l'ombre portée de la haute paroi verticale qui filterait tout droit vers le quai.

Vers le bout de la jetée, la construction se complique ...[63]

But this already sufficiently *compliqué* to make the point. The published English translation of this passage is as follows:

The pier, now quite close, towered several yards above the deck. The tide must have been out. The landing slip from which the ship would be boarded revealed the smoother surface of its lower section, darkened by the water and half-covered with greenish moss. On closer inspection, the stone rim drew almost imperceptibly closer.

The stone rim – an oblique, sharp edge formed by two intersecting perpendicular planes: the vertical embankment perpendicular to the quay and the ramp leading to the top of the pier – was continued along its upper side at the top of the pier by a horizontal line extending straight toward the quay.

The pier, which seemed longer than it actually was as an effect of perspective, extended from both sides of this base line in a cluster of parallels describing, with a precision accentuated even more sharply by the morning light, a series of elongated planes alternately horizontal and vertical: the crest of the massive parapet that protected the tidal basin from the open sea, the inner wall of the parapet, the jetty along the top of the pier, and the vertical embankment that plunged straight into the water of the harbor. The two vertical surfaces were in shadow, the other two brilliantly lit by the sun – the whole breadth of the parapet and all of the jetty save for one dark narrow strip: the shadow cast by the parapet. Theoretically, the reversed image of the entire group could be seen reflected in the harbor water, and, on the surface, still within the same play of parallels, the shadow cast by the vertical embankment extending straight toward the quay.[64]

The translator has not made things easier for us by translating *plus lointain* as 'longer', and by using only three English words (*pier, quay* and *jetty*) to translate four French words (*jettée, quai, digue, chausée*) – and not using them consistently, either, translating *jettée* as both 'pier' and 'jetty', and *quai* as both 'pier' and 'quay'. But one can only sympathize with anyone engaged on this task. An obvious procedure for a translator would be to make a sketch or diagram of the harbour, but when I invited students, and subsequently some colleagues in the French Department of my university, to do this, none of them succeeded. The description simply doesn't come together into a visualizable whole.

The last word on metonymic excess may be left to Jorge Luis Borges, who in his story 'Funes, the Memorious', describes a man who, after the shock of an accident, is able to perceive everything that is happening around him and unable to forget anything.

> We, at one glance, can perceive three glasses on a table; Funes, all the leaves and tendrils and fruit that make up a grape vine. He knew by heart the forms of the southern clouds at dawn on 30 April 1882, and could compare them in his memory with the mottled streaks on a book in Spanish binding he had only seen once and with the outlines of the foam raised by an oar in the Rio Negro the night before the Quebracho uprising.[65]

Funes inhabits a world of intolerable specificity and his time and energy are wholly absorbed by the interminable and futile task of classifying all the data of his experience without omission or generalization:

> He was the solitary and lucid spectator of a multiform world which was instantaneously and almost intolerably exact. ... I suspect, nevertheless, that he was not very capable of thought. To think is to forget a difference, to generalize, to abstract. In the overly replete world of Funes there were nothing but details, almost contiguous details.[66]

SHORT CIRCUIT

[...] I suggested that at the highest level of generality at which we can apply the metaphor/metonymy distinction, literature itself is metaphoric and nonliterature is metonymic. The literary text is always metaphoric in the sense that when we interpret it we apply it to the world as a total metaphor. This process of interpretation assumes a gap between the text and the world, between art and life, which postmodernist writing characteristically tries to short-circuit in order to administer a shock to the reader and thus resist assimilation into conventional categories of the literary. Ways of doing this include: combining in one work violently contrasting modes – the obviously fictive and the apparently factual; introducing the author and the question of authorship into the text; and exposing conventions in the act of using them. These ploys are not in themselves discoveries of the postmodernist writers – they are to be found in prose fiction as far back as *Don Quixote* and *Tristram Shandy* – but they appear so frequently in postmodernist writing, and are pursued to such lengths as to constitute, in combination with the other devices we have surveyed, a distinctively new development.

Vladimir Nabokov, a transitional figure between modernism and post-modernism, teasingly introduced himself (and his wife) on the perimeter of his fictions as early as his second novel *King, Queen, Knave*, originally published in Russian in 1928. As the coils of the intrigue tighten around the distracted hero, Franz, at a German seaside resort, he notices a vacationing couple talking a language he does not understand and carrying a butterfly net (something of a private joke, this, in 1928, when Nabokov was not yet the world's most famous lepidopterist):

> He thought that they glanced at him and fell silent for an instant. After passing him they began talking again; he had the impression they were discussing him, and even pronouncing his name. It embarrassed, it incensed him, that this damned happy foreigner hastening to the beach with his tanned, pale-haired, lovely companion, knew absolutely every-thing about his predicament.[67]

In *Pale Fire* (1962) Nabokov plays off the metaphoric and metonymic modes against each other with typical cunning. The novel consists of a poem and a commentary. Normally a poem is fictional and a commentary factual, as verse is a metaphorical and prose a metonymic medium. In *Pale Fire*, however, the prose commentary is more obviously fictive than the poem, in the sense that the commentator Kinbote is a madman suffering from the delusion that he is the exiled monarch of a Ruritanian kingdom called Zembla, while John Shade's poem is a meditation upon entirely credible personal experience. A measure of Kinbote's insanity is the way he perversely and absurdly interprets Shade's poem as a tissue of allusions to his own fantasy; but it would be an over-simplification to say that Nabokov demonstrates the difference between illu-sion and reality by this opposition between Kinbote and Shade. For one thing, Kinbote's evocation of Zembla has an imaginative power and eloquence which makes us all too eager to suspend our disbelief, and beside it Shade's world seems less interesting. For another, Shade himself is a fiction, an illusion created by a 'real' author, Nabokov, whose well-known personal history corresponds far more closely to Kinbote's than to Shade's. Even the murder of Shade, which, within the limits of the book was 'in fact' committed by an escaped criminal who mistook Shade for the judge who sentenced him, but which Kinbote represents as the error of an assassin sent to kill the exiled king of Zembla, has an origin in Nabokov's own experience, for his father was murdered by political assassins who were attacking someone else.[68] Teasing allusions to the author persist in Nabokov's subsequent novels.

In the last but one of J. D. Salinger's stories about the Glass family, 'Seymour: an Introduction', the narrator, Buddy Glass, mentions that he has written two other stories about his brother Seymour – 'Raise High the Roofbeam, Carpenters' (which is no surprise to the reader of the sequence) and 'A Nice Day for Bananafish', which I think *is* a surprise. For 'Bananafish' had no identified narrator, and appeared years before in a collection of *Nine Stories* (1953) by J. D. Salinger, seven of which did not concern the Glass family. Buddy goes on to claim authorship of one of these seven stories, and to refer to a novel of his that sounds very like Salinger's best-seller, *The Catcher in the Rye* (1951). Further on, Buddy refers to criticism of his work and rumours about his private life that are much the same as those provoked by Salinger himself. These revelations have a disorientating effect on the reader. The fiction that Buddy Glass is the author of 'Seymour: an Introduction' is made logically dependent upon the supposition that the J. D. Salinger who we thought wrote 'Bananafish' was the pen name of Buddy Glass, but of course J. D. Salinger's name appears on the title page of both books. Compelled to face the question, who is real, Buddy Glass or J.D. Salinger, common sense tells us the answer, but the rhetoric works in the opposite direction. This deliberate entangling of the myths of the Glass family and the Caulfield family with Salinger's personal history is typical of his later work, where he plays sly games with the reader's assent, stepping up the fictionality of the events as he damps down the literariness of the manner in which he describes them. Purporting to tell us a 'true' family history, and dropping heavy hints that he is the same person as J. D. Salinger, Buddy yet insists again and again on the autonomy of art and the irrelevance of biographical criticism. An extravagantly transcendental philosophy of life involving the endorsement of miracles and extra-sensory perception is put forward in terms of studied homeliness, wrapped around with elaborate qualifications, disclaimers, nods and winks, and mediated in a style that, for all its restless rhetorical mannerism, is strikingly lacking in any kind of 'poetic' resonances. As Ihab Hassan, one of the few critics to have placed Salinger in a postmodernist context, has observed: 'Ungainly, prolix, allusive, convoluted, tolerant of chance, whimsy, and disorder, these narratives define a kind of anti-form. Their impertinent exhortations of reader and writer undercut the authority of the artistic act.'[69]

In their play with the ideas of illusion, authorship and literary convention, however, Nabokov and Salinger maintain a precarious poise. Their narratives wobble on the edge of the aesthetic, but never quite fall off. Modes are mixed, but a certain balance, or symmetry, is preserved. The same is true of Doris Lessing, whose *The Golden Notebook* (1962) and *Briefing For a Descent into Hell* (1971) have certain features in common with their work – the Chinese-box authorship puzzle, for instance, and the reality fantasy contrast in which the fantasy is more potent than the reality. Present-day American writers are often more slapdash, or less inhibited, in mixing up fact and fiction, life and art. Brautigan's *Trout Fishing in America*, for instance, has many signs of being an unstructured autobiography. The text frequently refers us to the photograph of the author on the front cover, and includes a great many factual documents – letters, recipes, bibliographies, etc. But it also contains extravagantly fictitious episodes such as the one in which the narrator buys a used trout stream from the Cleveland Wrecking Yard:

It was stacked in piles of various lengths: ten, fifteen, twenty feet, etc. There was one pile of hundred foot lengths. There was also a box of scraps. I went up close and looked at the lengths of stream. I could see some trout in them. ... It looked like a fine stream. I put my hand in the water. It was cold and felt good.[70]

This fantastic event is narrated in a style of sober realism, just as the more banal events in the book are elaborated with fantastic similes. Brautigan leaves to the reader the task of integrating these totally disparate modes of writing. Plainly, he is not bothered.

Kurt Vonnegut uses an apparently artless, improvised mixing of modes to more deliberate thematic effect in *Slaughterhouse 5* (1969). Vonnegut happened to be a prisoner of war in Dresden at the time of the air raid which destroyed it at the end of World War II, and was employed in digging some of the 130,000 incinerated corpses out of the rubble. For years, he confides in his first chapter, he has been trying to make this lump of raw experience into a novel; but such novels have a way of covertly celebrating what they outwardly deplore and being turned into movies with parts for Frank Sinatra and John Wayne. The only way to write an anti-war novel is to write an anti-novel. 'It has to be so short and jumbled and jangled because there is nothing intelligent to say about a massacre.'[71] *Slaughterhouse 5* is a *bricolage* of fragments, short passages that are grim, grotesque and whimsical by turns, which describe the experiences of the very two-dimensional hero, Billy Pilgrim: his war-experiences (which bear a close resemblance to Vonnegut's) his civilian life as a married man and successful optometrist (domestic and social comedy) and his delusions of having been abducted by aliens from the planet Tralfamadore (science-fiction parody). Billy finds the Tralfamadorian concept of time as a field of simultaneous events, from which we are free to select, an answer to the problem of meaningless death which is instanced on almost every page of *Slaughterhouse 5* (invariably accompanied by the laconic comment, 'So it goes') for according to this doctrine (perhaps a parody of Christianity) 'we will all live for ever no matter how dead we may sometimes seem to be.' This concept also provides a justification for the drastic dislocation of chronology in the book, which prevents the reader from locating himself on a narrative line or settling into a single mood, and jumbles together disparate experiences in a way that imitates the incongruities and disjunctions of modern history. Nor are the various planes of the narrative – autobiographical, fictional, fantastic – kept insulated from each other. At his first German prison camp, for instance, Billy Pilgrim and his fellow American POWs are welcomed by a contingent of British veterans who provide a feast that makes the half-starved Americans violently ill. The latrine is crammed with these unfortunates.

An American near Billy wailed that he had excreted everything but his brains. Moments later he said, 'There they go; there they go.' He meant his brains.

That was I. That was me. That was the author of this book.[72]

This statement has an interesting double effect. On the one hand it reminds us that the story has an autobiographical, documentary origin, that the author 'was there', and therefore that the narrative is 'true'. On the other hand it simultaneously reminds us that Billy Pilgrim and the author belong to different planes of reality, that we are reading a book, a story, which (whatever its specific proportions of fiction to fact) is necessarily a highly conventionalized, highly artificial construction, and necessarily at a considerable distance from 'the way it was'.

In *Breakfast of Champions*, Vonnegut brings himself as composing author into the 'time present' of the narrative – for example:

> 'Give me a Black and White and water,' [Wayne] heard the waitress say, and Wayne should have pricked up his ears at that. That particular drink wasn't for any ordinary person. That drink was for the person who had created all Wayne's misery to date, who could kill him or make him a millionaire or send him back to prison or do whatever he damn well pleased with Wayne. That drink was for me.[73]

This is what the Russian Formalists called 'baring the device' carried to an extreme, and it is a persistent feature of postmodernist writing.

> The droplets rain from the eaves. The shadow of a cloud dims the snow dazzle. George Washington crosses the Delaware on the walls. I sit at my desk, making this up...

Thus Ronald Sukenick, in 'What's Your Story?'[74] 'I wander the island, inventing it,' begins Robert Coover's story 'The Magic Poker', in which his skill in evoking scenery and generating mystery and suspense is constantly undermined by declarations of his own manipulating presence – the narrator revealed as author:

> Bedded deep in the grass, near the path up to the first guest cabin, lies a wrought-iron poker. It is long and slender with an intricately worked handle, and it is orange with rust. It lies shadowed, not by trees, but by the grass that has grown up wildly around it. I put it there.[75]

'Another story about a writer writing a story! Another regressus ad infinitum! Who doesn't prefer art that at least overtly imitates something other than its own processes? That doesn't continually proclaim, "Don't forget I'm an artifice!" That takes for granted its mimetic nature instead of asserting it in order (not so slyly after all) to deny it, or vice versa?' That is a quite common complaint about the kind of writing I have surveyed in this chapter (especially among British reviewers and critics) but this particular expression of it occurs in a text by one of the most elaborately and ingeniously selfconscious of all postmodernist writers, John Barth;[76] and in context will give little comfort to partisans of traditional realism, one variety of which is amusingly parodied in the following passage:

C flung away the whining manuscript and pushed impatiently through
the french windows leading to the terrace from his oak-wainscotted study.
Pausing at the stone balustrade to light his briar he remarked through a
lavender cascade of wisteria that lithe-limbed Gloria, Gloria of timorous
eye and militant breast, had once again chosen his boat wharf as her
basking place.[77]

The way the narrative tracks its subject through spatial and temporal contiguities with obsessive attention to redundant detail is well-caught, and the
characterization of Gloria makes effective fun of the realistic writer's reliance
on synecdoche.

The 'manuscript' in this passage is the story itself, entitled 'Life-Story', the
trace of a writer's attempts to write a story about a writer who has come to
suspect that the world is a fiction in which he is a character – a hypothesis
which, if confirmed, would affect both writers, indeed all writers, including
Barth. The process of trying to make a story out of this *donnée* provokes various
pronouncements about the theory of fiction such as the one quoted above,
which seem to be comments upon the fiction but which prove to be part of the
fiction. 'Life-Story' is a metafiction cleverly constructed to outmanoeuvre critics
of metafiction, since the metafictional frame is continually being absorbed into
the picture. This 'regressus in infinitum' is finally arrested by the device of the
short-circuit:

To what conclusion will he come? He'd been about to append to his own
tale inasmuch as the old analogy between Author and God, novel and
world, can no longer be employed unless deliberately as a false analogy,
certain things follow: 1) fiction must acknowledge its fictitiousness and
metaphoric invalidity or 2) choose to ignore the question or deny its
relevance or 3) establish some other, acceptable relation between itself, its
author, its reader. Just as he finished doing so, however, his real life and
imaginary mistresses entered his study; 'It's a little past midnight' she
announced with a smile; 'do you know what that means?'[78]

The interruption reveals to him that 'he could not after all be a character in a
work of fiction inasmuch as such a fiction would be of an entirely different
character from what he thought of as fiction', and the birthday kiss his wife
bestows upon him obscures his view of his manuscript and makes him 'end his
ending story endless by interruption, cap his pen'.[79] Barth himself has referred
to postmodernist writing as 'the literature of exhausted possibility' – or, more
chicly, 'the literature of exhaustion',[80] and has praised Borges for demonstrating 'how an artist may paradoxically turn the felt ultimacies of our time
into material and means for his work – *paradoxically* because by doing so he
transcends what had appeared to be his refutation'.[81] Certainly, in seeking
'some other … relation between itself, its author, its reader' than that of
previous literary traditions, postmodernist writing takes enormous risks – risks

of abolishing itself, if ultimately successful, in silence, incoherence or what Fiedler calls 'the reader's passionate [i.e. non-aesthetic] apprehension and response'.[82] I would certainly not claim that all the texts surveyed in this chapter are equally interesting and rewarding: postmodernist writing tends to be very much a hit-or-miss affair. But many of these books and stories are imaginatively liberating to a high degree, and have done much to keep the possibilities of writing open in the very process of asserting that the most familiar ones are closed. If this assertion were really made good, however – if postmodernism really succeeded in expelling the idea of order (whether expressed in metonymic or metaphoric form) from modern writing, then it would truly abolish itself, by destroying the norms against which we perceive its deviations. A foreground without a background inevitably becomes the background for something else. Postmodernism cannot rely upon the historical memory of modernist and antimodernist writing for its background, because it is essentially a rule-breaking kind of art, and unless people are still trying to keep the rules there is no point in breaking them, and no interest in seeing them broken.

NOTES

1. Samuel Beckett, *More Pricks Than Kicks* (Picador edn., 1974) p. 18.
2. *Ibid.* pp. 18–19.
3. *Ibid.* p. 16.
4. *Ibid.* p. 17. The allusion is to the use of the fish as a symbol for Christ by the early Christians.
5. *Ibid.* p. 11.
6. *Ibid.* p. 13.
7. *Ibid.* p. 19.
8. See above p. 138.
9. Beckett, *Murphy* (1963) p. 5.
10. *Ibid.* pp. 52–3.
11. Beckett, *Watt* (1963) p. 67.
12. *Ibid.* pp. 71–2.
13. *The Unnamable in Three Novels By Samuel Beckett* (New York, 1965) pp. 394–5.
14. Donald Barthelme, *Snow White* (Bantam edn. New York, 1968) p. 129.
15. Hugh Kenner, *A Reader's Guide to Samuel Beckett* (1973) p. 94.
16. Joseph Conrad, 'Henry James: an appreciation', quoted by Alan Friedman *The Turn of the Novel* (New York, 1966) p. 77.
17. Muriel Spark, *Not To Disturb* (1971) p. 61.
18. John Barth, *Lost in the Funhouse* (Harmondsworth, 1972) p. 117.
19. Richard Brautigan, *A Confederate General from Big Sur* (Picador edn., 1973) p. 116.
20. Richard Brautigan, *Trout Fishing In America* (Picador edn., 1972) p. 150.
21. *Ibid.* p. 151.
22. See Leslie Fiedler. *The New Mutants, Partisan Review* Autumn 1956. Reprinted in Bernard Bergonzi, ed. *Innovations* (1900) pp. 23–45 and the same author's 'Cross the Border – Close that Gap; Postmodernism', *American Literature Since 1900* (1975) ed. Marcus Cunliffe. pp. 344–66.
23. Frank Kermode, 'Objects, Jokes and Art' in *Continuities* (New York, 1968) p. 23.
24. Fiedler, 'Cross the Border etc.' p. 348.
25. Kermode, *op. cit.* p. 20.

26. Samuel Beckett, *The Unnamable, op. cit.* p. 357.
27. Leonard Michaels, *I Would Have Saved Them If I Could* (New York, 1975) p. 137.
28. Quoted by Tony Tanner in *City of Words: American Fiction 1950–1970* (1971) p. 191.
29. Gore Vidal, *Myra Breckinridge* (1968) and *Myron* (1975).
30. John Barth, *Giles Goat-Boy* (1967) p. 672.
31. Jorge Luis Borges, *Labyrinths* (Harmondsworth, 1970) p. 37.
32. *Ibid.* p. 51.
33. Beckett, *Watt* p. 200.
34. Beckett, *Molloy* (1966) pp. 73–9.
35. Beckett, *Murphy* p. 68.
36. *Ibid.* pp. 43–4.
37. Joseph Heller, *Catch 22* (Corgi edn. 1964) p. 16.
38. Ronald Sukenick, *98.6* (New York, 1975) p. 167.
39. Raymond Federman, *Double or Nothing* (Chicago, 1971) p. 85.
40. Leonard Michaels, *I Would Have Saved Them If I Could* pp. 117–18.
41. *Ibid.* pp. 59–60.
42. Donald Barthelme, 'Edward and Pia', *Unspeakable Practices, Unnatural Acts* (Bantam edn. New York, 1969) p. 75.
43. Barthelme, 'Will You Tell Me?', *Come Back, Dr Caligari* (Boston, 1964) p. 47.
44. In 'See The Moon'. Quoted, and amusingly discussed by the author, in *The New Fiction: Interviews with Innovative American Writers* by Joe David Bellamy (1974) pp. 53–5.
45. Barthelme, *Come Back, Dr Caligari* pp. 90–4.
46. Quoted by Tony Tanner, *op. cit.* p. 126.
47. See *The Novelist at the Crossroads* pp. 13–14 and 166–70.
48. Barthelme, 'A Film', *Sadness* (Bantam edn. New York, 1972) p. 78.
49. Brautigan, *Trout Fishing in America* pp. 7–8.
50. *Ibid.* p. 27.
51. *Ibid.* p. 31.
52. *Ibid.* p. 34.
53. *Ibid.* p. 39.
54. *Ibid.* p. 72.
55. *Ibid.* p. 80.
56. *Ibid.* p. 13.
57. *Ibid.* p. 43.
58. *Ibid.* p. 89.
59. *Ibid.* p. 129.
60. *Ibid.* p. 131.
61. *Ibid.* p. 148.
62. Roman Jakobson, 'Two Aspects of Language' p. 80.
63. Alain Robbe-Grillet, *Le Voyeur* (Paris, 1955) pp. 11–12.
64. Alain Robbe-Grillet, *The Voyeur*, translated by Richard Howard (1959) pp. 6–7.
65. Jorge Louis Borges, *Labyrinths* p. 92.
66. Quoted by Tony Tanner in *City of Words* p. 41. The translation differs slightly from that of the Penguin *Labyrinths*, and I have preferred to quote it in this instance because the word 'contiguous' is used.
67. Vladimir Nabokov, *King, Queen, Knave* (1968) p. 259.
68. Nabokov, *Speak, Memory* (Pyramid edn., New York, 1968) p. 143.
69. Ihab Hassan, *The Dismemberment of Orpheus: Toward a Postmodernist Literature* (New York, 1971) p. 251.
70. Brautigan, *Trout Fishing in America* pp. 142–3.
71. Kurt Vonnegut, *Slaughterhouse 5* (1970) p. 17.
72. *Ibid.* p. 109.
73. Vonnegut, *Breakfast of Champions* (Panther edn., 1975) p. 179.

74. Reprinted in *Superfiction, or the American Story Transformed*, ed. Joe David Bellamy (New York, 1975) p. 254.
75. Robert Coover, *Pricksongs and Descants* (Picador edn., 1973) p. 15.
76. John Barth, *'Life-Story'*, *Lost in the Funhouse* p. 121.
77. *Ibid.* p. 122.
78. *Ibid.* pp. 131–2.
79. *Ibid.* p. 132.
80. John Barth 'The Literature of Exhaustion', *Atlantic* August 1967, p. 29.
81. *Ibid.* p. 32.
82. Leslie Fiedler, 'Cross the Border – Close that Gap' *op. cit.* p. 346.

WORKS CITED

Beckett, Samuel (1963) *Murphy*. London: Calder & Boyars.
Beckett, Samuel (1963) *Watt*. London: Calder & Boyars.
Beckett, Samuel (1966) *Molloy*. London: Calder & Boyars.
Bellamy, Joe David (1974) *The New Fiction: Interviews with Innovative American Writers*. Urbana, IL and London: University of Illinois Press.
Jakobson, Roman (1956) 'Two Aspects of Language and Two Types of Aphasic Disturbances', in Roman Jakobson and Morris Halle, *Fundamentals of Language*. The Hague: Mouton.
Kenner, Hugh (1973) *A Reader's Guide to Samuel Beckett*. London: Thames & Hudson.
Lodge, David (1971) *The Novelist at the Crossroads, and Other Essays on Fiction and Criticism*. London: Routledge & Kegan Paul.
Michaels, Leonard (1975) *I Would Have Saved Them if I Could*. New York: Farrar, Straus & Giroux.
Nabokov, Vladimir (1968) *King, Queen, Knave*. London: Weidenfeld & Nicolson.
Spark, Muriel (1971) *Not To Disturb*. London: Macmillan.
Tanner, Tony (1971) *City of Words: American Fiction 1950–1970*. London: Cape.
Vonnegut, Kurt (1970) *Slaughterhouse 5*. New York: Dell.

20

'CHANGE OF DOMINANT FROM MODERNIST TO POSTMODERNIST WRITING'

Brian McHale

I don't think the ideas were 'in the air' . . .; rather, all of us found ourselves at the same stoplights in different cities at the same time. When the lights changed, we all crossed the streets.
                                     – Steve Katz (in LeClair and McCaffery 1983: 227)

1. META-THEORETICAL PRELIMINARIES

Let me begin by laying my theoretical cards on the table. I assume that all definitions in the field of literary history, all acts of categorization or boundary-drawing, are *strategic*. That is, they are all made in view of some purpose on the definer's part; they are all *apropos* of something else – some other proposed categorization or literary-historical model, some perceived contradiction or shortcoming in the currently-accepted picture of literary history, some antici-pated gain in scope or tidiness. This view of literary periodization is, in fact, perfectly orthodox; it dates at least from A.O. Lovejoy's classic essay 'On the Discrimination of Romanticisms' (Lovejoy 1948). (For a recent restatement, see Ibsch 1977 [. . .]). Of course, not all literary historians have been equally willing, or able, to recognize the strategic character of their definitions and categories.

I further assume that the criterion of a good or superior definition is not its supposed approximation to some objective state of affairs 'out there,' but rather its *productiveness*.[1] A superior definition produces new insights, new

From Brian McHale (1986) 'Change of Dominant from Modernist to Postmodernist Writing', in Douwe Fokkema and Hans Bertens (eds), *Approaching Postmodernism*, papers presented at a workshop on postmodernism, 21–23 September 1984, University of Utrecht. Amsterdam and Philadelphia: John Benjamins.

connections, coherence of a different degree or kind; ultimately, it produces *more discourse*, in the form of follow-up research, new interpretations, criticisms and refinements of the model, counter-proposals, polemics. The best definition of all will be the one that is productive in this way and also takes explicitly into account its own strategic character, the one that is self-consciously rather than unconsciously strategic.

To put it differently: we as literary historians construct the objects of our descriptions in the very act of defining and describing them. We should try to construct *interesting* objects; and we should never forget that we are constructing rather than discovering them. This does not mean, by the way, that I am out of sympathy with the scientific aspirations of our discipline; after all, I teach in a department called in Hebrew *torat ha-sifrut*, 'science of literature,' and I subscribe to the perspective that that name implies. I am only asking that our science model itself on the theoretical sciences of our own day and not those of Newton's day. In contemporary physics, it is sometimes strategically advantageous to think of light as a wave, at other times to think of it as a particle. It makes perfectly good sense to ask, for instance, 'In what respects does light behave like a wave, in what respects does it behave like a particle?' or 'Under what circumstances is it more advantageous to think of light as a wave, under what circumstances is it more advantageous to think of it as a particle?' But the question, 'What is light *really*, wave or particle?' is meaningless. Analogously, it is sometimes advantageous to think of Romanticism as the strain of primitivism and naturalism in late-eighteenth and early-nineteenth century aesthetics (Joseph Warton's Romanticism), at other times to think of it as the strain of anti-naturalism and self-conscious artifice (German Romanticism), but it makes no sense to ask, 'What was Romanticism *really*?'

And the same goes for Postmodernism. Just as there are a number of romanticisms, in the plural, depending upon our strategic purpose in using the term, so there are a number of postmodernisms. Hans Bertens, in his contribution [to this workshop] has attempted to sort them out; his essay might have been titled, by analogy with Lovejoy's, 'On the Discrimination of Postmodernisms.' A positive outcome of such an essay in discrimination would be the compiling of a directory of the most productive definitions of Postmodernism, in which each entry was accompanied by an explicit statement of its strategic purpose, answering the question, 'Apropos of *what*?' This directory of postmodernisms, if it was complete and honest, would even include those definitions, such as Frank Kermode's (1968), which define Postmodernism right out of existence. And it would include the definition which I will propose below – not *the* definition of Postmodernism, but only one among the plurality of definitions in our directory of literary-historical strategies.

2. THE DOMINANT

What I have said about categories in the field of literary history also applies to the transhistorical categories of descriptive poetics. These, too, are strategic, defined in view of some purpose, apropos of something else. An example is the concept of the dominant, the tool I propose to use here in my account of Postmodernist writing. The *locus classicus* for this concept is, of course, Roman Jakobson's 1935 lecture in Czech, essentially recapitulating the insights of his Russian Formalist colleague Jurij Tynjanov. I quote the familiar English translation (from Matejka and Pomorska 1971):

> The dominant may be defined as the focusing component of a work of art: it rules, determines, and transforms the remaining components. It is the dominant which guarantees the integrity of the structure. ... In the evolution of poetic form it is not so much a question of the disappearance of certain elements and the emergence of others as it is the question of shifts in the mutual relationship among the diverse components of the system, in other words, a question of the shifting dominant (Matejka and Pomorska 1971: 105, 108).

This is obviously a composite definition, collapsing together two different contexts in Jakobson's lecture. One is the context of his discussion of the structure of individual texts; the other, his discussion of the structure of the literary system and its change over time. Pertinent to both contexts, the concept of the dominant is nevertheless slightly different in each, bearing on different types of elements and pitched at different levels of generalization. There are, in a sense, *two* dominants here, one at the level of the text, the other at the level of the system; or rather, more than two, for in this brief but typically dense lecture Jakobson also applies this concept of the dominant to the analysis of verse in general (where rhyme, meter, and intonation are dominant at different historical periods), of verbal art in general (where the aesthetic function is a transhistorical dominant), and of cultural history (painting is the dominant art-form in the Renaissance, music in the Romantic period, and so on). Jakobson's critics have sometimes complained that his dominant is not a single, unified concept, but more like a *bundle* of concepts. I agree; in my view, however, this is not a flaw but, on the contrary, a virtue. The flaw in Jakobson's lecture, if there is one, lies in its failure to state explicitly that there is no *one* dominant, but rather that the dominant is a 'floating' concept, applicable at different levels of analysis and over different ranges of phenomena. Confronting one and the same text, we may discern quite different dominants depending upon what question we are intent on answering. If we approach the text synchronically and in isolation, we may identify one dominant; if we approach it from the point of view of its position in the evolution of the literary system, we may identify a different dominant; if we analyse it as an example from the history of verse, we may discern yet another one; if as an example of verbal art in general, a fourth; and so on. In short, the dominant is a strategic category, and a good deal of misunderstanding might have been avoided if Jakobson had said so in so many words.

Since the issue at hand (namely, the definition of Postmodernism) involves problems of literary-historical periodization, it is the dominant as a category in literary evolution that particularly interests us right now. Here is some more of what Jakobson had to say about *this* dominant in his 1935 lecture:

> Within a given complex of poetic norms in general, or especially within the set of poetic norms valid for a given poetic genre, elements which were originally secondary become essential and primary. On the other hand, the elements which were originally the dominant ones becomes subsidiary and optional ... a poetic work [is] a structured system, a regularly ordered hierarchical set of artistic devices. Poetic evolution is a shift in this hierarchy. ...The image of ... literary history substantially changes; it becomes incomparably richer and at the same time more monolithic, more synthetic and ordered, than were the *membra disjecta* of previous literary scholarship (Matejka and Pomorska 1971: 108).

More monolithic? Surely this picture of a monolithic literary history contradicts what I just finished saying about multiplicity of dominants. Well, no, in fact it does not. For each particular angle of approach we adopt, each question we put to the text, we elicit from it an answer in the form of a particular hierarchical structure of elements, governed by a dominant; but as soon as we shift our ground, change our question, we elicit a different structure and a different dominant. If we ask of certain exemplary twentieth-century texts, 'What changes are involved in the transition from the system of Modernist writing to the system of Postmodernist writing?', we obtain an answer which is monolithic, or, as Jakobson goes on to say, synthetic and ordered. But this does not preclude our asking other questions and obtaining other syntheses and other orders – different monoliths, so to speak, ranged parallel to the first one.

By way of demonstrating the utility of Jakobson's concept for historical poetics, let us see how the dominant could have functioned to organize and unify one recent account of the Modernist literary system.

According to Douwe Fokkema (1982), a period code is a 'secondary model-ling system' (in Lotman's sense), capable of overriding the rules of the linguistic code. The signs of the period code are discernible at four different levels of analysis: that of macro-structural organizing principles; that of microstructure (the sentence level); that of thematics and denotation; and that of connotation (Fokkema 1982: 68–69). Fokkema describes the signs of the Modernist period code at these four levels, drawing on Gide's *Les Faux monnayeurs* and other texts by Joyce, Woolf, Mann, Proust, Musil and Valery Larbaud for his examples; for tactical reasons, which will become clear later, I have substituted examples from William Faulkner's *Absalom, Absalom!* (1936), another exemplary Modernist text (see Fokkema 1982: 69–72).

At the macrostructural level, Modernist fiction is characterized, according to Fokkema, by the provisional and hypothetical nature of the narrator's or lyrical subject's perspective. This is certainly the case in *Absalom*, where Quentin's and Shreve's knowledge of the Sutpen story depends upon unreliable (biased or under-informed) sources, notably Miss Rosa Coldfield, or has been handed down to them through a long chain of intermediaries, virtually guaranteeing some degree of garbling of the information. This same provisionality of perspective is also reflected at the micro-structural level. In the case of *Absalom*, sentence-level provisionality takes the form of adverbs of speculation or supposition (*maybe, probably, possibly*) and verbal auxiliaries expressing conditionality (*might, must*), which riddle certain passages of the text and fatally weaken the authority of the narrative.

Fokkema identifies themes of intellection and intellectual independence and detachment as being typical of Modernism. The semantic universe of Modernism, according to him, is organized around terms such as *detachment, awareness, observation*. Detachment is thematized in *Absalom*, where Quentin, the passive listener-observer, succeeds in maintaining an intellectual and emotional distance from what he hears and experiences until the novel's closing paragraph. His reconstruction of the South's tragic history occurs, significantly, at Harvard, geographically remote from the South, and in collaboration with an outsider, the Canadian Shreve. Faulkner's semantic universe in *Absalom* centers on the most fundamental of all verbs of intellection: *to think, to know*.

The connotative features of terms, Fokkema tells us, encoded in and through everyday uses of language, are reorganized by the period code through the process of collocation. In the Modernist period code, the familiar ascription of connotations of significance and insignificance or triviality is disturbed by the collocation of trivial happenings or details with highly-valued terms relating to awareness and observation. This sign of Fokkema's Modernist period code does not happen to be corroborated by *Absalom*, although it is certainly strongly in evidence in the texts by Woolf and Gide which he cites.

What can we say about this analysis of the Modernist period code? Principally, that as it now stands it amounts to little more than a heterogeneous catalogue, a collection of the *membra disjecta* which, according to Jakobson, constituted literary-historical scholarship before the advent of the concept of the dominant. We are left speculating about what common denominator might be shared by these, on the face of it, diverse signs, what connecting principle might bind them together – in short, what dominant 'guarantees the integrity' of the period code. Fokkema's analysis is a follow-the-dots puzzle, with all the dots in place and properly numbered, but the connecting line still to be drawn; and that line is the dominant.

3. TWO THESES

What the items in Fokkema's catalogue all have in common, it seems to me, is an *epistemological* element. Provisionality of perspective at the macrostructural and sentence levels, themes of intellection, revaluation of trivialities because of their involvement in acts of awareness – each of these Modernist features serves to focus our attention on epistemological issues.[2] This brings me to the first of my two theses:

THESIS 1. The dominant of Modernist writing is *epistemological*. That is, Modernist writing is designed to raise such questions as: what is there to be known? who knows it? how do they know it, and with what degree of certainty? how is knowledge transmitted from one knower to another, and with what degree of reliability? how does the object of knowledge change as it passes from knower to knower? what are the limits of knowledge? and so on.

I think there can be no doubt that Faulkner's *Absalom, Absalom!*, for example, has been designed to raise epistemological questions. Its logic is that of the detective story, the epistemological genre *par excellence*. Faulkner's protagonists, like characters in many classic Modernist texts – Henry James's and Joseph Conrad's, for instance – sift through the evidence of witnesses of different degrees of reliability in order to reconstruct and solve a 'crime' – except that in Faulkner's case the quotation-marks can be dropped from around the word crime, for there really is a murder-mystery to be solved here. *Absalom* foregrounds such epistemological themes as the accessibility and circulation of knowledge, the different structuring imposed on the 'same' knowledge by different minds, and the problem of 'unknowability' or the limits of knowledge. And it foregrounds these themes through the use of characteristically Modernist (epistemological) devices: the multiplication and juxtaposition of perspectives, the focalization of all the evidence through a single 'center of consciousness' (Quentin), virtuoso variants on interior monologue (especially in the case of Miss Rosa), and so on. Finally, in a typically Modernist mode, *Absalom* transfers the epistemological difficulties of its characters to its readers; its strategies of 'impeded form' (dislocated chronology, withheld or indirectly-presented information, difficult 'mind-styles,' and so on) *stimulate* for the reader the very same problems of accessibility, reliability, and limitation of knowledge that plague Quentin and Shreve (see Kinney 1978).

So Faulkner in *Absalom, Absalom!* practices a poetics of the epistemological dominant – Modernist poetics, in other words. Except perhaps in one chapter, where Modernist poetics threatens to break down, or more than threatens, actually *does* break down. In Chapter 8, Quentin and Shreve reach the limit of their knowledge of the Sutpen murder-mystery; nevertheless they go on, beyond reconstruction into pure speculation. The signs of the narrative act fall away, and with them all questions of authority and reliability. The text passes from mimesis of the various characters' narrations to unmediated diegesis, from characters 'telling' to the author directly 'showing' us what happened between Sutpen, Henry, and Bon. The murder-mystery is 'solved,' not, however, through epistemological processes of weighing evidence and making deductions, but through the imaginative projection of what *could* – and, the text insists, *must* – have happened. '*Shall I project a world?*' is Oedipa Maas' anguished cry when faced by the absolute limits of her knowledge in Pynchon's *The Crying of Lot 49* (1966). Quentin and Shreve project a world, apparently unanxiously. Abandoning the intractable problems of attaining to reliable knowledge of *our* world, they improvise a *possible world*; they *fictionalize*. (See Rimmon-Kenan 1978.)

In short, Chapter 8 of *Absalom, Absalom!* dramatizes the shift of dominant from problems of *knowing* to problems of *modes of being* – from an epistemological dominant to an *ontological* one.[3] At this point Faulkner's novel touches and perhaps crosses the boundary between Modernist and Postmodernist writing.

Let me extrapolate from this conclusion to the second of my two theses:

> THESIS 2. The dominant of Postmodernist writing is *ontological*. That is, Postmodernist writing is designed to raise such questions as: what is a world? what kinds of world are there, how are they constituted, and how do they differ? what happens when different kinds of world are placed in confrontation, or when boundaries between worlds are violated? what is the mode of existence of a text, and what is the mode of existence of the world (or worlds) it projects? how is a projected world structured? and so on.

The case of *Absalom, Absalom!* suggests that a kind of inner logic or inner dynamics governs the shift of dominant from Modernist to Postmodernist writing. Intractable epistemological uncertainty, it seems to suggest, becomes at a certain point ontological plurality or instability: push epistemological questions far enough and they 'tip over' into ontological questions. By the same token, push ontological questions far enough and they tip over into epistemological questions – the progression is not linear and one-way, but circular and reversible. The transition in the *opposite* direction, from an ontological dominant to an epistemological one, has actually happened once in the history of Western European writing, namely at the end of the seventeenth century, the period of the 'rise of the novel,' according to traditional literary histories. The great document of *that* transition is, of course, *Don Quixote*.[4]

4. FIVE CASE-STUDIES

Steve Katz said it better, and more briefly, in the remark I have cited as my epigraph. The logic of literary history brought writers in various cities – cities in Europe and Latin America as well as in North America – to a crosswalk; when the stoplights changed, they had one of two options, either to remain on this side and continue to practice a Modernist poetics of the epistemological dominant (as many of them did), or to cross to a Postmodernist poetics of the ontological dominant. The streets were different, but the *crossing* was the same.

Faulkner made that crossing in Chapter 8 of *Absalom Absalom!* This is an isolated event in his œuvre, however; he did not stay on the Postmodernist side of the street, but quickly returned to the practice of Modernism. So Faulkner is not very representative of the change that has occurred throughout Western literature in the years since the Second World War. The change of dominant appears in its most dramatic form in writers who in the course of their careers travel the entire trajectory from Modernist to Postmodernist poetics, marking in successive novels different stages of the crossing. I have chosen some of the more familiar writers of whom this is true: Samuel Beckett, Alain Robbe-Grillet, Carlos Fuentes, Vladimir Nabokov, and Robert Coover. (I could easily have included Thomas Pynchon as well, but I have written about his case elsewhere; see McHale 1979.)

BECKETT. Samuel Beckett makes the transition from Modernist to Postmo-dernist poetics in the course of his trilogy of novels of the early '50s, *Molloy* (1950/55), *Malone Dies* (1951/56), and *The Unnamable* (1952/59). *Molloy* juxtaposes two different, contrasting minds, Molloy's and Moran's, exposing them to (apparently) one and the same object-world, and thus allowing us to gauge their dissimilarity. This is a minimal structure of Modernist perspectivism – its *locus classicus* is the 'Nausicaa' chapter of Joyce's *Ulysses* – and Beckett has further reduced and stylized it, converting a minimal structure to a minimal*ist* one. But if Beckett in *Molloy* continues to practice a (stylized) Modernist poetics, it is not a straightforward or unruffled Modernism. There are difficul-ties with the structure of Beckett's world, incipient internal contradictions, threatened violations of the law of the excluded middle. In particular, it appears that Moran both is and is not identical with Molloy – a blurring of identities that tends to destabilize the projected world, and consequently to foreground its ontological structure. Here, we might say, Modernist poetics begins to *hae-morrhage*, to leak away – though not fatally, since it is still (barely) possible to recuperate these internal contradictions by invoking the model of the 'unreli-able narrator,' thus stabilizing the projected world and reasserting the episte-mological dominant of the text.

This hard-won stability is revoked in the opening pages of the trilogy's second volume, *Malone Dies*. Here Malone retroactively alters the ontological status of Molloy's and Moran's world by claiming to have been its author; with this gesture he places it between brackets or, better, *sous rature*, under erasure (see Derrida 1967: 31). Malone's claim to authorship of *Molloy* has the effect of foregrounding the act of projecting a world, of fictionalizing, as indeed do all his other acts of world-projection throughout the text. Malone's stories of Macmann (or Saposcat – the name-change is in itself a sign of Malone's authorial freedom) constitute a second, embedded ontological level, a world subordinated to and ontologically 'weaker' than the world Malone himself occupies. Of course, this embedded world is still recuperable in epistemological terms, as a reflection or extension of Malone's consciousness – until the end, that is. For at the end of the text the secondary world 'takes over': we 'descend' from Malone's world to the world of Macmann, but without ever reascending to Malone's world again, the text breaking off while we are still at the level of the secondary world. We are invited (by the novel's title, if nothing else) to construe this as a sign of the author's (Malone's) death *in medias res*, so to speak; nevertheless, an ambiguity lingers over this ending, leaving us to wonder which was the 'more real,' the world in which Malone lives and (presumably) dies, or the world which he has projected, and within which the text ends. In other words, there is here some *hesitation* between an epistemological dominant and an ontological dominant. *Both* epistemological *and* ontological questions seem to be raised by this text, but which focus of attention *dominates* depends upon how we look at the text. In this respect, *Malone Dies* recalls the figure/ground paradoxes of the Gestalt psychologists: looked at one way, the picture seems to represent (say) a goblet, looked at another way it represents two faces. Analogously, looked at one way, *Malone Dies* seems to be focused on epistemological issues, while looked at another way it seems to be focused on ontological issues. I would like to reserve for texts of this type – hesitant texts, goblet/face texts – the label of 'limit-Modernist,' on the model of Alan Wilde's 'late modernism' (Wilde 1981). (I do not claim any great advantage for my label over Wilde's – certainly it is no improvement from the point of view of elegance – except that it does manage to incorporate the notion of *cas-limite*, of teetering on the brink, that I wish to emphasize.)

The Unnamable duplicates the opening gambit of *Malone Dies*, with the unnamed and unnamable narrator claiming to have been the author of Malone's world, *and* of Molloy's, and indeed of all the worlds of Beckett's earlier fictions as well. Like Malone, the Unnamable projects worlds, but he displays greater freedom of ontological improvisation than Malone ever did, constructing, revising, deconstructing, abolishing, and reconstructing his characters (Basil/Mahood, Worm) and their worlds apparently at will. And he goes even further, extending the recursive structure of worlds-within-worlds 'upwards' as well as (like Malone) 'downwards.' That is, the Unnamable not only imagines characters, he also tries to imagine himself *as the character of someone else*. But who? First, he can only imagine an undifferentiated *they*, a chorus of voices constituting the discourse that he transmits to us, and that makes him exist for us; but then he speculates that surely *they*, in their turn, must be determined by some being ontologically superior even to them, whom he calls *the master*; but surely the master too, in his turn, must be determined by some still *more* superior being, some 'everlasting third party'...

In *The Unnamable* Beckett has, in effect, written a grotesque parody of St. Anselm's so-called 'ontological argument' for the existence of God. God is that than which no greater can be thought, said Anselm. Now if that than which no greater can be thought existed only in the mind, then a greater could still be thought after all, namely a being who existed in extramental reality. Therefore, so runs the syllogism, God must exist not only mentally but also in reality. The Unnamable parodies this astonishing feat of pulling-oneself-up-by-one's-own-ontological-bootstraps by showing that no matter how 'high' his imaginings go, no matter how many recursive authors and authors-above-authors and authors-above-authors-above-authors he projects, he can never get outside of his own imaginings to the reality of his ultimate creator. There is an absolute ontological 'ceiling' above the Unnamable's head which retreats as he approaches it. The ultimate creator, the God whom the Unnamable can never reach, is of course Samuel Beckett himself, and the retreating ceiling is the unbreachable barrier between the fictional world of the Unnamable and the real world which Samuel Beckett shares with us, his readers. In short, *The Unnamable* foregrounds the fundamental ontological discontinuity between the fictional and the real, and does so in such a way as to *model* the discontinuity between our own mode of being and that of whatever divinity we may wish there were.

ROBBE-GRILLET. Evidently the watershed between Modernist and Postmodernist poetics, which I have been describing, coincides rather closely with the one between the *nouveau* and the *nouveau nouveau roman*, a distinction regularly made in recent French criticism. Exactly how closely, I can demonstrate most conveniently from the case of Alain Robbe-Grillet, in some sense the exemplary *nouveau romancier*. His *La Jalousie* (1957), a 'classic' *nouveau roman*, is also, like Beckett's Molloy, a stylized Modernist novel, employing with extreme rigor the Modernist conventions of limited point of view – except, of course, that the character through whom the world of the novel is focalized has been effaced, leaving a gap where a center of consciousness should be. This gap is readily filled, however: from the textual evidence, the reader reconstructs the missing figure of the jealous husband who obsessively spies on his wife and her presumed lover. 'Completed' by the reader in this way, the novel becomes an example of a Modernist epistemological *topos*, that of the *voyeur*, whose narrow aperture of physical sight – here, the *jalousie* of the title – serves as a kind of objective correlative for limited point of view itself. The *locus classicus* is perhaps the opening episode of Proust's *Sodome et Gomorrhe* (1921), where Marcel spies upon the homosexual courtship of Charlus and Jupien; but voyeurism in its epistemological function also recurs throughout Henry James, especially in *The Sacred Fount* (1901).

Thus, though at first sight strange and intractable, *La Jalousie* actually puts up little resistance to a recuperation in epistemological terms. Or at least not from this quarter; for it *does* put up some resistance from another quarter, namely in its use of structures *en abyme* (most notoriously, the black's song). *Mise en abyme*, wherever it occurs, disturbs the orderly hierarchy of ontological levels (worlds within worlds), in effect *short-circuiting* the ontological structure, and thus foregrounding it. In other words, *mise en abyme* in *La Jalousie* constitutes, like the internal contradictions in *Molloy*, a haemorrhage of Modernist poetics – but, again as in *Molloy*, not a fatal one.

Resistance to recuperation is stronger in Robbe-Grillet's next novel, *Dans le Labyrinthe* (1959). This text is recuperable if we are willing to attribute the instability and inconsistency of its world to the consciousness of the dying soldier who is its protagonist. A number of critics have been willing to do so, most recently Christine Brooke-Rose (1981). But this is an 'expensive' reading, in the sense that it requires us to smooth over a good many difficulties and to repress the text's own resistance to being read this way, especially the resistance that comes from what we might call its 'Klein-bottle' structure. A Klein bottle is a three-dimensional figure whose inside surface is indistinguishable from its outside; similarly, inside and outside are indistinguishable in *Dans le Labyrinthe*, its secondary or embedded representations (viz., the engraving of 'The Defeat of Reichenfels') becoming the 'outside world,' its world in turn collapsing back into a secondary representation (a world within a world), which is thus *embedded in itself*. The ontological focus of this structure competes with the epistemological focus of the dying-soldier motif; but which dominates? I am suggesting, in other words, that *Dans le Labyrinthe* is, like *Malone Dies*, a text of limit-Modernism.

Klein-bottle paradoxes proliferate in *La Maison de rendez-vous* (1965), to the point where the projected world is completely destabilized. Here there is no identifiable center of consciousness through which we may attempt to recuperate the text's paradoxical changes of level and other inconsistencies. An exemplary *nouveau nouveau roman*, in short, demonstrating the 'practice of writing'; or, I would prefer to say, an exemplary Postmodernist text, governed by the ontological dominant and designed to dramatize ontological issues.

One good measure of the change of dominant in Robbe-Grillet's writing from *La Jalousie* through *La Maison de rendez-vous* is his treatment of *space*. *La Jalousie*, of course, is notorious for the obsessive precision with which it specifies the spatial disposition of objects in and around the African bungalow (e.g., the counting of the banana-trees). This precision obviously relates to the text's epistemological motifs; on the one hand, it serves to position the effaced center of consciousness; on the other, it enables us to infer aspects of the husband's psychological profile. In *Dans le Labyrinthe*, our loss of bearings as readers is paralleled by the soldier's loss of bearings in a city which is apparently uniform and repetitive. Urban space here is modular or *serial* (in the sense of 'serial music'), like the Law Courts in Kafka's *The Trial* or the infinitely-repeated hexagonal galleries of Borges' 'The Library of Babel' (which may well have been Robbe-Grillet's models). Finally, space in the 'Oriental port' (Hong Kong or Singapore or wherever it is supposed to be) of *La Maison de rendez-vous* is simply impossible, defying our attempts at orderly reconstruction. Here projected space has been overwhelmed by paradox; and this is true not only of the exterior spaces of the city, but also of the interior spaces of its buildings, for instance the tenement housing Edouard Manneret's flat, through which Kim the Eurasian girl traces an impossible, paradoxical itinerary.

FUENTES. The pattern I have been tracing can also be discerned in some of the writers of the so-called Latin-American 'boom.' My example is the career of the Mexican novelist Carlos Fuentes from *La Muerte de Artemio Cruz* (1962) through *Terra Nostra* (1975). *Artemio Cruz* and the novel which follows it, *Zona Sagrada* (1967), represent variants of the Modernist interior monologue novel, which focuses on the characteristic grid which each mind imposes on the outside world, or through which it assimilates the outside world. Each of these novels employs a different situational *topos* associated with the interior monologue convention, a different type of distortion of the mental grid. In the case of *Artemio Cruz*, this is the deathbed monologue *topos*, to which *Malone Dies*, incidentally, also belongs, and which may be traced back through Broch's *Death of Virgil* and Hemingway's 'Snows of Kilimanjaro' ultimately to Tolstoj's 'Ivan Ilič.' The deathbed *topos* has been complicated or aggravated in *Artemio Cruz* by the presence of the Modernist (and subsequently Postmodernist) theme of the multiplicity of the self, dramatized here through the fragmentation of the monologue into three discontinuous monologues each using a different grammatical person. The model for this may well be Dos Passos' *U.S.A.* trilogy (1930–36), where in several places the 'same' experience is attributed both to a third-person fictional character and to an autobiographical persona who is sometimes a first-person subject, sometimes a second-person self-addressee.

The interior monologue of *Zona Sagrada* belongs to the *topos* of the mad monologuist, the speaker who progressively becomes, or is progressively revealed to be, insane. This type of interior monologue situation dates at least from Edgar Allan Poe (e.g., 'The Tell-Tale Heart', 'The Black Cat'), and enters mainstream Modernist poetics especially through the neo-gothic mad monologuists of Faulkner (e.g., Darl Bundren in *As I Lay Dying*, Quenting Compson in *The Sound and the Fury*; but see also Septimus Warren Smith in Virginia Woolf's *Mrs. Dalloway*). Fuentes' use of this *topos* here is complicated by the presence of the epistemological theme *par excellence*, the theme of illusion and reality; the monologuist's madness expresses itself through his obsession with his film-star mother and the disparity (or lack of it) between her 'real' self and her public and cinematic 'image.'

Cambio de Piel (1967) is Fuentes' limit-Modernist text. In it he adapts the ontological structure of the fantastic, a genre which he had already exploited in a 'straight' fantastic story, 'Aura' (1962). The fantastic genre (in a broad sense, not in the narrow sense of Todorov 1970) involves a confrontation between two worlds whose basic physical norms are mutually incompatible. A miracle is 'another world's intrusion into this one,' according to a character in Pynchon's *The Crying of Lot 49*, and it is precisely the miraculous in this sense of the term that constitutes the ontological structure of the fantastic genre. Miracles do happen in *Cambio de Piel* – sympathetic magic, the resurrection of the dead – but Fuentes is careful to leave a loophole by framing the fantastic story within the discourse of a mad monologuist. On its closing pages we learn that the text has been produced by one Freddy Lambert, inmate of an insane asylum. As in the German Expressionist film *The Cabinet of Dr. Caligari*, which uses this same strategy (and to which *Cambio de Piel* actually alludes), the fantastic is recuperated at the last possible moment and converted into a subjective delusion; the ontological structure of 'another world's intrusion into this one' collapses into an epistemological structure, that of the uncanny (in Todorov's sense). We may well wonder, as in the case of Robbe-Grillet's *Dans le Labyrinthe*, whether such a recuperation is not after all too 'expensive,' whether it does not foreclose a bit too abruptly on the fantastic elements and their ontological dominant.

Fuentes' adaptation and integration of peripheral or sub-literary ontological genres continues and reaches its peak in *Terra Nostra*. This novel is, along with Pynchon's *Gravity's Rainbow* (1973), one of the paradigmatic texts of Postmodernist writing, literally an anthology of Postmodernist themes and devices. Here Fuentes again exploits the conventions of the fantastic, as well as those of science fiction and the historical novel. Science fiction, we might say, is to Postmodernism what detective fiction was to Modernism: it is the ontological genre *par excellence* (as the detective story is the epistemological genre *par excellence*), and so serves as a source of materials and models for Post-modernist writers (including William Burroughs, Kurt Vonnegut, Italo Calvino, Pynchon, even Beckett and Nabokov). The pertinence of the historical novel to Postmodernism, by contrast, is not so immediately obvious, and needs some explaining.

All historical novels, even the most traditional, typically involve some violation of ontological boundaries. For instance, they often claim 'transworld identity' (see Eco 1979) between characters in their projected worlds and real-world historical figures, e.g., Napoleon or Richard Nixon. Traditional historical novels strive to suppress these violations, to hide the ontological 'seams' between fictional projections and real-world facts. They do so by tactfully avoiding contradictions between their versions of historical figures and the familiar facts of these figures' careers, and by making the background norms governing their projected worlds conform to accepted real-world norms. *Terra Nostra*, by contrast, foregrounds its ontological seams by systematically transgressing these rules of its genre. Here familiar facts are tactlessly contradicted – Columbus discovers America a full century too late, Philip II of Spain marries Elizabeth of England, and so on – and the projected world is governed by fantastic norms. Fuentes thus converts the historical novel into a medium for raising ontological issues, as do other Postmodernist historical novelists, including Pynchon, Günter Grass, Robert Coover, Ishmael Reed, and Salman Rushdie.

One measure of the change of dominant in Fuentes' writing is the different treatments of the same motif in the Modernist novel *Zona Sagrada* and in *Terra Nostra*. This is the motif of the 'transhistorical party,' where characters apparently from disparate historical eras are brought together at the same time and place. Obviously a carnivalesque motif, in Baxtin's sense, it is also related to the typical Modernist motif of the party that assembles, or reassembles, all the characters of the novel at a single locus – for instance, the Guermantes party in *Le Temps retrouvé*, Clarissa's party in *Mrs. Dalloway*, or even the fiesta at Pamplona in *The Sun Also Rises*. In Fuentes' *Zona Sagrada*, the transhistorical party is epistemologically motivated, and implicated in the theme of illusion and reality: Guillermo, the narrator-protagonist, stumbles into such a party at his friend's Italian villa, only to find that things are not what they seem, and that the party is really only a movie set for one of his mother's films, the figures from different historical eras only actors in period costumes. In *Terra Nostra*, however, the party is real, Paris having been transformed into an immense transhistorical carnival by the appearance in its streets of time-travelers from past historical periods. This transhistorical partly, in short, has been modeled on a science-fiction *topos*, that of the 'time war' (see, e.g., Fritz Leiber's *The Big Time*, 1958, or Philip José Farmer's *To Your Scattered Bodies Go*, 1971). The motivation here is ontological, a confrontation between our world and a world whose norms permit time-travel.

Moreover, at the center of the transhistorical carnival of *Terra Nostra* stands another ontological motif, involving a different type of 'transworld identity' from the one that is characteristic of historical fiction. A number of characters gather to play poker, including Pierre Menard, Buendía, Oliveira, the cousins Sofía and Esteban, and Cuba Venegas. These characters have, of course, been 'lifted' from texts by *other* south-American 'boom' novelists – from Borges' 'Pierre Menard, Author of Don Quixote,' García Márquez's *Cien Años de Soledad*, Cortázar's *Rayuela*, Carpentier's *El Siglo de las Luces*, and Cabrera Infante's *Tres Tristes Tigres*, respectively. Here, in other words, we have a case of *intertextual* boundary-violation, transworld identity between characters belonging to different fictional worlds. Disparate, incommensurable worlds literally rub shoulders around this poker-table, creating a dense ontological 'knot,' as though the entire intertextual space of Latin-American Postmodernist writing had somehow been folded *into* the projected world of *Terra Nostra*. What conceivable space could such a poker-table occupy? Only the sort of space where fragments of a number of possible orders have been gathered together – the space which Michel Foucault (1966) has called a *heterotopia*.

NABOKOV. The crossover from Modernist to Postmodernist writing also occurs during the middle years of Vladimir Nabokov's American career, specifically in the sequence *Lolita* (1955), *Pale Fire* (1962), *Ada* (1969). Humbert Humbert of *Lolita* belongs, of course, to the tradition of radically unreliable Modernist narrators, joining the distinguished line that includes Dowell of Ford Madox Ford's *The Good Soldier* and Jason Compson of *The Sound and the Fury*, and whose founder, so to speak, is Dostoevskij's Underground Man (see Tamir-Ghez 1979). In *Pale Fire*, this familiar convention of narratorial unreliability has been pushed to the limit. Here we can be sure that the narrator is radically unreliable, but without being able to determine (as we still can in the case of Humbert Humbert) *in what ways* he is unreliable, or *to what degree*. Excluding minor variants, no fewer than *four* distinct hypotheses may be entertained about *Pale Fire* (see Rabinowitz 1977):

(1)   that Kinbote (or Botkin, or whatever his name is) is telling the truth and nothing but the truth: John Shade's poem 'Pale Fire' really is an allusive and heavily camouflaged biography of Kinbote himself, who secretly is none other than Charles the Beloved, exiled King of Zembla;

(2)   that Kinbote really is the exiled King of Zembla, and the Zemblan part of his story is true, but that he is deluded in believing that Shade's poem in any way reflects the events of his own life;

(3)   that Kinbote is really a Russian émigré academic named Botkin, the whole of the king of Zembla's adventures, possibly the very Kingdom of Zembla itself, having been hallucinated by Botkin (on this hypothesis, needless to say, Shade's poem *certainly* has nothing to do with the Zemblan story);

(4)   that *everything* – Zembla and its king, John Shade and his poem – has been concocted by someone who is neither Shade nor Kinbote/Botkin. By whom, then? Well, by Vladimir Nabokov at one level, it goes without saying; but ought we perhaps to reconstruct some intermediary figure who stands between the biographical Nabokov and the substance of *Pale Fire*, or is there insufficient warrant for this?

Pale Fire, in other words, is a text of absolute epistemological uncertainty: we know that something is happening here but we don't know what it is, as Bob Dylan said of Mister Jones. Inevitably, epistemological doubt as total as this has ontological consequences as well; in particular, the Kingdom of Zembla flickers in and out of existence, depending upon which hypothesis we choose to entertain (it exists according to hypotheses 1 and 2, but not according to 3 and 4). Thus, we not only hesitate among hypotheses, but also between an epistemological and an ontological focus, making *Pale Fire* a text of limit-Modernism, perhaps the paradigmatic limit-Modernist novel.

Epistemological preoccupations continue to be visible in *Ada*: the Modernist theme of memory, the device of joint narration by Van and Ada, comically dramatizing the disparity between two perspectives on the same objective 'facts,' and so on. Nevertheless, the dominant has unmistakably been shifted away from these preoccupations in this text, and it is above all the strange, familiar-yet-alien make-up of the projected world that engrosses our attention, memory and perspectivism having been firmly displaced to the background. The world of *Ada* can be seen as the convergence of two ontological structures, one based on a science fiction *topos*, the other extrapolated from the conventions of the *roman à clef*. On the one hand, the Antiterra of *Ada*, with its displaced and superimposed spaces, its skew place-names, and its oddly juggled chronology, incorporates the parallel-world *topos* of such science-fiction novels as Philip K. Dick's *The Man in the High Castle* (1962): this is our world as it *might have been* if at certain branchings in history's garden of forking paths some path *other* than the one which produced our world had been chosen. Alternatively, Nabokov's Antiterra can be seen as a sort of ontological variant on the *roman à clef*, in which Nabokov's complicated multi-national and multi-lingual autobiography has been, in effect, encoded in the structure of the projected world. Thus, all three of Nabokov's 'nations' – Russia, France, the United States – have been superimposed on a single geographical space, the 'Estotiland' of *Ada*, while three peak periods in his life – the pre-Revolutionary years of his childhood, the years of his young manhood in the 1920s, and the years of his greatest postwar success – have been telescoped into a single present. Either way we look at it, *Ada* represents a case of sheer ontological improvisation more radical than anything Quentin and Shreve attempt in *Absalom, Absalom!*

COOVER. Robert Coover's career, too, corresponds to the by-now familiar pattern of change of dominant. His first novel, *The Origin of the Brunists* (1966), deploys the repertoire of Modernist devices – multiple focalization and juxtaposed perspectives, interior monologue, and so on – in a perfectly orthodox, if perhaps somewhat mechanical, way. As in classic Modernist texts, these devices function to express epistemological themes, here stated with particular explicitness. Coover's themes are essentially those of Berger's and Luckmann's *The Social Construction of Reality* – subtitled, it will be recalled, *A Treatise in the Sociology of Knowledge* – which appeared, interestingly, the same year as *Origin of the Brunists* (something in the air?). In effect, *Brunists* recounts the process of consolidation of what Berger and Luckmann would call a new 'subuniverse of meaning' – i.e., a breakaway religious sect – from the solipsistic private world views of an assortment of mystics, paranoiacs, and cranks. This process is evaluated form the normative viewpoint of the newspaperman Tiger Miller, a pluralist and relativist, but also a spokesman for 'paramount reality,' to use Berger's and Luckmann's term, the shared world of normal social interaction. 'Not the void within and ahead,' thinks Tiger on the novel's closing pages, 'but the immediate living space between two;' not, in other words, the self-contained and totalizing 'esoteric enclave' (Berger and Luckmann again) of the Brunist cult, but the paramount reality of our everyday life with others, here and now.

Just as Nabokov in *Pale Fire* pushes the unreliable narrator convention of *Lolita* to its limit, so Coover pushes the epistemological themes of *Origin of the Brunists* to their limit – and beyond – in his next novel, *The Universal Baseball Association, Inc., J. Henry Waugh, Prop.* (1968). *Brunists* sticks to the central area of Berger's and Luckmann's epistemological problematics, namely the tension between paramount reality and subuniverses of meaning. *J. Henry Waugh* shifts to the fringes of that area, focusing on one of the strategies of temporary (or, in this case, permanent) *withdrawal* from paramount reality, a topic pursued by Stanley Cohen and Laurie Taylor, sociologists following very much in the footsteps of Berger and Luckmann, in their book *Escape Attempts: The Theory and Practice of Resistance to Everyday Life* (1976). Cohen and Taylor actually cite Coover's J. Henry Waugh as an example of permanent escape from paramount reality into what they call an 'activity enclave,' namely the table-top baseball game that Waugh designs and obsessively plays in private. Waugh is the novel's center of consciousness, and we witness from inside, so to speak, his progressively deeper absorption in the solipsistic world of the game, his increasing alienation from the everyday concerns of 'real life.' Thus, we are very near here to the mad monologuist *topos* exemplified by Guillermo of Fuentes' *Zona Sagrada*. However, just at the point where Waugh's obsession escalates into outright madness, the text itself goes mad, or so it would appear: the signs of Waugh's framing consciousness fall away, Waugh himself disappears from the text, and the world-within-the-world of Waugh's baseball game acquires an independent reality, even a history, becoming in effect a freestanding world of its own. In this astonishing final chapter, *J. Henry Waugh* duplicates the breakthrough in Chapter 8 of Faulkner's *Absalom, Absalom!* or the closing pages of Beckett's *Malone Dies*. With this gesture of pure ontological improvisation, it crosses over from a Modernist poetics of the epistemological dominant to a Postmodernist poetics of the ontological dominant.

In subsequent writings, Coover has extended and consolidated his practice of Postmodernist poetics. His collection *Pricksongs and Descants* (1969), for instance, amounts to a mini-anthology of ontological motifs and devices. Granted, several of the texts it contains were written before *J. Henry Waugh*; nevertheless, it seems significant that these texts were not actually gathered together into a book until *after* the breakthrough to Postmodernism had been dramatized in *J. Henry Waugh*. *Pricksongs* includes a number of revisionist and parodic adaptations of fairy-tale and Bible-story ontologies ('The Door', 'The Magic Poker', 'The Gingerbread House', 'The Brother', 'J.'s Marriage'), a strategy used by other Postmodernist writers as well, including Donald Barthelme (e.g., *Snow White*, 1967) and Angela Carter (e.g., *The Bloody Chamber*, 1979). It also contains several self-contradictory or self-canceling fictions ('The Magic Poker', 'The Elevator', 'Quenby and Ola, Swede and Carl', 'The Babysitter'), worlds under erasure that realize the possibilities inherent in Beckett's trilogy or in Borges' 'The Garden of Forking Paths,' in the process laying bare the ontological structure of the fictional text.[5] Coover's *The Public Burning* (1977) resembles Fuentes' *Terra Nostra* in its (ab)use of the conventions of the historical novel for ontological purposes. Like Fuentes, Coover here systematically contradicts well-known historical facts (e.g., Vice-President Richard Nixon is made to attempt the seduction of Ethel Rosenberg on the eve of her execution), and grafts historical characters onto a fantastic world, a mismatching of norms dramatized by Richard Nixon's sodomization (!) by the mythological Uncle Sam. The climactic scene of the carnivalesque public execution in Times Square constitutes an ontological knot like the poker-game of *Terra Nostra*, although on a larger scale. Here characters of different and incompatible ontological statuses – real-world historical figures, corporate trade-marks (e.g., Betty Crocker) and national symbols (e.g., Uncle Sam), purely fictional characters – have been gathered together in an impossible, heterotopian locus which is also, according to Coover, 'the ritual center of the Western World.'

5. CONCLUSION: APROPOS OF WHAT?

To recapitulate, then: I have proposed to define Postmodernist writing as contemporary writing governed or characterized by the ontological dominant, or (which is the same thing) the contemporary practice of a poetics of the ontological dominant. This, as I said at the outset, is a strategic definition, 'merely' instrumental, and only one of (no doubt) many possible definitions of Postmodernism. That it is a good one in my sense, i.e. a productive one, I hope the preceding case-studies have demonstrated. At any rate, as a strategic definition it ought also to be self-conscious, answering the question, 'Apropos of what?' It ought, in other words, to be accompanied by an explicit statement of the purpose(s) for which it was designed.

The purposes of my definition of Postmodernism are, as nearly as I can make out, the following:

(1) to capture the intuition of a sharp *discontinuity* between Modernist poetics and a certain range of contemporary practice (although by no means all of it). This is not, of course, the only intuition about contemporary writing that one might want to capture. It runs dead counter, for instance, to Frank Kermode's intuition (which we all no doubt share in part) of the *continuity* between Modernism and the contemporary writing which he insists we must call 'neo-modernist' (Kermode 1968: 24). Kermode tends to efface the boundary between Modernism and Postmodernism precisely because he wishes to keep as clear and sharp as possible the earlier boundary that marked the onset of Modernism. Conversely, my definition aims to clarify and sharpen the Modernist/Postmodernist boundary, but at the cost of effacing the earlier boundary. This, it appears, is the price one must pay.

(2) to formulate a satisfactory common denominator or connecting principle for the widest possible range of contemporary devices, themes, and *topoi*. This is in preference to the purpose of formulating a more heterogeneous, although possibly more exhaustive, catalogue, of which Fokkema's Modernist period code is an example.

(3) to include the widest possible range of contemporary movements of avant-grade writing, national 'schools,' and individual writers – without, however, shrinking from the necessity of sometimes having to exclude writers or movements that have usually been included in the Postmodernist canon. Thus, for example, it seems to me that my definition will exclude Nathalie Sarraute, William Gaddis, Manuel Puig, John Hawkes (except for *The Cannibal*, 1949, and possibly *Virginie*, 1982), and William H. Gass (except for *Willie Master's Lonesome Wife*, 1968) – all writers who have been regarded as Postmodernists.

6. POSTSCRIPT: SOME FALLACIES

Finally, I would like to take the opportunity to try to pre-empt certain fallacies that I suppose might arise from my treatment of Postmodernist writing:

(1) Postmodernist writing, as I understand it, does *not* embrace the entire range of contemporary innovative or avant-garde writing; it does not exhaust the field. The term 'Postmodernism' is not synonymous with 'innovative' or 'avant-garde.' It is still possible to be innovative or avant-garde while continuing to practice some contemporary version of Modernist (or limit-Modernist) poetics. This is the case with the writers I mentioned above as falling outside of my definition of Postmodernism: Sarraute, Gaddis, Puig, Hawkes, Gass, these are innovators and avant-gardists, without being Postmodernists.

(2) The crossover from Modernist to Postmodernist poetics is *not irreversible*, not a gate that swings one way only, even in a single writer's career (as I hope the example of Faulkner has made clear). It is possible to 'retreat' from Postmodernism to Modernism, or indeed to vacillate between the two. Thus, for example, Carlos Fuentes seems to have retreated from the Postmodernism of *Terra Nostra* to an epistemological thriller in *La Cabeza de la Hidra* (1978); similarly, Walter Abish's *How German Is It* (1980) represents a withdrawal from the Postmodernist poetics of his earlier fictions (*Alphabetical Africa*, 1974; *Minds Meet*, 1975; *In the Future Perfect*, 1977).

(3) The decision to label a text Postmodernist as distinct from Modernist is independent, so far as I am concerned, from any decisions about its aesthetic superiority or inferiority. (Do I really need to insist upon this, at this late date? Yes, probably.) The label 'Postmodernist' is not, in my usage, an automatic commendation (nor is it, by the same token, an automatic *condemnation*!). A Postmodernist text is not necessarily aesthetically superior (or inferior) to a Modernist text simply because it *is* Postmodernist, and we are free (say) to rate Coover's limit-Modernist text *J. Henry Waugh* more highly than his Postmodernist text *The Public Burning* on aesthetic grounds – or vice-versa, of course.

NOTES

1. In discussion of this paper, Jean Galard observed that my criterion of productiveness belongs to the conceptual framework of Modernism, so that in effect I am building up a distinction between Modernism and Postmodernism on the basis of theoretical principles derived from Modernism, not from Postmodernism. In the background of this remark stands, of course, Lyotard's (1979) view of Postmodernism as a general cultural phenomenon, a 'condition.' To Galard's objection I really have no adequate defense. I could, for instance, simply dissociate myself from Lyotard's view of Postmodernism. Or I could reply that there is no *a priori* reason why one should *not* use Modernist theoretical perspectives in describing Postmodernism. But neither of these moves seems quite satisfactory. Perhaps the best I can do is to fall back on psychological *preference* (which plays a larger role in our practice of the 'science of

literature' than we might care to admit; see Tsur 1975); personally, I *prefer* the productive to the restrained (or whatever the opposite category would be).

2. In a subsequent publication, Fokkema, in collaboration with Elrud Ibsch, has filled in the gap in his 1982 paper, actually specifying epistemology as the Modernist dominant (Fokkema and Ibsch 1984). I regard this as important independent corroboration of my view – truly independent, since I was unaware of Fokkema's and Ibsch's book (and could not have read it even if I had been aware of it, due to my ignorance of Dutch).

3. It would probably be wise to try to clear up right at the outset my use of the term *ontology*, and thus head off some possible misunderstandings. 'Ontology' has passed into the discourse of literary criticism from philosophical discourse, especially that of Heidegger, and usually pertains to attempts to 'ground' our world in some stable or determinate order of being. In the criticism of Postmodernist writing, it typically turns up in the context of Postmodernism's alleged *undermining* of all attempts at ontological grounding [...] I wish to dissociate myself from this use of 'ontology.' *My* 'ontology' derives (as I hope the case-studies below will make clear) from the use of the term in poetics, above all by Roman Ingarden (1931, 1937; cf. Falk 1981) and by Thomas Pavel and others who have adapted concepts from modal logic ('possible worlds') to the description of fictional worlds (Pavel, 1975, 1979, 1980, 1981a, 1981b, 1982, 1983; see also Eco 1979). For a working definition, let me cite Pavel: an ontology is 'a theoretical description of a universe' (1981b: 234). The operative word here, from my point of view, is the indefinite article: a description of *a* universe, not of *the* universe; that is, of *any* universe, potentially of a *plurality* of universes. In other words, to 'do ontology' in this perspective is not necessarily to seek some grounding for *our* universe; it might just as well involve the description of *other* universes, including 'possible' and fictional ones. To put it another way: the difference between *the* universe and *a* universe is precisely what the Postmodernist critics mean when they talk about the undermining of ontology.

4. In the discussion of this paper, the philosopher Willem van Reijen protested that one cannot raise epistemological questions without immediately raising ontological questions, and vice-versa. I could not agree more: the ontological questions raised by Postmodernist texts immediately prompt epistemological questions, just as the epistemological questions raised by Modernist texts, immediately prompt ontological ones. Nevertheless, I stick by my notion of the dominant. The dominant, in effect, determines the *order* in which the questions must be raised: the ontological dominant forces us to *notice* the ontological questions, and vice-versa for the epistemological dominant. I think it significant that van Reijen had to use the language of *temporality* to describe the inseparability of the two sets of questions: 'immediately after' raising one kind of question, the other kind arises. This is an inevitable consequence of the temporality and linearity of all discourse, of course. Even a philosopher who knows that these two sets of questions exist, so to speak; *simultaneously* has no choice but to raise them *consecutively*, since the nature of discourse (even philosophical discourse) does not permit us to ask two questions at exactly the same moment. In this respect, as in many others, literary discourse only heightens and exaggerates what is normally the case in non-literary uses of language: that is, it *slows down* the process, increasing the time lag between the asking of one question and the asking of the next, even if the second is in some sense inseparable from the first.

Let me disgress here to remark that my two theses are not designed to be 'original,' but quite the contrary, to capture intuitions in very general circulation, although nowhere (to my knowledge) explicitly formulated. There is already, I think, a rather widespread consensus about the epistemological dominant in Modernist writing; I have already mentioned Fokkema and Ibsch 1984 (see note 2), and could add Krysinski 1981 as further corroboration. There is also some consensus that this dominant has changed, that epistemology has been (or is being) superseded as a focus of attention. Here some recent remarks by Ronald Sukenick, in an interview with

Larry McCaffery (February 1981), seem pertinent:

> McCAFFERY: ... one of the defining features of postmodern fiction [seems to be] its emphasis on cognition, epistemology, pattern-making, rather than the ego-oriented fiction of, say, American fiction in the 1950s.
> SUKENICK: I agree, although maybe this issue is already established now as something we can take for granted. ... That's one of those issues that we don't have to concentrate on anymore. We assume that now, and are free to investigate other things.
> McCAFFERY: When you say that 'we assume *that* now,' do you mean that writers today don't have to deal with epistemological issues anymore, in the same way that your generation of writers assumed that depth psychology, at least temporarily, didn't need further exploration?
> SUKENICK: Not exactly. Contemporary fiction still has to deal with the issue, just the way fiction always has to deal with ego psychology. But it doesn't have to *focus* on it necessarily.
> (LeClair and McCaffery 1983: 286).

Others who have written about the shift away from the epistemological dominant in comparable terms include Wilde 1981 and Higgins 1984, where the label 'post-cognitive' is proposed for innovative contemporary art – a very near neighbor to 'post-epistemological.' Higgins' term also indicates, however, the *absence* of consensus about what comes *after* the epistemological dominant: after all, the word 'post-cognitive' only tells us what the new art is *not*, it does not tell us what the new art is. Among those who have come closest to defining the Postmodernist dominant in my terms, i.e. in terms of ontology, are Hutcheon 1980, Wilde 1981, and Brooke-Rose 1981; see my review of Wilde and Brooke-Rose (McHale 1982).

5. See Ingarden's account of the ontological 'irridescence' or 'opalescence' of objects projected by ambiguous sentences, a quality of ontological oscillation that may even extend to entire fictional worlds:

> It may ... happen that ambiguity is sustained in a number of sentences with a certain consistency; then this opalescence applies to an entire sphere of objects, so that, in a manner of speaking, two different worlds are struggling for supremacy, with neither of them capable of attaining it (Ingarden 1931: 254).
>
> Ingarden assumed, however, that ontological structures such as this belonged to the background or subliminal level of the text, and could never be brought into the foreground and made to function aesthetically as a focus of interest. He failed to allow for texts such as Coover's 'Magic Poker' or 'The Babysitter,' or those of the Surfictionists Federman and Sukenick, which *do* make aesthetic capital of the ontological structure of the text; he failed, in short, to predict or imagine Postmodernism.

REFERENCES

Berger, Peter L. and Thomas Luckmann. 1966. *The Social Construction of Reality: A Treatise in the Sociology of Knowledge*. Garden City, N.Y.: Doubleday.
Bronzwaer, W.J.M., D.W. Fokkema and Elrud Ibsch. 1977. *Tekstboek algemene literatuurwetenschap*. Baarn: Ambo.
Brooke-Rose, Christine. 1982. *A Rhetoric of the Unreal: Studies in Narrative and Structure, Especially of the Fantastic*. Cambridge and London: Cambridge University Press.
Cohen, Stanley and Laurie Taylor. 1976. *Escape Attempts: The Theory and Practice of Resistance to Everyday Life*. Harmondsworth: Penguin, 1978.

Derrida, Jacques. 1967. *De la grammatologie*. Paris: Minuit.

Eco, Umberto. 1979. '*Lector in Fabula*: Pragmatic Strategy in a Metanarrative Text,' in *The Role of the Reader: Explorations in the Semiotics of Texts*: 200–266. Bloomington and London: Indiana University Press.

Falk, Eugène H. 1981. *The Poetics of Roman Ingarden*. Chapel Hill: University of North Carolina Press.

Fokkema, D.W. 1982. 'A Semiotic Definition of Aesthetic Experience and the Period Code of Modernism,' *Poetics Today* 3, 1: 61–79.

Fokkema, Douwe and Elrud Ibsch. 1984. *Het Modernisme in de Europese letterkunde*. Amsterdam: Arbeiderspers.

Foucault, Michel. 1966. *Les Mots et les choses*. Paris: Gallimard.

Higgins, Dick. 1984. *Horizons: The Poetics and Theory of the Intermedia*. Carbondale and Edwardsville: Southern Illinois University Press.

Hutcheon, Linda. 1980. *Narcissistic Narrative: The Metafictional Paradox*. London: Methuen, 1984.

Ibsch, Elrud. 1977. 'Periodiseren: de historische ordening van literaire teksten,' in Bronzwaer *et al.* 1977: 284–297.

Ingarden, Roman. 1931. *The Literary Work of Art*. Evanston: Northwestern University Press, 1973.

——. 1937. *The Cognition of the Literary Work of Art*. Evanston: Northwestern University Press, 1973.

Jakobson, Roman. 1971. 'The Dominant,' in Matejka and Pomorska 1971: 105–110.

Kermode, Frank. 1968. *Continuities*. London: Routledge and Kegan Paul.

Kinney, Arthur F. 1978. *Faulkner's Narrative Poetics: Style as Vision*. Amherst: University of Massachusetts Press.

Krysinski, Wladimir. 1981. *Carrefour de signes: Essais sur le roman moderne*. The Hague: Mouton.

LeClair, Tom and Larry McCaffery. 1983. *Anything Can Happen: Interviews with American Novelists*. Urbana, Chicago, London: University of Illinois Press.

Lovejoy, Arthur O. 1948. 'On the Discrimination of Romanticisms,' in *Essays in the History of Ideas*. Baltimore: Johns Hopkins University Press.

Lyotard, Jean-François. 1979. *La Condition postmoderne: Rapport sur le savoir*. Paris: Minuit.

Matejka, Ladislav and Krystyna Pomorska. 1971. *Readings in Russian Poetics: Formalist and Structuralist Views*. Cambridge, Mass. and London: MIT Press.

McHale, Brian. 1979. 'Modernist Reading, Post-Modern Text: The Case of *Gravity's Rainbow*,' *Poetics Today* 1, 1–2: 85–110.

——. 1982. 'Writing about Postmodern Writing,' *Poetics Today* 3, 3: 211–227.

Pavel, Thomas. 1975. ' "Possible Worlds" in Literary Semantics.' *Journal of Aesthetics and Art Criticism* 34: 165–176.

——. 1979. 'Fiction and the Causal Theory of Names,' *Poetics* 8, 1–2: 179–191.

——. 1980. 'Narrative Domains,' *Poetics Today* 1, 4: 105–114.

——. 1981a. 'Ontological Issues in Poetics: Speech Acts and Fictional Worlds,' *Journal of Aesthetics and Art Criticism* 40: 167–178.

——. 1981b. 'Tragedy and the Sacred: Notes Towards a Semantic Characterization of a Fictional Genre,' *Poetics* 10, 2–3: 231–242.

——. 1982. 'Fiction and the Ontological Landscape,' *Studies in Twentieth Century Literature* 6, 1–2: 149–163.

——. 1983. 'The Borders of Fiction,' *Poetics Today* 4, 1: 83–88.

Rabinowitz, Peter. 1977. 'Truth in Fiction: A Reexamination of Audiences,' *Critical Inquiry* 4: 121–141.

Rimmon-Kenan, Shlomith. 1978. 'From Reproduction to Production: The Status of Narration in *Absalom, Absalom!*' *Degrés* 16: f–f19.

Tamir-Ghez, Nomi. 1979. 'The Art of Persuasion in Nabokov's *Lolita*,' *Poetics Today* 1, 1–2: 65–83.

Todorov, Tzvetan. 1970. *Introduction à la littérature fantastique*. Paris: Seuil.
Tsur, Reuven. 1975. 'Two Critical Attitudes: Quest for Certitude and Negative Capability,' *College English* 36: 776–88.
Wilde, Alan. 1981. *Horizons of Assent: Modernism, Postmodernism, and the Ironic Imagination*. Baltimore and London: Johns Hopkins University Press.

21

FROM A *POETICS OF POSTMODERNISM*

Linda Hutcheon

I

Clearly, then, the time has come to theorize the term [postmodernism], if
not to define it, before it fades from awkward neologism to derelict cliché
without ever attaining to the dignity of a cultural concept.

Ihab Hassan

Of all the terms bandied about in both current cultural theory and contemporary writing on the arts, postmodernism must be the most over- and under-
defined. It is usually accompanied by a grand flourish of negativized rhetoric:
we hear of discontinuity, disruption, dislocation, decentring, indeterminacy,
and antitotalization. What all of these words literally do (precisely by their
disavowing prefixes – *dis, de, in, anti*) is incorporate that which they aim to
contest – as does, I suppose, the term *post*modernism itself. I point to this simple
verbal fact in order to begin 'theorizing' the cultural enterprise to which we
seem to have given such a provocative label. Given all the confusion and
vagueness associated with the term itself (see Paterson 1986), I would like to
begin by arguing that, for me, postmodernism is a contradictory phenomenon,
one that uses and abuses, installs and then subverts, the very concepts it
challenges – be it in architecture, literature, painting, sculpture, film, video,
dance, TV, music, philosophy, aesthetic theory, psychoanalysis, linguistics, or
historiography. These are some of the realms from which my 'theorizing' will

From Linda Hutcheon (1988) *A Poetics of Postmodernism: History, Theory, Fiction*. London:
Routledge.

proceed, and my examples will always be specific, because what I want to avoid are those polemical generalizations – often by those inimical to postmodernism: Jameson (1984a), Eagleton (1985), Newman (1985) – that leave us guessing about just what it is that is being called postmodernist, though never in doubt as to its undesirability. Some assume a generally accepted 'tacit definition' (Caramello 1983); others locate the beast by temporal (after 1945? 1968? 1970? 1980?) or economic signposting (late capitalism). But in as pluralist and fragmented a culture as that of the western world today, such designations are not terribly useful if they intend to generalize about all the vagaries of our culture. After all, what does television's 'Dallas' have in common with the architecture of Ricardo Bofill? What does John Cage's music share with a play (or film) like *Amadeus*?

In other words, postmodernism cannot simply be used as a synonym for the contemporary (cf. Kroker and Cook 1986). And it does not really describe an international cultural phenomenon, for it is primarily European and American (North and South). Although the concept of *modernism* is largely an Anglo-American one (Suleiman 1986), this should not limit the poetics of *postmodernism* to that culture, especially since those who would argue that very stand are usually the ones to find room to sneak in the French *nouveau roman* (A. Wilde 1981; Brooke-Rose 1981; Lodge 1977). And almost everyone (e.g. Barth 1980) wants to be sure to include what Severo Sarduy (1974) has labelled – not postmodern – but 'neo-baroque' in a Spanish culture where 'modernism' has a rather different meaning.

I offer instead, then, a specific, if polemical, start from which to operate: as a cultural activity that can be discerned in most art forms and many currents of thought today, what I want to call postmodernism is fundamentally contradictory, resolutely historical, and inescapably political. Its contradictions may well be those of late capitalist society, but whatever the cause, these contradictions are certainly manifest in the important postmodern concept of 'the presence of the past.' This was the title given to the 1980 Venice Biennale which marked the institutional recognition of postmodernism in architecture. Italian architect Paolo Portoghesi's (1983) analysis of the twenty facades of the 'Strada Novissima' – whose very newness lay paradoxically in its historical parody – shows how architecture has been rethinking modernism's purist break with history. This is not a nostalgic return; it is a critical revisiting, an ironic dialogue with the past of both art and society, a recalling of a critically shared vocabulary of architectural forms. 'The past whose presence we claim is not a golden age to be recuperated,' argues Portoghesi (1983, 26). Its aesthetic forms and its social formations are problematized by critical reflection. The same is true of the postmodernist rethinking of figurative painting in art and historical narrative in fiction and poetry (see Perloff 1985, 155–71): it is always a critical reworking, never a nostalgic 'return.' Herein lies the governing role of irony in postmodernism. Stanley Tigerman's dialogue with history in his projects for family houses modelled on Raphael's palatial Villa Madama is an ironic one: his miniaturization of the monumental forces a rethinking of the social function of architecture – both then and now [...].

Because it is contradictory and works within the very systems it attempts to subvert, postmodernism can probably not be considered a new paradigm (even in some extension of the Kuhnian sense of the term). It has not replaced liberal humanism, even if it has seriously challenged it. It may mark, however, the site of the struggle of the emergence of something new. The manifestations in art of this struggle may be those almost undefinable and certainly bizarre works like Terry Gilliam's film, *Brazil*. The postmodern ironic rethinking of history is here textualized in the many general parodic references to other movies: *A Clockwork Orange, 1984*, Gilliam's own *Time Bandits* and Monty Python sketches, and Japanese epics, to name but a few. The more specific parodic recalls range from *Star Wars'* Darth Vadar to the Odessa Steps sequence of Eisenstein's *Battleship Potemkin*. In *Brazil*, however, the famous shot of the baby carriage on the steps is replaced by one of a floor cleaner, and the result is to reduce epic tragedy to the bathos of the mechanical and debased. Along with this ironic reworking of the history of film comes a temporal historical warp: the movie is set, we are told, at 8:49 am, sometime in the twentieth century. The decor does not help us identify the time more precisely. The fashions mix the absurdly futuristic with 1930s styling; an oddly old-fashioned and dingy setting belies the omnipresence of computers – though even they are not the sleekly designed creatures of today. Among the other typically post-modern contradictions in this movie is the co-existence of heterogenous filmic genres: fantasy Utopia and grim dystopia; absurd slapstick comedy and tragedy (the Tuttle/Buttle mix-up); the romantic adventure tale and the political documentary.

While all forms of contemporary art and thought offer examples of this kind of postmodernist contradiction, this book (like most others on the subject) will be privileging the novel genre, and one form in particular, a form that I want to call 'historiographic metafiction.' By this I mean those well-known and popular novels which are both intensely self-reflexive and yet paradoxically also lay claim to historical events and personages: *The French Lieutenant's Woman, Midnight's Children, Ragtime, Legs, G., Famous Last Words*. In most of the critical work on postmodernism, it is narrative – be it in literature, history, or theory – that has usually been the major focus of attention. Historiographic metafiction incorporates all three of these domains: that is, its theoretical self-awareness of history and fiction as human constructs (historio*graphic* meta*fic*tion) is made the grounds for its rethinking and reworking of the forms and contents of the past. This kind of fiction has often been noticed by critics, but its paradigmatic quality has been passed by: it is commonly labelled in terms of something else – for example as 'midfiction' (Wilde 1981) or 'paramodernist' (Malmgren 1985). Such labeling is another mark of the inherent contradictori-ness of historiographic metafiction, for it always works *within* conventions in order to subvert them. It is not just metafictional; nor is it just another version of the historical novel or the non-fictional novel. Gabriel García Márquez's *One Hundred Years of Solitude* has often been discussed in exactly the contradictory terms that I think define postmodernism. For example Larry McCaffery sees it as both metafictionally self-reflexive and yet speaking to us powerfully about real political and historical realities: 'It has thus become a kind of model for the contemporary writer, being self-conscious about its literary heritage and about the limits of mimesis ... but yet managing to reconnect its readers to the world outside the page' (1982, 264). What McCaffery here adds as almost an after-thought at the end of his book, *The Metafictional Muse*, is in many ways my starting point.

Most theorists of postmodernism who see it as a 'cultural dominant' (Jameson 1984a, 56) agree that it is characterized by the results of late capitalist dissolution of bourgeois hegemony and the development of mass culture (see Jameson 1984a [via Lefebvre 1968]; Russell 1980; Egbert 1970; Calinescu 1977). I would agree and, in fact, argue that the increasing uniformization of mass culture is one of the totalizing forces that postmodernism exists to challenge. Challenge, but not deny. But it does seek to assert difference, not homogeneous identity. Of course, the very concept of difference could be said to entail a typically postmodern contradiction: 'difference,' unlike 'otherness,' has no exact opposite against which to define itself. Thomas Pynchon allegorizes otherness in *Gravity's Rainbow* through the single, if anarchic, 'we-system' that exists as the counterforce of the totalizing 'They-system' (though also impli-cated in it). Postmodern difference or rather differences, in the plural, are always multiple and provisional.

Postmodern culture, then, has a contradictory relationship to what we usually label our dominant, liberal humanist culture. It does not deny it, as some have asserted (Newman 1985, 42; Palmer 1977, 364). Instead, it contests it from within its own assumptions. Modernists like Eliot and Joyce have usually been seen as profoundly humanistic (e.g. Stern 1971, 26) in their paradoxical desire for stable aesthetic and moral values, even in the face of their realization of the inevitable absence of such universals. Postmodernism differs from this, not in its humanistic contradictions, but in the provisionality of its response to them: it refuses to posit any structure or, what Lyotard (1984) calls, master narrative – such as art or myth – which, for such modernists, would have been consolatory. It argues that such systems are indeed attractive, perhaps even necessary; but this does not make them any the less illusory. For Lyotard, postmodernism is characterized by exactly this kind of incredulity toward master or metanarratives: those who lament the 'loss of meaning' in the world or in art are really mourning the fact that knowledge is no longer primarily narrative knowledge of this kind (1984, 26). This does not mean that knowledge somehow disappears. There is no radically new paradigm here, even if there is change.

[...]

III

Unfortunately, 'postmodern' is a term *bon à tout faire*. I have the impression that it is applied today to anything the user happens to like. Further, there seems to be an attempt to make it increasingly retroactive: first it was apparently applied to certain writers or artists active in the last twenty years, then gradually it reached the beginning of the century, then still further back. And this reverse procedure – continues; soon the postmodern category will include Homer.

Umberto Eco

When Charles Newman attempts to denigrate the 'essence' of the postmodern strategy by characterizing it as one of assimilating 'voraciously (though rarely systematically) while simultaneously repudiating assimilation' (1985, 28), he has, in fact, put his finger on precisely what characterizes postmodernism: contradiction and a move toward antitotalization. The same is true when Charles Russell calls postmodernism 'an art of criticism, with no message other than the need for continuous questioning. It is an art of unrest, with no clearly defined audience other than those predisposed to doubt and to search' (in Russell 1981, 58). Russell intends this as a criticism of the postmodern, for (at this early stage in his theorizing) he would prefer to see in it a new romantic individualism and originality as mediated through modernist transcendence, a move 'beyond doubt and distrust toward inspired vision' (5). But this kind of move is not part of the postmodernist enterprise, as he saw later. As the very label of 'historiographic metafiction' is intended to suggest, postmodernism remains fundamentally contradictory, offering only questions, never final answers. In fiction, it combines what Malcolm Bradbury (1973, 15) has called 'argument by poetics' (metafiction) with 'argument by historicism' (historiographic) in such a way as to inscribe a mutual interrogation within the texts themselves.

We have seen that the contradictions that characterize postmodernism reject any neat binary opposition that might conceal a secret hierarchy of values. The elements of these contradictions are usually multiple; the focus is on differences, not single otherness; and their roots are most likely to be found in the very modernism from which postmodernism derives its name (or rather, from the 'ideal type notion' of modernism that has resulted from successive canonizations – Huyssen 1986, 53). Many critics have pointed out the glaring contradictions of modernism: its élitist, classical need for order and its revolutionary formal innovations (Kermode 1971, 91); its 'Janus-faced' anarchistic urge to destroy existing systems combined with a reactionary political vision of ideal order (Daiches 1971, 197); its compulsion to write mixed with a realization of the meaninglessness of writing (in the work of Beckett or Kafka); its melancholy regret for the loss of presence and its experimental energy and power of conception (Lyotard 1986, 30–1). In fact, Terry Eagleton sees as a positive characteristic of modernism the fact that it retains its contradictions:

'between a still ineluctable bourgeois humanism and the pressures of a quite different rationality, which, still newly emergent, is not even able to name itself' (1985, 70). Postmodernism challenges some aspects of modernist dogma: its view of the autonomy of art and its deliberate separation from life; its expression of individual subjectivity; its adversarial status *vis-à-vis* mass culture and bourgeois life (Huyssen 1986, 53). But, on the other hand, the postmodern clearly also developed out of other modernist strategies: its self-reflexive experimentation, its ironic ambiguities, and its contestations of classic realist representation.

However, I would argue not only that postmodernism, like modernism, also retains its own contradictions, but also that it foregrounds them to such an extent that they become the very defining characteristics of the entire cultural phenomenon we label with that name. The postmodern is in no way absolutist; it does not say that 'it is both impossible and useless to try and establish some hierarchical order, some system of priorities in life' (Fokkema 1986, 82). What it does say is that there are all kinds of orders and systems in our world – *and* that we create them all. That is their justification and their limitation. They do not exist 'out there', fixed, given, universal, eternal; they are human constructs in history. This does not make them any the less necessary or desirable. It does, however, as we have seen, condition their 'truth' value. The local, the limited, the temporary, the provisional are what define postmodern 'truth' in novels like John Banville's *Kepler* or Christa Wolfe's *Cassandra*. The point is not exactly that the world is meaningless (Wilde 1981, 148), but that any meaning that exists is of our own creation.

In fiction, it is self-reflexivity that works to make the paradoxes of post-modernism overt and even defining. Many have argued that all art possesses some of these devices of self-reference and that they function in much the same way:

> Even the most 'realistic' of works use such conventions because, rather than trying to 'take us in' (that is, to delude us), they prefer to show us how close they have come to doing so, how marvellously verisimilar their illusion is: one cannot appreciate the verisimilar without being aware that it is not the thing itself.
>
> (Krieger 1982, 101; see too 1976, 182–3)

No language, in other words, is really 'self-effacing'; all is to some degree 'self-apparent,' to use Jerome Klinkowitz's terms (1984, 14). Postmodernism, in this perspective, would just be a more self-conscious and overt manifestation of the basic paradox of aesthetic form.

But there are other postmodern contradictions that are less generalizable. While much art uses irony and parody to inscribe and yet critique the discourses of its past, of the 'already-said,' postmodernism is almost always double-voiced in its attempts to historicize and contextualize the enunciative situation of its art. Black American culture has been defined as one of 'double consciousness'

(W. E. B. DuBois 1973, 3) in which black and white, slave and master cultures are never reconciled, but held in a doubled suspension. Some types of feminism have argued much the same sort of relationship between female and male culture. The next chapter [in *A Poetics of Postmodernism*] will investigate how both of these social forces have had their impact on postmodernism, and how its contradictory double- or multiple-voicing is one of the manifestations of this impact.

There are many forms that this paradoxical identity of the postmodern can take. One of the most interesting involves the actual reception of postmodernism. Douwe Fokkema has argued that it is 'sociologically limited to mostly academic readers interested in complicated texts' (1986, 81). (For a similar argument re modernism, see Todd 1986, 79.) But if that is true, how do we account for the fact that *The Name of the Rose, The French Lieutenant's Woman, Ragtime, Midnight's Children, Flaubert's Parrot*, and so many other historiographic metafictions have been prominent on the best-sellers' lists in both Europe and North America? One of the contradictions of postmodernism, I would argue, is that it does indeed 'close the gap' that Leslie Fiedler (1975) saw between high and low art forms, and it does so through the ironizing of both. Think of the ironic mixtures of religious history and the detective story in *The Name of the Rose* or of war documentary and science fiction in *Slaughterhouse-Five*. Woody Allen's films (see D'Haen 1986; 226) also close this gap by paradoxically using both familiar movie staples (love, anxiety, sex) and also sophisticated parodic and metafictional forms (for example in *Play it Again, Sam* or *The Purple Rose of Cairo*). Postmodernism is both academic and popular, élitist and accessible.

One of the ways in which it achieves this paradoxical popular-academic identity is through its technique of installing and then subverting familiar conventions of both kinds of art. E. L. Doctorow has claimed that he had to give up trying to write *The Book of Daniel* with the usual realist narrative concern for transition that is characteristic of the nineteenth-century novel (and popular fiction) (in Trenner 1983, 40), yet he self-consciously has his narrating character both exploit and undercut that very structural concern for continuity. In its contradictions, postmodernist fiction tries to offer what Stanley Fish (1972, xiii) once called a 'dialectical' literary presentation, one that disturbs readers, forcing them to scrutinize their own values and beliefs, rather than pandering to or satisfying them. But as Umberto Eco has reminded us, postmodern fiction may seem more open in form, but constraint is always needed in order to feel free (in Rosso 1983, 6). This kind of novel self-consciously uses the trappings of what Fish calls 'rhetorical' literary presentation (omniscient narrators, coherent characterization, plot closure) in order to point to the humanly constructed character of these trappings – their arbitrariness and conventionality. This is what I mean by the typically contradictory postmodern exploitation and subversion of the familiar staples of both realist and modernist fiction.

307

We have seen that when postmodern architects showed the world their wares at that Venice Biennale in 1980, they chose as their banner the motto: 'the presence of the past.' This obvious paradox offers a conjoining of performance in the present and recording of the past. In fiction, this contradiction is played out in terms of parody and metafiction versus the conventions of realism. The metafictionally present modern narrator of Fowles's *The French Lieutenant's Woman* jars with and parodies the conventions of the nineteenth-century novelistic tale of Charles, Sarah, and Ernestina. The various Chinese boxes of narrators and fiction-makers (Fowles, the narrator, his persona, Charles, and finally Sarah) enact the novel's themes of freedom and power, of creation and control. The multiple parodies of specific Victorian novels (by Thackeray, George Eliot, Dickens, Froude, Hardy) are matched by more generic ironic play on nineteenth-century authoritative narrating voices, reader address, and narrative closure.

This complex and extended parody is not, however, just a game for the academic reader. It is overtly intended to prevent any reader from ignoring both the modern and the specifically Victorian social, as well as aesthetic, contexts. We are not allowed to say either that this is 'only a story' or that it is 'only about the Victorian period.' The past is always placed critically – and not nostalgically – in relation with the present. The questions of sexuality, of social inequality and responsibility, of science and religion, and of the relation of art to the world are all raised and directed both at the modern reader and the social and literary conventions of the last century. The plot structure of *The French Lieutenant's Woman* enacts the dialectic of freedom and power that is the modern existentialist and even Marxist answer to Victorian or Darwinian determinism. But it requires that historical context in order to interrogate the present (as well as the past) through its critical irony. Parodic self-reflexiveness paradoxically leads here to the possibility of a literature which, while asserting its modernist autonomy as art, also manages simultaneously to investigate its intricate and intimate relations with the social world in which it is written and read.

This kind of contradiction is what characterizes postmodern art, which works to subvert dominant discourses, but is dependent upon those same discourses for its very physical existence: the 'already-said.' Yet, I think it is wrong to see postmodernism as defined in any way by an 'either/or' structure. As we shall see in more detail in Chapter 12, it is not a case of its being either nostalgically neoconservative or radically antihumanist in its politics (Foster 1985, 121). It is, actually, both and neither. Certainly it is marked by a return to history, and it does indeed problematize the entire notion of historical knowledge. But the reinstalling of memory is not uncritical or reactionary, and the problematization of humanist certainties does not mean their denial or death. Postmodernism does not so much erode our 'sense of history' and reference (Foster 1985, 132), as erode our old sure sense of what both history and reference meant. It asks us to rethink and critique our notions of both.

Both theorists and artists have recognized that paradox can often reek of compromise. Witness video artist Douglas Davis's view:

> If I want to address my art to the world, I must address it through the system, as must everyone else. It this sounds suspiciously like liberalism and compromise, so be it: liberalism and compromise is the only way any true revolutionary has ever worked, save through the sword.
>
> (1977, 22)

Certainly *The French Lieutenant's Woman* would corroborate such a view of contradiction as compromise, but not compromise in the sense of avoidance of questioning or of creating a new and alternate unifying interpretative totality. Postmodernism exploits, but also undermines, such staples of our humanist tradition as the coherent subject and the accessible historical referent, and this may well be what is so irritating about it for Eagleton and Jameson. The contested concepts of artistic originality and 'authenticity' and of any stable historical entity (such as 'the worker') would appear to be central to their Marxist master narrative. The postmodern blurring of firm distinctions is probably, by definition, anathema to Marxist dialectical reasoning, as it is to any Habermasian position of Enlightenment rationality. Both of these influential positions of opposition to postmodernism are founded on the kind of totalizing meta-narratives (Lyotard 1984) that postmodernism challenges – that is, at once uses and abuses. I would argue, along with Nannie Doyle and others, that what is positive, not negative, about postmodernism is that it does not attempt to hide its relationship to consumer society, but rather exploits it to new critical and politicized ends, acknowledging openly the 'indissoluble relation between cultural production and its political and social affiliations' (Doyle 1985, 169).

Postmodern discourses assert both autonomy and worldliness. Likewise, they participate in both theory and praxis. They offer a collective, historicized context for individual action. In other words, they do not deny the individual, but they do 'situate' her/him. And they do not deny that collectivity can be perceived as manipulation as well as activism: witness Pynchon's and Rushdie's novels of paranoia. The postmodern is not quite an avant-garde. It is not as radical or as adversarial. In Charles Russell's view (1985), the avant-garde is self-consciously modern and subject to socio-cultural change. The same is true of the postmodern, but this valuing (fetishizing?) of innovation is conditioned by a re-evaluation of the past which puts newness and novelty into perspective. The avant-garde is also seen as critical of the dominant culture and alienated from it in a way that the postmodern is not, largely because of its acknowledgement of its unavoidable implication in that dominant culture. At the same time, of course, it both exploits and critically undermines that dominance. In short, the postmodern is not as negating (of the past) or as Utopic (about the future) as is, at least, the historical or modernist avant-garde. It incorporates its past within its very name and parodically seeks to inscribe its criticism of that past.

These contradictions of postmodernism are not really meant to be resolved, but rather are to be held in an ironic tension. For example in John Fowles's *A Maggot*, there are an amazing number of such unresolved and unresolvable paradoxes. On a formal level, the novel holds in tension the conventions of history and fiction (specifically, of romance and science fiction). One of its main narrative structures is that of question and answer (a lawyer's questioning of witnesses), a structure that foregrounds the conflicts between truth and lies, differing perceptions of truth, facts and beliefs, and truth and illusion. The transcribing clerk believes there are two truths: 'One that a person believes is truth; and one that is truth incontestable' (1985, 345), but the entire novel works to problematize such binary certainty. The contradictory tensions recur in the twentieth-century narrator/historian's emphasizing of his distance from the 1736 action of his plot. The two major antagonists, the male lawyer Ayscough and the prostitute-turned-Dissenter Rebecca Lee are established as each other's opposite: in gender, class, education, religion. They come to represent reason versus instinct, male versus female, even left versus right hemispheres of the brain.

In this novel there are still other unresolved thematic contradictions: the absent 'hero,' known as His Lordship, is both a scientist and a believer in theories of the physical world that are 'more phantasics than probable or experimental truths' (188). Christianity and paganism are also played off against each other constantly in the novel, and the narrator's interest in Dissenters, especially the Shakers, comes from the fact that they too have been perceived in contradictory ways: 'Orthodox theologians have always despised the sect's doctrinal naïvety; orthodox priests, its fanaticism; orthodox capitalists, its communism; orthodox communists, its superstition; orthodox sensualists, its abhorrence of the carnal; and orthodox males, its striking feminism' (450). The different and the paradoxical fascinate the postmodern.

So too do the multiple and the provisional. In the course of the novel, the titular 'maggot' is defined as 'the larval stage of a winged creature; as is the written text, at least in the writer's hope' (unpaginated prologue, signed by Fowles). We are also told from the start that the word signifies a whim or quirk. Within the plot, maggots are associated with death (260) and with fancy (277). The title's full contradictory force comes from Rebecca's description of the large white object in the cave as a 'great swollen maggot ... tho' not' (355). The challenging of certainty, the asking of questions, the revealing of fiction-making where we might have once accepted the existence of some absolute 'truth' – this is the project of postmodernism.

Ihab Hassan sees the oppositional paradox of postmodernism as lying in 'its fanatic will to unmaking,' on the one hand, and, on the other, 'the need to discover a 'unitary' sensibility' (1982, 265). I see this paradox as less oppositional than provisional; I see it, instead, as an inscribing and undercutting of *both* any unitary sensibility *and* any disruptive will to unmake, for these are equally absolutist and totalizing concepts. Postmodernism is characterized by energy derived from the rethinking of the value of multiplicity and provision-ality; in actual practice, it does not seem to be defined by any potentially paralyzing opposition between making and unmaking. This is the energy (if also logical inconsistency) we get from those cohesive challenges to coherence in the work of Foucault or Lyotard (see Roth 1985, 107). Postmodernist discourses – both theoretical and practical – need the very myths and conventions they contest and reduce (Watkins 1978, 222); they do not necessarily come to terms with either order of disorder (cf. Wilde 1981, 10), but question both in terms of each other. The myths and conventions exist for a reason, and postmodernism investigates that reason. The postmodern impulse is not to seek any total vision. It merely questions. If it *finds* such a vision, it questions how, in fact it *made* it.

IV

> The great modern achievements were wagers which made gestures, invented methods, but laid no foundations for a future literature. They led in the direction of an immensity from which there was bound to be a turning back because to go further would lead to a new and completer fragmentation, utter obscurity, formlessness without end.
>
> *Stephen Spender*

History has proved Spender wrong, for in postmodernism we see the results of those wagers and they have not taken the form he imagined. The debate over the definition of both modernism and postmodernism has now been going on for years (see Fokkema 1984, 12–36). There is little firm agreement on their limiting dates, their defining characteristics, even the players in this game. Instead of trying to delimit either, I would like to look at the configuration of concerns in each that could help us define a poetics of postmodernism in its relation to modernism. In other words, I do not want to enter into the arguments of evaluation; nor do I want to set the one enterprise against the other. The entire issue of binary oppositions like this one needs rethinking. What inevitably happens is that one – either modernism or postmodernism – gets privileged over the other.

One of the most influential of postmodern theorists, Ihab Hassan, is fond of creating parallel columns that place characteristics of the one next to their opposite characteristics in the other, usually making clear his preference for the postmodern. But this 'either/or' thinking suggests a resolution of what I see as the unresolvable contradictions within postmodernism. For example I would see it less as a case of postmodern play versus modernist purpose, as Hassan claims (1982, 267–8), than as a case of play with purpose. The same is true of all his oppositions: postmodernism is the *process* of making the *product*; it is *absence* within *presence*, it is *dispersal* that needs *centering* in order to *be* dispersal; it is the *ideolect* that wants to be, but knows it cannot be, the *master code*; it is *immanence* denying yet yearning for *transcendence*. In other words, the postmodern partakes of a logic of 'both/and,' not one of either/or.' And, not surprisingly, those who privilege the modernist over the postmodernist also work in similar oppositional binary terms (Graff 1979; Eagleton 1985; Newman 1985).

As I have already mentioned, the major danger in setting up this kind of structure is that of creating 'straw men' in order to make one's point more clearly. For instance when we read that modernism's concept of time is inescapably linear' and 'ideally controllable' (Calinescu 1983, 284), we wonder what happened to those experimental works of Woolf, Joyce, Eliot, and others we think of as modernists. Did modernism really abandon *intracultural dialogue*' (Calinescu 1983, 275, his italics)? What about *The Waste Land* or *Finnegans Wake*? No matter which 'ism' is preferred, both it and its antagonist run the risk of this kind of reduction. And no two critics seem to agree on which reductions to make. Jameson (1984b) sees modernism as oppositional and marginal – what I take as important defining characteristics of the *post*modern. He offers no proof why modernism is somehow exempt from implication in mass culture. (Andreas Huyssen – 1986, viii – suggests that it is because of its elitism that attempted to transcend that mass culture.) Nor does he offer any reason why he sees postmodernism in particular as the dominant aesthetic of consumer society Jameson 1984b, 197). In this book, I will be arguing that such reasons must be given and that, in defining postmodernism, it is necessary to be as specific and explanatory as possible.

It is all too easy to reject, as does John Barth, all notions of postmodernism based on its being an extension, intensification, subversion, or repudiation postmodernism (1980, 69). But modernism literally and physically haunts postmodernism, and their interrelations should not be ignored. Indeed there appear to be two dominant schools of thought about the nature of the interaction of the two enterprises: the first sees postmodernism as a total break from modernism and the language of this school is the radical rhetoric of rupture; the second sees the postmodern as an extension and intensification of certain characteristics of modernism.

The radical break theory depends upon firm binary oppositions that operate on the formal, philosophical, and ideological levels. On the formal level postmodern surface is opposed to modernist depth (Wilde 1981, 43; Sontag 1967), and the ironic and parodic tone of postmodernism contrasts with the seriousness of modernism (Graff 1979, 55; Zurbrugg 1986, 78). It is easy to see which half is being privileged here, though it usually is not quite as clear when the oppositions are between chaos and order or contingency and coherence (Bradbury 1983, 160; 185). This last point is often made in terms of the difference between the modernist use of myth as a structuring device in the work of, for instance, Mann, Pavese, or Joyce (see Begnal 1973; Beebe 1972, 175; 1974, 1,076) and the postmodern ironic contesting of myth as master narrative in the novels of Barth, Reed, or Morrison, where there is no consolation of form or consensual belief (Lyotard 1986, 32–3). Modernism has been seen as creating its own form of aesthetic authority in the face of a center that was not holding (Hassan 1985, 59; Josipovici 1977, 109), but if that point is made, it usually entails claiming that postmodernism is to be defined as anarchic, in complicity with chaos, accepting of uncertainty and confusion (Wilde 1981, 44). Postmodern skepticism is presented as the refutation and rejection of modernism's heroism (Wilde 1981, 132–3). Instead of this kind of opposition, I would argue that what postmodernism does is use and abuse these characteristics of modernism in order to install a questioning of *both* of the listed extremes.

Related to these formal and tonal distinctions between the two are differences in philosophical intent. But even here there is little agreement. One group (McHale 1987; Wilde 1981) sees modernism as epistemological in its focus, while postmodernism is ontological. The other group just reverses the adjectives (Krysinski 1981; McCaffery 1982; Russell 1974). Again, I would argue that the contradictions of postmodernism cannot be described in 'either/or' terms (especially if they are going to be reversible!). Historiographic metafiction asks both epistemological and ontological questions. How do we know the past (or the present)? What is the ontological status of that past? Of its documents? Of our narratives?

For some critics, this philosophical issue is also an ideological one. The postmodern's epistemological break from modernism is seen by some as linked to an important new role it is to play in 'worldly practices' (Radhakrishnan 1983, 34). This is precisely what Jameson accuses postmodernism of in a *negative* sense: he sees it as too involved in the economic system of late capitalism, too institutionalized (1984a, 56). It does not share, he says, modernism's repudiation of the Victorian bourgeoisie. But perhaps it questions any such easy repudiation, and does so in the light of its acknowledgements of its own inescapable ideological implication in precisely the contemporary situation of late capitalism.

It is worth recalling that this same modernism has also been accused of cultural élitism and hermeticism, political conservatism, alienating theories of the autonomy of art, and a search for transcendent, ahistorical dimensions of human experience (Russell 1981, 8). It would not be difficult to figure out what postmodernism challenges and what attempts at change it offers in the stead of such a list: cultural democratizing of high/low art distinctions and a new didacticism, potentially radical political questioning, contextualizing theories of the discursive complexity of art, and a contesting of all ahistorical and totalizing visions. In fact Charles Russell argues precisely this:

> postmodern literature recognizes that all perception, cognition, action, and articulation are shaped, if not determined, by the social domain. There can be no simple opposition to culture, no transcendent perspective or language, no secure singular self-definition, for all find their meaning only within a social framework.

(1985, 246)

Clearly it all depends on who is valorizing what in this kind of theory of an epistemic break between the modern and the postmodern.

The other school of thought argues a relationship of continuity or extension between the two. For David Lodge, they share a commitment to innovation and to a critique of tradition, even if the manifestations of these shared values differ (1977, 220–45). On a formal level, modernism and postmodernism are said to share self-reflexivity (Fokkema 1984, 17), fragmentation (Newman 1985, 113), and a concern for history (literary and social) (Thiher 1984, 216–19). Certainly postmodern works have turned to modernist texts – often in different media – in their parodic play with convention and history. Peter Maxwell Davies has used Joyce's Cyclops episode in *Ulysses* as the model for his *Missa super L'Homme Armé* and Gordon Crosse's Second Violin Concerto uses Nabokov's *Pale Fire* for structural inspiration. Saura's flamenco film of *Carmen* invokes and comments upon both Bizet's opera and Mérimée's story.

On a more theoretical level, some critics see postmodernism as raising the same kinds of issues as modernism: investigating the cultural assumptions underlying our models of history (Josipovici 1977, 145) or challenging the entire western humanistic tradition (Spanos 1972, 147). Others argue that the ironic distance that modernism sets up between art and audience is, in fact, intensified in postmodernism's 'double-distancing' (Hayman 1978, 34–6). For others, postmodern fiction completes modernism's break with traditional realism and bourgeois rationalism (Graff 1975), just as postmodern poetry is seen as continuing the modernist challenge to romantic self-transcendence, though its stress on the local and topical does contest modernist impersonality (Altieri 1973, 629).

As this last example suggests, the continuity model is not without its necessary alterations and exceptions. My own response is probably typically postmodernist in its acceptance of both models, for I see as one of the many contradictions of postmodernism that it can both self-consciously incorporate and equally self-consciously challenge that modernism from which it derives and to which it owes even its verbal existence. There has been a certain move in criticism (see Pütz 1973, 228; Butler 1980, 138; Bertens 1986, 47–8; Todd 1986, 105–6) to distinguish between two types of postmodernism: one that is non-mimetic, ultra-autonomous, anti-referential, and another that is historically *engagé*, problematically referential. I would argue that only the latter properly defines postmodernism, according to the model developed here (based on postmodern architecture). The former presents many difficulties, not the least of which are logical ones. Can language and literature *ever* be totally non-mimetic, non-referential, and still remain understandable as literature? This is a theoretical problem that the radical rhetoric of antirepresentation usually ignores. Can there ever really be a total 'loss of meaning' in art (Graff 1973, 391)? Would we still call it art? Is there anything to which we cannot grant meaning?

The attempt to make the label 'postmodernist' describe these extremes of modernist aestheticism is, I believe, a mistaken one. Much contemporary metafiction is indeed almost solely concerned with its own artifice, its own aesthetic workings. But self-reflexivity has a long history in art, and, in fact, the label of 'self-begetting novel' has been used to describe both modernist fiction and the New Novel (Kellman 1980). The postmodernist art I have been and will be describing in this book is historical and political in a way that much metafiction is not. It cannot be described as removing representation and replacing it with textual materiality (Klinkowitz 1985, 192). Nor does it unquestioningly accept the act of fiction-making as a humanist stay against chaos (Alter 1975; Hutcheon 1980; Christensen 1981).

It is the French New and also the New New Novel, along with American surfiction, that are most often cited by critics as examples of postmodernist fiction. But by my model, they would, instead, be examples of late modernist extremism. Others have taken this stand as well: Spanos (1972, 165); Mellard (1980); Wilde (1981, 144); Butler (1980, 132). Modernist hermeticism and autotelic reflexivity characterize much surfiction and its theorizing. Raymond Federman (as both surfictionist and theorist) claims that his extreme metafiction represents an effort to reinstate things and the world in their proper places, but somehow in a purer state. The way he speaks of surfiction betrays his modernist and almost romantic bias: it is 'the kind of fiction that constantly renews our faith in man's imagination and not in man's distorted vision of reality' (1981, 7). Fiction is 'an autonomous art form in its own right' (9). No contradictory and interrogating postmodernist discourse could speak with such authority and certainty.

Postmodern fiction challenges both structuralist/modernist formalism and any simple mimeticist/realist notions of referentiality. It took the modernist novel a long time to win back its artistic autonomy from the dogma of realist theories of representation; it has taken the postmodernist novel just as long to win back its historicizing and contextualizing from the dogma of modernist aestheticism (which would include the hermeticism and ultra-formalism of the 'textes' of *Tel Quel*, for example). What I want to call postmodernism in fiction paradoxically uses and abuses the conventions of both realism and modernism, and does so in order to challenge their transparency, in order to prevent glossing over the contradictions that make the postmodern what it is: historical and metafictional, contextual and self-reflective, ever aware of its status as discourse, as a human construct.

[...]

WORKS CITED

Alter, Robert (1975) *Partial Magic: The Novel as a Self-Conscious Genre*. Berkeley, CA: University of California Press.

Altieri, Charles (1973) 'From Symbolist Thought to Immanence: The Ground of Postmodern American Poetics', *boundary 2*, 1 (3): 605–41.

Barth, John (1980) 'The Literature of Replenishment: Postmodernist Fiction', *Atlantic Monthly*, 245 (1): 65–71.

Beebe, Maurice (1972) 'Ulysses and the Age of Modernism', James Joyce Quarterly, 10, Fall: 172–88.

Beebe, Maurice (1974) 'What Modernism Was', Journal of Modern Literature, 3 (5): 1065–84.

Begnal, Michael H. (1973) 'James Joyce and the Mythologizing of History', in Stanley Weintraub and Philip Young (eds), Directions in Literary Criticism. University Park, PA: Pennsylvania State University Press, pp. 211–19.

Bertens, Hans (1986) 'The Postmodern Welanschauung and its Relation with Modernism: An Introductory Survey', in Douwe Fokkema and Hans Bertens (eds), Approaching Postmodernism. Amsterdam and Philadelphia: John Benjamins, pp. 9–51.

Bradbury, Malcolm (1973) Possibilities: Essays on the State of the Novel. London, Oxford and New York: Oxford University Press.

Bradbury, Malcolm (1983) The Modern American Novel. Oxford and New York: Oxford University Press.

Brooke-Rose, Christine (1981) A Rhetoric of the Unreal: Studies in Narrative and Structure, Especially of the Fantastic. Cambridge and New York: Cambridge University Press.

Butler, Christopher (1980) After the Wake: An Essay on the Contemporary Avant-Garde. Oxford: Oxford University Press.

Calinescu, Matei (1977) Faces of Modernity. Bloomington, IN: Indiana University Press.

Calinescu, Matei (1983) 'From the One to the Many: Pluralism in Today's Thought', in Ihab Hassan and Sally Hassan (eds), Innovation/Renovation: New Perspectives on the Humanities. Madison, WI: University of Wisconsin Press, pp. 263–88.

Caramello, Charles (1983) Silverless Mirrors: Book, Self and Postmodern American Fiction. Tallahassee, FL: University Presses of Florida.

Christensen, Inger (1981) The Meaning of Metafiction: A Critical Study of Selected Novels by Sterne, Nabokov, Barth and Beckett. Bergen and Oslo: Universitetsforlaget.

D'Haen, Theo (1986) 'Postmodernism in American Fiction and Art', in Douwe Fokkema and Hans Bertens (eds), Approaching Postmodernism. Amsterdam and Philadelphia: John Benjamins, pp. 211–31.

Daiches, David (1971) 'Politics and the Literary Imagination', in Ihab Hassan (ed.), Liberations: New Essays on the Humanities in Revolution. Middletown, CT: Wesleyan University Press, pp. 100–16.

Davis, Douglas (1977) Artculture: Essays on the Post-Modern. New York: Harper & Row.

Doyle, Nannie (1985) 'Desiring Dispersal: Politics and the Postmodern', Subjects/Objects, 3: 166–79.

DuBois, W. E. B. (1973) The Souls of Black Folk: Essays and Sketches. Millwood, NY: Kraus-Thomson.

Eagleton, Terry (1985) 'Capitalism, Modernism and Postmodernism', New Left Review, 152: 60–73.

Egbert, Donald D. (1970) Social Radicalism and the Arts. New York: Knopf.

Federman, Raymond (1981) 'Surfiction: Four Propositions in Form of an Introduction', in Raymond Federman (ed.), Surfiction: Fiction Now and Tomorrow, 2nd edn. Chicago, IL: Swallow.

Fiedler, Leslie (1975) 'Cross the Border – Close that Gap', in Marcus Cunliffe (ed.), American Literature Since 1900. London: Sphere.

Fish, Stanley (1972) Self-Consuming Artefacts: The Experience of Seventeenth-Century Literature. Berkeley, CA: University of California Press.

Fokkema, Douwe (1984) Literary History, Modernism, and Postmodernism. Amsterdam and Philadelphia: John Benjamins.

Fokkema, Douwe (1986) 'The Semantic and Syntactic Organization of Postmodernist Texts', in Douwe Fokkema and Hans Bertens (eds), *Approaching Postmodernism*. Amsterdam and Philadelphia: John Benjamins, pp. 81–98.

Foster, Hal (1985) *Recodings: Art, Spectacle, Cultural Politics*. Port Townsend, WA: Bay Press.

Fowles, John (1985) *A Maggot*. Toronto: Collins.

Graff, Gerald (1973) 'The Myth of the Postmodernist Breakthrough', *TriQuarterly*, 26: 383–417.

Graff, Gerald (1975) 'Babbitt at the Abyss: The Social Context of Postmodern American Fiction', *TriQuarterly*, 33: 305–37.

Graff, Gerald (1979) *Literature Against Itself*. Chicago, IL: University of Chicago Press.

Hassan, Ihab (1975) *Paracriticisms: Seven Criticisms of the Times*. Urbana, IL: University of Illinois Press.

Hassan, Ihab (1982) *The Dismemberment of Orpheus: Towards a Postmodern Literature*, 2nd edn. Madison, WI: University of Wisconsin Press.

Hayman, David (1978) 'Double-Distancing: An Attribute of the "Post-Modern" Avant-Garde', *Novel*, 12 (1): 33–47.

Hutcheon, Linda (1980) *Narcissistic Narrative: The Metafictional Paradox*. Waterloo, Ontario: Wilfred Laurier University Press.

Huyssen, Andreas (1986) *After the Great Divide: Modernism, Mass Culture, Postmodernism*. Bloomington, IN: Indiana University Press.

Jameson, Fredric (1984a) 'Postmodernism or the Cultural Logic of Late Capitalism', *New Left Review*, 146, July–August: 53–93.

Jameson, Fredric (1984b) 'Periodizing the Sixties', in Sohnya Sayres, Anders Stephanson, Stanley Aronowitz and Frederic Jameson (eds), *The 60s Without Apology*. Minneapolis: *Social Text* and University of Minnesota Press.

Josipovici, Gabriel (1977) *The Lessons of Modernism and Other Essays*. London: Macmillan.

Kellman, Steven G. (1980) *The Self-Begetting Novel*. London: Macmillan.

Kermode, Frank (1971) 'Revolution: The Role of the Elders', in Ihab Hassan (ed.), *Liberations: New Essays on the Humanities in Revolution*. Middletown, CT: Wesleyan University Press, pp. 87–99.

Klinkowitz, Jerome (1984) *The Self-Apparent World: Fiction as Language/Language as Fiction*. Carbondale, IL: Southern Illinois University Press.

Klinkowitz, Jerome (1985) *Literary Subversions: New American Fiction and the Practice of Criticism*. Carbondale and Edwardsville, IL: Southern Illinois University Press.

Krieger, Murray (1976) *Theory of Criticism: A Tradition and Its System*. Baltimore, MD: Johns Hopkins University Press.

Krieger, Murray (1982) 'Poetic Presence and Illusion II: Formalist Theory and the Duplicity of Metaphor', in William V. Spanos, Paul A. Bové and Daniel O'Hara (eds), *The Question of Textuality: Strategies of Reading in Contemporary American Criticism*. Bloomington, IN: Indiana University Press, pp. 95–122.

Kroker, Arthur and Cook, David (1986) *The Postmodern Scene: Excremental Culture and Hyper-Aesthetics*. Montreal: New World Perspectives.

Krysinski, Wladimir (1981) *Carrefour des signes: Essais sur le roman moderne*. The Hague: Mouton.

Lefebvre, Henry (1968) *La Vie quotidienne dans le monde moderne*. Paris: Gallimard.

Lodge, David (1977) *The Modes of Modern Writing: Metaphor, Metonymy, and the Typology of Modern Literature*. London: Edward Arnold.

Lyotard, Jean-François (1984) *The Postmodern Condition: A Report on Knowledge*. Minneapolis, MN: University of Minnesota Press.

Lyotard, Jean-François (1986) *Le Postmodern expliqué aux enfants: Correspondance 1982–1985*. Paris: Galilée.

McCaffery, Larry (1982) *The Metafictional Muse*. Pittsburgh, PA: University of Pittsburg Press.

McHale, Brian (1987) *Postmodernist Fiction*. London: Routledge.

Malmgren, Caryl Darryl (1985) *Fictional Space in the Modernist and Postmodernist American Novel*. Lewisburg, PA: Bucknell University Press.

Mellard, James M. (1980) *The Exploded Form: The Modernist Novel in America*. Urbana, IL: University of Illinois Press.

Newman, Charles (1985) *The Post-Modern Aura: The Act of Fiction in an Age of Inflation*. Evanston, IL: Northwestern University Press.

Palmer, Richard E. (1977) 'Postmodernity and Hermeneutics', *boundary 2*, 5 (2): 363–93.

Paterson, Janet (1986) 'Le Roman "postmoderne": mise au point et perspectives', *Canadian Review of Comparative Literature*, 13 (2): 238–55.

Perloff, Marjorie (1985) *The Dance of the Intellect: Studies in the Poetry of the Pound Tradition*. Cambridge: Cambridge University Press.

Portoghesi, Paolo (1983) *Postmodern: The Architecture of the Postindustrial Society*. New York: Rizzoli.

Pütz, Manfred (1973) 'The Struggle of the Postmodern: Books on a New Concept in Criticism', *Kritikon Litterarum*, 2: 225–37.

Radhakrishnan, Rajagoplan (1983) 'The Post-Modern Event and the End of Logocentrism'. *boundary 2*, 12 (1): 33–60.

Rosso, Stephano (1983) 'A Correspondence with Umberto Eco', *boundary 2*, 12 (1): 1–13.

Roth, Martin (1985) 'Some Comments on Foucault's *History of Madness*', *Paragraph*, 5: 103–7.

Russell, Charles (1974) 'The Vault of Language: Self-Reflexive Artifice in Contemporary American Fiction', *Modern Fiction Studies*, 20 (3): 349–59.

Russell, Charles (1980) 'The Context of the Concept', in Harry R. Garvin (ed.), *Romanticism, Modernism, Postmodernism*. Lewisburg, PA: Bucknell University Press; London: Associated University Press, pp. 181–93.

Russell, Charles (1981) (ed.) *The Avant-Garde Today: An International Anthology*. Urbana, IL: University of Illinois Press.

Russell, Charles (1985) *Poets, Prophets, and Revolutionaries: The Literary Avant-garde from Rimbaud through Postmodernism*. New York and Oxford: Oxford University Press.

Sarduy, Severo (1974) 'El barroco y el neobarocco', in César Fernández Moreno (ed.), *América Latina en su Literatura*. Buenos Aires: Siglo XXI, pp. 167–84.

Sontag, Susan (1967) *Against Interpretation and Other Essays*. New York: Dell.

Spanos, William V. (1972) 'The Detective and the Boundary: Some Notes on the Postmodern Literary Imagination', *boundary 2*, 1 (1): 147–68.

Stern, Daniel (1971) 'The Mysterious New Novel', in Ihab Hassan (ed.), *Liberations: New Essays on the Humanities in Revolution*. Middletown, CT: Wesleyan University Press, pp. 22–37.

Suleiman, Susam Rubin (1986) 'Naming a Difference: Reflections on "Modernism versus Postmodernism" in Literature', in Douwe Fokkema and Hans Bertens (eds), *Approaching Postmodernism*. Amsterdam and Philadelphia: John Benjamins, pp. 255–70.

Thiher, Allen (1984) *Words in Reflection: Modern Language Theory and Postmodern Fiction*. Chicago, IL: University of Chicago Press.

Todd, Richard (1986) 'The Presence of Postmodernism in British Fiction: Aspects of Style and Selfhood', in Douwe Fokkema and Hans Bertens (eds), *Approaching Postmodernism*. Amsterdam and Philadelphia: John Benjamins, pp. 99–117.

Trenner, Richard (ed.) (1983) *E. L. Doctorow: Essays and Conversations*. Princeton, NJ: Ontario Review Press.

Watkins, Evan (1978) *The Critical Act: Criticism and Community.* New Haven, CT and London: Yale University Press.

Wilde, Alan (1981) *Horizons of Assent: Modernism, Postmodernism, and the Ironic Imagination.* Baltimore, MD: Johns Hopkins University Press.

Zurbrugg, Nicholas (1986) 'Postmodernity, *Métaphore manquée*, and the Myth of the Trans-avant-garde', *Substance*, 48: 68–90.

POSTMODERN GENRE
22

FROM *THE DOOMED DETECTIVE*

Stephano Tani

In his essay 'Literaturnyj Fakt,' Tynjanov writes that 'a [literary] epoch always selects its necessary materials, but it is the use of these materials that specifically characterizes the epoch the whole essence of a new construction can be in the new use of old techniques, in their new constructive meaning.'[1] One can examine in this light the detective fictional techniques used in the anti-detective novel; it is actually how they are used and, indeed, which of them are used that clarifies the meaning of the new fictional form and creates distinctions among the anti-detective novels themselves.

A conventional detective story is a fiction in which an amateur or professional detective tries to discover by rational means the solution of a mysterious occurrence – generally a crime, usually a murder. This definition implies the presence of at least three invariable elements: the detective, the process of detection, and the solution. Besides these basic elements other characteristics typical of detective fiction and useful for definition of the anti-detective novel are: a mystery or a crime to unravel; suspense (the interaction between detection and solution as it plays with the expectations of the reader); delay of the solution (normally caused by a first false solution planted by the criminal or caused by a mistake on the part of the detective). For our present purposes, however, the crucial elements of the genre are detective, detecting process, and solution; they are chronologically sequential in the fiction and can change or

From Stephano Tani (1984) *The Doomed Detective: The Contribution of the Detective Novel to Postmodern American and Italian Fiction.* Carbondale and Edwardsville, IL: Southern Illinois University Press.

subvert its meaning if used in a new way. The solution is the most important element since it is the final and fulfilling link in the detective novel's sequence, the one that gives sense to the genre and justifies its existence. So it is to the solution that the anti-detective novelist devotes his attention; he anticipates the solution in the narrative sequence (Gardner's *The Sunlight Dialogues*), fulfills it only partially (Sciascia's *A ciascuno il suo*), denies it (Pynchon's *The Crying of Lot 49*), nullifies it (Hjortsberg's *Falling Angel*), or parodies it (Calvino's *Se una notte d'inverno un viaggiatore*).

The twist of the final element is prepared for by an elaboration of the two others (detective and detection), which does not thoroughly follow the rules of the conventional detective novel yet does not subvert the meaning of the fiction either. The detective of the anti-detective story no longer has the detachment of a M. Dupin. Unwillingly, he gets emotionally caught in the net of his detecting effort and is torn apart between the upsurge of feelings and the necessity for rationality (Laurana in *A ciascuno il suo*; Oedipa in *The Crying of Lot 49*; Clumly in *The Sunlight Dialogues*; Harry Angel in *Falling Angel*). The detective's relationship with the mystery or with the crime cannot be impersonal any more, suggesting that something unexpected (not an unexpected solution) awaits the reader at the end of the fiction. In the hard-boiled school, detection could become a personal existential quest, but not to the point of being unfulfilled (as it is in *The Crying of Lot 49*) or fulfilled in a thoroughly unconventional way ('La muerte y la brújula,' *Les Gommes*).

It is the more or less radical treatment of the solution that distinguishes different kinds of anti-detective novels; the treatment of the old form creates the new content. All the other elements must seem apparently unchanged so that the fiction at the beginning can be identified by the reader as a detective novel and reveal itself as a negation of the genre only at the end. Thus what in an anti-detective novel seems suspense that promises fulfillment actually proves unfulfilled suspense by the end of the reading, while the delay of the solution becomes nonsolution; even the nature of the crime or mystery often acquires during the development of the detection disturbing and unusual connotations, as in *The Crying of Lot 49*. Conventions hence become deceitful clues planted by the writer to rouse the attention of the reader before disappointing his expectations; conventions are paradoxically functional in the disintegration of the genre.

We can distinguish three different techniques for handling the solution; these techniques correspond to three kinds of anti-detective fiction.

1) *INNOVATION:* an early solution disappoints the reader and then an unexpected final one puzzles him (*The Sunlight Dialogues*), or a solution does not imply the punishment of the culprit (*A ciascuno il suo*), or a solution is found by chance (*Il nome della rosa*). These novels are characterized by a social preoccupation related to the crime and its causes. This social preoccupation is totally foreign to the 'British' kind, but is already present in the hard-boiled school. In general, the conventional rules of detective fiction are freely used or twisted but not subverted; some partially satisfying solution is still present.

2) *DECONSTRUCTION:* the opposite constructive principle is fulfilled; instead of a solution there is a suspension of the solution. The novel frustratingly ends a few pages before the denouement, after having teased the reader into a wild goose chase throughout the fiction by planted and inconsequential clues (*The Crying of Lot 49*); the suspension of the solution can leave the reader in total darkness (*The Crying of Lot 49*), or intimate a solution (Sciascia's *Todo modo*), or give a mocking solution that is rationally unacceptable (Hjortsberg's *Falling Angel*). The crime is seen as a conspiracy by a secret organization ruling and perverting society; the investigation is experienced by the detective as an existential quest; both are emphasized at this level – the truly postmodern one that subverts the conventional detective novel's rules. Here the postmodern imagination often plays an important part in the form of 'black humor' and 'new gothicism.'

3) *METAFICTION:* these novels are only in a very general way anti-detective novels. They emphasize that 'book-conscious-of-its-bookness' aspect typical also of the puzzle-like British detective fiction. Here the detection is present in the relation between the writer who deviously writes ('hides') his own text and the reader who wants to make sense out of it (who 'seeks' a solution). A similar 'hide-and-seek' relation corresponds within the fiction. In fact *Se una notte d'inverno un viaggiatore* (*If on a winter's night a traveler*) by Calvino presents a relation between writer and reader outside and within the fiction: 1) writer (Calvino) deviously writing (hiding the solution of) the text and real reader trying to make sense out of it (seeking the solution); 2) fictional 'writer' (Marana, the translator-forger) forging and interrupting the texts within the text (hiding their conclusions) and two fictional readers trying to make sense out of them (seeking their conclusions). These relations can also be simplified by the absence of fictional readers as in Nabokov's *Pale Fire*: 1) writer (Nabokov) deviously writing (hiding the solution of) the text and real reader trying to make sense out of it (seeking the solution); 2) fictional 'writer' (Kinbote, the commentator-distorter) distorting the text within the text (the poem 'Pale Fire') by his comment. Parody and 'intertextual detection,' a metafictional preoccupation that has been lately predominant in the growth of the postmodern imagination,' are typical of this third and very flexible kind of anti-detective novel.

These categories are intentionally overlapping and by no means rigid and definitive. It is obvious that a novel that is primarily deconstructive, such as *The Crying of Lot 49*, in which there is no solution, is also a novel that neither implies the punishment of the culprit nor the triumph of justice; in this sense it also satisfies some features of innovative anti-detective fiction. Characteristic features themselves may vary in intensity within a category; for example, *The Crying of Lot 49* is much more a deconstructive anti-detective novel than *Todo modo*, as in the former there is a total suspension of the solution, while in the latter some hint is given. Likewise, the relation criminal detective/writer-reader typical of the metafictional anti-detective novel is present in any text where there is a 'dialogue' (implicit or not) between reader and writer (for example, in the famous Ellery Queen's interruptions, in which he challenged the reader to find the solution before the end of the novel as by that moment he had all the elements in hand). Thus one of *The Crying of Lot 49's* metafictional hints resides in its third-person narrator who reminds us continuously that it is not Oedipa who is telling her story but someone else who could even be the Tristero (if we like to remain within the fiction) but who is actually Thomas Pynchon (who is anyway for all of us a name as mysterious and unsubstantial as Tristero itself). The fact is that the voice narrating *The Crying of Lot 49* plays with us, as does any other third-person narrator; this in other cases would be an obvious fact, but in a complicated novel like *The Crying of Lot 49* it adds a further dimension to its imperviousness. At any rate, it should by now be clear that any category 'implies' – although with an intensity varying according to the novel concerned – quite a few characteristics of other categories.

What also connects innovative, deconstructive, and metafictional anti-detective novels is a teasing, puzzle-like relation between the text and the reader, which gets more overt and sophisticated as one goes from the first to the third treatment of the solution. This relation replaces and changes the function of the conventional suspense, since the reader gets involved in the mystery and in the detection to be only partially or not at all rewarded by a plausible denouement.

Just as these anti-detective modes renew the conventional use of solution and suspense, they also alter the relation to time, which in traditional detective fiction is repetitive and predetermined, but in some deconstructive anti-detective novels is non-repetitive and open.

The traditional detective novel presents a reconstruction of the past and ends when this reconstruction has been fulfilled. To reconstruct the past is to go back to a point (the one of the crime) about which the detective is concerned. There must be a fixed point; otherwise the regression in time would be infinite. So to go back in time is equal to finding a criminal, to unravelling a mystery.'[2]

There is no free time in a detective novel: the present is employed to explain the past, the past has already happened before the story started, and the future is not even taken into account. The detective 'wins' the past, unravels it, but only to be doomed to go backwards in time in the next story. If it is a detective-fiction serial, he must repeat the same process over and over, and it is perhaps because of his continuous frequenting of the past, because of his living in the past, that he never ages in the present. Nero Wolfe and Hercule Poirot are always the same, impervious to passing time. Their next victory, which is by no means unexpected (the reader knows from the beginning that they will eventually solve the mystery), represents just a slight variation in a repetitive formula; victory is private and ephemeral since it concerns only a few people and never transcends the puzzle-like ratiocination of the case. Neither Nero Wolfe nor Hercule Poirot, however, can refuse to win, since the solution is fundamental to the genre in which they are imprisoned; they cannot lose as they cannot have a complete and final victory.[3] Like Sisyphus, they are doomed to roll the stone of detection up to the top of the hill over and over. To have to repeat the discovery ultimately means that no discovery is final, no discovery is a solution but rather a tendency, an approximation, since the past is full of unsolved mysteries waiting for their detective.

By contrast, in the deconstructive anti-detective novel, the inanity of the discovery is brought to its climax in the nonsolution, which unmasks a tendency toward disorder and irrationality that has always been implicit within detective fiction (i.e., both parallel and intersecting Poesque and non-Poesque currents). The detective in the deconstructive anti-detective novel does not solve the mystery and so avoids the trap of repetition (serialization). The anti-detective is like the Kierkegaardian ironist who knows that the only way to remain free (not imprisoned in the fiction and its serialization) and somehow superhuman is to choose not to choose (not to solve the mystery), since choice is a limitation of freedom and of the power of creativity as it turns the potential into the actual. To choose not to choose is the widest choice the anti-detective can make, because to let the mystery exist does not restrict his freedom to a single choice and, at the same time, potentially implies all solutions without choosing any. The anti-detective arrives reluctantly at this non-solution, however, forced to it by the proliferation of meanings (clues) in the events he goes through; at the same time, even if unwillingly, he or she (Oedipa Maas in *The Crying of Lot 49*) still transcends in a single sweep the honorable but limited victories of an endless career (Poirot), since here, too, not to choose is to allow all outcomes.

It is interesting that the detective's discovery is about the past, while we think of discovery always in terms of the future, as giving us a knowledge that will make us progress into the future. This is what we think in relation to scientific discoveries. The detective is supposed to use a scientific method, but he applies it to a discovery in the past. The point is that a discovery is not about finding something really new but, rather, about finding a missing link, something that already existed and we did not know about (or about which we had only a vague notion). America had always been there, waiting for a Columbus. Ultimately, both for some detectives and anti-detectives, to discover is 'to recollect in tranquillity' their double's emotions, to find out about their own past, of which they are not aware (Hjortsberg's *Falling Angel*). Even for a serialized detective like Maigret, to find a criminal means to identify with him, to drench himself in the environment of the murder and wait patiently for an epiphany that will solve the mystery.

The detective is a scientist, but a particular kind of scientist, a humanist, an archaeologist. In fact both the detective and the archaeologist 'dig out,' and their reconstruction is only partial, limited to *what is left after* (after the end of a civilization, after a murder). The detective can discover why Mrs. Smith killed her husband, where and how, but, of course, he will never be able to stop Mrs. Smith because the murder has already happened.

It is now possible to see how a set of elements typical of mythology (mirror, labyrinth, and map) recurs both at a literal and at a symbolic level in some early anti-detective fiction (especially in Borges' stories such as 'La muerte y la brújula' and in the French *nouveau roman*) and how it contributes to relate time to the development of the detecting process. In fact, if the detective is an 'archeologist,' he is also a map-maker, a maker of meaning (of solution), who turn into rational symbols something that he cannot take hold of, because he cannot relive the past, but only piece together what is left of it, which can be cigarette butts, overthrown furniture, a corpse in the living room. Objects are important to him, as they are all potential clues.

Theseus, the map-maker, went through the labyrinth Daedalus made. Getting through the labyrinth and finding the exit was to Theseus what finding the solution, making sense out of the past in the flowing of time, is for the detective. If the detective is the map-maker (the maker of a solution), the present time is the mirror-maker, since every present moment flows away from the time of the murder, changes and distorts the image of that past: a cigarette butt is kicked away by someone who perhaps is also busy setting back the overthrown furniture or moving the corpse. The labyrinth of the past 'mirrored' (distorted, changed, removed) in the present is the best ally of the murderer. The murderer was not the maker of the labyrinth (the maker of the labyrinth is of course the flowing of time which, as it makes things past, I will simply call 'the past'), but he gave it a dimension; freezing a point in time by the murder, he fixed how far in 'mapping' the past the detective must go.

It seems hardly necessary to stress the importance of mirrors, labyrinths, and maps in Borges' fiction.[4] The *nouveau roman* also contains this pattern, although it declares itself antisymbolical and antimythological. This pattern relates detecting process and time: the detective tries to map the labyrinth (the mystery, the murder) fighting through the distorted view available in the present (the mirror). The novel is thus simplified in a tension between the distortion of the past due to the flowing of present time (mirror) and the mapping of that past attempted by the detective. The flowing of present time (present – mirror-maker) maker) makes occurrences past, that is, mysterious and irretrievable (past = labyrinth-maker); the silent presence of things, witnesses of the mystery, may help the detective, the map-maker, to 'map' the labyrinth (the mystery, the crime), to find a solution (solution = map) by following an Ariadne's thread, a lead, throughout the labyrinth. These mythical symbols work at more than one level.

The mirror that the detective has to crash through to get to the past is also the prefiguration of the 'double,' the detective's reflection who is the criminal he is looking for (Poe's 'William Wilson,' Hjortsberg's *Falling Angel*, Robbe-Grillet's *Les Gommes*, Butor's *L'emploi du temps*). The mirror is also the deceiving reproduction of multiform reality, and, as such, it appears as a forewarning in the first lines of *L'emploi du temps*: '[T]he dark windowpane [of the train compartment was] covered on the outside with raindrops, myriad tiny *mirrors* each reflecting a quivering particle of feeble light that drizzled down from the grimy ceiling.'[5]

An actual map as a symbolic and objective representation of the place where the anti-detective novel is set (and the prefiguration, ironical or not, of the success of the detective as 'map-maker,' maker of a solution) is often offered to the reader in the first page of the novel as it often used to in the old-style British mystery (Robbe-Grillet's *La Jalousie*, Butor's *L'emploi du temps*, Ollier's *La Mise en Scène*).[6] The novel setting objectively represented in the map is often opposed to a 'mirror.' I call the 'mirror' the distortion of the novel setting by the narrator. This occurs no matter how objective his narration appears (the obsessive camera-eye description of the house where the action takes place by the third person narrator of *La Jalousie*; in *L'emploi du temps* the narrator's description of Bleston, the mapped town, as an evil, eerie place). In Borges' 'La muerte y la brújula,' the map of the city is a crucial element in the fatal detection performed by Lönnrot (the detective as 'map-maker'). More generally, many of Borges' titles emphasize the shape (the 'mapping') of objects or of environments: 'Las ruinas circulares' ('The Circular Ruins'), 'El jardín de senderos que se bifurcan' ('The Garden of Forking Paths'), 'La forma de la espada' ('The Shape of the Sword').[7]

Time itself becomes a mirror-image, emphasizing specularity and repetition; everything ends (almost) as it has started (Butor's *L'emploi du temps*, Ollier's *La Mise en Scène*, Robbe Grillet's *La Jalousie* and *Dans le labyrinthe*)[8] while the static plot and the detailed, obsessive descriptions of the objects as surfaces in the environment give the reader an objective correlative of patterned, impenetrable repetition, that is, the sense of the labyrinth (*L'emploi du temps*, *La Mise en Scène*, *La Jalousie*, *Dans le labyrinthe*). Labyrinths are present in Borges' 'detective' stories; an actual one in 'Abejacán el Bojarí, muerto en su laberinto' ('Ibn Hakkan al-Bokhari, Dead in His Labyrinth'),[9] and a literary one in 'El jardín de senderos que se bifurcan' ('The Garden of Forking Paths').

The narrator of *L'emploi du temps*, Revel, burning the map of Bleston, the town locus of the novel, gives himself up to the inscrutable labyrinth Bleston represents for him. The detective novel he has been reading, *Le Meurtre de Bleston (Bleston Murder)* perfectly mirrors something that is going to happen to him: an occurrence in which he is the unaware (but to what degree unaware?) accomplice of an attempted murder he describes in his journal. The journal in the novel and the detective novel (*Le Meurtre de Bleston*) in the novel are interacting and so are the time in which the journal is written and the time of the occurrences it describes, and we have again a game of mirrors.

We will see how also in some recent anti-detective novels the elements of the labyrinth-mirror-map pattern can be traced either at a symbolic or at a literal level. In Sciascia's *Todo modo* the 'mirror' is symbolic for the detective-murderer duality, while there is an actual drawing, a 'map,' which leads the narrator to the solution of the mystery. In Eco's *Il nome della rosa (The Name of the Rose)* all three elements are actually present and also stand for the chronological development of the detecting process: labyrinth – the mystery to unravel; mirror – the distortion, the false solution; map – the solution. The three elements – especially the map – may be found even in traditional detective fiction, perhaps because they are generally evocative of mystery.

All these terms, of course, can be undermined or perverted – a fact of which Poe seems to have had at least an inkling. In 'The murders in the Rue Morgue' it turns out that there was not, technically, a murder; in several of his nondetective tales, as in 'Ligeia,' the narrator leaves us with a false, solution; and in the detective story-like tale 'William Wilson' the seeming solution destroys the solver, while in *The Narrative of Arthur Gordon Pym of Nantucket* the solution of the (nondetective) mystery is withheld. But since Poe's time the world has changed. The madness and self-contradiction of the narrator has become general, a quality of the universe in which the detective struggles.

NOTES

1. Jurij N., Tynjanov, 'Literaturnyj Fakt,' *Poetika, Istorija Likeratory, Kiro* (Moscow: Nauka, 1977), p. 259.
   This statement by Tynjanov recalls one made by William Barrett in *Irrational Man: A Study in Existential Philosophy* (Garden City N.Y.: Doubleday, 1958): 'Every age projects its own image of man into its art' (p. 52). Also, Barrett argues that recent art is 'concerned, in any case, simply with the destruction of the traditional image of man,' so that nothingness has become 'one of the chief themes in modern art literature' (p. 54). These general observations, when applied to our topic, explain the postmodern destruction of the traditional image of the detective as a detached and successful man. In fact, as we will see, the detective of the anti-detective novel gets emotionally involved in the mystery and often fails to solve it. The detective novel structure itself is destroyed in the anti-detective novel which, in the deconstructive category, offers no solution: nothingness, acceptance of the mystery, becomes its chief theme. Indeed Barrett's work shows throughout that existentialism, as a philosophy stressing the limits of human reason and the consequent acceptance of 'nothingness,' prepares for the nonsolution of the anti-detective novel.
2. The Freudian adaptation of the Oedipus myth may be used to illustrate this concept of time in detective fiction. Theoretically conceived, the Freudian construct recalls the Dupin paradox: the detective and the criminal depend upon, or 'invent' each other. The Freudian construct might be expressed as follows: to the detective, to find (and perhaps kill) the culprit is to find (and perhaps kill) a father, since the fiction in which he exists is generated by a crime, and without a criminal the detective would not exist otherwise. The fiction does indeed end when the detective finds the 'father'; the quest has been fulfilled and, after his descent into the past, the detective comes back into the present to explain to a skeptical audience his successful reconstruction of things past.
3. See Guido Carboni, 'Un matrimonio ben riuscito? Note sul giallo d'azione negli USA,' *Calibano 2* (Rome: Savelli, 1978), p. 118.
4. See for example Ana Maria Barrenechea, *Borges, the Labyrinth Maker* (New York: New York University Press, 1965).
5. Michel Butor, *Passing Time*, translated from the French by Jean Stewart (New York: Simon & Schuster, 1960), p. 3. Original title: *L'emploi du temps* (Paris: Les Editions de Minuit, 1956). Italics mine. One of the very few *nouveaux romans* in which 'form and surfaces' do not suffocate 'substance and life.'
6. Claude Ollier's *La Mise en Scène* (Paris: Les Editions de Minuit, 1958) is not available in English. Alain Robbe-Grillet's *La Jalousie*, published by Les Editions de Minuit in 1957, has been translated into English (*Two Novels by Robbe-Grillet, Jealousy & In the Labyrinth* [New York: Grove Press, 1965]).

7. 'La muerte y la brújula,' 'La ruinas circulares,' 'El jardín de senderos que se bifurcan,' 'La forma de la espada' belong to the collection of short stories *Ficciones* (Buenos Aires: Editorial Sur, 1944), published in English under the same title (New York: Grove Press, 1962).

8. *Dans le labyrinthe* by Alain Robbe-Grillet was published by Les Editions de Minuit in 1959; for English translation see note 6.

9. 'Abenjacán el Bojarí, muerto en su laberinto' belongs to the collection of short stories *El Aleph* (Buenos Aires: Editorial Losada, 1949), published in English under the title *The Aleph & Other Stories* (New York: Dutton, 1979).

PART IV
POSTMODERN POLITICS

POSTMODERN POLITICS: INTRODUCTION

The essays and extracts in this final section cover a broader range of issues than the previous sections. All of them, though, deal in diverse ways with the question of politics – politics, that is, in a general sense, not confined to matters of government but to other questions of discourse, power, authority and ethics.

The point is not that politics should be regarded as a self-contained issue which is dealt with only in those postmodern novels or works of criticism which choose to. The extracts in the reader so far reflect the tendency for theorists of postmodernism to be divided – and to a large extent be willing to divide themselves – into those who 'approve' of postmodernism (e.g. Hutcheon, McHale, Sontag, Eco, Fiedler) and those who do not (Jameson, Huyssen, Graff, Howe). In the end, this reminds us that postmodernism always comes down to politics, even when a theorist is not explicit about, or even aware of, the political motivations behind his or her theory. This is something we need to bear in mind as we assess the contribution of individual theorists to the overall debate. To fully understand Daniel Bell's definition of postindustrialism, for example, we need to be aware that he is, as Jürgen Habermas has said, a 'neo-conservative' who is concerned with ensuring 'norms arise in a society which will limit libertinism, re-establish the ethic of discipline and work' and 'put a brake on the levelling caused by the social welfare state so that the virtues of individual competition for achievement can again dominate'. For Bell the answer is 'religion tied to a faith in tradition' (Habermas, 1983: 6–7). What Habermas's insight reminds us of is that none of the definitions of the postmodern we have so far come across are made from a disinterested position. The logic is something often addressed explicitly by postmodern theory: there can no objective totalising overview of a phenomenon provided as if 'from outside'; everyone is *implicated* in what they talk about. Like Habermas, though, many of the theorists of postmodernism are aware of this fact, and attempt explicitly to link their discussions of postmodernism to wider political objectives.

The reason I cited Bell is that, as a right-wing theorist who figures prominently in the postmodern debate, he is in a small minority. In the overwhelming majority of cases, 'wider political objectives' mean Marxist ones. Most of the major defining statements of the postmodern have been delivered from a broadly left-wing perspective: Jameson is a card-carrying Marxist, Lyotard and Baudrillard two recovering Marxists. The virtual omnipresence of Marxism in the postmodern debate is partly because, as a prime 'suspicious theory' (which seeks to unmask the inequities in the way things seem by pointing to the 'reality' beneath), it is a major shaping force behind theory and criticism as a whole over the last few decades. As Dick Hebdige has pointed out (Hebdige, 1988), it makes sense to see postmodernism as opposed to Marxism as much as it is to modernism, for postmodernism destablises the very things – notions of social order, teleology, the subject – which Marxism holds dear.

But while Marxism has always been central to the debate about postmodernism, in the 1980s and 1990s, in tune with wider patterns within contemporary critical theory, the postmodernism debate opens out to include political concerns beyond class, ideology or capitalism. The extracts in this section deal with the question of 'the political' in ways that address more generally political or ethical concerns raised in postmodern treatments of history, representation, gender and race. Though some of the writers (notably Morris and hooks) deal with the question of the politics of postmodern *theory*, others explore the question which has frequently been asked of postmodern art and culture: does its emphasis on self-reflexivity and irony fatally limit its political dimension? The case against postmodern art in this respect is neatly summarised by David Harvey, when he wonders in *The Condition of Postmodernity* whether postmodernism

> with its emphasis on the ephemerality of *jouissance*, its insistence upon the impenetrability of the other, its concentration on the text rather than the work, its penchant for deconstruction bordering on nihilism, its preference for aesthetics over ethics, takes matter too far. It takes them beyond the point where any coherent politics are left, while that wing of it that seeks a shameless accommodation with the market puts it firmly in the tracks of an entrepreneurial culture that is the hallmark of reactionary conservatism. (Harvey, 1989: 116)

The first three extracts provide some measure of continuity with the previous part in that they all engage with the question of formalism. First is a chapter from Linda Hutcheon's *The Politics of Postmodernism* (1989), a follow-up to *A Poetics of Postmodernism* (1988) of sorts, which covers much of the same ground, though with a wealth of different examples drawn from fiction and photography. The difference from its predecessor is suggested by the title: the book more heavily emphasises the political implications of Hutcheon's understanding of postmodernism as a contradictory, double entity. The extracts included here do this by defining (again, as the concept is introduced in *A Poetics of Postmodernism*) a category of fiction which has come to be a crucial one in studies of postmodernism and the novel, 'historiographic metafiction'. This is essentially a self-reflexive version of a long established fictional genre, the historical novel. In telling the story of a quest into the past, or by juxtaposing a story in the past and a story in the present day, historiographic metafiction raises questions about how we 'write' – or construct – 'history'. Thus it shows us that history is not a given, but something which always comes to us mediated through *text*. Although the conventional rhetoric suggests otherwise, historiography, the writing of history, is subject to the same laws as the writing of fiction, i.e. one implicated subject, the writer, selects and interprets events from the past, and organises them into a coherent narrative.

Historiographic metafiction is one of the most common types of contemporary fiction, especially in Britain, where it has been the key product in a kind of boom industry within the 'literary' novel, featuring prominently on the shortlists of most literary prizes. Examples include John Fowles's *The French Lieutenant's Woman* (1969), Graham Swift's *Waterland* (1982), D. M. Thomas's *The White Hotel* (1981), Salman Rushdie's *Midnight's Children* (1981), Julian Barnes's *Flaubert's Parrot* (1986), A. S. Byatt's *Possession* (1990) and, most recently, *English Passengers* (2000) by Matthew Kneale – a kind of roll call of some of the most significant British novels in the late twentieth century. No doubt partly because of the influence of Hutcheon's work, the form has come to seem almost like a 'canon' of postmodern fiction – an alternative, we might say, to the other great postmodernist canon made up of earlier writers like Borges, Barth, Barthelme, Coover, Gass and Pynchon. As Hutcheon says, historiographic metafiction is a form of metafiction which retains a strong referential (or realist) function, something which perhaps accounts for its popularity. Indeed the very popularity of the genre testifies to a serious concern with history in contemporary culture, which gives an answer to some of the critiques of postmodernism levelled by theorists such as Jameson, and supports Hutcheon's main point in the extracts which follows. Postmodernism's critiques of history do not suggest an incredulity towards history, but that we no longer believe in history as something we can all agree upon. Historiographic metafictions do not seek to deny that events in the past happened or that they are important in shaping how we are today; the problem is in 'accessing' these events and determining precisely how they have shaped the present.

The faith Hutcheon places in the capacity of contemporary literary form to function as political critique is shared by Thomas Docherty in his essay 'Postmodern Characterization: The Ethics of Alterity'. Like some of the pieces in Part III Docherty's piece is a detailed study of how postmodern fiction *works* – particularly in contrast to realist narrative – but rather than developing an overall typology he confines himself to one key feature, character. He starts by outlining the ideology of character which operated in classic realist narrative: the human being is presented as essential and autonomous, and thus, 'while seeming to grant some measure of independence and a democratic equality to the individual, actually serves to proffer a normative role for the individual in a specific social formation'. Postmodern characterisation, by contrast, gives us a view of subjectivity as always *in process*, endlessly deferred, 'about-to-be'. Its metafictional portrayal of character both demystifies the process of character-isation and also makes the reader unable to impose a final definition on a particular character's identity. Thus the 'imperialism' of realist characterisation – where author and reader know exactly who a particular character is and thereby 'place' him/her socially – is frustrated. Ultimately for Docherty this is a question of ethics, for postmodern characterisation allows us fully to appreciate the otherness (alterity) of people, as we are prevented from reducing them to versions of the same (us).

One of the starting points of Paul Maltby's *Dissident Postmodernists: Barthelme, Coover, Pynchon* is the inadequacy of formalist approaches to postmodern fiction. While rightly pointing to its concern with 'the "fiction-ality" of meaning (i.e. the perception that the "real", history, or nature can only be apprehended in narrative form, that is, as "stories")' postmodern 'neo-formalism' overlooks the fact that this theme does not figure in the same way in every postmodern text. Specifically, some novels grasp this problem in *political* terms, while others do not. Maltby argues that a purely formalist concern with self-reflexivity does not have the required socio-historical perspective to answer the question, 'why should the fictionality of meaning become a major issue at a particular time, in a particular place (i.e. late-capitalist America)?'

This is the question Maltby's own study attempts to answer, by engaging in his own kind of politicised formalism. He differentiates what he calls a 'dissident' current with postmodern fiction from an 'introverted' current. Where the governing impulse of the introverted kind of novel is to explore how all meaning is produced through text, dissident postmodernism – and he uses the work of Donald Barthelme, Robert Coover and Thomas Pynchon to exemplify this – is a set of writing strategies which can expose and confront the powerful ways in which late capitalism has changed the nature and function of *language* in postmodernity. The linguistic implications of late capitalism Maltby outlines are, surprisingly, seldom considered in theories of postmodern fiction, and include: 'the erosion of the "public sphere"; the diffusion of concept-poor discourses which limit social understanding; the enlargement of the state's propaganda apparatuses; the corporate management of mass com-munications; the ideological ascendancy of functionalist discourses' (Maltby, 1991: 1). One of these features, 'attenuated language', is considered in the extracts I have chosen, along with Maltby's expression of his misgivings about the formalist bent to postmodern theory, his definition of the category 'dissident postmodernism' and a reading of Robert Coover's novel *The Public Burning*.

The extracts from Meaghan Morris and bell hooks both interrogate the politics of postmodernism from the perspective of two of the most important areas within contemporary theory, feminism and postcolonialism. On the surface it seems that both discourses should find something valuable in the postmodern debate, as postmodernism emphasises – as Docherty's article here makes clear – the value of challenging established authority and emphasising difference. Indeed this was the assumption behind two of the first serious considerations of the relation between feminism and the postmodern: Craig Owens's 'The Discourse of Others: Feminists and Postmodernism' (Owens, 1983) and Andreas Huyssen's 'After the Great Divide' (see Part I). Both men wondered why feminists hadn't so far been keen to join their cause to that of postmodernism. Many feminist theorists have tried to answer this question. Sandra Harding, for example, has argued that feminism can only go so far in throwing out Enlightenment ideals (though Enlightenment assumptions and prejudices are another matter), for, like Marxism, it is by definition committed to some of these values, such as emancipation (Harding, 1990: 99). Bonnie Zimmerman argues something similar in relation to literary form: most women writers, however explicit their feminism, remain committed 'to realism, to creating an authentic female voice, and to portraying authentic female experience' (Zimmerman, 1986: 186).

Instead of trying to provide an answer, however, the article by Meaghan Morris included here takes issue with the very *question* posed by the likes of Owens and Huyssen. Asking why so few female writers have sought to become directly involved in the postmodernism debate is 'perhaps the latest version of the "why have there been no great women artists (mathematicians, scientists ...)?" conundrum'. Of course, as English courses in universities continually point out, there *are* women artists, and good ones, at each point throughout history. It's just that to be recognised as 'great' they have to be actively isolated by critics from the masculine frame that limits them: they have to be judged on grounds other than those set out by masculine views of art. Something similar has occurred with the postmodernism debate, argues Morris. Key texts by women which have helped shape the postmodern debate have been excluded from the critical canon simply because they do not *explicitly* address the question of postmodernism or conform to the particular parameters to the discussion which have been set by male theorists.

The question of inclusion and exclusion is also central to bell hooks's article 'Postmodern Blackness' – perhaps because, like Morris, her work is located more in the discipline of cultural studies than in literature. hooks is more ambivalent about postmodernism because of the question of race. Postmodernism, she argues, is useful to African-Americans because it is a powerful tool with which to reconceptualise identity in the wake of outdated versions of subjectivity that disenfranchise black people. At the same time, though, it is unfortunate that its philosophy attempts to eliminate the idea of a unified subject at precisely the point when the black subject – via the emergence of popular cultural forms like rap music – is beginning to feel 'unified' and autonomous for the first time. Furthermore, the postmodern argument about difference has involved imposing another form of homogeneity – at least implicitly – on the idea of the subject: the *black* subject is ignored. Ironically, though, we might say that hooks's essay itself falls into this trap – indicating the complexity of dealing head on with political questions of inclusion and exclusion when it comes to postmodernism: she criticises postmodernism without stating which thinkers she is referring to.

In his essay 'The Postcolonial and the Postmodern' (1992) Kwame Anthony Appiah also argues for the value of preserving – and clarifying – the differences between postmodernism and postcolonialism. The point of the article is encapsulated in the rhetorical question it poses: does the 'post' in postcolonial mean the same as the 'post' in postmodernism? The essay subtly (Appiah's style of argument is more exploratory rather than decisive, to suit his theme) argues that there is a point at which democracy becomes 'dangerous' because it eliminates crucial differences.

Donna Haraway's 'A Manifesto for Cyborgs: Science, Technology, and Socialist Feminism in the 1980s' is a hugely influential piece of work, whose influence is not confined to postmodernism. Nevertheless postmodernism (though she seldom mentions it) is central to Haraway's essay, both in relation to its subject and its self-reflexive style. Before the beginning of the passage from which the following extract is taken Haraway describes her objective as the construction of 'an ironic political myth faithful to feminism, socialism and materialism' (Haraway, 1990: 191). In a note which appeared beside the essay when it was reprinted in Linda J. Nicholson's important collection of essays *Feminism/Postmodernism* (Nicholson, 1990) Haraway expands further, explaining that the essay 'originated as a response to a call for political thinking about the 1980s from socialist-feminist points of view, in hopes of deepening our political and cultural debates in order to renew commitments to fundamental social change in the face of the Reagan years. The cyborg manifesto tried to find a feminist place for connected thinking and acting in profoundly contradictory worlds' (Haraway, 1990: 191). Haraway's strategy is ironic, then, because it embraces the contradictory elements of postmodernism in order to try and present a coherent political course of action for feminism. Specifically this means taking the sci-fi metaphor of the cyborg – half human, half machine – and using it as a model for the project of transcending the conventional nature/culture binary which has tended to underpin the gender positions which operate in our culture (woman = nature, man = culture). As a 'creature in a postgender world' the cyborg embodies irony and contradiction, and eludes certainty. Haraway thus overcomes the concern Harding voices about the contradictory relationship of feminism and Enlightenment values in a simple, ironic way: by embracing it.

Veronica Hollinger describes Haraway's essay as partly an exercise in science fiction, partly feminist polemic. Her own essay, 'Cybernetic Deconstructions:

336

Cyberpunk and Postmodernism', switches the focus back to literature by considering another of postmodernism's typical genres, cyberpunk – the genre Fredric Jameson has called 'the supreme *literary* expression, if not of postmodernism, then of late capitalism itself' (Jameson, 1991: 419 n1). The kind of world presented in Haraway's essay, she argues, the world of the cyborg, means that it is not just the technology that has evolved since the old days of science fiction, but the human being too. More precisely, her contention is that the 'original trope' of sci-fi – of a world where the human and the inhuman (technology) clash – is no longer tenable. This accounts for the emergence of cyberpunk, a form which updates science fiction, in order to consider 'the technological ramifications of experience, within late-capitalist, post-industrial, media-saturated Western society' (Hollinger, 1992: 30).

For Jameson, cyberpunk is 'as much an expression of transnational corporate realities as it is of global paranoia itself' (Jameson, 1991: 38). The final essay in this section, Patrick O'Donnell's 'Engendering Paranoia in Contemporary Narrative', looks at the concern with paranoia within the contemporary novel in a broader range of texts than simply one genre. The plots and characters in contemporary fiction are symptomatic of what he calls 'cultural paranoia', 'a way of seeing the multiple stratifications of reality, virtual and material, as interconnected or networked' (O'Donnell, 1992: 182). Conspiracy theory enables individuals to deal with 'the mystified, hegemonic enactments of power' which are a key part of the late capitalist system. Drawing connections between disparate unconnected aspects of contemporary life becomes a political act, bringing groups of people together in order to gain 'visible identity as unified subjects'.

Among the American writers O'Donnell cites to state his case are the ones who might be regarded as the two most canonical postmodern novelists, Thomas Pynchon and Don DeLillo respectively. Though Pynchon's output is fairly small, his novels, especially *The Crying of Lot 49* and *Gravity's Rainbow*, have been explored in relation to postmodernism from the earliest days of the debate, while DeLillo's texts deal explicitly with some of the concerns of the postmodern condition: simulation, celebrity culture, late capitalism. Can it be a coincidence that the two novelists perhaps most associated with postmodernism are also both preoccupied with paranoia? While this sounds like a paranoid question (O'Donnell's essay, like Jameson's, is acutely aware of the similarities between the roles of critic and cultural paranoiac, who both draw connections between apparently unconnected things) it is surely related to the fact that paranoia foregrounds precisely the same questions about the fictionality of reality and the problems of interpretation which are central to postmodernism.

WORKS CITED

Foster, Hal (ed.) (1983) *The Anti-Aesthetic*. Port Townshend, WA: Bay Press. Later reprinted (1985) as *Postmodern Culture*. London: Pluto Press.

Habermas, Jürgen (1983) 'Modernity – an Incomplete Project', in Hal Foster (ed.), *The Anti-Aesthetic*. Port Townshend, WA: Bay Press. Later reprinted (1985) as *Postmodern Culture*. London: Pluto Press, pp. 3–15.

Haraway, Donna (1990) 'A Manifesto for Cyborgs: Science, Technology, and Socialist Feminism in the 1980s', in Linda J. Nicholson (ed.), *Feminist/Postmodernism*. London: Routledge, pp. 190–233.

Harding, Sandra (1990) 'Feminism, Science, and the Anti-Enlightenment Critiques', in Linda J. Nicholson (ed.), *Feminism/Postmodernism*. London: Routledge, pp. 157–76.

Harvey, David (1989) *The Condition of Postmodernity: An Enquiry into the Origins of Cultural Change*. Oxford: Blackwell.

Hebdige, Dick (1988) *Hiding in the Light: On Images and Things*. London: Routledge.

Hollinger, Veronica (1990) 'Cybernetic Deconstructions: Cyberpunk and Postmodernism', *Mosaic*, 23 (2): 29–44.

Jameson, Fredric (1991) *Postmodernism, or the Cultural Logic of Late Capitalism*. London and New York: Verso.

Maltby, Paul (1991) *Dissident Postmodernists: Barthelme, Coover, Pynchon*. Philadelphia, PA: University of Pennsylvania Press.

Nicholson, Linda J. (ed.), *Feminism/Postmodernism*. London: Routledge.

Owens, Craig (1983) 'The Discourse of Others', in Hal Foster (ed.), *The Anti-Aesthetic*. Port Townshend, WA: Bay Press. Later reprinted (1985) as *Postmodern Culture*. London: Pluto Press.

Zimmerman, Bonnie (1986) 'Feminist Fiction and the Postmodern Challenge', in Larry McCaffery (ed.), *Postmodern Fiction: A Bio-Bibliographical Guide*. New York and London: Greenwood Press, pp. 175–88.

POLITICS AND FICTIONALITY
23

FROM *THE POLITICS OF POSTMODERNISM*

Linda Hutcheon

DE-NATURALIZING THE NATURAL

Like every great word, 'representation/s' is a stew. A scrambled menu,
it serves up several meanings at once. For a representation can be an
image – visual, verbal, or aural. ... A representation can also be a
narrative, a sequence of images and ideas. ... Or, a representation can
be the product of ideology, that vast scheme for showing forth the world
and justifying its dealings.

(Stimpson 1988: 223)

Postmodern representation is self-consciously all of these – image, narrative,
product of (and producer of) ideology. It is a truism of sociology and cultural
studies today to say that life in the postmodern world is utterly mediated
through representations and that our age of satellites and computers has gone
well beyond Benjamin's 'Age of Mechanical Reproduction' and its particular
philosophical and artistic consequences and moved into a state of crisis in
representation. Nevertheless, in literary and art critical circles there is still a
tendency to see postmodern theory and practice either as simply replacing
representation with the idea of textuality or as denying our intricate involvement with representation, even though much postmodern thought has disputed
this tendency: think of Derrida's statements about the inescapability of the logic
of representation, and Foucault's problematization, though never repudiation,
of our traditional modes of representation in our discourses of knowledge.

From Linda Hutcheon (1989) *The Politics of Postmodernism*. London and New York: Routledge.

I suppose the very word 'representation' unavoidably suggests a given which the act of representing duplicates in some way. This is normally considered the realm of mimesis. Yet, by simply making representation into an issue again postmodernism challenges our mimetic assumptions about representation (in any of its 'scrambled menu' meanings): assumptions about its transparency and common-sense naturalness. And it is not just postmodern *theory* that has provoked this rethinking. Take, for instance, Angela Carter's story, 'The Loves of Lady Purple.' The plot details are derived from literalizations of these same mimetic assumptions – and their politics. It begins as the story of a master puppet-maker. The more life-like his marionettes can be made to seem, the more 'god-like' he becomes (Carter 1974: 23). He is said to speculate 'in a no-man's limbo between the real and that which, although we know very well it is not, nevertheless seems to be real' (23). He makes puppets which 'cannot live' yet can 'mimic the living' and even 'project signals of signification.' The precise imitation of these representations is said to be 'all the more disturbing because we know it to be false' (24). His 'didactic vedette,' Lady Purple, is such a success that she is said to have 'transcended the notion she was dependent on his hands and appeared wholly real and yet entirely other' (26). She did not so much imitate as distill and intensify the actions of real women: 'and so she could become the quintessence of eroticism, for no woman born would have dared be so blatantly seductive' (26–7).

The handbills advertising her show speak of her 'unappeaseable appetites,' for she is said to have once been a famous (living) prostitute who, 'pulled only by the strings of lust' (Carter 1974: 28), was reduced to this puppet status. The prostitute's tale is the narrative represented in the show. What Carter's text reveals is that women (as prostitutes, in particular) are never real; they are but representations of male erotic fantasies and of male desire, 'a metaphysical abstraction of the female' (30). Lady Purple was figuratively a puppet even in her living incarnation; she was always 'her own replica' (33) in a sense. The short story ends with the puppet returning to life, sucking her master's breath and drinking his blood. But what does she do with her new-found life and freedom? The only thing she can do: she heads for the brothel in the town. The question we are left with is: 'had the marionette all the time parodied the living or was she, now living, to parody her own performance as a marionette?' (38). But there is another question too: to what extent are all representations of women 'the simulacra of the living' (25)? While there are obvious references in this story to Hoffman's 'Sandman' story and thus to Freud's Uncanny, to Pygmalion and even to Mozart (Lady Purple is called 'Queen of Night'), there is clearly a more contemporary allusion here to Jean Baudrillard's theory of the postmodern simulacrum.

In an article entitled 'The precession of simulacra,' Baudrillard argued that today the mass media have neutralized reality by stages: first they *reflected* it; then they *masked* and perverted it; next they had to *mask its absence*; and finally they produced instead the *simulacrum* of the real, the destruction of meaning and of all relation to reality. Baudrillard's model has come under attack for the metaphysical idealism of its view of the 'real,' for its nostalgia for pre-mass-media authenticity, and for its apocalyptic nihilism. But, as Carter's story suggests, there is a more basic objection to his assumption that it is (or was) ever possible to have unmediated access to reality: have we ever known the 'real' except through representations? We may see, hear, feel, smell, and touch it, but do we *know* it in the sense that we give meaning to it? In Lisa Tickner's succinct terms, the real is '*enabled to mean* through systems of signs organized into discourses on the world' (Tickner 1984: 19). This is obviously where the politics of representation enters for, according to the Althusserian view, ideology is a production of representations. Our common-sense presuppositions about the 'real' depend upon how that 'real' is described, how it is put into discourse and interpreted. There is nothing natural about the 'real' and there never was – even before the existence of mass media.

This said, it is also true that – whatever the naivety of its view of the innocent and stable representation once possible – Baudrillard's notion of the simulacrum has been immensely influential. Witness the unacknowledged but none the less real debt to it in Jameson's own version of pre-mass-media nostalgia:

> In the form of the logic of the image or the spectacle of the simulacrum, everything has become 'cultural' in some sense. A whole new house of mirrors of visual replication and of textual reproduction has replaced the older stable reality of reference and of the non-cultural 'real'.
>
> (Jameson 1986: 42)

What postmodern theory and practice together suggest is that everything always was 'cultural' in this sense, that is, always mediated by representations. They suggest that notions of truth, reference, and the non-cultural real have not ceased to exist, as Baudrillard claims, but that they are no longer unproblematic issues, assumed to be self-evident and self-justifying. The postmodern, as I have been defining it, is not a degeneration into 'hyperreality' but a questioning of what reality can mean and how we can come to know it. It is not that representation now dominates or effaces the referent, but rather that it now self-consciously acknowledges its existence as representation – that is, as interpeting (indeed as creating) its referent, not as offering direct and immediate access to it.

This is not to say that what Jameson calls 'the older logic of the referent (or realism)' (1986: 43) is not historically important to postmodernist representation. In fact, many postmodern strategies are openly premised on a challenge to the realist notion of representation that presumes the transparency of the medium and thus the direct and natural link between sign and referent or between word and world. Of course, modernist art, in all its forms, challenged this notion as well, but it deliberately did so to the detriment of the referent, that is, by emphasizing the opacity of the medium and the self-sufficiency of the signifying system. What postmodernism does is to denaturalize both realism's transparency and modernism's reflexive response, while retaining (in its typically complicitously critical way) the historically attested power of both. This is the ambivalent politics of postmodern representation.

With the problematizing and 'de-doxifying' of both realist reference and modernist autonomy, postmodern representation opens up other possible relations between art and the world: gone is the Benjaminian 'aura' with its notions of originality, authenticity, and uniqueness, and with these go all the taboos against strategies that rely on the parody and reappropriation of already existing representations. In other words, the history of representation itself can become a valid subject of art, and not just its history in high art. The borders between high art and mass or popular culture and those between the discourses of art and the discourses of the world (especially history) are regularly crossed in postmodern theory and practice. But it must be admitted that this crossing is rarely done without considerable border tension.

As we shall see in later chapters, postmodern photography's parodic appropriation of various forms of mass-media representation has come under severe attack by the (still largely modernist) art establishment. The equivalent on the literary scene has been the hostile response of some critics to the mixing of historical and fictive representation in historiographic metafiction. It is not that the fact of the mixing is new: the historical novel, not to mention the epic, should have habituated readers to that. The problem seems to reside in its manner, in the self-consciousness of the fictionality, the lack of the familiar pretence of transparency, and the calling into question of the factual grounding of history-writing. The self-reflexivity of postmodern fiction does indeed foreground many of the usually unacknowledged and naturalized implications of narrative representation. In *The Politics of Reflexivity*, Robert Siegle lists some of these:

> the codes by which we organize reality, the means by which we organize words about it into narrative, the implications of the linguistic medium we use to do so, the means by which readers are drawn into narrative, and the nature of our relation to 'actual' states of reality.
>
> (Siegle 1986: 3)

Siegle further argues that textual reflexivity itself is 'highly charged ideologically precisely because it denaturalizes far more than merely literary codes and pertains to more than the aesthetic "heterocosm" to which some theorists might wish to restrict it' (11). In other words, a self-reflexive text suggests that perhaps narrative does not derive its authority from any reality it represents, but from 'the cultural conventions that define both narrative and the construct we call "reality"' (225). If this is so, the mixing of the reflexively fictional with the verifiably historical might well be doubly upsetting for some critics. Historiographic metafiction represents not just a world of fiction, however self-consciously presented as a constructed one, but also a world of public experience. The difference between this and the realist logic of reference is that here that public world is rendered specifically as discourse. How do we know the past today? Through its discourses, through its texts – that is, through the traces of its historical events: the archival materials, the documents, the narratives of witnesses and historians. On one level, then, postmodern fiction merely makes overt the processes of narrative representation – of the real or the fictive and of their interrelations.

TELLING STORIES: FICTION AND HISTORY

In *Postmodernist Fiction*, Brian McHale has noted that both modernist and postmodernist fiction show an affinity for cinematic models, and certainly the work of Manuel Puig or Salman Rushdie would support such a claim. But historiographic metafiction, obsessed with the question of how we can come to know the past today, also shows an attraction to photographic models – and to photographs – either as physically present (in Michael Ondaatje's *Coming Through Slaughter*) or as the narrativized trappings of the historical archive (in Timothy Findley's *The Wars*, Maxine Hong Kingston's *China Men*, or Gayl Jones's *Corregidora*). In raising (and making problematic) the issue of photographic representation, postmodern fiction often points metaphorically to the related issue of narrative representation – its powers and its limitations. Here, too, there is no transparency, only opacity. The narrator in John Berger's novel *G.* tries to describe an actual historical and political event, but ends up in despair: 'Write anything. Truth or untruth, it is unimportant. Speak but speak with tenderness, for that is all that you can do that may help a little. Build a barricade of words, no matter what they mean' (Berger 1972: 75). The politics of narrative representation can apparently sometimes be of limited efficacy when it comes to the representation of politics.

It is not surprising that this should be the case, especially with historical representation, for the question of historiography's representational powers is a matter of current concern in a number of discourses but most obviously, perhaps, in historiographic metafiction. Roa Bastos's *I the Supreme* is a typical, if extreme, example of this. El Supremo (Jośe Gaspar Rodríguez Francia) did exist and did rule Paraguay from 1814 to 1840, but the novel we read opens with a story about the instability of even a dictator's power over his self-representation in the documents of history: he discovers that his decrees are frequently parodied so well and so thoroughly that 'even the truth appears to be a lie' (Roa Bastos 1986: 5) and the competence of the scribe to whom the dictator 'dictates' his text is suspect. This novel disorients its readers on the level of its narration (who speaks? is the text written? oral? transcribed?), its plot and temporal structures, and even its material existence (parts of the text are said to have been burned): 'Forms disappear, words remain, to signify the impossible. No story can ever be told' (11), especially, perhaps, the story of absolute power.

'I the Supreme' and *I the Supreme* equally distrust history's ability and will to convey 'truth': 'The words of power, of authority, words above words, will be transformed into clever words, lying words. Words below words' (Roa Bastos 1986: 29). Historians, like novelists, are said to be interested not in 'recounting the facts, but [in] recounting that they are recounting them' (32). Yet the text does provide a narrative of the historical past of Paraguay, albeit one recounted in anachronistic wording that underlines the present time of the recounting to the (doubly dictated-to) scribe who writes down what he is told to. Or does he? He openly admits to not understanding the meaning of what he transcribes, and, therefore, to misplacing words, to writing 'backwards' (35). The text metafictionally includes even a reference to Roa Bastos and his novel: 'One or another of those émigré-scribblers will doubtless take advantage of the impunity of distance and be so bold as to cynically affix his signature' to the text we read (35). And so he does.

I the Supreme is a novel about power, about history-writing, and about the oral tradition of story-telling. It thematizes the postmodern concern with the radically indeterminate and unstable nature of textuality and subjectivity, two notions seen as inseparable: 'I must dictate/write; note it down somewhere. That is the only way I have of proving that I still exist' (Roa Bastos 1986: 45). Writing here is not 'the art of tracing flowery figures' but that of 'deflowering signs' (58). Or, as the text explicitly states: 'This is representation. Literature. Representation of writing as representation' (60). However, the power of literary representation is as provisional as that of historiography: 'readers do not know if they [Don Quixote and Sancho Panza] are fables, true stories, pretended truths. The same will come to pass with us. We too will pass for real-unreal beings' (60).

The entire novel is full of such remarks about representation – in the narratives of both fiction and history. The 'Final Compiler's Note' states:

> The reader will already have noted that, unlike ordinary texts, this one was read first and written later. Instead of saying and writing something new, it merely faithfully copies what has already been said and composed by others. ... [T]he re-scriptor declares, in the words of a contemporary author, that the history contained in these *Notes* is reduced to the fact that the story that should have been told in them has not been told. As a consequence, the characters and facts that figure in them have earned, through the fatality of the written language, the right to a fictitious and autonomous existence in the service of the no less fictitious and autonomous reader.
>
> (Roa Bastos 1986: 435)

This is postmodern de-naturalizing – the simultaneous inscribing and subverting of the conventions of narrative.

Coinciding with this kind of challenge in the novels themselves, there have been many theoretical examinations of the nature of narrative as a major human system of understanding – in fiction, but also in history, philosophy, anthropology, and so on. Peter Brooks (1984: xii) has claimed that with the advent of romanticism, narrative became a dominant mode of representation, though one might wonder what the status of the classical epic and the Bible might be. He is likely right to say, however, that in the twentieth century there has been an increasing suspicion of narrative plot and its artifice, yet no diminishing of our reliance on plotting, however ironized or parodied (7). We may no longer have recourse to the grand narratives that once made sense of life for us, but we still have recourse to narrative representations of some kind in most of our verbal discourses, and one of the reasons may be political.

Lennard Davis describes the politics of novelistic narrative representation in this way: 'Novels do not depict life, they depict life as it is represented by ideology' (Davis 1987: 24). Ideology – how a culture represents itself to itself – 'doxifies' or naturalizes narrative representation, making it appear as natural or common-sensical (25); it presents what is really *constructed* meaning as something *inherent* in that which is being represented. But this is precisely what postmodern novels like Peter Ackroyd's *Chatterton* or Roa Bastos's *I the Supreme* or Graham Swift's *Waterland* are about. And in none of these cases is there ever what Jameson associates with the postmodern: 'a repudiation of representation, a "revolutionary" break with the (repressive) ideology of story-telling generally' (Jameson 1984: 54). This misconception shows the danger of defining the postmodern in terms of (French or American) anti-representational late modernism, as so many do. In these novels, there is no dissolution or repudiation of representation; but there *is* a problematizing of it.

Historiographic metafiction is written today in the context of a serious contemporary interrogating of the nature of representation in historiography. There has been much interest recently in narrative – its forms, its function, its powers, and its limitations – in many fields, but especially in history. Hayden White has even asserted that the postmodern is 'informed by a programmatic, if ironic, commitment to the return to narrative as one of its enabling pre-suppositions' (White 1987: xi). If this is the case, his own work has done much to make it so. Articles like 'The value of narrativity in the representation of reality' have been influential in raising questions about narrative representation and its politics in both history and literature. From a different angle, the work of Dominick LaCapra has acted to de-naturalize notions of historical documents as representations of the past and of the way such archival traces of historical events are used within historiographic and fictive representations. Documents are not inert or innocent, but may indeed have 'critical or even potentially transformative relations to phenomena "represented" in them' (LaCapra 1985: 38). [...]

Of course, it is not just historiographic theory that has deconstructed narrative representation. Feminist thought, such as that of Teresa de Lauretis, has done much to deconstruct it as well. It has explored how 'narrative and narrativity ... are mechanisms to be employed strategically and tactically in the effort to construct other forms of coherence, to shift the terms of representation, to produce the conditions of representability of another – and gendered – social subject' (de Lauretis 1987: 109). Narrative is indeed a 'socially symbolic act,' as Jameson claims, but it is also the outcome of social interaction. In the work of

Maxine Hong Kingston or Gayl Jones, story-telling is not presented as a privatized form of experience but as asserting a communicational bond between the teller and the told within a context that is historical, social, and political, as well as intertextual.

The same is true in the postmodern fiction of Salman Rushdie or Gabriel García Márquez. It is not simply a case of novels metafictionally revelling in their own narrativity or fabulation; here narrative representation – story-telling – is a historical and a political act. Perhaps it always is. Peter Brooks argues: 'We live immersed in narrative, recounting and reassessing the meaning of our past actions, anticipating the outcome of our future projects, situating ourselves at the intersection of several stories not yet completed' (1984: 3). In Fowles's *The French Lieutenant's Woman*, the hero does just this – at great length – and the contemporary narrator interrupts to forestall our objections in the name of a kind of postmodern mimesis of process, reminding us that we too do this constantly. While it is undoubtedly true that modernism had already challenged the conventions of what could/should be narrated and had already explored the limits of narrative's ability to represent 'life,' it is postmodern culture at large that may have become 'novelistic.' As Stephen Heath has argued, it mass-produces narratives (for television, radio, film, video, magazines, comic books, novels), thereby creating a situation in which we must consume 'the constant narration of the social relations of individuals, the ordering of meanings for the individual in society' (Health 1982: 85). Perhaps this is why story-telling has returned – but as a problem, not as a given.

It is still a truism of anti-postmodernist criticism that this return has been at the expense of a sense of history. But perhaps it just depends on your definition of history – or History. We may indeed get few postmodern narrative representations of the heroic victors who have traditionally defined who and what made it into History. Often we get instead both the story and the story-telling of the non-combatants or the losers: the Canadian Indians of Rudy Wiebe's *The Temptations of Big Bear* of Leonard Cohen's *Beautiful Losers*; the women of Troy in Christa Wolf's *Cassandra*; the blacks of South Africa or America in the work of J.M. Coetzee, André Brink, Toni Morrison, or Ishmael Reed.

Equally interesting are the postmodern attempts to go beyond the traditional representational forms of both fictional and historical narration: Patrick Süskind's *Perfume* offers the fictionalized history of eighteenth-century France in all its *olfactory* glory, though it must do so through verbal representations of the physical sense that narrative so rarely records. The novel offers the sense of smell as the vehicle not only for its historical and social contextualizing but also for its metafictional commentary, since this is the tale of Jean-Baptiste Grenouille, the product of French peasant misery who is born an 'abomination' – with no bodily odor himself, but with the most discerning nose in the world. The story's narrator is omniscient and controlling, as well as being our contemporary and in complicity with us as readers. He uses this power and position to emphasize from the start the limits of his (and our) language. As a boy Grenouille has trouble learning the words of things that have no smell: 'He could not retain them, confused them with one another, and even as an adult used them unwillingly and often incorrectly: justice, conscience, God, joy, responsibility, humility, gratitude, etc. – what these were meant to express remained a mystery to him' (Süskind 1986: 25). This may not be surprising, perhaps, for the protagonist of a novel subtitled: *The Story of a Murderer*.

Grenouille is constantly aware of the discrepancy between the 'richness of the world perceivable by smell' and 'the poverty of language' (Süskind 1986: 26). The narrator suggests that this linguistic impoverishment accounts for our normal inability to make anything other than gross distinctions in the 'smellable world' (125). The text links the failure of language to Grenouille's creativity as the distiller and creator of the greatest perfumes in the world, and yet, as readers, we can never forget that we know of this only through the very language of the novel. The postmodern paradox of inscription and subversion governs the metafictive reflexivity. It also structures the plot, for this is a novel about power: the power the poor peasant was not born into; the power he acquires in serving others with his gifts (as a master of scents); the power to kill (for the perfect scent); the power that perfect scent wields over others. His executioners and the crowd gathered to witness justice done to this multiple murderer suddenly fall into an ecstatic orgy of love for their victim – when he applies the 'perfume' distilled from the murdered girl who had possessed the most powerful smell in the world: 'A power stronger than the power of money or the power of terror or the power of death: the invincible power to command the love of mankind' (252).

Perfume points to the absence of the representation of the sense of smell in historical, social, or fictional narratives. The olfactory density of the novel – recounted through verbal representation, of course – is historically specific and accurate and also socially significant. This is historiographic metafiction, fictionalized history with a parodic twist. The form this twist takes may vary from novel to novel, but it is always present: Mario Vargas Llosa's *The War of the End of the World* represents the history of the 1896 Canudos War in northeastern Brazil, but its parody shows how traditional narrative models – both historiographical and fictional – that are based on European models of continuous chronology and cause-and-effect relations are utterly inadequate to the task of narrating the history of the New World.

Such a clashing of various possible discourses of narrative representation is one way of signalling the postmodern use and abuse of convention that works to 'de-doxify' any sense of the seamlessness of the join between the natural and the cultural, the world and the text, thereby making us aware of the irreducible ideological nature of every representation – of past or present. This complexity of clashing discourses can be seen in many historiographic metafictions. In Angela Carter's 'Black Venus,' [...] the discourses of male erotic representation of woman and those of female and colonial self-representations are juxtaposed with a certain political efficacy. Similarly, confrontations between contemporary narrators and their narrated historical contexts occur in novels as diverse as Banville's *Doctor Copernicus* and Fowles's *The French Lieutenant's Woman* or *A Maggot*.

In challenging the seamless quality of the history/fiction (or world/art) join implied by realist narrative, postmodern fiction does not, however, disconnect itself from history or the world. It foregrounds and thus contests the conventionality and unacknowledged ideology of that assumption of seamlessness and asks its readers to question the processes by which we represent our selves and our world to ourselves and to become aware of the means by which we *make* sense of and *construct* order out of experience in our particular culture. We cannot avoid representation. We *can* try to avoid fixing our notion of it and assuming it to be transhistorical and transcultural. We can also study how representation legitimizes and privileges certain kinds of knowledge – including certain kinds of historical knowledge. As *Perfume* implies, our access through narrative to the world of experience – past or present – is always mediated by the powers and limits of our representations of it. This is as true of historiographical narrative as it is of fictional.

In his review article, 'The question of narrative in contemporary historical theory,' Hayden White outlines the role assigned to narrative representation in the various schools of thought about the theory of history. Given that narrative has become problematic in historiography as well as fiction, what is interesting is that the same issues arise: narrative representation as a mode of knowledge and explanation, as unavoidably ideological, as a localizable code. One way of outlining some of these parallel concerns would be to look at a historiographic metafiction that directly addresses the intersection of the debates about representation in both the novel and history: Graham Swift's *Waterland*, a didactic fictive lesson or a meditation on history – or both. No historical characters populate this book, but it is a profoundly historical work none the less, in both form and content.

Its first (unattributed) epigraph conditions our entry into the novel and prepares us for the 'de-doxifying' of narrative representation that it proceeds to enact: '*Historia*, ae, f. I. inquiry, investigation, learning. 2.a) a narrative of past events, history, b) any kind of narrative: account, tale, story.' The novel's action opens in the 'fairy tale' landscape of the fen country of England, a land so flat that it drives its inhabitants either to 'unquiet' or to telling stories, especially to calm the fears of children. This is a land 'both palpable and unreal' (Swift 1983: 6), an apt, self-reflexive setting for any fiction. The narrator, Tom Crick, comes from a family that has the 'knack for telling stories' of all kinds: true or made up, believable or unbelievable – 'stories which were neither one thing nor another' (1–2). This is a fitting description, too, of *Waterland* itself.

However, the second chapter is called 'About the end of history.' It is addressed to the second-person plural 'Children' by Crick, their history teacher, who has spent his life trying to 'unravel the mysteries of the past' (Swift 1983: 4), but who is now to be retired because of some personal embarrassment, though the official reason is that his school is 'cutting back on history.' Crick's response is to defend his discipline – and his personal past: 'sack *me*, don't dismiss what I stand for. Don't banish my history' (18). But his students seem little interested in his subject; for them history is a 'fairy tale' (5) and they prefer to learn of the 'here and now' of a world threatened by nuclear annihilation. From the opening pages of the novel, both history-telling and story-telling are thus linked to fear.

They are also connected to the marshy, reclaimed land of the fen country, primarily through the major historical metaphor of the novel: 'Silt: which shapes and undermines continents; which demolishes as it builds; which is simultaneous accretion and erosion; neither progress nor decay' (Swift 1983: 7). A more perfect image of postmodern paradox would be hard to find. In terms of history, the allegorical, slow 'process of human siltation' is contrasted with that of revolution and of 'grand metamorphoses.' To Crick, reality is what the monotonous fens provide: reality is 'that nothing happens.' Historiography's causality is only a construct: 'How many of the events of history have occurred for this or for that reason, but for no other reason, fundamentally, than the desire to make things happen? I present to you History, the fabrication, the diversion, the reality-obscuring drama. History, and its near relative, Histor-ionics' (34). He would like to replace the heroes of history with the silenced crowds who do the 'donkey-work of coping with reality' (34).

Nevertheless, Crick realizes that we all imitate 'the grand repertoire of history' in miniature and endorse 'its longing for presence, for feature, for purpose, for content' (Swift 1983: 34–5) in order to convince ourselves that reality means something. He himself attributes his becoming a history teacher to the tales his mother told him when he was afraid of the dark as a child. Later, when he wanted 'an Explanation,' he studied history as an academic discipline, only to 'uncover in this dedicated search more mysteries, more fantasticalities, more wonders and grounds for astonishment' (53). In other words, as it had begun for him, history continues to be 'a yarn': 'History itself, the Grand Narrative, the filler of vacuums, the dispeller of fears of the dark' (53).

The story Crick actually tells us and the 'Children' is one that is overtly fictive history, and we get to watch the fictionalizing process at work. At one point we are told: 'History does not record whether the day of Thomas's funeral was one of those dazzling mid-winter Fenland days' (Swift 1983: 70), but fourteen pages later, Thomas's funeral takes place under a definitely dazzling sky. Crick is aware of this creative, constructive process. At one point he stops: 'Children, you are right. There are times when we have to disentangle history from fairy-tale. ... History, being an accredited sub-science, only wants to know facts. History, if it is to keep on constructing its road into the future, must do so on solid ground' (74) – something his slippery fen-country tale often seems to lack. Swift manages to raise the issue of narrative employment and its relation to both fictionality and historiography at the same time as he begins his problematiza-tion of the notion of historical knowledge. Crick tells his students: 'When you asked, as all history classes ask, as all history classes should ask, what is the point of history? Why history? Why the past?' he feels he can reply: 'Isn't this seeking of reasons itself inevitably an historical process, since it must always work backwards from what came after to what came before?' (92).

The study of history – that 'cumbersome but precious bag of clues' – involves inquiry that attempts to 'uncover the mysteries of cause and effect' (Swift 1983: 92), but most of all it teaches us 'to accept the burden of our need to ask why' (93). That process of asking becomes more important than the details of historiography: 'the attempt to give an account, with incomplete knowledge, of actions themselves undertaken with incomplete knowledge' (94). As he later says, 'History: a lucky dip of meanings. Events clude meaning, but we look for meanings' (122) and we create them.

Tom Crick is in some ways an allegorical representation of the postmodern historian who might well have read, not just Collingwood, with his view of the historian as storyteller and detective, but also Hayden White, Dominick LaCapra, Raymond Williams, Michel Foucault, and Jean-François Lyotard. The debates about the nature and status of narrative representation in historical discourse coincide and are inextricably intertwined with the challenges offered by historiographic metafiction. Yet we have seen that postmodern fiction is typically denounced as dehistoricized, if not ahistorical, especially by Marxist critics. In the light of fiction like *Waterland* or *Midnight's Children* or *Ragtime* this position would seem difficult to maintain. Of course, the problematized histories of postmoderanism have little to do with the single totalizing History of Marxism, but they cannot be accused of neglecting or refusing engagement with the issues of historical representation and knowledge.

Among the consequences of the postmodern desire to denaturalize history is a new self-consciousness about the distinction between the brute *events* of the past and the historical *facts* we construct out of them. Facts are events to which we have given meaning. Different historical perspectives therefore derive different facts from the same events. Take Paul Veyne's example of Louis XIV's cold: even though the cold was a royal one, it was not a political event and therefore it would be of no interest to a history of politics, but it could be of considerable interest for a history of health and sanitation in France (Veyne 1971: 35). Postmodern fiction often thematizes this process of turning events into facts through the filtering and interpreting of archival documents. Roa Bastos's *I the Supreme* presents a narrator who admits to being a compiler of discourses and whose text is woven out of thousands of documents researched by the author. Of course, documents have always functioned in this way in historical fiction of any kind. But in historiographic metafiction the very process of turning events into facts through the interpretation of archival evidence is shown to be a process of turning the traces of the past (our only access to those events today) into historical representation. In so doing, such postmodern fiction underlines the realization that 'the past is not an "it" in the sense of an objectified entity that may either be neutrally represented in and for itself or

projectively reprocessed in terms of our own narrowly "presentist" interests'
(LaCapra 1987: 10). While these are the words of a historian writing about
historical representation, they also describe well the postmodern lessons about
fictionalized historical representation.

The issue of representation in both fiction and history has usually been dealt
with in epistemological terms, in terms of how we know the past. The past is not
something to be escaped, avoided, or controlled – as various forms of modernist
art suggest through their implicit view of the 'nightmare' of history. The past is
something with which we must come to terms and such a confrontation involves
an acknowledgement of limitation as well as power. We only have access to the
past today through its traces – its documents, the testimony of witnesses, and
other archival materials. In other words, we only have representations of the
past from which to construct our narratives or explanations. In a very real sense,
postmodernism reveals a desire to understand present culture as the product of
previous representations. The representation of history becomes the history of
representation. What this means is that postmodern art acknowledges and
accepts the challenge of tradition: the history of representation cannot be
escaped but it can be both exploited and commented on critically through
irony and parody [...]. The forms of representation used and abused by this
paradoxical postmodern strategy can vary – from the parodic and historic
architectural forms in Peter Ackroyd's *Hawksmoor* that mirror and structure
the novel's intricate narrative representation (itself parodic and historic) to the
strangely transcribed oral histories of the post-nuclear-holocaust world of
Russell Hoban's *Riddley Walker*, where the narratives of the past exist but
are, in the text's words, 'changet so much thru the years theyre all bits and blips
and all mixt up' (Hoban 1980: 20).

As this kind of novel makes clear, there are important parallels between the
processes of history-writing and fiction-writing and among the most problematic of these are their common assumptions about narrative and about the
nature of mimetic representation. The postmodern situation is that a 'truth is
being told, with "facts" to back it up, but a teller constructs that truth and
chooses those facts' (Foley 1986: 67). In fact, that teller – of story or history –
also constructs those very facts by giving a particular meaning to events. Facts
do not speak for themselves in either form of narrative: the tellers speak for
them, making these fragments of the past into a discursive whole. The 'true'
story of the historical gangster, Jack Diamond, that we read in William
Kennedy's *Legs* is shown to be a postmodern compromised one from its very
title: 'Legs' is the protagonist's public label, the name the newspapers give him.
In Jack's words: 'All the garbage they ever wrote about me is true to people who
don't know me' (Kennedy 1975: 245) – that is to say, to people like us. Brian
McHale calls this kind of work a 'revisionist historical novel' (McHale 1987:
90) because he feels it revises and reinterprets the official historical record and
transforms the conventions of historical fiction. I would rather put this
challenge in terms of a de-naturalizing of the conventions of representing the

past in narrative – historical and fictional – that is done in such a way that the politics of the act of representing are made manifest.

One of the clearest examples of this process self-consciously at work is (ironically) a novel by a Marxist critic who has accused postmodern fiction of being ahistorical: Terry Eagleton's *Saints and Scholars*. The introductory note to the novel asserts that the story is 'not entirely fantasy.' Some of the characters are real, as are some of the events, but most of the rest is invented. This becomes evident in the first chapter, a fictionalized historical account of the last hours of Irish revolutionary James Connolly before he is executed in Kilmainham gaol on 12 May 1916. But the account ends with a remark that engenders the rest of the fiction to follow:

> But history does not always get the facts in the most significant order, or arrange them in the most aesthetically pleasing pattern. Napoleon survived the battle of Waterloo, but it would have been symbolically appropriate if he had been killed there. Florence Nightingale lingered on until 1910, but this was an oversight on history's part.
>
> (Eagleton 1987: 10)

So the narrator arrests the bullets of the firing squad in mid-air in order to 'prise open a space in these close-packed events through which Jimmy may scamper, blast him out of the dreary continuum of history into a different place altogether' (10).

The plot action eventually comes to settle around a cottage on the west coast of Ireland where gather, thanks to irony and chance, a wondrous collection of historical and fictional excentrics: 'A Scottish Irishman [Connolly], an Irish Hungarian [Leopold Bloom], an anglicized Austrian [Ludwig Wittgenstein], and a Russian [Nicolai Bakhtin, Mikhail's brother]' (Eagleton 1987: 131–2). Though some are real and others fictional, all characters work to problematize the very distinction: Nicolai Bakhtin is said to be exceedingly extravagant but nevertheless historically real, and the others think he is 'an entirely fictional character, and the only real thing about him was that he knew it (30). When he later tells the fictive Leopold Bloom that the notion of individuality is a 'supreme fiction,' Joyce's character replies: 'You might be a bleeding fiction. . . . You look pretty much like one to me. I happen to be real. I think I'm just about the only real person here' (135).

The novel's metafictionality operates through many such parodic intertextual echoes. To offer another instance: Bakhtin asks Connolly about the success of the Easter Rising because he is eager to know whether he is 'in the presence of a world-historical figure' (Eagleton 1987: 94) – Lukács's term for the real personages found within historical fiction. The text's self-reflexivity also functions on the level of language and this is where Wittgenstein fits in. But what is also made clear is that Wittgenstein's famous linguistic theories are the direct product of his personal history, and particularly of his national history as a Viennese and his racial history as a Jew. When he (characteristically) tries to convince Connolly that the limits of his language are the limits of his world, the orator and man of action replies: 'What do you propose instead? That we should languish in the prison-house of language ...?' (114). The echo of the title of Jameson's book, *The Prison-House of Language*, is not just a clever move in some literary-critical recognition game: it invokes the entire context of Marxist criticism's (and Eagleton's own) stand against the reflexivity of language and narrative in the name of politics. This is important because *Saints and Scholars* attempts to reconcile these seemingly opposing positions – as indeed does much historiographic metafiction.

Eagleton's novel ends with another deferral of those firing-squad bullets heading for Connolly's body: 'When the bullets reached him he would disappear entirely into myth, his body nothing but a piece of language, the first cry of the new republic' (Eagleton 1987: 145). Of course, we *do* only know Connolly today primarily from pieces of language, the traces and texts of the past. Eagleton wants to do more than problematize this epistemological reality, though. He offers as well a new way of representing history – not derived from the official accounts of the victors, but taken from the unofficial, usually unrecorded perspective of the victims of history. The novel's densely detailed descriptions of the life of the poor and the working class in Dublin are accompanied by analyses of the causes of the misery: the economic and political maneuverings of imperialist Britain. The plot contrasts a Viennese Jew's desire to be 'hiding from history' (84) with an Irish revolutionary leader's view that to be free 'you have to remember' (128), tell your own story, and represent yourself: 'A colonial territory was a land where nothing happened, where you reacted to the narrative of your rulers rather than created one of your own' (104). Talk is all that is left to 'a race bereft of its history' (104) but talk – 'discourse' – is a kind of action: 'Discourse was something you did. ... The Irish had never fallen for the English myth that language was a second-hand reflection of reality' (105). Obviously, neither did the postmodern.

This is the kind of novel that works toward a critical return to history and politics *through* – not despite – metafictional self-consciousness and parodic intertextuality. This is the postmodernist paradox, a 'use and abuse' of history that Nietzsche, when considering that subject, never contemplated. In Roland Barthes's terms, we are shown that there is 'nothing natural anywhere, nothing but the historical' anywhere (Barthes 1977: 139) [...].

WORKS CITED

Barthes, Roland (1977) *Roland Barthes by Roland Barthes*. New York: Hill & Wang.
Berger, John (1972) *G.* New York: Pantheon.
Brooks, Peter (1984) *Reading for the Plot: Design and Intention in Narrative*. New York: Random House.
Carter, Angela (1974) *Fireworks: Nine Profane Pieces*. London: Quartet Books.
Davis, Lennard J. (1987) *Resisting Novels: Ideology and Fiction*. New York and London: Methuen.

de Lauretis, Teresa (1987) *Technologies of Gender: Essays on Theory, Film, and Fiction.* Bloomington, IN: Indiana University Press.

Eagleton, Terry (1987) *Saints and Scholars.* London and New York: Verso.

Foley, Barbara (1986) *Telling the Truth: The Theory and Practice of Documentary Fiction.* Ithaca, NY and London: Cornell University Press.

Heath, Stephen (1982) *The Sexual Fix.* London: Macmillan.

Hoban, Russell (1980) *Riddley Walker.* London: Picador.

Jameson, Fredric (1984) 'The Politics of Theory: Ideological Positions in the Postmodernism Debate', *New German Critique*, 33: 53–65.

Jameson, Fredric (1986) 'On Magic Realism in Film', *Critical Inquiry*, 12 (2): 301–25.

Kennedy, William (1975) *Legs.* Harmondsworth: Penguin.

LaCapra, Dominick (1985) *History and Criticism.* Ithaca, NY: Cornell University Press.

LaCapra, Dominick (1987) *History, Politics, and the Novel.* Ithaca, NY: Cornell University Press.

McHale, Brian (1987) *Postmodernist Fiction.* London: Routledge.

Roa Bastos, Augustos (1986) *I the Supreme.* New York: Aventura.

Siegle, Robert (1986) *The Politics of Reflexivity: Narrative and the Constitutive Poetics of Culture.* Baltimore, MD and London: Johns Hopkins University Press.

Stimpson, Catherine R. (1988) 'Nancy Reagan Wears a Hat: Feminism and its Cultural Consensus', *Critical Inquiry*, 14 (2): 223–43.

Süskind, Patrick (1986) *Perfume: The Story of Murderer.* New York: Knopf.

Swift, Graham (1983) *Waterland.* London: Heinemann.

Tickner, Lisa (1984) 'Sexuality and/in Representation: Five British Artists', in *Difference: On Representation and Sexuality* (Catalogue). New York: New Museum of Contemporary Art, pp. 19–30.

Veyne, Paul (1971) *Comment on écrit l'histoire.* Paris: Seuil.

White, Hayden (1987) *The Content of the Form: Narrative Discourse and Historical Representation.* Baltimore, MD and London: Johns Hopkins University Press.

24

'THE ETHICS OF ALTERITY'

Thomas Docherty

...I do beguile
The thing I am by seeming otherwise

(Shakespeare)

It is by now a commonplace that postmodern fiction calls into question most of
the formal elements of narrative that an earlier mode took for granted. The
notion of 'character' is no exception; like the political dissidents of some
totalitarian regimes, 'characters' have begun to disappear. But 'disappearance'
has itself become a crucial component of postmodern characterization, and is
not merely the result of an 'assault upon character' (Maddox 1978). In all
former understandings of the process of characterization in narrative, one
simple dichotomy prevails: appearance versus reality. Reading character has
always been a process whereby the reader learns to probe and bring to light the
murky depths of individual essences. He/she reads the visible presentation of
character as a mere 'index of implications'; the process of reading involves the
revelation of those implications, the 'depths' or idiosyncracies of particular,
individuated characters. It is thus that 'character', as an element distinguishable
from the narrative, is produced. Under the influence of existentialist philosophy, however, the notion of an essential reality in postmodern narrative has
consistently been called into question. The result, in characterological terms, is
twofold: firstly, 'appearance versus reality' as a paradigm is replaced by
'appearance versus disappearance'; secondly, character never *is*, but is always

From Thomas Docherty (1991) 'Postmodern Characterization: The Ethics of Alterity', in Edmund
J. Smyth (ed.), *Postmodernism and Contemporary Fiction*. London: Batsford.

about-to-be, endlessly deferred. This elusiveness of character, it is often suggested, makes postmodern narrative in some sense 'unreadable', and many readers find it tedious in its disappointment of their characterological expectations. Lennard J. Davis explores this view; but his response to it is not to suggest, as have many other recent critics (Bayley 1960; Harvey 1965; Swinden 1973), that the novel or narrative is somehow inherently bound up with an interest in character or 'human being' as an axiomatic given. On the contrary, Davis argues, like Zeraffa (1969), that the paradigmatic shift in postmodern characterization and the resultant 'unreadability' of narratives demonstrate that 'the very idea of character in the novel is itself ideological' (Davis 1987: 107), by which he means to suggest that character, and the interest in these 'essential individuals', is historically and culturally specific, the product of a particular ideological moment.

Two views on the history of narrative are in contention here. The first offers a historicist 'argument of periodicity' which charts various changes in the history of narrative. This argument goes that, once upon a time, there were novels with plots, ethnographic setting and recognizable individuals known as characters; this was at a moment when the individual was becoming interesting in and of him/herself for religious and political reasons (a dominance of individualistic Protestantism and a nascent capitalism). Then the Industrial Revolution took place and characters entered into a strife-ridden relation with an environment, being characters only to the extent that they circumvented the dehumanizing effects of the mechanics of plot and the determinacy of ethnographic setting (Taine 1873–1908). At a yet later moment, characters became archetypal models, as authors 'looked within', in Woolf's celebrated phrase (Woolf 1929: 189), to describe the life of the human psyche in itself and in general. Finally, in the postmodern period, they disappear altogether and narratives become boring. This is a neat history, but wrong in its theoretical orientation, for it assumes that there was indeed a time when individuals did exist as some essence which was not always already an ideological construction. A more radical view, as Jameson suggests, is

> what one might call the poststructuralist position ... not only is the bourgeois individual subject a thing of the past, it is also a myth; it *never* really existed in the first place; there have never been autonomous subjects of that type. Rather, this construct is merely a philosophical and cultural mystification which sought to persuade people that they 'had' individual subjects and possessed this unique personal identity. (Jameson 1983)

In a West, at least, which is witnessing the resurgence of a particular earlier moment of capitalist development and its concomitant 'values', there is an obvious ideological reason for stimulating this nostalgic desire for an earlier historical moment when 'we were all individuals', and for an earlier mode of narrative which seemingly celebrated that individuality. But this latter and more radical view allows us to suggest that postmodern narrative and the types of characterization that proceed in it simply 'lay bare' the techniques and problems of character which have in fact *always* existed in narrative. Postmodern narrative, in its demystifying revelation of the technical elements of fictional characterization, allows for a radical rereading of the history of narrative, calling into question the supposed certainties of the individuated essences of characters in an earlier fiction dominated by the 'appearance versus reality' paradigm.

1 THE EVASION OF HISTORY: CHARACTER, EMPIRE, IDENTITY

Prose narrative consolidates in a specific form known as the 'novel' in the eighteenth century, an age which represented itself as one of Reason and Enlightenment, when an ideology of liberalism stressed the importance of individualism (though not of specific individuals) in the social formation. Conventionally, the novel is thought to respond to this by recognizing the importance of the individual, and hence focusing on specific individual characters. But these characters are also the site of the dramatization of 'enlightenment'; as such, they become the models of a particular manifestation of what the age and ideology considers as 'reasonable'. The novel, typically, organizes itself around a plot in which an individual character stands at a tangent to his/her society (and is thus 'interesting' or extra-ordinary), and proceeds to the reconciliation of society and individual in a movement which identifies the interests of both and which reveals those interests to be reasonable and now self-evident, because brought to light.

While operating as a critique of a social formation, the novel orientates the reader through the *point de repère* of a recognizable character; and, given the necessity of having this character stand out, it in turn usually becomes the main centre of interest. The character, as our way into the hypothesized world of the fiction, becomes its main message too. It would clearly be fallacious to suggest that 'character' did not appear in writing prior to this historical moment; however, it was only during the Enlightenment that it came to have this central, organizing dominance as the model for 'individuality' in a social formation, as a recognizable and exemplary 'type'.

This age is also, crucially, the age which saw the invention of a specific category of primary relevance to character in the novel, for it was during this century that the concept of 'human nature' was invented. Foucault has argued that 'man is only a recent invention, a figure not yet two centuries old, a new wrinkle in our knowledge [who] will disappear again as soon as that knowledge has discovered a new form' (Foucault 1974: xxiii). The delineaments of this new form are now being traced in postmodern modes of narrative and characterization.

The construction of 'human nature' in the eighteenth century went hand in hand with the supervention of antiquity: it represented the 'ancients' winning the 'battle of the books' and the battle of competing philosophies against the 'moderns', and was thus a major defeat of a 'modernity'. The ancient tradition, in the form of a continuity hypothesized from antiquity, suggested that the

eighteenth-century state of affairs and state of understanding had
Len the case. To this extent, it was supposed to be *natural*, non-secular
storical. The concept of Enlightenment, that very metaphor, enacts the
ich is axiomatic to the novel and its characters, for it claims simply to
sible a latent nature that was always there. The corollary of this, of
course, is that there *is* an essential nature which is located in the human being
which makes him/her able to be in conformity with the wider 'natural'
environment, or social formation. 'Man', according to this argument, is always
and everywhere the same, at the most fundamental of levels; 'man' has simply to
be brought from his darkness into enlightenment. If we transpose these
metaphors of light and dark, we arrive at a 'white mythology': 'the white
man takes his own mythology, Indo-European mythology, his own *logos*, that
is, the *mythos* of his idiom, for the universal form of that he must still wish to
call Reason' (Derrida 1982: 213). If humanity is always and everywhere the
same, traditional and non-secular rather than geographically and historically
culture-specific, a justification is provided for the excesses of imperialism: in
principle, the oppressed is being 'enlightened', granted a position in the social
formation of the colonialist, who of course assumes his own 'enlightenment', an
enlightenment supposedly guaranteed by a rationalist epistemology and a
traditionalist antiquarianism. Further, the coining of 'human nature' also
allows for the construction of a cultural form whose task it is to dramatize
the bringing to light of this mysterious truth of human being. In prose narrative,
character accordingly becomes understood theoretically as an allegorical type:
not only 'individual' but also, as in the tradition of bourgeois democracy,
'representative' (Watt 1957; Josipovici 1971).

It is here, of course, that many critics have identified a radical potential in the
form of the novel (Swingewood 1975; Orwell 1962; Williams 1970; Eagleton
1976; Zeraffa 1969), for it seems to be inherent to the novel that a certain
democratic importance is afforded the individual within a dominant social
formation. But another way of looking at this suggests that the novel thus
understood, as a bourgeois liberal-democratic form, is a primary locus of
bourgeois values and of the regularization, legitimation, even normalization
of certain bougeois codes, together with the assimilation of other, contrary
codes and practices which remain silenced or which are shown to be 'unreasonable' by the novel and its characters.

Thus, the notion of character as locus of the revelation of an essential human
nature provides a form which, while seeming to grant some measure of
independence and a democratic equality to the individual, actually serves to
proffer a normative role for the individual in a specific social formation: in
short, the novel's characters enact certain practices as socially *normative*.
Thus, for example, Defoe's Robinson Crusoe can 'express' his innermost self in
his construction of life on his island; but no matter how this is done in its
detail, the text works to legitimize the practices of the same economic
individualism which bolsters the imperialist and colonialist expansion of trade

routes (Watt 1957: 69ff). *Moll Flanders*, similarly, may perform a critique of the social codes which lead to her criminality; but the text and its central character simply reiterate the legitimization of the notion of private property. To take a later example, Jane Austen's novels, while certainly granting a huge central importance to individual women characters as the main centre of attention and interest, simply operate to legitimize the bourgeois marriage and family which marginalized women in the first place.

If the novel is a conservative art-form, then it is so primarily because of the way in which its characters have been theorized and understood, as representative examples of human nature. Reading character in this way involves a simple *anagnorisis*: characterization enacts a scene of recognition in which the reader discovers, essentially, the 'truth' of him/herself reflected in the character, or, as we say, 'identifies' with the character (Davis 1987: 124ff). The reader 'discovers' a nature or essence of character which was always already known by that reader, for he/she shares in its 'human nature'. Thus, such a theoretical notion of the 'truth of identity', in the revelation of an essential human nature through characters in narrative, circumvents cultural specificity and historical difference: since human nature is, by definition, always and everywhere the same, and since 'most great novels exist to reveal and explore character' (Harvey 1965: 23), then an eighteenth-century fiction seems to exist to reveal and explore fundamentally the same thing as a late twentieth-century fiction.

Prior theoretical understanding of character as locus of an essential identity has worked to legitimize a particular, non-secular understanding of human being, of what it is to be a human in a specific social formation. With an eighteenth-century optimism, this understanding assumes that, in the relations between individuals and the social formation which they construct and which constructs them, 'whatever IS, is 'RIGHT'' (Pope 1975: 515), or at least that to change things would be 'unreasonable', 'unenlightened', or simply criminally 'illegitimate'. But if character is anything in narrative, it is a locus of temporal difference. While it could be argued that portraiture or photography is, in its essentials, an art of simultaneity, its product to be perceived 'at once' and in space, it is certainly the case that narrative is sequential, that its constituent elements, including characterization, come as a piecemeal process and in a fragmentary mode. Postmodern narrative makes this abundantly clear, for it insists on offering the merest fragments of character, without ever allowing for a fully coherent construction of an identifiable whole; it is, as it were, like a series of torn photographs, a photo-montage; and frequently, of course, in its narcissistic self-consciousness (Hutcheon 1980), it offers fragmentary portraits of the artist or writer. Postmodern narrative stresses the 'difference' from which an 'identity' is always recuperated or salvaged in prior theorizations of the process of characterization; that earlier notion is concerned with establishing and identifying a finished *product*, the character as named and identified individual; this postmodern mode establishes the differences which are revealed as the 'characterization' progresses as *process*, without ever managing to establish a final product.

Some modernist narratives take this 'heterogeneity' of character, the notion of character as process, into account. While a writer such as Lawrence thought that he was mining a seam of essential reality in character (Lawrence 1958: 75) Woolf was examining, often in a wilfully incoherent mode, the ambiguities offered by characters who never actually acted but were always 'between the acts'. She was interested in characterization as a process whereby the supposed essence of character always escaped, where characters were somehow never fully there, like the ghostly Mrs Ramsay in *To the Lighthouse* or the character, such as it is, of Percival in *The Waves*. Woolf's novels are largely about the process whereby the relations between characters always escape reification; they are largely about the *failure* to write a 'character' as the bearer of some essential truth of human nature, and an interest in character is replaced by an examination of the mobile and fluid inter-relations among shadowy half-articulated figures. Similar arguments could be advanced concerning, for instance, Mann's delineation of the relations between Aschenbach and Tadzio in *Death in Venice* (1912); another crucial example would be Proust's *A la recherche du temps perdu* (1913–27) in which, despite the autobiographical impctus, the text tells us little of the 'essence' of Marcel, replacing that by a series of shifting relations with Swann, Albertine, Saint-Loup and so on. In the later example, the reader reaches, at the 'close' of the novel, a hypothetical under-standing of Marcel; but, as the novel ends at the point where Marcel becomes a writer and can now write the text which has just been read, the reading exercise has, logically, to be repeated, but at a different level of understanding: the 'identity' which the reader proposes for Marcel at the close of the novel is itself to undergo a differential epistemological shift in a reiteration of the reading of the character.

Even in these modernist experiments, however, it is to be stressed that character is still organized around the basic notion of anagnorisis or re-cognizability: the individual characters can, at some level, be 'known', cognized and recognized. Theorists of character have always made a distinction between characters in novels and persons in a 'life' which is supposed to be constitutively different from textual semiotics. This distinction, fundamentally, hinges on the opposition between ontology and epistemology. As Davis puts it, in a formulation which echoes Bayley:

> Personality is what living beings have. Our personalities may not be coherent; they may not be readily understood by us; they may be mis-interpreted or not even accessible to others; but they are what we refer to when we refer to ourselves. 'Character' on the other hand is what people in novels have. They are characters with characteristics. (Davis 1987: 111)

Personality is purposeless and complex; character is purposeful and simple, a small set of definable and essentially *knowable* traits. Personalities have a degree of existential contingency, lacking in characters who merely enact functions in organized plots and delimited locations. Where personality is an ontological category, character is an epistemological one. If character has been most frequently construed as the medium through which we gain access to the world of the social formation being elaborated in a text, then it is important that it be epistemologically comprehensible. If this medium becomes as seemingly contingent as personalities in the different ontological level of 'real life' or history, if it becomes inconsistent or fundamentally shadowy and unknowable, unrecognizable, then there enters a confusion between categories. What has been assumed by a reader to be an epistemological category begins to operate in the manner of an ontological one: the 'fictionality' of the text and its characters is called into question and there arises a confusion about the relative ontological status of characters, on the one hand, and readers or authors, on the other. It is this confusion that we see most frequently entertained in postmodern narrative.

The confusion can take either of two orientations. On the one hand, it can operate in a conservative mode, whereby 'characters' are 'raised' to the level of personalities, without the text ever casting any doubts upon that ontological category itself. This would be the case, for instance, in a text such as *Daniel Martin* by John Fowles (1977), where Fowles introduces what Hamon calls *personnages-referentiels* (Hamon 1977: 122–3) – that is, proper names from the realm of history – and where these names or *personnages* are introduced at the same level as the other fictive 'characters' in the text. In *Daniel Martin*, the critic Kenneth Tynan appears as a 'character', with the result of confusion or eradicating the ontological distinction between such a 'personality' and the 'characters' of, say, Daniel or Jenny in that text. A similar working of the same manoeuvre is to be found in cases where a character, introduced in one text, reappears, perhaps in a minor role, in another. This happens, for example, in the novels of Alison Lurie where 'Leonard Zimmern' figures in a central role in *The War Between The Tates* (1974) and reappears in a more peripheral role in *Foreign Affairs* (1985). This 'character' appears to transcend the limitations of a role in one plot, and the illusion is created that what seemed to operate at the epistemological level of character now begins to operate as if it were at the ontological level of personality.

On the other hand, the confusion of character and personality can take a more radical dimension, whereby the result is the calling into question of the ontological status of author and reader. In this case, personality becomes transfigured as nothing more or less than a nexus of semiotic signification: persons in history become equated with characters as the effects of textuality, and become signifiers devoid of a signified. This view is elaborated by Federman when he argues that:

> the people of fiction, the fictitious beings, will also no longer be well-made characters who carry with them a fixed identity, a stable set of social and psychological attributes – a name, a situation, a profession, a condition,

etc. The creatures of the new fiction will be as changeable, as illusory, as nameless, as unnamable, as fraudulent, as unpredictable as the discourse that makes them. This does not mean, however, that they will be mere puppets. On the contrary their being will be more genuine, more complex, more true-to-life in fact, because they will not appear to be simply what they are; they will be what they are: word-beings . . . That creature will be, in a sense, present to his own making, present to his own absence.

(Federman 1975: 12–13)

When characters become as contingent as personalities in this way, the result is that they 'participate in the fiction only as a grammatical being' (Federman 1975: 13), and become aware of their purely linguistic or textual status, precisely to the extent that they are incoherent, self-contradictory, contingent as personality. The category of personality, then, is radically questioned, and the validity of its claims to an ontological status doubted. The most obvious examples of this would be texts such as Sorrentino's *Mulligan Stew* (1981), the 'magic realism' of Márquez's *Autumn of the Patriarch* (1978), or Ronald Sukenick's *98.6* (1975) where 'Ron' operates firstly, as a seemingly coherent medium on the fiction, and then proceeds to become inconsistent, incoherent and the merest empty signifier whose 'meaning' constantly varies in a thoroughly contingent manner. In cases such as this, what was taken as an ontological category becomes an epistemological problem.

The problem raised by this category confusion in postmodern characterization can be properly articulated in Heideggerian terms as a question of 'fundamental ontology and the search for the human place'. That mode of understanding character (the 'pre-modernist' mode, so to speak) is almost entirely epistemological. It renders 'other people' fundamentally knowable, offering the reader the illusion of having a position from which his/her own identity is guaranteed through its distinction from a basically knowable and recognizable 'otherness' or alterity. The epistemological steadiness or predictability of 'character' in this older mode grants the reader a position of security in his/her own identity, an identity which is of a different ontological status from that of the character and which transcends that lower status. In short, it offers the illusion of a control over the characters, whereby the reader can place or locate them in the plot not only in relation to each other, but also in relation to the reader's own position, a position which, in transcending the hypothetical world of the characters, offers the illusion of omniscience and its corollary, omnipotence. This situation is precisely akin to a mode of imperialist control of the Other in which, by pretending to 'know' the Other fully and comprehensibly, a Self can assure itself of its own truths and status. To this extent, 'reasonable' characters in the paradigmatic plot of enlightenment share that eighteenth-century predilection for the imperialist or colonialist control not only of other places, but also of other 'positions' (cf. Davis 1987: 52ff); in novelistic terms, this translates into control of other 'points of view' or, in short, of other characters. It is this imperialism of reading character which the more radical problematization of the ontological status of the reader, such as we have it in postmodern characterization, begins to challenge. It does so by problematizing the 'human place', by converting 'position' into 'disposition' or, to put this in poststructuralist terms, by displacing the reader and deconstructing the relation which obtains between reader and character.

[…]

In narratological terms, character is nothing other than the potential for story, for the releasing of temporality and sequence, or, in short, for narrative itself. This is outlined by Todorov in his suggestion that character be understood as 'homme-récit' (Todorov 1971: 81–2). *Vivre*, then, is *raconter*; or, as Foucault would have it, social formations and the very concept of identity are formed through the interplay of discourses. But the postmodern turning of this involves the multiplication of identities and the consequent fragmentation of the phenomenological subject-position which is afforded the reader in a text such as *La Jalousie* and its modernist precursors. Instead of offering the reading subject a specific or identifiable single ontological place, a 'clearing' in which a supposedly non-temporal identity can be established, postmodern narrative not only renders the reader of the status of textual discourse, making him/her the merest effect of the interplay of linguistic discourses, it also 'dis-positions' the reader, produces a *number* of conflicting positions from which the narrative is to be read.

The most basic manner in which this attack on the singularity of the human's 'place' is carried out is through the elaboration of a multiplicity of conflicting narratives, or 'hommes-récits'. In Robbe-Grillet's *Dans le labyrinthe*, for instance, each mention of the 'character' of the soldier operates as the release for another narrative beginning, often a narrative which contradicts the one which was in sequence before it. If the reader is using this character in a mode similar to the *je-néant* in *La Jalousie*, then the effect is to replace the elaboration of a particular, specifiable place for the reading subject with a non-specific, non-identifiable sequence of changing positions, or dispositions. This is the situation described by Borges in his story: 'The Garden of Forking Paths'. Here, Stephen Albert ponders Ts'ui Pên's labyrinthine manuscripts. He imagines the way in which Ts'ui Pên might have realized the task of writing an infinite, unending book, and can come up with nothing better than the circular text (such as Proust's *A la recherche*, Gide's *Les Faux-monnayeurs* and Joyce's *Finnegans Wake*), until he lingers on a particular sentence in the manuscript:

> I lingered, naturally, on the sentence: *I leave to the various futures (not to all) my garden of forking paths*. Almost instantly, I understood: 'the garden of forking paths' was the chaotic novel; the phrase 'the various futures (not to all)' suggested to me the forking in time, not in space. A broad rereading of the work confirmed the theory. In all fictional works,

each time a man is confronted with several alternatives, he chooses one and eliminates the others; in the fiction of Ts'ui Pên, he chooses – simultaneously – all of them. *He creates*, in this way, diverse futures, diverse times which themselves also proliferate and fork. Here, then, is the explanation of the novel's contradictions. Fang, let us say, has a secret; a stranger calls at his door; Fang resolves to kill him. Naturally, there are several possible outcomes: Fang can kill the intruder, the intruder can kill Fang, they both can escape, they both can die, and so forth. In the work of Ts'ui Pên, all possible outcomes occur; each one is the point of departure for other forkings. (Borges, *Labyrinths* 1978: 51)

Some postmodern narratives are like this hypothetical fiction. While modernist and earlier modes of narrative and characterization offer the reader a set of spatial relations (a plot) in and through which he/she finds a specific identity or place from which to know the fiction and its characters, postmodern narrative offers a proliferation of such positions, denying priority to any of them. This is the case in the heavily overplotted fictions of Pynchon, where the introduction – or eruption – of a character's name is the signal for another plot or for a further disorienting turn in an already complex baroque intrigue, as in Pynchon's own self-parody, 'The Courier's Tragedy', in the midst of *The Crying of Lot 49* (1966).

The temporal disposition or dislocation of the reading subject described here is itself dramatized as the material of Calvino's *If on a Winter's Night a Traveller* (1979), where because of a series of errors at the binder's, various hypothesized 'novels' are interleaved with each other. The position or disposition (*ethos*) of 'the Reader' is itself the subject of the narrative, for he/she has constantly to shift his/her position and expectations, as he/she shifts from one text to another. The reader, then, becomes multiple, as Calvino introduces 'other' readers of the various novels and provides dialogue and debate among them all. This multiplication of the reader is an analogue of what happens to characterization in postmodern narrative generally. All that Calvino has done is to take the initial sentence of a hypothetical text, split it up into its various component phrases, and propose each such phrase as the beginning of a new narrative, a narrative which is released by the phrase and by its introduction if not of a character, then at least of a position from which the text is understood and read. This fragmentation of a narrative, its multiplication into a series of seemingly unrelated and disconcertingly different narratives, generates at the same time a multiplicity of positions for the reading subject; but each such position is now strictly different from those that go before and after. 'The Reader', as a supposedly single, essential identity, disappears, and is replaced by a series of 'dispositions', shifts of position from which the text can be understood. The reader, then, is, as it were, released into the temporality of narrative, shifting position at every instant of reading Calvino's text. As Jip 'n' Zab suggest at the start of Brooke-Rose's *Xorandor* (1987), 'One, it's important to be two'

(Brooke-Rose 1987: 7), and in this novel the 'character' of Xor7 (itself a pun on 'Exocet') also becomes multiple, hovering uncertainly between computer and Lady Macbeth whose lines it picks up and plays back.

While 'pre-modern' characterization (which also includes modernist modes) is concerned with the production of identity, postmodern narrative fractūres such a homogeneity in both the 'characters' and the reading subject. Postmodern narrative seeks to circumvent the phenomenological elaboration of a definable spatial relation obtaining between a transcendent ontological reading subject and an equally fixed and non-historical object of that reader's perception, the 'character'. Earlier modes of characterization are related to the imperialist and colonialist impetus of the appropriation of space, and the grounds on which a position of intentional authority is afforded an imperial Self through its 'knowledge' of and understanding of an oppressed characterological or epistemological Other. Postmodern characterization disturbs this position by the interjection of a temporal component in the process of reading character, replacing the notion of 'position' with that of the poststructuralist displacement or 'disposition'. In short, postmodern characterization seeks to return the dimension of history which earlier modes of characterization, or of the theoretical understanding of character as 'identity' or 'essence', deny.

That denial of history in earlier theorizations of character is accompanied by a denial of politics. The bias of the novel, since its moment of inception, towards biography is obvious. The central characters of such fiction are interesting for criticism precisely to the extent that they are the locus of an anagnorisis, some moment of recognition or of turning and troping of the character. This is what passes for the supposedly temporal development of character in earlier modes of reading character. Such anagnorisis does not offer any fundamental change or 'disposition' in the reading of character; but even if it did (as earlier theory suggests), then it has the vital corollary of identifying change in the novel as something which always happens at the level of the individual rather than in the wider socio-political formation itself. Davis writes:

> Ideologically speaking ... character gives readers faith that personality is, first, understandable, and second, capable of rational change. As part of the general ideology of middle-class individualism, the idea that the subject might be formed from social forces and that change might have to come about through social change is by and large absent from novels. Change is always seen as effected by the individual. (Davis 1987: 119)

This reduction of politics to morality is entirely in keeping with a liberalism which operates precisely on the suppression of history (replacing this with eternal, immanent 'truths' of human nature) and the elimination of politics (replaced with 'values'). Postmodern characterization offers a challenge to this, with implications that go far beyond the realm of mere aesthetic predilections.

2 A DIFFERENT ECONOMY

Postmodern characterization advances an attack on the notion of identity, or of an essential Selfhood which is not traduced by a temporal dimension which threatens that Self with heterogeneity. In short, it leads to the elaboration of 'characters' (if they can still be called such, given their confusing ontological status) whose existence (rather than essence) is characterized by *difference* (rather than identity). Postmodern figures are always differing, not just from other characters, but also from their putative 'selves'. Whereas earlier characters were present-to-themselves, or, to put this in existentialist terms, finally reduced to the status of an essential selfhood and thus reified as *en-soi*, postmodern characters always dramatize their own 'absence' from themselves.

Postmodern characters most typically fall into incoherence: character-traits are not repeated, but contradicted; proper names are used, if at all, inconsistently; signposts implying specific gender are confused; a seemingly animate character mutates into an inanimate object, and so on. At every stage in the representation of character, the finality of the character, a determinate identity for the character, is deferred as the proliferation of information about the character leads into irrationality or incoherence and self-contradiction. There is never a final point at which the character can be reduced to the status of an epistemologically accessible essential quality or list of qualities and 'properties'. What is at stake in this is the entire notion of 'representation'. As in most art-forms and cultural practices, the postmodern impetus is almost synonymous with the questioning of representation (for example, Lyotard, 1984).

Following in the wake of an existentialist philosophical tradition, many postmodern characterizations seem to argue that there is always a discrepancy between the character who acts and the character who watches him/herself acting. There is, as it were, a temporal distance between agency and self-consciousness regarding that agency, a fine example of which is Barth's fiction, 'Menelaiad' (Barth 1969). This text enacts the continual deferral of coincidence between the narrating subject and the subject narrated, even though these are ostensibly identical, 'Menelaus'; as a result, 'Menelaus', paradoxically, is 'identified' or, better, characterized as that which is always differing from himself. There is a series of confusions about the ontological presence of the character, such that at any moment in the text when it seems that 'Menelaus' *is* somewhat, immediately a difference is produced and an alternative or new narrative is released.

The voice of Menelaus (for that is all there is in this tale) begins to relate the story of his life to Telemachus, Peisistratus and a hypothesized listener (actually, of course, the reader). During the tale, he tells of meeting Helen, who demanded the tale of his life; within this tale, now on a different level and in a different temporal frame, he met Proteus, who asked for the tale of his life, and so on. There are, then, a number of 'hommes-récits' identified in the figure of Menelaus; but this fiction begins precisely to unravel or untangle that identity, to release all the different figures, masquerading under the identical proper name which supposedly offers them a non-temporal, non-historical identity, and produces a multi-layered narrative. In characterological terms, the result is that the consciousness that identifies itself as 'Menelaus' is always out of step or non-identical with the voice of Menelaus and with the actions which Menelaus supposedly performed. The very telling of the tale of his life, an act which is supposed to proffer and guarantee identity, in fact produces this radical *décalage* or self-difference as the constituent of 'Menelaus's being. Menelaus is, as it were, never fully present to himself; every time he identifies himself, he has to do so by adverting to a different Menelaus, one who exists in a different temporal and narrative frame and one who exists, therefore, at a different ontological level from the narrating consciousness. Worse than this, within one of the tales Menelaus indicates his fully temporal predicament. He changes places and times every time he tries to fix or identify himself, as is fully seen in his encounter with Proteus. Menelaus is, if anything, the character as Heideggerian *Dasein*; the 'being' of Menelaus, such as it is, is endlessly deferred, endlessly seeming otherwise and reiterating itself in a different figuration. Its identity is characterized by this potentially endless differing from itself, the perpetual deferring of an essential Selfhood: 'the thing I am' is replaced or, indeed, constituted, by a 'seeming otherwise'. The character is constantly disappearing from its own surface, constantly escaping the parameters which the text implies for its figuration: in short, the character is constantly 'being there', constantly evading the fixity of a definite or identifiable and single 'place' for itself. To this extent, it becomes the merest series of instantiations of subjectivity, rather than a characterological selfhood; it has no place, but a series of *dis*positions, as the parameters of its figuration shift and metamorphose in temporal sequence.

There is a difficulty with the very notion of 'representation' of a character whose condition is that it is never present to itself in the first place but always 'ec-statically' escaping the constraints of self-presence (Docherty 1983). But it is precisely here that the politics of a 'different economy', or an economy of difference, can enter in a consideration of postmodern characterization.

[...]

[...] Postmodern narrative enacts the character as *Dasein*, the character who constantly escapes the fixity of identity by existing in the temporal predicament whereby the assumed or desired totality of a real Self is endlessly 'dispositioned', always a 'being *there*', as opposed to a being here, a being present to itself. This is not so much a character, more a series of 'appearances' which do not act as the cover for a 'deeper' reality, for it is that very notion of a material or essential reality which postmodern characterization denies. At best, the progression of a postmodern narrative cannot move from appearance to the enlightenment of a reality, but only from appearance to disappearance to *different* appearance and so on. In such characterization, the idea of a reciprocity, whereby the character is seen as a representative of the self of the historical reader, becomes impossible, since it is precisely this notion of a totalized real and essential selfhood which the texts deny. The simplicity of a seemingly 'democratic' mode of characterization, based upon a liberal individualism and the category of 'representation', is called into question. Postmodern narrative reveals that it is not simply the case that earlier modes of reading fiction reduce the political to the moral; more importantly, in their delineation of social and political formations through the medium of 'representative' characters, they confuse a political category of representation with an aesthetic mode of mimesis. Criticism has always prioritized this aesthetic component, in its endless discussion of 'well-rounded' or 'vividly realised' or 'fully depicted' characters in fiction; in short, there has been a dangerous 'aestheticisation of politics' (Benjamin 1973).

But postmodern narrative does not easily reverse this orientation. Instead, it introduces, through its mode of characterization, the category of *ethics*. The reader of postmodern narrative, as allegorized in Calvino's *If on a Winter's Night a Traveller*, is fully implicated in the proliferation of narratives. However, unlike the reader of earlier fiction, he/she is denied the possibility of producing a totalized self for the characters being processed in the reading; the totality of a supposedly enlightened truth or real essence of character is denied as a result of the proliferation of narratives which contradict such a totality. This also means that postmodern narrative attacks the possibility of the reader him/herself becoming a fully enlightened and imperialist subject with full epistemological control over the fiction and its endlessly different or altered characters. In order to read postmodern narrative at all, the reader must give up such a singular position, for he/she will be endlessly 'disposed', displaced, in figuring a number of different narratives and different characters. He/she has to be seduced from one position into many positions, has to give up a quasi-authorial position of a supposed access to the singular truth of character and move into a series of *dispositions* in trying to deal with the proliferating narratives. The reader is denied access to a totalizing narrative which will allow him/her to define and identify him/herself against the stable 'other' of a mysterious character. Rather, the reader replaces such a totalized and enlightened narrative, proposing access to a singular, monotheistic Truth, with the multiplicity of different local narratives, having no claims on truth in any absolute sense at all. The reader becomes nothing more or less than an excuse for the proliferation of further narratives, further dispositions. The reader becomes as imbricated in a temporal or historical predicament as the characters in postmodern narrative, and, like those characters, has no access to a totalized narrative of a true or essential Selfhood according to which he/she orients his/her present being. The reader's 'temporality' or historical condition in the act of reading postmodern characterization is itself characterized by the notion of disposition, of being seduced or disposed from one position to another in the construction and deconstruction of a series of narratives. In this, there is no final or overall, single position which would allow for a systematic ranging of the narratives; there is only an economy which, in its basic orientation to heterogeneity, endlessly produces more and more different narratives. Where the economy of identity produces a single totalized narrative, that of the Self, it also arrests the temporality of narrative and the notion of temporal change which is axiomatic to narrative; postmodern characterization keeps the narrative going.

In so doing, postmodern narrative lures a reader into 'disposition', a translation of the Greek word *ethos*. To this extent, the category of the ethical is introduced; and through this, which involves the reader in the search for 'the good' (as opposed to subscription to a monotheistic Truth), the political does in fact return. As MacIntyre (1967: 129) indicates, there is a distinction between the ethical and the political, but it cannot be drawn too sharply. Postmodern narrative of characterization, in attacking not only the notion of a Self but also the dichotomy on which it is based (interior 'reality' versus external 'appearance'), eradicates the distinction between the ethical and the political. To read postmodern characterization is to reintroduce the possibility of politics, and importantly of a genuinely historical political change, into the act of reading; and this reintroduction is generated from the category of the ethical, the disposition of the reading subject.

3 SEEMING OTHERWISE

What is at stake in postmodern characterization is, firstly, the confusion of the ontological status of the character with that of the reader; secondly, the decentring of that reader's consciousness, such that he/she is, like the character, endlessly displaced and 'differing'; and thirdly, the political and ethical implication of this 'seeming otherwise', shifting from appearance to different appearance in the disappearance of a totalized Selfhood. The reading subject in postmodern characterization is, thus, exactly like Kristeva's notion of the 'subject-in-process', a subject whose very subjectivity is itself endlessly deferred, endlessly differing. The explicit political dimension of reading postmodern characterization is now clear: it involves a marginalization of the reader from a centralized or totalized narrative of Selfhood, thus rendering the reading subject-in-process as the figure of the *dissident*. Among her types of dissident, Kristeva locates both the experimental writer, working with the 'diaspora of those languages that pluralize meaning and cross all national and linguistic barriers', and, crucially, *women*: 'And sexual difference, women: isn't that another form of dissidence?' (Kristeva 1986: 299, 296) What these two groups share is the impetus towards marginalization and indefinition; they are in a condition of 'exile' from a centred identity of meaning and its claims to a totalized law or truth. Exile is itself a form of dissidence, since it involves the marginalization or decentring of the Self from all positions of totalized or systematic law (such as imperialist nation, patriarchal family, monotheistic language), and 'if meaning exists in the state of exile, it nevertheless finds no incarnation, and is ceaselessly produced and destroyed in geographical or discursive transformations' (Kristeva 1986: 298).

In experimental writing, the major source of such exile and its consequential political disposition towards dissidence is in the questioning of the system of language itself (though this is not easily distinguished from the concerns of empire, family and so on). Postmodern characterization, construed as a writing in and from exile, serves to construct the possibility, perhaps for the first time, of elaborating the paradigmatic reader of these new novels as feminized. Woman, as 'that which cannot be represented, that which is not spoken, that which remains outside naming and ideologies' (Kristeva 1986: 163), is always 'dispositioned' towards otherness, alterity. To read postmodern characterization is to begin to construct the ethics of alterity, to discover what it means to speak always from the political disposition of the Other.

WORKS CITED

Barth, John (1969) *Lost in the Funhouse*. London.
Bayley, John (1960) *The Characters of Love*. London.
Benjamin, Walter (1973) *Illuminations*. London.
Borges, Jorge Luis (1978) *Labyrinths*. London.
Brooke-Rose, Christine (1987) *Xorandor*. London.
Davis, Lennard J. (1987) *Resisting Novels: Ideology and Fiction*. New York and London.
Derrida, Jacques (1982) *Margins of Philosophy*. Brighton.
Docherty, Thomas (1983) *Reading (Absent) Character*. Oxford.
Eagleton, Terry (1976) *Criticism and Ideology*. London.
Federman, Raymond (ed.) (1975) *Surfiction*. Chicago.
Foucault, Michel (1974) *The Order of Things*. London.
Hamon, Philippe (1977) 'Pour un statut sémiologique du personnage', in Roland Barthes (ed.), *Poétique du récit*. Paris.
Harvey, W. J. (1965) *Character and the Novel*. London.
Hutcheon, Linda (1980) *Narcissistic Narrative: The Metafictional Paradox*. London.
Jameson, Fredric (1983) 'Postmodernism and Consumer Society', in Hal Foster (ed.), *Postmodern Culture*. London.
Josipovici, Gabriel (1971) *The World and the Book*. London.
Kristeva, Julia (1986) *The Kristeva Reader*, ed. Toril Moi. London.
Lawrence, D. H. (1958) *Selected Letters*, ed. D. Trilling. New York.
Lyotard, Jean-François (1984) *The Postmodern Condition: A Report on Knowledge*. Minneapolis, MN.
MacIntyre, Alastair (1967) *A Short History of Ethics*. London.
Maddox, James H. Jnr (1978) *Joyce's* Ulysses *and the Assault upon Character*. New Brunswick, NJ.
Orwell, George (1962) *Inside the Whale*. London.
Pope, Alexander (1975) *Poems*, ed. J. Butt. London.
Swinden, Patrick (1973) *Unofficial Selves*. London: Macmillan.
Swingewood, Alan (1975) *The Novel and Revolution*. London.
Taine, Hyppolyte (1873–1908) *History of English Literature*, 4 vols. Edinburgh.
Todorov, Tzvetan (1971) *Poétique de la prose*. Paris.
Watt, Ian (1957) *The Rise of the Novel*. London.
Williams, Raymond (1970) *The English Novel From Dickens to Lawrence*. London.
Woolf, Virginia (1929) *The Common Reader* (Second Series). London.
Zerrafa, M. (1969) *V*. London.

25

FROM *DISSIDENT POSTMODERNISTS*

Paul Maltby

There is a tendency in literary studies to speak of 'modernism' and 'postmodernism' *tout court*. Yet as rubrics they are a source of vagueness and ambiguity. It is a commonplace that the prefix 'post-' in 'postmodernism' may be read as denoting a relationship with modernism which is one either of succession or of supersession. But there is another problem of terminology which is less often noted. The use of modernism and postmodernism as monolithic categories conceals a process of discrimination which may frame our reading of a text. For there are, of course, *several* currents of modernist and postmodernist writing, and our perception of the political significance of a postmodernist text can depend on whichever current of writing has been selected to serve as the normative model of modernism. Thus, for Terry Eagleton, 'It is as though postmodernism is [...] a sick joke at the expense of [...] revolutionary avant-gardism insofar as it is the avant-garde practices of Mayakovsky (or Tzara or Breton) which are invoked as the normative model of modernism (Eagleton 1985, p. 60). Yet, for Leslie Fiedler, postmodernism is 'subversive,' a blow to the 'elitism' or 'concealed class bias' of a modernism he identifies with Eliot and Joyce – a current of writing sometimes referred to as 'high' modernism (Fiedler [1968] 1975). And it is this latter, largely anglophone, modernism (which, typically, also includes Faulkner, Woolf, and Wallace Stevens) that critics most often invoke to signify modernism *in toto*.

From Paul Maltby (1991) *Dissident Postmodernists: Barthelme, Coover, Pynchon*. Philadelphia, PA: University of Philadelphia Press.

The need to differentiate between currents of postmodernist fiction will be discussed later. Suffice to say here, a problem as fundamental to postmodernist writing as the 'fictionality' of meaning (i.e., the perception that the 'real,' history, or nature can only be apprehended in narrative form, that is, as 'stories') does not, as we shall see, have the same implications for, say, Barth, Nabokov, and Gass, as for Barthelme, Coover, and Pynchon. Yet, all too often, we find these names indiscriminately bracketed together.

Further problems arise from discussions of postmodernist fiction that automatically take modernism as their principal point of reference. In response to the perception that the 'real' is fundamentally non-significant, postmodernist writers have developed an aesthetics of 'self-reflexiveness,' that is, a mode of fiction which investigates the very process of signification or meaning-production. In particular, literary-narrative conventions like plotting, use of metaphor, and omniscient narrator are parodied so as to expose their role in the fabrication of meaning; so as to present the text as a fiction-making apparatus. Narration (literary, historical, philosophical, etc.) and naming are revealed as inherently fictionalizing activities. Thus Malcolm Bradbury observes the postmodernist insistence on 'the utter fictionality of *all* attempts at naming, structuring, and ordering experience' (Bradbury 1983, p. 159). And Mas'ud Zavarzadeh has remarked upon the emergence of 'noninterpretive narrative forms' which embody 'the contemporary writer's approach to the world-as-it-is, free from any imposed scheme of meaning or extracted pattern of significance' (Zavarzadeh 1976, p. 4).

It is the postmodernist preoccupation with the fictionality of meaning which inevitably invites contrasts with (if I may generalize) the high-modernist faith in totalizing meaning-systems, such as those founded on cultural tradition. (It is the basis for these contrasts that I take to be the principal rationale for speaking of a *post*-modernist fiction.) Recall Eliot's observations on *Ulysses*, whose 'mythic method' he held up as an exemplary model for modern writing: 'a way of controlling, of ordering, of giving a shape and significance to the immense panorama of futility and anarchy which is contemporary history' (quoted in Russell 1985, p. 11). Many commentaries are grounded in this fundamental contrast between 'high' modernism's striving to impose a scheme of meaning on the world (e.g., Stevens' 'Idea of Order,' Eliot's Tradition, Joyce's Mythology) and postmodernism's ironic questioning of the very possibility of meaning. David Lodge provides a concise, graphic account of the matter:

> modernism, which for all its formal experiment and complexity held out to the reader the promise of meaning, if not of *a* meaning. 'Where is the figure in the carpet?' asks a character in Donald Barthelme's *Snow White*, alluding to the title of a story by Henry James that has become proverbial among critics as an image of the goal of interpretation; 'Where is the figure in the carpet? Or is it just ... carpet?' A lot of postmodernist writing implies that experience is just carpet, and that whatever meaningful

patterns we discern in it are wholly illusory, comforting fictions. (Lodge 1977, p. 43)

This is an illuminating comparison, yet it is also typical of the prevalent tendency to define postmodernist fiction primarily in terms of its relationship to modernism. The following statements, all by eminent critics, exhibit this tendency: 'postmodernist fiction tends to attack, undermine, parody, or otherwise call into question certain characteristic assumptions of modernist fiction' (Hite 1983, p. 4); 'Once we have identified the respective dominants of the modernist or postmodernist systems, we are in a good position to begin describing the dynamics of the change by which one system emerges from and supplants the other' (McHale 1987, pp. 10–11); 'the world view of the Postmodernists is built [...] on a polemics against Modernism' (Fokkema 1986, p. 83). To be sure, postmodernist fiction embodies a critique of the formal conventions and epistemology of literary modernism (but then it also embodies a critique of literary realism, and there is a case to be made for speaking of an 'antirealist' rather than a 'postmodernist' fiction).[1] However, I want to question the invocation of modernism as the *principal point of reference* for situating and making sense of post modernist fiction.

An approach to postmodernism which uses modernism, that is, the Anglo-American 'high' modernism of, roughly, 1915–30, as the main point of reference tends inevitably to understand the critical thrust of this fiction as chiefly *retrospective*. That is to say, this approach explains postmodernist fiction as, primarily, a response (ironic, deconstructive) to the narrative forms and epistemology of an earlier, literary-cultural paradigm. But, while acknowledging this retrospectiveness as a feature of, perhaps, all postmodernist fiction, there is an oppositional current of this fiction which is best thought of as, in the first instance, 'circumspective.' By this I mean a response to or, more accurately, a critical engagement with, surrounding or contemporaneous discourses (including literary narrative forms and the meaning-systems they embody); precisely, the discourses of postmodern culture. 'Postmodernism' need not only be read as an invitation to situate postmodernist fiction in relation to modernism; it may be read as an invitation to situate it in relation to *postmodernity*, to our experience of postmodern culture.

In the 1960s a number of critics, notably Leslie Fiedler, Ihab Hassan, and Susan Sontag, welcomed postmodernism as a species of subversive writing. It was understood as the literature of a 'time of Endings' (Fiedler 1975, p. 365), challenging the social hierarchies and oppressive meaning-systems of a supposedly moribund bourgeois culture. Hassan sees postmodernist fiction as an 'Antinomian' attack on 'reason and history, science and society,' as an expression of 'Anarchy' and an impulse to 'decreation' (Hassan 1971, pp. 27, 29). And for Sontag, with Burroughs and Beckett, among others, in mind, 'contemporary artists [...] share the same disdain for the "meanings" established by bourgeois-rationalist culture, indeed for culture itself in the familiar sense.

[They proclaim ...] a harsh despair and perverse vision of apocalypse ...'
(Sontag 1983, p. 203). Fiedler situates postmodernist fiction in an era he
defines as 'apocalyptic, anti-rational, blatantly romantic and sentimental'; a
time when 'the Dream, the Vision, *ekstasis* [...] have again become the avowed
goals of literature' (Fiedler 1975, pp. 345, 364). These critics were writing at
an explosive moment of protest and dissent – the moment, that is, of an
insurgent counterculture. Perhaps their focus on the apocalyptic strain in
postmodernist fiction reflected the belief, common at the time, in the exhaustion and imminent demise of 'bourgeois-rationalist culture.' In this respect, my
reading of this fiction will be almost diametrically opposed to theirs. Suffice to
say here, I shall read it (but for one or two texts) as a literature responsive not
to a 'time of Endings' but to a time marked by the *consolidation* of 'bourgeois-
rationalist culture.'

In his landmark essay (from which I have just quoted), 'Cross the Border –
Close that Gap' (1968), Fiedler observes that the postmodernist writer has
turned to popular art forms to draw on their 'Mythical' and 'Visionary' potential (p. 362). The art forms in question are those targeted for the mass market,
typically forms like the 'western,' 'science fiction,' and 'pornography.' Fiedler
contends that insofar as it exploits the motifs and conventions of these subgenres, postmodernism resists evaluation in the terms of the 'class bias'
inscribed in the literary Establishment's 'high'/'low' criteria. The 'Aristocratic
conceptions of art' which have led critics to canonize 'high' modernists like
Eliot, Joyce, and Proust, have been superseded: 'a closing of the gap between
elite and mass culture is precisely the function of the novel now' (p. 351).
Postmodernism subverts class-based norms:

> The notion of one art for the 'cultured,' i.e., the favored few in any given
> society – in our own chiefly the university educated, and another sub-art
> for the 'uncultured,' i.e., an excluded majority [... is] an invidious
> distinction proper only to a class-structured community. [...] Pop Art
> is, whatever its overt politics, *subversive:* a threat to all hierarchies insofar
> as it is hostile to order and ordering in its own realm. (pp. 359–60)

How valid is the claim that (literary) postmodernism is democratizing, that it
annuls the class-based distinction between 'high' art and mass culture? One
might ask of two of the writers cited by Fiedler, namely Barth and Nabokov,
precisely *whom* do they address? Surely one has to be intellectually prepared
for works like *Lost in the Funhouse* or *Pale Fire*, not to mention, say, *V*, *Snow
White*, and *Pricksongs and Descants*. These are 'self-reflexive' works which
depend upon the reader's prior knowledge of the narrative conventions which
they exploit, parody, and subvert. Whether or not these works sell well, they
speak, first and foremost, to the minority sensibility of the college educated.
Indeed, what Fiedler describes as the 'academicism' of the 'Age of T.S. Eliot'
survives in the sense that many postmodernist writers are, or have been,
university writers-in-residence or professors of literature: for example, Barth,

Barthelme, Coover, Gass, Hawkes, Nabokov, Sukenick, and Vonnegut. The fact is, postmodernist fiction has an institutional base, an enclosed cultural milieu, which from Fiedler's standpoint looks positively élitist. However, to argue that this fiction addresses only an educationally privileged few is not to imply that it has little or no subversive value; rather, it is to recognize that the claim for its subversiveness cannot rest on the thesis that postmodernism 'closes a class [. . .] gap' (p. 359).

Finally, Fiedler assumes that postmodernist fiction assimilates mass-market subgenres *uncritically* (nowhere in his essay does he suggest otherwise). This may be true of some early postmodernist writing. However, in many of the postmodernist texts discussed later, we shall see how subgenres are incorporated within an oppositional framework which exposes and contests their ideological content.

The formal complexity of postmodernist writing has given a new lease of life to formalist criticism. Unquestionably, some of the most distinguished and valuable studies of this fiction are formalist. Robert Scholes, David Lodge, Douwe Fokkema, Brian McHale, and Christine Brooke-Rose are among those who have theorized a poetics or rhetoric of postmodernism. McHale and Lodge, for example, have ingeniously exploited Jakobson's structuralist concepts in their constructions of postmodernism. McHale has built a 'descriptive poetics' around the concept of the 'shifting dominant,' explaining the change from modernist to postmodernist fiction in terms of the periodic shift in the literary system's hierarchy of artistic devices (whereby dominant devices become subsidiary and vice versa) (McHale 1987, pp. 3–25). Lodge, perceiving literary history as a pendulum movement between what Jakobson has identified as the 'metaphoric' and 'metonymic' poles of language, explains postmodernism as a violation of Jakobson's 'law' that 'there is nowhere for discourse to go except between these two poles' (Lodge 1977, pp. 42–43). My concern here is to outline the problematic of what I have broadly defined as 'neo-formalist' criticism and note the kind of questions it does not address (which is less to find fault with this criticism than to indicate its conceptual limits).

In *Fiction and the Figures of Life*, William Gass censures those who 'continue to interpret novels as if they were philosophies themselves [. . .] middens from which may be scratched important messages for mankind; they have predictably looked for content, not form' (Gass 1980, p. 25). Interpretation is a misconceived goal and criticism must focus on the text's formal properties, its figures, syntax, and design. A preoccupation with form follows from Gass's conception of fiction as an autonomous 'verbal world.' We are enjoined to stop thinking of fiction as ancillary to the task of reflecting reality, for, as Gass puts it in a memorable aphorism, 'There are no descriptions in fiction, there are only constructions' (p. 17). Scholes makes a similar point: 'All writing, all composition is construction. We do not imitate the world, we construct versions of it. There is no mimesis, only poiesis. No recording. Only constructing' (Scholes

1975, p.7). Literature which incorporates this critical perspective, that is, which self-consciously renounces any pretensions to mimesis and projects itself as a purely verbal fabrication, is called by Gass, Scholes, and others 'metafiction.' Many of the writers discussed under this rubric are also identified as post-modernist, for example, Barth, Barthelme, Coover, Gass, Nabokov, and Pynchon. However, 'metafiction' has a much wider compass than 'postmodern-ism' and is generally used to denote *any systematically self-reflexive* work of fiction, that is to say, fiction which investigates and exposes the processes of its own construction and, by implication, the codes and shifting parameters of 'literature.' Hence Cervantes, Sterne, Barth, and Barthelme may all be defined as metafictional but only the latter two are postmodernist.

Critics who adopt the term 'metafiction' invariably take as their starting point Gass's definition, which labels as metafiction those literary texts 'in which the forms of fiction serve as the material upon which further forms may be imposed' (Gass 1980, p. 25). It is a helpful and perceptive formulation but there is a problem in that it implies an intertextuality that is purely literary. To be sure, it is in this sense that the texts of, say, Barth, Nabokov, and Gass, which above all interact with other (usually earlier) literary forms, are metafictional. However, there is also a strain of postmodernist writing, which includes the work of Barthelme, Coover, and Pynchon, whose texts interact not only with literary but often with *nonliterary* forms of discourse. This kind of intertextuality tends to be oppositional in orientation; it works to lay bare and combat the ideologies inscribed in, for example, pop-cultural, scientific, and political discourse. For this type of postmodernism, 'metafiction,' as it is usually defined, is an inappropriate term. Furthermore, while postmodernism may be conceived as relating the fiction in question to a postmodern culture or postmodernity, metafiction, as a term, altogether lacks sociohistorical reference.

Around 1969–70, the neo-formalist approach to postmodernist fiction was invigorated by an input of structuralist ideas. There are, to be sure, striking correspondences between, for instance, Barthes's ideas on literature – for example, literature conceived as an interplay of codes rather than a medium of representation; the call for a mode of writing which privileges *discours* over *histoire* – and the thinking of Gass, Soholes, and other critics. (The concepts of structuralism/post-structuralism have undoubtedly been of value in articulating the linguistic-philosophical concerns of postmodernist writers, but we should not necessarily assume that these writers were structuralists/post-structuralists *avant la lettre*. The precise connections – theoretical and temporal – between post-Saussurean theory and postmodernism need to be researched.) However, the structuralist influence has also worked to reinforce the neo-formalist tendency to fetishize the text, to abstract the word from the world. The problem of the fictionality of meaning may serve to illustrate a limitation of this tendency. Thus, while this criticism may examine the formal implications of this problem, for example, the self-reflexive focus on the factitiousness and arbitrariness of the narrative conventions on which meaning is shown to rest, it does not address a question like: Why should the fictionality of meaning become a major issue at a particular time, in a particular place (i.e., in late-capitalist America)? The problem is that such a question cannot be adequately, if at all, posed by the discourses of neoformalism. No coherent model of postmodern culture underpins neoformalist studies of postmodernist fiction. In these studies, the fictionality of meaning is an issue rarely examined beyond its aesthetic and epistemological implications. And yet our very idea of fictionality has been enlarged and enriched by sociological inquiries into the nature of postmodern culture. For example, note the pervasive discourses of commodity aesthetics where the illusion (the false promises and fraudulent claims) of use-value becomes detached from use-value itself (Haug 1986, pp. 16–17); note the simulated realities of a media society, 'the generation by models of a real without origin or reality: a hyperreal' (Baudrillard 1983, p. 2). An explanation of the postmodernist writer's preoccupation with fictionality requires, *inter alia*, acknowledgment of his/her situation in a culture pervaded by illusory use-values and simulacra.

The dominant, neo-formalist strain of criticism generally precludes readings of postmodernist fiction as an oppositional current of writing. However, there are, of course, critics who have identified strands of postmodernist fiction as adversarial literature. Linda Hutcheon, for example, has proposed the category of 'historiographic metafiction,' instanced by such works as Reed's *Mumbo Jumbo* and Doctorow's *Ragtime*. This fiction operates through a subversive, highly self-reflexive use of parody. It ironically or paradoxically incorporates into its very structure the forms of historical narratives in order to destabilize them 'from within' – exposing them as purely social constructs and contesting their ideological closures. 'To adapt Barthes's general notion of the "doxa" as public opinion or the "Voice of Nature" and consensus, postmodernism works to "de-doxify" our cultural representations and their undeniable political import' (Hutcheon 1987, pp. 12, 21; 1989, p. 3). And Charles Russell has discussed the 'avant-garde strategies of aesthetic disruption' whereby Burroughs, Pynchon, Coover, and Sukenick, among others, attempt to demystify and deconstruct the social codes in which subjective identity is seen to be enfolded. It is a project which 'shift[s] the previous social context of rebellion to the social text of ideology' (Russell 1985, p. 253).

Both Hutcheon and Russell, who have contributed much to the idea of an adversarial postmodernist fiction, are, like myself, interested in the latter as a critique and contestation of hegemonic discourse. However, their arguments lack an account, not to say a systematic analysis, of the conjuncture or moment (late capitalist? postindustrial?) at which this fiction is written. Hence, a fundamental question is not addressed: What developments, *historically specific* to our society, have given rise to a mode of fiction that is so preoccupied with language as a political issue? In the subsequent pages, I shall discuss a number of social changes – identified later as distinctively *late-capitalist* developments – which, I shall argue, have been instrumental in raising consciousness of the political implications of language.

[...]

Attenuated language

Lefebvre sees language, at the late-capitalist stage of its evolution, as an attenuated medium. He has identified a substitution of 'signals' for 'signs,' a process which, he argues, 'eliminate[s] all other dimensions of language and meaning such as symbols and significant contrasts' and gives rise to 'a general sense of meaninglessness' because the subject can no longer articulate or totalize his/her experiences. The shift from signs to signals has the effect of eliding mediating thought processes and so enhancing control over behavior: 'signals provide practical systems for the *manipulation* of people ...' (Lefebvre 1971, pp. 39, 62). And William Burroughs has commented on a specific aspect of language attenuation. In an interview, he has observed that: 'An essential feature of the Western control machine is to make language as non-pictorial as possible, to separate words as far as possible from objects or observable processes' (Burroughs 1970, p. 98). And elsewhere, he remarks on 'the feat of prose abstracted to a point where no image track occurs' (Burroughs 1968a, p. 27). For Burroughs, our intellectual purchase on reality is weakened when the language at our disposal chiefly comprises abstract, imageless words. Finally, Marcuse has argued that language forms have emerged which limit consciousness to nonantagonistic modes of understanding; which render language incapable of expressing negation. He identifies a public discourse notable for its use of 'syntactical abridgment,' as in the propensity for acronyms and catchphrases. It is a syntax which erodes the critical 'space' between the parts of a sentence by condensing subject and predicate (Marcuse 1966, pp. 86–87). This results in propositions such as 'the Free World' or 'the clean bomb,' which come across as 'self-validating, hypnotic formulas.' It is a mode of discourse which impedes conceptual thought; which 'serves as a vehicle of coordination and subordination,' an 'irreconcilably anti-critical and anti-dialectical language' which 'absorbs ... the negative oppositional elements of Reason' (pp. 96–97). Evidently, for Marcuse, this (perceived) deadening of the critical impulse in language facilitates the integration of the subject into the social order. And while, to be sure, he has also identified points of resistance to the 'established universe of discourse,' noting the linguistic counter-practices of subcultural groups (Marcuse 1966, p. 86; 1969 pp. 34–36), his analysis of the prevailing state of language is overwhelmingly pessimistic.

Certainly, postmodern culture is marked by a preponderance of conceptually impoverished discourses that inhibit reflection and lack the perspectives necessary for critical analysis of the social order. Anyone can observe the impact on language of the phenomenal profit-motivated expansion of mass-media broadcasting and publishing. Fulfillment of the twin objectives of maximal marketability and rapid product-turnover demands the construction of easily consumable language forms like the pop lyric, the teen romance, or the tabloid story. Hence, much of the time, we receive discourse in the emaciated forms of catchphrases, clichés, and platitudes. There is a marked preference in television and radio shows for bland, frictionless talk, for conversation purged of critical and provocative content. Of much greater concern is the increasing tendency toward cosmeticized political discourse whereby issues are reduced to competing slogans inspired by the mesmerizing jingles of advertising.

All this is not to suggest that the prevalence of attenuated discourse *necessarily* renders the subject more susceptible to social incorporation (nor is it to suggest that in pre-postmodern times everyday language was animated by a critical impulse or was experienced as if endowed with a plenitude of meaning); my only concern here is to indicate certain changes in the field of discourse and to note how dissident thinkers have responded to them. However, I would add that we must not lose sight of the contradiction that although banalized and trivialized forms of language may have usurped much of our cultural space, at the same time, late-capitalist publics are information-conscious to a degree that is historically unprecedented. (One need only consider the insatiable demand for education and news or the phenomenal growth of the 'knowledge industry.') The value placed on concept- or information-rich discourse would suggest that, in general, publics do not 'consume' conceptually impoverished discourse unself-consciously or complacently. And, indeed, there is a growing awareness of the potential to develop media forms which promote knowledge, reflection, and critical debate. The necessary resources – for example, interactive communication technologies, data banks, media expertise – already exist in abundance and only await the conditions for their universal mobilization.

DISSIDENT POSTMODERNIST FICTION

I have argued that in the 1960s and early 1970s there was a prodigious enlargement of the notion of the political within the sphere of language. I noted, in particular, that a conception of language as a medium of social integration was a vital element in the dissident thought of this period. Furthermore, I sought to ground that conception of language in political, cultural, and other developments that have transformed the field of language and communications. And I have indicated that these developments are specific to, or more advanced under, late capitalism. These points will provide a framework for a discussion of the texts in the case studies which follow shortly – texts which I shall now identify as 'dissident postmodernist.'

Now, I want to distinguish between two tendencies in American postmodernist fiction: a 'dissident' tendency, exemplified not only by the work of Barthelme, Coover, and Pynchon, but also by that of Burroughs, DeLillo, Acker, and Reed; and an 'introverted' tendency, exemplified by the work of Nabokov, Gass, and, intermittently, Barth, among others. By way of a preliminary observation, I shall say that dissident postmodernist fiction embodies that enlarged notion of the political within the sphere of language as discussed above. And it is from this standpoint that I shall read the fiction of Nabokov and others as introverted – a literary tendency whose exploration of language barely registers its political dimensions. (Of course, from other standpoints, the work of Nabokov et al. may be evaluated without the negative undertone it has here.) This is not to propose hard and fast categories in which any postmodernist text can be instantly placed. Indeed, almost any literary text may be read as addressing, however marginally or obliquely, some political implications of language. Ultimately, the difference between these tendencies is best thought of as one of degree: the dissident tendency may be distinguished from the introverted by its *heightened perception* of the politics of language.

The problem of the 'fictionality' of meaning will serve to highlight the above distinction. For the postmodernist writer, the 'real' is essentially non-significant (it does not speak for itself), and the search for meaning, the endeavor to interpret the world, is perceived as a process of fictionalizing reality, of 'storifying' it. It is understood that extra-discursive referents – historical events, social processes, natural phenomena – can only be apprehended in narrative form, never in their pure, naked state, that is, 'as they really are.' Postmodernist writers respond to the problem of the fictionality of meaning by, *inter alia*, composing texts which mock, interrogate, and subvert the 'classical' realist-empiricist assumption that language can reflect or render 'things as they really are.' (I say '*classical* realist'; I do not suppose that all works classified as 'realist' aim persistently at a faithful transcription of reality or are unconscious of the problem of meaning as outlined above.) Their primary strategy is to use language in a self-reflexive, as opposed to self-effacing, fashion in order to demonstrate the operation of narrative codes in the constitution of meaning. It is a strategy that often results in word games which work to parody reality as subject to uncontrollable textualization.

However, the problem of the fictionality of meaning does not in every respect have the same implications for all postmodernist writers. Consider some texts of introverted tendency. The narrator of Barth's 'Lost in the Funhouse,' one of a collection of stories about the inescapability of storytelling, observes: 'The climax of the story must be its protagonist's discovery of a way to get through the funhouse. But he has found none, may have ceased to search' (Barth 1969, p. 96). We are all lost in the funhouse of fiction-making and there is no way out. Like Borges's Library, the funhouse is our textualized universe. In 'Menelaiad,' Menelaus exclaims in despair: ' "When will I reach my goal through its cloaks of story? How many veils to naked Helen?" ' (Barth, p. 144). 'Menelaiad' progresses as one story enframes a second which, in turn, enframes a third and so on, thereby suggesting, as the quotation marks multiply, that reality is but a framework of infinitely nesting narratives. Finally, 'Pale Fire' is a poem, a patently literary artifact (meticulously constructed in rhyming pairs of iambic pentameters) that reflects self-consciously on the powers of linguistic invention: 'playing a game of worlds,' building 'Empires of rhyme.' This text, moreover, is the object of study of another text, an overblown 'Commentary' of nearly two hundred pages by one Charles Kinbote. But this 'apparatus criticus,' against Kinbote's express intentions, becomes the 'monstrous semblance of a novel' (Nabokov 1973, p. 71) – *Pale Fire* itself, but also Nabokov's parody of historical romance fiction. (Kinbote, who may be a king in exile or just a deranged émigré scholar, reads the poem as a coded biography of *his* escapades as king of 'Zembla' – a mock-Ruritania of palace plots, secret passageways, and courtly love affairs.) In this way, Nabokov suggests that there is no direct passage from language to the real; rather, cognition is caught up in an interplay of texts.

These 'introverted' instances of postmodernist writing explore the individual ego's experience of entrapment in webs of narrative fiction. Typically, in this strain of fiction, the narrator-subjects are scholars, recluses, or fantasists, remote from street level, meditating from within an enclosed, monadic environment. (This is also a notable feature of Gass's stories – see Gass 1981 – and of course the *ficciones* of the master architect of hermetic spaces – Borges.) Here, the problem of the fictionality of meaning finds no grounding in social and historical conditions. On the other hand, for dissident postmodernist writers, the problem of meaning has a contextual dimension insofar as they perceive language as bearing the imprint of the institutions, projects, and conflicts in which it is imbricated. To be sure, these writers are acutely conscious of meaning as 'narrative.' But they are also conscious of meaning as imbued with the tensions of power-relations and conflicting value-systems. Thus Pynchon contextualizes the problem of the fictionality of meaning so that our 'delusional systems' and 'stories, all false, about who we are' cannot be understood without reference to a social order which 'bring[s] the State to live in the muscles of your tongue' (Pynchon 1978, p. 384). Or consider this observation by Barthelme expressed in the form of an imaginary conversation: ' "Madelaine," I say kindly to her over lunch, "semiotics is in a position to claim that no phenomenon has any ontological status outside its place in the particular information system from which it draws its meaning, and therefore, all language is finally groundless [. . .]" "Yes," says Madelaine kindly [. . .], "but some information systems are more enforceable than others." Alas, she's right' (Barthelme 1985, p. 44). Dissident postmodernists, unlike the introverted ones, explore the political and ideological implications of the fictionality of meaning. Their writing illuminates the institutional parameters of meaning-systems; it reveals how the latter operate in force fields of power-relations; how, through the medium of ideology, meaning-systems are connected to established political structures. In short, while both introverted and dissident tendencies explore 'the world within the word' (Gass 1978), as a rule, only the dissident tendency explores the word in the world.

The tendency to grasp the problem of the fictionality of meaning in political terms is one instance of what I have identified as a defining feature of dissident postmodernist fiction: its enlarged notion of the political within the sphere of language. A second instance of this, in which the first will be seen to be implied, is the focal point of this study: a *heightened perception of language as a medium of social integration*. This perception is not evident in all dissident postmodernist texts, but it is very much in the foreground of texts by, among others, Burroughs, DeLillo, Acker, and Reed, in addition to texts by Barthelme, Coover, and Pynchon. The dissident postmodernists' perception of language as a powerful medium of integration necessarily concerns them *qua* language-users; for, it need hardly be said, they are *implicated* in language both professionally as writers and generally as members of a speech community. The question then arises: Is an independent, critical standpoint within late-capitalist society possible? It is a question which haunts this fiction and which explains its self-conscious reflection on the limits of artistic autonomy.

Dissident modernists and postmodernists share the anxiety that communication is necessarily on terms established by the social order, such that to speak at all may be to surrender one's autonomy. Hence the problem of speaking in one's own voice becomes a theme in both currents of writing. Stephen Dedalus, the Irish protagonist of Joyce's *Portrait*, speaks for Joyce when, after an exchange with the dean of English studies, he reflects:

> The language in which we are speaking is his before it is mine [...] His language, so familiar and so foreign, will always be for me an acquired speech. I have not made or accepted its words. My voice holds them at bay. My soul frets in the shadow of his language. (Joyce 1960, p. 189)

The passage expresses Joyce's unease at having to speak in the alien tongue of a colonial power (i.e., imperial Britain). And, a little later the link between language and colonial subjection is made explicit: '– My ancestors threw off their language and took another, Stephen said. They allowed a handful of foreigners to subject them' (p. 202). But Joyce, in company with other literary (high) modernists, believed in a transhistorical plane of meaning, a judgmental standpoint *outside* of society's web of discourses, premised on the assumption that consciousness transcends language. Indeed, this faith in a transcendent consciousness is reflected in the novel's recurring image of flight, as in this famous passage: 'When the soul of a man is born in this country there are nets flung at it to hold it back from flight. You talk to me of nationality, language, religion. I shall try to fly by those nets' (p. 203). For Joyce, there is a space beyond language to which the individual consciousness, privileged as the origin and legislator of meaning, can exile itself and 'forge' a pure, non-alienating discourse. (And for modernists like Joyce, Stevens, and Yeats this is precisely the task of the artist – the artist exalted as a God-like 'artificer.') In short, he affirmed the modernist view of consciousness as an autonomous source of meaning and hence upheld the possibility of speaking in one's own voice. Contrast this position with that of Burroughs, fifty years later:

> That is the entry gimmick of The Death Dwarfs: supersonic imitation and playback so you think it is your own voice – (do you own a voice?) they invade The Right Centers which are The Speech Centers and they are in the right – in the right – in thee write – 'Right' – 'I'm in the right – in the right – You know I'm in the right so long as you hear me say inside your right centers "I am in the right." ' (Burroughs 1968b, p. 75)

Clearly, for Burroughs, the subject is compelled to speak on alien terms. Language inscribes ('in the write') a perspective on reality which is 'right' both in the sense that it is approved by the social order and, by the latter's standards, in that it seems obviously correct. Consciousness, far from transcending language, is perceived to be enclosed by it: 'What scared you all into time? into body? into shit? I will tell you: "the word." Alien Word "the." "The" word of Alien Enemy imprisons "thee" in Time. In Body. In shit' (Burroughs 1968b, p. 10). Dissident postmodernists communicate the experience of entrapment in language with much greater insistence and desperation than is generally found in modernism. They are far less confident about the possibility of achieving an autonomous critical perspective in their work.

The forms a dissident literature may usefully assume cannot be divorced from prevailing conceptions of power. A rough contrast between turn-of-the-century naturalism and dissident postmodernism may serve to illustrate the point. Where writers like Sinclair and London saw power as concentrated in a property-owning class, it was possible to write fiction in a confrontational mode; the target was plainly objective. Such fiction, operating directly and overtly as an indictment of society, typically assumed a documentary/didactic form as in *The Jungle* (1906) or *The Iron Heel* (1907). In contrast, dissident postmodernists conceive of power as *diffused* through the cultural sphere, in particular, through language, the very material with which the writer works. Language is deeply distrusted, so that, for example, for Barthelme:

> The question is, what is the complicity of language in the massive crimes of fascism, Stalinism, or (by implication) our own policies in Viet Nam? In the control of societies by the powerful and their busy functionaries? If these abominations are all in some sense facilitated by, made possible by, language, to what degree is that language ruinously contaminated? (Barthelme 1985, p. 42)

Given the dissident postmodernists' perception of language as a site of power, we can see why fiction in the confrontational mode seems to be of less strategic value than formerly, and we can begin to theorize, instead, the strategic value of the mode of writing itself.

Most critics identify postmodernist writing as typically 'self-reflexive.' The problem with this term is that it suggests no more than a mode of writing that examines and exposes the processes of its own composition, thereby revealing its meaning as the construct of so many (literary) codes and conventions. One might be forgiven, therefore, for thinking of self-reflexive writing as a rather sterile, cerebral kind of game, a tediously self-obsessed literature. However, as most critics who use the term would surely agree, self-reflexive fiction does not only reflect on the role of literature in the constitution of meaning. Rather, it suggests, sometimes using literature as a paradigm, that *any* sign-system constitutes meaning; it is understood that meaning is wholly or in part (depending on one's view) the 'effect' of the system's rules and codes which order signifiers into narratives. For the sake of accuracy, then, I prefer to speak of a 'sign-reflective' rather than 'self-reflexive' fiction.

Sign-reflective techniques of writing divert our attention away from story to the processes of signification.[2] Typically, there is a focus on the textual play of forms, plots, and tropes, and the way they mediate our relationship to the 'real' or, at least, to the signified. (Pynchon, for example, foregrounds authorial plotting as one such mediation.) This form of writing is a medium particularly suited to the complex task of probing the relationship between language and meaning. Moreover, with specific reference to the current of postmodernist fiction identified here as dissident, we can now begin to think of *its* sign-reflectiveness as the very property which enables it to perform a contestatory function within a substantially eroded critical space; as the very property which guarantees this fiction a measure of autonomy. We may think of sign-reflective writing as discourse to the second power or metadiscourse; discourse which, insofar as it lays bare the very processes of signification, permits a degree of disengagement from the sign-systems in which the writer is necessarily implicated. This disengagement is a desired objective when the prevailing discourses, including the conventions and motifs of established literary discourse, are perceived as fraudulent, mendacious, mystificatory, or hollow. Sign-reflectiveness is the strategy whereby lost critical distance is, albeit provisionally, redeemed. [...]

READING THE PUBLIC BURNING

The time frame of Coover's third novel, *The Public Burning*, is strictly limited to the three days in 1953 leading up to the electrocution of the Rosenbergs. Yet, by means of his critical engagement with the terms in which the Rosenbergs were vilified and arraigned at the climax of the McCarthy era, Coover interrogates and contests the master codes through which postwar America's perceptions of politics and society are mediated. However, many studies of the novel by Coover specialists convey scarcely a hint of its adversarial force. Indeed, the theoretical frameworks of commentaries tend all too often to foreclose on a political reading of the book.

One approach to *The Public Burning* privileges the book's *mythic* frame of reference. Exponents of this approach (e.g., Hume 1979, LeClair 1982, Ramage 1982) focus attention on the motifs of the sacrificial victim, the Manichaean duel, the orgiastic rite – motifs which, to be sure, figure prominently in this and other works by Coover, notably *The Origin of the Brunists, The Universal*

Baseball Association, and *A Political Fable*. However, readings which thematize the novel's mythic perspectives tend to marginalize its sociohistorical perspectives. There is not a single reference to the Cold War in myth-centered readings by Kathryn Hume, Thomas LeClair, and John Ramage; this is not surprising when myth, in Coover's book, is understood to supplant history.[3] In contrast, my point of entry into the novel will be the thematic context of cold war history, with attention focused on the Cold War presented as a regime of discourse.

Another critical approach to *The Public Burning* yields what might be termed the 'fabulationist' account of the novel. This account highlights Coover's model of man as a fiction-maker or fabulator through an examination of a central theme of the book: the fictional status of *all* 'historical' (documentary, factual) narrative. Hence, in commentaries on *The Public Burning*, Robert Scholes speaks of 'fabulative history' (Scholes 1979, p. 206), Larry McCaffery of 'history-as-artifice' (McCaffery 1982, p. 87). To be sure, Coover illuminates history or, more precisely, historiography, as 'fabulation' or 'artifice.' Indeed, in some important respects, Coover's views on writing history echo those of meta-historians like Hayden White. Speaking of 'the extent to which "invention" plays a part in the historian's operations' (White 1975, p. 7), White examines the 'fictive' elements inherent in the types of explanation provided by historical narrative. For example, 'explanation by employment' is 'the way by which a sequence of events fashioned into a story is gradually revealed to be a story of a particular kind,' that is, a history invested with the plot structure of, say, a 'Tragedy' or 'Comedy' (p. 7). White also explores what he sees as the unavoidable mediation of metaphor, metonymy and other tropes in the construction of historical accounts: 'All historical narratives presuppose figurative characterizations of the events they purport to represent and explain,' a view which prompts a conception of 'the historical text as a literary artifact' (White 1978b, p. 56; see also White 1978a). Now critics like McCaffery and Scholes read *The Public Burning* as an exemplary work of metafiction precisely insofar as it 'foregrounds' the artificiality of historiographical conventions; they recognize' its epistemological challenge to our (Enlightenment/positivist) faith in the possibility of an objective grasp of history. Accordingly they privilege the following passage as the *locus classicus* of the novel (where Coover's Richard Nixon, endeavoring to sort out the ambiguities and contradictions in documents relating to the Rosenberg spy case, reflects on his confusion):

> What was fact, what intent, what was framework, what was essence? Strange the impact of History, the grip it had on us, yet it was nothing but words. Accidental accretions for the most part, leaving most of the story out. We have not yet begun to explore the true power of the Word, I thought. What if we broke all the rules, played games with the evidence, manipulated language itself, made History a partisan ally? Of course, the Phantom [Coover's personification of communism] was already onto this, wasn't he? Ahead of us again. (Coover 1978, p. 172: Hereafter PB)

Yet this passage is not just about history-as-fiction, not just about the *primacy* of 'art' and 'fabulation' (Scholes) or the 'fiction-making process' (McCaffery) in the writing of history; such remarks are in need of qualification. Insofar as this key passage explicitly connects historical discourse with power and political strategy (i.e., making a 'partisan' use of history through the manipulation of language and evidence), it summarizes Coover's preoccupation with *political and ideological mediations* in the 'fictionalizing' of history. The problem with the 'fabulationist' account of *The Public Burning* is that it is bound to a conception of metafiction as purely epistemological critique; a conception which does not embrace the adversarial potential of 'metafictional' (or sign-reflective) writing. As we shall see, Coover's sign-reflective techniques work to undermine the authority of hegemonic historical narratives by exposing and contesting the ideology inscribed in them.[4]

The book's emphasis on the idea that history can only be apprehended in narrative form necessarily threatens the validity of any political reading of history proposed by its author; for such a reading, within the novel's sign-reflective framework, becomes just one more narrative construct or fiction. As Raymond Mazurek observes in an essay on Coover's novel: '. . . the analysis of history as text displaces an analysis of history' (Mazurek 1982, p. 40).[5] This is a valid point, but perhaps Mazurek might moderate his criticism if he was to consider whether there are other reasons besides Coover's perception of history-as-text that inhibit or disable a political reading or critique of recent American history. Such a critique implies a faith in the tenability of a critical standpoint outside of the established order of meaning. However, in our discussion of postmodernism (a concept absent from Mazurek's study), it was observed that the dissident postmodernist writer has little confidence in the possibility of a truly autonomous critical perspective. This attitude was seen to be derived from a view of postmodern consciousness as unable to transcend, or at least entirely free itself, from society's hegemonic codes. Accordingly, the narrative of *The Public Burning*, like the narratives of the Barthelme stories discussed earlier, is almost exclusively mediated through the consciousness of minds (Nixon's, The Times Square crowds') enclosed within the prevailing ideologies. (Of course, in its sign-reflective dimension, the novel transcends the horizons of Nixon's or the cold war public's mindset. But the sign-reflective frame of the narrative does not in itself constitute a standpoint from which Coover can offer a critical analysis or political reading of recent American history.)

Second, it is not purely at the abstract level of discourse theory that the problem of writing history is raised in the novel. Careful attention to the text will show that the problem is almost always raised in contexts which illuminate its *political* implications, particularly in the chronologically and socially specific context of American cold war politics. The novel offers insights into the role of some of America's ideologically and politically dominant institutions – the press, the legal system, the Republican party, the FBI – in the propagation of cold war historical narratives and their promotion to hegemonic status. And while these insights probably fall short of Mazurek's idea (never specified) of an adequate political reading of cold war America, they nevertheless constitute a significant historical analysis of the role of privileged institutions in the production of 'truth.' In any event, the adversarial power of the book surely need not depend on a developed political analysis of recent American history. Rather, that power resides primarily in the novel's forceful deconstruction and de-mythification of the ruling historical narratives of cold war America – subversive operations which do not depend on some independent critical discourse but on the strength of formal, sign-reflective techniques.

[...]

NOTES

1. It is the forms and philosophical assumptions of literary realism that, more often than those of modernism, seem to be the prime target of postmodernist deconstruction and parody. Indeed, postmodernist fiction abounds with metafictional statements in which authors explicitly question the codes and presuppositions of realism. In *V*, for example, Pynchon speaks of 'eyes clear enough to see past the fiction of continuity, the fiction of cause and effect, the fiction of a humanized history endowed with "reason"' (Pynchon 1975, p. 306). In *Pale Fire*, Nabokov writes: ' "reality" is neither the subject nor the object of true art which creates its own special reality having nothing to do with the average "reality" perceived by the communal eye' (Nabokov 1973, p. 106). Moreover, recall that, from a strictly chronological standpoint, American postmodernist fiction follows a long phase of *non-modernist* literature. (There is an uneven development in the American arts. In painting, for example, the modernist impulse persists well into the 1950s in the form of abstract expressionism against whose 'élitism' and 'esotericism' the Pop Art of the 1960s may be read as an ironic response. Literary history, however, does not run a parallel course.) By the late 1930s, after Dos Passos and Faulkner had completed their major work, the modernist impulse in American narrative fiction was largely spent. It was outlived and/or followed by a variety of fictional forms (e.g., naturalist or 'existentialist') which generally adhered to realist conventions of narrative continuity, story, and plot and focused on problems of self-definition and existential crisis. This moment of American fiction (1940s and 1950s) may be represented by works like Mailer's *The Naked and the Dead*, Bellow's *The Victim*, Ellison's *The Invisible Man*, and Salinger's *The Catcher in the Rye*.
2. Barthes says of the contemporary novel that 'it aims to transpose narrative from the purely constative plane, which it has occupied until now, to the performative plane, whereby the meaning of an utterance is the very act by which it is uttered: today, writing is not "telling" but saying that one is telling and assigning all the referent ("what one says") to this act of locution' (Barthes 1977, p. 114).
3. For example, LeClair observes: '[Coover's] anthropological perspective suggests history is a fiction, perhaps finer-gauged than most yet without finality. But it is by stretching fact past "faction" to myth that Coover obviates history and makes *The Public Burning* a major achievement of conscience and imagination' (quoted in Hume 1979, p. 147). And Ramage writes: 'Not until the last hundred pages or so of *The Public Burning* does the veneer of history wear away sufficiently that the pentimento of myth can move into the foreground and make everything "perfectly clear"' (Ramage 1982, p. 62).
4. It ought to be said that there is nothing in the novel to suggest that Coover believes that overcoming ideology will grant us unmediated access to the truth; he sticks to the position that there is a radical separation between the discursive specification of

events and the events themselves; that history is inevitably 'received' in textual form.

5. It must be said that Coover's reader learns little about the economic and political motives behind the Cold War. For a perceptive analysis of these motives, see especially Chomsky 1984, pp. 24–58.

WORKS CITED

Barth, John (1969) *Lost in the Funhouse, Fiction for Print, Tape, Live Voice*. London: Secker & Warburg [orig. pub. 1968].

Barthelme, Donald (1985) 'Not-Knowing', in Allen Wier and Don Hendrie, Jr (eds), *Voice-Lust. Eight Contemporary Fiction Writers on Style*. Lincoln, NE: University of Nebraska Press, pp. 37–50.

Barthes, Roland (1977) *Image-Music-Text*, ed. and trans. Stephen Heath. London: Fontana.

Baudrillard, Jean (1983) *Simulations*, trans. P. Foss, P. Patton and P. Beitchman. New York: Semiotext(e).

Bradbury, Malcolm (ed.) (1983) *The Modern American Novel*. Oxford: Oxford University Press.

Burroughs, William (1968a) *The Ticket That Exploded*. London: Calder & Boyars [orig. pub. 1962].

Burroughs, William (1968b) *Nova Express*. London: Granada [orig. pub. 1964].

Burroughs, William (1970) *The Job*. London: Jonathan Cape.

Chomsky, Noam (1984) 'The United States: from Greece to El Salvador', in Noam Chomsky, Jonathan Steele and John Gittings, *Superpowers in Collision*. Harmondsworth: Penguin.

Coover, Robert (1978) *The Public Burning*. Harmondsworth: Penguin [orig. pub. 1977].

Eagleton, Terry (1985) 'Capitalism, Modernism and Postmodernism', *New Left Review*, 152, July–August: 60–72.

Fiedler, Leslie (1968) 'The New Mutants', in B. Bergonzi (ed.), *Innovations*. London: Macmillan.

Fiedler, Leslie (1975) 'Cross the Border – Close that Gap: Postmodernism', in Marcus Cunliffe (ed.), *Amerian Literature since 1900*. London: Barrie & Jenkins, pp. 344–66 [orig. pub. 1968].

Fokkema, Douwe (1986) 'The Semantic and Syntactic Organization of Post-modernist Texts', in Douwe Fokkema and Hans Bertens (eds), *Approaching Postmodernism*. Amsterdam and Philadelphia, PA: John Benjamins, pp. 81–95.

Gass, William (1978) *The World within the Word*. New York: Knopf.

Gass, William (1980) *Fiction and the Figures of Life*. Boston, MA: Godine [orig. pub. 1970].

Gass, William (1981) *In the Heart of the Country*. Boston: Godine [orig. pub. 1968].

Hassan, Ihab (1971) 'POSTmodernISM', *New Literary History*, III (1), Autumn: 5–30.

Haug, W. F. (1986) *Critique of Commodity Aesthetics*, trans. Robert Bock. Cambridge: Polity Press [orig. pub. 1971].

Hite, Molly (1983) *Ideas of Order in the Novels of Thomas Pynchon*. Columbus, OH: Ohio State University Press.

Hume, Kathryn (1979) 'Robert Coover's Fictions: The Naked and the Mythic', *Novel*, Winter: 127–48.

Hutcheon, Linda (1987) 'Beginning to theorize postmodernism', *Textual Practice*, 1 (1) Spring: 10–31.

Hutcheon, Linda (1989) *The Politics of Postmodernism*. London: Routledge.

Joyce, James (1960) *A Portrait of the Artist as a Young Man*. Harmondsworth: Penguin [orig. pub. 1916].

LeClair, Thomas (1982) 'Robert Coover, *The Public Burning*, and the Art of Excess', *Critique*, 23 (3), Spring: 5–27.

Lefebvre, Henri (1971) *Everyday Life in the Modern World*, trans. Sacha Rabinovitch. London: Allen Lane [orig. pub. 1968].

Lodge, David (1977) 'Modernism, Antimodernism and Postmodernism', *New Review*, 4 (38), May: 39–44.

McCaffery, Larry (1982) *The Metafictional Muse*. Pittsburgh, PA: University of Pittsburgh Press.

McHale, Brian (1987) *Postmodernist Fiction*. London: Methuen.

Marcuse, Herbert (1966) *One-Dimensional Man*. Boston: Beacon Press [orig. pub. 1964].

Marcuse, Herbert (1969) *An Essay on Liberation*. London: Allen Lane.

Mazurek, Raymond (1982) 'Metafiction, the Historical Novel, and Coover's *The Public Burning*', *Critique*, 23 (3), Spring: 29–41.

Nabokov, Vladimir (1973) *Pale Fire*. Harmondsworth: Penguin [orig. pub. 1962].

Pynchon, Thomas (1975) *V*. London: Pan/Picador [orig. pub. 1963].

Pynchon, Thomas (1978) *Gravity's Rainbow*. London: Pan/Picador [orig. pub. 1973].

Ramage, John (1982) 'Myth and Monomyth in Coover's *The Public Burning*', *Critique*, 23 (3), Spring: 29–41.

Russell, Charles (1985) *Poets, Prophets and Revolutionaries*. New York: Oxford University Press.

Scholes, Robert (1975) *Structural Fabulation*. Notre Dame, IN: University of Notre Dame Press.

Scholes, Robert (1979) *Fabulation and Metafiction*. Urbana, IL: University of Illinois Press.

Sontag, Susan (1983) 'The Aesthetics of Silence', in *A Susan Sontag Reader*. Harmondsworth: Penguin, pp. 181–204 [orig. pub. 1967].

White, Hayden (1975) *Metahistory: The Historical Imagination in Nineteenth-Century Europe*. Baltimore, MD: Johns Hopkins University Press [orig. pub. 1973].

White, Hayden (1978a) *Tropics of Discourse*. Baltimore, MD: Johns Hopkins University Press.

White, Hayden (1978b) 'The Historical Text as Literary Artifact', in R. Canary and H. Kozicki (eds), *The Writing of History*. University of Wisconsin Press, pp. 41–62.

Zavarzadeh, Mas'ud (1976) *The Mythopoeic Reality*. Urbana, IL: University of Illinois Press.

FEMINISM AND POSTMODERNISM
26

'FEMINISM, READING, POSTMODERNISM'

Meaghan Morris

[...]

In a number of recent discussions of postmodernism, a sense of intrigue develops around a presumed absence – or withholding – of women's speech in relation to what has certainly become one of the boom discourses of the 1980s. Feminists in particular, in this intrigue, have had little or nothing to say about postmodernism. This very curious *doxa* emerges from texts by male critics referring primarily to each other commenting on the rarity of women's speech.

In 1983, in a text commenting on his own 'remarkable oversight' in ignoring the question of sexual difference in his previous critical practice, Craig Owens noted 'the fact that few women have engaged in the modernism/postmodernism debate'.[1] In an essay first published the following year, Andreas Huyssen – warmly agreeing with Owens that feminist work in art, literature and criticism has been 'a measure of the vitality and energy' of postmodern culture – nonetheless found it 'somewhat baffling that feminist criticism has so far largely stayed away from the postmodernism debate which is considered not to be pertinent to feminist concerns'.[2]

Both of these critics stressed the complexity and importance of a feminist contribution to what *they*, in turn, wished to describe as a 'postmodern' culture. Owens in particular was careful to disclaim any desire to efface the specificity of feminist critique, and to insist that his own project was to consider the implications of an *intersection* of feminism and postmodernism.

From Meaghan Morris (1988) 'Feminism, Reading, Postmodernism', *The Pirate's Fiancée: Feminism, Reading, Postmodernism*. London and New York: Verso.

More recently, however, Jonathan Arac stated baldly in his Introduction to *Postmodernism and Politics*:

> ...*almost no women have figured in the debate*, even though many analysts include current feminism among the features of postmodernity. Nancy Fraser's important feminist critique of Habermas ('What's Critical') stands nearly alone (see also Kristeva), although Craig Owens and Andrew Ross have effectively situated feminist work by women in relation to postmodernism.[3]

In the bibliography which concludes Arac's Introduction, very few women do figure beside Fraser and Kristeva: five, to be precise, out of more than seventy individual and collaborative authorial entries. One of the five is Virginia Woolf. Another is Hannah Arendt.[4] Any bibliography, it is true, must be exclusive. This one is, when it comes to gender, *very* exclusive.

The interesting question, I think, is not whether feminists have or have not written about postmodernism, or whether they should have (for despite the 'baffled' expectation, the hope, perhaps, of eventual *fiançailles*, there is no suggestion here that feminism in any sense *needs* postmodernism as complement or supplement).[5] My question is rather under what conditions women's work *can* 'figure' currently in such a debate. There is general agreement between the male critics I've cited that 'feminist work *by women*' can figure when appropriately framed ('effectively situated') by what has mainly been, apparently, a man's discourse. But by what criteria does feminist work by women come to figure, or *not* to figure when it comes raw-edged, without a frame?

Common sense suggests that perhaps all that is meant by these remarks is that few women so far have written articles explicitly entitled 'Feminism and Postmodernism'; or that few have written analyses focussed on the standard (male) referents of present debate – Habermas, Lyotard, Rorty, Jameson, Huyssen, Foster, Owens, and so on. If we accept that this is true (or that many of the texts that fulfil these conditions are quite recent) then perhaps feminists have merely been busy doing other things. It would be hard to deny that in spite of its heavy (if lightly acknowledged) borrowings from feminist theory, its frequent celebrations of 'difference' and 'specificity', and its critiques of 'Enlightenment' paternalism, postmodernism as a publishing phenomenon has pulled off the peculiar feat of re-constituting an overwhelmingly male pantheon of proper names to function as ritual objects of academic exegesis and commentary. It would be easy to shrug away a presumed feminist noninvolvement with postmodernism as a wise avoidance by women of a singularly ponderous, phallo-centred conversation – and to point out with Michèle Le Doeuff that the position of faithful reader to the great male philosopher is one that women have good reason to approach with caution. Many feminist criticisms of theories of postmodernism have occurred, in fact, in passing, in the context of saying something else as well.

Yet the matter is not quite so simple. *If* it is true that few women have explicitly inscribed their work in relation to postmodernism (and I am sceptical of such claims, since they tend to present the limits and biasses of our local reading habits as a satisfactory survey of the state of the world), it should also be true that only male writers who *do* so inscribe their work then come to 'figure' in the debate.

Yet in Arac's bibliography, we find numerous figures whose contribution could only strictly be described as formative, enabling and/or indirect: Adorno and Horkheimer, Derrida, Heidegger, Lacan, Foucault (not to mention Althusser, Perry Anderson, Lukács and Raymond Williams). Their work can only be part of a debate about postmodernism when 'effectively situated' in relation to it by subsequent commentary and citation. But a formative or indirect role in postmodernism has been willingly accorded, by men cited by Arac, to feminism. Why then, alongside the names of those men, do we not find references to (for example) the closely and critically associated work of Catherine Clément, Hélène Cixous, Luce Irigaray, Shoshana Felman, Jane Gallop, Sarah Kofman, Alice Jardine, Michéle Le Doueff, Gayatri Chakravorty Spivak, or Jacqueline Rose?

One could continue this line of questioning. For example, it might be argued that the 'enabling' male figures have at least explicitly theorized 'modernity', and so provide the bases for thinking postmodernity. But then not only would my brief list of women recur with even greater insistence, but it would need immediate expansion: Janet Bergstrom, Mary Anne Doane, Elizabeth Grosz, Barbara Johnson, Donna Haraway, Teresa de Lauretis, Angela McRobbie, Patricia Mellencamp, Tania Modleski, Nancy K. Miller, Naomi Schor, Kaja Silverman, Judith Williamson . . . (many of whom have had, in fact, quite a bit to say about postmodernism). Furthermore, if the 'politics' in the conjunction of *Postmodernism and Politics* authorizes the figuring under that rubric of the work of a Perry Anderson – then surely we might also expect to find listed works by Nancy Hartsock, Carole Pateman, Juliet Mitchell or Chantal Mouffe?

At this point, however, it becomes difficult to keep restricting my own enquiries to the names of (mostly white and Western) women. In the first and last sentence of his introductory text, Arac invokes 'the world' as the context of criticism. So why would a bibliography of 'postmodernism and *politics*' today still privilege only the great names of Western Marxism and their American academic heirs – at the expense of new theorizations of politics and culture by writers differently placed in histories of racism and colonialism? Rasheed Araeen, Homi K. Bhabha, Eduardo Galeano, Henry Louis Gates Jr, Geeta Kapur, Trinh T. Minh-ha, Nelly Richard . . . After all, if postmodernism really has defined a useful sphere for political debate, it is because of the awareness it can foster that its 'world' is finally not so small, so clearly 'mapped'.

It is, as a Derridean might observe, all a matter of border lines and frames. Any bibliography 'frames', as it defines, its field of representation. But the paradox of the frame does not prevent us from asking, in relation to any instance of framing, where and why a line is drawn. As John Frow has argued in *Marxism and Literary History*, the paradox of the frame is most useful precisely for framing a political project of working on 'the limits of reading'.

In reading the limits of Arac's bibliography, it becomes particularly difficult to determine the difference between an act of re-presenting a presupposed historical not-figuring of women in postmodernism debates, and an act of re-*producing* the not-figuring, not counting, of women's work, by 'simple' omission (writing it out of history, by writing its absence into history).

I have a similar difficulty with the more sensitive comments of Owens and Huyssen. Why do women artists and feminist theorists count *as* postmodernist (and as objects of commentary) for Owens, but not as 'engaging' in a debate? Doesn't this distinction return us precisely to that division between a (feminized) object-language and a (masculine) metalanguage that feminist theory has taught us to question for its political function, rather than for its epistemological validity? How can Huyssen simply cite and confirm what Owens says, while conceding that crucial aspects of postmodernism now would be 'unthinkable'[6] without the impact of feminist thought?

After all, it is Huyssen himself who has stressed in his feminist reading of 'Mass Culture as Woman: Modernism's Other' that male authors' preoccupation with imaginary femininity 'can easily go hand in hand with the exclusion of real women from the literary enterprise'.[7] Following Huyssen, then, a 'male' postmodernism could be seen as renewing one of the inaugural gestures (in Lyotard's sense) of modernism: inscribing its 'bafflement' by an imaginary, 'absent', silent femininity, while erasing and silencing the work of real women in the history and practice of the theoretical enterprise.

Given the persistence of the figure of women as mass culture (the irony of modernism), it is no accident that a debate about a presumed silence and absence of women has already taken place in relation to the work on popular culture that is in turn a component of postmodernism.[8] But the bafflement about women that besets both is also perhaps the latest version of the 'why have there been no great women artists (mathematicians, scientists …)?' conundrum – a badly posed question that assumes a negative response to a previous question, which remains, by default, unasked and unexamined.

How can this happen again? Again, there are some obvious responses that feminists might make. We could say that 'feminist theory' has come to function in academic publishing as a limiting category to a certain extent. It's now too easy to assume that if a text is labelled 'feminist' theory, then it can't properly 'count' or 'figure' as anything else ('woman's sphere', again). We could adopt a complacent paranoia, and assume that the male pantheon of postmodernism is merely a twilight of the gods – the last ruse of the patriarchal University trying for power to fix the meaning, and contain the damage, of its own decline. Or we could claim, probably with some justice if much brutality, that in spite of many rhetorical flourishes from men about their recognition and acceptance of feminism's 'contribution' to cultural and political theory, not very many men have really read extensively, or kept on reading, very many women's books and essays – particularly those published off the fast-track of prestige journals, or in strictly feminist contexts. The bottom line of any working bibliography is not, after all, a frame, but a practical prerequisite: you have to know it to use it.

The problem that interests me, however, is rather the difficulty that a feminist critic now faces in *saying* something about this – in trying to point out, let alone come to terms with, what seems to be a continued, repeated, basic *exclusion* of women's work from a highly invested field of intellectual and political endeavour. What women writer wants to say, in 1987, that men still aren't reading feminist work?; that women are being 'left out again'?; thus running the risk of being suspected of talking about herself ('if she writes about women's experiences, especially the unpleasant ones, declare her hysterical or "confessional"').[9]

In addressing the myth of a postmodernism still waiting for its women we can find an example of a genre, as well as a discourse, which in its untransformed state leaves a woman no place from which to speak, or nothing to say. For by resorting to the device of listing 'excluded' women, women excluded for no obvious reason except that given by the discourse – their gender – I have positioned myself in a speech-genre all too familiar in everyday life, as well as in pantomime, cartoons, and sitcoms: the woman's complaint, or *nagging*. One of the defining generic rules of 'nagging' is unsuccessful repetition of the same statements. It is unsuccessful, because it blocks change: nagging is a mode of repetition which fails to produce the desired effects of difference that might allow the complaint to end. In this it is quite close to what Anne Freadman, in her analysis of *Indiana*, calls the lament: a 'powerless text'. (A conventional comic scenario goes: she nags, he stops listening, nothing changes, she nags). Yet there is always a change of sorts implied by repetition: in this case, her 'place' in speech becomes, if not strictly nonexistent, then insufferable – leaving frenzy or silence as the only places left to go. It is an awesome genre, and I am not sure, I confess, how to transform it.

A traditional method has always been for the nagger somehow to lose interest, and so learn to change her subject (and her addressee). One possibility in this context is to follow up Dana Polan's suggestion that postmodernism is a 'machine for producing discourse'.[10] Polan argues that as the input to this machine begins to determine what it is possible to say in its name, so it becomes increasingly difficult to generate as output anything non-repetitive. Participants in a postmodernism debate are 'constrained' to refer back to previous input, and to take sides in familiar battles on a marked-out, well-trodden, terrain ('Habermas v. Lyotard', for example). The solution to feminist complaint might then be a simple one – switch position from nagger to nagged, then switch off.

But assuming a calculated deafness to discussion about postmodernism is not much of a solution for feminist women. To choose to *accept* a given constraint is not to challenge, overcome or transform anything. Besides, one of the fascinating paradoxes of the postmodernism machine is precisely how difficult it can be to switch it off (or switch off to it). Many of its best operators (Lyotard and Baudrillard, for example) have tried, and failed. As a discourse which runs on a 'paradoxical concern with its own lateness', as Andrew Ross points out (in one of the few essays relating feminism to postmodernism without attributing silence to women),[11] postmodernism has so far proved compatible with, rather than vulnerable to, vast quantities of input about its obsolescence or imminent breakdown.

A different response worth making would be, it seems to me, to make a generically feminist gesture of reclaiming women's work, and women's names, as a context *in* which debates about postmodernism might further be considered developed transformed (or abandoned).

[...]

NOTES

1. Craig Owens, 'Feminists and Postmodernism', in Hal Foster, ed., *The Anti-Aesthetic: Essays on Postmodern Culture*, Washington 1983, p. 61.
2. Andreas Huyssen, *After the Great Divide: Modernism, Mass Culture, Postmodernism*, Indiana 1986, pp. 198–99.
3. Jonathan Arac, ed., *Postmodernism and Politics*, Manchester 1986, p. xi. [Morris's emphasis.]
4. The others are Rosalind Coward (as co-author with John Ellis); Sally Hassan (as coeditor with Ihab Hassan); and Laura Kipnis, for one article.
5. For discussions of the problems of an intersection between feminism and postmodernism (and responses to Craig Owens' essay), see Barbara Creed, 'From Here to Modernity – Feminism and Postmodernism', *Screen*, vol. 28, no. 2, 1987, pp. 47–67, and Elspeth Probyn, 'Bodies and Anti-bodies: Feminism and the Postmodern', *Cultural Studies*, vol. 1, no. 3, 1987, pp. 349–60.
6. *After the Great Divide*, p. 220.
7. Ibid., p. 45.
8. See papers in Colin MacCabe, ed., *High Theory/Low Culture: Analyzing Popular Television and Film*, Manchester 1986.
9. Joanna Russ, *How To Suppress Women's Writing*, London 1983, p. 66.
10. Dana Polan, 'Postmodernism As Machine', paper to the Australian Screen Studies Association, Sydney, December 1986.
11. Andrew Ross, 'Viennese Waltzes', *Enclitic*, vol. 8, nos. 1–2, 1984, p. 76.

27

'A MANIFESTO FOR CYBORGS: SCIENCE, TECHNOLOGY AND SOCIALIST FEMINISM IN THE 1980s'

Donna Haraway

AN IRONIC DREAM OF A COMMON LANGUAGE FOR WOMEN
IN THE INTEGRATED CIRCUIT

[...]

A cyborg is a cybernetic organism, a hybrid of machine and organism, a creature of social reality as well as a creature of fiction. Social reality is lived social relations, our most important political construction, a world-changing fiction. The international women's movements have constructed 'women's experience,' as well as uncovered or discovered this crucial collective object. This experience is a fiction and fact of the most crucial, political kind. Liberation rests on the construction of the consciousness, the imaginative apprehension, of oppression, and so of possibility. The cyborg is a matter of fiction and lived experience that changes what counts as women's experience in the late twentieth century. This is a struggle over life and death, but the boundary between science fiction and social reality is an optical illusion.

Contemporary science fiction is full of cyborgs – creatures simultaneously animal and machine, who populate worlds ambiguously natural and crafted. Modern medicine is also full of cyborgs, of couplings between organism and machine, each conceived as coded devices, in an intimacy and with a power that was not generated in the history of sexuality. Cyborg 'sex' restores some of the lovely replicative baroque of ferns and invertebrates (such nice organic

From Donna Haraway (1985) 'A Manifesto for Cyborgs: Science, Technology and Socialist Feminism in the 1980s', *Socialist Review*, 15, (80); reprinted in Linda J. Nicholson (ed.) (1990) *Feminism/Postmodernism*. London: Routledge.

prophylactics against heterosexism). Cyborg replication is uncoupled from organic reproduction. Modern production seems like a dream of cyborg colonization of work, a dream that makes the nightmare of Taylorism seem idyllic. Modern war is a cyborg orgy, coded by C^3I, command-control-communication-intelligence, an $84 billion item in 1984's U.S. defense budget. I am making an argument for the cyborg as a fiction mapping our social and bodily reality and as an imaginative resource suggesting some very fruitful couplings. Foucault's biopolitics is a flaccid premonition of cyborg politics, a very open field.

By the late twentieth century, our time, a mythic time, we are all chimeras, theorized and fabricated hybrids of machine and organism; in short, we are cyborgs. The cyborg is our ontology; it gives us our politics. The cyborg is a condensed image of both imagination and material reality, the two joined centers structuring any possibility of historical transformation. In the traditions of Western science and politics – the tradition of racist, male-dominant capitalism; the tradition of progress; the tradition of the appropriation of nature as resource for the productions of culture; the tradition of reproduction of the self from the reflections of the other – the relation between organism and machine has been a border war. The stakes in the border war have been the territories of production, reproduction, and imagination. This chapter is an argument for pleasure in the confusion of boundaries and for responsibility in their construction. It is also an effort to contribute to socialist-feminist culture and theory in a postmodernist, nonnaturalist mode and in the utopian tradition of imagining a world without gender, which is perhaps a world without genesis, but maybe also a world without end. The cyborg incarnation is outside salvation history. Nor does it mark time on an Oedipal calendar, attempting to heal the terrible cleavages of gender in oral symbiotic utopia or post-Oedipal apocalypse. As Zoe Sofoulis argues in her unpublished manuscript on Lacan, Klein, and nuclear culture, *Lacklein*, the most terrible and perhaps the most promising monsters in cyborg worlds are embodied in non-Oedipal narratives with a different logic of repression, which we need to understand for our survival.

The cyborg is a creature in a postgender world; it has no truck with bisexuality, pre-Oedipal symbiosis, unalienated labor, or other seductions to organic wholeness through a final appropriation of all the powers of the parts into a higher unity. In a sense, the cyborg has no origin story in the Western sense; a 'final' irony since the cyborg is also the awful apocalyptic telos of the West's escalating dominations of abstract individuation, an ultimate self untied at last from all dependency, a man in space. An origin story in the Western humanist sense depends on the myth of original unity, fullness, bliss, and terror, represented by the phallic mother from whom all humans must separate, the task of individual development and of history, the twin potent myths inscribed most powerfully for us in psychoanalysis and Marxism. Hilary Klein has argued that both Marxism and psychoanalysis, in their concepts of labor and of individuation and gender formation, depend on the plot of original unity out of which difference must be produced and enlisted in a drama of escalating domination of woman/nature. The cyborg skips the step of original unity, of identification with nature in the Western sense. This is its illegitimate promise that might lead to subversion of its teleology as Star Wars.

The cyborg is resolutely committed to partiality, irony, intimacy, and perversity. It is oppositional, utopian, and completely without innocence. No longer structured by the polarity of public and private, the cyborg defines a technological polis based partly on a revolution of social relations in the oikos, the household. Nature and culture are reworked; the one can no longer be the resource for appropriation or incorporation by the other. The relationships for forming wholes from parts, including those of polarity and hierarchical domination, are at issue in the cyborg world. Unlike the hopes of Frankenstein's monster, the cyborg does not expect its father to save it through a restoration of the garden, that is, through the fabrication of a heterosexual mate, through its completion in a finished whole, a city and cosmos. The cyborg does not dream of community on the model of the organic family, this time without the Oedipal project. The cyborg would not recognize the Garden of Eden; it is not made of mud and cannot dream of returning to dust. Perhaps that is why I want to see if cyborgs can subvert the apocalypse of returning to nuclear dust in the manic compulsion to name the Enemy. Cyborgs are not reverent; they do not remember the cosmos. They are wary of holism, but needy for connection – they seem to have a natural feel for united front politics, but without the vanguard party. The main trouble with cyborgs, of course, is that they are the illegitimate offspring of militarism and patriarchal capitalism, not to mention state socialism. But illegitimate offspring are often exceedingly unfaithful to their origins. Their fathers, after all, are inessential.

I will return to the science fiction of cyborgs at the end of the chapter, but now I want to signal three crucial boundary breakdowns that make the following political fictional (political scientific) analysis possible. By the late twentieth century in United States, scientific culture, the boundary between human and animal, is thoroughly breached. The last beachheads of uniqueness have been polluted, if not turned into amusement parks – language, tool use, social behavior, mental events. Nothing really convincingly settles the separation of human and animal. Many people no longer feel the need of such a separation; indeed, many branches of feminist culture affirm the pleasure of connection with human and other living creatures. Movements for animal rights are not irrational denials of human uniqueness; they are clear-sighted recognition of connection across the discredited breach of nature and culture. Biology and evolutionary theory over the last two centuries have simultaneously produced modern organisms as objects of knowledge and reduced the line between humans and animals to a faint trace re-etched in ideological struggle or professional disputes between life and social sciences. Within this framework, teaching modern Christian creationism should be fought as a form of child abuse.

Biological-determinist ideology is only one position opened up in scientific culture for arguing the meanings of human animality. There is much room for radical political people to contest for the meanings of the breached boundary.[1] The cyborg appears in myth precisely where the boundary between human and animal is transgressed. Far from signaling a walling off of people from other living things, cyborgs signal disturbingly and pleasurably tight coupling. Bestiality has a new status in this cycle of marriage exchange.

The second leaky distinction is between animal-human (organism) and machine. Pre-cybernetic machines could be haunted; there was always the specter of the ghost in the machine. This dualism structured the dialogue between materialism and idealism that was settled by a dialectical progeny called spirit or history, according to taste. But basically machines were not self-moving, self-designing, autonomous. They could not achieve man's dream, only mock it. They were not man, an author of himself, but only a caricature of that masculinist reproductive dream. To think they were otherwise was paranoid. Now we are not so sure. Late twentieth-century machines have made thoroughly ambiguous the difference between natural and artificial, mind and body, self-developing and externally designed, and many other distinctions that used to apply to organisms and machines. Our machines are disturbingly lively, and we ourselves frighteningly inert.

Technological determinism is only one ideological space opened up by the reconceptions of machine and organism as coded texts through which we engage in the play of writing and reading the world.[2] 'Textualization' of everything in poststructuralist, postmodernist theory has been damned by Marxists and socialist feminists for its utopian disregard for lived relations of domination that ground the 'play' of arbitrary reading.[3] It is certainly true that postmodernist strategies, like my cyborg myth, subvert myriad organic wholes (e.g., the poem, the primitive culture, the biological organism). In short, the certainty of what counts as nature – a source of insight and a promise of innocence – is undermined, probably fatally. The transcendent authorization of interpretation is lost and with it the ontology grounding Western epistemology. But the alternative is not cynicism or faithlessness, that is, some version of abstract existence, like the accounts of technological determinism destroying 'man' by the 'machine' or 'meaningful political action' by the 'text.' Who cyborgs will be is a radical question; the answers are a matter of survival. Both chimpanzees and artifacts have politics, so why shouldn't we?[4]

The third distinction is a subset of the second: The boundary between physical and nonphysical is very imprecise for us. Pop physics books on the consequences of quantum theory and the indeterminacy principle are a kind of popular scientific equivalent to the Harlequin romances as a marker of radical change in American white heterosexuality: They get it wrong, but they are on the right subject. Modern machines are quintessentially microelectronics devices: They are everywhere and they are invisible. Modern machinery is an irreverent upstart god, mocking the Father's ubiquity and spirituality. The silicon chip is a surface for writing; it is etched in molecular scales disturbed only by atomic noise, the ultimate interference for nuclear scores. Writing, power, and technology are old partners in Western stories of the origin of civilization, but miniaturization has changed our experience of mechanism. Miniaturization has turned out to be about power; small is not so much beautiful as preeminently dangerous, as in Cruise missiles. Contrast the TV sets of the 1950s or the news cameras of the 1970s with the TV wristbands or hand-sized video cameras now advertised. Our best machines are made of sunshine; they are all light and clean because they are nothing but signals, electromagnetic waves, a section of a spectrum. These machines are eminently portable, mobile – a matter of immense human pain in Detroit and Singapore. People are nowhere near so fluid, being both material and opaque. Cyborgs are ether, quintessence.

The ubiquity and invisibility of cyborgs is precisely why these Sunshine Belt machines are so deadly. They are as hard to see politically as materially. They are about consciousness – or its simulation.[5] They are floating signifiers moving in pickup trucks across Europe, blocked more effectively by the witch-weavings of the displaced and so unnatural Greenham women, who read the cyborg webs of power very well, than by the militant labor of older masculinist politics, whose natural constituency needs defense jobs. Ultimately, the 'hardest' science is about the realm of greatest boundary confusion, the realm of pure number, pure spirit, C^3I, cryptography, and the preservation of potent secrets. The new machines are so clean and light. Their engineers are sun worshipers mediating a new scientific revolution associated with the night dream of post industrial society. The diseases evoked by these clean machines are 'no more' than the minuscule coding changes of an antigen in the immune system, 'no more' than the experience of stress. The 'nimble' fingers of 'Oriental' women, the old fascination of little Anglo-Saxon Victorian girls with dollhouses, and women's enforced attention to the small take on quite new dimensions in this world. There might be a cyborg Alice taking account of these new dimensions. Ironically, it might be the unnatural cyborg women making chips in Asia and spiral dancing in Santa Rita jail after an antinuclear action whose constructed unities will guide effective oppositional strategies.

So my cyborg myth is about transgressed boundaries, potent fusions, and dangerous possibilities which progressive people might explore as one part of needed political work. One of my premises is that most American socialists and feminists see deepened dualisms of mind and body, animal and machine, idealism and materialism in the social practices, symbolic formulations, and physical artifacts associated with high technology and scientific culture. From *One-Dimensional Man to The Death of Nature*,[6] the analytic resources developed by progressives have insisted on the necessary domination of technics and recalled us to an imagined organic body to integrate our resistance. Another of my premises is that the need for unity of people trying to resist worldwide intensification of domination has never been more acute. But a slightly perverse shift of perspective might better enable us to contest for meanings, as well as for other forms of power and pleasure in technologically mediated societies.

From one perspective, a cyborg world is about the final imposition of a grid of control on the planet, about the final abstraction embodies in a Star Wars apocalypse waged in the name of defense, about the final appropriation of women's bodies in a masculinist orgy of war.[7] From another perspective, a cyborg world might be about lived social and bodily realities in which people are not afraid of their joint kinship with animals and machines, not afraid of permanently partial identities and contradictory standpoints. The political struggle is to see from both perspectives at once because each reveals both dominations and possibilities unimaginable from the other vantage point. Single vision produces worse illusions than double vision or many-headed monsters. Cyborg unities are monstrous and illegitimate; in our present political circumstances, we could hardly hope for more potent myths for resistance and recoupling. I like to imagine the Livermore Action Group, LAG, as a kind of cyborg society, dedicated to realistically converting the laboratories that most fiercely embody and spew out the tools of technological apocalypse, and committed to building a political form that actually manages to hold together witches, engineers, elders, perverts, Christians, mothers, and Leninists long enough to disarm the state. Fission Impossible is the name of the affinity group in my town. (Affinity: related not by blood but by choice, the appeal of one chemical nuclear group for another, avidity.)[8]

FRACTURED IDENTITIES

It has become difficult to name one's feminism by a single adjective – or even to insist in every circumstance upon the noun. Consciousness of exclusion through naming is acute. Identities seem contradictory, partial, and strategic. With the hard-won recognition of their social and historical constitution, gender, race, and class cannot provide the basis for belief in 'essential' unity. There is nothing about being 'female' that naturally binds women. There is not even such a state as 'being' female, itself a highly complex category constructed in contested sexual scientific discourses and other social practices. Gender, race, or class consciousness is an achievement forced on us by the terrible historical experience of the contradictory social realities of patriarchy, colonialism, racism and capitalism. Who counts as 'us' in my own rhetoric? Which identities are available to ground such a potent political myth called 'us', and what could motivate enlistment in this collectivity? Painful fragmentation among feminists (not to mention among women) along every possible fault line has made the concept of woman elusive, an excuse for the matrix of women's dominations of each other. For me – and for many who share a similar historical location in white, professional, middle-class, female, radical, North American, mid-adult bodies – the sources of a crisis in political identity are legion. The recent history for much of the U.S. Left and the U.S. feminism has been a response to this kind of crisis by endless splitting and searches for a new essential unity. But there has also been a growing recognition of another response through coalition – affinity, not identity.[9]

Chela Sandoval, from a consideration of specific historical moments in the formation of the new political voice called women of color, has theorized a hopeful model of political identity called 'oppositional consciousness,' born of the skills for reading webs of power by those refused stable membership in the social categories of race, sex, or class.[10] 'Women of color,' a name contested at its origins by those whom it would incorporate, as well as a historical consciousness marking systematic breakdown of all the signs of Man in Western traditions, constructs a kind of postmodernist identity out of otherness, difference, and specificity. This postmodernist identity is fully political, whatever might be said about other possible postmodernisms. Sandoval's oppositional consciousness is about contradictory locations and heterochronic calendars, not about relativisms and pluralisms.

Sandoval emphasizes the lack of any essential criterion for identifying who is a woman of color. She notes that the definition of the group has been by conscious appropriation of negation. For example, a chicana or a U.S. black woman has not been able to speak as a woman or as a black person or as a chicano. Thus, she was at the bottom of a cascade of negative identities, left out of even the 'privileged' oppressed authorial categories called 'women and blacks,' who claimed to make the important revolutions. The category 'woman' negated all nonwhite women; 'black' negated all nonblack people, as well as all black women. But there was also no 'she,' no singularity, but a sea of differences among U.S. women who have affirmed their historical identity as U.S. women of color. This identity marks out a self-consciously constructed space that cannot affirm the capacity to act on the basis of natural identification, but only on the basis of conscious coalition, of affinity, of political kinship.[11] Unlike the 'woman' of some streams of the white women's movement in the United States, there is no naturalization of the matrix, or at least this is what Sandoval argues is uniquely available through the power of oppositional consciousness.

Sandoval's argument has to be seen as one potent formulation for feminists out of the worldwide development of anti-colonialist discourse, that is, discourse dissolving the West and its highest product – the one who is not animal, barbarian, or woman: that is, man, the author of a cosmos called history. As Orientalism is deconstructed politically and semiotically, the identities of the Occident destabilize, including those of its feminists.[12] Sandoval argues that 'women of color' have a chance to build an effective unity that does not replicate the imperializing, totalizing revolutionary subjects of previous Marxisms and feminisms which had not faced the consequences of the disorderly polyphony emerging from decolonization.

[...]

I do not know of any other time in history when there was greater need for political unity to confront effectively the dominations of race, gender, sexuality, and class. I also do not know of any other time when the kind of unity we might help build could have been possible. None of 'us' have any longer the symbolic or material capability of dictating the shape of reality to any of 'them.' Or at least 'we' cannot claim innocence from practicing such dominations. White women, including Euroamerican socialist feminists, discovered (i.e., were forced kicking and screaming to notice) the noninnocence of the category 'woman.' That consciousness changes the configuration of all previous categories; it denatures them as heat denatures a fragile protein. Cyborg feminists have to argue that 'we' do not want any more natural matrix of unity and that no construction is whole. Innocence, and the corollary insistence on victimhood as the only ground for insight, has done enough damage. But the constructed revolutionary subject must give late twentieth-century people pause as well. In the fraying of identities and in the reflexive strategies for constructing them, the possibility opens up for weaving something other than a shroud for the day after the apocalypse that so prophetically ends salvation history.

[...]

In another context, the French theorist Julia Kristeva claimed women appeared as a historical group after World War II, along with groups like youth. Her dates are doubtful, but we are now accustomed to remembering that as objects of knowledge and as historical actors, 'race' did not always exist, 'class' has a historical genesis, and 'homosexuals' are quite junior. It is no accident that the symbolic system of the family of man – and so the essence of woman – breaks up at the same moment that networks of connection among people on the planet are unprecedentedly multiple, pregnant, and complex. 'Advanced capitalism' is inadequate to convey the structure of this historical moment. In the Western sense, the end of man is at stake. It is no accident that woman disintegrates into women in our time. Perhaps socialist feminists were not substantially guilty of producing essentialist theory that suppressed women's particularity and contradictory interests. I think we have been, at least through unreflective participation in the logics, languages, and practices of white humanism and through searching for a single ground of domination to secure our revolutionary voice. Now we have less excuse. But in the consciousness of our failures, we risk lapsing into boundless difference and giving up on the confusing task of making partial, real connection. Some differences are playful; some are poles of world historical systems of domination. Epistemology is about knowing the difference.

THE INFORMATICS OF DOMINATION

In this attempt at an epistemological and political position, I would like to sketch a picture of possible unity, a picture indebted to socialist and feminist principles of design. The frame for my sketch is set by the extent and importance of rearrangements in worldwide social relations tied to science and technology. I argue for a politics rooted in claims about fundamental changes in the nature of class, race, and gender in an emerging system of world order analogous in its novelty and scope to that created by industrial capitalism; we are living through a movement from an organic, industrial society to a polymorphous, information system – from all work to all play, a deadly game. Simultaneously material and ideological, the dichotomies may be expressed in the following chart of transitions from the comfortable old hierarchical dominations to the scary new networks I have called the informatics of domination:

Representation	Simulation
Bourgeois novel, realism	Science fiction, postmodernism
Organism	Biotic component
Depth, integrity	Surface, boundary
Heat	Noise
Biology as clinical practice	Biology as inscription
Physiology	Communications engineering
Small group	Subsystem
Perfection	Optimization
Eugenics	Population Control
Decadence, *Magic Mountain*	Obsolescence, *Future Shock*
Hygiene	Stress management
Microbiology, tuberculosis	Immunology, AIDS
Organic division of labor	Ergonomics/cybernetics of labor
Functional specialization	Modular construction
Reproduction	Replication
Organic sex role specialization	Optimal genetic strategies
Biological determinism	Evolutionary inertia, constraints
Community ecology	Ecosystem
Racial chain of being	Neo-imperialism, United Nations humanism
Scientific management in home/factory	Global factory/electronic cottage
Family/market/factory	Women in the integrated circuit
Family wage	Comparable worth
Public/private	Cyborg citizenship
Nature/culture	Fields of difference
Cooperation	Communications enhancement
Freud	Lacan
Sex	Genetic engineering
Labor	Robotics
Mind	Artificial intelligence
World War II	Star Wars
White capitalist patriarchy	Informatics of domination

This list suggests several interesting things.[13] 'First, the objects on the right-hand side cannot be coded as 'natural,' a realization that subverts naturalistic coding for the left-hand side as well. We cannot go back ideologically or materially. It's not just that 'god' is dead; so is the 'goddess.' Or both are revivified in the worlds charged with microelectronic and biotechnological politics. In relation to objects like biotic components, one must think not in terms of essential properties, but in terms of design, boundary constraints, rates of flows, systems logics, costs of lowering constraints. Sexual reproduction is one kind of reproductive strategy among many, with costs and benefits as a function of the system environment. Ideologies of sexual reproduction can no longer reasonably call on notions of sex and sex role as organic aspects in natural objects like organisms and families. Such reasoning will be unmasked as irrational, and ironically corporate executives reading *Playboy* and anti-porn radical feminists will make strange bedfellows in jointly unmasking the irrationalism.

[...]

This kind of analysis of scientific and cultural objects of knowledge which have appeared historically since World War II prepares us to notice some important inadequacies in feminist analysis which has proceeded as if the organic, hierarchical dualism ordering discourse in the West since Aristotle still ruled. They have been cannibalized, or as Zoe Sofia (Sofoulis) might put it, they have been 'techno-digested.' The dichotomies between mind and body, animal and human, organism and machine, public and private, nature and culture, men and women, primitive and civilized are all in question ideologically. The actual situation of women is their integration/exploitation into a world system of production/reproduction and communication called the informatics of domination. The home, work place, market, public arena, the body itself – all can be dispersed and interfaced in nearly infinite, polymorphous ways, with large consequences for women and others – consequences that themselves are very different for different people and which make potent oppositional international movements difficult to imagine and essential for survival. One important route for reconstructing socialist-feminist politics is through theory and practice addressed to the social relations of science and technology, including crucially the systems of myth and meanings structuring our imaginations. The cyborg is a kind of disassembled and reassembled, postmodern collective and personal self. This is the self feminists must code.

Communications technologies and biotechnologies are the crucial tools recrafting our bodies. These tools embody and enforce new social relations for women worldwide. Technologies and scientific discourses can be partially understood as formalizations, that is, as frozen moments, of the fluid social interactions constituting them, but they should also be viewed as instruments for enforcing meanings. The boundary is permeable between tool and myth, instrument and concept, historical systems of social relations and historical anatomies of possible bodies, including objects of knowledge. Indeed, myth and tool mutually constitute each other.

[. . .]

THE HOMEWORK ECONOMY

The 'New Industrial Revolution' is producing a new worldwide working class, as well as new sexualities and ethnicities. The extreme mobility of capital and the emerging international division of labor are intertwined with the emergence of new collectivities and the weakening of familiar groupings. These developments are neither gender- nor race-neutral. White men in advanced industrial societies have become newly vulnerable to permanent job loss, and women are not disappearing from the job rolls at the same rates as men. It is not simply that women in third-world countries are the preferred labor force for the science-based multinationals in the export-processing sectors, particularly in electronics. The picture is more systematic and involves reproduction, sexuality, culture, consumption, and production. In the prototypical Silicon Valley, many women's lives have been structured around employment in electronics-dependent jobs, and their intimate realities include serial heterosexual monogamy, negotiating child care, distance from extended kin or most other forms of traditional community, a high likelihood of loneliness and extreme economic vulnerability as they age. The ethnic and racial diversity of women in Silicon Valley structures a microcosm of conflicting differences in culture, family, religion, education, and language.

Richard Gordon has called this new situation the homework economy.[14] Although he includes the phenomenon of literal homework emerging in connection with electronics assembly, Gordon intends 'homework economy' to name a restructuring of work that broadly has the characteristics formerly ascribed to female jobs, jobs literally done only by women. Work is being redefined as both literally female and feminized, whether performed by men or women. To be feminized means to be made extremely vulnerable; able to be disassembled, reassembled, exploited as a reserve labor force; seen less as workers than as servers; subjects to time arrangements on and off the paid job that make a mockery of a limited work day; leading an existence that always borders on being obscene, out of place, and reducible to sex. De-skilling is an old strategy newly applicable to formerly privileged workers. However, the homework economy does not refer only to large-scale de-skilling, nor does it deny that new areas of high skill are emerging, even for women and men previously excluded from skilled employment. Rather, the concept indicates that factory, home, and market are integrated on a new scale and that the places of women are crucial – and need to be analyzed for differences among women and for meanings for relations between men and women in various situations.

The homework economy as a world capitalist organizational structure is made possible by (not caused by) the new technologies. The success of the attack on relatively privileged, mostly white men's unionized jobs is tied to the power of the new communications technologies to integrate and control labor despite extensive dispersion and decentralization. The consequences of the new technologies are felt by women both in the loss of the family (male) wage (if they ever had access to this white privilege) and in the character of their own jobs, which are becoming capital-intensive, for example, office work and nursing.

The new economic and technological arrangements are also related to the collapsing welfare state and the ensuing intensification of demands on women to sustain daily life for themselves as well as for men, children, and old people. The feminization of poverty – generated by dismantling the welfare state, by the homework economy where stable jobs become the exception, and sustained by the expectation that women's wage will not be matched by a male income for the support of children – has become an urgent focus. The causes of various women-headed households are a function of race, class, or sexuality; but their increasing generality is a ground for coalitions of women on many issues. That women regularly sustain daily life partly as a function of their enforced status as mothers is hardly new; the kind of integration with the overall capitalist and progressively war-based economy is new. The particular pressure, for example, on U.S. black women, who have achieved an escape from (barely) paid domestic service and who now hold clerical and similar jobs in large numbers, has large implications for continued enforced black poverty with employment. Teenage women in industrializing areas of the third world increasingly find themselves the sole or major source of a cash wage for their families, while access to land is ever more problematic. These developments must have major consequences in the psychodynamics and politics of gender and race.

[...]

This is the context in which the projections for worldwide structural unemployment stemming from the new technologies are part of the picture of the homework economy. As robotics and related technologies put men out of work in 'developed' countries and exacerbate failure to generate male jobs in third-world 'development' and as the automated office becomes the rule even in labor-surplus countries, the feminization of work intensifies. Black women in the United States have long known what it looks like to face the structural underemployment ('feminization') of black men, as well as their own highly vulnerable position in the wage economy. It is no longer a secret that sexuality, reproduction, family, and community life are interwoven with this economic structure in myriad ways which have also differentiated the situations of white and black women. Many more women and men will contend with similar situations, which will make cross-gender and race alliances on issues of basic life support (with or without jobs) necessary, not just nice.

[...]

Another critical aspect of the social relations of the new technologies is the reformulation of expectations, culture, work, and reproduction for the large scientific and technical work force. A major social and political danger is the formation of a strongly bimodal social structure, with masses of women and men of all ethnic groups, but especially people of color, confined to a homework economy, illiteracy of several varieties, and general redundancy and impotence, controlled by high-tech repressive apparatuses ranging from entertainment to surveillance and disappearance. An adequate socialist-feminist politics should address women in the privileged occupational categories and particularly in the production of science and technology that constructs scientific-technical discourse, processes, and objects.[15]

[...]

WOMEN IN THE INTEGRATED CIRCUIT

Let me summarize the picture of women's historical locations in advanced industrial societies, as these positions have been restructured partly through the social relations of science and technology. If it was ever possible ideologically to characterize women's lives by the distinction of public and private domains – suggested by images of the division of working-class life into factory and home, of bourgeois life into market and home, and of gender existence into personal and political realms – it is now a totally misleading ideology, even to show how both terms of these dichotomies construct each other in practice and in theory. I prefer a network ideological image, suggesting the profusion of spaces and identities and the permeability of boundaries in the personal body and in the body politic. 'Networking' is both a feminist practice and a multinational corporate strategy – weaving is for oppositional cyborgs.

So let me return to the earlier image of the informatics of domination and trace one vision of women's 'place' in the integrated circuit, touching only a few idealized social locations seen primarily from the point of view of advanced capitalist societies: Home, Market, Paid Work Place, State, School, Clinic-Hospital, and Church. Each of these idealized spaces is logically and practically implied in every other locus, perhaps analogous to a holographic photograph. I want to suggest the impact of the social relations mediated and enforced by the new technologies in order to help formulate needed analysis and practical work. However, there is no 'place' for women in these networks, only geometries of differences and contradiction crucial to women's cyborg identities. If we learn how to read these webs of power and social life, we might learn new couplings, new coalitions. There is no way to read the following list from a standpoint of 'identification,' of a unitary self. The issue is dispersion. The task is to survive in diaspora.

[...]

The only way to characterize the informatics of domination is as a massive intensification of insecurity and cultural impoverishment, with common failure of subsistence networks for the most vulnerable. Since much of this picture interweaves with the social relations of science and technology, the urgency of a socialist-feminist politics addressed to science and technology is plain. There is much now being done, and the grounds for political work are rich. For example, the efforts to develop forms of collective struggle for women in paid work, like District 925 of the SEIU (Service Employees International Union) should be a high priority for all of us. These efforts are profoundly tied to technical restructuring of labor processes and reformations of working classes. These efforts also are providing understanding of a more comprehensive kind of labor organization, involving community, sexuality, and family issues never privileged in the largely white male industrial unions.

The structural rearrangements related to the social relations of science and technology evoke strong ambivalence. But it is not necessary to be ultimately depressed by the implications of late twentieth-century women's relation to all aspects of work, culture, production of knowledge, sexuality, and reproduction. For excellent reasons, most Marxisms see domination best and have trouble understanding what can only look like false consciousness and people's complicity in their own domination in late capitalism. It is crucial to remember that what is lost, perhaps especially from women's points of view, is often virulent forms of oppression, nostalgically naturalized in the face of current violation. Ambivalence toward the disrupted unities mediated by high-tech culture requires not sorting consciousness into categories of 'clear-sighted critique grounding a solid political epistemology' versus 'manipulated false consciousness,' but subtle understanding of emerging pleasures, experiences, and powers with serious potential for changing the rules of the game.

There are grounds for hope in the emerging bases for new kinds of unity across race, gender, and class, as these elementary units of socialist-feminist analysis themselves suffer protean transformations. Intensifications of hardship experienced worldwide in connection with the social relations of science and technology are severe. But what people are experiencing is not transparently clear, and we lack sufficiently subtle connections for collectively building effective theories of experience. Present efforts – Marxist, psychoanalytic, feminist, anthropological – to clarify even 'our' experience are rudimentary.

[. . .]

CYBORGS: A MYTH OF POLITICAL IDENTITY

I want to conclude with a myth about identity and boundaries which might inform late twentieth-century political imaginations. I am indebted in this story to writers like Joanna Russ, Samuel Delany, John Varley, James Tiptree, Jr., Octavia Butler, and Vonda McIntyre.[16] These are our storytellers exploring what it means to be embodied in high-tech worlds. They are theorists for cyborgs. Exploring conceptions of bodily boundaries and social order, the anthropologist Mary Douglas should be credited with helping us to consciousness about how fundamental body imagery is to world view and so to political language.[17] French feminists like Luce Irigaray and Monique Wittig, for all their differences, know how to write the body, how to weave eroticism, cosmology, and politics from imagery of embodiment, and especially for Wittig, from imagery of fragmentation and reconstitution of bodies.[18]

[...]

Contrary to Orientalist stereotypes of the 'oral primitive,' literacy is a special mark of women of color, acquired by U.S. black women as well as men through a history of risking death to learn and to teach reading and writing. Writing has a special significance for all colonized groups. Writing has been crucial to the Western myth of the distinction of oral and written cultures, primitive and civilized mentalities, and more recently to the erosion of that distinction in postmodernist theories attacking the phallogocentrism of the West, with its worship of the monotheistic, phallic, authoritative, and singular work, the unique and perfect name.[19] Contests for the meanings of writing are a major form of contemporary political struggle. Releasing the play of writing is deadly serious. The poetry and stories of U.S. women of color are repeatedly about writing, about access to the power to signify, but this time that power must be neither phallic nor innocent. Cyborg writing must not be about the Fall, the imagination of a once-upon-a-time wholeness before language, before writing, before Man. Cyborg writing is about the power to survive not on the basis of original innocence, but on the basis of seizing the tools to mark the world that marked them as other.

The tools are often stories, retold stories, versions that reverse and displace the hierarchical dualisms of naturalized identities. In retelling origin stories, cyborg authors subvert the central myths of origin of Western culture. We have all been colonized by those origin myths, with their longing for fulfillment in apocalypse. The phallogocentric origin stories most crucial for feminist cyborgs are built into the literal technologies–technologies that write the world, biotechnology and microelectronics – that have recently textualized our bodies as code problems on the grid of C^3I. Feminist cyborg stories have the task of recoding communication and intelligence to subvert command and control.

Figuratively and literally, language politics pervade the struggles of women of color, and stories about language have a special power in the rich contemporary writing by U.S. women of color. For example, retellings of the story of the indigenous woman Malinche, mother of the mestizo 'bastard' race of the new world, master of languages, and mistress of Cortés, carry special meaning for Chicana constructions of identity. Cherríe Moraga in *Loving in the War Years* explores the themes of identity when one never possessed the original language, never told the original story, never resided in the harmony of legitimate heterosexuality in the garden of culture, and so cannot base identity on a myth or a fall from innocence and right to natural names, mother's or father's.[20] Moraga's writing, her superb literacy, is presented in her poetry as the same kind of violation as Malinche's mastery of the conqueror's language – a violation, an illegitimate production, that allows survival. Moraga's language is not 'whole';

it is self-consciously spliced, a chimera of English and Spanish, both conqueror's languages. But it is this chimeric monster, without claim to an original language before violation, that crafts the erotic, competent, potent identities of women of color. Sister Outsider hints at the possibility of world survival not because of her innocence, but because of her ability to live on the boundaries, to write without the founding myth of original wholeness, with its inescapable apocalypse of final return to a deathly oneness that Man has imagined to be the innocent and all-powerful Mother, freed at the End from another spiral of appropriation by her son. Writing marks Moraga's body, affirms it as the body of a woman of color, against the possibility of passing into the unmarked category of the Anglo father or into the Orientalist myth of 'original illiteracy' of a mother that never was. Malinche was mother here, not Eve before eating the forbidden fruit. Writing affirms Sister Outsider, not the Woman-before-the-Fall-into-Writing needed by the phallogocentric Family of Man.

Writing is preeminently the technology of cyborgs, etched surfaces of the late twentieth century. Cyborg politics is the struggle for language and the struggle against perfect communication, against the one code that translates all meaning perfectly, the central dogma of phallogocentrism. That is why cyborg politics insist on noise and advocate pollution, rejoicing in the illegitimate fusions of animal and machine. These are the couplings which make Man and Woman so problematic, subverting the structure of desire, the force imagined to generate language and gender, and so subverting the structure and modes of reproduction of Western identity, of nature and culture, of mirror and eye, slave and master, body and mind. 'We' did not originally choose to be cyborgs, but choice grounds a liberal politics and epistemology that imagines the reproduction of individuals before the wider replications of 'texts.'

[...]

To recapitulate, certain dualisms have been persistent in Western traditions; they have all been systemic to the logics and practices of domination of women, people of color, nature, workers, animals – in short, domination of all constituted as others, whose task is to mirror the self. Chief among these troubling dualisms are self/other, mind/body, culture/nature, male/female, civilized/primitive, reality/appearance, whole/part, agent/resource, maker/made, active/passive, right/wrong, truth/illusion, total/partial, God/man. The self is the One who is not dominated, who knows that by the service of the other; the other is the one who holds the future, who knows that by the experience of domination, which gives the lie to the autonomy of the self. To be One is to be autonomous, to be powerful, to be God; but to be One is to be an illusion and so to be involved in a dialectic of apocalypse with the other. Yet, to be other is to be multiple, without clear boundaries, frayed, insubstantial. One is too few, but two are too many.

High-tech culture challenges these dualisms in intriguing ways. It is not clear who makes and who is made in the relation between human and machine. It is not clear what is mind and what is body in machines that resolve into coding practices. Insofar as we know ourselves in both formal discourse (e.g., biology) and in daily practice, (e.g., the homework economy in the integrated circuit), we find ourselves to be cyborgs, hybrids, mosaics, chimeras. Biological organisms have become biotic systems, communications devices like others. There is no fundamental, ontological separation in our formal knowledge of machine and organism, of technical and organic. The replicant Rachel in the film *Blade Runner* stands as the image of a cyborg culture's fear, love, and confusion.

One consequence is that our sense of connection to our tools is heightened. The trance state experienced by many computer users has become a staple of science-fiction film and cultural jokes. Perhaps paraplegics and other severely handicapped people can (and sometimes do) have the most intense experiences of complex hybridization with other communication devices.[21] Anne McCaffrey's profeminist *The Ship Who Sang* explored the consciousness of a cyborg, hybrid of girl's brain and complex machinery, formed after the birth of a severely handicapped child. Gender, sexuality, embodiment, skill: All were reconstituted in the story. Why should our bodies end at the skin or include at best other beings encapsulated by skin? From the seventeenth century till now, machines could be animated – given ghostly souls to make them speak or move or to account for their orderly development and mental capacities. Or organisms could be mechanized – reduced to body understood as resource of mind. These machine/organism relationships are obsolete, unnecessary. For us, in imagination and in other practice, machines can be prosthetic devices, intimate components, friendly selves. We don't need organic holism to give impermeable wholeness, the total woman and her feminist variants (mutants?). Let me conclude this point by a very partial reading of the logic of the cyborg monsters of my second group of texts, feminist science fiction.

The cyborgs populating feminist science fiction make very problematic the statuses of man or woman, human, artifact, member of a race, individual identity, or body. Katie King clarifies how pleasure in reading these fictions is not largely based on identification. Students facing Joanna Russ for the first time, students who have learned to take modernist writers like James Joyce or Virginia Woolf without flinching, do not know what to make of *The Adventures of Alyx of The Female Man*, where characters refuse the reader's search for innocent wholeness while granting the wish for heroic quests, exuberant eroticism, and serious politics. *The Female Man* is the story of four versions of one genotype, all of whom meet, but even taken together do not make a whole, resolve the dilemmas of violent moral action, nor remove the growing scandal of gender. The feminist science fiction of Samuel Delany, especially *Tales of Neverÿon*, mocks stories of origin by redoing the neolithic revolution, replaying the founding moves of Western civilization to subvert their plausibility. James Tiptree, Jr., an author whose fiction was regarded as particularly manly until her 'true' gender was revealed, tells tales of reproduction based on nonmammalian technologies like alternation of generations or male brood pouches and male nurturing. John Varley constructs a supreme cyborg in his arch-feminist exploration of Gaea, a mad goddess-planet-trickster-old-woman-technological device on whose surface an extraordinary array of post cyborg symbioses are spawned. Octavia Butler writes of an African sorcerers pitting her powers of transformation against the genetic manipulations of her rival (*Wild Seed*), of time warps that bring a modern U.S. black woman into slavery where her actions in relation to her white master-ancestor determine the possibility of her own birth (*Kindred*), and of the illegitimate insights into identity and community of, an adopted cross-species child who came to know the enemy as self (*Survivor*). In her recent novel, *Dawn* (1987), the first installment of a series called *Xenogenesis*, Butler tells the story of Lilith lyapo, whose personal name recalls Adam's first and repudiated wife and whose family name marks her status as the widow of the son of Nigerian immigrants to the United States. A black woman and a mother whose child is dead, Lilith mediates the transformation of humanity through genetic exchange with extraterrestrial lovers/rescuers/destroyers/genetic engineers, who reform earth's habitats after the nuclear holocaust and coerce surviving humans into intimate fusion with them. It is a novel that interrogates reproductive, linguistic, and nuclear politics in a mythic field structured by late twentieth-century race and gender.

Because it is particularly rich in boundary transgressions, Vonda McIntyre's *Superluminal* can close this truncated catalogue of promising and dangerous monsters who help redefine the pleasures and politics of embodiment and feminist writing. In a fiction where no character is 'simply' human, human status is highly problematic. Orca, a genetically altered diver, can speak with killer whales and survive deep ocean conditions, but she longs to explore space as a pilot, necessitating bionic implants jeopardizing her kinship with the divers and cetaceans. Transformations are effected by virus vectors carrying a new developmental code, by transplant surgery, by implants of microelectronic devices, by analogue doubles, and by other means. Laenea becomes a pilot by accepting a heart implant and a host of other alternations allowing survival in transit at speeds exceeding that of light. Radu Dracul survives a virus-caused plague on his outerworld planet to find himself with a time sense that changes the boundaries of spatial perception for the whole species. All the characters explore the limits of language, the dream of communicating experience, and the necessity of limitation, partiality, and intimacy even in this world of protean transformation and connection. *Superluminal* stands also for the defining contradictions of a cyborg world in another sense; it embodies textually the intersection of feminist theory and colonial discourse in the science fiction I have alluded to in this essay. This is a conjunction with a long history that many first world feminists have tried to repress, including myself in my readings of *Superluminal* before being called to account by Zoe Sofoulis, whose different location in the world system's informatics of domination made her acutely alert to the imperialist moment of all science-fiction cultures, including women's science fiction. From an Australian feminist sensitivity, Sofoulis remembered more readily McIntyre's role as writer of the adventures of Captain Kirk and Spock in 'Star Trek' than her rewriting the romance in *Superluminal*.

Monsters have always defined the limits of community in Western imaginations. The centaurs and Amazons of ancient Greece established the limits of the centered polis of the Greek male human by their disruption of marriage and boundary pollutions of the warrior with animality and woman. Unseparated twins and hermaphrodites were the confused human material in early modern France who grounded discourse on the natural and supernatural, medical and legal, portents and diseases – all crucial to establishing modern identity.[22] The evolutionary and behavioral sciences of monkeys and apes have marked the multiple boundaries of late twentieth-century industrial identities. Cyborg monsters in feminist science fiction define quite different political possibilities and limits from those proposed by the mundane fiction of Man and Woman.

There are several consequences to taking seriously the imagery of cyborgs as other than our enemies. Our bodies, ourselves – bodies are maps of power and identity. Cyborgs are no exceptions. A cyborg body is not innocent; it was not born in a garden; it does not seek unitary identity and so generates antagonistic dualisms without end (or until the world ends); it takes irony for granted. One is too few, and two is only one possibility. Intense pleasure in skill, machine skill, ceases to be a sin, but an aspect of embodiment. The machine is not an it to be animated, worshiped, and dominated. The machine is us, our processes, an aspect of our embodiment. We can be responsible for machines; they do not dominate or threaten us. We are responsible for boundaries; we are they. Up till now (once upon a time), female embodiment seemed to be given, organic, necessary; female embodiment seemed to mean skill in mothering and its metaphoric extensions. Only by being out of place could we take intense pleasure in machines and then with excuses that this was organic activity after all, appropriate to females. Cyborgs might consider more seriously the partial, fluid, sometimes aspect of sex and sexual embodiment. Gender might not be global identity after all, even if it has profound historical breadth and depth.

The ideologically charged question of what counts as daily activity, as experience, can be approached by exploiting the cyborg image. Feminists have recently claimed that women are given to dailiness, that women more than men somehow sustain daily life, and so have a privileged epistemological position potentially. There is a compelling aspect to this claim, one that makes visible unvalued female activity and names it as the ground of life. But the ground of life? What about all the ignorance of women, all the exclusions and failures of knowledge and skill? What about men's access to daily competence, to knowing how to build things, to take them apart, to play? What about other embodiments? Cyborg gender is a local possibility taking a global vengeance. Race, gender, and capital require a cyborg theory of wholes and parts. There is no drive in cyborgs to produce total theory, but there is an intimate experience of boundaries, their construction and deconstruction. There is a myth system waiting to become a political language to ground one way of looking at science and technology and challenging the informatics of domination – in order to act potently.

One last image: organisms and organismic, holistic politics depend on metaphors of rebirth and invariably call on the resources of reproductive sex. I would suggest that cyborgs have more to do with regeneration and are suspicious of the reproductive matrix and of most birthing. For salamanders, regeneration after injury, such as the loss of a limb, involves regrowth of structure and restoration of function with the constant possibility of twinning or other odd topographical productions at the site of former injury. The regrown limb can be monstrous, duplicated, potent. We have all been injured, profoundly. We require regeneration, not rebirth, and the possibilities for our reconstitution include the utopian dream of the hope for a monstrous world without gender.

Cyborg imagery can help express two crucial arguments in this essay: (1) the production of universal, totalizing theory is a major mistake that misses most of reality, probably always, but certainly now; (2) taking responsibility for the social relations of science and technology means refusing an anti-science metaphysics, a demonology of technology, and so means embracing the skillful task of reconstructing the boundaries of daily life, in partial connection with others, in communication with all of our parts. It is not just that science and technology are possible means of great human satisfaction, as well as a matrix of complex dominations. Cyborg imagery can suggest a way out of the maze of dualisms in which we have explained our bodies and our tools to ourselves. This is a dream not of a common language, but of a powerful infidel heteroglossia. It is an imagination of a feminist speaking in tongues to strike fear into the circuits of the super savers of the New Right. It means both building and destroying machines, identities, categories, relationships, spaces, stories. Although both are bound in the spiral dance, I would rather be a cyborg than a goddess.

[...]

NOTES

1. Useful references to left and/or feminist radical science movements and theory and to biological/biotechnological issues include Ruth Bleier, *Science and Gender: A Critique of Biology and Its Themes on Women* (New York: Pergamon, 1984); Ruth Bleier, ed., *Feminist Approaches to Science* (New York: Pergamon, 1986); Sandra Harding, *The Science Question in Feminism* (Ithaca, NY: Cornell University Press, 1986); Anne Fausto-Sterling, *Myths of Gender* (New York: Basic Books, 1985); Stephen J. Gould, *Mismeasure of Man* (New York: Norton, 1981); Ruth Hubbard, Mary Sue Henifin, Barbara Fried, eds., *Biological Woman, the Convenient Myth* (Cambridge, MA: Schenkman, 1982); Evelyn Fox Keller, *Reflections on Gender and Science* (New Haven, CT: Yale University Press, 1985); R. C. Lewontin, Steve Rose, and Leon Kamin, *Not in Our Genes* (New York: Pantheon, 1984); *Radical Science Journal* (from 1987, *Science as Culture*), 26 Freegrove Road, London N7 9RQ; *Science for the People*, 897 Main St., Cambridge, MA 02139.
2. Starting points for left and/or feminist approaches to technology and politics include Ruth Schwartz Cowan, *More Work for Mother: The Ironies of Household*

Technology from the Open Hearth to the Microwave (New York: Basic Books, 1983); Joan Rothschild, *Machina ex Dea: Feminist Perspectives on Technology* (New York: Pergamon, 1983); Sharon Traweek, *Beantimes and Lifetimes: The World of High Energy Physics* (Cambridge, MA: Harvard University Press, 1988); R. M. Young and Les Levidov, eds., *Science, Technology, and the Labour Process*, Vols. 1–3 (London: CSE Books); Joseph Weizenbaum, *Computer Power and Human Reason* (San Francisco: Freeman, 1976); Langdon Winner, *Autonomous Technology: Technics Out of Control as a Theme in Political Thought* (Cambridge, MA: MIT Press, 1977); Langdon Winner, *The Whale and the Reactor* (Chicago: Chicago University Press, 1986); Jan Zimmerman, ed., *The Technological Woman: Interfacing with Tomorrow* (New York: Praeger, 1983); Tom Athanasiou, 'High-tech Politics. The Case of Artificial Intelligence,' *Socialist Review*, No. 92, 1987, pp. 7–35; Carol Cohn, 'Nuclear Language and How We Learned to Pat the Bomb,' *Bulletin of Atomic Scientists*, June 1987, pp. 17–24; Terry Winograd and Fernando Flores, *Understanding Computers and Cognition: A New Foundation for Design* (New Jersey: Ablex, 1986); Paul Edwards, 'Border Wars: The Politics of Artificial Intelligence,' *Radical America*, Vol. 19, No. 6, 1985, pp. 39–52; *Global Electronics Newsletter*, 867 West Dana St., #204, Mountain View, CA 94041; *Processed World*, 55 Sutter St., San Francisco, CA 94104; *ISIS*, Women's International Information and Communication Service, P.O. Box 50 (Cornavin), 1211 Geneva 2, Switzerland, and Via Santa Maria dell'Anima 30, 00186 Rome, Italy. Fundamental approaches to modern social studies of science that do not continue the liberal mystification that it all started with Thomas Kuhn, include: Karin Knorr-Cetina, *The Manufacture of Knowledge* (Oxford: Pergamon, 1981); K. D. Knorr-Cetina and Michael Mulkay, eds., *Science Observed: Perspectives on the Social Study of Science* (Beverly Hills, CA: Sage, 1983); Bruno Latour and Steve Woolgar, *Laboratory Life: The Social Construction of Scientific Facts* (Beverly Hills, CA: Sage, 1979); Robert M. Young, 'Interpreting the Production of Science,' *New Scientist*, Vol. 29, March 1979, pp. 1026–1028. More is claimed than is known about room for contesting productions of science in the mythic/material space of 'the laboratory'; the 1984 Directory of the Network for the Ethnographic Study of Science, Technology, and Organizations lists a wide range of people and projects crucial to better radical analysis; available from NESSTO, P.O. Box 11442, Stanford, CA 94305.

3. Fredric Jameson, 'Post Modernism, or the Cultural Logic of Late Capitalism,' *New Left Review*, July/August 1984, pp. 53–94. See Marjorie Perloff, ' "Dirty" Language and Scramble Systems,' *Sulfur* Vol. 2, 1984, pp. 178–183; Kathleen Fraser, *Something (Even Human Voices) in the Foreground, a Lake* (Berkeley, CA: Kelsey St. Press, 1984). For feminist modernist/postmodernist cyborg writing, see *How(ever)*, 871 Corbett Ave., San Francisco, CA 94131.

A provocative, comprehensive argument about the politics and theories of post-modernism is made by Fredric Jameson, who argues that postmodernism is not an option, a style among others, but a cultural dominant requiring radical reinvention of left politics from within; there is no longer any place from without that gives meaning to the comforting fiction of critical distance. Jameson also makes clear why one cannot be for or against postmodernism, an essentially moralist move. My position is that feminists (and others) need continuous cultural reinvention, post-modernist critique, and historical materialism; only a cyborg would have a chance. The old dominations of white capitalist patriarchy seem nostalgically innocent now: They normalized heterogeneity, e.g., into man and woman, white and black. 'Advanced capitalism' and postmodernism release heterogeneity without a norm, and we are flattened, without subjectivity, which requires depth, even unfriendly and drowning depths. It is time to write *The Death of the Clinic*. The clinic's methods required bodies and works; we have texts and surfaces. Our dominations don't work by medicalization and normalization anymore; they work by networking, communications redesign, stress management. Normalization gives way to automation, utter redundancy. Michel Foucault's *Birth of the Clinic, History of Sexuality,* and *Discipline and Punish* name a form of power at its moment of implosion. The discourse of biopolitics gives way to technobabble, the language of the spliced substantive; no noun is left whole by the multinationals. These are their names, listed from one issue of *Science*: Tech-Knowledge, Genentech, Allergen, Hybritech, Compupro, Genen-cor, Syntex, Allelix, Agrigenetics Corp., Syntro, Codon, Repligen; Micro-Angelo from Scion Corp., Percom Data, Inter Systems, Cyborg Corp., Statcom Corp., Intertec. If we are imprisoned by language, then escape from that prison-house requires language poets, a kind of cultural restriction enzyme to cut the code; cyborg heteroglossia is one form of radical culture politics.

4. Frans de Waal, *Chimpanzee Politics: Power and Sex among the Apes* (New York: Harper & Row, 1982); Langdon Winner, 'Do artifacts have politics?' *Daedalus* (Winter 1980): 121–136.

5. Jean Baudrillard, *Simulations,* trans. P. Foss, P. Patton, P. Beitchman (New York: Semiotext(e), 1983). Jameson ('Postmodernism,' p. 66) points out that Plato's definition of the simulacrum is the copy for which there is no original, i.e., the world of advanced capitalism, of pure exchange. See *Discourse 9,* Spring/Summer 1987, for a special issue on technology (Cybernetics, Ecology, and the Postmodern Imagination).

6. Herbert Marcuse, *One-Dimensional Man* (Boston: Beacon Press, 1964); Carolyn Merchant, *Death of Nature* (San Francisco: Harper & Row, 1980).

7. Zoe Sofia, 'Exterminating Fetuses,' *Diacritics,* Vol. 14, No. 2, Summer 1984, pp. 47–59, and 'Jupiter Space' (Pomona, CA: American Studies Association, 1984).

8. For ethnographic accounts and political evaluations, see Barbara Epstein, 'The Politics of Prefigurative Community: The Non-Violent Direction Action Movement,' *The Year Left,* forthcoming, and Noel Sturgeon, qualifying essay on feminism, anarchism, and nonviolent direct-action politics, University of California, Santa Cruz, 1986. Without explicit irony, adopting the spaceship earth/whole earth logo of the planet photographed from space, set off by the slogan 'Love Your Mother,' the May 1987 Mothers and Others Day action at the nuclear weapons testing facility in Nevada nonetheless took account of the tragic contradictions of views of the earth. Demonstrators applied for official permits to be on the land from officers of the Western Shoshone tribe, whose territory was invaded by the U.S. government when it built the nuclear weapons test ground in the 1950s. Arrested for trespassing, the demonstrators argued that the police and weapons facility personnel, without authorization from the proper officials, were the trespassers. One affinity group at the women's action called themselves the Surrogate Others, and in solidarity with the creatures forced to tunnel in the same ground with the bomb, they enacted a cyborgian emergence from the constructed body of a large, nonheterosexual desert worm.

9. Powerful developments of coalition politics emerge from 'third world' speakers, speaking from nowhere, the displaced center of the universe, earth: 'We live on the third planet from the sun' – *Sun Poem* by Jamaican writer Edward Kamau Braithwaite, review by Nathaniel Mackey, *Sulfur,* Vol. 2, 1984, pp. 200–205. *Home Girls,* ed. Barbara Smith (New York: Kitchen Table Women of Color Press, 1983), ironically subverts naturalized identities precisely while constructing a place from which to speak called home. See Bernice Reagan, 'Coalition Politics, Turning the Century,' pp. 356–368. Trinh T. Minh-ha, ed., 'She, the Inappropriate/d Other,' *Discourse* Vol. 8, Fall/Winter 1986–1987.

10. Chela Sandoval, 'Dis-Illusionment and the Poetry of the Future: The Making of Oppositional Consciousness,' Ph.D. qualifying essay, University of California, Santa Cruz, 1984.

11. bell hooks, *Ain't I a Woman?* (Boston: South End Press, 1981); bell hooks, *Feminist Theory: From Margin to Center* (Boston: South End Press, 1984); Gloria Hull,

Patricia Bell Scott, and Barbara Smith, eds., *All the Women Are White, All the Men Are Black, But Some of Us Are Brave: Black Women's Studies* (Old Westbury, NY: Feminist Press, 1982). Toni Cade Bambara, *The Salt Eaters* (New York: Vintage/Random House, 1981), writes an extraordinary postmodernist novel, in which the women of color theater group, The Seven Sisters, explores a form of unity. Elliott Butler-Evans, *Race, Gender, and Desire: Narrative Strategies and the Production of Ideology in the Fiction of Toni Cade Bambara, Toni Morrison and Alice Walker*, Ph.D. Dissertation, University of California, Santa Cruz, 1987.

12. On Orientalism in feminist works and elsewhere, see Lisa Lowe, 'Orientation: Representations of Cultural and Sexual "Others," ' Ph.D. thesis, University of California, Santa Cruz; Edward Said, *Orientalism* (New York: Pantheon, 1978). Chandra Talpade Mohanty, 'Under Western Eyes: Feminist Scholarship and Colonial Discourse.' *Boundry* Vol. 2, No. 12, and Vol 3, No. 13, 1984, pp. 333–357; 'Many Voices, One Chant: Black Feminist Perspectives,' *Feminist Review*, Vol. 17, Autumn 1984.

13. My previous efforts to understand biology as a cybernetic command-control discourse and organisms as 'natural-technical objects of knowledge' are 'The High Cost of Information in Post-World War II Evolutionary Biology,' *Philosophical Forum*, Vol. 13, Nos. 2–8, 1979, pp. 206–237; 'Signs of Dominance: From a Physiology to a Cybernetics of Primate Society,' *Studies in History of Biology*, Vol. 6, 1983, pp. 129–219; 'Class, Race, Sex, Scientific Objects of Knowledge: A Socialist-Feminist Perspective on the Social Construction of Productive Knowledge and Some Political Consequences,' *Women in Scientific and Engineering Professions*, ed. Violet Haas and Carolyn Perucci (Ann Arbor, MI: University of Michigan Press, 1984), pp. 212–229.

14. For the homework economy and some related arguments: Richard Gordon, 'The Computerization of Daily Life, the Sexual Division of Labor, and the Homework Economy,' paper delivered at the Silicon Valley Workshop Group conference, 1983; Richard Gordon and Linda Kimball, 'High-Technology, Employment and the Challenges of Education,' *SVRG Working Paper*, No. 1, July 1985; Judith Stacey, 'Sexism by a Subtler Name? Postindustrial Conditions and Postfeminist Consciousness in the Silicon Valley,' *Socialist Review*, no. 96, 1987, pp. 7–30; *Women's Work, Men's Work*, ed. Barbara F. Reskin and Heidi Hartmann (Washington, DC: National Academy of Sciences Press, 1986); *Signs*, Vol. 10, No. 2, 1984, special issue on women and poverty; Stephen Rose, *The American Profile Poster: Who Owns What, Who Makes How Much, Who Works Where, and Who Lives With Whom?* (New York: Pantheon, 1986); Patricia Hill Collins, 'Third World Women in America,' and Sara G. Burr, 'Women and Work,' ed. Barbara K. Haber, *The Women's Annual. 1981* (Boston: G. K. Hall, 1982); Judith Gregory and Karen Nussbaum, 'Race against Time: Automation of the Office,' *Office: Technology and People*, Vol. 1, 1982, pp. 197–236; Frances Fox Piven and Richard Cloward, *The New Class War: Reagan's Attack on the Welfare State and Its Consequences* (New York: Pantheon, 1982); Microelectronics Group, *Microelectronics: Capitalist Technology and the Working Class* (London: CSE, 1980); Karin Stallard, Barbara Ehrenreich, and Holly Sklar, *Poverty in the American Dream* (Boston: South End Press, 1983) including a useful organization and resource list.

15. For crucial guidance for thinking about the political/cultural implications of the history of women doing science in the United States see *Women in Scientific and Engineering Professions*, ed. Violet Haas and Carolyn Perucci (Ann Arbor, MI: University of Michigan Press, 1984); Sally Hacker, 'The Culture of Engineering: Women, Workplace, and Machine,' *Women's Studies International Quarterly*, Vol. 4, No. 3, 1981, pp. 341–353; Evelyn Fox Keller, *A Feeling for the Organism* (San Francisco: Freeman, 1983); National Science Foundation, *Women and Minorities in Science and Engineering* (Washington, DC: NSF,

1988); Margaret Rossiter, *Women Scientists in America* (Baltimore, MD: Johns Hopkins University Press, 1982); Londa Schiebinger, 'The History and Philosophy of Women in Science: A Review Essay,' *Signs*, Vol. 12, No. 2, 1987, pp. 305–332.

16. Katie King, 'The Pleasure of Repetition and the Limits of Identification in Feminist Science Fiction: Reimaginations of the Body after the Cyborg,' California American Studies Association, Pomona, 1984. An abbreviated list of feminist science fiction underlying themes of this essay: Octavia Bulter, *Wild Seed, Mind of My Mind, Kindred, Survivor*; Suzy McKee Charnas, *Motherlines*; Samuel Delany, *Tales of Neverÿon*; Anne McCaffery, *The Ship Who Sang, Dinosaur Planet*; Vonda McIntyre, *Superluminal, Dreamsnake*; Joanna Russ, *Adventures of Alyx. The Female Man*; James Tiptree, Jr., *Star Songs of an Old Primate. Up the Walls of the World*; John Varley, *Titan, Wizard, Demon*.

17. Mary Douglas, *Purity and Danger* (London: Routledge & Kegan Paul, 1966), *Natural Symbols* (London: Cresset Press, 1970).

18. French feminisms contribute to cyborg heteroglossia. Carolyn Burke, 'Irigaray through the Looking Glass,' *Feminist Studies*, Vol. 7, No. 2, Summer 1981, pp. 288–306; Luce Irigaray, *Ce sexe qui n'en est pas un* (Paris: Minuit, 1977); L. Irigaray, *Et l'une ne bouge pas sans l'autre* (Paris: Minuit, 1979); *New French Feminisms*, ed. Elaine Marks and Isabelle de Courtivron (Amherst, MA: University of Massachusetts Press, 1980); *Signs*, Vol. 7, No. 1, *Autumn* 1981, special issue on French feminism; Monique Wittig, *The Lesbian Body*, trans. David LeVay (New York: Avon, 1975; *Le corps lesbien*, 1973). See especially *Feminist Issues: A Journal of Feminist Social and Political Theory*, 1 (1980), and Claire Duchen, *Feminism in France: From May '68 to Mitterand* (London: Routledge Kegan & Paul, 1986).

19. Jacques Derrida, *Of Grammatology*, trans. and introd. G. C. Spivak (Baltimore, MD: Johns Hopkins University Press, 1976), especially part II, 'Nature, Culture, Writing'; Claude Levi-Strauss, *Tristes Tropiques*, trans. John Russell (New York: Criterion Books, 1961), especially 'The Writing Lesson'; Henry Louis Gates, 'Writing "Race" and the Difference It Makes,' in 'Race,' Writing and Difference, special issue of *Critical Inquiry*, Vol. 12, No. 1, Autumn 1985, pp. 1–20; *Cultures in Contention*, ed. Douglas Kahn and Diane Neumaier (Seattle: Real Comet Press, 1985); Walter Ong, *Orality and Literacy: The Technologizing of the World* (New York: Methuen, 1982); Cheris Kramarae and Paula Treichler, *A Feminist Dictionary* (Boston: Pandora, 1985).

20. Cherríe Moraga, *Loving in the War Years* (Boston: South End Press, 1983). The sharp relation of women of color to writing as theme and politics can be approached through 'The Black Woman and the Diaspora: Hidden Connections and Extended Acknowledgments.' An International Literacy Conference, Michigan State University, October 1985; *Black Women Writers: A Critical Evaluation*, ed. Mari Evans (Garden City, NY: Doubleday/Anchor, 1984); Barbara Christian, *Black Feminist Criticism* (New York: Pergamon, 1985); *The Third Woman: Minority Women Writers of the United States*, ed. Dexter Fisher (Boston: Houghton Mifflin, 1980); several issues of *Frontiers*, especially vol. 5, 1980, 'Chicanas en el Ambiente Nacional' and Vol. 7, 1983, 'Feminisms in the Non-Western World'; Maxine Hong Kingston, *China Men* (New York: Knopf, 1977); *Black Women in White America: A Documentary History*, ed. Gerda Lerner (New York: Vintage, 1973); Paula Giddings, *When and Where I Enter: The Impact of Black Women on Race and Sex in America* (Toronto: Bantam, 1985); *This Bridge Called My Back: Writings by Radical Women of Color*, ed. Cherríe Moraga and Gloria Anzaldua (Watertown, MA: Persephone, 1981); *Sisterhood Is Global*, ed. Robin Morgan (Garden City, NY: Anchor/Doubleday, 1984). The writing of white women has had similar meanings: Sandra Gilbert and Susan Gubar, *The Madwoman in the Attic* (New Haven, CT: Yale University Press, 1979); Joanna Russ, *How to Suppress Women's Writing* (Austin, TX: University of Texas Press, 1983).

21. The convention of ideologically taming militarized high technology by publicizing its applications to speech and motion problems of the disabled-differently abled takes on a special irony in monotheistic, patriarchal, and frequently anti-Semitic culture when computer-generated speech allows a boy with no voice to chant the Haftorah at his bar mitzvah. See Vic Sussman, 'Personal Technology Lends a Hand,' *Washington Post Magazine*, Nov. 9, 1986, pp. 45–46. Making the always context-relative social definitions of 'abledness' particularly clear, military high-tech has a way of making human beings disabled by definition, a perverse aspect of much automated battlefield and Star Wars R&D. See John Noble Welford, 'Pilot's Helmet Helps Interpret High Speed World,' *New York Times*, July 1, 1986, pp. 21, 24.

22. Page DuBois, *Centaurs and Amazons* (Ann Arbor, MI: University of Michigan Press, 1982); Lorraine Daston and Katharine Park, 'Hermaphrodites in Renaissance France,' ms., n.d.; Katharine Park and Lorraine Daston, 'Unnatural Conceptions: The Study of Monsters in 16th and 17th Century France and England,' *Past and Present*, No. 92, August 1981, pp. 20–54. The word *monster* shares its root with the verb *to demonstrate*.

IS THE 'POST' IN POSTCOLONIAL THE SAME AS THE 'POST' IN POSTMODERN?

28

'POSTMODERN BLACKNESS'

bell hooks

Postmodernist discourses are often exclusionary even as they call attention to, appropriate even, the experience of 'difference' and 'Otherness' to provide oppositional political meaning, legitimacy, and immediacy when they are accused of lacking concrete relevance. Very few African-American intellectuals have talked or written about postmodernism. At a dinner party I talked about trying to grapple with the significance of postmodernism for contemporary black experience. It was one of those social gatherings where only one other black person was present. The setting quickly became a field of contestation. I was told by the other black person that I was wasting my time, that 'this stuff does not relate in any way to what's happening with black people.' Speaking in the presence of a group of white onlookers, staring at us as though this encounter were staged for their benefit, we engaged in a passionate discussion about black experience. Apparently, no one sympathized with my insistence that racism is perpetuated when blackness is associated solely with concrete gut level experience conceived as either opposing or having no connection to abstract thinking and the production of critical theory. The idea that there is no meaningful connection between black experience and critical thinking about aesthetics or culture must be continually interrogated.

My defense of postmodernism and its relevance to black folks sounded good, but I worried that I lacked conviction, largely because I approach the subject cautiously and with suspicion.

From bell hooks (1991) 'Postmodern Blackness', in *Yearning: Race, Gender and Cultural Politics*. London: Turnaround Books.

Disturbed not so much by the 'sense' of postmodernism but by the conventional language used when it is written or talked about and by those who speak it, I find myself on the outside of the discourse looking in. As a discursive practice it is dominated primarily by the voices of white male intellectuals and/or academic elites who speak to and about one another with coded familiarity. Reading and studying their writing to understand postmodernism in its multiple manifestations, I appreciate it but feel little inclination to ally myself with the academic hierarchy and exclusivity pervasive in the movement today.

Critical of most writing on postmodernism, I perhaps am more conscious of the way in which the focus on 'Otherness and difference' that is often alluded to in these works seems to have little concrete impact as an analysis or standpoint that might change the nature and direction of postmodernist theory. Since much of this theory has been constructed in reaction to and against high modernism, there is seldom any mention of black experience or writings by black people in this work, specifically black women (though in more recent work one may see a reference to Cornel West, the black male scholar who has most engaged postmodernist discourse). Even if an aspect of black culture is the subject of postmodern critical writing, the works cited will usually be those of black men. A work that comes immediately to mind is Andrew Ross's chapter 'Hip, and the Long Front of Color' in *No Respect: Intellectuals and Popular Culture*; while it is an interesting reading, it constructs black culture as though black women have had no role in black cultural production. At the end of Meaghan Morris' discussion of postmodernism in her collection of essays *The Pirate's Fiancée: Feminism and Postmodernism*, she provides a bibliography of works by women, identifying them as important contributions to a discourse on postmodernism that offer new insight as well as challenging male theoretical hegemony. Even though many of the works do not directly address postmodernism, they address similar concerns. There are no references to works by black women.

The failure to recognize a critical black presence in the culture and in most scholarship and writing on postmodernism compels a black reader, particularly a black female reader, to interrogate her interest in a subject where those who discuss and write about it seem not to know black women exist or even to consider the possibility that we might be somewhere writing or saying something that should be listened to, or producing art that should be seen, heard, approached with intellectual seriousness. This is especially the case with works that go on and on about the way in which postmodernist discourse has opened up a theoretical terrain where 'difference and Otherness' can be considered legitimate issues in the academy. Confronting both the absence of recognition of black female presence that much postmodernist theory re-inscribes and the resistance on the part of most black folks to hearing about real connection between postmodernism and black experience, I enter a discourse, a practice, where there may be no ready audience for my words, no clear listener, uncertain then, that my voice can or will be heard.

During the sixties, black power movement was influenced by perspectives that could easily be labeled modernist. Certainly many of the ways black folks addressed issues of identity conformed to a modernist universalizing agenda. There was little critique of patriarchy as a master narrative among black militants. Despite the fact that black power ideology reflected a modernist sensibility, these elements were soon rendered irrelevant as militant protest was stifled by a powerful, repressive postmodern state. The period directly after the black power movement was a time when major news magazines carried articles with cocky headlines like 'Whatever Happened to Black America?' This response was an ironic reply to the aggressive, unmet demand by decentered, marginalized black subjects who had at least momentarily successfully demanded a hearing, who had made it possible for black liberation to be on the national political agenda. In the wake of the black power movement, after so many rebels were slaughtered and lost, many of these voices were silenced by a repressive state; others became inarticulate. It has become necessary to find new avenues to transmit the messages of black liberation struggle, new ways to talk about racism and other politics of domination. Radical postmodernist practice, most powerfully conceptualized as a 'politics of difference,' should incorporate the voices of displaced, marginalized, exploited, and oppressed black people. It is sadly ironic that the contemporary discourse which talks the most about heterogeneity, the decentered subject, declaring breakthroughs that allow recognition of Otherness, still directs its critical voice primarily to a specialized audience that shares a common language rooted in the very master narratives it claims to challenge. If radical postmodernist thinking is to have a transformative impact, then a critical break with the notion of 'authority' as 'mastery over' must not simply be a rhetorical device. It must be reflected in habits of being, including styles of writing as well as chosen subject matter. Third world nationals, elites, and white critics who passively absorb white supremacist thinking, and therefore never notice or look at black people on the streets or at their jobs, who render us invisible with their gaze in all areas of daily life, are not likely to produce liberatory theory that will challenge racist domination, or promote a breakdown in traditional ways of seeing and thinking about reality, ways of constructing aesthetic theory and practice. From a different standpoint, Robert Storr makes a similar critique in the global issue of *Art in America* when he asserts:

> To be sure, much postmodernist critical inquiry has centered precisely on the issues of 'difference' and 'Otherness.' On the purely theoretical plane the exploration of these concepts has produced some important results, but in the absence of any sustained research into what artists of color and others outside the mainstream might be up to, such discussions become rootless instead of radical. Endless second guessing about the latent imperialism of intruding upon other cultures only compounded matters, preventing or excusing these theorists from investigating what black, Hispanic, Asian and Native American artists were actually doing.

Without adequate concrete knowledge of and contact with the non-white 'Other,' white theorists may move in discursive theoretical directions that are threatening and potentially disruptive of that critical practice which would support radical liberation struggle.

The postmodern critique of 'identity,' though relevant for renewed black liberation struggle, is often posed in ways that are problematic. Given a pervasive politic of white supremacy which seeks to prevent the formation of radical black subjectivity, we cannot cavalierly dismiss a concern with identity politics. Any critic exploring the radical potential of postmodernism as it relates to racial difference and racial domination would need to consider the implications of a critique of identity for oppressed groups. Many of us are struggling to find new strategies of resistance. We must engage decolonization as a critical practice if we are to have meaningful chances of survival even as we must simultaneously cope with the loss of political grounding which made radical activism more possible. I am thinking here about the postmodernist critique of essentialism as it pertains to the construction of 'identity' as one example.

Postmodern theory that is not seeking to simply appropriate the experience of 'Otherness' to enhance the discourse or to be radically chic should not separate the 'politics of difference' from the politics of racism. To take racism seriously one must consider the plight of underclass people of color, a vast majority of whom are black. For African-Americans our collective condition prior to the advent of postmodernism and perhaps more tragically expressed under current postmodern conditions has been and is characterized by continued displacement, profound alienation, and despair. Writing about blacks and postmodernism, Cornel West describes our collective plight:

> There is increasing class division and differentiation, creating on the one hand a significant black middle-class, highly anxiety-ridden, insecure, willing to be co-opted and incorporated into the powers that be, concerned with racism to the degree that it poses constraints on upward social mobility; and, on the other, a vast and growing black underclass, an underclass that embodies a kind of walking nihilism of pervasive drug addiction, pervasive alcoholism, pervasive homicide, and an exponential rise in suicide. Now because of the deindustrialization, we also have a devastated black industrial working class. We are talking here about tremendous hopelessness.

This hopelessness creates longing for insight and strategies for change that can renew spirits and reconstruct grounds for collective black liberation struggle. The overall impact of postmodernism is that many other groups now share with black folks a sense of deep alienation, despair, uncertainty, loss of a sense of grounding even if it is not informed by shared circumstance. Radical postmodernism calls attention to those shared sensibilities which cross the boundaries of class, gender, race, etc., that could be fertile ground for the construction of empathy – ties that would promote recognition of common commitments, and serve as a base for solidarity and coalition.

Yearning is the word that best describes a common psychological state shared by many of us, cutting across boundaries of race, class, gender, and sexual practice. Specifically, in relation to the post-modernist deconstruction of 'master' narratives, the yearning that wells in the hearts and minds of those whom such narratives have silenced is the longing for critical voice. It is no accident that 'rap' has usurped the primary position of rhythm and blues music among young black folks as the most desired sound or that it began as a form of 'testimony' for the underclass. It has enabled underclass black youth to develop a critical voice, as a group of young black men told me, a 'common literacy.' Rap projects a critical voice, explaining demanding, urging. Working with this insight in his essay 'Putting the Pop Back into Postmodernism,' Lawrence Grossberg comments:

> The postmodern sensibility appropriates practices as boasts that announce their own – and consequently our own – existence, like a rap song boasting of the imaginary (or real – it makes no difference) accomplishments of the rapper. They offer forms of empowerment not only in the face of nihilism but precisely through the forms of nihilism itself: an empowering nihilism, a moment of positivity through the production and structuring of affective relations.

Considering that it is as subject one comes to voice, then the postmodernist focus on the critique of identity appears at first glance to threaten and close down the possibility that this discourse and practice will allow those who have suffered the crippling effects of colonization and domination to gain or regain a hearing. Even if this sense of threat and the fear it evokes are based on a misunderstanding of the postmodernist political project, they nevertheless shape responses. It never surprises me when black folks respond to the critique of essentialism, especially when it denies the validity of identity politics by saying, 'Yeah, it's easy to give up identity, when you got one.' Should we not be suspicious of postmodern critiques of the 'subject' when they surface at a historical moment when many subjugated people feel themselves coming to voice for the first time. Though an apt and oftentimes appropriate comeback, it does not really intervene in the discourse in a way that alters and transforms.

Criticisms of directions in postmodern thinking should not obscure insights it may offer that open up our understanding of African-American experience. The critique of essentialism encouraged by postmodernist thought is useful for African-Americans concerned with reformulating outmoded notions of identity. We have too long had imposed upon us from both the outside and the inside a narrow, constricting notion of blackness. Postmodern critiques of essentialism which challenge notions of universality and static over-determined identity within mass culture and mass consciousness can open up new possibilities for the construction of self and the assertion of agency.

Employing a critique of essentialism allows African-Americans to acknowledge the way in which class mobility has altered collective black experience so that racism does not necessarily have the same impact on our lives. Such a critique allows us to affirm multiple black identities, varied black experience. It also challenges colonial imperialist paradigms of black identity which represent blackness one-dimensionally in ways that reinforce and sustain white supremacy. This discourse created the idea of the 'primitive' and promoted the notion of an 'authentic' experience, seeing as 'natural' those expressions of black life which conformed to a pre-existing pattern or stereotype. Abandoning essentialist notions would be a serious challenge to racism. Contemporary African-American resistance struggle must be rooted in a process of decolonization that continually opposes re-inscribing notions of 'authentic' black identity. This critique should not be made synonymous with a dismissal of the struggle of oppressed and exploited peoples to make ourselves subjects. Nor should it deny that in certain circumstances this experience affords us a privileged critical location from which to speak. This is not a re-inscription of modernist master narratives of authority which privilege some voices by denying voice to others. Part of our struggle for radical black subjectivity is the quest to find ways to construct self and identity that are oppositional and liberatory. The unwillingness to critique essentialism on the part of many African-Americans is rooted in the fear that it will cause folks to lose sight of the specific history and experience of African-Americans and the unique sensibilities and culture that arise from that experience. An adequate response to this concern is to critique essentialism while emphasizing the significance of 'the authority of experience.' There is a radical difference between a repudiation of the idea that there is a black 'essence' and recognition of the way black identity has been specifically constituted in the experience of exile and struggle.

When black folks critique essentialism, we are empowered to recognize multiple experiences of black identity that are the lived conditions which make diverse cultural productions possible. When this diversity is ignored, it is easy to see black folks as falling into two categories: nationalist or assimilationist, black-identified or white-identified. Coming to terms with the impact of postmodernism for black experience, particularly as it changes our sense of identity, means that we must and can rearticulate the basis for collective bonding. Given the various crises facing African-Americans (economic, spiritual, escalating racial violence, etc.), we are compelled by circumstance to reassess our relationship to popular culture and resistance struggle. Many of us are as reluctant to face this task as many non-black postmodern thinkers who focus theoretically on the issue of 'difference' are to confront the issue of race and racism.

Music is the cultural product created by African-Americans that has most attracted postmodern theorists. It is rarely acknowledged that there is far greater censorship and restriction of other forms of cultural production by black folks – literary, critical writing, etc. Attempts on the part of editors and publishing houses to control and manipulate the representation of black culture, as well as the desire to promote the creation of products that will attract the widest audience, limit in a crippling and stifling way the kind of work many black folks feel we can do and still receive recognition. Using myself as an example, that creative writing I do which I consider to be most reflective of a postmodern oppositional sensibility, work that is abstract, fragmented, non-linear narrative, is constantly rejected by editors and publishers. It does not conform to the type of writing they think black women should be doing or the type of writing they believe will sell. Certainly I do not think I am the only black person engaged in forms of cultural production, especially experimental ones, who is constrained by the lack of an audience for certain kinds of work. It is important for postmodern thinkers and theorists to constitute themselves as an audience for such work. To do this they must assert power and privilege within the space of critical writing to open up the field so that it will be more inclusive. To change the exclusionary practice of postmodern critical discourse is to enact a postmodernism of resistance. Part of this intervention entails black intellectual participation in the discourse.

In his essay 'Postmodernism and Black America,' Cornel West suggests that black intellectuals 'are marginal – usually languishing at the interface of Black and white cultures or thoroughly ensconced in Euro-American settings.' He cannot see this group as potential producers of radical postmodernist thought. While I generally agree with this assessment, black intellectuals must proceed with the understanding that we are not condemned to the margins. The way we work and what we do can determine whether or not what we produce will be meaningful to a wider audience, one that includes all classes of black people. West suggests that black intellectuals lack 'any organic link with most of Black life' and that this 'diminishes their value to Black resistance.' This statement bears traces of essentialism. Perhaps we need to focus more on those black intellectuals, however rare our presence, who do not feel this lack and whose work is primarily directed towards the enhancement of black critical consciousness and the strengthening of our collective capacity to engage in meaningful resistance struggle. Theoretical ideas and critical thinking need not be transmitted solely in written work or solely in the academy. While I work in a predominantly white institution, I remain intimately and passionately engaged with black community. It's not like I'm going to talk about writing and thinking about postmodernism with other academics and/or intellectuals and not discuss these ideas with underclass non-academic black folks who are family, friends, and comrades. Since I have not broken the ties that bind me to underclass poor black community, I have seen that knowledge, especially that which enhances daily life and strengthens our capacity to survive, can be shared. It means that critics, writers, and academics have to give the same critical attention to nurturing and cultivating our ties to black community that we give to writing articles, teaching, and lecturing. Here again I am really talking about cultivating habits of being that reinforce awareness that knowledge can be disseminated and shared on a number of fronts. The extent to which knowledge is made available, accessible, etc. depends on the nature of one's political commitments.

Postmodern culture with its decentered subject can be the space where ties are severed or it can provide the occasion for new and varied forms of bonding. To some extent, ruptures, surfaces, contextuality, and a host of other happenings create gaps that make space for oppositional practices which no longer require intellectuals to be confined by narrow separate spheres with no meaningful connection to the world of the everyday. Much postmodern engagement with culture emerges from the yearning to do intellectual work that connects with habits of being, forms of artistic expression, and aesthetics that inform the daily life of writers and scholars as well as a mass population. On the terrain of culture, one can participate in critical dialogue with the uneducated poor, the black underclass who are thinking about aesthetics. One can talk about what we are seeing, thinking, or listening to; a space is there for critical exchange. It's exciting to think, write, talk about, and create art that reflects passionate engagement with popular culture, because this may very well be 'the' central future location of resistance struggle, a meeting place where new and radical happenings can occur.

WORKS CITED

Grossberg, Lawrence (1988) 'Putting the Pop Back into Postmodernism', in Andrew Ross (ed.), *Universal Abandon: The Politics of Postmodernism*. Minneapolis, MN: University of Minnesota Press, pp. 167–90.

Morris, Meaghan (1991) *The Pirate's Fiancée: Feminism and Postmodernism*. London and New York: Verso.

Ross, Andrew (1989) *No Respect: Intellectuals and Popular Culture*. New York: Routledge.

Storr, Robert (ed.) (1989) 'The Global Issue: A Symposium', *Art in America*, 77 (7).

West, Cornel (1987) 'Postmodernism and Black America', *Zeta Magazine*, 1: 27–9.

29

'THE POSTCOLONIAL AND THE POSTMODERN'

Kwame Anthony Appiah

[...]

Let me begin with the most-obvious and surely one of the most-often remarked features of Jean-François Lyotard's account of postmodernity: the fact that it is a meta-narrative of the end of meta-narratives.[1] To theorise certain central features of contemporary culture as *post* anything, is, of course, inevitably to invoke a narrative, and, from the Enlightenment on, in Europe and European-derived cultures, that 'after' has also meant 'above and beyond' and to step forward (in time) has been *ipso facto* to *progress*.[2] Brian McHale announces in his recent *Postmodernist Fiction*: 'As for the prefix POST, here I want to emphasize the element of logical and historical *consequence* rather than sheer temporal *posteriority*. Postmodernism follows *from* modernism, in some sense, more than it follows *after* modernism. ... Postmodernism is the posterity of modernism, this is tautological...'[3]

My point then, is not the boring logical point that Lyotard's view – in which, in the absence of 'grand narratives of legitimation', we are left only local legitimations, immanent in our own practices – might seem to presuppose a 'grand narrative of legitimation' of its own, in which justice turns out to reside, unexcitingly, in the institutionalisation of pluralism: it is rather that his analysis seems to feel the need to see the contemporary condition as over-against an immediately anterior set of practices and as going beyond them. Lyotard's postmodernism – his theorisation of contemporary life as postmodern – is *after*

From Kwame Anthony Appiah (1992) 'The Postcolonial and the Postmodern', in *In My Father's House: Africa and the Philosophy of Culture*. London: Methuen.

modernism because it rejects aspects of modernism. And in this repudiation of one's immediate predecessors (or, more especially, of their theories of themselves) it recapitulates a crucial gesture of the historic avant-grade: indeed, it recapitulates the crucial gesture of the modern 'artist'; in that sense of modernity characteristic of sociological usage in which it denotes 'an era that was ushered in via the Renaissance, rationalist philosophy and the Enlightenment, on the one hand, and the transition from the absolutist state to bourgeois democracy, on the other';[4] in that sense of 'artist' to be found in Trilling's account of Arnold's *Scholar Gypsy*, whose 'existence is intended to disturb us and make us dissatisfied with our habitual life in culture...'.[5]

This straining for a contrast – a modernity or a modernism to be *against* – is extremely striking given the lack of any plausible account of what distinguishes the modern from the postmodern that is distinctively formal. In a recent essay, Fredric Jameson grants at one point, after reviewing recent French theorisings (Deleuze, Baudrillard, Debord) that it is difficult to distinguish formally the postmodern from high modernism:

> indeed, one of the difficulties in specifying postmodernism lies in its symbiotic or parasitical relationship to [high modernism]. In effect with the canonization of a hitherto scandalous, ugly, dissonant, amoral, antisocial, bohemian high modernism offensive to the middle classes, its promotion to the very figure of high culture generally, and perhaps most importantly, its enshrinement in the academic institution, postmodernism emerges as a way of making creative space for artists now oppressed by those henceforth hegemonic categories of irony, complexity, ambiguity, dense temporality, and particularly, aesthetic and utopian monumentality.[6]

Jameson's argument in this essay is that we must characterise the distinction not in formal terms – in terms, say, of an 'aesthetic of *textuality*', or of 'the eclipse, finally, of all depth, especially historicity itself', or of the ' "death" of the subject', or the '*culture of the simulacrum*', or 'the society of the spectacle'[7] – but in terms of 'the social functionality of culture itself'.

> [H]igh modernism, whatever its overt political content, was oppositional and marginal within a middle-class Victorian or philistine or gilded age culture. Although postmodernism is equally offensive in all the respects enumerated (think of punk rock or pornography), it is no longer at all 'oppositional' in that sense; indeed, it constitutes the very dominant or hegemonic aesthetic of consumer society itself and significantly serves the latter's commodity production as a virtual laboratory of new forms and fashions. The argument for a conception of postmodernism as a periodizing category is thus based on the presupposition that, even if *all* the formal features enumerated above were already present in the older high modernism, the very significance of those features changes when they become a cultural *dominant* with a precise socio-economic functionality.[8]

It is the 'waning' of the 'dialectical opposition' between high modernism and mass culture – the commodification, and, if I may coin a barbarism, the de-oppositionalisation, of those cultural forms once constitutive of high modernism – that Jameson sees as key to understanding the postmodern condition.

There is no doubt much to be said for Jameson's theorising of the postmodern. But I do not think we shall understand what is common to all the various postmodernisms if we stick within Jameson's all-subsuming vision. The commodification of a fiction, a stance, of oppositionality that is saleable precisely because its commodification guarantees for the consumer that it is no substantial threat was, indeed, central to the cultural role of 'punk rock' in Europe and America. But what, more than a word and a conversation, makes Lyotard and Jameson competing theorists of the *same* postmodern?

I do not – this will come as no surprise – have a definition of the postmodern to put in the place of Jameson's or Lyotard's: but there is now a rough consensus about the structure of the modern/postmodern dichotomy in the many domains – from architecture to poetry to philosophy to rock to the movies – in which it has been invoked. In each of these domains there is an antecedent practice that laid claim to a certain exclusivity of insight and in each of them postmodernism is a name for the rejection of that claim to exclusivity, a rejection that is almost always more playful – though not necessarily less serious – than the practice it aims to replace. That this will not do as a *definition* of postmodernism follows from the fact that in each domain this rejection of exclusivity takes up a certain specific shape, one that reflects the specificities of its setting.

To understand the various postmodernisms this way is to leave open the question of how their theories of contemporary social, cultural and economic life relate to the actual practices that constitute that life; to leave open, then, the relations between postmodern*ism* and postmodern*ity*. Where the practice is theory – literary or philosophical – postmodernism as a *theory* of postmodernity can be adequate only if it reflects to some extent the realities of that practice, because the practice is itself fully theoretical. But when a postmodernism addresses, say, advertising or poetry, it may be adequate as an account of them even if it conflicts with their own narratives, their theories of themselves. For, unlike philosophy and literary theory, advertising and poetry are not largely *constituted* by their articulated theories of themselves.

It is an important question *why* this distancing of the ancestors should have become so central a feature of our cultural lives. And the answer, surely, has to do with the sense in which art is increasingly commodified. To sell onself and one's products as art in the marketplace, it is important, above all, to clear a space in which one is distinguished from other producers and products – and one does this by the construction and the marking of differences.

It is this that accounts for a certain intensification of the long-standing individualism of post-Renaissance art-production: in the age of mechanical reproduction aesthetic individualism – the characterisation of the art-work as belonging to the *oeuvre* of an individual – and the absorption of the artist's life into the conception of the work can be seen precisely as modes of identifying objects for the market. The [African] sculptor of [an ornamental] bicycle, by contrast, will not be known by those who buy this object; his individual life will make no difference to its future history. (Indeed, he surely knows this, in the sense in which one knows anything whose negation one has never even considered.) Nevertheless, there is *some*thing about the object that serves to establish it for the market: the availability of Yoruba culture and of stories about Yoruba culture to surround the object and distinguish it from 'folk-art' from elsewhere. [...]

[...]

If postmodernism is the project of transcending some species of modernism – which is to say some relatively self-conscious self-privileging project of a privileged modernity – our *neo-traditional* sculptor of the 'Man with a Bicycle' is presumably to be understood, by contrast, as pre-modern; i.e. traditional. (I am supposing, then, that being neo-traditional is a way of being traditional; what work the 'neo' does is matter I shall take up again briefly later.) And the sociological and anthropological narratives of tradition through which he or she came to be so theorised is dominated, of course, by Weber.

Weber's characterisation of traditional (and charismatic) authority *in opposition* to rational authority is in keeping with his general characterisation of modernity as the rationalisation of the world; and he insisted on the significance of this characteristically Western process for the rest of humankind. The introduction to *The Protestant Ethic* begins: 'A product of modern European civilization, studying any problem of universal history, is bound to ask himself to what combination of circumstances the fact should be attributed that in Western civilization, and in Western civilization only, cultural phenomena have appeared which (as we like to think) lie in a line of development having universal significance and value.'[9]

Now, there is certainly no doubt that Western modernity now has a universal *geographical* significance. The Yoruba bicyclist – like Sting and his Amerindian chieftains of the Amazon rain forest or Paul Simon and the Mbaqanga musicians of *Graceland* – is testimony to that. But, if I may borrow someone else's borrowing, the fact is that the Empire of Signs strikes back, Weber's 'as we like to think' reflects his doubts about whether the Western *imperium* over the world was as clearly of universal *value* as it was certainly of universal *significance*; and postmodernism surely fully endorses his resistance to this claim. The bicycle enters our museums to be valued by us (David Rockefeller tells *how* it is to be valued); but just as the *presence* of the object reminds us of this fact, its *content* reminds us that the trade is two-way.

I want to argue that to understand our – our human – modernity we must first understand why the rationalisation of the world can no longer be seen as the tendency either of the West or of history, why, simply put, the modernist characterisation of modernity must be challenged. To understand our world is to reject Weber's claim for the rationality of what he called rationalisation and his projection of its inevitability; it is, then, to have a radically post-Weberian conception of modernity.

We can begin with a pair of familiar and helpful caricatures: Thomas Stearns Eliot is against the soullessness and the secularisation of modern society, the reach of Enlightenment rationalism into the whole world. He shares Weber's account of modernity and more straightforwardly deplores it. Le Corbusier is in favour of rationalisation – a house is a 'machine for living in'; but he, too, shares Weber's vision of modernity. And, of course, the great rationalists – the believers in a transhistorical reason triumphing in the world – from Kant on, are the source of Weber's Kantian vision. Modernism in literature and architecture and philosophy – the account of modernity that, on my model, *post-modernism* in these domains seeks to subvert – may be for reason or against it: but in each domain rationalisation – the pervasion of reason – is seen as the distinctive dynamic of contemporary history.

But the beginning of postmodern wisdom is to ask whether Weberian rationalisation is in fact what has happened. For Weber, charismatic authority – the authority of Stalin, Hitler, Mao, Guevara, Nkrumah – is anti-rational; yet modernity has been dominated by just such charisma. Secularisation seems hardly to be proceeding: religions grow in all parts of the world; more than 90 per cent of North Americans still avow some sort of theism; what we call 'fundamentalism' is as alive in the West as it is in Africa and the Middle and Far Easts; Jimmy Swaggart and Billy Graham have business in Louisiana and California as well as in Costa Rica and in Ghana.

What we can see in all these cases, I think, is not the triumph of Enlightenment capital-R Reason – which would have entailed exactly the end of charisma and the universalisation of the secular – not even the penetration of a narrower instrumental reason into all spheres of life, but what Weber mistook for that: namely, the incorporation of all areas of the world and all areas of even formerly 'private' life into the money economy. Modernity has turned every element of the real into a sign, and the sign reads 'for sale'; and this is true even in domains like religion where instrumental reason would recognise that the market has at best an ambiguous place.

If Weberian talk of the triumph of instrumental reason can now be seen to be a mistake, what Weber thought of as the disenchantment of the world – that is the penetration of a scientific vision of things – describes at most the tiny – and in the United States quite marginal – world of the higher academy and a few islands of its influence. The world of the intellectual *is*, I think, largely disenchanted (even theistic academics largely do not believe in ghosts and ancestor-spirits); and fewer people (though still very many) suppose the world to be populated by the multitudes of spirits of earlier religion. Still, what we have seen in recent times in the United States is not secularisation – the end of religions – but their commodification; and with that commodification religions have reached further and grown – their markets have expanded – rather than dying away.

Postmodernism can be seen, then, as a new way of understanding the multiplication of distinctions that flows from the need to clear oneself a space; the need that drives the underlying dynamic of cultural modernity. Modernism saw the economisation of the world as the triumph of reason; postmodernism rejects that claim, allowing in the realm of theory the same multiplication of distinctions we see in the cultures it seeks to understand.

[...]

I have been exploring how modernity looks from the perspective of the Euro-American intellectual. But how does it look from the postcolonial spaces inhabited by the 'Man with a Bicycle?' I shall speak about Africa, with confidence *both* that some of what I have to say will work elsewhere in the so-called Third World *and* that, in some places, it will certainly not. And I shall speak first about the producers of these so-called neo-traditional artworks and then about the case of the African novel, because I believe that to focus exclusively on the novel (as theorists of contemporary African cultures have been inclined to do) is to distort the cultural situation and the significance within it of postcoloniality.

I do not know when the 'Man with a Bicycle' was made or by whom; African art has, until recently, been collected as the property of 'ethnic' groups, not of individuals and workshops, so it is not unusual that not one of the pieces in the *Perspectives* show was identified in the 'Checklist' by the name of an individual artist, even though many of them are twentieth-century (and no one will have been surprised, by contrast, that most of them *are* kindly labelled with the name of the people who own the largely private collections where they now live). As a result I cannot say if the piece is literally postcolonial, produced after Nigerian independence in 1960. But the piece belongs to a genre that has certainly been produced since then: the genre that the catalogue calls *neo-traditional*. And, simply put, what is distinctive about this genre is that it is produced for the West.

I should qualify. Of course, many of the buyers of first instance live in Africa, many of them are juridically citizens of African states. But African bourgeois consumers of neo-traditional art are educated in the Western style, and, if they want African art, they would often rather have a 'genuinely' traditional piece: by which I mean a piece that they believe to be made precolonially, or at least in a style and by methods that were already established precolonially. And these buyers are a minority. Most of this art, which is *traditional* because it uses actually or supposedly precolonial techniques, but is *neo* – this, for what it is worth, is the explanation I promised earlier – because it has elements that are recognisably from the colonial or postcolonial in reference, has been made for Western tourists and other collectors.

The incorporation of these works in the West's world of museum culture and its art-market has almost nothing, of course, to do with postmodernism. By and large, the ideology through which they are incorporated is modernist: it is the ideology that brought something called 'Bali' to Artaud, something called 'Africa' to Picasso, and something called 'Japan' to Barthes. (This incorporation as an official Other was criticised, of course, from its beginnings: Oscar Wilde once remarked that 'the whole of Japan is a pure invention. There is no such country, no such people.'[10]) What *is* postmodernist is Vogel's muddled conviction that African Art should not be judged 'in terms of [someone else's] traditional criteria'. For modernism, primitive art was to be judged by putatively *universal* aesthetic criteria; and by these standards it was finally found possible to value it. The sculptors and painters who found it possible were largely seeking an Archimedean point outside their own cultures for a critique of a Weberian modernity. For *post*modernisms, by contrast, these works, however they are to be understood, cannot be seen as legitimated by culture- and history-transcending standards.

What is useful in the *neo-traditional* object as a model – despite its marginality in most African lives – is that its incorporation in the museum-world (while many objects made by the same hands – stools for example – live peacefully in non-bourgeois homes) reminds one that in Africa, by contrast, the distinction between high culture and mass culture, insofar as it makes sense at all, corresponds, by and large, to the distinction between those with and those without Western-style formal education as cultural consumers.

The fact that the distinction is to be made this way – in most of sub-Saharan Africa excluding the Republic of South Africa – means that the opposition between high-culture and mass-culture is available only in domains where there is a significant body of Western formal training: and this excludes (in most places) the plastic arts and music. There are distinctions of genre and audience in African musics, and for various cultural purposes there is something that we call 'traditional' music that we still practise and value; but village and urban dwellers alike, bourgeois and non-bourgeois, listen, through discs and, more importantly, on the radio, to reggae, to Michael Jackson, and to King Sonny Adé.

And this means that by and large the domain in which it makes most sense is the one domain where that distinction is powerful and pervasive: namely in African writing in Western languages. So that it is here that we find, I think, a place for consideration of the question of the *post*coloniality of contemporary African culture.

Postcoloniality is the condition of what we might ungenerously call a *comprador* intelligentsia: of a relatively small, Western-style, Western-trained, group of writers and thinkers, who mediate the trade in cultural commodities of world capitalism at the periphery. In the West they are known through the Africa they offer; their compatriots know them both through the West they present to Africa and through an Africa they have invented for the world, for each other and for Africa.

All aspects of contemporary African cultural life – including music and some sculpture and painting, even some writings with which the West is largely not familiar – have been influenced – often powerfully – by the transition of African societies *through* colonialism, but they are not all in the relevant sense *post*colonial. For the *post* in postcolonial, like the *post* in postmodern, is the *post* of the space-clearing gesture I characterised earlier: and many areas of contemporary African cultural life – what has come to be theorised as popular culture, in particular – are not in this way concerned with transcending – with going beyond – coloniality. Indeed, it might be said to be a mark of popular culture that its borrowings from international cultural forms are remarkably insensitive to – not so much dismissive of as blind to – the issue of neocolonialism or 'cultural imperialism'. This does not mean that theories of postmodernism are irrelevant to these forms of culture: for the internationalisation of the market and the commodification of art-works are both central to them. But it *does* mean that these artworks are not understood by their producers or their consumers in terms of a postmodern*ism*: there is no antecedent practice whose claim to exclusivity of vision is rejected through these artworks. What is called 'syncretism' here is made possible by the international exchange of commodities, but is not a consequence of a space-clearing gesture.

Postcolonial intellectuals in Africa, by contrast, are almost entirely dependent for their support on two institutions: the African university – an institution whose intellectual life is overwhelmingly constituted as Western – and the Euro-American publisher and reader. (Even when these writers seek to escape the West – as Ngugi was Thiong'o did in attempting to construct a Kikuyu peasant drama – their theories of their situation are irreducibly informed by their Euro-American formation. Ngugi's conception of the writer's potential in politics is essentially that of the avant-garde; of left modernism.)

Now this double dependence on the university and the Euro-American publisher means that the first generation of modern African novels – the generation of Achebe's *Things Fall Apart* and Laye's *L'Enfant noir* – were written in the context of notions of politics and culture dominant in the French and British university and publishing worlds in the 1950s and '60s. This does not mean that they were like novels written in Western Europe at that time: for part of what was held to be obvious both by these writers and by the high culture of Europe of the day was that new literatures in new nations should be anti-colonial and nationalist. These early novels seem to belong to the world of eighteenth- and nineteenth-century literary nationalism: they are theorised as the imaginative recreation of a common cultural past that is crafted into a shared tradition by the writer; they are in the tradition of Scott, whose *Minstrelsy of the Scottish Border* was intended, as he said in the preface, to 'contribute somewhat to the history of my native country; the peculiar features of whose manners and character are daily melting and dissolving into those of her sister and ally'. The novels of this first stage are thus realist legitimations of nationalism: they authorise a 'return to traditions' while at the same time recognising the demands of a Weberian rationalised modernity.

From the later sixties on, these celebratory novels of the first stage become rarer: Achebe, for example, moves from the creation of a usable past in *Things Fall Apart* to a cynical indictment of politics in the modern sphere in *A Man of the People*. But I should like to focus on a francophone novel of the later sixties, a novel which thematises in an extremely powerful way many of the questions I have been asking about art and modernity: I mean, of course, Yambo Ouologuem's *Le Devoir de violence*. This novel, like many of this second stage, represents a challenge to the novels of this first stage: it identifies the realist novel as part of the tactic of nationalist legitimation and so it is – if I may begin a catalogue of its ways-of-being-*post*-this-and-that – *postrealist*.

Now, postmodernism is, of course, postrealist also. But Ouologuem's post-realism is surely motivated quite differently from that of such postmodern writers as, say, Pynchon. Realism naturalises: the originary 'African novel' of Chinua Achebe – *Things Fall Apart* – and of Camara Laye – *L'Enfant noir* – is 'realist'. So Ouologuem is against it, rejects – indeed, assaults – the conventions of realism. He seeks to delegitimate the forms of the realist African novel, in part, surely, because what it sought to naturalise was a nationalism that, by 1968, had plainly failed. The national bourgeoisie that took on the baton of rationalisation, industrialisation, bureaucratisation in the name of nationalism, turned out to be a kleptocracy. Their enthusiasm for nativism was a rationalisation of their urge to keep the national bourgeosies of other nations – and particularly the powerful industrialised nations – out of their way. As Jonathan Ngaté has observed '... *Le Devoir de violence* ... deal[s] with a world in which *the efficacy* of the call to the Ancestors as well as the Ancestors themselves is seriously called into question'.[11] That the novel is in this way postrealist allows its author to borrow, when he needs them, the techniques of modernism: which, as we learned from Fred Jameson, are often also the techniques of postmodernism. [...]

Christopher Miller's discussion – in *Blank Darkness* – of *Le Devoir de violence* focuses usefully on theoretical questions of intertextuality raised by the novel's persistent massaging of one text after another into the surface of its own body. The book contains, for example, a translation of a passage from Graham Greene's 1934 novel *It's a Battlefield* (translated and improved, according to some readers); and borrowings from Maupassant's *Boule de suif* (hardly an unfamiliar work for francophone readers; if this latter is a theft, it is the adventurous theft of the kleptomaniac, who dares us to catch him at it).

And the book's first sentence artfully establishes the oral mode – by then an inevitable convention of African narration – with words that Ngaté rightly describes as having the 'concision and the striking beauty and power of a proverb'[12] ... and mocks us in this moment because the sentence echoes the beginning of André Schwartz-Bart's decidedly un-African 1959 holocaust novel *Le Dernier des justes*; an echo that more substantial later borrowings confirm.[13]

> Our eyes drink the flash of the sun, and, conquered, surprise themselves by weeping. Maschallah! oua bismillah! ... An account of the bloody adventure of the niggertrash – dishonour to the men of nothing – *could easily begin in the* first half of this *century; but the true history of* the Blacks *begins* very much *earlier*, with the Saifs, in the year 1202 of our era, in the African kingdom of Nakem ...

> *Our eyes* receive the light of dead stars. A biography of my friend Ernie *could easily begin in the* second quarter of the 20th *century; but the true history of* Ernie Lévy *begins* much *earlier*, in the old anglican city of York. More precisely: on the 11 March 1185.

The reader who is properly prepared will expect an African holocaust; and these echoes are surely meant to render ironic the status of the rulers of Nakem as descendants of Abraham El Héït, 'le Juif noir'.[14]

The book begins, then, with a sick joke at the unwary reader's expense against nativism: and the assault on realism is – here is my second signpost – postnativist; this book is a murderous antidote to a nostalgia for *Roots*. As Wole Soyinka has said in a justly well-respected reading: 'the Bible, the Koran, the historic solemnity of the griot are reduced to the histrionics of wanton boys masquerading as humans'.[15] It is tempting to read the attack on history here as a repudiation not of roots but of Islam, as Soyinka does when he goes on to say:

> A culture which has claimed indigenous antiquity in such parts of Africa as have submitted to its undeniable attractions is confidently proven to be imperialist; worse, it is demonstrated to be essentially hostile to the indigenous culture ... Ouologuem pronounces the Moslem incursion into black Africa to be corrupt, vicious, decadent, elitist and insensitive. At the least such a work functions as a wide swab in the deck-clearing operation for the commencement of racial retrieval.[16]

But it seems to me much clearer to read the repudiation as a repudiation of national history; to see the text as postcolonially postnationalist as well as anti- (and thus, of course, post-) nativist. (Indeed, Soyinka's reading here seems to be driven by his own equally representative tendency [...] to read Africa as race and place into everything.) Raymond Spartacus Kassoumi – who is, if anyone is, the hero of this novel – is, after all, a son of the soil, but his political prospects by the end of the narrative are less than uplifting. More than this, the novel explicitly thematises, in the anthropologist Shrobenius – an obvious echo of the name of the German Africanist Frobenius, whose work is cited by Senghor – the mechanism by which the new elite has come to invent its traditions through the 'science' of ethnography: 'Saif made up stories and the interpreter translated, Madoubo repeated in French, refining on the subtle-ties to the delight of Shrobenius, that human crayfish afflicted with a groping mania for resuscitating an African universe – cultural autonomy, he called it, which had lost all living reality; ... he was determined to find metaphysical meaning in everything. .... African life, he held, was pure art ...'[17] At the start we have been told that 'there are few written accounts and the versions of the elders diverge from those of the griots, which differ from those of the chroniclers'.[18] Now we are warned off the supposedly scientific discourse of the ethnographers.[19]

Because this is a novel that seeks to delegitimate not only the form of realism but the content of nationalism, it will to that extent seem to us misleadingly to be postmodern. *Mis*leadingly, because what we have here is not postmodern*ism* but postmodernis*ation*; not an aesthetics but a politics, in the most literal sense of the term. After colonialism, the modernisers said, comes rationality; that is the possibility the novel rules out. Ouologuem's novel is typical of this second stage in that it is not written by someone who is comfortable with and accepted by the new elite, the national bourgeoisie. Far from being a celebration of the nation, then, the novels of the second stage – the postcolonial stage – are novels of delegitimation: rejecting the Western *imperium*, it is true; but also rejecting the nationalist project of the postcolonial national bourgeoisie. And, so it seems to me, the basis for that project of delegitimation is very much not the postmodernist one: rather, it is grounded in an appeal to an ethical universal; indeed it is based, as intellectual responses to oppression in Africa largely are based, in an appeal to a certain simple respect for human suffering, a fundamental revolt against the endless misery of the last thirty years. Ouologuem is hardly likely to make common cause with a relativism that might allow that the horrifyingly new-old Africa of exploitation is to be understood – legitimated – in its own local terms.

Africa's postcolonial novelists – novelists anxious to escape neocolonialism – are no longer committed to the nation; and in this they will seem, as I have suggested, misleadingly postmodern. But what they have chosen instead of the nation is not an older traditionalism but Africa – the continent and its people. This is clear enough, I think, in *Le Devoir de violence*; at the end of the novel Ouologuem writes: 'Often, it is true, the soul desires to dream the echo of happiness, an echo that has no past. But projected into the world, one cannot help recalling that Saïf, mourned three million times, is forever reborn to history beneath the hot ashes of more than thirty African republics.'[20] If we are to identify with anyone, *in fine*, it is with 'la négraille' – the niggertrash, who have no nationality. For these purposes one republic is as good – which is to say as bad – as any other. If this postulation of oneself as African – and neither as of this-or-that allegedly precolonial ethnicity nor of the new nation states – is implicit in *Le Devoir de violence*, in the important novels of V. Y. Mudimbe, *Entre les eaux, Le Bel Immonde* – recently made available in English as *Before the Birth of the Moon* – and *L'Écart*, this postcolonial recourse to Africa is to be found nearer the surface and over and over again.[21]

There is a moment in *L'Écart*, for example, when the protagonist, whose journal the book is, recalls a conversation with the French girlfriend of his student days – the young woman on whom he reflects constantly as he becomes involved with an African woman.

> 'You can't know, Isabelle, how demanding Africa is.'
>
> 'It's important for you, isn't it?'
>
> 'To tell you the truth, I don't know ... I really don't ... I wonder if I'm not usually just playing around with it.'
>
> 'Nara ... I don't understand. For me, the important thing is to be myself. Being European isn't a flag to wave.'
>
> 'You've never been wounded like ...'
>
> 'You're dramatising, Nara. You carry your African-ness like a martyr. ... That makes one wonder ... I'd be treating you with contempt if I played along with you.'
>
> 'The difference is that Europe is above all else an idea, a juridical institution ... while Africa ...'
>
> 'Yes? ...'
>
> 'Africa is perhaps mostly a body, a multiple existence ... I'm not expressing myself very well.'[22]

This exchange seems to me to capture the essential ambiguity of the post-colonial African intellectual's relation to Africa. [...]

Postrealist writing; postnativist politics; a *transnational* rather than a *national* solidarity. And pessimism: a kind of *post*optimism to balance the earlier enthusiasm for *The Suns of Independence*. Postcoloniality is *after* all this: and its *post*, like postmodernism's, is also a *post* that challenges earlier legitimating narratives. And it challenges them in the name of the suffering victims of 'more than thirty republics'. But it challenges them in the name of the ethical universal; in the name of *humanism*, 'le gloire pour l'homme'. And on that ground it is not an ally for Western postmodernism but an agonist: from which I believe postmodernism may have something to learn.

For what I am calling humanism can be provisional, historically contingent, anti-essentialist (in other words, postmodern) and still be demanding. We can surely maintain a powerful engagement with the concern to avoid cruelty and pain while nevertheless recognising the contingency of that concern.[23] Maybe, then, we can recover within postmodernism the postcolonial writers' humanism – the concern for human suffering, for the victims of the postcolonial state (a concern we find everywhere: in Mudimbe, as we have seen; in Soyinka's *A Play of Giants*; in Achebe, Farrah, Gordimer, Labou Tansi – the list is difficult to complete) – while still rejecting the master-narratives of modernism. This human impulse – an impulse that transcends obligations to churches and to nations – I propose we learn from Mudimbe's Landu.

But there is also something to reject in the postcolonial adherence to Africa of Nara, the earlier protagonist of Mudimbe's *L'Écart*: the sort of Manicheanism that makes Africa '*a body*' (nature) against Europe's juridical reality (culture) and then fails to acknowledge – even as he says it – the full significance of the fact that Africa is also '*a multiple existence*'. *Entre les eaux* provides a powerful postcolonial critique of this binarism: we can read it as arguing that if you postulate an either-or choice between Africa and the West, there is no place for you in the real world of politics, and your home must be the otherworldly, the monastic retreat.

If there is a lesson in the broad shape of this circulation of cultures, it is surely that we are all already contaminated by each other, that there is no longer a fully autochthonous pure-African culture awaiting salvage by our artists (just as there is, of course, no American culture without African roots). And there is a clear sense in some postcolonial writing that the postulation of a unitary Africa over against a monolithic West – the binarism of Self and Other – is the last of the shibboleths of the modernisers that we must learn to live without.

Already in *Le Devoir de violence*, in Ouologuem's withering critique of 'Shrobéniusologie', there were the beginnings of this postcolonial critique of what we might call 'alterism', the construction and celebration of oneself as Other. '… that's how Negro art was baptised "aesthetic" and hawked – hey! – in the imaginary universe of "life-giving exchanges"!'[24] Ouologuem writes; and then, after describing the fantasmatic elaboration of some interpretative mumbo-jumbo 'invented by Saif', he announces that '… Negro art created its patent of nobility from the folklore of mercantile spirituality, hey, hey, hey …'.[25] Shrobenius, the anthropologist, as apologist for 'his' people; a European audience that laps up this exoticised other; African traders and producers of African Art, who understand the necessity to maintain the 'mysteries' that construct their product as 'exotic'; traditional and contemporary elites who require a sentimentalised past to authorise their present power: all are exposed in their complex and multiple mutual complicities.

> '… witness the splendour of its art – the true face of Africa is the grandiose empires of the Middle Ages, a society marked by wisdom, beauty, prosperity, order, nonviolence, and humanism, and it is here that we must seek the true cradle of Egyptian civilisation.'
>
> Thus drooling, Shrobenius derived a twofold benefit on his return home: on the one hand, he mystified the people of his own country, who in their enthusiasm raised him to a lofty Sorbonnical chair, while on the other hand he exploited the sentimentality of the coons, only too pleased to hear from the mouth of a white man that Africa was 'the womb of the world and the cradle of civilisation'.
>
> In consequence the niggertrash donated masks and art treasures by the ton to the acolytes of 'Shrobeniusology'.[26]

A little later, Ouologuem articulates more precisely the interconnections of Africanist mystifications with tourism, and the production, packaging and marketing of African artworks.

An Africanist school harnessed to the vapours of magico-religious, cosmological, and mythical symbolism had been born: with the result that for three years men flocked to Nakem – and what men! – middle-men, adventurers, apprentice bankers, politicians, salesmen, conspirators – supposedly 'scientists', but in reality enslaved sentries mounting guard before the 'Shrobeniusological' monument of Negro pseudo-symbolism.

Already it had become more than difficult to procure old masks, for Shrobenius and the missionaries had had the good fortune to snap them all up. And so Saif – and the practice is still current – had slapdash copies buried by the hundredweight, or sunk into ponds, lakes, marshes, and mud holes, to be exhumed later on and sold at exorbitant prices to unsuspecting curio hunters. These three-year-old masks were said to be charged with the weight of four centuries of civilisation.[27]

Ouologuem here forcefully exposes the connections we saw earlier in some of David Rockefeller's insights into the international system of art-exchange, the international art-world: we see the way in which an ideology of disinterested aesthetic value – the 'baptism' of 'negro art' as 'aesthetic' – meshes with the international commodification of African expressive culture; a commodification which requires, by the logic of the space-clearing gesture, the manufacture of otherness. (It is a significant bonus that it also harmonises with the interior decor of modern apartments.) Shrobenius, '[c]e marchand-confectionneur d'idéologie' – this marketer-manufacturer of ideologies – the ethnographer allied with Saif – image of the 'traditional' African ruling caste – has invented an Africa that is a body over against Europe, the juridical institution; and Ouologuem is urging us vigorously to refuse to be thus Other.[28]

Sara Suleri has written recently, in *Meatless Days*, of being treated as an 'Otherness-machine' – and of being heartily sick of it.[29] If there is no way out for the postcolonial intellectual in Mudimbe's novels, it is, I suspect, because *as* intellectuals – a category instituted in black Africa by colonialism – we are always at risk of becoming Otherness-machines. It risks becoming our principal role. Our only distinction in the world of texts to which we are latecomers is that we can mediate it to our fellows. This is especially true when postcolonial meets postmodern; for what the postmodern reader seems to demand of its Africa is all-too-close to what modernism – as documented in William Rubin's 'Primitivism' exhibit of 1985 – demanded of it. The role that Africa – like the rest of the Third World – plays for Euro-American postmodernism – like its better-documented significance for modernist art – must be distinguished from the role postmodernism might play in the Third World; what that might be it is, I think, too early to tell. And what happens will happen not because we pronounce upon the matter in theory, but out of the changing everyday practices of African cultural life.

For all the while, in Africa's cultures, there are those who will not see themselves as Other. Despite the overwhelming reality of economic decline, despite unimaginable poverty; despite wars, malnutrition, disease and political instability, African cultural productivity grows apace: popular literatures, oral narrative and poetry, dance, drama, music, and visual art all thrive. The contemporary cultural production of many African societies – and the many traditions whose evidences so vigorously remain – is an antidote to the dark vision of the postcolonial novelist.

And I am grateful to James Baldwin for his introduction to the 'Man with a Bicycle'; a figure who is, as Baldwin so rightly saw, polygot – speaking Yoruba and English, probably some Hausa and a little French for his trips to Cotonou or Cameroon; someone whose 'clothes do not fit him too well'. He and the other men and women amongst whom he mostly lives suggest to me that the place to look for hope is not just to the postcolonial novel – which has struggled to achieve the insights of a Ouologuem or Mudimbe – but to the all-consuming vision of this less anxious creativity. It matters little who it was made *for*; what we should learn from is the imagination that produced it. The 'Man with a Bicycle' is produced by someone who does not care that the bicycle is the Whiteman's invention – it is not there to be Other to the Yoruba Self; it is there because someone cared for its solidity; it is there because it will take us further than our feet will take us; it is there because machines are now as African as novelists ... and as fabricated as the kingdom of Nakem.[30]

NOTES

1. Jean-François Lyotard, *The Postmodern Condition: A Report on Knowledge*.
2. 'Post-' thus images in modernity the trajectory of 'meta' in classical metaphysics. Originating in the editorial glosses of Aristotelians wishing to refer to the books 'after' the Philosopher's books on nature (physics), this 'after' has also been translated into an 'above and beyond'.
3. Brian McHale, *Postmodernist Fiction*, p. 5.
4. Scott Lash, 'Modernity or Modernism? Weber and Contemporary Social Theory', p. 355.
5. Lionel Trilling, *The Opposing Self: Nine Essays in Criticism*, p. xiv.
6. Fredric Jameson, *The Ideologies of Theory: Essays 1971–1986*, Vol. II: *Syntax of History*, pp. 178–208; p. 195.
7. Jameson, *The Ideologies of Theory: Essays 1971–1986*, Vol. II, p. 195.
8. Jameson, *The Ideologies of Theory: Essays 1971–1986*, Vol. II, p. 195; 196.
9. *The Protestant Ethic and the Spirit of Capitalism*, p. 13.
10. 'The Decay of Lying: An Observation' in *Intentions*, p. 45.
11. Jonathan Ngaté, *Francophone African Fiction: Reding a Literary Tradition*, p. 59.
12. Ngaté, *Francophone African Fiction: Reading a Literary Tradition*, p. 64.
13. Ngaté's focus on this initial sentence follows Aliko Songolo 'The Writer, The Audience And The Critic's Responsibility: The Case Of *Bound To violence*' cited by Ngaté, *loc cit.*
14. Ouologuem, *Le Devoir de violence*, p. 12.
15. Soyinka, *Myth, Literature and the African World*, p. 100.
16. Soyinka, *Myth, Literature and the African World*, p. 105.
17. *Bound to Violence* translated by Ralph Manheim, p. 87. 'Saïf fabula et l'interprète traduisit, Madoubo répéta en français, raffinant les subtilités qui faisaient le

bonheur de Shrobénius, écrevisse humaine frappée de la manie tâtonnante de vouloir ressusciter, sous couleur d'autonomie culturelle, un univers africain qui ne correspondait à plus rien de vivant; ... il voulait trouver un sens métaphysique à tout ... Il considérait que la vie africaine était art pur ...' Ouologuem, *Le Devoir de violence*, p. 102.

18. Ouologuem, *Bound to Violence*, p. 6.

19. Here we have the literary thematisation of the Foucauldian *Invention of Africa* that is the theme of Valentin Mudimbe's important recent intervention.

20. *Bound to Violence*, pp. 181–2. 'Souvent il est vrai, l'âme veut rêver l'écho sans passé du bonheur. Mais, jeté dans le monde, l'on peut s'empêcher de songer que Saïf, pleuré trois millions de fois, renaît sans cesse a l'Histoire, sous les cendres chaudes de plus de trente Républiques africaines. ...' Ouologuem, *op. cit.*, p. 207.

21. It would be interesting to speculate on how to account for an apparently similar trend in African-American writing and cultural theory.

22. 'Tu ne peux savoir, Isabelle, l'exigence de l'Afrique. – C'est important pour toi, n'est-ce pas? – A vrai dire, je ne sais pas ... [...] – Nara ... Je ne comprends pas. Pour moi, l'important, c'est d'être moi. Etre européenne n'est pas un pavillon. – 'Tu n'as jamais été blessé comme ... – Tu dramatises, Nara. Tu portes ton africanité comme un martyre ... Ça donne à penser ... Je te mépriserais si j'entrais dans ton jeu. – La différence, Isabelle, la différence, c'est que l'Europe est avant tout une idée, une institution juridique ... alors l'Afrique ... – Oui? ... – L'Afrique est peut-être surtout un corps, une existence multiple ... Je m'exprime mal ...' Mudimbe, *L'Écart* p. 116.

23. See Richard Rorty's *Contingency, Irony and Solidarity*.

24. '...voilà l'art nègre baptisé "esthétique" et marchandé – oye! – dans l'univers imaginaire des "échanges vivifiants"' Ouologuem, *Le Devoir de violence*, p. 110.

25. '[l]'art nère se forgeait ses lettres de noblesse au folklore de la spiritualité mercantiliste, oye oye oye ...' Ouologuem, *Le Devoir de violence*, p. 110.

26. Ouologuem, *Bound to Violence*, pp. 94–5. ' "... témoin: la splendeur de son art –, la grandeur des empires du Moyen Age constituait le visage vrai de l'Afrique, sage, belle, riche, ordonnée, non violente et puissante tout autant qu'humaniste – berceau même de la civilisation égyptienne."

Salivant ainsi, Shrobéhius, de retour au bercail, en tira un double profit: d'une part, il mystifia son pays, qui, enchanté, le jucha sur une haute chair sorbonicale, et, d'autre part, il exploita la sentimentalité négrillarde – par trop heureuse de s'entendre dire par un Blanc que "l'afrique était ventre du monde et berceau de civilisation."

La négraille offrit par tonnes, conséquemment et gratis, masques et trésors artistiques aux acolytes de la "shrobéniusologie", Ouologuem, *Le Devoir de violence*, p. 111.

27. *Bound to Violence*, pp. 95–6. 'Une école africaniste ainsi accrochée aux nues du symbolisme magico-religieux, cosmologique et mythique, était née: tant et si bien que durant trois ans, des hommes – et quels hommes!: des fantoches, des aventuriers, des apprentis banquiers, des politiciens, des voyageurs, des conspirateurs, des chercheurs – "scientifiques", dit-on, en vérité sentinelles asservies, montant la garde devant le monument "shrobéniusologique" du pseudo-symbolisme nègre, accoururent au Nakem.

Déjà, l'acquisition des masques anciens était devenue problématique depuis que Shrobénius et les missionnaries connurent le bonheur d'en acquérir en quantité. Saïf donc – et la pratique est courante de nos jours encore – fit enterrer des quintaux de masques hâtivement exécutés à la ressemblance des originaux, les engloutissant dans des mares, marais, étangs, marécages, lacs, limons – quitte à les exhumer quelque temps après, les vendant aux curieux et profanes à prix d'or. Ils étaient, ces masques, vieux de trois ans, *chargés* disait-on, *du poids de quatre siècles de civilisation.*' Ouologuem, *Le Devoir de violence*, p. 112.

28. Ouologuem, *Le Devoir de violence*, p. 111.
29. Sara Suleri, *Meatless Days*, p. 105.
30. I learned a good deal from trying out earlier versions of these ideas at an N.E.H. Summer Institute on 'The Future of the Avant-Garde in Postmodern Culture' under the direction of Susan Suleiman and Alice Jardine at Harvard in July 1989; at the African Studies Association (under the sponsorship of the Society for African Philosophy in North America) in November 1989, where Jonathan Ngaté's response was particularly helpful; and, as the guest of Ali Mazrui, at the Braudel Center at S.U.N.Y. Binghamton in May 1990. As usual, I wish I knew how to incorporate more of the ideas of the discussants on those occasions.

WORKS CITED

Jameson, Fredric (1988) *The Ideologies of Theory: Essays 1971–1986. Vol. II: Syntax of History*. London: Routledge.

Lash, Scott (1990) 'Modernity or Modernism? Weber and Contemporary Social Theory', in *Sociology of Postmodernism*. London: Routledge, pp. 130–3.

Lyotard, Jean-François (1984) *The Postmodern Condition: A Report on Knowledge*. Minneapolis: University of Minnesota Press.

McHale, Brian (1987) *Postmodernist Fiction*. London: Methuen.

Masterman, Margaret (1970) 'The Nature of a Paradigm', in I. Latakos and A. Musgrave (eds), *Criticism and the Growth of Knowledge*. Cambridge: Cambridge University Press, pp. 59–89.

Mudimbe, Valentin (1979) *L'écart: récit*. Paris: Présence africaine.

Mudimbe, Valentin (1988) *The Invention of Africa: Gnosis, Philosophy and the Order of Knowledge*. Bloomington, IN: Indiana University Press.

Ngaté, Jonathan (1988) *Francophone African Fiction: Reading a Literary Tradition*. Trenton, NJ: Africa World Press.

Ouologuem, Yambo (1968) *Le Devoir de violence*. Paris: Seuil.

Ouologuem, Yambo (1986) *Bound to Violence*, trans. Ralph Manheim. London: Heinemann Educational.

Rorty, Richard (1989) *Contingency, Irony and Solidarity*. Cambridge: Cambridge University Press.

Soyinka Wole (1990) *Myth, Literature and the African World*. Cambridge: Cambridge University Press.

Suleri, Sara (1990) *Meatless Days*. London: Collins.

Trilling, Lionel (1955) *The Opposing Self: Nine Essays in Criticism*. London: Secker & Warburg.

Vogel, Susan (ed.) (1987) *Perspectives on African Art*. New York: Center for African Art.

Weber, Max (1965) *The Protestant Ethic and the Spirit of Capitalism*, trans. Talcott Parsons. London: Allen & Unwin.

Wilde, Oscar (1905) 'The Decay of Lying', in *Intentions*. New York: Brentano's.

TECHNOLOGY AND PARANOIA
30

'CYBERNETIC DECONSTRUCTIONS: CYBERPUNK AND POSTMODERNISM'

Veronica Hollinger

If, as Fredric Jameson has argued, postmodernism is our contemporary cultural dominant ('Logic' 56), so equally is technology 'our historical context, political and personal,' according to Teresa de Lauretis: 'Technology is now, not only in a distant, science fictional future, an extension of our sensory capacities; it shapes our perceptions and cognitive processes, mediates our relationships with objects of the material and physical world, and our relationships with our own or other bodies' (167). Putting these two aspects of our reality together, Larry McCaffery has recently identified science fiction as 'the most significant evolution of a paraliterary form' in contemporary literature (xvii).

Postmodernist texts which rely heavily on science-fiction iconography and themes have proliferated since the 1960s, and it can be argued that some of the most challenging science fiction of recent years has been produced by mainstream and vangardist rather than genre writers. A random survey of postmodernist writing which has been influenced by science fiction – works for which science-fiction writer Bruce Sterling suggests the term 'slipstream' ('Slipstream') – might include, for example, Richard Brautigan's *In Watermelon Sugar* (1968), Monique Wittig's *Les Guérillères* (1969), Angela Carter's *Heroes and Villains* (1969), J.G. Ballard's *Crash* (1973), Russell Hoban's *Riddley Walker* (1980), Ted Mooney's *Easy Travel to Other Planets* (1981), Anthony Burgess's *The End of the World News* (1982), and Kathy Acker's *Empire of the Senseless* (1988).

From Veronica Hollinger (1990) 'Cybernetic Deconstructions: Cyberpunk and Postmodernism', *Mosaic*, vol. 23, no. 2, pp. 29–44.

Not surprisingly, however, the specific concerns and esthetic techniques of postmodernism have been slow to appear in genre science fiction, which tends to pride itself on its status as a paraliterary phenomenon. Genre science fiction thrives within an epistemology which privileges the logic of cause-and-effect narrative development, and it usually demonstrates a rather optimistic belief in the progress of human knowledge. Appropriately, the space ship was its representative icon during the 1940s and '50s, the expansionist 'golden age' of American science fiction. Equally appropriately, genre science fiction can claim the realist novel as its closest narrative relative; both developed in an atmosphere of nineteenth-century scientific positivism and both rely to a great extent on the mimetic transparency of language as a 'window' through which to provide views of a relatively uncomplicated human reality. When science fiction is enlisted by postmodernist fiction, however, it becomes integrated into an esthetic and a world-view whose central tenets are an uncertainty and an indeterminacy which call into question the 'causal interpretation of the universe' and the reliance on a 'rhetoric of believability' which virtually define it as a generic entity (Ebert 92).

It is within this conflictual framework of realist literary conventions played out in the postmodernist field that I want to look at cyberpunk, a 'movement' in science fiction in the 1980s which produced a wide range of fictions exploring the technological ramifications of experience within late-capitalist, post-industrial, media-saturated Western society. 'Let's get back to the Cyberpunks,' Lucius Shepard recently proposed in the first issue of *Journal Wired* (1989), one of several non-academic periodicals devoted to contemporary issues in science fiction and related fields; 'Defunct or not, they seem to be the only revolution we've got' (113).

Cyberpunk was a product of the commercial mass market of 'hard' science fiction; concerned on the whole with near-future extrapolation and more or less conventional on the level of narrative technique, it was nevertheless at times brilliantly innovative in its explorations of technology as one of the 'multiplicity of structures that intersect to produce that unstable constellation the liberal humanists call the "self"' (Moi 10). From this perspective, cyberpunk can be situated among a growing (although still relatively small) number of science-fiction projects which can be identified as 'anti-humanist.' In its various deconstructions of the subject – carried out in terms of a cybernetic breakdown of the classic nature/culture opposition – cyberpunk can be read as one symptom of the postmodern condition of genre science fiction. While science fiction frequently problematizes the oppositions between the natural and the artificial, the human and the machine, it generally sustains them in such a way that the human remains securely ensconced in its privileged place at the center of things. Cyberpunk, however, is about the breakdown of these oppositions.

This cybernetic deconstruction is heralded in the opening pages of what is now considered the quintessential cyberpunk novel – we might call it 'the c-p limit-text' – William Gibson's *Neuromancer* (1984). Gibson's first sentence – 'The sky above the port was the color of television, tuned to a dead channel' (3) – invokes a rhetoric of technology to express the natural world in a metaphor which blurs the distinctions between the organic and the artificial. Soon after, Gibson's computer-cowboy, Case, gazes at 'the chrome stars' of shuriken, and imagines these deadly weapons as 'the stars under which he voyaged, his destiny spelled out in a constellation of cheap chrome' (12). Human bodies too are absorbed into this rhetorical conflation of organism and machine: on the streets of the postmodern city whose arteries circulate information, Case sees 'all around [him] the dance of biz, information interacting, data made flesh in the mazes of the black market ...' (16). The human world replicates its own mechanical systems, and the border between the organic and the artificial threatens to blur beyond recuperation.

If we think of science fiction as a genre which typically foregrounds human action *against* a background constituted by its technology, this blurring of once clearly defined boundaries makes cyberpunk a particularly relevant form of science fiction for the post-industrial present. Richard Kadrey, himself a (some-time) cyberpunk writer, recently noted the proliferation of computer-based metaphors – 'downtime,' 'brain dump' and 'interface,' for example – which are already used to describe human interaction ('Simulations' 75). We can read cyberpunk as an analysis of the postmodern *identification* of human and machine.

Common to most of the texts which have become associated with cyberpunk is an overwhelming fascination, at once celebratory and anxious, with technology and its immediate – that is, *unmediated* – effects upon human being-in-the-world, a fascination which sometimes spills over into the problematizing of 'reality' itself. This emphasis on the potential interconnections between the human and the technological, many of which are already gleaming in the eyes of research scientists, is perhaps the central 'generic' feature of cyberpunk. Its evocation of popular/street culture and its valorization of the socially margin-alized, that is, its 'punk' sensibility, have also been recognized as important defining characteristics.

Sterling, one of the most prolific spokespersons for the Movement during its heyday, has described cyberpunk as a reaction to 'standard humanist liberalism' because of its interest in exploring the various scenarios of humanity's potential interfaces with the products of its own technology. For Sterling, cyberpunk is 'post-humanist' science fiction which believes that 'technological destruction of the human condition leads not to futureshocked zombies but to hopeful monsters' ('Letter' 5,4).

Science fiction has traditionally been enchanted with the notion of transcendence, but, as Glenn Grant points out in his discussion of *Neuromancer*, cyberpunk's 'preferred method of transcendence is through technology' (43). Themes of transcendence, however, point cyberpunk back to the romantic trappings of the genre at its most conventional, as does its valorization of the (usually male) loner rebel/hacker/punk who appears so frequently as its central character. Even Sterling has recognized this, concluding that 'the proper mode of critical attack on cyberpunk has not yet been essayed. Its truly dangerous element is incipient Nietzschean philosophical fascism: the belief in the Overman, and the worship of will-to-power' ('Letter' 5).

It is also important to note that not all the monsters it has produced have been hopeful ones; balanced against the exhilaration of potential technological transcendence is the anxiety and disorientation produced in the self/body in danger of being absorbed into its own technology. Mesmerized by the purity of technology, Gibson's Case at first has only contempt for the 'meat' of the human body and yearns to remain 'jacked into a custom cyberspace deck that projected his disembodied consciousness into the consensual hallucination that was the matrix' (5). Similarly, the protagonist of K.W. Jeter's *The Glass Hammer* (1987) experiences his very existence as a televised simulation. The postmodern anomie which pervades *The Glass Hammer* demonstrates that Sterling's defense of cyberpunk against charges that it is peopled with 'future-shocked zombies' has been less than completely accurate.

'In virtual reality, the entire universe is your body and physics is your language,' according to Jaron Lanier, founder and CEO of VPL Research in California; 'we're creating an entire new reality' (qtd. in Ditlea 97–98).

Gibson's *Neuromancer*, the first of a trilogy of novels which includes *Count Zero* (1986) and *Mona Lisa Overdrive* (1988), is set in a near-future trash-culture ruled by multi-national corporations and kept going by black-market economies, all frenetically dedicated to the circulation of computerized data and 'the dance of biz' (16) which is played out by Gibson's characters on the streets of the new urban overspill, the Sprawl. The most striking spatial construct in *Neuromancer*, however, is neither the cityscape of the Sprawl nor the artificial environments like the fabulous L-5, Freeside, but 'cyberspace,' the virtual reality which exists in simulated splendor on the far side of the computer screens which are the real center of technological activity in Gibson's fictional world. Scott Bukatman describes cyberspace as 'a new and decentered spatiality ... which exists parallel to, but outside of, the geographic topography of experiential reality' (45). In a fascinating instance of feedback between science fiction and the 'real' world, Autodesk, a firm researching innovations in computerized realities in Sausalito, California, has recently filed for trademark protection of the term 'cyberspace' which it may use as the name for its new virtual reality software (Ditlea 99). Jean Baudrillard's apocalyptic commentary seems especially significant here: 'It is thus not necessary to write science fiction: we have as of now, here and now, in our societies, with the media, the computers, the circuits, the networks, the acceleration of particles which has definitely broken the referential orbit of things' ('The Year 2000' 36).

Along with the 'other' space of cyberspace, *Neuromancer* offers alternatives to conventional modalities of human existence as well: computer hackers have direct mental access to cyberspace, artificial intelligences live and function within it, digitalized constructs are based on the subjectivities of humans whose 'personalities' have been downloaded into computer memory, and human bodies are routinely cloned.

This is Sterling's post-humanism with a vengeance, a post-humanism which, in its representation of 'monsters' – hopeful or otherwise – produced by the interface of the human and the machine, radically decenters the human body, the sacred icon of the essential self, in the same way that the virtual reality of cyberspace works to decenter conventional humanist notions of an unproblematical 'real.'

As I have noted, however, cyberpunk is not the only mode in which science fiction has demonstrated an anti-humanist sensibility. Although radically different from cyberpunk – which is written for the most part by a small number of white middle-class men, many of whom, inexplicably, live in Texas – feminist science fiction has also produced an influential body of anti-humanist texts. These would include, for example, Joanna Russ's *The Female Man* (1975), Jody Scott's *I, Vampire* (1984), and Margaret Atwood's *The Handmaid's Tale* (1985), novels which also participate in the postmodernist revision of conventional science fiction. Given the exigencies of their own particular political agendas, however, these texts demonstrate a very different approach to the construction/deconstruction of the subject than is evident in the technologically-influenced post-humanism of most cyberpunk fiction.

Jane Flax, for example, suggests that 'feminists, like other postmodernists, have begun to suspect that all such transcendental claims [those which valorize universal notions of reason, knowledge, and the self] reflect and reify the experience of a few persons – mostly white, Western males. These transhistoric claims seem plausible to us in part because they reflect important aspects of the experience of those who dominate our social world' (626). Flax's comments are well taken, although her conflation of all feminisms with postmodernism tends to oversimplify the very complex and problematical interactions of the two that Bonnie Zimmerman has noted. Moreover, in a forthcoming essay for *Extrapolation*, I have argued that most feminist science fiction rather supports than undermines the tenets of liberal humanism, although 'changing the subject' of that humanism, to borrow the title of a recent study by Nancy K. Miller.

We can also include writers like Philip K. Dick, Samuel R. Delany and John Varley within the project of anti-humanist science fiction, although these writers are separated from cyberpunk not only by chronology but also by cyberpunk's increased emphasis on technology as a constitutive factor in the development of postmodern subjectivity. Darko Suvin also notes some of the differences in political extrapolation between cyberpunk and its precursors: 'in between Dick's nation-state armies or polices and Delany's Foucauldian micro-politics of bohemian groups, Gibson [for example] has – to my mind more realistically – opted for global economic power-wielders as the arbiters of peoples [sic] lifestyles and lives' (43).

In 'Prometheus as Performer: Toward a Posthumanist Culture?' Ihab Hassan writes: 'We need first to understand that the human form – including human desire and all its external representations – may be changing radically, and thus must be re-visioned. We need to understand that five hundred years of human-ism may be coming to an end, as humanism transforms itself into something that we must helplessly call posthumanism' (205).

Sterling's *Schismatrix* (1986) is one version of 'posthumanity' presented as picaresque epic. Sterling's far-future universe – a rare construction in the cyberpunk 'canon' – is one in which countless societies are evolving in countless different directions; the Schismatrix is a loose confederation of worlds where the only certainty is the inevitability of change. Sterling writes that 'the new multiple humanities hurtled blindly toward their unknown destinations, and the vertigo of acceleration struck deep. Old preconceptions were in tatters, old loyalties were obsolete. Whole societies were paralyzed by the mind-blasting vistas of absolute possibility' (238). Sterling's protagonist, a picaresque hero for the postmodern age, 'mourned mankind, and the blindness of men, who thought that the Kosmos had rules and limits that would shelter them from their own freedom. There were no shelters. There were no final purposes. Futility, and freedom, were Absolute' (273).

Schismatrix is a future history different from many science-fiction futures in that what it extrapolates from the present is the all-too-often ignored/denied/repressed idea that human beings will be different in the future and will continue to develop within difference. In this way, *Schismatrix* demonstrates a familiarly post-structuralist sensibility, in its recognition both of the potential anxiety *and* the potential play inherent in a universe where 'futility, and freedom, [are] Absolute.'

Sterling's interest in and attraction to the play of human possibility appears as early as his first novel, *Involution Ocean* (1977). In this story (which reads in some ways like a kind of drug-culture post-*Moby-Dick*), the protagonist falls into a wonderful vision of an alien civilization, in a passage which, at least temporarily, emphasizes freedom over futility: 'There was an incredible throng, members of a race that took a pure hedonistic joy in the possibilities of surgical alteration. They switched bodies, sexes, ages, and races as easily as breathing, and their happy disdain for uniformity was dazzling. ... It seemed so natural, rainbow people in the rainbow streets; humans seemed drab and antlike in comparison' (154).

This is a far cry from the humanist anxieties which have pervaded science fiction since the nincteenth century. Consider, for example, the anxiety around which H. G. Wells created *The Time Machine* (1895): it is 'de-humanization,' humanity's loss of its position at the center of creation, which produces the tragedy of the terminal beach, and it is, to a great extent, the absence of the human which results in the 'abominable desolation' (91) described by Wells's Time Traveller. Or consider what we might term the 'trans-humanism' of Arthur C. Clarke's *Childhood's End* (1953), in which a kind of transcendental mysticism precludes the necessity of envisioning a future based on changing technologies, social conditions and social relations. Greg Bear's more recent *Blood Music* (1985) might be read, from this perspective, as a contemporary version of the same transcendental approach to human transformation, one based on an apocalyptic logic which implies the impossibility of any change in the human condition *within history*. *Blood Music* is especially interesting in this context, because its action is framed by a rhetoric of science which would seem to repudiate any recourse to metaphysics. Darko Suvin has noted, however, that it functions as 'a naïve fairytale relying on popular wishdreams that our loved ones not be dead and that our past mistakes may all be rectified, all of this infused with rather dubious philosophical and political stances' (41).

'Certain central themes spring up repeatedly in cyberpunk,' Sterling points out in his preface to the influential short-fiction collection, *Mirrorshades: The Cyberpunk Anthology*. 'The theme of body invasion: prosthetic limbs, implanted circuitry, cosmetic surgery, genetic alteration. The even more powerful theme of mind invasion: brain-computer interfaces, artificial intelligence, neurochemistry – techniques radically redefining the nature of humanity, the nature of the self' (xiii).

The potential in cyberpunk for undermining concepts like 'subjectivity' and 'identity' derives in part from its production within what has been termed 'the technological imagination'; that is, cyberpunk is hard science fiction which recognizes the paradigm-shattering role of technology in post-industrial society. We have to keep in mind here, of course, that the Movement has become (in)famous for the adversarial rhetoric of its ongoing and prolific self-commentary which, in turn, functions as an integral part of its overall production as a 'movement.' We should be careful, for this reason, not to confuse claims with results. The anti-humanist discourse of cyberpunk's frequent manifestoes, however, strongly supports de Lauretis's contention that 'technology is our historical context, political and personal' (167). As I have suggested, this context functions in cyberpunk as one of the most powerful of the multiplicities of structures which combine to produce the postmodern subject.

Thus, for example, the characters in Michael Swanwick's *Vacuum Flowers* (1987) are subjected to constant alterations in personality as the result of programming for different skills or social roles – metaphysical systems grounded on faith in an 'inner self' begin to waver. Human bodies in Gibson's stories, and even more so in Sterling's, are subjected to shaping and re-shaping, the human

CYBERNETIC DECONSTRUCTIONS'

form destined perhaps to become simply one available choice among many; notions of a human nature determined by a 'physical essence' of the human begin to lose credibility (for this reason, many behavioral patterns defined by sexual difference become irrelevant in these futures). Thus Rudy Rucker can offer the following as a chapter title in *Wetware*: 'Four: In Which Manchile, the First Robot-Built Human, Is Planted in the Womb of Della Taze by Ken Doll, Part of Whose Right Brain Is a Robot Rat.'

We must also recognize, however, that 'the subject of the subject' at the present time has given rise to as much anxiety as celebration (anxiety from which the postmodernist theorist is by no means exempt). The break-up of the humanist 'self' in a media-saturated post-industrial present has produced darker readings which cyberpunk also recognizes. Fredric Jameson, whose stance *vis-à-vis* the postmodern is at once appreciative and skeptical, has suggested that fragmentation of subjectivity may be the postmodern equivalent of the modernist predicament of individual alienation ('Cultural Logic' 63). Pat Cadigan's 'Pretty Boy Crossover' (1985), for example, raises questions about the effects of simulated reality upon our human sense of self as complete and inviolable. In her fictional world, physical reality is 'less efficient' than computerized simulation, and video stars are literally video programs, having been 'distilled … to pure information' (89, 88) and downloaded into computer matrices. Cadigan's eponymous Pretty Boy is tempted by the offer of literally eternal life within the matrix and, although he finally chooses 'real' life, that reality seems to fade against the guaranteed 'presence' of its simulation. Bobby, who has opted for existence as simulation, explains the 'economy of the gaze' which guarantees the authenticity of the self in this world: 'If you love me, you watch me. If you don't look, you don't care and if you don't care I don't matter. If I don't matter, I don't exist. Right?' (91).

'Pretty Boy Crossover' offers this succinct observation about the seductive power of simulated reality: 'First you see video. Then you wear video. Then you eat video. Then you *be* video' (82).

In K.W. Jeter's *The Glass Hammer*, being is *defined* by its own simulation. *The Glass Hammer* is one of the most self-conscious deconstructions of unified subjectivity produced in recent science fiction, and one which dramatizes (in the neurotic tonalities familiar to readers of J.G. Ballard) the anxiety and schizophrenia of the (technologically-produced) postmodern situation. In *The Glass Hammer* the break-up of the 'self' is narrated in a text as fragmented as its subject (subject both as protagonist and as story). Jeter's novel is a chilling demonstration of the power of simulated re-presentation to construct 'the real' (so that it functions like a cyberpunk simulacrum of the theories of Jean Baudrillard). It 'narrates' episodes in the life of Ross Schuyler, who watches the creation of this life as a video event in five segments. There is no way to test the accuracy of the creation, since the self produced by memory is as unreliable a re-presentation as is a media 'bio.' As Schuyler realizes: 'Just because I was there – that doesn't mean anything' (59).

The opening sequence of *The Glass Hammer* dramatizes the schizophrenia within the subjectivity of the protagonist:

> Video within video. He watched the monitor screen, seeing himself there, watching. In the same space ... that he sat in now ...
> He watched the screen, waiting for the images to form. Everything would be in the tapes, if he watched long enough. (7)

Like Schuyler himself, the reader waits for the images to form as s/he reads the text. Episodes range over time, some in the past(s), some in the present, some real, some simulated, many scripted rather than 'novelized,' until the act of reading/watching achieves a kind of temporary coherence. It is this same kind of temporary coherence which formulates itself in Schuyler's consciousness, always threatening to dissolve again from 'something recognizably narrative' into 'the jumbled, half-forgotten clutter of his life' (87).

What takes place in *The Glass Hammer* may also be read as a deconstruction of the opposition between depth and surface, a dichotomy which is frequently framed as the familiar conflict between reality and appearance. Jeter reverses this opposition, dramatizing the haphazard construction of his character's 'inner self' as a response to people and events, both real and simulated, over time. The displacement of an 'originary' self from the text places the emphasis on the marginal, the contingent, the re-presentations (in this case electronically produced) which actually create the sense of 'self.' Jeter's technique in *The Glass Hammer* is particularly effective: the reader watches the character, and watches the character watching himself watching, as his past unfolds, not as a series of memories whose logical continuity guarantees the stability of the ego, but as an entertainment series, the logical continuity of which is the artificial re-arrangement of randomness to *simulate* coherence.

Near the outset of Case's adventures in *Neuromancer*, Gibson's computer cowboy visits the warehouse office of Julius Deane, who 'was one hundred and thirty-five years old, his metabolism assiduously warped by a weekly fortune in serums and hormones.' In Deane's office, 'Neo-Aztec bookcases gathered dust against one wall of the room where Case waited. A pair of bulbous Disney-styled table lamps perched awkwardly on a low Kandinsky-look coffee table in scarlet-lacquered steel. A Dali clock hung on the wall between the bookcases, its distorted face sagging to the bare concrete floor' (12).

In this context, it is significant that the 'average' cyberpunk landscape tends to be choked with the debris of both language and objects; as a sign-system, it is overdetermined by a proliferation of surface detail which emphasizes the 'outside' over the 'inside.' Such attention to detail – recall Gibson's nearly compulsive use of brand names, for example, or the claustrophobic clutter of his streets – replaces the more conventional (realist) narrative exercise we might call 'getting to the bottom of things'; indeed, the shift in emphasis is from a symbolic to a surface reality.

In a discussion of *Neuromancer*, Gregory Benford observes that 'Gibson, like Ballard, concentrates on surfaces as a way of getting at the aesthetic of an age.' This observation is a telling one, even as it misses the point. Benford concludes that Gibson's attention to surface detail 'goes a long way toward telling us why his work has proved popular in England, where the tide for several decades now has been to relish fiction about surfaces and manners, rather than the more traditional concerns of hard SF: ideas, long perspectives, and content' (19).

This reliance on tradition is perhaps what prevents Benford, whose own 'hard science fiction' novels and stories are very much a part of science fiction's humanist tradition, from appreciating the approach of writers like Gibson and Jeter. The point may be that, in works like *Neuromancer* and *The Glass Hammer*, surface *is* content, an equation which encapsulates their critique – or at least their awareness – of our contemporary 'era of hyperreality' (Baudrillard, 'Ecstasy' 128). In this context, the much-quoted opening sentence of *Neuromancer*, with its image of the blank surface of a dead television screen, evokes the anxiety of this new era. Istvan Csicsery-Ronay, for example, sees in cyberpunk the recognition that 'with the computer, the problem of identity is moot, and the idea of reflection is transformed in to [sic] the algorithm of replication. SF's computer wipes out the Philosophical God and ushers in the demiurge of thought-as-technique' (273).

Like much anti-humanist science fiction, cyberpunk also displays a certain coolness, a kind of ironically detached approach to its subject matter which precludes nostalgia or sentimentality. This detachment usually discourages any recourse to the logic of the apocalypse, which, whether positive (like Clarke's) or negative (like Wells's), is no longer a favored narrative move. Jameson and Sterling (representatives of 'high theory' and 'low culture' respectively?) both identify a waning interest in the scenarios of literal apocalypse: Jameson perceives in the postmodern situation what he calls 'an inverted millennarianism, in which premonitions of the future ... have been replaced by the senses of the end of this or that' ('Cultural Logic' 53); in his introduction to Gibson's short-story collection, *Burning Chrome*, Sterling comments that one 'distinguishing mark of the emergent new school of Eighties SF [is] its boredom with the Apocalypse' (xi).

This is supported by Douglas Robinson, in his *American Apocalypses*, when he concludes that 'antiapocalypse – not apocalypse, as many critics have claimed – is the dominant topos of American postmodernism' (xvi). In a discussion of Derrida's discourse on apocalypse, Robinson argues that 'the apocalyptic imagination fascinates Derrida precisely as the 'purest' form, the most mythical expression or the most extreme statement of the metaphysics of presence' (251n1).

One reason for this tendency to abandon what has been a traditional science fiction topos may be the conviction, conscious or not, that a kind of philosophical apocalypse has already occurred, precipitating us into the dis-ease of postmodernism. Another reason may be the increased commitment of anti-humanist science fiction to the exploration of changes that will occur – to the self, to society and to social relations – in time; that is, they are more engaged with historical processes than attracted by the jump-cuts of apocalyptic scenarios which evade such investment in historical change. Cyberpunk, in particular, has demonstrated a keen interest in the near future, an aspect of its approach to history which discourages resolution-through-apocalypse.

In a discussion of 'the cybernetic (city) state,' Scott Bukatman has argued that as a result of the tendency in recent science fiction to posit 'a reconception of the human and the ability to interface with the new terminal experience . . . terminal space becomes a legitimate part of human (or post-human) experience' (60). In many cases, however, science-fiction futures are all too often simply representations of contemporary cultural mythologies disguised under heavy layers of futuristic make-up.

The recognition of this fact provides part of the 'meaning' of one of the stories in Gibson's *Burning Chrome* collection. 'The Gernsback Continuum' humorously ironizes an early twentieth-century futurism which could conceive of no real change in the human condition, a futurism which envisioned changes in 'stuff' rather than changes in social relations (historical distance increases the ability to critique such futures, of course). In Gibson's story, the benighted protagonist is subjected to visitations by the 'semiotic ghosts' of a future which never took place, the future, to borrow a phrase from Jameson, 'of one moment of what is now our own past' ('Progress' 244). At the height of these 'hallucinations,' he 'sees' two figures poised outside a vast city reminiscent of the sets for films like *Metropolis* and *Things to Come*:

> [the man] had his arm around [the woman's] waist and was gesturing toward the city. They were both in white. . . . He was saying something wise and strong, and she was nodding. . . .
> . . . [T]hey were the Heirs to the Dream. They were white, blond, and they probably had blue eyes. They were American. . . . They were smug, happy, and utterly content with themselves and their world. And in the Dream, it was *their* world. . . .
> It had all the sinister fruitiness of Hitler Youth propaganda. (32–33)

Gibson's protagonist discovers that 'only really bad media can exorcise [his] semiotic ghosts' (33) and he recovers with the help of pop culture productions like *Nazi Love Motel*. 'The Gernsback Continuum' concludes with the protagonist's realization that his dystopian present could be worse, 'it could be perfect' (35).

Gibson's story is not simply an ironization of naïve utopianism; it also warns against the limitations, both humorous and dangerous, inherent in any vision of the future which bases itself upon narrowly defined ideological systems which take it upon themselves to speak 'universally,' or which conceive of themselves as 'natural' or 'absolute.' David Brin's idealistic *The Postman* (1985), for example, is a post-apocalyptic fiction which closes on a metaphorical note 'of innocence, unflaggingly optimistic' (321), nostalgically containing itself within the framework of a conventional humanism. Not surprisingly, its penultimate chapter concludes with a re-affirmation of the 'natural' roles of men and women:

> And always remember, the moral concluded: Even the best men – the heroes – will sometimes neglect to do their jobs.
> *Women, you must remind them, from time to time.* ... (312)

Compare this to Gibson's description of the Magnetic Dog Sisters, peripheral characters in his story, 'Johnny Mnemonic' (1981), also collected in *Burning Chrome*: 'They were two meters tall and thin as greyhounds. One was black and the other white, but aside from that they were as nearly identical as cosmetic surgery could make them. They'd been lovers for years and were bad news in a tussle. I was never quite sure which one had originally been male' (2).

Another story in the same collection, 'Fragments of a Hologram Rose,' uses metaphors of the new technology to express the indeterminate and fragmented nature of the self: 'A hologram has this quality: Recovered and illuminated, each fragment will reveal the whole image of the rose. Falling toward delta, he sees himself the rose, each of his scattered fragments revealing a whole he'll never know. ... But each fragment reveals the rose from a different angle ...' (42).

Gibson's rhetoric of technology finally circumscribes all of reality. In his second novel, *Count Zero* (1986), there is an oblique but pointed rebuttal of humanist essentialization, which implicitly recognizes the artificiality of the Real. Having described cyberspace, the weirdly real 'space' that human minds occupy during computer interfacing, as 'mankind's unthinkably complex consensual hallucination' (44), he goes on to write the following:

> 'Okay,' Bobby said, getting the hang of it, 'then what's the matrix? ... [W]hat's cyberspace?'
> 'The world,' Lucas said. (131)

It is only by recognizing the consensual nature of socio-cultural reality, which includes within itself our definitions of human nature, that we can begin to perceive the possibility of change. In this sense, as Csicsery-Ronay suggests (although from a very different perspective), cyberpunk is 'a paradoxical form of realism' (266).

Csicsery-Ronay also contends that cyberpunk is 'a legitimate international artistic style, with profound philosophical and aesthetic premises,' a style captured by films such as *Blade Runner* and by philosophers such as Jean

Baudrillard; 'it even has, in Michael Jackson and Ronald Reagan, its hyperreal icons of the human simulacrum infiltrating reality' (269).

Lucius Shepard concludes his 'requiem for cyberpunk' by quoting two lines from Cavafy's 'Waiting for the Barbarians': 'What will we do now that the barbarians are gone? / Those people were a kind of solution' (118).

Cyberpunk seemed to erupt in the mid-80s, self-sufficient and full-grown, like Minerva from the forehead of Zeus. From some perspectives, it could be argued that this self-proclaimed Movement was nothing more than the discursive construction of the collective imaginations of science-fiction writers and critics eager for something/anything new in what had become a very conservative and quite predictable field. Now that the rhetorical dust has started to settle, however, we can begin to see cyberpunk as itself the product of a multiplicity of influences from both within and outside of genre science fiction. Its writers readily acknowledge the powerful influence of 1960s and '70s New Wave writers like Samuel R. Delany, John Brunner, Norman Spinrad, J.G. Ballard and Michael Moorcock, as well as the influence of postmodernists like William Burroughs and Thomas Pynchon. The manic fragmentations of Burroughs's *Naked Lunch* and the maximalist apocalypticism of Pynchon's *Gravity's Rainbow* would seem to have been especially important for the development of the cyberpunk 'sensibility.' Richard Kadrey has even pronounced *Gravity's Rainbow* to be cyberpunk *avant la lettre*' the best cyberpunk novel ever written by a guy who didn't even know he was writing it' ('Cyberpunk' 83). Equally, Delany has made a strong case for feminist science fiction as cyberpunk's 'absent mother,' noting that 'the feminist explosion – which obviously infiltrates the cyberpunk writers so much – is the one they seem to be the least comfortable with, even though it's one that, much more than the New Wave, has influenced them most strongly, both in progressive and in reactionary ways ...' (9).

Due in part to the prolific commentaries and manifestoes in which writers like Sterling outlined/analyzed/defended their project(s) – usually at the expense of more traditional science fiction – cyberpunk helped to generate a great deal of very useful controversy about the role of science fiction in the 1980s, a decade in which the resurgence of fantastic literature left much genre science fiction looking rather sheepishly out of date. At best, however, the critique of humanism in these works remains incomplete, due at least in part to the pressures of mass market publishing as well as to the limitations of genre conventions which, more or less faithfully followed, seem (inevitably?) to lure writers back into the power fantasies which are so common to science fiction. A novel like Margaret Atwood's *The Handmaid's Tale*, for instance, produced as it was outside the genre market, goes further in its deconstruction of individual subjectivity than do any of the works I have been discussing, except perhaps *The Glass Hammer*.

Gibson's latest novel, *Mona Lisa Overdrive*, although set in the same universe as *Neuromancer* and *Count Zero*, foregrounds character in a way which necessarily mutes the intensity and multiplicity of surface detail which is so marked a characteristic of his earlier work. Sterling's recent and unexpected *Islands in the Net* (1988) is a kind of international thriller which might be read as the depiction of life *after* the postmodern condition has been 'cured.' Set in a future after the 'Abolition' (of nuclear warfare), its central character, Laura Webster, dedicates herself to the control of a political crisis situation which threatens to return the world to a global state of fragmentation and disruptive violence which only too clearly recalls our own present bad old days. Sterling's 'Net' is the vast information system which underlies and makes possible the unity of this future world and his emphasis is clearly on the necessity for such global unity. Although, in the final analysis, no one is completely innocent – Sterling is too complex a writer to structure his forces on opposite sides of a simple ethical divide – the movement in *Islands in the Net* is away from the margins toward the center, and the Net, the 'global nervous system' (15), remains intact.

As its own creators seem to have realized, cyberpunk – like the punk ethic with which it was identified – was a response to postmodern reality which could go only so far before self-destructing under the weight of its own deconstructive activities (not to mention its appropriation by more conventional and more commercial writers). That final implosion is perhaps what Jeter accomplished in *The Glass Hammer*, leaving us with the image of a mesmerized Schuyler futilely searching for a self in the videoscreens of the dystopian future. It is clearly this aspect of cyberpunk which leads Csicsery-Ronay to conclude that 'by the time we get to cyberpunk, reality has become a case of nerves. ... The distance required for reflection is squeezed out as the world implodes: when hallucinations and realia collapse into each other, there is no place from which to reflect' (274). For him, 'cyberpunk is ... the apotheosis of bad faith, apotheosis of the postmodern' (277). This, of course, forecloses any possibility of political engagement within the framework of the postmodern.

Here cyberpunk is theorized as a symptom of the malaise of postmodernism, but, like Baudrillard's apocalyptic discourse on the 'condition' itself, Csicsery-Ronay's analysis tends to underplay the positive potential of re-presentation and re-visioning achieved in works like *Neuromancer* and *Schismatrix*. Bukatman, for example, has suggested that the function of cyberpunk 'neuro-manticism' is one appropriate to science fiction in the postmodern era: the *reinsertion* of the human into the new reality which its technology is in the process of shaping. According to Bukatman, 'to dramatize the terminal realm means to somehow insert the figure of the human into that space to experience it *for us*. ... Much recent science fiction stages and restages a confrontation between figure and ground, finally constructing a new human form to interface with the other space and cybernetic reality' (47–48).

The postmodern condition has required that we revise science fiction's original trope of technological anxiety – the image of a fallen humanity controlled by a technology run amok. Here again we must deconstruct the human/machine opposition and begin to ask new questions about the ways in which we and our technologies 'interface' to produce what has become a *mutual* evolution. It may be significant that one of the most brilliant visions of the potential of cybernetic deconstructions is introduced in Donna Haraway's merger of science fiction and feminist theory, 'A Manifesto for Cyborgs: Science, Technology, and Socialist Feminism in the 1980s,' which takes the rhetoric of technology toward its political limits: 'cyborg unities are monstrous and illegitimate,' writes Haraway; 'in our present political circumstances, we could hardly hope for more potent myths for resistance and recoupling' (179).

WORKS CITED

Acker, Kathy (1988) *Empire of the Senseless*. New York: Grove.

Atwood, Margaret (1986) *The Handmaid's Tale*. Toronto: McCelland.

Ballard, J. G. (1985) *Crash* [1975]. London Triad/Panther.

Baudrillard, Jean (1983) 'The Ecstasy of Communication', in Hal Foster (ed.), *The Anti-Aesthetic: Essays on Postmodern Culture*, trans. John Johnston. Port Townsend, WA: Bay, pp. 12–34.

Baudrillard, Jean (1987) 'The Year 2000 Has Already Happened', in Arthur Kroker and Marilouise Kroker (eds), *Body Invaders: Panic Sex in America*, trans. Nai-Fei Ding and Kuan Hsiog Chen. Montreal: New World Perspectives, pp. 35–44.

Bear, Greg (1985) *Blood Music*. New York: Ace.

Benford, Gregory (1988) 'Is Something Going On?', *Mississippi Review*, 47/48: 8–23.

Brautigan, Richard (1968) *In Watermelon Sugar*. New York: Dell.

Brin, David (1985) *The Postman*. New York: Bantam.

Bukatman, Scott (1989) 'The Cybernetic (City) State: Terminal Space Becomes Phenomenal', *Journal of the Fantastic in the Arts*, 2: 43–63.

Burgess, Anthony (1982) *The End of the World News*. Markham, ON: Penguin.

Burroughs, William (1959) *Naked Lunch*. New York: Grove.

Cadigan, Pat 'Pretty Boy Crossover' (1985), in *The 1987 Annual World's Best SF*. Donald A. Wollheim (ed.), New York: DAW, pp. 82–93.

Carter, Angela (1972) *Heroes and Villains* [1969]. London: Pan.

Clarke, Arthur C. (1953) *Childhood's End*. New York: Ballantine.

Csicsery-Ronay, Istvan (1988) 'Cyberpunk and Neoromanticism', *Mississippi Review*, 47/48: 266–78.

Delany, Samuel R. (1988) 'Some *Real* Mothers: An Interview with Samel R. Delaney by Takayuki Tatsumi', *Science-Fiction Eye*, 1: 5–11.

de Lauretis, Teresa (1980) 'Signs of Wo/ander', in Teresa de Lauretis, Andreas Huyssen and Kathleen Woodward (eds), *The Technological Imagination*. Madison, WI: Coda, pp. 159–74.

Ditlea, Steve (1989) 'Another World: Inside Artificial Reality', *P/C Computing*, November: 90–102.

Ebert, Teresa L. (1980) 'The Convergence of Postmodern Innovative Fiction and Science Fiction: An Encounter with Samuel R. Delaney's Technotopia', *Poetics Today*, 1: 91–104.

Flax, Jane (1987) 'Postmodernism and Gender Relations in Feminist Theory', *Signs: Journal of Women in Culture and Society*, 12: 621–43.

Gibson, William (1968) *Mona Lisa Overdrive*. New York: Bantam.

Gibson, William (1981) 'The Gernsback Continuum', in *Burning Chrome*. New York: Ace, pp. 23–35.

Gibson, William (1981) 'Johnny Mnemonic', in *Burning Chrome*. New York: Ace, pp. 1–22.

Gibson, William (1984) *Necromancer*. New York: Berkley.

Gibson, William (1986) *Count Zero*. New York: Arbor House.

Gibson, William (1987) 'Fragments of a Hologram Rose' [1972], in *Burning Chrome*. New York: Ace, pp. 36–42.

Grant, Glenn (1990) 'Transcendence Through Détournement in William Gibson's *Neuromancer*', *Science Fiction Studies*, 17: 41–9.

Haraway, Donna (1989) 'A Manifesto for Cyborgs: Science, Technology, and Socialist Feminism in the 1980s' [1985], in Elizabeth Weed (ed.), *Coming to Terms: Feminism, Theory, Politics*. New York: Routledge, pp. 173–204.

Hassan, Ihab (1977) 'Prometheus as Performer: Toward a Posthumanist Culture?', in Michel Benamou and Charles Caramello (eds), *Performance in Postmodern Culture*. Madison, WI: Coda, pp. 201–17.

Hoban, Russell (1988) *Riddley Walker* [1982]. London: Pan.

Hollinger, Veronica (1990) 'Feminist Science Fiction: Breaking Up the Subject', *Extrapolation*, 31: forthcoming.

Jameson, Fredric (1984) 'Postmodernism, or The Cultural Logic of Late Capitalism', *New Left Review*, 146: 53–94.

Jameson, Fredric (1984) 'Progress versus Utopia, or Can We Imagine the Future?', in Brian Wallis (ed.), *Art After Modernism: Rethinking Representation*. New York: New Museum of Contemporary Art, pp. 239–52.

Jeter, K. W. (1997) *The Glass Hammer*. New York: Signet.

Kadrey, Richard (1989) 'Simulations of Immortality', *Science Fiction Eye*, 1: 74–6.

Kadrey, Richard (1989) 'Cyberpunk 101 Reading List', *Whole Earth Review*, 63: 83.

MacCaffery, Larry (ed.) (1986) 'Introduction', in *Postmodern Fiction: A Bio-Bibliographical Guide*. Westport, CT: Greenwood, pp. xi–xxviii.

Miller, Nancy K. (1988) 'Changing the Subject: Authorship, Writing, and the Reader', in Teresa de Lauretis (ed.), *Feminist Studies/ Critical Studies*. Bloomington, IN: Indiana University Press, pp. 102–20.

Moi, Toril (1985) *Sexual/ Textual Politics: Feminist Literary Theory*. New York: Methuen.

Mooney, Ted (1981) *Easy Travel to Other Planets*. New York: Ballantine.

Pynchon, Thomas (1974) *Gravity's Rainbow* [1973]. New York: Bantam.

Robinson, Douglas (1985) *American Apocalypses The Image of the End of the World in American Literature*. Baltimore, MD: Johns Hopkins University Press.

Rucker, Rudy (1988) *Wetware*. New York: Avon.

Russ, Joanna (1975) *The Female Man*. New York: Bantam.

Scott, Jody (1984) *I, Vampire*. New York: Ace.

Shepard, Lucius (1989) 'Waiting for the Barbarians', *Journal Wired*, 1: 187.

Sterling, Bruce (1981) Preface to *Burning Chrome*. New York: Ace, pp. ix–xii.

Sterling, Bruce (1986) *Schismatrix*. New York. Ace.

Sterling, Bruce (1987) 'Letter from Bruce Sterling', *REM*, 71: 4–7.

Sterling, Bruce (1988) *Involution Ocean* [1977]. New York: Ace.

Sterling, Bruce (1988) Preface to *Mirrorshades: The Cyberpunk Anthology*. New York: Ace, pp. ix–xvi.

Sterling, Bruce (1989) 'Slipstream' *Science Fiction Eye*, 1: 77–80.

Sterling, Bruce (1998) *Islands in the Net*. New York: Arbor House.

Swanwick, Michael (1987) *Vacuum Flowers*. New York: Arbor.

Suvin, Darko (1989) 'On Gibson and Cyberpunk SF', *Foundation*, 46: 40–51.

Wells, H. G. (1968) *The Time Machine* [1895], in *The Time Machine and The War of the Worlds*. New York: Fawcett, pp. 25–98.

Wittig, Monique (1985) *Les Guérillères* [1969], trans. David Le Vay. Boston: Beacon.

Zimmerman, Bonnie (1986) 'Feminist Fiction and the Postmodern Challenge', in Larry McCaffery (ed.), *Postmodern Fiction: A Bio-Bibliographical Guide*. Westport, CT: Greenwood, pp. 175–88.

$$31$$

'ENGENDERING PARANOIA IN CONTEMPORARY NARRATIVE'

Patrick O'Donnell

Paranoia is one of the more prominent issues taken up by contemporary North American novelists since 1960. Writers as divergent in matters of style and subject as Norman Mailer, Philip Roth, Joseph Heller, Robert Coover, Thomas Pynchon, Diane Johnson, Joseph McElroy, John Barth, Kathy Acker, Saul Bellow, Marge Piercy, Don DeLillo, William Gaddis, Ishmael Reed, and Margaret Atwood have represented paranoid characters, communities, schemes, and lifestyles; history, technology, religion, patriarchy, and bureaucracy have all been viewed as motivated systems that oppress the masses and disenfranchise the preterite. Of course, to generate a list of writers who, despite their differences, seem mysteriously to agree to represent *paranoia* as a way of knowing or acting in their fiction is a paranoid act, especially if one were to argue that this is the result of the operation of some manipulated cultural paradigm (conceived by whom? enforced by what agency?). Paranoia, like power after Foucault, ranges across the multi-discursivity of contemporary existence; it is as present in most of the current debates over canonicity and cultural literacy as it was in the debates about the 'domino theory' that took place during the Vietnam War and that recur with disturbing frequency in American foreign policy.

For the purposes of this essay, I will refer to *cultural paranoia* as an intersection of contiguous lines of force – political, economic, epistemological, ethical – that make up a *dominant reality* (or *episteme*, or *paradigm*, or *habitus*, or *structure of feeling*) empowered by virtue of the connections to be made

From Patrick O'Donnell (1992) 'Engendering Paranoia in Contemporary Narrative', *boundary 2*, 19, (1): pp. 181–204.

between materiality, as such, and the fictional representations or transformations of that materiality which come to affect its constitution.[1] In my definition, cultural paranoia is not content but method: a way of seeing the multiple stratifications of reality, virtual and material, as interconnected or networked. In essence, this is to use a paranoid method (seeking the meeting point between political and epistemological lines of force) to elucidate the paranoia of contemporary narrative. However limited and self-enclosed it may be, looking at paranoia in this way partially reveals (and partially conceals) the nature of the compact and the engendering of paranoia as an element that partakes of and informs a contemporary American ideology.

Since paranoia has so much to do with the mystified, hegemonic enactments of power, the representation of paranoia in the artificial plots of fiction can, indeed, be seen as a site where epistemology and ideology meet. As a way of knowing, paranoia is a mode of perception that notes the connectedness between things in a hyperbolic metonymizing of reality. It can be conflated with – is the mirror image of – the more blatant monolithic and incorporative aspects of 'late capitalism,' defined by Fredric Jameson as a 'world system' whose features include the emergence of 'transnational business[,] ... the new international division of labor, a vertiginous new dynamic in international banking and the stock exchanges (including enormous Second and Third World debt), new forms of media interrelationship (very much including transportation systems such as containerization), computers and automation, the flight of production to Third World areas.'[2] The conflation of epistemology and politics in cultural paranoia is particularly pressing, as I will show, when apparent forms of resistance to political or narrative systems actually comply with the evolving story of hegemony. The romanticized opposition to cultural domination, for example, in which the individual perceives him- or herself to be part of a community of underground men and women opposed to the dominant culture, becomes, in novels of cultural paranoia, the disguised infiltration of that culture into every hidden corner of contemporary existence. There is complicity here, as well as connection. In the work of four male writers – Norman Mailer's *Executioner's Song*, Thomas Pynchon's *Crying of Lot 49*, Don DeLillo's *Running Dog*, and Joseph McElroy's *Lookout Cartridge* – I will discuss these manifestations of paranoia as means to transforming information into knowledge and to formulating identity as part of a paranoid community. Alternatively, Diane Johnson's work, *The Shadow Knows*, poses a critique of the neat fit between cultural domination and paranoid preterition, our Puritan inheritance.[3] In the comparisons I draw between these authors, I will suggest how cultural paranoia arises from the construction of the 'knowing' subject negotiated within our social and political economies.

1

In his revisionary view of Foucauldian notions of power, Jean Baudrillard writes of the 'transparency principle' operative in a culture that pursues the

following set of edicts: 'Let everything be produced, be read, become real, visible, and marked with the sign of effectiveness; let everything be transcribed into force relations, into conceptual systems or into calculable energy; let everything be said, gathered, indexed and registered. ... Ours is a culture of "monstration" and demonstration.'[4] In this arena of the 'hyperreal,' where information is capital, where performance replaces interpretation, and where the most valued form of mystification is the exultation of the obvious, what I educe in work-in-progress to be the manifestation of cultural paranoia in contemporary narrative finds its true home.[5] If, following Baudrillard, everything is visible and marked by or transcribed into capitalized relations of force and energy, then paranoia becomes the means by which connections are forged between disparate material realms: everything is known; everything is related; the anecdotal becomes the conspiratorial; accident becomes design. Further, paranoia, under these conditions, can be viewed as the binding force of the nation or the community: What brings people together, as it were, is the sense that they are the wary participants in an unfolding historical plot over which they have no control, but through which they gain visible identity as historically unified subjects.

[...]

2

Within the realm of the obvious, saturated by information overload, the paranoid subject is disempowered by virtue of the all-encompassing plots and systems that surround her; paradoxically, she is empowered as one in a growing army capable of reading the signs of these plots and power relations, not to resist or escape them but to formulate an ironic, streetwise attitude toward them. One knows she is part of a series of orchestrated events over which she has no control, but knowing it confers a kind of legitimacy upon the knower: she can be manipulated but she can't be fooled about being manipulated; she is always prepared for the revelation of deeper plots, more layered conspiracies.

This description approximates the situation of Oedipa Maas, protagonist of Thomas Pynchon's *The Crying of Lot 49*. In the novel, Oedipa, co-executor of the vast Pierce Inverarity empire, slowly discovers that her powers of dispensation have been accompanied by both an insider's knowledge of an oppositional postal system and a cluster of marginalized communities – from Inamorati Anonymous, for those who are addicted to love and, thus, must live as isolates, to AC-DC, the Alameda County Death Cult. Increasingly sensitive to and suspicious of the proliferation of signs indicative of Trystero, a vast conspiratorial umbrella under which all the plots and sects she encounters operate, Oedipa drives the freeways of southern California and looks out upon endless suburbs that resemble Mailer's Provo: 'a vast sprawl of houses which had grown up all together, like a well-tended crop, from the dull brown earth; and she thought of the time she'd opened a transistor radio to replace a battery and seen her first printed circuit.'[6] In a Walpurgisnacht of revelations, she walks the streets of San Francisco observing the sign of the Trystero (a muted post horn) as the city lies spread out, anatomized: 'The city was hers ... she had safe passage tonight to its far blood's branchings, be they capillaries too small for more than peering into, or vessels mashed together in shameless municipal hickeys, out on the skin for all but tourists to see' (*TCL49*, 117).

Oedipa is trapped in the hermeneutic circle, arguably, the philosopher's trope for paranoia. She either possesses secret knowledge of an increasingly obvious conspiracy – thus assisting in its construal – and is the victim of sinister global machinations stretching across a millennium, or she is just another crazy housewife in suburban America victimized by a patriarchal culture that forces her to such extremes in the quest for articulation. She awaits, even as the novel ends, some final, apocalyptic revelation, 'the direct, epileptic Word, the cry that might abolish the night' (*TCL49*, 118), and, a true child of the fifties, she is admirably prepared for her role in Pynchon's sardonic conflation of conservative politics and academic training: 'Where were secretaries James and Foster and Senator Joseph, those dear daft numina who'd mothered over Oedipa's temperate youth? In another world. ... Among them they had managed to turn the young Oedipa into a rare creature indeed, unfit for marches and sit-ins, but just a whiz at pursuing strange words in Jacobean texts' (*TCL49*, 104). In these characterizations, Oedipa becomes what might be termed the paranoid Cold War subject formed within the cybernetic economy of contemporary America. Literate, suspicious, and sensitive (like any good New Critic) to the subtleties of paradox and ambiguity, the more information Oedipa gathers, the more connections she finds, confirming her sense that she is part of some tangled network of linkages whose origins and ends ever recede into obfuscation as the information mounts. She is part of something bigger, and she appears to be taken in at the end – as are many of Pynchon's readers – by the promise of some singular revelation that will explain it all as she awaits the voice of the prophetic auctioneer, Loren Passerine, about to announce the sale of a lot of forged postage stamps.[7] Placed within this hushed roomful of buyers, shills, and hermeneuts (in a typical Pynchonian contradiction, a community of insiders – the power elite – oddly similar in its constitution to the preterite communities she has discovered in the streets), Oedipa is about to fulfill the promise of her upbringing: a daughter of Joe McCarthy, Oedipa will hear the word and fulfill the destiny of 'the true paranoid for whom all is organized in spheres joyful or threatening about the central pulse of [her]self' (*TCL49*, 128–29).

Pynchon's infamous 'ambiguity' prevents us from stabilizing any further the arcing contradictions of his vision in *The Crying of Lot 49* – a vision which, growing more complex in the encyclopedic narratives of *Gravity's Rainbow* and *Vineland*, thus accruing more material and information, has become the basis for an academic industry.[8] In a replay of the modern/postmodern dialectic, *The Crying of Lot 49* moves between the obfuscated mysteries of modernist symbolic depth and the surfaces of the contemporary 'hyperreal.' The inherent indeterminacies of this movement are analogous to Oedipa's confusion about whether she is really part of a labyrinthine plot or just making it all up: ambiguity and confusion, within the regime of a totalizing cultural paranoia and its attendant political consequences, comply with its advancement.[9] In Pynchon's contradictorily patent and suppressed engendering of paranoia, Oedipa is aptly named as the female questor in pursuit of the truth; she reduplicates, rather than subverts, the oedipal desire for a singular truth and an origin to the order of things. And Pynchon, himself, has taken on the peculiar role he assigns Oedipa in *The Crying of Lot 49*. Both a cult figure and a best-selling author, both liminal and at the center of that manifestation of the dominant culture labeled (by some) postmodernism, he has disappeared as an intentionality into the interpretive plots constructed for him by 'well-meaning' critics. It is perfectly consistent with the logic of cultural paranoia that his invisibility as a public personality has served as an enticement for the proliferation of 'information' about Pynchon, including apocryphal stories about his youth, insider's gossip about his travels and his next novel, and privately circulated annotations to his works. Here, networks of communication and communities of informational exchange are formed around the conservation of the text and the mystified authorial source of the text's plots. Intentionally or not, he may be said in this way to foster paranoia, as well as to fabulate it.

The novels of Don DeLillo do not indulge in Pynchon's transitionally late modernist enjambments of ambiguity and circuitry; rather, as Tom LeClair has argued, DeLillo writes the novel of information systems, of Baudrillard's 'hyperreal,' where everything is visible and on the surface.[10] The tone of such works as *Libra, White Noise, The Names*, and *Running Dog* is jaded and anxious: yes, everything is connected; yes, we are part of plots and systems of capital and informational exchange over which we have no control; no, there is nothing we can do about it, at least not in the usual senses of political engagement or resistance. In *Running Dog*, DeLillo presents the reader with an assemblage of crosshatched plots, secret agents, politicians, collectors of erotic art, and, supposedly, a secret pornographic film recording Hitler's sexual exploits during his last days in the bunker. All are red herrings in DeLillo's demystification of the romance of secrecy: even the film of Hitler is a failure, as it records the maniac dictator at a children's birthday party playing the role of an avuncular clown. The monstrosity of this historical recording (these children are the ones who will die in the parental murder-suicides of the final moments in the bunker) is lost upon those who would vend it. Since this is the age of over-exposure and pornography, the film is, Baudrillard would claim, just another example of the overwhelming 'order of visible and calculable phenomena: objects, machines, sexual acts, or gross national product.'[11] Everybody wants to see the formerly hidden, the opaque 'private life' exposed; no one wants to see Hitler acting within a normalized familial framework: 'Pornography is there,' Baudrillard suggests, 'only to reactivate th[e] lost referent in order to prove a *contrario*, by its grotesque hyperrealism, that there is however some *real* sex somewhere.'[12]

The case is put clearly in a conversation between Moll Robbins, the female lead of *Running Dog* and a parodic recapitulation of Oedipa Maas, and Glen Selvy, a secret agent with multifarious political connections:

> 'What is it like, secrecy? The secret life. I know it's sexual. I want to know this. Is it homosexual?'
> 'You're way ahead of me,' he said.
> 'Isn't that why the English are so good at espionage? Or why they seem so good at it, which comes to the same thing. Isn't it rooted in national character?'
> 'I didn't know the English controlled world rights.'
> 'To what?'
> 'Being queer,' he said.
> 'No, I'm saying the link is there. That's all. Tendency finds an outlet. I'm saying espionage is a language, an art, with sexual sources and coordinates. Although I don't mean to say it so Freudianly.'
> 'I'm open to theorizing,' he said. 'What else do you have?'
> 'I have links inside links. This is the age of conspiracy.'
> 'People have wondered.'
> 'This is the age of connections, links, secret relationships.'[13]

In an age when sexuality is organized according to lines of force ('sources and coordinates'), even incorporated, secrecy is reconfigured as the obvious – the 'always already' known – waiting to be mapped; 'hiddenness' becomes merely the precondition for materialization. In this corporate environment, every form of human activity, including subversion and 'theorizing,' aspires to the condition of espionage. In this system, as we know from John LeCarré's sinister and cynical novels, patriotic and political affiliations are merely the cover for articulation and positioning within a single, vast 'language' or monolithic system of communication devoted to obfuscating (in the contained processes of encoding and deciphering) the transparency of its signs.

As Baudrillard suggests, the hyperbolic referentiality and connectedness of a novel like *Running Dog* is due, in part, to a desire for 'the real,' for the materiality, or 'worldliness,' that lies behind all of the information. Like Baudrillard, DeLillo conceives of contemporary reality as a palimpsest of representations, so that, in the novel, any quest for the 'real' Hitler results in the accumulation of the unprofitable representations of him that remain. In this and all of his novels, DeLillo seemingly offers an escape or alternative to the monolithic reign of cultural paranoia, just as Mailer offers oral consensus as complicit response to the machinery of the state, or as Pynchon offers modernist ambiguity as a countereffect to postmodern cybernetic binarity. If everything is a matter of representation, the novel might argue, then perhaps (again, conceiving of paranoia as an epistemological issue) how we see representations can transform the nature of what Baudrillard terms the *reality effect*.

In *Running Dog*, a senator enmeshed in political conspiracies remarks to Moll that the moderator of a television show upon which he has recently been interviewed is 'all image. . . . He's a bunch of little electronic dots, that's all he is' (*RD*, 31). The senator unwittingly suggests that one might undermine the overwhelming effects of televised images by regarding them not as reality, not even as representations of reality, but as what they are materially – transmissions of colored, electronic dots. DeLillo suggests that the de-totalization of representation, the replacement of the paranoid, macroscopic 'hyperreal' with what Guattari and Deleuze refer to as the 'rhizomic' or 'molecular,' the breaking down of the image into a series of 'particles that do not divide without changing in nature,' whose 'movements are Brownian' and whose 'quantities are intensities, differences in intensity' might be seen as an alternative to the paranoid activities of making connections in a punning reversal of 'networking.'[14] But, of course, we are culturally constrained to connect any dots we might see floating about; moreover, the dominance of the orders of representation in *Running Dog* (itself a form of representation in a late capitalist culture wherein its author is becoming more famous, more familiar as a representation, because of the success of his critiques of representation) suggests that the perceptual variations of de-totalization – essentially, parodies of representation – will be quickly reincorporated into another image connected with other images, providing a 'view' of the real. Hence, DeLillo and Pynchon implicitly define the activity of subjectivity within paranoid political and epistemological orders as a form of resistance to totalization, but the very nature of the resistance itself – for Pynchon, preterition, for DeLillo, molecularization – is homologous to the formation of the repressive orders in the first place.

In Joseph McElroy's *Lookout Cartridge*, as in *Running Dog*, there is a futile quest for a missing film, purportedly a montage of 'English life' rendered by the American filmmakers Cartwright and Daggar DiGorro. Cartwright, the novel's protagonist, searches for the experimental film amidst a labyrinthine assemblage of characters and plots, recalling its disjointed sequences: a softball game played by American expatriates in an English park; a meeting of druids at Stonehenge; the social activities of a weekend at a circular English country house; a conversation between an American draft dodger and an anonymous friend in a bare room; the antics of vacationing Brits in Corsica. As Cartwright recounts the filming of each scene, he realizes that Dagger, who has also disappeared, has managed the casting and production in such a way that the same characters appear in widely scattered shots, seemingly, 'meeting' in the film to exchange secret messages. Cartwright begins to suspect that Daggar is using the film as a way of communicating with co-conspirators in a political plot that may involve anything from the hiding of American war resisters to a terrorist attack upon a roomful of singing schoolchildren.

The outlines of *Lookout Cartridge* are familiar within the terms of cultural paranoia: Cartwright, like Oedipa Maas, processes masses of unassimilated information (about the Mayan calendar, Cartherwood's explorations of Central America, techniques of film editing, Bunel's engineering feats, the nature of liquid crystals) only to discover that everything is connected to everything else, and that he is the subject or victim of a monolithic scheme whose ends, even and especially in acts of resistance, he unwittingly advances. While Pynchon and DeLillo portray, respectively, ambiguity and parody as forms of complicitous narrative resistance, McElroy fragments the narrative process itself, thereby framing the forced juxtapositions, displacements, and de-contextualizations of the avant-garde within the schematic of cultural paranoia. Cartwright's function in the novel is that of a 'lookout cartridge,' a technological advance over Mailer's author/transcriber, which, apparently, indiscriminately records everything within its range without filtering out background noise. While this allows for the possibility of random information and noise to seep through, for pure chance connections and patterns to emerge (the illusion created by a Pollock composition), Cartwright suggests that even the most spontaneous upsurge of event, text, noise, or response into the 'inchoate' will result in design or geometry:

> And at this instant, hearing Sub [Cartwright's friend] come out of the kitchen and stand on the threshold of the littered living room and not speak, I found that though my power to prove my feeling about computers – about miles of memory, or abstract numbers switched out of the blue into the real angular turns of a machine or the actual relation of two electric currents – stirred inchoate though contained inside a circle of broken connections that could get long or short or acquire right angles and stern diagonals while being still this circle of known emotions and words and people, my power to turn that inchoate into a statement was, as if half unwilled, finding itself in the new movements after the ruin of the film that my pulses from moment to moment were deciding to make.[15]

The style of this passage is characteristic of McElroy's novel: loose, rambling, and syntactically skewed. Yet, we see that Cartwright insists on the 'half unwilled' systematizing of the instinctual, as if the human mind is constrained to convert the casual into the causal, the pulsings of spontaneity into statement and decision, as if, in short, it were a computer generating and assembling random numbers.

In ways more extreme than Pynchon or Mailer – the former relying upon postmodern indeterminacy, the latter upon the romance of consensus to cheat or 'humanize' paranoia – McElroy, in *Lookout Cartridge*, portrays a thoroughly hegemonic universe, where the mirroring of human cognitive processes in technology (and vice versa) is so complete that it is impossible to tell where the mind ends and the machine begins. This cybernetic rendering of contemporary reality is familiar enough at this point with such cultural manifestations as the movie *Robocop* or Transformers, children's toys that can be converted from machine, to warrior, to machine again.[16] In the end, Cartwright finds pieces of the film and destroys them, possibly as a futile protest against the novel's tangled plots and against those who cultivate them, those for whom the film has served as code and courier. Cartwright concludes with a reflection about the contaminating, oddly non-egotistical nature of his retrospective paranoia: The 'initial system highly improbably would indeed have yielded increasing probabilities, things coming together … but only if that system had to begin with one system and not many systems which I had to forget in the living, and whose multiple impingements I had easily imagined operating through me in the chance of my life but operating through this impure semiconductor like many parts of *me* or as through one terminal albeit moving. But that was not the case' (*LC*, 525). For Cartwright, there is not one Trystero but an infinite number of plots crisscrossing each other, and not one Oedipa upon whom the whole plot impinges but hundreds of Oedipas working at different states of awareness on the local level. Things do not come together in *Lookout Cartridge*, yet the novel suggests that this de-centered form of para-noia, like the avant-garde film, serves analogous sinister ends because dominant political and ideological processes can proceed apace while the forces of resistance are relegated to the micropolitical tier. McElroy's novel equates epistemological specialization to complicity with assimilative cultural and political forces. In the narrowed range of the specialist's angle of vision (that of the scientist, anthropologist, or literary critic), it appears that he is at the center of overlapping conspiracies, or that he is peering through layered complexities and getting at the underlying order of things; meanwhile, to personify, the larger political processes grind on, all too content to leave him the field.

I have been arguing that in these four dense, encyclopedic, highly allusive works, paranoia is represented as a way of coming to terms with a complex reality, but that the perceptual orders which evolve within the arena of our contemporary imperialistic and incorporative cultural environment will reflect, as what is materially 'there,' its overarching designs; the nature and specificity of the designs themselves are inevitably obscured by the size and intricacy of the revealed plot or plots. What are, in fact, 'literary' alternatives to the formation or finalization of plots – counterplot, heteroglossia, ambiguity, fragmentation, and encyclopedic inflation – result in the advancement of the plot. If the plot is, at once, narrative, economic, and political (and the works I have been discussing clearly insist on the conflation of these), then the double bind of the contem-porary episteme I have been calling *cultural paranoia* becomes apparent. Traditional ways of knowing and perceiving, 'deconstructed' in these recent novels, are shown to accommodate a political process – in the great American tradition of consensus – that assimilates, capitalizes, and homogenizes in the very obfuscation of that process all that falls outside its purview. So much, we might say, for the touted radicalism of the avant-garde, 'multi-voicedness,' the pragmatic 'realism' of oral consensus and communities of belief, or the self-consciousness of experimental metafiction, were it not that these authors, arguably, forge a tautology to tell a truth about what that tautology does not include.

3

An alternative version of the causes and effects of contemporary cultural paranoia exists in Diane Johnson's largely ignored *The Shadow Knows*. In this work, Johnson, a Victorian scholar and author of several novels, a series of biographical sketches depicting the 'lesser lives' of several nineteenth-century women, and a biography of Dashiell Hammett, portrays a woman continually beset by fears that she is about to be murdered. N., as the narrator refers to herself, is a recently divorced mother of four young children living in a low-rent housing district of north Sacramento and is pursuing a graduate degree in linguistics. In the midst of an affair with a married man, Andrew, N. is suddenly beleaguered with threats from an unknown assailant: the door to her house is battered with an ax, the window of her car is covered with vomit, and her companion and housekeeper, Ev, is physically assaulted in a laundry room. *The Shadow Knows* – a preemptory rejoinder to recent misogynist affirmations of the nuclear family in films such as *Fatal Attraction* and *Someone to Watch Over Me* – recounts a week in N.'s life during which she is compelled to come to terms with the embodiment of her anxieties about her identity as one who knows and sees the magnitude of her victimization.

N., who reveals her married name to be Hexam, suggestive of her paranoia (she is 'hexed') and her role as a victimized woman (reminiscent of Lizzie Hexam of Dickens's *Our Mutual Friend*), does believe that there is a plot to murder her. As the novel unfolds, she runs through the list of suspects – her ex-husband, her ex-maid Osella, who has been making obscene phone calls to her, Andrew's wife, and her best friend Bess – and so exposes her troubled personal life to the scrutiny of the reader, who is implicitly asked to take on the role of confessor while verifying that there is, indeed, something going on here. The novel proceeds through a series of personal disasters that neither confirm nor deny N.'s status as a paranoid victim: Ev dies suddenly of pancreatitis (though N. believes she has been murdered); N. miscarries the child she has conceived with Andrew; after a series of indecisive moves, Andrew returns to his wife; Bess confesses to N. that she has, for years, hated her and resented her supposedly promiscuous activities. Johnson's novel has all of the earmarks of a soap opera, a genre whose conventions inscribe the putative feminine desire to be violated; hence, in the end, N.'s fears are 'confirmed' not by murder but by rape. *The Shadow Knows* thus brings to bear upon the phenomena of paranoia several leading questions: how is paranoia gendered and engendered? Where and how, in its range, do the 'personal' and the 'political' meet? In the case of N., is it a defense against external evils or the projection of guilt and self-victimizing desire?

These questions suggest that *The Shadow Knows*, unlike the other novels I've discussed, 'personalizes' paranoia by taking the issue of paranoia out of the realm of the consensual hyperreal and converting it into what may appear, on the surface, to be a rather outdated existentialist dialectic moving between the 'inner' and 'outer' life. Johnson, however, makes this conversion in such a way as to suggest that the projections of passion, longing, revenge, jealousy, and hatred found in this disturbing novel both disguise and abet the cultural forces that lie behind the victimization of women. Variously stereotyped by friends, relatives, neighbors, and police as 'the other woman,' the promiscuous divor- cée, the careless mother, the hysteric, N. is enclosed in a threatening environ- ment that takes its revenge upon any woman who resists its normalizing processes by pressuring its victims into the state of paranoia where hegemonic reality and marginalized inwardness are so split up, so separated, that the 'paranoid' can only engage in the 'narcissistic' activity of bringing them back together – at times, violently.

N., faced with extreme circumstances, resorts to what Julia Kristeva terms a 'paranoid-type mechanism' that is 'the inevitable product of . . . a denial of the sociosymbolic contract and its counterinvestment as the only means of self- defense in the struggle to safeguard an identity.'[17] Thus, N. is continually marked for exhibitions of abjection and hysteria that further separate her from the existing order and that designate her as victim or paranoid: she screams at the 'Famous Inspector' (the police detective assigned to investigate Ev's death) that Ev has been murdered when all evidence points to the contrary; she hemorrhages from a miscarriage in a public parking lot. The manifestations of N.'s paranoia involve recurrent incidents where inwardness and exteriority are brought to meet, where what is intuited or imagined and what is 'real' coincidentally or prophetically merge. The condition of separation forced upon her (when a neighbor suggests she spend her money fixing up the outside of her house, not the inside, for the sake of property values; when N. declares that 'outside I am a round-faced little woman with round breasts and toes, sur- rounded by round babies; I look like a happy moon – now who would have thought that I am riddled and shot through invisibly with desperate and sordid passions, raging passions and egotism, insecurity and lust?'[18]) results in its opposite. Thus, N. cites as evidence of the 'interrelation among passions and things unceasing' her, seemingly, ludicrously exaggerated violent passion with Andrew: 'When we were first in love [we] wrecked each other's houses. It was peculiar. I mean physically wrecked them with crowbars and such, and it seemed quite natural and called-for' (*SK*, 28). She looks out for (or she 'makes up,' or naturalizes) the 'interrelation among passions and things unceasing' with increasing anticipation as the evidence mounts that someone is planning an act of violence against her. By the time of her rape she is relieved that the violence is not as bad as what she had been expecting: 'I don't know. I felt happy. Anything bad can happen to the unwary, and when life sends you the *coup de grâce* you have a way of knowing. So I felt better then, thinking well, that was the *coup de grâce* and here I still am' (*SK*, 276). This is the rhetoric of a survivor in a paranoid system that has so thoroughly converted her to that system that she will remain content (now that the 'worst' has happened) with her liminal status. N. 'becomes herself' in the end, but her identity is that of the shadow, otherness beat into airy thinness, inside and outside joined in the shadow's single dimension, outrage transformed into the street wisdom of the 'spiritually sly':

> I feel better. You can change; a person can change. I feel myself different already and to have taken on the thinness and lightness, like a ghost slipping out from his corporeal self and stealing invisibly across the lawn while the body he has left behind meantime smiles stolidly as usual and nobody notices anything different. You can join the spiritually sly, I mean. Well, maybe I'm making too much of this. I mean your eyes get used to the dark, that's all, and also if nothing else you learn to look around you when you get out of your car in a dark garage. (*SK*, 277)

The Shadow Knows thus critiques the romance of that complicitous, 'marginalized' identity (Gilmore, Oedipa Maas, Selvy) that is fostered in the male paranoid novels I have mentioned. It stands as a judgment upon the paranoid system it represents – a system that disguises its inclusions so well that N.'s alteration to the status of shadow could be conceived as revolutionary. As countercritique to the binary versions of cultural paranoia projected by DeLillo, McElroy, and Pynchon, Johnson's novel warrants that N.'s paranoia arises out of gender-specific anxieties transformed into a series of cultural relations that then, at a later stage, become homogenized into the all-powerful conspiracy that represses the preterite in Pynchon, or the nomadic in McElroy. What stands in *The Executioner's Song* as the transparent text upon which is inscribed a primary function of cultural paranoia – the exchange of women's bodies – is brought to the fore of Johnson's novels as the engendering element of cultural paranoia. Johnson engages the 'before' of cultural paranoia, one of its founding moments; in so doing, she reveals the underlying motives of a system of mastery that encourages paranoia and offers epistemology as resistance to it.

In a telling moment, N. reflects upon not her own anxiety but what she refers to as 'that inchoate masculine fear' that leads to the resentment of bad mothers and other 'abnormal' versions of womanhood:

> A smirk of comprehension and disgust overspreads the features of the Famous Inspector: this is a neglectful, a resentful mother he is dealing with, the sort that gets murdered all the time and the children put in foster homes, usually a good thing, too. Ah, it is not reason which congeals the wellsprings of the Famous Inspector's sympathy, but that he is a man. It is that inchoate masculine fear they all have. Where does it come from? It must be that sometime in his life every little baby boy, rosy in his bath,

looking up past the warm, strong arms of his mother into her eyes, one time sees there a strangeness which suddenly reveals to him that she is not him, she is not even like him but is another creature of another race, and however much this terrible recognition may be obscured by subsequent pats, hugs, kisses, coos, years and years of love and encouragement – the terror and isolation of that moment, and the fear of it returning, remain forever. (SK, 37)

In stark contrast to McElroy's representation of 'the inchoate,' Johnson's narrator engenders paranoia as the male response to the alien that the mother represents. Fear of the utter isolation contained in this moment of rupture between pre-oedipal mother and oedipal son, terror at the thought of its return, leads to the homogeneous system of suppression that attempts to border off all of those who recall this differential instant in their lives and beings by converting them into hysterics and paranoids. Kristeva suggests that this moment of separation 'preconditions the binding of language which is already syntactical'; therefore, 'the common destiny of the two sexes, men and women,' is that 'certain biofamilial conditions and relationships [i.e., those of the "nuclear family"] cause women (and notably hysterics) to deny this separation and the language which ensues from it, whereas men (notably obsessionals) magnify both and, terrified, attempt to master them.'[19] This is precisely the situation in The Shadow Knows, where N. attempts to erase the separation between 'inside' and 'outside' through paranoid confirmations. These confirmations are, in turn, guaranteed by the male system of discipline and control represented by the Famous Inspector, whom society has put in charge of separating good women from bad, hysterics from 'normal' women, thus reinstating and mastering the distance between feeling and event that N. attempts to overcome.

Kristeva suggests that to live in this system is to live with the myth of the archaic mother (that woman who existed before the terrifying instant of male recognition and who lives on in alienated versions of femininity). Indeed, the climactic scene of The Shadow Knows portrays the huge Osella performing a striptease at a night club while several of the novel's principals, gathered together for the moment of revelation, look on. This, not so fancifully, might be said to be the ambiguous unwritten moment that Oedipa awaits at the end of The Crying of Lot 49, or what is portrayed in the secreted films of Lookout Cartridge and Running Dog, save that, in this scene, the recognition is concretized, disambiguated, and de-mythologized. Johnson portrays what lies behind paranoia in the spectacle of Osella's body: black, grossly overweight, violent (for it appears to N. that Osella is responsible for Ev's death), Osella is the embodiment of 'otherness,' brought under control and theatricalized for the consumption of the fascinated audience. As N. remarks, 'The naked Osella makes everything clear' (SK, 262). In this crucial scene, the moment of separation is reenacted and contained as Osella receives the mythic investment of the archaic mother, but now she is objectified, her bizarreness (in the Club Zanzibar) zoned off and normalized, for she is soon to be a star in Las Vegas:

> The naked Osella, a sight at first so horrifying and then so immensely fascinating that the people watching all drew in their breath. ... But Osella did nothing at all, merely radiantly stood which was enough, with the light gleaming down on the folds of her body, on her tremendous breasts. She seemed to have been oiled, for she shone so; one saw nothing but the gleaming immense breasts lying across her huge belly, breasts astoundingly full and firm like zeppelins overhead. (*SK*, 267)

For Mailer, Pynchon, DeLillo, and McElroy, paranoia is a kind of logical desire: an attempt to make order out of chaos, to make or see connections, and then to resist mimetically the discourse of mastery. In each instance, however, the form resistance takes to the system that represses otherness merely replicates that system. Even more disturbingly, what appear to be resistant *mis*representations of a prevailing linguistic order homologous to the dominant political order – modern/postmodern gestures of hyperrealism, polyglossia, ambiguity, fragmentation, epistemological magnification – are shown to be cooperative resistances that relegate the problem to the realm of hermeneutics. Johnson, too, sees this as the condition of contemporary cultural paranoia, but in *The Shadow Knows* she makes it clear that these forms of verbal resistance or misrepresentation and their entailing of analogous political oppositions are part of a network of sexual and racial differences that the paranoid system always works to erase or contain. For her, paranoia, in addition to being a narratological or epistemological issue – a way of seeing or ambiguating what is seen, a totalized vision or a fragmentation of that vision, a matter of faithfully transcribing the story or disguising one's arrangements – is a political issue, where enforced cultural relations stemming from anxieties about difference and otherness result in specific consequences for women. In *The Shadow Knows*, a novel filled with scenes of violence toward women, a black woman is possibly murdered, and her murder is ignored because N., a paranoid, is the only person who wishes to pursue the issue. Ev's corpse is a stark contrast to Osella's living body, but they are both made objects in the system of terror and domination that passes for middle-class culture in Johnson's novel. For Johnson's protagonist, nameless and lacking identity, paranoia is not so much a matter of seeing – for she sees clearly enough – as it is of surviving warily and invisibly in an unrelentingly threatening environment. N.'s shadowy transformation in the novel's concluding pages is only the obverse of Osella's presence on the stage: theatricalized or underground, star or paranoid, these strange women are precisely placed. These consequences are not, as the Famous Inspector insists of Ev's murder, in another Dickensian echo reminiscent of another story about a 'little' woman (*Little Dorrit*), 'nobody's fault.' These consequences are, Johnson's novel powerfully argues, no accident.

NOTES

1. The familiar terms I cite here are lifted at large from a heterogeneous assortment of social and critical texts/authors: thus, *episteme* comes from Foucault: *paradigm* from Kuhn; *habitus* from Bourdieu; and *structure of feeling* from Raymond Williams. What is interesting in this assortment is the number of terms that have, of necessity, it seems, been invented to describe a cultural dominant; conceivably, doing so is, in itself, a paranoid activity that assumes there is one or more forms of thought and action that can be said to characterize a culture. Tautologically, these ways of thinking about thought and action – much as they critique whatever forms of cultural and discursive dominance they describe – are (self-admittedly, for many of these critics) produced by and within them. This, I will argue, is also the case for those novels I discuss that both critique paranoia, or represent it as liminal, 'outside the system,' and, at the same time, *produce* paranoia.
2. Fredric Jameson, *Postmodernism, or, The Cultural Logic of Late Capitalism* (Durham: Duke University Press, 1991), xix.
3. Sacvan Bercovitch, *The Puritan Origins of the American Self* (New Haven: Yale University Press, 1975). This work provides a comprehensive analysis of 'Puritan' identity and its historical lineaments.
4. Jean Baudrillard, *Forget Foucault*, trans. Nicole Dufresne (New York: Semiotext(e), 1987), 21–22.
5. Tentatively entitled *Always Connect: Cultural Paranoia in Contemporary American Fiction*. At this point, I do not trace the representation of paranoia in psychoanalytic theory since Freud's 'Schreber' case; rather, I argue, in a limited sense, that it is the representation of a cultural perception of subject–object relations. Later work on this project, however, will attempt to make more explicit connections between cultural paranoia and the homophobia inherent in the Freudian representations of paranoia. The classic reflection on paranoia as a form of cultural representation can be found in Richard Hofstadter's 'The Paranoid Style in American Politics,' in *The Paranoid Style in American Politics and Other Essays* (New York: Alfred A. Knopf, 1965), 3–40.
6. Thomas Pynchon, *The Crying of Lot 49* (1966; reprint, New York: Harper & Row, 1986), 24; hereafter cited in my text as *TCL49*.
7. For an example of an interpretation of *The Crying of Lot 49* which argues that Oedipa is on the verge of a sacred revelation, see Edward Mendelson, 'The Sacred, the Profane, and *The Crying of Lot 49*,' in *Individual and Community: Variations on a Theme in American Fiction*, ed. Kenneth Baldwin and David Kirby (Durham: Duke University Press, 1976), 182–222.
8. Thomas Schaub's *Pynchon: The Voice of Ambiguity* (Urbana: University of Illinois Press, 1981) offers the most far-reaching discussion of ambiguity in Pynchon.
9. I am indebted here to Donald Pease's arguments concerning the relation between modernist versions of indeterminacy and the 'Cold War consensus' in his *Visionary Compacts: American Renaissance Writings in Cultural Context* (Madison: University of Wisconsin Press, 1987), 7–12.
10. See Tom LeClair, *In the Loop: Don DeLillo and the Systems Novel* (Urbana: University of Illinois Press, 1987).
11. Baudrillard, *Forget Foucault*, 22.
12. Baudrillard, *Forget Foucault*, 15n. (Baudrillard's emphasis).
13. Don Delillo, *Running Dog* (1978; reprint, New York: Vintage, 1979), 111; hereafter cited in my text as *RD*.
14. Gilles Deleuze and Félix Guattari, *A Thousand Plateaus: Capitalism and Schizophrenia*, trans. Brian Massumi (Minneapolis: University of Minnesota Press), 33.
15. Joseph McElroy, *Lookout Cartridge* (1974; reprint, New York: Carroll & Graf, 1985), 214; hereafter cited in my text as *LC*.

16. For fascinating discussions of the cybernatization of contemporary literature and material culture, see Gabrielle Schwab, 'Cyborgs and Intertexts: On Postmodern Phantasms of the Body and Mind,' in *Intertextuality and Contemporary American Fiction*, ed. Patrick O'Donnell and Robert Con Davis (Baltimore: Johns Hopkins University Press, 1989), 191–213; and Donna Haraway, *Simians, Cyborgs, and Women: The Reinvention of Nature* (New York: Routledge, 1991).

17. Julia Kristeva, 'Women's Time,' in *Feminist Theory: A Critique of Ideology*, ed. Nanneri O. Keohane, Michelle Z. Rosaldo, and Barbara C. Gelpi (Chicago: University of Chicago Press, 1982), 46.

18. Diane Johnson, *The Shadow Knows* (New York: Alfred A. Knopf, 1975), 8; hereafter cited in my text as *SK*.

19. Kristeva, 'Women's Time,' 41.

NAMES INDEX

SUBJECT INDEX

abstraction, 197–8
absurdism, 135
advertising, development in
postmodern era, 43
agonistics, 75, 88n8
alienation, 25
alteritism, 441
alterity
in characterisation, 333–4
effects on characterisation,
369–70
ambiguity, and ontology,
298n5
America *see* United States
anagnorisis, 359, 360, 364,
365
animal-human organisms, and
machines, breakdown of
distinctions between, 399
anti-detective fiction, 224
anti-detective novels
characterisation, 320–7
deconstruction of detective
novels, 327n1
as representative of
existentialism in
postmodernism, 170–6
see also detective novels;
novels
antinomianism, 198, 204
anxiety, 25
apocalypticism, unimportance
in cyberpunk, 455–6
architects, role in
postmodernism, 54–5
architecture
economics, 23
historicism, 27, 28

and postmodernism, 21,
302, 308: use of irony,
113–16; use of pluralism,
116, 117
Aristotelianism
rejection by
postmodernism, 169,
172: literary aspects,
170–6
art
African art:
commodification, 441–3;
and the
neo-traditional, 434–5
commodification, 431–2,
441–3
concept as experience
without understanding,
209–10
functional changes in
postmodernism,
134–5
modern art, 118–19
modernist art, and
representation, 341
postmodern art, 117–18:
contradictory nature,
308–9
art industry, twentieth-century
developments as
symptoms of
postmodernism, 46
art literature, and nothingness,
327n1
art market, as hedge against
inflation, 52
artistic selection, as basics of
novel writing, 212

artists
role, 430
treatment of in
postmodernism,
139–40
see also authors
arts
intermedia arts and their
treatment of audiences
and the artists,
139–40
role, 154, 158–9
audiences, treatment of in
postmodernism, 139
authors
development in
postmodernism, 141–7
impingement into the story,
in Beckett's work,
253–4
introduction into own
fiction, 270–4
see also artists
avantgarde, 15, 17, 111, 112,
189–90, 430
and postmodernism, 60,
61–4, 65–8, 71n7,
309

Balkanisation, 122–3
Baroque, 117
Borges's views, 146, 147
Big Other (Lacan), 121
black culture, and
postmodernism,
421–8
boredom, 160
brat pack fiction, 224